Pluralism and Diversity in Ireland

PLURALISM AND DIVERSITY IN IRELAND

Iolrachas agus Éagsúlacht in Éirinn

Prejudice and Related Issues in Early 21ˢᵗ Century Ireland

MICHEÁL MAC GRÉIL

Foreword by
Éamon Ó Cuív, TD

THE COLUMBA PRESS

First published in 2011 by
THE COLUMBA PRESS
55A Spruce Avenue, Stillorgan Industrial Park,
Blackrock, Co. Dublin

Cover by Bill Bolger
Origination by Teresa Hunt
Printed in Ireland by Crotare, Dublin

ISBN 978 1 85607 737 8

*This book is dedicated to the
emancipation of the Travelling People,
Ireland's indigenous ethnic minority.*

Pluralism and Diversity in Ireland

Table of Contents

Chapter Twenty-One

Foreword
by
Éamon Ó Cuív, TD
Iar-Aire Rialtais (Former Government Minister)

Understanding society with all its complexities is, perhaps, the greatest challenge facing government and administrators.

Information, of course, is one of the keys. Today, the government minister, the political practitioner, and the administrator have oceans of information available to them on a daily basis. It comes not only through mass media but also in specialised reports, ranging from economic statistics produced by government departments and independent institutions to expressions of expert opinion in book and other forms.

To make beneficial use of all this information it is necessary, indeed essential, to identify quickly that which is of strategic importance. One has to "see the wood for the trees", so to speak, to separate the transient from the information that reveals long-term trends in society. To do otherwise is to waste valuable time.

Dr Mac Gréil in his book has arranged his sociological information in strategic frameworks which make it easier to understand, absorb and interpret. The information here reveals the heart of our national reality. Another defining characteristic of the work is the **linear** nature of the surveys conducted by Dr Mac Gréil. We have here, for the first time in our history, reliable, systematic reporting on the values, attitudes, interests and outlooks that obtain in our society, **examined for trends over the very long period of thirty-five years.**

This is a most valuable aid to policymakers, administrators, students, academics and even writers who attempt to describe the realities and relationships of society. Dr Mac Gréil describes and measures attitudes towards ethnic minorities and other societal categories. You can read here how society in Ireland regards, for example, the Travelling People, women, Irish Speakers, people from Northern Ireland, and our various neighbours in Europe. Changes in attitudes occurring over a long period of time are measured.

This is no instant poll performed over the telephone for tomorrow's or next Sunday's newspaper. The basis is an up-to-an-hour-long, face-to-face interview conducted by trained interviewers employed by the Economic and Social Research Institute. The sample of over 1,000 was sufficiently large to allow for fine analysis of subsidiary variables, grouping respondents under a number of categories including Education, Occupational Status, Social Class Position, Gender etc. We can be sure that we have here a reliable and accurate account of the attitudes prevalent in our society in 2007-08 and of long-term trends.

When Dr Micheál Mac Gréil approached me and my colleague Michael McDowell in relation to his proposal to conduct a further survey on prejudice and tolerance in Ireland we were, as Government Ministers, very interested. As Minister with responsibility for the Irish Language, I was interested in a detailed sociological examination of the place of the language in today's society. Michael McDowell and I, as Minister for Justice and Equality and Minister for Community respectively, were particularly interested in the survey in relation to various groups in our society. In particular we were interested in finding out the current position of Travellers in our society and the attitudes of society to the many people who have come to live in our State in the last 20 years. This period has seen the greatest influx ever in peacetime of non-Irish people into our country. Up to 10% of our population are now migrants.

This in-migration could have caused major tensions in our society and it was vital to know whether the policies followed to date were facilitating the integration of the *"new Irish"* into our society and if there was a threat of ethnic and racial discord here.

Generally speaking, the survey indicates a high level of acceptance of our new communities although there is a surprising result in that the attitudes of young adults are less positive than those of older age groups. Policymakers should now examine this issue further and consideration should be given to highlighting the importance of interculturalism and racial tolerance in the CSP Programme in schools.

In relation to the Travelling People, the results are both good and bad. On one hand a considerable minority (18.2%) would refuse citizenship to Travellers and on the other hand, more tolerance towards Travellers is indicated by the increasing number of people (39.6%) who would welcome a

Traveller into the family. What this particular survey shows is that there is considerable work to be done before the Travelling People are considered truly equal by many in our society.

In his chapter "Irish Political Attitudes", Dr Mac Gréil chronicles our changing attitudes towards northern Unionists. The percentage willing to accept "Unionists to kinship" increased from 34.4% in 1988-89 to 62.2% in 2007-08. The percentage who would deny citizenship to Unionists dropped from 13.4% to 7.9% over the same period. This, of course, reflects, at least in part, the new, more equitable arrangements made for government in Northern Ireland. The inclusion of all Irish people as equals in the Irish national community or nation is a fundamental republican principle in the tradition of Wolfe Tone.

Another area of interest to me is, of course, the Irish language. It is not possible in a few short lines to express an adequate appreciation of Dr Mac Gréil's chapter, "The Irish Language". This chapter and, indeed, the chapter, "Theory and Methodology", should be required reading for all who make and/or implement policies in respect of Irish, be they in political parties, government departments, government agencies or in voluntary Irish language organisations including *naíonraí* and *gaelscoileanna*. I would extend that recommendation to include in their reading the special report, *The Irish Language and the Irish People,* which was published in 2009 and which is a more detailed analysis based on the 2007-08 survey.

Some of our politicians, administrators and mass-media commentators seem to believe that the aspirations for the restoration of Irish are and should be a thing of the past. The study shows that support for Irish in the adult population is maintained at an unwavering 93%. It is difficult to think of any other issue in public life on which there is such a depth of agreement.

In relation to Irish, there is the primary motivation of any society-wide learning of a second language – the social status of the language compared to that of the dominant language. It can be measured in several ways. One measure is the social status or position in society of speakers of the language. Dr Mac Gréil's report shows by several measures that the status of speakers of Irish is very high indeed in Irish society. Irish Speakers are an in-group in Irish society. They are very near the very top of the list of categories of people who would be accepted into kinship by the respondents.

The book is a treasure trove of organised information on many other aspects of Irish attitudes and prejudices – Religious Attitudes and Practices, Authoritarianism and Social Anomie, Irish Political Attitudes, The Irish Family and Attitudes towards Women, Irish Attitudes towards the British, Attitudes towards Northern Ireland, Ethnic Prejudice and Irish Ethnic Self-Identity, Ethnic, Ethnico-Racial and Racial Social Distance and much, much more.

I am delighted that the Government has funded part of this monumental work. For the policymaker, the academic, the student, the journalist or anyone interested in understanding the social dynamic of Irish society, this book will be a constant reference source for many years to come and I have no doubt that it will be consulted on an ongoing basis.

Pluralism and Diversity in Ireland tells us how things are. I know that the earnest wish of the author is that this book would be not just a reference source as to how things are, but an important building block in devising evidence-based policies to make Ireland a more pluralist, tolerant and caring society and a better place in which to live. If it succeeds in this regard, the author, along with his colleagues who produced this monumental tome, will feel the work was very well worth the effort.

Let me end by hoping that Dr Mac Gréil's long and energetic career will go on well into the future and continue to inspire and inform us.

Go dtuga Día saol fada dhó.

23ú Marta 2011   Éamon Ó Cuív, TD

Author's Preface and Acknowledgements

Preface

Social Prejudice is a particular type of negative disposition or attitude towards persons who are perceived to belong to a category or group, and are seen or felt to be less desirable in themselves because of their membership of that category or group. Unlike negative attitudes that are based on personal experience and rational judgement and are open to change, social prejudice tends to be rigid and inflexible and resistant to change. A greater understanding of the social situation, unbiased rearing of the young, strict control of incitement to hatred, and conditions conducive to favourable interpersonal and intergroup contact are among the most effective conditions of greater social tolerance in society.

The main aim of ***Pluralism and Diversity in Ireland*** is to contribute to a reduction in social prejudice and to replace it with intergroup tolerance. The current text is based on a national survey of intergroup attitudes carried out in the Republic of Ireland from November 2007 to March 2008. Two previous major surveys were undertaken and reported on by the same author in 1972-73 (Greater Dublin area) and in 1988-89 (Republic of Ireland). More or less the same questions were used in each of the three surveys. This has enabled the researcher to monitor significant changes in Irish social prejudice over thirty-five years, which is very valuable in assessing the impact of sociocultural change on the people's intergroup attitudes.

One of the positive latent functions or consequences of researching and publishing the state of social prejudice is to weaken its grip in society. *A prejudice exposed is a prejudice undermined!* It is a universal phenomenon and is present in various guises, i.e. class, ethnic, political, racial, religious, sexist and social. It is basically **a hate attitude** which has led to incredible atrocities throughout history, not least over the past eighty years in Europe and elsewhere.

In addition to the systematic exposure of social prejudice through the findings of survey research, it is proposed **to interpret and discuss** the results throughout the text as well as in the final chapter. This is done without compromising the scientific rigour of the findings. The ongoing normative commentary is included in the text to enhance the attainment of the main aim of this research (as outlined above). Obviously, normative commentary can be challenged by readers from different theoretical and ideological points of view.   Such challenges are always welcome.

It is the view of the present author that **integrated pluralism** is the most equitably human solution to a modern society composed of cultural and religious diversity.   Such a model of integration respects, protects and even promotes cultural diversity while, at the same time, guaranteeing intergroup equality.   It represents diversity **without** segregation or involuntary assimilation.   Chapter Three deals with the conceptual and theoretical frameworks deemed relevant to the diagnosis and explanation of different levels of prejudice and tolerance in society.

A **descriptive summary** of the main findings is presented in Chapters Nineteen and Twenty.   Because of the heavy concentration of statistical data and findings presented through the main body of the text, i.e. Chapters Four to Eighteen, readers are advised to go through the text, concentrating on one chapter at a time.   The findings are presented in a fairly clear and, hopefully, non-intimidating manner.   The tables represent a considerable range of information and findings, collected from 1,015 respondents over an average interview time of forty minutes (replying to pre-coded questions – see Appendix A, pages 615-632).

It will be clear from the findings that the overall results of this research have been quite positive.   *The level of intergroup tolerance has increased substantially between 1988-89 and 2007-08.*   Among the causes which were anticipated or hypothesised for such dramatic improvement in social tolerance were the following, i.e.

(i)   the satisfactory outcome of the Northern Ireland Peace Process;
(ii)   the increase in social and economic security between 1995 and 2008;
(iii)   the positive impact of the in-migration of workers resulting in favourable contact.

Other contributions which were expected to reduce social prejudice were greater participation in education, an increase in foreign travel, and the rise of urbanisation and related changes.   The relatively higher social prejudice score of the **younger age** (18 to 25 years) sub-variable questioned some of the positive influences of greater educational achievement at the complete second-level and with third-level experience.   This anomaly requires further research (see pages 156-160).

The levels of intolerance or prejudice towards a number of categories at the end of the rank-order list, i.e. from 39th to 51st on Table No. 19.1 (page 515) are well above acceptable scores. The position of **Travellers**, for example, is one of relatively high social prejudice. A special chapter is devoted to the attitudes towards them in Irish society. While there was a substantial increase in the percentages willing "to admit members of the Travelling community into the family" (at 39.6%), there was also a significant proportion of respondents prepared "to deny them citizenship" (at 18.2%). The latter is an intolerable percentage! (See Chapter Thirteen.)

Chapters Sixteen and Seventeen deal with areas integrally related to intergroup attitudes and relations, namely, the **Irish Language** and **Religion**. Cultural and religious pluralism are basic to most modern societies with diverse ethnic and religious categories. The experience of modern Ireland bears out the need to respect religious and cultural diversity in a pluralist manner.

In regard to the findings concerning the Irish Language, there is a real basis for optimism. The level of positive aspirations in relation to Irish continues to be overwhelming at 93% in favour of its preservation or revival. Reasonable competence at 47% is the highest since the Great Famine, while the level of regular use is too low at 23%. The growing degree of ambiguity in relation to the people's ethnic self-identity may, in part, be due to less use of Irish and also to a weaker level of identity with one's religion and community.

The decline in religious practice has been substantial since 1988-89 in the Republic of Ireland. Attitudes towards religious categories, while improved, were very varied. The position of **Muslims** was disappointing, while the attitudes towards **Jews** did not improve as much as was anticipated, probably due to their association with the Israeli-Palestinian troubles. The negative correlation between education and religiosity is a matter of concern in that it can result, by default, in a rise of religious fundamentalism (with its possible links with prejudice).

Attitudes towards **Northern Ireland** and the **British** have confirmed the progress achieved by the *Belfast Agreement (1998)* and the *Saint Andrew's Agreement (2006)*. The findings clearly point to a significant 'peace dividend' following years of division and strife. **Sexism** and **anti-feminism** are measured in Chapter Fourteen and raise interesting questions about progress towards further gender equality in Ireland. The level of **homophobia** in Irish society had greatly reduced between 1988-89 and 2007-08.

Authoritarianism and **Social Anomie** are key phenomena in explaining the level of social prejudice in society. The former represents a personality trait conducive to closed-mindedness. The latter is a social condition discerned by the French sociologist, Emile Durkheim, which results in a sense of normlessness. Both correlate with social prejudice very significantly. The present author recommends that serious research into the causes of these two important measures is required in order to find out how to reduce them and in the interests of greater social tolerance. The levels of 'authoritarianism' and 'social anomie' in Irish society are still moderately high.

Chapters Six to Nine deal with **ethnic, ethnico-racial** and **racial prejudice** in the Republic of Ireland. In all, there are twenty-nine stimulus categories covered under this broad classification. They are subdivided into four specific sets of categories, i.e. (i) *Irish, British and American categories (9)*; (ii) *Continental European nationalities (9);* (iii) *African, Asian and Racial categories (7)*; and (iv) *Middle-East categories (4).*

The level of social distance (*Bogardus Scale*) towards each of the different categories is measured, analysed and discussed. One of the optimistic findings was the overall increase in closeness to which members of the various categories are admitted. An important indirect finding for the Middle-East categories is the **urgent need** for effective dialogue between **Christians, Jews** and **Muslims**. The process of secularisation in public affairs in the Middle-East, if not accompanied by such dialogue, is likely to aggravate the situation rather than reconcile it!

It will be clear to the reader that this book contains a considerable amount of tabulated information. Every effort has been made to present as comprehensive a set of findings as possible, publishing individual findings for **each** stimulus category and scale. The new technique of **presenting extracts** from the bigger Tables in the body of the text should help the reader in discerning the patterns emerging. Hopefully, this will help to make the reader's task less intimidating. The overall analysis in Chapter Twenty-One tries to examine correlations between personal variables and different types of social prejudice, and suggest areas for research.

Acknowledgements

Every social researcher is indebted primarily to **the respondents**, 1,015 in this case, who voluntarily gave of up to an hour of their time to take part in the interview. Thanks are also due to the staff of the ESRI Survey Division and the interviewers, under Dr Dorothy Watson's direction, who carried out the fieldwork on behalf of the author.

A key person in the statistical processing and analysis of the data has been **Fergal Rhatigan, M.Soc.Sc.**, Senior Research Officer of the 2007-08 survey (research) project. He was most competent, conscientious and methodical in his work over two years. **Maria Woulfe** and **Teresa Hunt** have been responsible for the preparation and presentation of the various drafts of the main text and the three monographs published on the Irish Language, Religion and the Travelling People. The author is also grateful to **an tOllamh Seán Ó Riain**, Department of Sociology, NUI Maynooth, for his administrative backup and supervision over three years, i.e. since March 2008.

The principal sponsor of this project has been the **Government** (Departments of *Community, Rural and Gaeltacht Affairs* and of *Justice, Equality and Law Reform*). The support of the **Irish Jesuit Province**, by enabling the author to work on the project full-time for four years, i.e. from 2007 to 2011, is also acknowledged. The contribution of **The Atlantic Philanthropies** provided valuable financial support towards the completion of the text and its preparation for publication. Thanks are due to the Grants' Office in the NUI Maynooth for administering the various grants.

The author acknowledges the value of other authors and researchers quoted in the text. The **data sets** of both the 1988-89 and the 2007-08 national surveys are made available for the use of future survey research into intergroup attitudes. The data will be deposited in the Irish Social Science Data Archive (ISSDA), Geary Institute, UCD, Belfield, Dublin 4.

Help with the proofreading of the different reports and the main text was professionally given by Angela Burt (Portfolio Proofreading Services) and the late Diarmuid Ó Luanaigh. The critical readers who read and improved the draft text included Rev. Derek Cassidy, SJ, Joseph P. Mulholland (USA) and Maolsheachlainn Ó Caollaí. The author acknowledges the valuable work of critical readers and proofreaders.

Thanks are due to Liam Killion of **Crotare Printing Ltd**. for printing the text and to Seán Ó Baoill of **The Columba Press** for publishing the book *Pluralism and Diversity in Ireland.* The author apologises for any errors which may have avoided detection.

The author's special thanks are due to **Éamon Ó Cuív, TD** for his ongoing support for this research and for writing the **Foreword** to this book. His encouragement and assistance in this project have been most important.

Finally, the text was drafted and written in **Loughloon, Westport, Co. Mayo**, away from the busy coming and going of the society about which it reports. I wish to thank my family for allowing me to use the old Loughloon cottage as a research and writing office over the years. This 'haven' was sustained because of the support of my family, kind neighbours and Jesuit colleagues.

Guím dea-ghuí ar ghach léitheoir. Tá súil agam go mbainfear sásamh agus misneach as an leabhar seo a seolfar in Earrach na Bliana 2011 agus go gcuirfidh sé leis an sprioc atá le léamh sa teideal, **Iolrachas agus Éagsúlacht in Éirinn**.

Micheál Mac Gréil, s.j.
Loch Chluain, (Loughloon)
Cathair na Mart, (Westport)
Co. Mhaigh Eo. (Co. Mayo)

31ú Marta 2011

CHAPTER I
Introduction

Intergroup attitudes are both a cause and a result of intergroup behaviour and constitute a central determining factor in the nature and level of social integration. Social prejudice is a special type of intergroup attitude which tends to be hostile, negative, rigid and based on negative stereotypes of members of particular groups and categories. Such attitudes lead to negative discrimination of members or groups who are objects of prejudice in society. Attitudes have their causes in the actual situation as well as in the personality and are rooted in society and the people's culture.

The present author has been engaged in measuring social prejudice and tolerance for most of his academic life, i.e. since 1963, while he was a student in Louvain, Belgium. There he learned from older Jesuits about the horrors of the Nazi Regime and visited the Concentration Camp in Dachau, near Munich. As stated in *Prejudice in Ireland Revisited (1996)*, he was appalled on "seeing the real evidence of the persecution of the Jews, Russians, Gypsies, Homosexuals and others, including a number of German Jesuits who opposed the xenophobic slaughter". A question raised by one of his Jesuit professors, i.e. *"How was it possible for a civilised society (like the Germans) to permit the practice of such blatant inhumanity towards fellow human beings?"*, decided for him (the present author) that he would devote his academic and other endeavours to seeking an answer to the professor's question! This book is a further contribution towards getting the answer.

It became obvious after a short time that the understanding and exposure of social prejudice were the complex keys to that answer. It also became clear that an important way to undermine social prejudice in public was to expose it through careful and methodical research. Social Prejudice is a universal phenomenon which has played a most destructive role throughout the history of humanity. It is likely to continue to impede the advance of a just and fair society unless the people are aware of it and are willing to replace it with tolerance.

In the short term, prejudice is perceived to be functional and is often an implicit expression of the rationalisation of discrimination leading to

1

social inequality. When discrimination is formally endorsed by custom and by law it is defined as segregation. The removal of legal support from 'segregation' in society is defined as desegregation. Although informal discrimination may continue, desegregation is, nevertheless, an essential prerequisite to the process of changing ingrained prejudices into positive social attitudes. *Minority rights' legislation* is a most effective method of removing and preventing discrimination and segregation in society. Such legislation is necessary in all human societies throughout the world. Favourable contact between members of different categories of people is seen to be one of the most effective ways of replacing social prejudice with positive intergroup attitudes.

1.1 Measuring and Monitoring Intergroup Attitudes:
This book reports on the findings of a comprehensive national survey of intergroup attitudes and related issues carried out in the Republic of Ireland between November 2007 and March 2008. An interview-questionnaire was completed by 1,015 respondents. The average length of the interview was forty minutes. The fieldwork was carried out by the Economic and Social Research Institute (ESRI), on commission. The sample was weighted to coincide as closely as possible with the distribution of population in the *2006 Census Report*. A breakdown of the sample interviewed is given in Table No. 1.1 and confirms its representativeness in the case of major variables. (See Table No. 13.1, pages 298-300 below, col. 3.)

The two types of standard (personal) variables given in Table No. 1.1 are 'ordinal' and 'nominal' variables. *Ordinal Variables* have a 'more-than/less-than' quantitative relation between the sub-variables. In the case of such variables it is possible to establish product-moment correlations, which help to provide causal explanations for the different scores in relation to 'dependent variables', e.g. measures of social prejudice. *Nominal Variables* lack a 'more-than/less-than' relation between the sub-variables, e.g. gender. The information provided by such variables is useful for descriptive and geographic reasons.

The following profile of the eighteen year-olds and over corresponds closely (within the margins of error) with the actual distribution of the adult population in the *2006 Census of Population Report* in the case of variables which are comparable. In instances of a cell being fewer than 40 in number, it is not taken as a viable sub-sample. The level of confidence required for statistically significant variations between sub-samples is *Chi Square* P<0.05 or being not due to chance in fewer than one-in-twenty cases.

Table No. 1.1: Profile of Sample

Ordinal Variables			Nominal Variables	
(a) Age	**Actual**	**Cum.**	**(f) Gender**	**Actual**
1. 18 – 25 years	16.6%	16.6%	Males	49.4%
2. 26 – 40 years	32.0%	48.6%	Females	50.6%
3. 41 – 56 years	24.3%	73.0%	Total Number	1,015
4. 57 – 70 years	17.5%	90.5%	**(g) Marital Status**	
5. 71 years plus	9.5%	100.0%	1. Single/Never Married	35.3%
Total Number	1,015	---	2. Married	46.6%
(b) Area of Birth			3. Separated/Divorced	4.3%
1. City (100,000+)	41.3%	41.3%	4. Permanent Relationship	7.0%
2. Large Town (10,000-99,999)	11.7%	53.0%	5. Widowed	6.7%
3. Town (1,500-9,999)	13.0%	66.0%	Total Number	1,015
4. Rural/Village	34.0%	100.0%	**(h) Place of Rearing (in Rep. of Irl.)**	
Total Number	1,014	---	1. Dublin City/County	31.0%
(c) Education			2. Rest of Leinster	20.1%
1. Primary or Less	11.6%	11.6%	3. Munster	29.0%
2. Incomplete Second-Lev.	25.8%	37.3%	4. Connaught/Ulster	19.9%
3. Complete Second-Level	25.1%	62.5%	Total Number	796
4. Third-Level	37.5%	100.0%	**(i) Province of Residence**	
Total Number	1,015	---	1. Border/Midlands/West	26.8%
(d) Occupational Status			2. Dublin	28.3%
1. Unskilled/Semi-Skilled	24.1%	24.1%	3. Mid-East/South-East	21.7%
2. Skilled/Routine Non-Man.	38.2%	62.3%	4. Mid-West/South-West	23.3%
3. Inspectional/Supervisory	15.5%	77.7%	Total Number	1,005
4. Professional/Senior Exec.	22.3%	100.0%	**(j) Religious Affiliation**	
Total Number	859	---	1. Roman Catholic	89.6%
(e) Social Class Position			2. C. of I./Methodist/Presbyterian	2.3%
Class I: 'Upper Class'	4.5%	4.5%	3. Other Christian	2.1%
Class II: 'Upper Middle'	16.3%	20.8%	4. Other Religion	2.7%
Class III: 'Middle-Middle'	26.9%	47.8%	5. No Religion	3.3%
Class IV: 'Working Class'	42.4%	90.1%	Total Number	1,013
Class V: 'Lower Class'	9.9%	100.0%	**(k) Ethnic Origin (where born)**	
Total Number	855	---	1. Ireland	84.2%
			2. United Kingdom	6.9%
Note: **Social Class Position** is based on the Hollingshead method which combines **Educational Standard** reached and **Occupational Status** achieved. Each criterion is divided into **seven** grades and multiplied by **4** and **7** respectively (see Table No. 8.14 page 189 below)			3. Other Europe	5.3%
			4. Asia	1.3%
			5. Africa	1.1%
			6. U.S.A.	0.5%
			7. Other	0.6%
			Total Number	1,015

The general detail of the actual interviewing operation, i.e. the fieldwork was quite positive as recorded in Table No. 1.2 below:

Table No. 1.2: Interview Details

(a) Place of Interview:		(d) Respondents' Reception	Actual	Cumul.
1. Living room and/or Kitchen	70.8%	1. Excellent	41.8%	
2. Hallway	13.4%	2. Very Good	26.5%	85.1%
3. Doorstep	13.4%	3. Good.	16.6%	
4. Other	2.6%	4. Fair	8.3%	
Total Number	1,011	5. Fair, Improving later	3.1%	11.4%
(b) Amount of Explanation Needed:		6. Cool	2.5%	
1. General Introduction Only	48.5%	7. Hostile	1.0%	3.5%
2. General Introduction + Explanation	28.3%	Total Number	1,011	
3. General Introduction + Clarification	23.2%	(e) Number of Visits:	Actual	Cumul.
Total Number	1,009	1. First Visit	38.1%	38.1%
(c) Previous Knowledge of Survey:		2. Second Visit	32.1%	70.3%
1. Had not heard of survey/Did not know	95.2%	3. Third Visit	20.0%	90.3%
2. Heard of person previously interviewed	3.0%	4. Fourth Visit	7.6%	97.9%
3. Heard from other sources	1.8%	5. Fifth Visit	1.1%	99.0%
Total Number	995	6. Sixth to Ninth Visit	1.0%	100.0%
		Total Number	999	

The value of the above information is to give the reader reassurance of the voluntary nature of the interview which took on average forty minutes. Such details are also useful to future social survey researchers and interviewers of the actual requirements of the operation. The objective selection of the sample was organised by the ESRI and interviewers were assigned the names in their various localities or districts.

Most of the material researched in the 2007-08 survey has been included in two previous major surveys of intergroup relations in the **Republic of Ireland**, i.e. the Greater Dublin Survey of 1972-73 and a National Survey carried out in 1988-89. The findings of these two surveys were published in 1977[1] and 1996[2] respectively. Because of the replication of the questions asked in the previous two surveys it is possible *to monitor changes in prejudices* in Ireland over a period of thirty-six years. Between 1972 and 2008, Ireland and the world witnessed many significant social, political and

---

[1] Mac Gréil, Micheál, *Prejudice and Tolerance in Ireland*, Dublin, College of Industrial Relations, 1977 and New York, Praeger, 1980.
[2] Mac Gréil, Micheál, *Prejudice in Ireland Revisited*, Maynooth, St Patrick's College, 1996 and 1997.

religious changes. The period marks the time of Ireland's membership of the European Union. It also covers most of the recent 'Troubles' in Northern Ireland and the move to joint-rule within Northern Ireland.

The 1970s, 1980s and early 1990s were times of low gainful employment, high emigration and the State's preoccupation with the pursuit of a satisfactory solution to the 'Troubles' in Northern Ireland. *The collapse of the 'Berlin Wall'* in 1989 and the fall of the Soviet Union had repercussions on socio-political views in Ireland as witnessed with the rise of **neo-liberalism,** especially during the decade 1997 to 2007 when Ireland experienced a substantial rise in material wealth and economic development resulting in the economy 'over-heating' in some departments. This coincided with *the international banking crisis* and widespread economic recession in the autumn of 2008, which triggered a global economic and financial crisis. Ireland, with its open economy, was to feel the brunt of this crisis in a most severe manner.

The economic expansion of mid-1990s to 2006 resulted in a large increase in the labour force and the in-migration of workers from outside the Republic of Ireland. From the point of view of intergroup relations, *the change* from being largely an *emigrant society* to becoming an *immigrant society* (which followed the rise of socio-economic prosperity between the mid-1990s and 2006) was most significant. The findings of this text report the impact of in-migration on prejudice and tolerance in the Republic of Ireland.

This also marked the rise of the economic institution to 'the pivotal position' in Irish society (which was possible once a viable settlement was reached in Northern Ireland). Over a period of ten years **the workforce increased** from 1.3 million in 1996 to over two million. Despite the relatively large young Irish workforce, who were relatively highly qualified, there was a significant decline in Irish blue-collar workers as a proportion of that workforce. Irish youth were focussing on white-collar and professional occupations. This led to greater dependence on in-migration of manual workers (skilled, semi-skilled and unskilled).

Ireland has also been affected by developments and social and cultural changes throughout the world over the past number of decades. Among the changes it is possible to include:

1) International travel both from and to Ireland has greatly increased and has been facilitated by the greater access to countries and the reduction in the cost of air and sea travel;

2) The process of globalisation of goods and labour has resulted in inter-ethnic familiarisation and contact.   Socio-political developments, such as the expansion of the European Union and attempts to integrate it more interdependently, have influenced Irish patterns of intergroup interaction;

3) As already noted, changes in the workforce, i.e. decline in agriculture and the manufacturing industry in the so-called developed world and the rise in services' jobs, have taken place in the Republic of Ireland over the forty years since the 1960s;

4) The rise in participation in third-level education by men and women which has been quite substantial;

5) An area of change to have taken place over the past thirty years has been the rise in women taking up full-time gainful employment outside the home with consequent effects on fertility, family life and economic growth;

6) The expansion and changes in communication constitute the area of social change which has affected modern society and influences intergroup relations;

7) The decline in religious practice and the growth of religious indifference, especially among the younger people, and a rise in materialism and consumerism;

8) The decline in the importance and function of the family and community; and

9) The growth in urbanisation with the substantial increase in inter-regional imbalance.

These nine areas of social change have been exceptionally evident in modern Ireland and are likely to have had an impact on our intergroup attitudes and prejudices.

1.2 In-Migration of Workers:
When the State set about renewing its housing stock and preparing accommodation for in-migrants and a significant national increase in population, it was forced to recruit its extra blue-collar workers from Eastern Europe and elsewhere abroad.   Some former Irish emigrants returned to fill the new vacancies and got involved in construction at home in Ireland. Nursing and other services were in need of additional workers from abroad.

A significant and substantial increase in wealth and material standard of living was experienced. The proportion of citizens and others born outside the Republic of Ireland in 2006 was 15%. This changed the ethnic make-up of Irish society to the extent that a minority of people of different cultural, ethnic, racial, religious and social backgrounds were now present in most Irish urban populations. The building and catering trades recruited significant numbers of migrant workers.

While the proportion of non-Irish or those not born to Irish parents has so far remained a relatively small percentage of the State's population (see Table No. 2.1, page 17), their visibility in Irish society has become quite clear. In the case of a number of ethnic and racial categories measured in previous surveys, respondents had not met members in Ireland. They were responding to groups they had read about or met abroad. This time it will be possible to measure the impact of meeting members of these categories living and working in Ireland. *It will be shown that actual contact in the favourable environment of fellow workers has contributed to **an increase in ethnic and racial tolerance** and a reduction in ethnic and racial prejudice.* These are encouraging findings.

Improvement in tolerance and a reduction in prejudice, unfortunately, do not mean that ethnic and racial prejudice has been replaced by positive attitudes by the majority of respondents in the case of a number of minorities. As will be pointed out in the text, prejudices can both **increase** and **decrease** depending on the degree of unfavourable or favourable social and cultural environment at a particular time. Not all change is progressive, hence the need for continuous vigilance and effective enforcement of minority rights' legislation. The socio-cultural factors which affect changes in prejudice and tolerance are varied and will be examined in the course of the various chapters. At times of economic downturn, attitudes can become more negative towards the 'outsider' because of insecurity, frustration and displaced aggression against him or her, i.e. 'scapegoating'.

1.3 General Outline of Text:
The general outline of topics dealt with in the text is as follows:
- (a)   Minorities in the Republic of Ireland;
- (b)   Methodology and Theoretical Approach;
- (c)   Social Distance in the Republic of Ireland;
- (d)   Rationalisation and Intergroup Definition;
- (e)   Ethnic, Ethnico-Racial and Racial Prejudice;

(f)   Ethnic Prejudice;
(g)   Racial Prejudice;
(h)   Attitudes toward Northern Ireland;
(i)   Irish Attitudes towards the British;
(j)   Prejudice towards Social Categories;
(k)   The Irish Travelling People;
(l)   The Irish Family and Attitudes towards Women;
(m)   Political Attitudes and Opinions;
(n)   The Irish Language;
(o)   Religious Attitudes and Practices;
(p)   Authoritarianism and Social Anomie;
(q)   Summary of Findings.

The questionnaire is largely a replication of the questions asked in 1972-73 and in 1988-89 (see Appendix A).   There have been a number of changes, i.e. omissions and additions, due to the changing socio-cultural situation in 2007-08 and to constraints imposed by limited financial resources and a five-fold increase in the cost of the fieldwork between 1988-89 and 2007-08.   The exclusion of the voters' register as a source for the selection of a national random sample in 2007-08 added to the costs of the fieldwork.

1.4 Primary Field Research:
As stated in Chapter I of *Prejudice in Ireland Revisited*[3], this book "reports on primary field-research" and deals with relatively little secondary analysis. Such secondary references are chosen to compare and contrast the findings analysed in the text.   The primacy of fieldwork is the text's main contribution to research into intergroup attitudes and prejudices as Irish society grows more pluralist in its demographic composition[4].   The principal sponsors of this project, i.e. the **Departments of Community, Rural and Gaeltacht Affairs** and of **Justice, Equality and Law Reform**, were keen to find out the current state of intergroup attitudes in Ireland in the wake of the arrival of the recent members of other ethnic groups, i.e. migrant workers and their families.   Migrants had come to Ireland in search of

---

[3] Mac Gréil, Micheál, *Prejudice in Ireland Revisited*, Maynooth, St Patrick's College, Department of Social Studies, 1996, 97, page 5.

[4] It is intended to deposit the data of the 2007-08 survey in the archive of survey research for the use of future social researchers. Hopefully, a follow-up survey will be carried out in 2026-27 to monitor changes in Irish prejudices over the following eighteen years.   The data from the 1988-89 national survey will also be available in the archive.

employment from Great Britain, Eastern Europe, India, China, the Philippines, Africa and elsewhere abroad.

1.5 Old and New Minorities:

Since the influx of new minorities, Ireland's historical groups are examined in a broader context.   The main indigenous minorities would be the Travelling Community, different religious minorities, political groups and general categories, i.e. gender groups, social class groups, and others.   The arrival at a settlement to the Northern Ireland 'Troubles' in the 1990s has been a major and positive development for intergroup relations in the country.   It was providential that an agreement was signed in a time of economic security and relative prosperity.   The welcome Northern settlement will help Ireland in addressing the socio-economic challenges in the years ahead because of the constructive cooperation emerging from the *Good Friday Agreement in 1998* and subsequent developments.   It will be most interesting to evaluate the influence of the recent developments in Northern Ireland on the attitudes towards Northern Ireland and towards Britain, which were measured in the current (2007-08) and previous surveys in 1972-73 and in 1988-89.   At the times of the previous surveys the scene in Northern Ireland was tragic and violent.

The position of the **Travelling People** is examined once again in this book.   The Travellers constitute **0.5%** of the population of the Republic of Ireland or **22,369** persons.   They, in a sense, constitute an example of **apartheid** within the indigenous Irish population.   Their minority status in 1972-73 could be classified as one of *'lower caste'* (see Table No. 13.3, page 309).   This position had deteriorated further in 1988-89 to become the status of *'outcasts'*.   It will be shown that the findings of the 2007-08 survey have both improved and disimproved, i.e. more people **(39.6%)** would welcome Travellers as 'members of their family' while, at the same time, a substantial minority **(18.2%)** would 'deny them citizenship'.   This means that Travellers can no longer be classified as 'lower caste' but, at the same time, they are facing serious hostility and prejudice in their own country.   A special report on the current state of the Travelling People (based on the findings of the 2007-08 survey) was published in 2010[5].   Its main findings are included in this text also (see Chapter XIII).

---

[5] Mac Gréil, Micheál, *Emancipation of the Travelling People*, Maynooth, Survey & Research Unit, Dept. of Sociology, NUI Maynooth 2010.

1.6 The Irish Language and Irish Ethnic Self-Identity:

Because of the special significance of the Irish language as a basic ethnic symbolic system for the Irish people, the people's aspirations for, competence in, and use of the language were measured and monitored. A special report on the Irish language (based on the findings of the 2007-08 survey) was also published in 2009[6]. The main findings of that report are published in this book (see Chapter XVI).

It will be seen below that the current status of Irish is relatively high and there is overwhelming support in the national population for its preservation and revival. This new confidence in the people's own national language could be seen as a further weakening of our *'post-colonial attitudinal schizophrenia'* (see Mac Gréil 1996/97[7]), i.e. which is basically an inferiority complex *vis-à-vis* our former colonial masters. The importance of a good degree of confidence in our own cultural identity is a condition of inter-ethnic tolerance and pluralist integration. Being ashamed of one's own language and culture can contribute to prejudice and envy of those whose language and culture appear to be strong and firmly rooted. At the same time, it will be shown that there may be a degree of ambiguity in the majority of respondents' primary ethnic self-identity (see pages 164-6).

1.7 Religious Belief and Practice:

The link between religion and intergroup relations is basic. Religion can be both liberating and a source of intolerance. *Religious fundamentalism* can become a source of rationalisation which justifies the perception of minorities as inferior and even subhuman. Over the whole of recorded history, unwarranted persecution of minorities has often been justified in the name of fundamentalist religion. Religious fundamentalism is correlated with authoritarianism. Equally true has been the liberating role of religion in the promotion of human equality. Recent evidence has shown that religion (apart from fundamentalism) is generally a source of intergroup tolerance. Irreligious regimes such as **Nazi Germany** and **Stalinist Russia** have shown high levels of anti-Semitism, racism, ethnocentrism and other forms of prejudice, discrimination and merciless persecution by some extremely secular leaderships.

---

[6] Mac Gréil, Micheál, *The Irish Language and the Irish People*, MaNuad, Aonad Suirbhé agus Taighde, Ollscoil na hÉireann, MaNuad 2009.
[7] Mac Gréil, Micheál, *Prejudice in Ireland Revisited*, Maynooth, Survey and Research Unit, St Patrick's College, 1996, 97, pp 260/ff.

A special report of the findings of the religious variable surveyed in the 2007-08 survey has been published separately in 2009[8]. The relevant findings of that report are also included in this text (see Chapter XVII). It will be shown that there has been a *welcome reduction in prejudice* towards various religious categories, i.e. 'Agnostics', 'Atheists', 'Jews', 'Muslims', 'Protestants' and 'Roman Catholics'. The latter (Roman Catholics) are the largest demographically (89.6%) in the adult sample and would constitute statistically the 'dominant religious group' in the Republic. In the *Census Report of 2006*,[9] Roman Catholics made up 86.8% of the population or 92.4% of those declaring a religious affiliation in the Republic of Ireland.

The significance of religious tolerance in the Irish population is of special importance for two reasons, namely, the sad history of religious intolerance and the relatively high level of religiosity in the population. The religious group with the highest level of social distance towards it, i.e. the highest level of prejudice against them, are the members of the 'Muslim' minority. This is to be regretted because of the positive role 'Muslims' play in our society both as workers and as people who have strong family values. Our prejudice towards them, it would seem, is largely a vicarious prejudice absorbed from media stereotypes and association with the problems of the Middle East and the various high profile cases of Western-Arab conflict.

1.8 Social Anomie and Authoritarianism:

In every comprehensive national survey it is possible to find out many aspects of the people's psycho-socio-cultural profile. An examination of the many personal variables goes to explain variations in the level of prejudice. Two such traits are measured in this survey (as independent variables) which are also of interest in themselves, i.e. authoritarianism and social anomie.

Authoritarianism is a personality trait which is very closely correlated to social prejudice (see Adorno, *et al*[10]). This has been confirmed in the 1972-73 and the 1988-89 surveys carried out by the present author. The causes of authoritarianism are personal, social and cultural and

---

[8] Mac Gréil, Micheál, *The Challenge of Indifference: A Need for Religious Revival in Ireland*, Maynooth, Survey and Research Unit, Dept. of Sociology, NUI Maynooth, 2009.
[9] See *Census 2006 Report*, (2007).
[10] Adorno. T.W., Frenkel-Brunswick, E., Levinson, D.J., Sanford, R.W., (in collaboration with B. Aron, M.H. Levinson, and W. Morrow), *The Authoritarian Personality*, New York, Harpur, 1950.

are generally socio-culturally determined. There is no correlation between authoritarianism and intelligence. One of the best ways to prevent extreme social prejudice is by addressing the causes of authoritarianism in our education system and in the teaching of religion based on universal tolerance and respect and in the types of structures in society. Certain political ideologies seem to attract authoritarian leaders who seek uncritical followers.

Social anomie is a society-induced condition. The concept of 'social anomie' was developed by the eminent French sociologist, Emile Durkheim[11], to express *a sense of normlessness in the individual.* This has serious consequences for the person facing challenges in life. It is a measure of social and personal insecurity, arising from a sense of normlessness, which is accepted as a cause of social prejudice[12]. The causes of social anomie are largely to be found in rapid social change, the socialisation of the individual, the transmission of the basic norms of the culture, peer and social pressure and the influence of media. The internalisation of a moral code of behaviour by the individual and a commitment to it seems to be a way of reducing social anomie and pessimism in society. The rise of **suicide** in Irish society is likely to be correlated with the level of social anomie in recent years.

1.9 Other Personal Variables:
Other personal variables measured by the 2007-08 survey include: age, gender, educational achievement, occupational status, social-class position, social mobility, personal and household income, satisfaction with material standard of living, place of rearing and residence, political affiliation and competence in Irish and religiosity. Each of these variables provides valuable insights into the population of the Republic of Ireland at the beginning of the 21st century. It is intended to shed some light on each of them in the course of this text.

1.10 Conclusion:
It is hoped that the above paragraphs will help the reader to understand the context and general outline of the following text. The objective of the project is to measure and monitor Irish intergroup prejudice and tolerance and to continue exposing areas where the quality of life in Ireland is being

---

[11] Durkheim, Emile, *Suicide, a Study in Sociology*, New York, Free Press (1897), 1951.
[12] Srole, L. "Social Dysfunction, Personality and Social Distance Attitudes" paper read before *The American Sociological Society*, 1951.

greatly reduced by social prejudice in the hope that "a prejudice exposed is a prejudice undermined"!

Every serious social research project should add something of value to the reader's understanding of society and, thereby, enable him or her to cope more effectively with the day-to-day challenges of living in community – whether at work, enjoying leisure activities, at home with the family, worshipping one's God, or providing a voluntary public service. Social prejudice constricts the prejudiced and constrains those prejudiced against! It tends to destroy the 'victor' and the 'victim'!

This work marks *the third* in a series of social surveys of prejudice and tolerance, i.e. Greater Dublin Survey of 1972-73, National Survey of 1988-89 and the National Survey of 2007-08. The three survey reports are seen as 'benchmark' studies of prejudice in Ireland. It is to be hoped that the 'tradition' of monitoring Irish intergroup attitudes will continue in 2026-27 when it will be possible to confirm or reject the trends emerging from the findings of the 2007-08 National Survey. As our population becomes more pluralistically integrated (within and across our borders) it will be very necessary to be constantly on our guard against movements or developments which are conducive to bigotry or bias and discrimination against minorities within Irish society or relating to it. The present author is quite prepared "to hand-on the baton" of social survey researcher into prejudice and tolerance in Ireland in the years ahead and hopes that this text will contribute towards *"pluralist coexistence in Ireland"* for decades to come!

Every attempt has been made to present the findings in an objective manner according to the rules of survey research. The reader is given as much information as possible so that he or she can grasp the actual situation. The author's theoretical and other commentary can also be evaluated in the light of the evidence presented. Any shortcomings in the text are the author's. Hopefully, the reader will understand that total perfection in social research is well-nigh impossible. For the human scientist who reads this text, as stated already, the full data-files of the 1988-89 and 2007-08 national surveys will be available from the *Irish Social Science Data Archive (ISSDA)*[13].

---

[13] The ISSDA is "a joint initiative of University College Dublin and The Economic and Social Research Institute, Geary Institute, UCD, Belfield, *Baile Átha Cliath* 4, *Éire*".

Note: This text covers a wide range of topics, findings, commentaries and numerous statistical tables. An attempt has been made to construct chapters which can be read as separate units of findings and commentary. In this way the reader can select to focus on one topic at a time in such a way as to make the task of reading the whole text a gradual process. Hopefully, the final chapters, i.e. Chapters XIX, XX and XXI, will facilitate the bringing-together of the component units of findings and interpretations.

***

CHAPTER II
Minorities in the Republic of Ireland

The aim of the research which forms the main basis of this text, i.e. the 2007-08 national survey of intergroup attitudes and opinions, is *to describe, explore and explain the general prejudices of the people of the Republic of Ireland and to monitor changes in their ethnic, gender, political, racial, religious and social prejudices.* This means that the range of stimulus categories is likely to be wider than the current list of minorities resident in Ireland or encountered by every respondent in the national sample. Nevertheless, it is an important aspect of the level of social prejudice and tolerance as it relates to the extent to which respondents are exposed to *actual* contact with members of various minorities. Many respondents could have had contact with minorities when abroad or read or heard about them. Irish people, through emigration and foreign missionaries, have benefited from vicarious contact with a wide range of ethnic groups. The influence of foreign missionary contact with minorities in Africa, Asia, South and Central America and elsewhere has been beneficial as was shown in the 1972-73 findings[1].

Part I – Demographic Breakdown of Ethnic Minorities in Ireland

During the period since the previous survey of intergroup attitudes, i.e. 1988-89 to 2007-08, there has been a very significant change in the demographic make-up of the national population in relation to the coming to Ireland to work and stay of new ethnic, racial, religious and social minorities. Since 1901 (and before) the Republic of Ireland suffered from a continuous outflow of emigrants until a brief period in the 1970s (1971-81) when there was a net in-migration of **10,389** in a population of **2,978,248**, due to economic activity generated at home and poor socio-economic growth in Great Britain. Most of those who came to the Republic of Ireland in the 1970s were Irish emigrants returning home. This welcome change in population unfortunately reversed to a severe emigration loss of **20,606** during the decade 1981-91.

The size of the non-Irish resident population in the Republic of Ireland has changed substantially since 1991 **(6.1%)** to 1996 **(7.0%)** to 2002

---

[1] Mac Gréil, Micheál, *Prejudice and Tolerance in Ireland*, Dublin, CIR, 1977, page 246.

(10.4%)[2].   The proportion of non-Irish-born residents grew to **15%** in 2006[3].   It should be noted that a substantial percentage of immigrants to the Republic of Ireland prior to 1996 were born to emigrant Irish parents in the United Kingdom and to Irish parents in Northern Ireland.   Within Ireland there had been a degree of cross-border social (geographic) mobility during the period of the Troubles 1969-94.   Because of the division of Ireland in 1922, persons born in Northern Ireland and living in the Republic of Ireland (and *vice versa*) would be classified as those 'Irish-born outside the State'.

As stated in Chapter I, the demographic change which had taken place in the 1990s and the first seven years of the 21st century has been a most significant factor as regards intergroup attitudes.   Since *the contact* between those who came into Ireland would be *largely favourable*, i.e. they would become fellow-workers and, thereby, contribute to the nation's growth of prosperity, *it has been hypothesised that this would lead to a reduction in ethnic and racial prejudice and an increase in tolerance in the adult population.*   Also, the fact that the period between the mid-1990s and the time of the survey, i.e. November 2007 until March 2008, had been one of marked socio-economic security and this would also contribute to an increase in intergroup tolerance.   The relatively low level of tolerance in the 1988-'89 survey findings was, in part, explained by the socio-economic insecurity of the population due to high unemployment in the 1980s coupled with relatively high inflation[4].   The combination of greater socio-economic security and favourable contact with migrant workers coming to the Republic of Ireland should contribute to greater ethnic, racial and social tolerance.

The ethnic composition of the population of the Republic of Ireland is given in Table No. 2.1 below:

---

[2] McGinnity, F., O'Connell, P.J., Quinn, E. and Williams, J., *Migrants' Experience of Racism and Discrimination in Ireland*, Dublin ESRI, 2006, pp 2-5.
[3] *Report of 2006 Census*, Dublin, 2007.
[4] Mac Gréil, Micheál, *Prejudice in Ireland Revisited*, Maynooth, Survey and Research Unit, St Patrick's College, pp. 355ff.

Table No. 2.1:
Ethnic Composition of the Population of the Republic of Ireland – 2006

State / Country of Birth	Number	Percentage
1. Republic of Ireland	3,559,384	85.3%
2. Northern Ireland	50,172	1.2%
(Total Ireland)	**(3,609,556)**	**(86.5%)**
3. Great Britain	221,609	5.3%
4. Western Europe (EU)	45,496	1.1%
5. Eastern Europe (Incl. Non-EU)	140,003	3.4%
6. Other Non-EU Countries	8,726	0.2%
7. Africa	42,764	1.0%
8. Asia	55,628	1.3%
9. America (North, Central & South)	38,301	0.9%
10. Australia and New Zealand	9,017	0.2%
11. Other Countries	913	0.02%
Total	4,172,013	99.92%

Source: *Census 2006 Report,* Dublin 2007.

When those born in Ireland and residents born in Great Britain are added, one gets **91.8%.** Since most British-born living in Ireland are likely to be from families of Irish emigrants, this makes the Republic of Ireland overwhelmingly of Irish origin. Apart from migrants from Western and Eastern Europe, the spread of other ethnic groups is fairly thin, i.e. 1.3% or lower from any single Continent. Sometimes the impression is given that the influx of foreign migrants is much greater than it is on the ground. Talk about their being a threat to the jobs of the 'natives' is greatly exaggerated. It is, therefore, very important to present the actual figures and percentages as given on Table No. 2.1 to clarify the rumour and quell the fears of those who stir up hostility to the migrant worker when times get economically tough!

The change in migration patterns between 1996 and 2006 is very clear from Table No. 2.2 below. This decade embraces the so-called 'Celtic Tiger' period.

Table No. 2.2:
Change in Migration by Place of Birth – 1996-2006

Place of Birth	1996	2006	Change in Population	
			Number	Per Cent
1. Republic of Ireland	3,344,919	3,559,384	+214,465	+6.4%
2. Northern Ireland	39,567	50,172	+10,605	+26.8%
(Total Ireland)	(3,384,486)	(3,609,556)	(+225,070)	(+6.6%)
3. Great Britain	151,081	221,609	+70,528	+46.7%
4. Western Europe (EU)	19,232	45,496	+26,264	+136.6%
5. Other (Mainly Eastern) European Countries	3,605	148,729	+145,124	+4,025.6%
6. Elsewhere Abroad	38,139	146,623	+108,484	+284.4%
Total	3,596,543	4,172,013	+575,470	+16.0%

Source: *Census 2006 Report*, (2007), Dublin.

Few countries have ever experienced such an extraordinary change in in-migration and succeeded in integrating the relatively massive expansion in the influx of foreign-born people in the relatively short period of ten years. The State, both centrally and locally, achieved a most successful feat in accommodating such a relatively large increase, i.e. the rapid expansion of basic infrastructure and services to meet the needs of so many in so short a period of time. Social historians will study this period of socio-economic achievement as a case study of success, at least in the short term!

The unfortunate downturn in the economy in late 2008 could tend to overshadow what a relatively small and young State succeeded in doing in integrating so much expansion with no major social breakdown. This book is examining the effects of this increase in in-migration on intergroup attitudes (prejudice and tolerance) in the population. It will be shown that the Irish people became less prejudiced and more tolerant towards the various ethnic groups and categories who became in-migrants to the Republic of Ireland between 1996 and 2007-08. Normally, critics (the present author included) point to the failures in our society in the hope of bringing about improvements. Research into social prejudice tends to focus on weaknesses in human relationships. At the same time, when a people collectively (statutory and voluntary) succeed in integrating such an increase in population, as examined in Table No. 2.2 above, it would be wrong not to put its achievement on record. Hopefully, a serious research and analysis of the factors that made it possible will be undertaken and the archives are preserved for such a study. Of course, the tolerance of the people and their openness towards the stranger will feature as part of that study.

The distribution of migrants throughout the State was a positive feature of the in-migration in many ways. It prevented large ghettoes and it enabled the Irish people and the migrants to get to know each other better in favourable contexts. Table No. 2.3 gives a summary breakdown of the level of distribution of the in-migrant population. It should be noted and anticipated that normally the highest concentration of in-migrant workers would centre on locations or communities with suitable job opportunities. The following table examines the distribution of in-migrants proportionate to the population of each province. An interesting pattern emerges from Table No. 2.3:

Table No. 2.3:
Provincial Distribution of In-Migrants in 2006 by Place of Birth

Place of Birth	Province of Residence				Total Population
	Leinster	Munster	Connaught	Ulster	
1. Republic of Ireland	1,920,254 (53.9%)	1,005,067 **(28.2%)**	416,961 (11.7%)	217,102 (6.1%)	3,559,584 (99.9%)
2. Northern Ireland	25,646 (51.1%)	5,441 (10.8%)	4,602 (9.2%)	14,483 **(28.9%)**	50,172 (100.0%)
(Total Ireland)	(1,945,900) (53.9%)	(1,010,508) **(28.0%)**	(421,563) (11.7%)	(231,585) **(6.4%)**	(3,609,556) (100.0%)
3. Great Britain	99,033 (44.7%)	66,079 **(29.8%)**	37,689 **(17.0%)**	18,808 **(8.5%)**	221,609 (100.0%)
4. Poland	35,487 **(56.2%)**	18,180 **(28.8%)**	7,239 (11.5%)	2,184 (3.5%)	63,090 (100.0%)
5. Lithuania	15,338 **(61.8%)**	4,841 (19.5%)	2,005 (8.1%)	2,624 **(10.6%)**	24,808 (100.0%)
6. Other EU	49,021 **(62.2%)**	19,190 (24.3%)	7,809 (9.9%)	2,790 (3.5%)	78,810 (99.9%)
7. Other Europe	19,915 **(72.4%)**	5,149 (18.7%)	1,763 (6.4%)	690 (2.5%)	27,517 (100.0%)
8. U.S.A.	11,749 (46.7%)	7,105 **(28.2%)**	4,662 **(18.5%)**	1,665 **(6.6%)**	25,181 (100.0%)
9. Africa	30,368 **(71.0%)**	8,184 (19.1%)	3,049 (7.1%)	1,145 (2.7%)	42,764 (99.9%)
10. Asia	40,713 **(73.2%)**	9,426 (16.9%)	4,002 (7.2%)	1,487 (2.7%)	55,628 (100.0%)
11. Other Countries	13,716 **(59.5%)**	4,773 (20.7%)	3,791 **(16.4%)**	770 (3.3%)	23,050 (99.9%)
Total	2,261,258 **(54.2%)**	1,153,435 **(27.6%)**	493,572 **(11.8%)**	263,748 **(6.3%)**	4,172,013 (99.9%)

Note: Percentages above average are in **bold**.
Source: Census 2006 Report.

Despite the substantial dispersion of the in-migrants, there is an obvious concentration in the province of **Leinster**, where the main economic activity took place during the 'Celtic Tiger' decade. **Connaught** and **Ulster's** share of in-migrants reflect the lower than national average rate of economic growth. The main proportionate concentration of in-migrants from **Africa** and **Asia** are in Leinster while those from **Great Britain** and the **United States of America** opted for the other provinces. This would reflect the areas in Ireland from which Irish emigrants left in large numbers in the past. The highest proportion of residents reared in Northern Ireland were obviously living in the three counties of Ulster, i.e. Cavan, Donegal and Monaghan. This is, in part, probably as a result of 'Troubles' over the years in parts of Northern Ireland.

The prominence of in-migration from Eastern European countries was facilitated by the expansion of the EU in 2004 and the decision of the Irish Government to open its doors to workers from the new member-States. The relatively few migrants from countries outside the EU was partly due to the 'fortress policy' of the Brussels's administration to restrict those seeking work and economic improvement to the 'developed' economies of the EU. This policy was rather ironic in the case of Ireland and other European countries whose sons and daughters had been *economic migrants* to North America, Australia and New Zealand for over a century! "Eaten bread was soon forgotten"!

Part II – Experience of Ethnic Minorities in Ireland

The policy of the Irish Government to spread the in-migration around the country (as evident from Table No. 2.3 above) prevented, as noted earlier, over-concentration in particular local communities in general. This should have a positive impact overall and prevent the impression of 'swamping' which gives an exaggerated impression of the proportion of the population who makes up the in-migrants. It also prevents the build-up of large ghettoes of foreigners which lead to the minimum degree of integration and less favourable contact. This is not to deny the need for foreign workers and in-migrants to have the support of fellow-country people with whom to socialise and maintain their legitimate pluralist identity. The Irish emigrants needed such support when they emigrated to Britain, the United States and elsewhere. Many, if not most, of the recent in-migrants to the Republic of Ireland had the additional problem of language differences (which most of the Irish did not have when they emigrated to English-speaking countries). Support of fellow countrymen and countrywomen is necessary and understandable at least for one or two generations. It is good to see the emergence of ethnic shops and clubs, which accommodate migrant workers and their families in Ireland. Facilities for worship are also very important especially for those of the Orthodox, Muslim and other religions not served in the Republic heretofore.

An area of potential discrimination is that of workers' rights, i.e. pay and conditions. This is particularly true of immigrants from outside the European Union. Trade unions and others have expressed concern about the control of individual employers over certain categories of work, e.g. domestic service, horticulture, construction, and others.

The special study (referred to already) carried out in the Republic of Ireland by McGinnity, O'Connell, Quinn and Williams (2006) on behalf of the Economic and Social Research Institute for the European Union Monitoring Centre on Racism and Xenophobia has interesting findings in relation to perceived racism and discrimination by immigrants in October 2005. This was a time of very successful economic development in Ireland. The report was entitled *Migrants' Experience of Racism and Discrimination in Ireland.* The in-migrants were classified under five categories[5].

Table No. 2.4:   Non-EU Migrants Sample

	Total Number		Asylum Seekers		Work Permits	
1. Black & Other South/Central African	301	(27.6%)	271	(64.5%) **90.0%**	30	(4.5%) **10.0%**
2. White South/Central African	38	(3.5%)	3	(0.7%) **7.9%**	35	(5.2%) **92.1%**
3. North African	66	(6.1%)	49	(11.7%) **74.2%**	17	(2.5%) **25.8%**
4. Asian	424	(38.9%)	49	(11.7%) **11.6%**	375	(56.1%) **88.4%**
5. Non-EU East European	260	(23.9%)	48	(11.4%) **18.5%**	212	(31.7%) **81.5%**
Total Sample	1,089	(100.0%)	420	(38.6%)	669	(61.4%)

Source: McGinnity, *et al*.   *Note*: Percentages **in bold** added.

The above categories excluded "EU and American nationals, all illegal immigrants, most refugees, migrants on student visas, migrants on work authorisation visas and dependants of legal residents"[6]. To the extent that the above distribution is an accurate representation of the actual numbers of asylum seekers and those with work permits can only be gauged from Table No. 2.1 (page 17 above). The racialist lesson of the distribution

---

[5] McGinnity, O'Connell, Quinn and Williams, *Op. Cit.*
[6] *Ibid*, Page 13.

J164203

21

of asylum seekers by category is fairly stark, i.e. Black and other South/Central Africans are **90%** asylum seekers and only **10%** with work permits, while White South/Central Africans are **7.9%** asylum seekers and **92.1%** with work permits. On the face of it there seems to be a greater reluctance to give permits to Black in-migrants (in contrast to the total distribution of 27.6%)!

It is also noteworthy that the North Africans are also predominantly asylum-seekers at **74.2%**. The 'principle of racial propinquity' seems to be operating! It will be confirmed in Chapter IV that this principle is also present in the 2007-08 survey where **81.3%** of the national sample would welcome *'Euro-Americans'* (i.e. White Americans) into the family through marriage and only **52.7%** would welcome *'Afro-Americans'* (i.e. Black Americans) into kinship (see Table No. 4.1, pages 62-4). Such racism is insidious and invidious!

Another interesting feature of the McGinnity, *et al*, survey is the type of situations where asylum seekers and other in-migrants experienced racism[7] and discrimination[8]. "Harassment on the street and in public transport" as well as "harassment at work" were the most prevalent forms of unwarranted counter-behaviour.

Table No. 2.5: Experience of Racism and Discrimination

Percentage of Respondents	Specified Occasions
1. 30 – 35%	Harassment on the street and public transport
	Harassment at work
2. 20 – 25%	Missed job
3. 15 – 20%	Badly treated by emigration services
	Badly treated in shop or restaurant
	Missed promotion
	Harassed by neighbour
	Denied credit / loan
	Denied housing
4. 10 – 15%	Badly treated by social services
	Badly treated by health care
	Refused entry to restaurant
	Badly treated by Gardaí
	Victim of violent crime
5. 5 – 10%	Badly treated by employment services
6. 0 – 5%	Refused entry to shop

Source: McGinnity *et al,* Fig. 5.1, page 33.

---

[7] The use of the concept 'racism' is **not precise** in the McGinnity *et al* report, i.e. it seems to include ethnocentrism as well as racism, which is to be discouraged in the pursuit of accurate and precise conceptual frameworks.

[8] *Ibid*, see Figure 5.1, page 33.

When evaluating Table No. 2.5, it is important to keep in mind the percentage of respondents who recorded the different forms of discrimination. Public harassment "on the streets and public transport" is ignorant and irresponsible and should be monitored closely by Gardaí, Church leaders and the 'critical' media commentators. **Intergroup relations** should become part of the curriculum of primary and second-level schools to remove the ignorance dimension of the problem.

"Harassment at work" is also to be regretted. The important roles of trade unions and of management in this area cannot be exaggerated. At around 33% or one-third of respondents, this level of discrimination and hostile ridicule is intolerable. It is poor thanks for the contribution to the wealth of Irish society made by our migrant workers! Over 20% of respondents in the special study felt they "missed jobs" because of prejudice against them. This is very serious and unjust.

One of the findings of the special study carried out by McGinnity *et al*[9] was that immigrants to Ireland were highly educated:

> "Overall, over half of the sample of this survey had attended tertiary education, and these findings are consistent with previous research on the educational attainment of immigrants" (see Barrett *et al*[10]) ... The most highly educated group are 'East Europeans', seventy-one percent of whom attended tertiary education."[11]

The relatively high educational achievement standards of the immigrants in the sample of the current 2007-08 survey is given on Table No. 8.9, page 169 below.

The reverse side of this influx of highly educated immigrants, many of whom come from poorer countries than Ireland, is *the serious loss to their countries of origin* of their valuable and necessary contribution to the development of the home communities. They must have become a serious *brain drain* on their societies of origin. In times of high emigration from Ireland, the development of local communities in this country suffered from the leaving of talented men and women and their making their contribution to the relatively strong communities in Britain, the United States, Australia

---

[9] *Op.Cit.*, page 25.
[10] Barrett, A., Bergin, A, and Duffy, D. "The Labour Market Characteristics and Labour Market Impact on Immigrants to Ireland", *ESRI Seminar Paper*, Dublin 2005.
[11] *Ibid.*, page 25

and elsewhere. Within Ireland the migration of talented people from the West of Ireland and the Midlands into the strong communities in Dublin and elsewhere has left Ireland with unbalanced regional development. The net beneficiary of worker migration is the host society while the society of origin remains the net loser. Of course, the remittances sent home by migrant workers is a valuable contribution to their families and communities, in times of material need. Ideally, highly qualified people should be encouraged to remain in their countries of origin and contribute to the social and economic development of those countries in times of economic weakness! They are best qualified to spearhead socio-economic development.

Where our in-migrants worked is reflective of the nature of the expansion in the Irish economy. The Immigrant Council of Ireland published a breakdown of the areas of employment of immigrants who received work permits between 1995 and 2005. The following Table tells where those from outside the EEA, i.e. outside the EU, were seeking employment:

Table No. 2.6:
Total and New Work Permits Issued 1995 – 2005[12]

Sector of Industry	Number	Percentage
1. Service Industry	14,571	42.8%
2. Catering	8,306	24.4%
3. Agriculture and Fisheries	3,701	10.9%
4. Medical and Nursing	2,469	7.3%
5. Industry	2,174	6.4%
6. Entertainment	963	2.8%
7. Domestic	772	2.3%
8. Education	717	2.1%
9. Sport	207	0.6%
10. Exchange Agreements	167	0.5%
Total	34,047	100.1%

Source: Department of Enterprise, Trade and Employment

---

[12] Immigrant Council of Ireland, *"Background Information and Statistics on Immigration to Ireland"*, June 2005.

According to Ruhs, a majority of work permits issued to Non-EU Nationals were "for employment in relatively low-skilled and/or low-wage occupations, especially in the service sector"[13] (quoted by the Immigration Council of Ireland document of June 2005). Non-European Nationals' work is quite visible in the services (including construction) and catering sector. Many are dealing with the public in shops, bars, restaurants, etc. Other non-EU nationals employed in hospitals are doctors and nurses with much favourable contact with Irish people. In recent years a number of priests, nuns and other religious ministers have come to work in Ireland and compensate for the decline in religious vocations at home in the Republic.

The role of the *media* (including the *Internet*) has been highlighted by Catherine Lynch in her European Network against Racism (ENAR) Report of 2007[14]. Her comment on the media's role is worth quoting:

> "The media can play a positive and negative role in the struggle against racism. In fact, the media is a key mechanism in bringing our attention to racist incidents and crime. It is also a powerful mechanism for the promotion of positive images of ethnic minority groups. … However, it can also play a negative role. In the Irish context this negative role has included scapegoating and inciting hatred against ethnic minority groups through scaremongering, biased and inaccurate reporting."

Part III – Sequential Cycle of Acting-Out Prejudice (Allport)

Before proceeding with the presentation and explanation of the findings, it may be worthwhile addressing the likely **effects** of social prejudice on the **behaviour** of the people. This highlights the urgency of addressing this negative phenomenon (prejudice) in Irish and other societies. The Allport sequential cycle of acting-out prejudice seems to the present author to be a valid assessment of the consequences of social prejudice.

Gordon Allport listed *"anti-locution"* as the first behavioural expression of social prejudice in a sequential five-stage path leading to

---

[13] Ruhs, M. *"Managing the Immigration and Employment of European Non-Nationals in Ireland"*, Dublin, Policy Institute, Trinity College Dublin, 2005.

[14] Lynch, Catherine, *ENAR Shadow Report: Racism* in Ireland*, Brussels, European Network Against Racism, 2008, pp 23/24. (*Note: The concept **racism** is not used in its strictly scientific sense but rather covers ethnocentrism and class prejudice.)

expulsion and genocide. The five stages of acting out social prejudice are as follows:

> Stage One: *"Anti-locution" or ridicule;*
> Stage Two: *"Avoidance" or shunning;*
> Stage Three: *"Discrimination" often confirmed by law or custom, i.e. "segregation";*
> Stage Four: *"Physical attack" or "roughing-up";*
> Stage Five: *"Extermination" or "expulsion"*[15].

1. Anti-Locution or Ridicule:

Probably the easiest stage at which to intervene is at stage one, i.e. *'Anti-locution'* or ridicule. Very strict enforcement of anti-defamation laws is critical. In the Republic of Ireland, the State has outlawed public utterances which are likely to lead to "incitement to hatred" against members of minorities. Such utterances may occur in the media, in the theatre or elsewhere. Negative ethnic or racial jokes spoken by comedians at 'gigs', in pubs or clubs are outlawed in Irish legislation[16], if they are likely to lead to 'incitement to hatred'.

People should be very careful at the informal level to avoid derogatory or belittling remarks about members of minorities. Negative stereotypes are circulated in this manner. Generalisations about negative behaviour and traits are often 'given legs' by careless talk. As justification one hears such phrases as: *"Sure everyone knows they are all at it!"* The use of 'everyone knows' is an attempt to give the impression of 'universal support' for the allegation. *'They are all at it'* is an attempt to ascribe the negative trait or behaviour, which may be true of a few, to all members of the minority. "Bad-mouthing" is quite a common expression of social prejudice. Even in the privileged area of the *Dáil* and *Seanad* debating, i.e. in Parliament, it is possible to hear 'anti-locution' and 'ridicule' about groups. The Irish were at the wrong end of such behaviour in the British House of Commons in the past. Catholics were the victims of venomous 'anti-locution' in the Irish Houses of Parliament in the 17th and 18th century[17].

---

[15] Allport, Gordon, *The Nature of Prejudice*, Boston, Beacon, 1954.
[16] *Prohibition of Incitement to Hatred Act, 1989.*
[17] Burke, William P., *Irish Priests in Penal Times 1660-1760*, Waterford, 1914.

English media in the nineteenth and early twentieth century have been notorious at times in its portrayal of the Irish peasants as atavistic, e.g. the magazine *Punch*. Some commentators today criticise the accepted practice of correctly describing different categories of people to avoid sexism, ethnocentrism, anti-Semitism, racism, etc., as unnecessary 'political correctness'. They are incorrect in such criticism because of the need to curtail anti-locution in the interest of pluralist integration. Some political cartoonists and others use racist physiognomic distortions to ridicule leaders, which is not to be commended.

2. Avoidance or Shunning:

The second stage in the sequential cycle of acting-out of social prejudice is *'avoidance' or shunning*. This has widespread negative consequences for members of minorities. It leads to involuntary 'ghettoisation' into areas of residence, usually in the most deprived sections of our towns and cities. It also affects access to normal education, since the parents of the dominant group may not wish their children to associate with minority parents' children. Jobs-stratification is also facilitated by the dominant posture of 'avoidance', e.g. the Chinese laundry workers in the United States in the early 20th century. 'Avoidance' in religious worship, even among Christians is part of the shunning process and contradicts the norm of universal charity proclaimed by Christian and other religions.

When 'anti-locution' is not curtailed, the public image of the minority becomes unattractive to the dominant group, and personal contact with members of the minority is greatly reduced. This is the opposite to favourable contact which is accepted by serious students of intergroup relations as *the most effective way of reducing and undermining prejudice*. Rumours and negative gossip about the minority members who have been shunned may begin to circulate which can give the minority an even dangerous reputation among the dominant group, who are made ignorant of their true traits and positive qualities, resulting from their (dominant group's) posture of 'avoidance', e.g. the distorted reputation of the Travelling People in Ireland who have been shunned for generations.

How to intervene to reduce or prevent 'avoidance' as a dominant posture is more difficult than curtailing 'anti-locution'. The cooperation of both statutory and voluntary bodies is necessary at the community level. Groups such as Churches and places of prayer and assembly can help by being inclusive. Sports and entertainment bodies should also be inclusive because talent crosses minority-dominant lines. With regard to education, housing, employment and participation in public life, it is very important that they are made inclusive by the State and Local Government.

It should be noted that separation of minority members from the dominant group can be a voluntary response (of the minority) in order to maintain cultural or religious pluralism and prevent involuntary assimilation with the dominant culture. This may be part of the requirements of maintaining integrated pluralism. Also, in times of immigration, migrants from different cultures need the support of each other to survive and overcome language and certain differences. This is especially true of first-generation migrants, e.g. the Irish in London and other cities in the past.

It is imperative that involuntary 'avoidance' (or 'shunning') of members of minorities is discontinued in the interests of good intergroup relations. The dominant group in society is obliged to seek to integrate all its minorities (without forcing assimilation). The creation of structural and other occasions conducive to 'favourable contact' is probably the best way everyone can contribute to non-avoidance. Any form of imposed stratification to facilitate avoidance should be outlawed in minority rights' legislation. Voluntary community-based groups such as religious, sports, cultural and environmental organisations need to be strictly inclusive, within the requirements of pluralism. Shunning and involuntary 'avoidance' was an integral part of the *Apartheid Regime* in South Africa prior to the emancipation of the 'Black and Coloured people'.

3. Discrimination and Segregation:
The third stage in the acting-out of the prejudice cycle is discrimination which could be defined as: *selective negative behaviour towards members of a minority group because of their membership of such a group or category.* The step from 'avoidance' to 'discrimination' is true of all situations of dominant-minority relations which have been studied to date, that is, where there is nothing effective being done to counter involuntary 'avoidance' and 'anti-locution'.

'Discrimination' takes place in two main areas of life, i.e. residence and employment. From these flow other forms of discrimination, namely, in education, recreation, political participation, religious practice, prohibited intermarriage and (when discrimination is sanctioned by law or custom, i.e. segregation) equal access to the law. Discrimination leads to 'lower class' and even 'underclass' status in society in the case of most minorities. This adds an extra type of prejudice to the members of the minorities be they ethnic, racial, religious, etc., i.e. *class prejudice.*

Minority-rights' legislation has improved over the past sixty years, since the discovery of the outrageous discrimination and segregation unearthed in Nazi Germany, Stalinist Russia, the Deep South of the United States, Apartheid in South Africa, and other less notorious situations. *The United Nations Charter of Human Rights* was a response to World War II. In Ireland we have had to suffer much, especially in Northern Ireland, from segregation against nationalists and Roman Catholics following the partition of the country in 1922 until the latter decades of the twentieth century. There are still very serious cases of segregation in a number of countries throughout the world, e.g. in Israel and certain Muslim countries and in other places with restrictive access to ruling elites. Segregation in the case of women is still a serious issue in large parts of the world.

When desegregation, i.e. the removal of legal sanctions for discrimination, takes place in a society, it is usually followed by minority-rights' legislation. This is a major step forward and an essential part of the protection of members of minorities. Of course, such changes in legislation need vigilant and conscientious enforcement by Gardaí and police and strict application in the courts. The courts have a key role in applying equality legislation in defence of minorities which, unfortunately, does not always happen. When the courts do not apply the law equally or police fail to enforce minority rights' legislation, persecution of vulnerable members of minorities is open to exploitation resulting in their deprivation. This raises a challenge to juries in criminal cases involving members of minorities.

Even when desegregation has taken place and the police and courts enforce and apply the law conscientiously, informal discrimination can and does continue in society. Our behaviour towards others is always influenced by our prejudices and our social preferences, hence the importance of raising awareness of attitudes which are prejudiced and the injustice of discrimination.

4. Physical Attack or Roughing-Up:

This is the fourth stage of Allport's sequential cycle of acting-out social prejudice, if 'anti-locution', 'avoidance' and 'discrimination' are not dealt with appropriately by responsible citizens of the dominant group in society. It is called physical attack or *'roughing-up'*. A classic example of this form of behaviour was that of the Ku Klux Klan in the Deep South of the United States when they visibly attacked Black People (behind the 'burning cross' and special garb or vestments) "to keep the 'niggers' in their place"! Here in Ireland there has been the occasional 'roughing-up' of a Travellers' campsite. In Germany, in the early days of the Nazi Regime, Jews were physically attacked in the ghettoes. 'Gay-bashing' is a classic expression of the acting-out of *homophobia* in society at the 'roughing-up' stage. For the vulnerable members of the minority it is often an experience similar to that of a *'reign of terror'*. The recent raids on the people of Gaza by the Israeli armoured army must have felt like being victims of *'reign of terror'*. The vulnerable Israelis suffering from indiscriminate rocket attacks from Hamas paramilitaries is also (but to a much lesser extent) an example of 'roughing-up'. The burning and destroying of people's houses or places of residence is another cowardly way of 'roughing-up'. The destruction of places of worship and the desecration of tombs and gravestones are typical examples of the brutal and callous behaviour called 'roughing-up'.

When such activity happens in a society, it is essential that effective and forceful intervention takes place promptly. In the Allport cycle this is the penultimate stage before 'extermination' and 'expulsion' of the minority. Failure to intervene by the State raises serious questions of dereliction of its duty to its citizens. International intervention to prevent physical attack of minorities when the State fails may be necessary, i.e. by the United Nations. There can be no compromise where people are being attacked physically because of who they are. The legitimacy of the State itself is at stake if it allows, much less engages in, the physical attack on minorities. The sad fact is that 'physical attack' on minority members and on their domestic property has been and, unfortunately, still is quite universal where dominant-minority relations are not equitably resolved. One of the obvious consequences for the dominant groups of their practising 'physical attack' on the minority, e.g. the anti-Nationalist/Catholic Riots in Belfast and Derry in 1969 and the Bloody Sunday murders in Derry in 1972, is the generation of a paramilitary response from the outraged members of the minority. At the end of the day, the 'dominant group' stands to lose even more than the 'minority' as a result of their toleration of 'physical attack' on the members of minorities.

5. Extermination or Expulsion:

The *final stage* of the acting-out of social prejudice is the *extermination or expulsion of the members of the minority from the country.* The great tragedy is that this has happened down through history. Even in biblical writings we see expulsion of peoples taking place from time to time. In the United States of America we had terrible examples of attempts to exterminate and to expel the Native Americans and to even glorify in their 'ethnic cleansing' to make way for the European occupiers and planters and their descendants. Most countries have experienced attempts of conquerors to invade their territory and replace the indigenous ethnic population with varied degrees of severity from *genocide* to *expulsion.* Ireland has had its history of invasions and plantations followed by ethnic cleansing, e.g. *the Cromwellian Act of Settlement in 1654.*

The horrific 'final solution' of the Nazi Government to exterminate the Jews was the most notorious example of genocide in recent history, which is aptly named as the *'Holocaust'.* It marked the final stage of the acting-out of Anti-Semitism in Germany. Most ethnic groups in the Balkan States have suffered expulsion, mainly for ethnico-religious reasons, over the past one hundred years. Inter-religious prejudice has been acted out more than once in this troubled area on the shores of the Adriatic Sea.

At last, today there is an acceptance of 'ethnic cleansing' and 'genocide' as crimes against humanity, which are sanctioned and tried by the International Court of Human Rights. Unfortunately, not every country has 'signed up' to this court, but most have. As it evolves and is seen not to be just a *Victors' Court*, it will gain universal credibility. Also, it does not apply the death penalty which gives it even greater credibility and a humane character. Ever since World War II, there has been a growing awareness of the evil of 'genocide' and 'ethnic cleansing'. Since the decolonisation of the British and other empires, there have been intertribal acts of expulsion and attempts at wholesale extermination. The African Continent has suffered from this post-colonial tragedy. The expansion of the Muslim religion into Central Africa and elsewhere in Eastern Europe and parts of Asia has, unfortunately, led to similar tragic episodes of attempted ethnic-cleansing and occasionally widespread extermination, both against Muslim people and by them against members of other religious beliefs. The intervention of Western military powers has not always been neutral, especially in the supply of conventional weapons of mass destruction to certain countries. The most honourable role has been played by the United Nations (whenever the major powers agreed).

6. Conclusion:

In conclusion, it is hoped that the above presentation of Allport's five-stage acting-out of social prejudice makes clear to the reader the need for every serious citizen to act to prevent the deterioration of the cycle before it becomes too late. *The rights of others must take precedence over any privileges.* Intervention by law and its rigorous enforcement and application are critical. Any ideology or religious doctrine that is incapable of coexistence with other political views or religions must be suspect. History has taught us all its lessons at an appalling human cost. With the presence of the United Nations Human Rights' Department, there is some hope that the Allport Cycle will become checked more effectively at its early stages. We in Ireland have made a significant contribution to that department through the numerous instances of our Defence Forces' intervention in Peace Missions and through the pro-peace leadership of Irish political leaders (of all main parties), not to mention the positive and courageous work of our former President, **Mary Robinson**, who served as the United Nations' Human Rights' Commissioner in the recent past.

The purpose of this text is to contribute to people's awareness of our social prejudices and to monitor changes in a wide range of biases against various minorities. Perhaps, at some stage, major research should be carried out on the **acting-out** of our prejudices in a systematic and objective manner. The above reflection on the acting-out of social prejudice has been included at this early stage in the text to alert the reader's attention to the vital seriousness of the quality of our intergroup attitudes which is the main subject of subsequent chapters.

***

CHAPTER III
Theory and Methodology

The following is largely an extract from Chapter II of *Prejudice in Ireland Revisited* by the current author. Some additions and omissions have been made where appropriate in the light of new developments in the field of sociology, social psychology and social anthropology. Also, the new socio-cultural environment in Ireland may require new concepts and theoretical explanations, i.e. based on serious empirical research.

Part I – Conceptual Framework

As in most areas of study in the human sciences there is an absence of unanimity among authors as to the definition of key concepts used in intergroup attitudes research. For that reason, therefore, it is imperative that the key concepts and terms used in this work are defined at this stage.

The function of a precise conceptual framework is to provide the reader and the researcher with a coherent set of terms which enable the accurate diagnosis of phenomena and provide the basis for research and categories for empirical measurement. Adherence to a more precise use of the concepts selected is also essential for the validity of the findings.

1.1 The Key Concepts Defined:
Prejudice is the principal concept of this study and is primarily classified as a (social) psychological topic. Few concepts have received so much attention from a wide range of social psychologists. Since prejudice is a particular type of **social attitude**, it is, therefore, necessary at this stage to attempt a comprehensive definition of social attitudes.

Because social attitudes have a strong social and cultural dimension, it is also necessary to attempt a definition of the concepts: **society** and **culture**. To complete the psycho-socio-cultural framework, it will also be necessary to define the concept: **personality**. These five terms, i.e. social attitude, social prejudice, society, culture and personality constitute the basic set of general concepts which are at the core of this study.

There are, in addition, a number of specific concepts which require some clarification for the reader at this stage. They fall into two categories, namely, *types* of social prejudice and intergroup *postures and responses*.

With regard to intergroup postures and responses, students of dominant-minority relations have noted a range of postures adopted by dominant groups and responses made by minority groups. **Dominant groups** are defined as *those collectivities or categories of people who exercise excessive and disproportionate degrees of power and influence over other groups living in the same society.* **Minority groups** are *those groups who exercise a degree of power and influence which is less than equity would require.* Dominant and minority groups are not classified according to numerical strength. A numerical majority can be a sociological minority group, e.g., the Black People in South Africa prior to their liberation.

The concepts to be included as *postures and/or responses* are: conflict, accommodation, avoidance, assimilation, amalgamation, discrimination, segregation, stratification and pluralism. Two other postures are also adopted from time to time in situations of intergroup conflicts, i.e. annihilation (genocide) and expulsion (transplantation or ethnic cleansing).

1.2 Definition of Social Prejudice:

Ann Weber in her text, *Social Psychology,* defines prejudice as: "an attitude (usually negative) about people based on their membership of a particular social group". (Weber, 1992, p.198) This very general and, at the same time, concise definition identifies prejudice as an attitude based on a perception of group membership. Weber goes on to state that prejudice "involves stereotyping, social categorisation of people, and acceptance of social norms that favour prejudice. Prejudice is acquired through learning, as part of normal socialization, and in developing social identity through group membership." (*Ibid*, p.211)

The American social psychologist, Gordon Allport, a leading authority on social prejudice, defined it thus:

> "An avertive or hostile attitude towards a person who belongs to a group, simply because he (she) belongs to that group, and is therefore presumed to have the objectionable qualities ascribed to that group....... It is an antipathy based on a faulty and inflexible generalisation." (Allport, 1954, pp. 8, 10)

Allport's definition adds a number of further points to Ann Weber's definition and description of prejudice, i.e.

(a) Avertive or hostile nature of the attitude;
(b) Presumption of the group's ascribed negative qualities defining the persons prejudiced against;
(c) Faulty and inflexible generalisation.

Elliot Aronson, in his highly acclaimed book, *The Social Animal* (3rd edition, 1980, pp. 195 ff), emphasises the role of generalisations or stereotyping in his definition of prejudice: "We will define prejudice as a hostile and negative attitude toward a distinguishable group based on generalisations derived from faulty or incomplete information." (Aronson, 1980, p.197)

The following operational definition draws together the notes of Allport's definition and that of a number of other authors:

Social prejudice is a hostile (antipathetic), rigid and negative attitude towards a person, group, collectivity or category, because of the negative qualities ascribed to the group, collectivity or category, based on faulty and stereotypical information and inflexible generalisations.

This summary definition is an adaptation of the one given in *Prejudice and Tolerance in Ireland* (Mac Gréil), p.9) [1]. The points made in relation to the 1977 definition are still valid although the scope is broadened somewhat. The operation of prejudice towards the *"group, collectivity or category"* is normally exercised in the case of social prejudice towards the individual, but there are incidents of prejudice being exercised towards the "group, collectivity or category" at one remove from a personal encounter. For example, a residential or community group's prejudice towards a group of Travellers, or towards Travellers as a collectivity or category without any contact with an individual Traveller.

The use of the phrase: *"based on faulty and stereotypical information"* instead of: "as a result of selective, obsolete and faulty evidence" has been seen to be a more accurate definition of the

---

[1] 1977 Summary Definition: "Social prejudice is a negative, hostile, rigid and emotional attitude towards a person simply because he/she is perceived to belong to a group and is presumed to possess the negative qualities ascribed to the group as a result of selective, obsolete and faulty evidence." (Mac Gréil, 1977, p.9)

rationalisation of prejudice. The new version re-emphasises Allport's emphasis on "faulty generalisation" and points to the fact that the actual person or group who happens to be the focus of the prejudice does not come into the reckoning in the situation. The justification to self, i.e., rationalisation of the prejudice, is founded in the "faulty and stereotypical information".

Finally, the addition of *"inflexible generalisations"* is added from Allport's definition. It reinforces the rigidity of prejudices as social attitudes. Unlike the negative attitudes which are responsive to changes in information and wants, prejudices are frequently change-resistant and can survive in spite of having no rational basis. Prejudices become deeply rooted in the culture and in the social structure – not to mention in the interpersonal response traits.

1.3 Definition of Social Attitudes:
Since social prejudice is a particular type of negative attitude, it shares most of the characteristics of attitudes. Few concepts in social psychology have received more attention than that of attitudes. Despite all that is written, it is not easy to decide on a clear and comprehensive definition of social attitudes. The approach adopted in this text is based mainly on a structural-functional understanding of social attitudes.

D.W. Rajecki in his book, *Attitudes* (1990), uses Allport's definition as the basic definitional course.

> "Gordon W. Allport, an eminent social psychologist, provided an early and comprehensive definition of attitudes. 'An attitude is a mental and neural state of readiness, organised through experience, exerting a directive or dynamic influence upon the individual's response to all objects and situations with which it is related'." (Allport, 1935) (Rajecki, 1990, p.4)

The extent to which this definition of over seventy years ago is still relevant is very obvious. The tens of thousands of books and articles written on attitudes (Rajecki 1990, p.7) in the meantime have not been able to add that much to the original Allport definition. It is clear from the above definition that an attitude is seen to be:

    (a)   A disposition, i.e., "a mental and neural state of readiness";
    (b)   The product of experience;
    (c)   An influence on behaviour, i.e., "exerting a directive or dynamic influence upon the individual's response to all objects and situations with which it is related".

1.3.a The Structural Approach: The approaches adopted to the definition of social attitudes in *Prejudice and Tolerance in Ireland* (Mac Gréil, 1977, pp. 11-28) were two-fold, i.e. structural and functional.   The structural definition may be defined as follows:

> *Attitudes are positive or negative dispositions towards foci composed of evaluations, feelings and behavioural tendencies.*

This proved to be a highly useful (operational) definition because of its measurable components.   It was also confirmed in the findings of the 1972-73 and 1988-89 surveys that there was a strong correlation between the valency of each of the components, especially in the case of more extreme attitudes, i.e., when evaluations of the focus were "bad", feelings towards it tended towards "dislike" of the object of the attitudes and there was a behavioural tendency to "hinder" or "attack" the focus.   Because of this internal consistency it was possible to assess the valency of the whole attitude from a measurement of one of its components. For instance, **social distance** or the closeness to which people were prepared to admit numbers of various ethnic, racial, religious, political or social groups, collectivities or categories was seen also as a measure of the **behavioural disposition** component of the attitudes and, thereby, also a measure of the whole attitude or prejudice toward the particular focus or stimulus category.

Roger Brown's descriptive definition of the concept "attitude" was included in the 1977 publication.   It too was quite comprehensive and worth repeating here:

> "An attitude has always a focus; it may be a person, a group, a nation, a product, anything whatever really.   When the focus is known to many as in the case of statesmen, ethnic groups, and nations, the corresponding attitude can be used for the comparative characterisation of many persons.   The dimension of characterisation extends from positive (or favourable) through neutrality to negative (or unfavourable). Persons are thought of as occupying positions on this dimension corresponding to their disposition to behave favourably or unfavourably towards the focus." (Brown, R., 1965, p. 420)
>
> (Mac Gréil, 1977, p. 11)

Figure No. 3.1 demonstrates the structural nature of attitudes and illustrates the valency of attitudes.

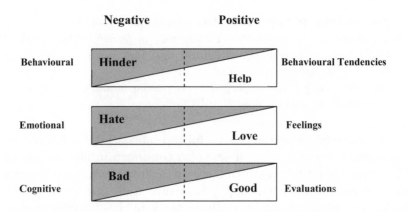

Figure No. 3.1: Components of Social Attitudes

Figure No. 3.1 highlights the valency of an attitude from positive to negative or favourable to unfavourable. The point made in Roger Brown's descriptive definition in relation to valency, i.e. "….. from positive (favourable) through neutrality to negative (unfavourable)…..", raises a question as to the nature of attitudinal neutrality. It is the contention of the present author that "neutrality" on the valency continuum is **not** a "zero point" but, rather, a situation where the positive and negative are **evenly balanced**.

1.3.b The Functional Approach: Katz, in his article "The Functional Approach to the Study of Attitudes" (*Public Opinion Quarterly*, 24, 1960) suggested four motivational functions that were performed by attitudes:

(1)   *"The adjustive function:* Essentially this function is a recognition of the fact that people strive to maximise the rewards in their external environment and to minimise the penalties….

(2)   *"The ego-defensive function:* The mechanism by which the individual protects his ego from his own unacceptable impulses and from the knowledge of threatening forces from without and the methods by which he reduces his anxieties created by such problems, are known as mechanisms of ego-defense…..

(3)   *"The value expressive function:* The function of giving positive expression of his central values and to the type of person he conceives himself to be…..

(4)   *"The knowledge function:* Individuals not only acquire beliefs in the interests of satisfying various specific needs; they also seek knowledge to give meaning to what would otherwise be an unorganised chaotic world….."

(Katz, 1960, pp. 163-204)

The four functions outlined by Katz provide a good insight into what the reasons are for people holding on to certain attitudes. They also show why people may change or refuse to change their attitudes.

1.3.c Attitudes and Behaviour: The link between attitudes and behaviour is quite a complex issue for a number of reasons. In the first place, attitudes are both pre-reflectional and pre-behavioural. They may have a structural and functional logic but they are really a-rational. They are primarily dispositions which are positive or negative. As such, they influence behaviour in a positive or negative manner. While **an attitude** is a pre-reflectional disposition, **an opinion** is a post-reflectional behavioural expression, which is likely to have been influenced by the former!

Since most people have a highly complex configuration of attitudes towards most major stimulus objects or categories, these attitudes have been informed by their functions and by the socio-cultural environment of the person. Not infrequently a person may possess mutually contradictory attitudes towards a focus. For example, a person with a very strong racialist prejudice against a Black person may, at the same time, have a strong Christian disposition towards all people as equal. These two mutually opposing attitudes to the Black person will, in all probability, result in a behavioural expression which will be neither strongly racialist nor strongly Christian. We have the case of Merton's "fair-weather liberal" who is not racialist but refuses to behave positively towards Black people so as not to offend wealthy White friends whom he/she sees as being financial allies. Political loyalty can also overturn or severely qualify behavioural expression of positive or negative attitudes, e.g. religious prejudice in Northern Ireland.

The link between attitudes and behaviour, is rarely, if ever, one-to-one. Neither is it non-existent. There is a higher correlation between strongly held (positive or negative) attitudes and their behavioural expression. For instance, a high level of anti-Traveller prejudice will make it unlikely that the people will permit proper living conditions in the community (nomadic or settled) for Travellers.

The link between attitudes and behaviour is also affected by a range of other factors such as "dissonance", "self-presentation", "self-perception" and "self-justification". (See Weber, 1992, pp. 132-34.)

In regard to dissonance, Weber points out that:

> "dissonance theory argues that mismatches among cognitive elements create dissonance, an arousing tension we are motivated to reduce. Unjustified behaviours are impossible to change once they have been enacted. Dissonant attitudes, however, are easier to alter: one need only change one's mind and the new attitude can be brought into line with the unalterable behaviour".

> (Weber, 1992, p.134)

This adoption of a new attitude to "go along with" certain behaviour patterns happens quite frequently in everyday life. The difference caused by the new attitude backing the behaviour is that it reinforces the latter continuing, as well as acting as a form of rationalisation or self-justification.

In relation to the changing of attitudes, it should be emphasised that it is *impossible to remove attitudes* once they exist, that is, without removing the focus of the attitudes. All we can do is *replace* our attitudes. For example, if a person has negative attitudes towards Travelling People, it is impossible to remove such attitudes as if the Travellers no longer existed for that person. The only way to change the situation is to replace the negative attitude with a positive one or one less negative. In other words, an *"attitudinal vacuum" is impossible*, as long as the focus is relevant.

The links between attitudes and behaviour have been highlighted over the years by many sociologists and social psychologists (W.I. Thomas, and F. Znaniecki, 1918, Vander Zanden, 1972, Merton 1957, Weber 1992) in the context of the *vicious-circle theory* and the *self-fulfilling prophecy theory*. The latter is often referred to as the *"definition of the situation" theory* which states that *our perception of and attitudes towards a social situation can actually lead to it changing to become as we define it*.

The *vicious-circle theory* sees a causal connection between the dominant groups' **attitudes** towards minorities leading to **behaviour** of the establishment and resulting in the **conditions** of living of the minority. Negative attitudes will inevitably lead to negative behaviour, which in turn results in a deterioration of the conditions of those against whom the negative attitudes are directed. (See Figure No. 13.2, page 301 – The Vicious-Circle Model.)

The worsening of the social and living conditions of those prejudiced against will reinforce and rationalise the negative attitudes. So, the vicious-circle theory operates and explains the deterioration of the overall position. The great thing about the vicious-circle theory is that *it works in the positive direction also*. For example, if attitudes toward Black people in the dominant group in Britain were to become positive, the behaviour and services would improve and the Black people would respond by improving their own education, housing, job opportunities and general conditions. This, in turn, would challenge the racialist attitudes and further strengthen positive behaviour.

Intervention at the second level of the vicious-circle refers directly to behavioural change. The role of **law** is central here. For that reason, a Minority Rights Act (regularly updated) which is fully enforced and seriously applied seems to be a *sine qua non* in any heterogeneous society wishing long-term equity and good intergroup relations.

There is the possibility of positive intervention to improve the actual material and cultural conditions of the minority. In modern societies, **the State** is the main source of the required resources to ensure a basic minimum standard of living in line with that prevailing in society for the time being. Voluntary agencies can also contribute in this regard. Once positive interventions take place at the three points of the circle, a self-generating dynamic should amplify the pace towards equality.

Finally, there are those authors who seem to disregard attitude and prejudice research (as pursued in this book) as somewhat distant. They would challenge the relevance of attitudes for behaviour and look upon them as *mere conceptual constructs*. Rajecki addresses this problem in Chapter Three of his book, *Attitudes* (2nd Edition 1990, pp. 77-106). The author sets the problematic thus:

> "...... By the late 1960s evidence had accumulated that attitudes and behaviour were often inconsistent. These findings provoked something of a crisis in the field, and the status of 'attitudes' as a useful concept was called into question by some. As a reaction to these theoretical concerns of the sixties, recent work on attitude-behaviour consistency has produced what appears to be a happy ending. By now we better understand when and why attitudes and behaviour are related, or not." (Rajecki, 1990, p. 77)

Some of the difficulties arising from the link between attitudes and behaviour have been explained earlier in Section 1.3c above (pages 39-41).

1.4 Related Concepts:
To complete the conceptual framework particular to this work, it may be worth giving a brief definition and comment on a number of related concepts.

Personality, Society and Culture:
All interpersonal and intergroup interaction is dependent on and reflects the personality, the social system and the culture. The human being is psycho-socio-cultural in all aspects of social interaction.

(i) Personality: It is not easy to get agreement on the definition of personality. Walter Mischel in his text, *Introduction to Personality* (3rd Edition, 1981), draws on the definitions of Allport (1961, p.28), Guilford, (1959, p.5) and McClelland (1951, p.69) and presents the following:

> " 'Personality' usually refers to the distinctive patterns of behaviour (including thoughts and emotions) that characterise each individual's adaptations to the situations of his or her life." (Mischel, 1981, p.2)

Gordon Allport's definition of personality focused on the internal psychological systems which determine an individual's personality as:

> "the dynamic organisation within the individual of those psychological systems that determine her/his characteristic, behaviour or thought." (Allport, 1961, p.28)

Personality is a product of socialisation and genetically inherited capacities. One's place in society and the accepted norms of the culture greatly influence the development of one's innate ability. Some psychologists, such as **Sigmund Freud**, place great emphasis on the inner developments of the personality while others, like **George H. Mead**, highlight the primary group social environment of the young person as the most important determinant of personality growth.

The different theories of personality are more complementary than contradictory in that they emphasise different features of human beings at different levels of explanation (Hayes, 1994, p.220).

(ii) Society: Most sociologists of note have attempted to define the concept 'society'. Talcott Parsons saw two essential requirements in a society, namely, that it be a "self-subsistent social system" and that it endure "beyond the life-span of the normal human individual" and continue in the next generation.

> "A social system of this type, which meets the essential functional prerequisites of long-term persistence from within its own resources, will be called a society. It is not essential to the concept of society that it should not in any way be empirically interdependent with other societies, but it should contain all the structural and function fundamentals of an independently subsisting social system."
>
> (Parsons, 1951, p.19)

This definition, despite its heady jargon and tight reasoning is very comprehensive. It refers to the relatively autonomous society or, in previous terms, *"sovereign state"* or *country*. The current moves towards European integration, by weakening the autonomy of Irish society, may soon raise the question – at what point do we cease to be a *"self-subsisting social system"?* Once that point is reached, if it ever happens, then we would become in Parsons' terms a territorial *"community"* or *mere province.*

The social system is operated by its members, or at least a significant proportion of them, conforming to those *basic norms* required for the satisfaction of society's and the members' needs. We are not free to ignore social norms necessary for the satisfaction of our collective and individual needs. These norms are, in the words of sociologist, Emile Durkheim, *"social facts"* which he defined in his book, *The Rules of Sociological Method* (1895, translations, 1938, 1964). The following was Durkheim's own definition of "social facts":

> "A social fact is every way of acting, fixed or not, capable of exercising on the individual an external constraint; or again, every way of acting which is general throughout a given society, while at the same time existing in its own right independent of its individual manifestations." (Durkheim, 1964 translation, p.13)

It should be added that there are some who would take an opposite and extreme view and say that society, as such, does not exist! This view is rejected by the present author.

(iii) Culture: Culture and society are integrally related. At its most basic level, culture is that which distinguishes human beings from all other forms of animal life, even that of the high primates. Culture is possible because of *human beings' capacity "to symbol."* (White 1959, pp. 6ff) It is possible to distinguish two definitions of the concept culture. One definition is what is meant when we use the concept in everyday life, while the other is what anthropologists and sociologists mean by the concept.

> "When we use the term in ordinary daily conversation, we often think of 'culture' as equivalent to the 'higher things of the mind' – art, literature, music and painting. As sociologists use it, the concept includes such activities, but also far more. Culture refers to the whole way of life of members of society. It includes how they dress, their marriage customs and family life, their patterns of work, religious ceremonies and leisure pursuits. It covers also the goods they create and which become meaningful for them – bows and arrows, ploughs, factories and machines, computers, books, dwellings." (Giddens, 1989, p.30)

The content of culture is essentially non-material, although it is dependent on material media and artefacts of the 'vehicles of culture'. The anthropologist, Mervin Harris, in his book, *Culture, People, Nature* (New York, Harper and Row, 1988), quotes (with approval) from **Sir Edward Burnett Tylor's** original definition of culture in his book, *Primitive Culture* (London, Murray, 1871), as follows:

> "Culture taken in its wide ethnographic sense is that complex whole which includes knowledge, belief, art, morals, law, customs and any other capabilities acquired by man as a member of society. The condition of culture among the various societies of mankind, insofar as it is capable of being investigated on general principles, is a subject apt for the study of laws of human thought and action". (Tylor, 1871, p.1; Harris, 1988, p.122)

Most definitions of the concept "culture" have been influenced by Tylor's definition. Building on this definition and that of other eminent authors (Malinowski, 1930; Benedict, 1935/1961; Kroeber, 1948; Kluckhohn, 1949/1971; Parsons 1954/64; Smelser, 1962) the present author, in the previous publication (1977), gave the following definition of culture.

> *"Culture is the interrelated set (configuration) of learned, created and borrowed beliefs, ideas, values, norms and symbolic meaningful systems, which characterise and influence the human behaviour of a people."* (Mac Gréil, 1977, p.181)

It can be seen from this definition that culture is a composite phenomenon whose content consists of "beliefs and ideas" (i.e. cognitive component), "values" (i.e. "ethical ideals"), "norms" (i.e. "shared expectations and obligations") or the specification of values for behaviour, and "symbolic meaningful systems", (i.e. language and rituals). These components of culture are non-material. Culture defines the "ethos" of a society and the "mentality" of its people. (Benedict 1935/1961, p. 32ff) The link between culture and social attitudes is given in Mac Gréil (1996), pages 24-5.

2. Types of Social Prejudice:

It is the basic tenet of this book that social prejudice is *a universal phenomenon with manifestations in attitudes towards various groups, collectivities and categories of human beings.* It has become common practice in the literature to categorise or classify types of social objects of prejudice into a number of distinct categories, namely, ethnic, political, racial, religious, sex or gender, and social. Religious prejudice is frequently subdivided into sectarianism and anti-Semitism. Sex or gender prejudice is also subdivided into sexism and homophobia. Ethnic prejudice, which is normally termed ethnocentrism, is occasionally referred to as xenophobia.

2.1 Ethnocentrism:

This concept refers to a belief or conviction that members of other nationalities or cultures are basically inferior to members of one's own nationality or culture, because of their nationality, culture or way of life. The definition given in *Prejudice and Tolerance in Ireland* was more specific, i.e.:

> "Ethnic prejudice consists of rigid, negative, hostile attitudes towards people who are defined as members of groups or categories that are perceived to differ from one's own group or category in matters of culture and nationality. It is basically a belief in the superiority of the members of one's own ethnic groups or categories." (Mac Gréil, 1977, p.263)

2.2 Political Prejudice:

This prejudice is against people defined as members of political parties, as upholders of certain political ideologies, and/or as committed to the pursuit of political goals or objectives in a manner not acceptable to the person's group. It is more than a rational objection to the party, ideology or political methodology. The following was proposed in the author's 1996 text (*Prejudice in Ireland Revisited*):

> "Political prejudice consists of rigid, negative, hostile attitudes towards people who are defined as members of political groups and categories that are perceived to differ from one's own political group or category in matters of party affiliation, ideological commitment and campaign methodology." (Mac Gréil, 1996, p.34)

Political prejudice is not to be confused with disagreement on political issues and questions but rather a rejection of **people** deemed to belong to certain political groups and categories, because of their political views. Disagreement can lead to a rejection of **views** while prejudice leads to a rejection of people.

2.3 Racialism/Racism:
There has been some divergence of opinion on the use of this concept (see Robert Miles, *Racism after "Race Relations"*, London, Routledge, 1993). There are those who seem to use it for groups or categories with ethnic and social characteristics. The present author is *not convinced of the utility of the broader use* of the concept and restricts its meaning to superficial physiognomic and genetically inherited visible body, facial features, eyes, hair, and skin traits.

The following descriptive definition from the 1977 text adequately defines the concept as used in this text:

> "The use of the concept 'racial attitudes' in this study is restricted to attitudes based on response to physical characteristics, i.e., visible features, e.g., colour, size, facial features, etc. Unlike ethnic attitudes which are in response to nationality or cultural characteristics, racial attitudes are, in themselves, a-cultural. Racial prejudice then, is a negative attitude towards persons because of their membership of groups or categories perceived to differ in physical characteristics from the perceiver. It is ultimately based on the belief that certain physical characteristics, such as size, skin, colour, etc., make a person innately superior or inferior." (Mac Gréil, 1977, p.288)

For further consideration of the concept of 'race', see Chapter IX, pages 193 - 198.

2.4 Religious Prejudice:
As already noted, one religious category has been isolated in the literature as a special prejudice, i.e. *"anti-Semitism"* or prejudice against Jews. Anti-Semitism is one of the most studied and researched forms of social prejudice because of the genocide against Jews by the German Third Reich and its collaborators during the Second World War in Europe and because of the very long history of persecution of Jews in the diaspora.

Religious prejudice in the broader context covers all religious affiliations and non-affiliations, as well as "agnostics" and "atheists".

Religious sectarianism is a form of segregation based on perceived religious affiliation or non-affiliation. The question of prejudice against all believers becomes an issue in a world where there are explicit or implicit ideological positions adopted in professedly atheistic societies and, at the informal level, in societies where absolutist secularist policies and attitudes lead to hostile postures towards religion.

The following is a tentative definition of religious prejudice which was proposed in the 1996 text, *Prejudice in Ireland Revisited,* by the present author:

> "Religious prejudice consists of rigid, negative, hostile attitudes towards people who are seen as members of religious or religion-related groups or categories which differ from the religious or religion-related group or category of the perceiver or who are perceived not to profess belief in or be members of any religious faith or category and are, because of their membership or non-belief, deemed to be inferior to one's own group or category members."
>
> (Mac Gréil, 1996, p.36)

Prejudice related to deeply held religious and ideological belief is one of the most dangerous of all prejudices and, probably, least amenable to pluralist integration. Religious prejudice is frequently used to give a so-called "spiritual" or absolutist rationalisation to other forms of prejudice and discrimination.

2.5 Sexism:

Elliot Aronson in *The Social Animal* (3rd edition, 1980) points to the facts pertaining to the constrained role of women in society and the need of society to face up to the subtle and less than subtle areas of sexist prejudice against women. As society becomes more aware "of the discrimination and stereotyping that occurs as a result of differential sex roles … sex-role stereotypes continue to crumble … as women widen their interests and enter new occupations the role perspectives for men are also becoming less restrictive." (Aronson, 1980, p.205)

John C. Brigham, in his text, *Social Psychology*, (1991) gives a very succinct definition of sexism, as follows:

> "Sexism can be defined as any attitude, action or institutional structure that subordinates a person because of his or her gender." (Brigham, 1991, p.462)

Sexism incorporates prejudice and discrimination **against males** as well as against females, although, in the present time, it is widely agreed that males have had a dominant role in major positions of authority and influence in many areas of Irish society, especially in the middle and upper classes. **Anti-male sexism** needs to be addressed seriously by social and psychological researchers.

2.6 Homophobia:

The attitude in society towards people deemed to be homosexual (gay or lesbian) in relation to their sexual orientation must be of concern to the student of intergroup relations. In recent years in Ireland, homosexual behaviour between consenting male adults over the age of seventeen years has been **decriminalised** after a long and arduous struggle through the Irish Courts and ultimately to the European Court of Human Rights, i.e. the Senator David Norris constitutional case, 1988.

It may be better to define it more generally as follows (as proposed in the 1996 text):

> Homophobic prejudice consists of rigid, negative, hostile attitudes towards people who are deemed to be homosexual and possess the negatively stereotypical qualities ascribed to homosexual people. (Mac Gréil, 1996, p.38)

2.7 Prejudice against Social Categories:

This is a general category covering *diverse stimulus categories* not covered by ethnic, political, racial, religious, sexist and homophobic prejudices. It includes a range of disadvantaged, disabled, class and 'socially unacceptable' categories. Each category will be treated as an application of the general definition of prejudice. Bias against the Travelling People in Ireland is an example of 'prejudice against a social category' which is of serious concern and leads to unnecessary suffering and discrimination of many people.

Part II – Theoretical Framework

1. Macrotheory:

The theoretical framework on which this research has been based has not differed greatly from that of the 1972-73 survey published in 1977 (*Prejudice and Tolerance in Ireland*) and the 1988-89 national survey published in 1996 (*Prejudice in Ireland Revisited*) which was derived in part from a study carried out in 1966 (*A Psycho-Socio-Cultural Theory of Prejudice*) by the same author.   The whole approach has been heavily influenced, at the macro level, by the structural-functional model of society and also by the theoretical reflections of the conflict structuralists.

Among the authors of the **structural-functional school** the following are included: Emile Durkheim (1893), Bronislaw Malinowski (1944), Alfred R. Radcliffe-Brown (1952), Talcott Parsons (1951), Leslie White (1959), Robert K. Merton (1957) and others.   The main authors of the **conflict school** would include Karl Marx (1845/6), Georg Simmel (1908), Robert E. Park (1921), Lewis Coser (1956), Ralf Dahrendorf (1959) and others.

Sociology passed through a reaction to structural-functionalism between the late 1960s and the mid 1980s, when "micro theorising" and alternative "macro theorising" held sway with numerous authors.   By the end of the 1980s there came the "**crisis of post-functionalism**", which in some circles spawned a **neo-functionalism revival** as well as worthy critical thinking by sociologists such as Michel Foucault (1970), Jürgen Habermas (1973), Harold Garfinkel (1967), and Anthony Giddens (1973).   During the 1990s we seemed to have been going through **a crisis in neo-Marxist structuralism** after almost a decade of post-functionalism.

2. The Momentum Model of Society:

As stated above, the theoretical roots of both the 1977 and the 1996 studies have been deeply planted in two structuralist schools, i.e. conflict and functional.   In line with the approaches of 1977 and 1996, neither school has been fully adopted.   Instead, a **new** theoretical model was proposed which enabled *a synthesis of both the conflict and equilibrium models.*

Based on a reflection on the fundamental nature of society as the *product of patterned interaction, that very interaction is seen as the very binding force of society*.   The nature of this interaction can be placed anywhere on the continuum from conflict to equilibrium, providing there is room for the minimum proportion of both forms of interaction.   *The momentum model* sees society in the perpetual process of *becoming* or *declining* but never fully being.   "*Societas semper reformanda."*

If one assumes that society is structured, and it would be against all the evidence to deny it, it is reasonable to expect that the two major forces at work within this dynamic structure are forces leading to conformity and consent *en route* to **social equilibrium** and forces of dissent and non-conformity leading to **social conflict**. A high level of social equilibrium leads to the satisfaction of the citizens' social and personal *"interests"* and can lead to long periods of social stability and prosperity as long as it can maintain overall conformity. When, however, there is a significant level of social conflict there is a greater sense of *"meaning"* and ideas of change and vision. The pursuit of "interests" and of "meaning" (in Max Weber's sense) seem to be the two primary needs of humans in society. But the real struggle is to achieve a balance between both[2]. In the 1977 text, an attempt was made to depict in diagrammatic form the co-existence in society of "equilibrium" and "conflict" and the dynamic tension between both. Figure No. 3.2 demonstrates the relative position of conflict and equilibrium in a society at any particular time in history.

Figure No. 3.2: The Vacillating Social Situation Model

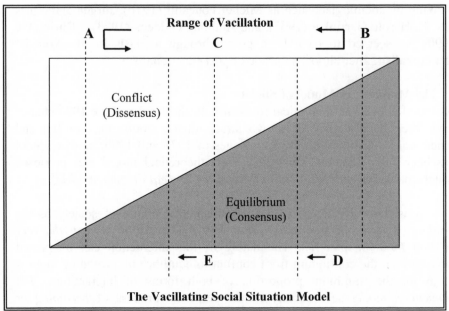

---

[2] See: Mac Gréil, Micheál, *Prejudice and Tolerance in Ireland*, Dublin, C.I.R., 1977, pages 4-5, 153-155.

There are two points on the continuum beyond which the social situation cannot go. Right of point B would mean so little space for ideas or conflict that society would be totally de-radicalised and under a benign or dictatorial regime where a perfectly organised bureaucratic system would only satisfy the material interests of the significant section of society. Dissent would be ruled out for all practical purposes. At such a state of imbalance between consensus and dissensus, a significant revolt, i.e. a rapid and radical change of values and norms, would be most likely with all safety valves closed. Once the forces of conflict gather momentum, the taste of freedom (of ideas and participation) becomes socially contagious and a new situation develops and, possibly, the old order of equilibrium weakens or loses its grip, or else concedes greater dissent, e.g. the collapse of East European centralist regimes.

At the other end of the spectrum or continuum, the level of dissent becomes so problematic that normal routine work is impossible. Preoccupation with ideas and revolution will not till the fields, rear the children, do the research, build the houses, provide for education, administer the welfare system, etc. If unchecked it can lead to anarchy. When point A (see Figure No. 3.2) is reached, the forces of equilibrium begin to assert themselves and a *process of routinisation and ideological de-radicalisation* begins to take place. The pendulum swings back with the gradual rise of administrators, bureaucrats, business people and priests replacing revolutionaries, charismatic idealists and prophets, e.g. post the *Good Friday Agreement* in Northern Ireland.

Probably the healthiest position is at point C where there is a balanced tension between the **prophetic** and the **priestly**, or between the **idealistic** and **bureaucratic**. Point D would represent a "right-of-centre" situation where there is more emphasis on "interests" than on ideas or "meaning". The left-of-centre situation at point E may be difficult to maintain, although it is a more stimulating place to live. A basic antinomy seems to exist between the pursuit of "ideas/meaning" and that of "interests/prosperity"!

The relevance of these theoretical reflections for the study of prejudice and intergroup attitudes and opinions is obvious. Our attitudes are very functional in relation to social conformity and dissent. Prejudices are part of our attitude configuration.

3. Middle-Range Social Psychological Theories:
At the middle range level of theory it will be contended that "authoritarianism" (Adorno *et al*, 1950) and "anomie" (Srole *et al*, 1956), (Merton, 1968), are correlated to prejudice scores.

3.1 Frustration-Aggression:
The social-psychological condition of "frustration" will be hypothesised again as a proximate cause of social prejudice, which is seen as a psychological form of displaced aggression. The frustration-aggression theory, with a strong Freudian background, has been developed by John Dollard (Dollard *et. al*, 1939). Insecurity, fear and anxiety (Maier 1961) are seen to be closely linked to frustration and, thereby, to social prejudice. Guilt is a psychological factor with strong links to prejudice (Allport, 1954).

3.2 Labelling and Stereotyping:
Labelling and stereotypes also play an important role in generating and reinforcing prejudice. Negative stereotypes become social stigmas against members of certain groups and categories. The authors who have contributed most to Labelling Theory include Erving Goffman (1963), Thomas Scheff (1966/1984), Edwin Lemert (1951) and others.

3.3 Scapegoating:
The psychological functions of providing meaning, social prestige, affiliation and pathological relief add further dimensions of explanation to the variations in the scale and subscale "prejudice scores". Under the context of *meaning* prejudice can provide acceptable popular reasons for meaningless situations and causes more people to resort to *scapegoating* (Simpson and Yinger, 1970). Certain minority groups are easily scapegoated and become the objects of displaced aggression, e.g., the scapegoating of Jews in times of economic and other crisis. The conditions under which scapegoating occurs have been outlined by sociologist Harry Johnson:

(1)   For some reason the true source of frustration and resentment cannot be attacked.

(2)   Some other object exists that is symbolically a connection with the source of frustration and is, therefore, a psychologically appropriate substitute as an object of aggression.

(3)   For some reason this substitute is less well protected against attack than the true source of resentment.

It is difficult to say whether these three conditions are sufficient as well as necessary for scapegoating to occur. At any rate, the syndrome is common." (Johnson: 1961, p. 595)

One of the functions of leaders (political, religious, business, etc.) is to become scapegoats for major failures in society. Unfortunately, removing the leader does not address the complete causes of the problem, although it may give a 'feel-good' solution to the people suffering from the situation.

3.4 Social Prestige:

Social prestige and prejudice have a complex relation. As a "reaction formation" response to serious social and cultural deprivation, prejudice can lead people to adopt strong anti-minority dispositions, e.g. the prejudice of the Ku Klux Klan against Black People, Jews and Roman Catholics. Demagogues have exploited this tendency of the insecure disadvantaged to displace their aggression towards available scapegoats. Adolf Hitler, in his book, *Mein Kampf*, gives status to the defeated German by pointing to the need for superiority over the Jews:

> "..... For a racially pure people (the Aryans) which is conscious of its blood can never be enslaved by the Jew. In this world he will forever be master over bastards and bastards alone...." (Hitler, 1933, p. 295)

3.5 In-group Cohesion *vs* Out-group Hostility:

Affiliation as a psychological function of prejudice is quite a serious issue. Affiliation is a dominant Western 'want' (Krech, Crutchfield and Ballachey 1962, p. 89-93).

> "Sometimes this affiliation want becomes overpowering – the all-important want of the individual. One can almost speak of a pathological affiliation want. Schachter (1959) has pointed out that a strong affiliation want may be related to anxiety....." (Krech, *et al*, 1962, p. 91)

Graham Sumner put forward the thesis that out-group hostility leads to in-group cohesion (Sumner, 1906, p. 12). Robert K. Merton qualifies Sumner's thesis:

> "He (Sumner) assumed, and his assumption has echoed an established truth on numerous occasions since his day, that immense loyalty to a group necessarily generates hostility to those outside the group." (Merton, 1957, p. 398)

Some political and religious leaders, in times of crisis, may use the tactics of generating a "common enemy" to unite the people behind a cause perceived to be under threat. Such support can be uncritical, prejudicial and hostile at times of intense intergroup strife and conflict. At the international level, there was a period of *'Anti-Communist' hysteria* in the propaganda with the purpose of creating Western solidarity. This seems to have abated in recent years.

3.6 The Apostate Complex:
This is one aspect of special interest, namely, the deep-seated complex relationship which people have had for groups which they may have left. The psychological residue of such former attachments, after membership of the group has been abandoned, may be the source of internal tension and external hostility towards the members, views and practices of the former group. Talcott Parsons seems to say that there can be a *"compulsive alienation"* towards one's former group after abandoning it for a new and, maybe, opposite-oriented group (Parsons, 1951, p. 255).

If one takes the example of a devout Catholic, who becomes a liberal atheist, or *vice versa,* or an active Communist who becomes an aggressive Capitalist, or *vice versa*, there is a likelihood in the case of such conversions of "over-identification" with one's new group and "compulsive alienation" towards the former group. This creates a high degree of tension because *we tend to be what we were as well as being what we are.* This is reinforced by the clash between old and new sets of friends. Also, we carry our past with us in our memories, in our interpersonal response traits, and so forth. This predicament may be called *The Apostate Complex*.

Robert K. Merton puts it very well in the context of "negative reference groups":

> "Full effective attachment to a former membership group need not, and perhaps typically does not, occur. It is then the case that former members of the group often convert it into a negative reference group towards which they are dependently hostile rather than simply indifferent. For precisely because the loss or rejection of membership does not promptly eradicate the former attachment to the groups, ambivalence rather than indifference is apt to result. This gives rise to what Parsons calls 'compulsive alienation', in this, an abiding and rigid rejection of the norms of the repudiated groups." (Merton, 1957, p. 295)

In a time of high ideological mobility and change of loyalties and commitment in terms of belief systems and political ideologies, this phenomenon may be more widespread than is realised.

3.7 Fear and Anxiety:

Anxiety may be defined as *a generalised state of chronic and unrealistic fear*. It can be caused by prolonged insecurity and a situation conducive to unresolved realistic fear due to factors outside one's control such as long-term unemployment, a breakdown in community social order, domestic disorganisation, community violence, and so forth.

Norman Maier's description of anxiety, quoted in the 1977 study (Mac Gréil, 1977, p.94), is worth requoting here:

> "In so far as the term anxiety indicates a state of generalised fear and not a reaction to some particular object in the environment, it fails to be goal-oriented and thus appears as a product of frustration. Likewise, in anxiety the object feared may give no clue as to the source of the danger." (Maier, 1961, p.131)

4. The 'Park-Cycle':

In addition to the macro- and middle-range theories discussed above, i.e., structural-functionalism, conflict structuralism and the combined functional-conflict momentum model, it was possible to seek explanation for variations in prejudice scores in other more middle-range theories and theoretical models.

A number of sociologists interested in the study of intergroup relations have adapted Park's Cycle with some success. These include Emory Bogardus (1930, pp.613 ff.), W. Brown (1934, pp.34-37), Clarence E. Glick (1955, pp. 219 ff.), Stanley Lieberson (1961, pp. 902-10), Brewton Berry (1965), Michael Banton (1967, pp. 304 ff.) and others. More recent writings on the sociology of intergroup relations have moved away from Park's four primary forms of intergroup interaction, i.e., "competition, conflict, accommodation and assimilation". The present author has found the Park approach most useful and relatively easy to apply to dominant-minority situations on the ground, while not agreeing that 'assimilation' is **necessarily** the final solution! As Michael Banton notes, it can be applied to all situations of intergroup interaction.

> "One virtue of this (Park's) theoretical framework is its refusal to treat race relations as different in any sociologically essential respect from relations between other sorts of groups. Park thought that patterns of race relations exemplified conflict, and to a lesser extent assimilation, but it is clear that many features could be counted as illustrations of accommodation and competition."
>
> (Banton (1967, p. 305)

Park devised the idea of a *"patterned-sequence-cycle"* which follows an irreversible order in minority-dominant relations, i.e.

1st Stage:	Contact;
2nd Stage:	Competition between members of both groups;
3rd Stage:	Accommodation;
4th Stage:	Assimilation. (Park 1926, pp. 196 ff)

This phased or staged development from the completely marginal status of the "arrived outsider" to adoption as one of the "dominant group" through assimilation was irreversible for Park. (See page 310 below.) Banton quotes Park in the course of his comment on the journey into society.

> "Another seminal idea linking the study of individual behaviour to social processes was his (Park's) notion of the 'marginal man'. In describing perhaps the most general process of all, Park maintained *'the race relations cycle which takes the form to state it abstractly of contact, competition, accommodation and eventual assimilation, is apparently progressive and irreversible' (Park 1950, p. 150)*. Peoples may for a time live side by side, preserving their distinctive cultures, but in the long run intermarriage will increase and the movement to assimilation will grow." (Banton 1967, p. 307)

At the time of Park's writing on the inevitable and irreversible move towards assimilation, it was generally accepted that cultural pluralism was neither possible nor maybe desirable. It was the famous "melting pot" era in the United States.[3] Since the 1960s, however, the assimilationists have been challenged, and the possibility of the *coexistence* of diverse cultural and religious groups on a basis of equality has been deemed desirable and possible, i.e. *integrated pluralism* for groups with cultural and religious differences (see page 311 below).

5. Dominant Group Postures and Minority Group Responses:
The interaction between dominant groups and the minority groups within society can be seen as a **"posture/response dialectic"**. It should be stated very clearly that this approach examines only the actual existential situation of a dominant and a minority group co-occupying the same society at different times in the history of their interaction. This does not, of course, ignore the background to the situations examined.

---

[3] Henry Pratt Fairchild in his book *Immigration* (1925) was seen by James Vander Zanden (1972, p.25) as an effective promoter of assimilation. See also Zangwill, Israel, *The Melting Pot: Drama in Four Acts*, New York, Macmillan, 1921.

Migration theory and history are essential dimensions to the explanation of the nature and state of intergroup relations. Robert Miles in his book *Racism after "Race Relations"* (1993) correctly draws attention to these dimensions. The Irish abroad have endured some of the "alienation" effects experienced by immigrants and migrants from other poorer countries around the world.

Returning to the **posture-response dialectic/paradigm**, Figure No. 3.3 gives the range of options and possibilities.

Figure No. 3.3: Dominant Posture/Minority Response Paradigm

Dominant Postures → Minority ↓ Responses	Annihilation 1.	Expulsion 2.	Segregation 3.	Stratification 4.	Assimilation 5.	Amalgamation 6.	Pluralism 7.
1. Avoidance (Withdrawal)	A	B	C	D	E	F	XXXXXXXXXX XXXXXXXXXX XXXXXXXXXX XXXXXXXXXX
2. Aggression (Conflict)	G	H	I	J	K	L	XXXXXXXXXX XXXXXXXXXX XXXXXXXXXX XXXXXXXXXX
3. Accommodation (Acceptance)	XXXXXXXXXX XXXXXXXXXX XXXXXXXXXX XXXXXXXXXX	XXXXXXXX XXXXXXXX XXXXXXXX XXXXXXXX	M	N	O	P	XXXXXXXXXX XXXXXXXXXX XXXXXXXXXX XXXXXXXXXX
4. Assimilation (Acculturation)	XXXXXXXXXX XXXXXXXXXX XXXXXXXXXX XXXXXXXXXX	XXXXXXXX XXXXXXXX XXXXXXXX XXXXXXXX	XXXXXXXXXX XXXXXXXXXX XXXXXXXXXX XXXXXXXXXX	XXXXXXXXXXX XXXXXXXXXXX XXXXXXXXXXX XXXXXXXXXXX	Q	XXXXXXXXXXX XXXXXXXXXXX XXXXXXXXXXX XXXXXXXXXXX	XXXXXXXXXX XXXXXXXXXX XXXXXXXXXX XXXXXXXXXX
5. Amalgamation (Miscegenation)	XXXXXXXXXX XXXXXXXXXX XXXXXXXXXX XXXXXXXXXX	XXXXXXXX XXXXXXXX XXXXXXXX XXXXXXXX	XXXXXXXXXX XXXXXXXXXX XXXXXXXXXX XXXXXXXXXX	XXXXXXXXXXX XXXXXXXXXXX XXXXXXXXXXX XXXXXXXXXXX	XXXXXXXXXX XXXXXXXXXX XXXXXXXXXX XXXXXXXXXX	R	XXXXXXXXXX XXXXXXXXXX XXXXXXXXXX XXXXXXXXXX
6. Pluralism (Coexistence)	XXXXXXXXXX XXXXXXXXXX XXXXXXXXXX XXXXXXXXXX	XXXXXXXX XXXXXXXX XXXXXXXX XXXXXXXX	XXXXXXXXXX XXXXXXXXXX XXXXXXXXXX XXXXXXXXXX	XXXXXXXXXXX XXXXXXXXXXX XXXXXXXXXXX XXXXXXXXXXX	XXXXXXXXXX XXXXXXXXXX XXXXXXXXXX XXXXXXXXXX	XXXXXXXXXXX XXXXXXXXXXX XXXXXXXXXXX XXXXXXXXXXX	S

In all, there are nineteen situations ranging from A, "avoiding annihilation" to S "mutual desire for pluralism". Generally speaking, in the case of A to P the initiative is in the hands of the dominant group. It is also possible to experience shift and changes in the postures of the dominant groups and in the responses of the minority groups over time.

An understanding of the behaviour patterns implied in the various "postures" and those predicted by the "responses" of the minorities should make it possible to explain and, in some instances, predict, the psychological, sociological and cultural (anthropological) outcome of the intergroup interaction. Space does not permit a detailed analysis and description of the parameters of each of the nineteen situations, i.e., from A to S. In the course of the text, reference can be made to the paradigm, when dealing with different groups, collectivities and categories, especially those classified as minorities. Each posture and response is examined further in Mac Gréil, Micheál (1996), *Prejudice in Ireland Revisited,* (pages 48-54).

The above ten postures and responses help to explain the volatility of intergroup relations, which can change in both a positive or negative manner depending on the wishes of the dominant groups and the responses of the minorities. Generally speaking, the nature of the dialectic or dialogue **is mostly determined by the dominant group**, which is invariably in a position to take the initiative in its own interests or apparent interests.

It is frequently said that there are "minority problems" in societies! This is a very symptomatic description of the situation. Usually intergroup relations are primarily "problems of the dominant groups"!

It is important to avoid **the trap of "victimology"**, i.e. focus on the victim's response and condition, which seeks the explanation of social problems in the deprived and weaker sections of society rather than in the privileged and more powerful beneficiaries of the social inequality. The *victimological approach* keeps the spotlight away from the dominant group, which is "structurally" responsible for the deprivation of the weak, through their (the dominant group's) superfluity of power and resources.

Note: **Measuring Social Prejudice**

Prejudice was measured in the 2007-08 National Survey (as in the two previous surveys of 1972-73 and 1988-89) by means of two types of scale, i.e. the *Bogardus Social Distance Scale* and *Likert-type scales*. The former measured the degree of closeness to which respondents would be prepared to admit members of fifty-one different ethnic, gender, political, racial, religious and social categories. The *Likert-type scales* were used to gauge attitudes (and opinions) towards: Black People, British, Northern Irish, Travellers and Women. Such scales were also used to find out levels of authoritarianism, social anomie and general tolerance (see Appendix A, pages 615-632).

***

CHAPTER IV
Social Distance in Ireland

The principal scale devised to measure social prejudice and tolerance in the 2007-08 national survey was the *Bogardus Social Distance Scale*. Some fifty-one 'stimulus categories' were selected and respondents were asked how close they were prepared to admit members of each of them. The level of closeness ranged from 'kinship' to 'debarring or deporting'.

Part I – Introduction

The *Bogardus Social Distance Scale* was also the main scale in the 1972-73 Greater Dublin and the 1988-89 National Survey. Forty-six of the fifty-nine stimulus categories measured in the 1988-89 survey were replicated in the 2007-08 one. Stimulus categories absent from the 1988-89 Bogardus Scale in the 2007-08 were: 'Heavy Drinkers', 'Iranians', 'Lithuanians', 'Palestinians' and 'Romanians'. The component of prejudice, i.e. a negative social attitude which the social distance scale measures, is *"behavioural tendency"* (See Figure No. 3.1, page 38 above).

The fifty-one stimulus categories of the 2007-08 survey could be classified into specific groups, i.e.:

(a) *Ethnic Categories (of White European and Middle-East origin)*: 'Arabs', 'British', 'Canadians', 'Dutch', 'English', 'French', 'Germans', 'Iranians', 'Israelis', 'Italians', 'Irish Speakers', 'Lithuanians', 'Northern Irish', 'Palestinians', 'Polish', 'Russians', 'Romanians', 'Scottish', 'Spaniards' and 'Welsh'.
(b) *Racial Categories*: 'Blacks' and 'Coloureds'.
(c) *Ethnico-Racial Categories*: 'Africans', 'Afro-Americans', 'Chinese', 'Euro-Americans', 'Indians', 'Nigerians' and 'Pakistanis'.
(d) *Religious Categories*: 'Agnostics', 'Atheists', 'Jews', 'Muslims', 'Protestants' and 'Roman Catholics'.
(e) *Political Categories*: 'Capitalists', 'Communists', 'Gardaí', 'Socialists', 'Trade Unionists' and 'Unionists'.
(f) *Social Categories*: 'Alcoholics', 'Drug Addicts', 'Gay People', 'Heavy Drinkers', 'People with Mental Disability', 'People with Physical Disability', 'Travellers', 'Unemployed', 'Unmarried Mothers' and 'Working Class'.

The above lists are based on notional categorisation. The results of a **special rationalisation scale** (which gives the principal reason why respondents refused to admit members of the above stimulus categories into a kinship relationship, i.e. "Would marry or welcome as a member of the family") result in a subjective classification of each category. The replies to the *rationalisation scale* confirm how the respondents define members of the various categories (see Table No. 5.1 below, pages 86-87).

Social distance has been measured by the *Bogardus Social Distance Scale*, which was devised by Emory Bogardus in 1925/26 to measure the attitudes (prejudices) towards ethnic and other minorities in the United States of America. The Bogardus Scale was adapted by the present author in 1965 to measure the attitudes of Irish-Americans and others of different ethnic background in Philadelphia and Cleveland in the United States[1] and in his three Irish surveys of 1972-73 (Dublin), 1988-89 (National)[2] and 2007-08 (National). In each of the surveys the adapted scale proved to have high **validity** and **reliability**.

The respondents were asked how close they would be willing to admit members of each category listed. A seven-point scale was suggested to the respondent as follows:

1. *"Would Marry or Welcome as a Member of My Family";*
2. *"Would Have as a Close Friend";*
3. *"Would Have as a Next-Door Neighbour";*
4. *"Would Work in the Same Workplace";*
5. *"Would Welcome as an Irish citizen";*
6. *"Would Have as a Visitor Only";*
7. *"Would Debar or Deport from Ireland".*

Respondents were asked to indicate the **closest** of the above seven levels of social distance to which they would be willing to admit members of each of the fifty-one stimulus categories. Respondents were given a **'prompt-card'** with the seven stages written out on it. Interviewers were instructed to encourage respondents to give their answer **briskly** in order to get the "first-feeling response" and avoid reflection on their answer (since our attitudes / prejudices are pre-reflectional and often inconsistent with the

---

[1] Mac Gréil, Micheál, *A Psycho-Socio-Cultural Theory of Prejudice* (unpublished M.A. Thesis), Kent, Kent State University, 1966. This thesis was directed by the late Prof. Chuck Hildebrandt, who continued to encourage and advise the present author in his further study and research into social prejudice. He also was instrumental in promoting Holocaust Museums in New England, USA.
[2] See Mac Gréil, *Prejudice in Ireland Revisited*, Maynooth, St Patrick's College, 1996, pages 63-4.

perception of our 'better' selves). The modifications in the wording of the stages were necessary to adapt to the current popular culture[3].

Part II – The Overall Social Distance Findings

The findings of the Bogardus Scale are presented on Table No. 4.1 in the **rank order** of the **'mean-social-distance'** (MSD) of each 'stimulus category'. The MSD ranges from **one**, which means 100% acceptance into the family and **seven** which would indicate 100% in favour of "debar or deport". 'In-groups' would score 1.500 or lower.

In addition to the mean-social-distance score, the position of the various groups is also assessed by their position on the **rank order** of such scores. When examining the results on Table No. 4.1 it is interesting to observe the most (and least) preferred stimulus categories. It is generally anticipated that they are ranked in accordance with the *'principle of propinquity'*, i.e. those closest to the respondent's culture, religion, political views, racial group, social class position, etc., would be placed in a more preferred position on the rank order of stimulus categories. When the 'principle of propinquity' is **not** honoured in the findings, there is something (negative or positive) influencing the standing of members of the 'stimulus category' in question, which merits comment.

Once again, the *Bogardus Social Distance Scale* has performed excellently in discerning the action or behavioural-tendency of the national random sample. Stimulus categories were presented in alphabetical order and the responses have pulled them into a rank-order that was largely anticipated. Categories under **1.500** mean-social-distance scores are classified as **'in-groups'** and represent an interesting array of the top fifteen and most favoured ones. They include 'people with physical disability', 'unmarried mothers' and 'unemployed', which is very reassuring and should enable the State to be generous in support of these minorities in our society. 'People with mental disability' were just outside the 'in-group' classification at 1.612, which is also indicative of a very favourable position or standing in Irish society today of those with either physical or mental disability. From these findings, a political party who supported services for those with disabilities would not lose electoral support as a result!

---

[3] Mac Gréil, Micheál, *Prejudice in Ireland Revisited*, Maynooth, St Patrick's College, 1996/97, pages 63-4.

Table No. 4.1:
Total Sample's Social-Distance Scores towards all Stimulus Categories (2007-08)

Rank Order	Stimulus Category	Kin-ship %	Friendship %	Neigh-bour %	Co-Worker %	Citizen %	Visitor %	Debar %	Mean Social Distance (1 – 7)	No.
1.	Roman Catholics	91.1	5.7 (96.8)	0.7 (97.5)	1.4 (98.9)	0.5 (99.4)	0.1	0.5	1.168	1,012
2.	Working Class	85.6	10.0 (95.6)	1.3 (97.1)	2.2 (99.2)	0.7 (99.9)	0.1	0.1	1.228	1,011
3.	People with Physical Disability	83.0	11.6 (94.6)	2.4 (97.0)	1.9 (98.9)	0.8 (99.7)	0.2	0.1	1.268	1,012
4.	Irish Speakers	84.4	8.6 (93.0)	1.4 (94.4)	3.0 (97.4)	1.2 (98.6)	1.4	0.1	1.324	1,010
5.	Unmarried Mothers	82.4	9.8 (92.2)	2.7 (94.9)	2.8 (97.7)	1.5 (99.2)	0.5	0.2	1.339	1,011
6.	Welsh	82.4	8.2 (90.6)	3.0 (93.6)	3.3 (96.9)	1.1 (98.0)	1.7	0.3	1.388	1,012
7.	Gardaí	81.4	8.9 (90.2)	4.4 (94.7)	2.4 (97.0)	1.2 (98.2)	1.0	0.8	1.392	1,012
8.	Euro-Americans*	81.3	9.1 (90.4)	2.4 (92.8)	3.3 (96.1)	1.8 (98.0)	1.7	0.3	1.416	1,010
9.	English	81.0	8.9 (89.9)	2.7 (92.6)	4.1 (96.7)	1.2 (97.9)	1.8	0.3	1.422	1,012
10.	Canadians	80.1	9.8 (89.9)	2.8 (92.7)	3.9 (96.6)	1.2 (97.8)	2.0	0.2	1.430	1,012
11.	Scottish	81.7	7.9 (89.6)	2.6 (92.2)	3.8 (96.0)	1.2 (97.1)	2.8	0.1	1.436	1,011
12.	Unemployed	80.9	8.0 (88.9)	4.0 (93.0)	2.2 (95.2)	2.7 (97.9)	1.7	0.5	1.446	1,011
13.	Protestants	78.4	10.1 (88.5)	4.2 (92.7)	2.7 (95.4)	2.1 (97.5)	1.9	0.7	1.4827	1,012
14.	French	78.5	10.3 (88.8)	3.5 (92.4)	3.5 (95.8)	0.8 (96.7)	2.9	0.5	1.4829	1,012
15.	British	77.2	12.2 (89.4)	3.0 (92.4)	3.2 (95.6)	1.6 (97.2)	2.2	0.6	1.488	1,010
16.	Trade Unionists	77.8	7.9 (85.8)	3.6 (89.4)	5.9 (95.3)	1.9 (97.2)	2.0	0.8	1.552	1,011
17.	Northern Irish	75.1	11.5 (86.6)	3.6 (90.2)	3.3 (93.5)	2.2 (95.7)	3.0	1.3	1.603	1,009
18.	People with Mental Disability	74.4	11.3 (85.7)	3.6 (89.3)	4.7 (94.0)	3.0 (96.9)	1.6	1.5	1.612	1,009
19.	Dutch	74.2	10.3 (84.4)	4.1 (88.6)	5.1 (93.7)	2.6 (96.3)	3.3	0.4	1.632	1,010
20.	Germans	73.9	10.2 (84.1)	5.0 (89.1)	4.7 (93.7)	1.7 (95.4)	3.9	0.7	1.644	1,010
21.	Spaniards	75.4	9.7 (85.1)	3.0 (88.1)	4.0 (92.1)	2.0 (94.1)	5.1	0.8	1.660	1,008
22.	Italians	73.0	10.6 (83.6)	4.1 (87.6)	4.8 (92.5)	2.4 (94.9)	3.3	1.8	1.703	1,010
23.	Polish	69.6	11.9 (81.5)	4.1 (85.6)	6.1 (91.7)	2.9 (94.6)	3.4	1.9	1.790	1,011
24.	Gay People	62.8	14.4 (77.2)	7.8 (85.0)	6.0 (91.1)	3.6 (94.7)	2.2	3.1	1.923	1,012

Rank Order	Table No. 4.1 Cont. Stimulus Category	Kin-ship %	Friendship %	Neigh-bour %	Co-Worker %	Citizen %	Visitor %	Debar %	Mean Social Distance (1 – 7)	No.
25.	Chinese	63.0	13.9 (76.9)	6.3 (83.2)	9.0 (92.2)	1.9 (94.1)	4.3	1.6	1.924	1,011
26.	Unionists	66.2	11.8 (78.0)	5.8 (83.8)	5.1 (88.9)	3.2 (92.1)	4.6	3.3	1.944	1,010
27.	Socialists	67.0	10.4 (77.4)	4.1 (81.5)	6.8 (88.4)	2.5 (90.9)	5.0	4.1	1.990	1,007
28.	Lithuanians	65.5	10.5 (76.0)	4.3 (80.3)	7.3 (87.6)	2.9 (90.5)	5.2	4.3	2.044	1,009
29.	Russians	63.9	10.5 (74.3)	5.3 (79.6)	7.1 (86.7)	3.2 (89.8)	6.8	3.4	2.091	1,005
30.	Coloureds	58.7	14.6 (73.3)	4.8 (78.1)	9.2 (87.3)	2.9 (90.2)	5.7	4.0	2.164	1,010
31.	Jews	60.7	12.0 (72.7)	6.6 (79.3)	6.3 (85.6)	2.9 (88.5)	6.6	4.9	2.179	1,009
32.	Indians	57.2	13.6 (70.8)	5.9 (76.7)	8.6 (85.3)	3.5 (88.8)	5.0	6.3	2.276	1,011
33.	Capitalists	60.8	8.3 (69.1)	5.9 (74.9)	8.9 (83.8)	4.4 (88.2)	5.4	6.4	2.297	1,007
34.	Afro-Americans**	52.7	17.1 (69.8)	6.6 (76.4)	6.9 (83.4)	4.7 (88.1)	7.3	4.6	2.342	1,013
35.	Blacks	52.6	17.4 (70.0)	6.7 (76.7)	7.0 (83.6)	4.3 (87.9)	6.4	5.7	2.348	1,011
36.	Atheists	52.5	16.1 (68.8)	7.7 (76.5)	6.6 (83.1)	6.0 (89.0)	3.7	7.3	2.373	1,003
37.	Africans	52.3	14.7 (67.1)	6.5 (73.6)	7.9 (81.5)	4.7 (86.2)	9.0	4.7	2.440	1,013
38.	Agnostics	50.3	14.5 (64.8)	7.8 (72.6)	6.9 (79.5)	6.2 (85.7)	5.8	8.4	2.554	1,002
39.	Romanians	55.6	9.4 (65.0)	6.2 (71.2)	7.0 (78.3)	5.0 (83.3)	6.7	10.0	2.566	1,008
40.	Heavy Drinkers	41.9	22.1 (64.0)	9.2 (73.2)	5.9 (79.1)	7.4 (86.4)	6.5	7.1	2.626	1,010
41.	Pakistanis	49.4	12.9 (62.3)	7.2 (69.5)	8.0 (77.5)	4.4 (81.9)	9.3	8.8	2.682	1,010
42.	Palestinians	49.4	13.4 (62.8)	6.8 (69.6)	7.0 (76.6)	4.3 (80.9)	8.8	10.3	2.709	1,010
43.	Nigerians	50.5	11.1 (61.6)	7.4 (69.0)	7.5 (76.5)	4.5 (81.0)	7.9	11.1	2.726	1,010
44.	Israelis	47.9	13.5 (61.4)	5.5 (67.0)	7.2 (74.1)	3.7 (77.8)	9.7	12.5	2.842	1,007
45.	Iranians	47.5	13.6 (61.1)	6.3 (67.5)	7.0 (74.5)	3.3 (77.8)	8.7	13.4	2.850	1,008
46.	Arabs	45.6	11.5 (57.1)	8.3 (65.5)	8.6 (74.1)	5.1 (79.2)	8.5	12.3	2.908	1,011
47.	Communists	45.9	10.1 (56.0)	8.2 (64.3)	9.4 (73.7)	6.6 (80.3)	7.6	12.1	2.920	1,007
48.	Alcoholics	32.7	21.2 (53.9)	13.7 (67.6)	6.8 (74.3)	11.2 (85.5)	6.7	7.8	2.937	1,009
49.	Travellers	39.6	13.8 (53.4)	8.3 (61.7)	8.0 (69.8)	12.1 (81.8)	8.9	9.3	3.030	1,010

Rank Order	Table No. 4.1 Cont. Stimulus Category	Kin-ship %	Friendship %	Neigh-bour %	Co-Worker %	Citizen %	Visitor %	Debar %	Mean Social Distance (1 – 7)	No.
50.	Muslims	42.9	11.6 (54.5)	8.4 (62.9)	7.9 (70.9)	6.0 (76.9)	8.6	14.6	3.066	1,010
51.	Drug Addicts	19.7	9.9 (29.6)	10.8 (40.4)	7.6 (48.0)	18.2 (66.3)	10.2	23.5	4.194	1,009

* 'Euro-Americans' refer to 'White Americans', which was on the questionnaire.
** 'Afro-Americans' refer to 'Black Americans', which was on the questionnaire.
Note: Cumulative percentages up to 'citizen' are in brackets.

When compared with the levels of 'social distance' in the 1988-89 national survey, it is clear that there has been a significant overall improvement in the level of tolerance towards practically all of the forty-six stimulus categories which have been replicated from the 1988-89 survey in the 2007-08 one.   This confirms the hypotheses that favourable contact and greater economic security contribute to a reduction in social prejudice (see changes in mean-social-distance scores on Table No. 4.2).   Positive changes are indicated by reductions in MSD scores.

Part III – Changes in Social Distance since 1988-89

The changes in the rank-ordering of the replicated 'stimulus categories' indicate a shift in the sample's preferences.   Table No. 4.2 gives the extent of these changes (for the forty-six replicated categories) in column three below.   Again, negative changes in mean-social-distance (MSD) indicate relative improvement of the status of the category, while an increase in a stimulus category's rank order would point to a relative disimprovement in its standing with the sample.

The Spearman rank-order correlation coefficient for the forty-six stimulus categories at *rho*=0.92[4] points to the very high degree of consistency in the people's preferences over the past eighteen or nineteen years.

---

[4] Spearman Rank-Order Correlation Coefficient between 1988-89 and 2007-08 results.
$Rho = 1 - \frac{6 \times \sum d^2}{N(N^2 - 1)} = 1 - \frac{6 \times 1,246}{46 \times 2,115} = 1 - \frac{7,476}{97,290} = 1 - .08 = 0.92$

Table No. 4.2:
Changes in Rank Order and in Mean Social Distance 1988-89 to 2007-08

Rank Order	Stimulus Category (by 2007-08 Rank Order)	Rank Order			Mean-Social-Distance		
		2007-08	1988-89	Change	2007-08	1988-89	Change
1st	Roman Catholics	1	1	0	1.168	1.057	+0.111
2nd	Working Class	2	2	0	1.228	1.210	+0.018
3rd	People with Physical Disab.	3	9	-6	1.268	1.581	-0.313
4th	Irish Speakers	4	4	0	1.324	1.287	+0.037
5th	Unmarried Mothers	5	15	-10	1.339	1.684	-0.345
6th	Welsh	6	13	-7	1.388	1.641	-0.296
7th	Gardaí	7	3	+4	1.392	1.267	+0.125
8th	Euro-Americans	8	7	+1	1.416	1.514	-0.098
9th	English	9	6	+3	1.422	1.475	-0.053
10th	Canadians	10	10	0	1.430	1.582	-0.152
11th	Scottish	11	11	0	1.436	1.592	-0.156
12th	Unemployed	12	5	+7	1.446	1.345	+0.101
13th	Protestants	13	14	-1	1.4827	1.6590	-0.1763
14th	French	14	16	-2	1.4829	1.8830	**-0.4001**
15th	British	15	8	+7	1.488	1.521	-0.033
16th	Trade Unionists	16	20	-4	1.552	2.022	**-0.470**
17th	Northern Irish	17	12	+5	1.603	1.637	-0.034
18th	People with Mental Disab.	18	19	-1	1.612	2.010	-0.398
19th	Dutch	19	17	+2	1.632	1.946	-0.314
20th	Germans	20	18	+2	1.644	1.994	-0.350
21st	Spaniards	21	21	0	1.660	2.252	**-0.592**
22nd	Italians	22	23	-1	1.703	2.239	**-0.536**
23rd	Polish	23	22	+1	1.790	2.315	**-0.525**
24th	Gay People	24	45	-21	1.923	3.793	**-1.870**
25th	Chinese	25	30	-5	1.924	3.009	**-1.085**
26th	Unionists	26	33	-7	1.944	3.084	**-1.140**
27th	Socialists	27	26	+1	1.990	2.650	**-0.660**
28th	Russians	28	28	0	2.091	2.882	**-0.791**
29th	Coloureds	29	27	+2	2.164	2.715	**-0.551**
30th	Jews	30	25	+5	2.179	2.599	**-0.420**
31st	Indians	31	35	-4	2.276	3.108	**-0.832**
32nd	Capitalists	32	24	+8	2.297	2.587	-0.290

Rank Order	Table No. 4.2 (cont'd.) Stimulus Category (by 2007-08 Rank Order)	Rank Order			Mean-Social-Distance		
		2007-08	1988-89	Change	2007-08	1988-89	Change
33rd	Afro-Americans	33	39	-6	2.342	3.212	**-0.870**
34th	Blacks	34	31	+3	2.348	3.019	**-0.671**
35th	Atheists	35	38	-3	2.373	3.152	**-0.779**
36th	Africans	36	29	+7	2.440	2.916	**-0.476**
37th	Agnostics	37	32	+5	2.554	3.021	**-0.467**
38th	Pakistanis	38	40	-2	2.682	3.404	**-0.722**
39th	Nigerians	39	37	+2	2.726	3.131	**-0.402**
40th	Israelis	40	36	+4	2.842	3.117	-0.272
41st	Arabs	41	42	-1	2.908	3.509	**-0.601**
42nd	Communists	42	44	-2	2.920	3.769	**-0.849**
43rd	Alcoholics	43	34	+9	2.937	3.105	-0.168
44th	Travellers	44	43	+1	3.030	3.681	**-0.651**
45th	Muslims	45	41	+4	3.066	3.420	-0.354
46th	Drug Addicts	46	46	0	4.194	4.798	**-0.604**
	Sample Average	-	-	-	1.805	2.204	-0.399

Note: Negative changes in MSD scores above sample average are in **bold**. (Negative MSD changes indicate a reduction in social prejudice and an increase in tolerance.)

The sample average of **-0.399** is a very significant and substantial reduction in social prejudice and marks a positive change in the overall attitudes of the sample. Obviously changes in the 'in-group' categories are less because of their relatively low mean-social-distance scores. The nine 'stimulus categories' recording the greatest reduction in prejudice are:

	Stimulus Category		M.S.D.	Rank-Order	Change
1.	'Gay People'	=	- 1.870	- 21	(45th to 24th)
2.	'Unionists'	=	-1.140	-7	(33rd to 26th)
3.	'Chinese'	=	-1.085	-5	(30th to 25th)
4.	'Afro-Americans'	=	-0.870	-6	(39th to 33rd)
5.	'Communists'	=	-0.849	-2	(44th to 42nd)
6.	'Indians'	=	-0.832	-4	(35th to 31st)
7.	'Russians'	=	-0.791	0	(28th to 28th)
8.	'Atheists'	=	-0.779	-3	(38th to 35th)
9.	'Pakistanis'	=	-0.722	-2	(40th to 38th)

Note: Each of these stimulus categories had relatively high MSD scores in the 1988-89 findings.

Each of the above 'stimulus categories' experienced a decrease of over 0.700 MSD score which is almost three-quarters of a stage on the Bogardus 1 – 7 (six stages) scale.   The improvement of the standing of **'Gay People'** has been most exceptional and marks a very significant drop in homophobic attitudes in Irish society.   They were also highest in the improvement in their MSD score and in their rank-order position, i.e. moved from 45th in 1988-89 to 24th in 2007-08, an improvement of twenty-one places.   There is, however, room for further improvement in Irish homophobic attitudes!

The improvement of the standing of **'Unionists'** in the findings on Table No. 4.2 is also very noteworthy and confirms the move towards mutual acceptance of people with diverse political aspirations in relation to the Northern Ireland question.   Their rank-order standing has also improved significantly (ahead of 'socialists' and 'capitalists' in the 2007-08 findings).

Irish social-distance scores in relation to 'Chinese', 'Afro-Americans', 'Indians' and 'Pakistanis' are very much improved and are indicative of a reduction in the relative 'racialist' as well as the 'ethnic' prejudices towards these categories.   All four stimulus categories improved their rank-order position.

The position of the 'Afro-Americans' when compared with the 'in-group' status of 'Euro-Americans' is still very problematic.   Perhaps, the election of **President Barack Obama** in the United States of America in November 2008 will help to remove the still unacceptable level of racial prejudice against 'Afro-Americans' in this country.   What is optimistic about the 2007-08 findings is that the changes are in the right direction, i.e. growth in racial tolerance.

The reduction of prejudice towards 'Communists', 'Russians' and 'Atheists' is also significant and substantial and to be welcomed.   From political, ethnic and religious points of view, these changes would facilitate better relations and greater dialogue with members of those three stimulus categories, who have been perceived as deviant and even demonised in some western societies in the past.

The above comments do not exhaust the significance of the changes in rank order and in mean-social-distance scores.   It is proposed to return to

Table No. 4.2 again when analysing the findings of the 'stimulus categories' under various groupings classified as: ethnic, ethnico-racial, political, racial, religious or social categories. It should also be noted that categories with relatively high MSD in the 1988-89 National Survey were likely to have the greatest change in scores (in the event of an overall increase in inter-group tolerance).

Part IV – Social Distance by 'Kinship' and 'Denial of Citizenship

The patterns of responses towards each 'stimulus category' vary according to overall classification and other factors. Table No. 4.3 presents, at a glance, not only the level of social distance, but also the pattern of responses, i.e. percentages "admitting to kinship" and "denying citizenship". A high percentage denying citizenship is very serious for members of the minorities in question and shows the need for strong *minority rights' legislation* and its enforcement without neglect. Gardaí and civil servants (dealing with Travellers, for instance) should be trained in the detection of offences against minority-rights' legislation. The protection of the law is more important for categories of people who are *a priori* deemed unworthy of Irish citizenship by a substantial minority of society, i.e. 10% plus.

The findings brought together on Table No. 4.3 show a very high Spearman Rank-Order Correlation Co-Efficient (Rho=0.99) between percentages 'welcoming into kinship' and the stimulus categories' mean-social-distance scores. This shows an internal consistency in the *Bogardus Social Distance Scale* and validates the mean-social-distance (MSD) scores as reliable indicators of how close respondents were prepared to admit members of the various 'stimulus categories'.

The highlighting of the percentages 'denying citizenship' shows the level of severe prejudice in the sample. As pointed out, to deny citizenship is a very intolerant behavioural tendency. The 'deny citizenship' percentage is made up by adding the score for "visitor only" and "debar/deport". Table No. 4.1 gives the breakdown of these two levels of social rejection. In the case of indigenous minorities, e.g. 'Travellers', or those with compulsive-behaviour problems, e.g. 'alcoholics' and 'drug addicts', relatively high percentages 'deny-citizenship' scores are to be regretted

Table No. 4.3: Overall Percentages 'Admit into Kinship' and 'Deny Citizenship'

R/O	Stimulus Category	Kinship	Deny Citizen'p	Mean Social Distance	R/O	Stimulus Category	Kinship	Deny Citizen'p	Mean Social Distance
1.	Roman Catholics	91.1	0.6	1.168	27.	Socialists	67.0	9.1	1.990
2.	Working Class	85.6	0.2	1.228	28.	Lithuanians	65.5	9.5	2.044
3.	People with Physical Dis.	83.0	0.3	1.268	29.	Russians	63.9	10.2	2.091
4.	Irish Speakers	84.4	1.5	1.324	30.	Coloureds	58.7	9.7	2.164
5.	Unmarried Mothers	82.4	0.7	1.339	31.	Jews	60.7	11.5	2.179
6.	Welsh	82.4	2.0	1.388	32.	Indians	57.2	11.3	2.276
7.	Gardaí	81.4	1.8	1.392	33.	Capitalists	60.8	11.8	2.297
8.	Euro-Americans	81.3	2.0	1.416	34.	Afro-Americans	52.7	11.9	2.342
9.	English	81.0	2.1	1.422	35.	Blacks	52.6	12.1	2.348
10.	Canadians	80.1	2.2	1.430	36.	Atheists	52.5	11.0	2.373
11.	Scottish	81.7	2.9	1.436	37.	Africans	52.3	13.7	2.440
12.	Unemployed	80.9	2.2	1.446	38.	Agnostics	50.3	14.2	2.554
13.	Protestants	78.4	2.6	1.4827	39.	Romanians	55.6	16.7	2.566
14.	French	78.5	3.4	1.4829	40.	Heavy Drinkers	41.9	13.6	2.626
15.	British	77.2	2.8	1.488	41.	Pakistanis	49.4	18.1	2.682
16.	Trade Unionists	77.8	2.8	1.552	42.	Palestinians	49.4	19.1	2.709
17.	Northern Irish	75.1	4.3	1.603	43.	Nigerians	50.5	19.0	2.726
18.	People with Mental Dis.	74.4	3.1	1.612	44.	Israelis	47.9	22.2	2.842
19.	Dutch	74.2	3.7	1.632	45.	Iranians	47.5	22.1	2.850
20.	Germans	73.9	4.6	1.644	46.	Arabs	45.6	20.8	2.908
21.	Spaniards	75.4	5.9	1.660	47.	Communists	45.9	19.7	2.920
22.	Italians	73.0	5.1	1.703	48.	Alcoholics	32.7	14.5	2.937
23.	Polish	69.6	5.3	1.790	49.	Travellers	39.6	18.2	3.030
24.	Gay People	62.8	5.3	1.923	50.	Muslims	42.9	23.2	3.066
25.	Chinese	63.0	5.9	1.924	51.	Drug Addicts	19.7	33.7	4.194
26.	Unionists	66.2	7.9	1.944					

because such intolerance **impedes** the necessary support they require to improve their conditions or rehabilitate themselves. The **irrationality** of social prejudice is highlighted most in the "denial of citizenship" scores! In the case of some categories it is possible to detect a degree of **polarisation** in the responses, i.e. relatively substantial percentages willing to "admit to kinship" and a significant percentage "denying citizenship" to stimulus categories, e.g. 'Nigerians', 'Israelis', 'Iranians', 'Communists', 'Travellers' and 'Muslims'.   In previous surveys it was found that stimulus categories with 'political' associations attracted such a pattern of polarisation in the social-distance responses[5], i.e. 'bi-modal' responses.

The overall findings of Tables Nos. 4.1, 4.2 and 4.3 indicate a significant and substantial improvement in the social distance of almost all of the stimulus categories when compared with those of 1988-89.   Despite this, the order of preference of the national sample is almost the same as it was, with a number of notable exceptions.   In assessing the findings of the *Bogardus Social Distance Scale*, the rank-order of preferences and the mean-social-distance scores are the principal measures which determine the level of social tolerance and prejudice towards members of the various 'stimulus categories'.

Part V – Diverse Prejudices!

1. Ethnic:

Returning to the notional classification of categories selected for inclusion in the 2007-08 national survey, it is interesting to evaluate how they were scored by the sample.   The **twenty Ethnic Categories** (mainly of White European and Middle-East background) were ranked and scored as follows (in rank order of preference):

Table No. 4.4:   Ethnic Social Distance

Stimulus Category	R/O (1-51)	MSD	Ethnic Rationalisation	Stimulus Category	R/O (1-51)	MSD	Ethnic Rationalisation
1. 'Irish Speakers'	4	(1.324)	19.2%	11. 'Spaniards'	21	(1.660)	32.4%
2. 'Welsh'	6	(1.388)	29.6%	12. 'Italians'	22	(1.703)	36.1%
3. 'English'	9	(1.422)	29.7%	13. 'Polish'	23	(1.790)	37.5%
4. 'Canadians'	10	(1.430)	37.2%	14. 'Lithuanians'	28	(2.044)	39.8%
5. 'Scottish'	11	(1.436)	32.3%	15. 'Russians'	29	(2.091)	36.0%
6. 'French'	14	(1.483)	42.0%	16. 'Romanians'	39	(2.566)	31.3%
7. 'British'	15	(1.488)	28.3%	17. 'Palestinians'	42	(2.709)	32.3%
8. 'Northern Irish'	17	(1.603)	21.0%	18. 'Israelis'	44	(2.842)	26.5%
9. 'Dutch'	19	(1.632)	41.6%	19. 'Iranians'	45	(2.850)	29.0%
10. 'Germans'	20	(1.644)	36.2%	20. 'Arabs'	46	(2.908)	25.5%

---

[5] Mac Gréil, Micheál, (1977), *Op.Cit.*, pp 204-5.

It is noteworthy that the rank-order position of the **'Northern Irish'** is not in accord with the *'principle of propinquity'*. If it were, it would be ranked **No. 2** (between the 'Irish Speakers' and the 'Welsh'). This is probably the result of the unfortunate partition of Ireland in the early 1920s and the sporadic and prolonged 'Troubles' at various times since that time. Much more **favourable contact** between people from the Republic of Ireland and from Northern Ireland should be promoted to correct the current 'social distance' anomaly!

The position of the 'Spaniards' and the 'Italians', at 11th and 12th, below the 'Dutch' and the 'Germans' (at 9th and 10th) also conflicts with the *'principle of propinquity'* (despite the minimal differences of scores). The Republic of Ireland is over 90% Roman Catholic in the *2006 Census Report*, when 'no religion' and 'not stated' are removed. This would give the population religious propinquity with 'Italians' and 'Spaniards'. Yet, we prefer predominantly Protestant Northern European peoples. Is this due to the vicarious influence of English preferences? Or do we prefer the non-Latin European cultures?

The four 'stimulus categories' at the end of the Ethnic Scale are all from the Middle East. The 'Palestinians' were preferred to the 'Israelis' in 2007-08 (even before the military onslaught on the Gaza Strip in 2008-09) which is quite significant. The 'Iranians' have practically the same mean-social-distance score as do the 'Israelis' who were just 0.008 lower. The position of 'Arabs' is also very close to the other three Middle-East categories. In the case of the four Middle-East categories, the pattern of social distance is bi-modal with over 45% "welcoming to the family" and between 19% and 22% willing to deny citizenship to members of each of the four 'stimulus categories'. This is as anticipated because of the political conflict in the area.

2. Racial:
The two racial 'stimulus categories' had behaved according to the racial propinquity principle, i.e. white respondents would be less prejudiced against 'Coloureds' than against 'Blacks'.

Table No. 4.5:   Racial Social Distance

Stimulus Category	R/O (1-51)	MSD	Ethnic Rationalisation	Racial Rationalisation
1. 'Coloureds'	30	(2.164)	(37.0%)	13.3%
2. 'Blacks'	35	(2.348)	(31.8%)	15.7%

Table No. 4.2 (pages 65-66) shows that both categories reduced their social distance by significant MSD scores, i.e. 'Coloureds' by **-0.551** and 'Blacks' by **-0.671**.   Their position on the rank order slipped from 27th to 29th in the case of 'Coloureds' and from 31st to 34th for 'Blacks'.   Both categories' rationalisation scale defines each as primarily **ethnic**.   The low racial rationalisation confirms the reduction of the 'racial' factor in Irish prejudice.

3. Ethnico-Racial:

The seven 'ethnico-racial' stimulus categories measured, recorded a wide range of mean-social-distance scores.

Table No. 4.6:   Ethnico-Racial Social Distance

Stimulus Category	R/O (1-51)	MSD	Ethnic Rationalisation	Racial Rationalisation
1. 'Euro-Americans'	8	(1.416)	31.2%	2.3%
2. 'Chinese'	25	(1.924)	38.2%	4.9%
3. 'Indians'	32	(2.276)	39.8%	4.7%
4. 'Afro-Americans'	34	(2.342)	33.3%	14.9%
5. 'Africans'	37	(2.440)	35.8%	7.9%
6. 'Pakistanis'	41	(2.682)	32.2%	3.7%
7. 'Nigerians'	43	(2.726)	36.1%	7.4%

The above list tells much about Irish racial and ethnic attitudes.   It will be shown from the rationalisation scale (Table No. 5.1, pages 86-87 below) that the racial factor is no longer that relevant as a perceived main reason for not welcoming these categories into 'kinship', that is, apart from 'Afro-Americans' whose rationalisation was 33.3% ethnic and 14.9% racial.

The difference between the mean-social-distance score of 'Afro-Americans' and 'Euro- Americans' are almost one stage (in the six-stage scale of 1 to 7), i.e. **2.342 – 1.426 = 0.926**.   Only **2.3%** adverted to the 'colour-factor' as the main reason for not welcoming 'Euro-Americans' into the family, while **14.9%** gave a racial reason for not welcoming 'Afro-Americans' to kinship. At a time when the 'primary election campaign' for the Democratic candidate was running in the **United States** between Barack Obama (an 'Afro-American') and other candidates was in full swing, the Irish people still recorded such a wide gap in their social-distance scores! At the same time, it should be noted that the current status of 'Afro-Americans' recorded a significant and a substantial improvement in *rank order of preference* since 1988-89, i.e. from 39th in 1988-89 to 33rd (-6) in 2007-08 (see Table No. 4.2, pages 65-66). The change in mean-social-distance score over the same period went from **3.212** in 1988-89 to **2.342** in 2007-08 **(-0.870)**. The great success of President Barack Obama could well narrow the gap further over the next twenty years.

The **'Chinese'** as an ethnico-racial category has succeeded in gaining a relatively high position on the rank order of preference in 25th out of 51 stimulus categories (see Table No. 4.1, pages 62-64 above). The change in mean-social-distance score was the third highest, i.e. from **3.009** in 1988-89 to **1.924** in 2007-08 **(-1.085)**. The international status of China as well as the admiration for the Chinese immigrants to Ireland seems to have impressed the Irish people in a most positive manner according to the findings of the 2007-08 survey.

The relative positions of the **'Indians'** and **'Pakistanis'** have improved significantly and substantially (see Table No. 4.2, pages 65-66). The positions of the **'Nigerians'** and the **'Africans',** having improved in mean-social-distance scores, have disimproved on the rank order of preference, i.e. 'Africans' have gone from 29th in 1988-89 to 36th in 2007-08 (+7) while the 'Nigerians' dropped two places from 37th in 1988-89 to 39th in 2007-08. Anecdotal evidence seems to point to *quite widespread negative stereotypes against African ethnic groups, especially the 'Nigerians'!* These are grossly unfair for the ordinary Nigerian trying to integrate into Irish society. The mass media should exercise greater vigilance in protecting members of the African minority from bigotry which leads to discrimination and inequality.

Despite the negative factors of the findings in regard to ethnico-racial stimulus categories, the overall reduction in social-distance scores since 1988-89 is to be affirmed and welcomed. Our ethnic and racial prejudices are less than they were twenty years ago and the experience of immigration has had a positive effect on our growth in tolerance.

4. Religious:
Overall changes in the case of six religious 'stimulus categories' are very noteworthy:

Table No. 4.7:   Religious Social Distance

Stimulus Category	Rank Order (1-51)	MSD	Religious Rationalisation
1. 'Roman Catholics'	1	(1.168)	11.8%
2. 'Protestants'	13	(1.483)	32.0%
3. 'Jews'	31	(2.179)	31.3%
4. 'Atheists'	36	(2.373)	46.4%
5. 'Agnostics'	38	(2.554)	38.7%
6. 'Muslims'	50	(3.066)	37.9%

The rank order of the religious variables shows a reversal of places for 'Agnostics' and 'Atheists'. In the previous two studies 'Agnostics' were preferred to 'Atheists'. 'Atheists' went from 38th to 35th (-3) while 'Agnostics' went from 32nd to 37th (+5) between 1988-89 and 2007-08 (see Table No. 4.2, pages 65-66). Mean-social-distance scores for 'Atheists' dropped from **3.152** in 1988-89 to **2.373** in 2007-08 which is more than three-quarters of a stage **(-0.779)**. 'Agnostics' also improved their social-distance scores from 3.021 to 2.554 over the nineteen years with slightly less than half a stage **(-0.467)**.

Both 'Roman Catholics' and 'Protestants' are 'in-groups', i.e. mean-social-distance score of less than 1.500, so great variations are not statistically possible. The position of 'Jews' has disimproved in the rank-order of preference, i.e., went from 25th in 1988-89 to 30th in 2007-08 (in Table No. 4.2, pages 65-66). This stimulus category's mean-social-distance score improved by **-0.420** since 1988-89. The problem of the standing of the **'Jews'** has been affected by the relatively unpopular position (44th out of 51) of the **'Israelis'** in the preferences of the Irish people. The current negative image of 'Israelis' has serious consequences for the possible revival of anti-Semitism, which would be very dangerous and unjust to the 'Jews'.

The current position of 'Muslims' as a stimulus category (with 23.2% willing to deny them citizenship) is a very serious reflection on the level of our universal tolerance of fellow human beings. How Irish people have come to entertain such hostile attitudes towards Muslims is largely based on the penetration of anti-Muslim stereotypical thinking from sources (media) outside Ireland. The one ray of hope in the above findings is the fact that, despite a drop in rank-order preference from 41st to 45th between 1988-89 and 2007-08, the mean-social-distance score improved by coming down from **3.420** in 1988-89 to **3.066** in 2007-08, i.e. **-0.354**. This, in itself, is a relatively significant change in the right direction. The whole population needs to become **more enlightened** in the positive tenets of the Muslim religion, which has given European civilisation so much since the time of the philosophers **Avicenna** and **Averroes**[6], not to mention the contribution of the **Moors** to European and Spanish civilisation. The medieval Christian philosopher, St. Thomas Aquinas, was greatly indebted to Averroes and other Muslim philosophers. On the ground in Ireland the Muslim communities are fitting-in in a positive and pluralist manner. Muslims have much to offer Irish society and Irish culture can also contribute to Muslim culture.

5. Political:

With regard to the political stimulus categories, it is clear that the list on page 59 represents a range of sub-categories ideological and occupational. Their rank order of preference is as follows:

Table No. 4.8:
Political Social Distance

Stimulus Category	Rank Order (1-51)	MSD	Political Rationalisation
1. 'Gardaí'	7	(1.392)	20.8%
2. 'Trade Unionists'	16	(1.552)	27.9%
3. 'Unionists'	26	(1.944)	35.9%
4. 'Socialists'	27	(1.990)	22.6%
5. 'Capitalists'	33	(2.297)	21.7%
6. 'Communists'	47	(2.920)	28.7%

---

[6] Footnote on Averroes: Ibn Rushd/Averroes (1126-1198) was an eminent philosopher and medical scientist. "The subject of harmony between reason and faith passed to the West through the works of Averroes ... He composed a number of philosophical works in Latin versions ... Averroes contributed to keeping Aristotelianism alive at a juncture of history when Aristotle was being relegated to oblivion in the rest of the Muslim world ... Averroes played a dominant role in the development of Christian Scholasticism through his commentaries on Aristotle ... The influence of Averroes was also felt among the Jews." (Chejne, Anwar G., *Muslim Spain: Its History and Culture*, Minneapolis, University of Minnesota Press, 1974, pages 327-332)

Gardaí (Irish Police) rank among the 'in-groups' in the Republic of Ireland, i.e. under MSD of 1.500. Their rank-order preference status had disimproved since 1988-89, i.e. slipped from 3rd to 7th, and the mean-social-distance increased slightly from 1.267 to 1.392 over the same period. Despite this slight slippage, it must be rare enough to have the national police force ranking among the country's in-groups. As most students of crime and deviance know, public support for the 'Gardaí' is something to be valued in a democracy. Aspects of perceived Garda behaviour or reporting which undermine this public confidence must be addressed. The slightly negative change in attitude by a minority should serve as a caution!

'Trade Unionists' as a stimulus category improved over the period since 1988-89. Their rank-order position went from 20th in 1988-89 to 16th in 2007-08, while their mean-social-distance score improved by almost half a stage on the Bogardus scale, i.e. **-0.470**. The Irish people seem to think highly of, or feel positive towards, Trade Unions. The strength of the 'white-collar' unions may be among the reasons why 'Trade Unions' have such high esteem among Irish adults. In the light of these findings, it is difficult to explain the ban on Trade Unions in some of the Irish and multinational companies operating in the Republic!

The very significant improvement in the social-distance scores towards **'Unionists'** has already been commented on. The rank-order position improved by seven places, i.e. from 33rd in 1988-89 to 26th in 2007-08 and 'Unionists' experienced the second highest improvement in social-distance scores, i.e. from **3.084** in 1988-89 to **1.944** in 2007-08, which is more than one whole stage on the scale, i.e. **-1.140**. This change endorses, in a most positive manner, the movement toward **peace and reconciliation** in Northern Ireland since 1988-89, especially, during the period from 1994 onwards. Mutual respect for different political views is essential to *the equitable and pluralist integration of Irish society* (in the Republic and in Northern Ireland and between the two administrative areas).

The position of the three ideological stimulus categories, 'Socialists', 'Capitalists' and 'Communists' is of interest. **'Capitalists'** dropped eight places in the rank order of preference between 1988-89 and 2007-08, i.e. from 24th to 32nd. They experienced a modest improvement in social-distance scores, i.e. from **2.587** in 1988-89 to **2.297** in 2007-08 **(-0.290)**. This drop in rank order happened before the failure of self-regulated international capitalism, which contributed to **the major economic**

recession in Ireland in late 2008, had become fully evident! Are people becoming more ambivalent towards some multinational corporate capitalists who have created great hardship in certain communities in the Republic of Ireland as a result of transfer of operations to countries with cheaper labour? Some of the intrinsic weakness of *Capitalism* may be blamed on individual capitalists by the media rather than addressing the structural source of modern economic and financial problems!

'**Communists**', although still low down on the rank order of preference, have experienced an improvement in standing from 44th in 1988-89 to 42nd in 2007-08. The improvement on the mean-social-distance scale has been very substantial, i.e. from **3.769** in 1988-89 to **2.920** in 2007-08 **(-0.849)**. The current survey had been completed just before 'the partial collapse of Capitalism' (as we know it) in Western Europe in 2008 and following. Are we in the eve of a major social revolution[7]? Has the free-market (self-regulated) international capitalist system proven dysfunctional?

'**Socialists**' as a stimulus category has maintained its position (dropping one place from 26th in 1988-89 to 27th in 2007-08) and improved its mean-social-distance scores by two-thirds of a stage, i.e. from **2.650** in 1988-89 to **1.990** in 2007-08 **(-0.660)**. 'Socialists' are now more popular than 'Capitalists' as a stimulus category in the Republic of Ireland. The negative publicity about the unregulated 'free market' is likely to damage further the image of the 'Capitalist' as a stimulus category! Are 'Socialists' being perceived as normal members of modern Ireland's *bourgeoisie* in the attitudes of respondents?

6. Social Categories:

The group of stimulus categories classified as social are quite a **diverse** group. The importance of our taking serious the public attitudes towards these groups is that some of them are dependent on the people's positive help to survive and improve their deprived conditions.

It is clear from the following Table (No. 4.9) that "Way of Life" rather than "Not Socially Acceptable" has been the main reason for not "Admitting to Kinship" for the majority of the 'Social Categories'. In some cases the 'Way of Life' may be perceived just as **different** while in other cases it would be **unacceptable**.

---

[7] By **social revolution** is meant a rapid and radical change in our socio-economic values and norms.

Table No. 4.9: Social Distance towards 'Social' Categories

Stimulus Category	Rank Order (1-51)	MSD	Not Socially Acceptable (Rationalisation)	Way of Life (Rationalisation)
1. Working Class	2	(1.228)	7.1%	(62.2%)
2. People with Physical Disability	3	(1.268)	6.9%	(68.0%)
3. Unmarried Mothers	5	(1.339)	7.0%	(59.7%)
4. Unemployed	12	(1.446)	7.2%	(53.7%)
5. People with Mental Disability	18	(1.612)	10.3%	(54.6%)
6. Gay People	24	(1.923)	11.2%	(74.5%)
7. Heavy Drinkers	40	(2.626)	24.5%	(65.1%)
8. Alcoholics	48	(2.937)	24.9%	(61.0%)
9. Travellers	49	(3.030)	17.8%	(63.7%)
10. Drug Addicts	51	(4.194)	30.3%	(59.6%)

Categories 1 to 5 are *in-groups* (or almost in-group in the case of 'People with Mental Handicap') in Irish society with an exceptionally high level of social acceptance. This is a very positive result and manifests a good level of tolerance towards people who need public support. This speaks well for the ethos of the people of the Republic of Ireland. The position of the 'Working Class' has been maintained at 2nd in rank order of preference since 1988-89. The standing of this category is fascinating, considering that almost half of the sample (47.8%) could be classified 'Upper Class' or 'Middle Class' (see Table No. 1.1, page 3).

The improvement of the rank-order preference of the **'People with Physical Disability'** is very noteworthy. They went from 9th in 1988-89 to 3rd in 2007-08 (see Table No. 4.2, pages 65-66). Their mean-social-distance score improved by almost one-third of a stage, i.e. from **1.581** in 1988-89 to **1.268** in 2007-08 **(-0.313)**. Coming from a relatively strong position (on the edge of 'in-group') to third lowest MSD in the whole list of stimulus categories is both significant and substantial. This must be one of the great success stories in attitude-change in Irish society and it reflects well on the people's priorities and respect for human life.

The improvement in the rank-ordering of **'Unmarried Mothers'** has been even greater than that of the 'People with Physical Handicap'. They moved ten places on the rank order of preference from 15th in 1988-89 to 5th

in 2007-08. Their mean-social-distance score improved by over one-third of a stage on the six-stage social-distance scale, i.e. from **1.684** in 1988-89 to **1.339** in 2007-08 **(-0.345)**. This marks an extraordinary and welcome change from the penal ostracisation of unmarried mothers in Victorian times and much later to the current level of tolerance expressed in these figures. Such positive attitudes should lead to domestic and public support for 'unmarried mothers' and their children. Some might interpret this change as a reduction in the status of marriage in contemporary Ireland. This is not necessarily so. Those who benefit most from the change are *the children* of unmarried mothers. The fact that 82.4% of the sample would welcome 'unmarried mothers' into the family enhances the chances of 'unmarried mothers' finding a husband of their choice, if they so wish! Probably, more importantly, it indicates greater support for the children from the unmarried mother's family of origin.

Although still among the 'in-group' stimulus categories, **'Unemployed'** slipped somewhat since 1988-89. They went from 5th in 1988-89 to 12th in 2007-08 and their mean-social-distance score disimproved by **+0.101**, i.e. from **1.345** in 1988-89 to **1.446** in 2007-08. After a period of almost full employment in the Republic of Ireland since 2002, some people were probably feeling that those out of work had not sought it! In 1988-89, the position was different. In the current (2011) position of unemployment, it is likely that the unemployed will become a more universal phenomenon. This would lead to their regaining their lost seven places on the rank order of preferences, should the question be put in late 2009!

'People with Mental Disability' have maintained their relatively high status in Irish society. At 1.612 they are just on the edge of 'in-group' status. The rank order of preference improved by one place since 1988-89, i.e. moved from 19th in 1988-89 to 18th in 2007-08. The improvement of their mean-social-distance scores was significant, i.e. from **2.010** in 1988-89 to **1.612** in 2007-08 **(-0.398)**. This is positive news for 'people with mental disability', their families and those dedicated to ensuring they have the best quality of life possible. It also shows an advance in enlightenment in relation to 'people with mental disability'.

The social standing of **'Gay People'** in Irish society has greatly improved over the period 1988-89 to 2007-08 (as already noted on page 65 above). This marks a significant and substantial decrease in **'homophobia'** and should lead to a better quality of life for 'Gay People' in Irish society. The move to decriminalise homosexual behaviour between consenting male adults seems to have contributed to greater tolerance. Considering that the Nazi Regime in Germany murdered 'Gay People' in the concentration camps in the 1940s and the long history of persecution of male homosexuals in most societies until relatively recently, the above trend is to be welcomed. These findings, however, leave no room for complacency. 'Gay People's' mean-social-distance at 1.923 is still significant. The trend is in the positive direction.

The next four 'stimulus categories', i.e. 'Heavy Drinkers', 'Alcoholics', 'Travellers' and 'Drug Addicts' are in a less favourable position in Irish society. 'Heavy Drinkers' were a new stimulus category included in the 2007-08 questionnaire. Both **'Heavy Drinkers'** and **'Alcoholics'** received a very negative response from the sample with one-quarter giving "not socially acceptable" as their reason for not welcoming members of each of these two stimulus categories into the family. The position of 'Alcoholics' dropped nine places in the rank order of preference – from 34th in 1988-89 to 43rd in 2007-08. The slight improvement in the mean-social-distance scores of 'Alcoholics' was much less than the sample average of -0.399 at **-0.168**, i.e. from **3.105** in 1988-89 to **2.937** in 2007-08. Both of these social categories probably are **victims of compulsive behaviour** and require the **support** of family and friends to change their drinking behaviour. The levels of social distance found in this survey are likely to **aggravate** their condition rather than help them.

The myth of the positive stereotype of the 'Heavy Drinker' has been shattered by the above figures. The commercialisation of leisure seems to have been exploited by the drinks' industry and drinks' retailers. Young people should avoid addiction to alcohol. Otherwise, they could lose social status in Ireland. The attitudes expressed in this survey would support more control on the availability, advertising and use of alcoholic drink in the Republic of Ireland, in the best interests of our young people. For instance, more than half of those seen as 'Heavy Drinkers' would find it more difficult to attract a spouse for life, i.e. be 'welcome into the family'!

There is a possibility of a tendency towards ostracisation of groups with the above results. The reasons of the relative deterioration in these attitudes of the national sample have been in all likelihood influenced by the frequent media reports of a substantial increase in **binge-drinking** and over-indulgence by young people in particular.   The more widespread availability of alcohol in off-licences and its effective advertising in Irish society must make it very difficult to abstain for those with a compulsive inclination to over-indulge in drinking alcoholic liquor.   Off-licences and food supermarkets (including 'filling stations') provide and even promote the sale of alcohol, contributing to a higher consumption of drink outside the controlled environment of the public house, hotel or licensed club.   This inevitably leads to widespread heavy drinking!

The position of **'Drug Addicts'** is very negative and counter-productive in the findings of Tables No. 4.1 and No. 4.2.   'Drug Addicts' are again **victims of compulsive behaviour** and often 'seduced' by ruthless 'drug pushers'.   There is much negativity and hostility expressed in the social-distance scores towards the stimulus category, 'Drug Addicts'. Almost one-third (30%) of the **80.3%** who would not "welcome them into the family" saw them as "not socially acceptable", which may be understandable because of the self-destructive nature of drug addiction. 'Drug Addicts' retained their position at the *bottom of the rank-order preferential list* (51st place).   On the positive side, there was a significant improvement on their mean-social-distance scores, i.e. from **4.798** in 1988-89 to **4.194** in 2007-08, i.e. **-0.604**.   While this latter improvement is evidence of growing enlightenment, the overall position of 'Drug Addicts' is dangerously precarious.   They are in need of serious professional support, which is made more difficult by the extreme negativity of the attitudes expressed above.

The standing of the **'Travellers'**[8] as a stimulus category is very negative and highly prejudicial.   Table No. 4.1 records a growing polarisation or 'bimodal' pattern in the social-distance scores.   It will be shown later (see Chapter XIII) that, while the percentages "admitting to family" improved from **13.5%** in 1988-89 to **39.6%** in 2007-08, i.e. a nominal increase of **25.1%** (which is to be welcomed), Travellers are placed at the negative end of the social-distance scale.   There was a nominal increase of **8.2%** who would deny Travellers Irish citizenship, i.e. from **10%** in 1988-89 to **18.2%** in 2007-08.   As will be stated in the special chapter below (see Chapter XIII below) this polarisation could have a

---

[8] See: Mac Gréil, Micheál, (2010), *Emancipation of the Travelling People*, Maynooth, Survey and Research Unit, Department of Sociology.

positive meaning. It could be a sign of Travellers' reaction to their plight in Irish society. Are Travellers beginning to stand up for their rights and are they experiencing counter-hostility from the community? It should not be forgotten that the total number of 'Travellers' in the Republic of Ireland is only 0.5% of the population, i.e. 22,369 persons in the *2006 Census of Population.*

Part VI – Conclusion

The **main general findings** of intergroup prejudice and tolerance are reported on in this chapter (IV), namely, the social-distance responses towards fifty-one stimulus categories. Social distance is a measure of **behavioural tendency**, which is one of the three components of social attitudes, i.e. the other two components being **evaluations** and **feelings.** Since there is consistency between the **valency** of the findings on the positive-negative continuum of each of the three components (with some rare exceptions) in relation to stimulus categories, it is reasonable to expect that the measurement of any one of the components gives a measure of the attitude itself. The fact that respondents were urged to give their "first reaction" to the question in relation to each of the stimulus categories ensured that the reply was "**pre-reflectional**"[9]. The scale used was the *Bogardus Social Distance Scale* which was also used in the 1972-73 Survey of Greater Dublin and the National Survey of 1988-89.

The overall findings on Table No. 4.1 were most revealing. Mean-social-distance scores (1 to 7) determined the rank-order of preference of the categories. The *'principle of propinquity'* seemed to operate in most cases resulting in a consistent manner, with notable exceptions, i.e. 'Northern Irish', 'Afro-Americans', 'Nigerians', 'Romanians, 'Travellers' and 'Pakistanis'. The changes in the **rank order** between 1988-89 and 2007-08 were minimal in the case of the forty-one of the forty-six stimulus categories which were replicated in the 2007-08 questionnaire. Social distance scores showed significant and substantial improvement (more than 0.200) for thirty-four of the forty-six categories. This marks a substantial reduction in social prejudice in the Republic of Ireland over seventeen years.

---

[9] Question 4a: *"People have different views about certain groups in society. I am going to read out a list of groups and I would like you to tell me for each group how close you would be willing to allow them. The idea is to get your **first reaction**. Therefore, it would be better if we went through the list **fairly quickly**."*

The nine stimulus categories to show greatest improvement in tolerance towards them (as indicated by MSD scores) were: 'Gay People' (-1.870), 'Unionists' (-1.140), 'Chinese' (-1.085), 'Afro-Americans' (-0.870), 'Communists' (-0.849), 'Indians' (-0.832), 'Russians' (-0.791), 'Atheists' (-0.779) and 'Pakistanis' (-0.722). Again, it must be pointed out that each of the above nine stimulus categories had relatively **high** mean-social-distance scores in the 1988-89 findings. Obviously, categories with high levels of tolerance (as expressed in **low** MSD scores) would not have had the possibility to improve very much. Nevertheless, the above changes are quite significant and point to the areas of growing tolerance, which are to be welcomed.

The two measures which were used in Table No. 4.3 were 'admit to kinship' and 'deny citizenship'. It is quite clear that the level of ethnic, racial, religious, political and social **endogamy** in Irish society is on the decrease when gauged by 'admit to kinship'. This may be due to the arrival of a new wave of globalisation, increased contact with categories from outside Ireland, a weakening of attachment to local community and the influence of the 'liberal' western media. The growth of European integration and the declaration of common European citizenship are likely to increase **international exogamy**.

The 'denial of citizenship' figures were still substantial for a number of categories. Twenty-two of the fifty-one stimulus categories recorded **over 10%** who would be denied their Irish citizenship (see Table No. 4.3, page 69). The ten categories with highest 'denial of citizenship' scores were: 'Drug Addicts' (33.7%), 'Muslims' (23.1%), 'Israelis' (22.2%), 'Iranians' (22.1%), 'Arabs' (20.8%), 'Communists' (19.7%), 'Jews' (19.5%), 'Pakistanis' (19.1%), 'Nigerians' (19.0%) and 'Travellers' (18.2%). The results are still disturbing at a time when an overall reduction in this **exclusion measure** was recorded. Six of the ten categories have Middle-East connections, two are social categories, one is political and another is ethnico-racial.

The fifty-one stimulus categories were divided into six groups, i.e. Ethnic, Racial, Ethnico-Racial, Religious, Political and Social. These groups of categories are based on a notional classification according to 'objective' characteristics. The twenty **ethnic** categories, for instance, consist of white European and Middle-East categories (including

'Canadians'). In the different Tables (Nos. 4.5, 4.6, 4.7, 4.8 and 4.9) the supporting **rationalisation percentages** are given.

The levels of closeness to which respondents were willing to admit members of the various stimulus categories in each of the groups are indicative of the people's **inclusiveness** and **exclusiveness.** They also reflect the myths and fables of the Irish people as well as the diffused biases picked up from the various foreign media (print and electronic). Prejudices and preferences have also been influenced by Ireland's long history of emigration, missionary work abroad, foreign travel for recreational purposes in recent times and the experience of being host to diverse visitors and in-migrants. The **Euro-centrism**, which was enhanced by the eighteenth century 'Enlightenment', is reflected in the findings of the above Tables. More specific analysis in later chapters will enable the reader to focus more closely on the various causes of the people's preferences.

***

CHAPTER V
Intergroup Definition

One of the most important pieces of information which the researcher must know when studying social prejudice and tolerance is how we define the minority group against which we are prejudiced. The rationalisation scale was devised in 1965[1] (by the present author) to find out what were the main reasons why respondents would not welcome members of various stimulus categories into kinship. This revealed their definition of the categories as objects of intergroup attitudes, i.e. as objects of distancing or negative prejudice.

Part I – Rationalisation Scale

Having completed the social-distance scale (see Table No. 4.1 above), respondents were asked the following question: *"Looking over your answers to this question, there are a number of categories which you would not welcome into kinship. Which of the following would you say was your main reason for placing them at the distance indicated?"*

A. Religious Beliefs and/or Practices	E. Economic Danger to Us
B. Racial – Colour of Skin, etc.	F. Not Socially Acceptable
C. Political Views and/or Methods	G. Way of Life
D. Nationality or Culture	H. Other (specify)

A **prompt card**, with the above eight possible reasons on it, was given to the respondent from which he or she was asked to select **one** as the principal reason why he or she would not welcome a member of the category into the family.

The reason for putting the above question to the respondents was to find out **their primary definition** of the category in question. As will be seen, this definition is quite different in many cases from the notional or

---

[1] Mac Gréil, Micheál, *A Psycho-Social-Cultural Theory of Prejudice* (1966), (unpublished M.A. Thesis), Kent (Ohio, USA), Kent State University, (1966).

'objective' classification of the categories listed. For instance, the rationalisation in relation to the Jews (which is notionally a religious category) was quite mixed, i.e. Rationalisation of 'Jews':

A.	Religious –	31.3%	E.	Economic Danger –	2.1%
B.	Racial –	0.7%	F.	Not Socially Acceptable –	3.6%
C.	Political –	5.7%	G.	Way of Life –	25.3%
D.	Nationality/Culture –	25.1%	H.	Other –	6.1%

In the minds of the respondents, 'Jews' were seen primarily as a *'religious'* category (31.3%) while a quarter saw them as *'cultural/national'* and a further 25% gave *'way of life'* as their reasons for not welcoming them into the family. The 'economic danger' stereotype was rejected, while a significant but small minority gave a 'political' reason.

Table No. 5.1:
General Rationalisation Scale
(Principal Reasons for Not Admitting to Kinship)

Rank Order	Stimulus Category (in Order of Preference)	Religious %	Racial %	Political %	Cultural Ethnic %	Economic %	Not Socially Acceptable %	Way of Life %	Other %	No.
1.	Roman Catholics	**11.8**	0.0	8.5	11.2	2.9	3.7	**41.8**	20.0	77
2.	Working Class	1.2	0.0	4.3	10.6	1.0	7.1	**62.2**	13.6	129
3.	People/Physical Dis.	0.1	0.0	2.4	6.7	1.2	6.9	**68.0**	14.7	152
4.	Irish Speakers	3.9	0.5	15.4	19.2	0.0	3.4	**44.4**	13.1	137
5.	Unmarried Mothers	1.3	0.2	3.5	10.6	5.8	7.0	**59.7**	11.9	167
6.	Welsh	2.0	0.4	2.6	29.6	4.1	1.9	**47.1**	12.3	160
7.	Gardaí	0.6	0.8	20.8	9.9	1.2	1.9	**50.5**	14.4	166
8.	Euro-Americans	2.0	2.3	4.2	31.2	2.2	1.1	**45.8**	11.2	173
9.	English	0.4	0.0	18.0	29.7	7.1	2.3	**33.5**	8.9	173
10.	Canadians	1.8	0.0	6.1	37.2	4.1	1.5	**38.9**	10.5	179
11.	Scottish	3.7	0.1	8.3	32.3	3.9	4.8	**35.3**	11.6	168
12.	Unemployed	0.7	0.1	9.0	6.5	13.2	7.2	**53.7**	9.7	174
13.	Protestants	**32.0**	0.6	8.5	17.0	1.5	1.5	29.5	9.4	199
14.	French	1.3	0.3	7.2	42.0	4.1	1.7	**34.2**	9.2	196
15.	British	2.7	0.1	16.5	28.3	4.3	2.5	**37.2**	8.4	209
16.	Trade Unionists	0.6	1.6	27.9	10.2	7.1	4.6	**38.3**	9.8	199
17.	Northern Irish	15.3	0.0	23.2	21.0	1.4	1.4	27.5	10.1	230
18.	People/ Mental Dis.	1.9	0.0	4.2	6.6	3.8	10.3	**54.6**	18.5	238
19.	Dutch	3.3	0.5	5.2	41.6	5.4	1.5	**33.8**	8.7	240
20.	Germans	3.8	0.5	7.8	36.2	6.1	4.0	**32.9**	8.7	242
21.	Spaniards	2.3	0.0	6.4	32.4	6.4	4.7	**38.6**	9.3	231
22.	Italians	2.8	0.4	6.0	36.1	2.2	6.5	**38.4**	7.6	247
23.	Polish	4.2	0.3	3.2	37.5	16.7	2.4	28.5	7.1	288
24.	Gay People	0.8	0.1	2.2	3.8	0.3	11.2	**74.5**	7.1	350

Rank Order	Table No. 5.1 Cont'd. Stimulus Category (in Order of Preference)	Religious %	Racial %	Political %	Cultural Ethnic %	Economic %	Not Socially Acceptable %	Way of Life %	Other %	No.
25.	Chinese	4.0	4.9	**7.9**	**38.2**	**7.7**	1.3	**29.6**	**6.4**	349
26.	Unionists	**11.4**	0.3	**35.9**	**12.5**	3.1	4.5	**26.5**	**5.8**	320
27.	Socialists	2.3	1.6	**22.6**	**14.5**	**8.6**	**7.1**	**37.2**	**6.2**	312
28.	Lithuanians	3.8	1.8	**5.1**	**39.8**	**13.1**	1.3	**28.6**	**6.4**	330
29.	Russians	**6.8**	0.6	**10.5**	**36.0**	**10.1**	3.2	**26.1**	**6.7**	344
30.	Coloureds	3.5	**13.3**	4.6	**37.0**	4.9	3.2	**26.8**	**6.7**	390
31.	Jews	**31.3**	0.7	**5.7**	**25.1**	2.1	3.6	**25.3**	**6.1**	381
32.	Indians	**10.0**	4.7	**5.8**	**39.8**	4.2	**5.1**	**25.3**	**5.1**	413
33.	Capitalists	2.9	0.0	**21.7**	**13.0**	**13.2**	**7.1**	**36.6**	**5.6**	372
34.	Afro-Americans	**5.9**	**14.9**	**6.4**	**33.3**	2.5	4.4	**26.1**	**6.4**	447
35.	Blacks	**6.8**	**15.7**	**6.9**	**31.8**	3.9	4.2	**23.8**	**6.9**	456
36.	Atheists	**46.4**	0.1	**7.8**	**9.1**	2.1	4.8	**24.3**	**5.4**	456
37.	Africans	**11.2**	**7.9**	4.2	**35.8**	**5.1**	3.0	**26.6**	**6.2**	455
38.	Agnostics	**38.7**	0.4	**9.7**	**10.1**	1.9	4.5	**30.7**	3.9	471
39.	Romanians	**7.3**	0.2	4.6	**31.3**	**9.7**	**8.7**	**33.7**	4.5	432
40.	Heavy Drinkers	0.4	0.4	0.6	2.6	3.0	**24.5**	**65.1**	3.4	554
41.	Pakistanis	**17.2**	3.7	**11.4**	**32.2**	3.1	2.8	**25.0**	4.7	494
42.	Palestinians	**16.7**	1.5	**16.7**	**32.3**	3.1	4.0	**21.0**	4.7	497
43.	Nigerians	**9.7**	**7.4**	**6.8**	**36.1**	**7.0**	**6.0**	**21.8**	**5.3**	478
44.	Israelis	**14.2**	0.9	**20.8**	**26.5**	4.6	**5.6**	**23.1**	4.4	506
45.	Iranians	**15.0**	2.0	**17.4**	**29.0**	3.8	**6.1**	**23.2**	3.5	515
46.	Arabs	**22.3**	3.0	**13.7**	**25.5**	4.3	**5.2**	**21.6**	4.3	331
47.	Communists	**16.6**	0.7	**28.7**	**11.5**	**9.9**	**5.6**	**22.2**	4.7	516
48.	Alcoholics	0.6	0.7	2.5	3.4	3.3	**24.9**	**61.0**	3.6	650
49.	Travellers	0.3	0.3	2.3	**9.6**	2.1	**17.8**	**63.7**	3.9	586
50.	Muslims	**37.9**	0.9	**14.1**	**13.1**	2.9	**5.0**	**23.0**	3.2	559
51.	Drug Addicts	0.0	0.1	1.7	2.6	3.8	**30.3**	**59.6**	1.8	796

Note: Percentages over 5% are **bold**.

The findings of the above Table (No. 5.1) merit patient examination and reveal the level of complexity of Irish people's primary definition of the various 'stimulus categories' presented. In the case of categories with high percentages admitting to kinship, i.e. with less than 200 who would not welcome members into the family, some of the cells can be very small.

The reason, 'Way of Life', can mean different things. For some it would refer to cultural lifestyle. Others would see 'Way of Life' as deviant behaviour patterns, while it can also refer to the culture of poverty and low standard of living. Because of this range of possible different meanings, there is a danger of it being used as a 'hold-all' category, both positive and negative.

Part II – Special Rationalisations

2.1 Racial:

The decline of *racial* as a reason for refusing a person into the family is to be welcomed, which means that the **Irish people are not explicitly racist** in the precise sense of the word except in the case of five categories with racial rationalisations over 5%, i.e. 'Afro-Americans' (14.9%), 'Coloureds' (13.3%), 'Blacks' (15.7%), 'Africans' (7.9%) and 'Nigerians' (7.4%). As is evident from the relatively low percentages, even in the case of 'Coloureds' and 'Blacks', Irish adults seem to have overcome the narrow racialism which has followed expansionist Europe over the past four hundred years. This change is a welcome sign. Out of the 51 stimulus categories only five recorded a score of over 5% for 'racial'.

Table No. 5.2: Racial Rationalisation

Stimulus Category	Racial Rationalisation 2007-08	Racial Rationalisation 1988-89 *	Change (A – B)
1. 'Blacks'	15.7%	46.2%	-30.5%
2. 'Afro-Americans'	14.9%	39.4%	-24.5%
3. 'Coloureds'	13.3%	49.6%	-36.3%
4. 'Africans'	7.9%	35.5%	-27.6%
5. 'Nigerians'	7.4%	32.5%	-25.1%
6. 'Chinese'	4.9%	17.0%	-12.1%
7. 'Indians'	4.7%	19.3%	-14.6%
8. 'Pakistani'	3.7%	24.8%	-21.1%
9. 'Arabs'	3.0%	12.9%	-9.9%
10. 'Israelis'	0.9%	5.9%	-5.0%

* *Source:* Mac Gréil (1996), *Prejudice in Ireland Revisited*, Maynooth, St Patrick's College, pages 74-5.

The popular use of the **racial concept** when referring to prejudice or discrimination against a wide range of ethnic, political, religious and social categories by commentators is inaccurate and unhelpful. Such loose use of the term 'racial' militates against emancipation of minorities in Ireland. For social integration purposes, it would be much wiser to move towards the erasing of the relevance of 'race' in intergroup relations[2].

---

[2] See Miller, Patrick H., (1998), "The Anatomy of Scientific Racism: Racialist Responses to Black Athletic Achievement", *The Journal of Sport History*, Vol. 25, No.1, 1998, page 140.

The very substantial decline in the racial rationalisation percentages between 1988-89 and 2007-08 are very significant.   They spell out in concrete figures the extent of such changes in intergroup perception.   This confirms the growth in explicit 'colour blindness' in the Republic of Ireland.

2.2 Economic:
The level of personal security of the sample (in general) was reflected in the relatively few who gave 'economic danger' as a reason for refusal to admit to kinship.   In order of perceived 'economic danger', the following extract is interesting.   It covers all 'stimulus categories' with 5% or higher 'economic' scores.

Table No. 5.3: Economic Rationalisation

	Stimulus Category	Economic Rationalisation 2007-08	1988-89		Stimulus Category	Economic Rationalisation 2007-08	1988-89
1.	'Polish'	16.7%	(0.9%)	9.	'Chinese'	7.7%	(1.5%)
2.5	'Capitalists' ⎱	13.2%	(25.6%)	10.5	'English' ⎱	7.1%	(1.4%)
2.5	'Unemployed' ⎰	13.2%	(19.5%)	10.5	'Trade Unionists' ⎰	7.1%	(18.6%)
4.	'Lithuanians'	13.1%	---	12.	'Nigerians'	7.0%	(0.6%)
5.	'Russians'	10.1%	(4.0%)	13.	'Spaniards'	6.4%	(1.5%)
6.	'Communists'	9.9%	(11.7%)	14.	'Germans'	6.1%	(1.1%)
7.	'Romanians'	9.7%	---	15.	'Dutch'	5.4%	(1.1%)
8.	'Socialists'	8.6%	(14.1%)	16.	'Africans'	5.1%	(1.2%)

Note: Percentages in brackets refer to 1988-89 Rationalisation Scale Scores.
(See: Mac Gréil, 1996, *Op.Cit.,* pages 74-5.)

The overall and relatively low level of perceived 'economic danger' as a "main reason" for refusing admission to the family is indicative of *the openness* of the sample to the external labour market.   At the same time, the above extract shows that Eastern European ethnic categories, who constituted the majority of recent 'in-migrants', i.e. 'Polish', 'Lithuanians', 'Russians' and 'Romanians', constitute four of the categories with substantial percentages.   In times of economic slowdown it is expected that these levels of rationalisation would **rise** and could cause intergroup difficulties.   When the above interviews were being carried out, the decline in job opportunities was not acute, although signs of an impending weakening of the global economy were being talked about.   The changes since the 1988-89 survey (in brackets) register the rise of in-migrant workers.   Categories which were economically neutral have taken on a new significance.

2.3 Political:
Political Rationalisation extended beyond the six (notional) political categories, i.e. 'Gardaí', 'Trade Unionists', 'Unionists', 'Socialists', 'Capitalists' and 'Communists'.   Thirty-six of the fifty-one 'stimulus categories' recorded a five per cent or higher political rationalisation.   The following extract from Table No. 4.9 gives the list of 'stimulus categories' scoring higher than 9.5% for 'political' as the main reason for not welcoming members into the family:

Table No. 5.4: Political Rationalisation

	Stimulus Category	Political Rationalisation 2007-08	1988-89		Stimulus Category	Political Rationalisation 2007-08	1988-89
1.	'Unionists'*	35.9%	(59.8%)	10.	'Iranians'	17.4%	---
2.	'Communists'*	28.7%	(27.4%)	11.	'Palestinians'	16.7%	---
3.	'Trade Unionists'*	27.9%	(39.8%)	12.	'British'	16.5%	(35.6%)
4.	'N. Irish'	23.2%	(42.6%)	13.	'Irish Speakers'	15.4%	(9.9%)
5.	'Socialists'*	22.6%	(39.2%)	14.	'Muslims'	14.1%	(2.6%)
6.	'Capitalists'*	21.7%	(18.1%)	15.	'Arabs'	13.7%	(5.6%)
7.5	'Gardaí' * ⎤	20.8%	(16.5%)	16.	'Pakistanis'	11.4%	(1.9%)
7.5	'Israelis' ⎦	20.8%	(11.7%)	17.	'Russians'	10.5%	(20.9%)
9.	'English'	18.0%	(31.6%)	18.	'Agnostics'	9.7%	(1.2%)

* Stimulus Categories notionally classified as Political Categories
Note: Percentages in brackets refer to Rationalisation Scores in the 1988-'89 survey. (See Mac Gréil, *Ibid.*)

The political rationalisation scores are, with notable exceptions, as anticipated and in line with the 1988-89 figures.   The politicisation of the Middle-Eastern ethnic categories, i.e. 'Israelis', 'Iranians', 'Palestinians', 'Arabs' and 'Pakistanis', and that of 'Muslims' in the intervening nineteen years, could be explained by the focus of the world media on the conflict in that region.   This assumes that 'Muslims' are identified with the 'Middle-East' in some way in the perception of the respondents, which is likely to cause this stimulus category to be placed less favourably in the rank order.

The perception of '**Socialists**' and '**Capitalists**' on the Rationalisation Scale (Table No. 5.1) is practically the same in the case of 'political' reasons for not welcoming members into the family, i.e. 22.6% and 21.7%

respectively.   This is in contrast to the rationalisation score of 1988-89 when 'Socialists' political score was 39.2% and 'Capitalists' registered less than half of that at 18.1%.   The fall of the **Berlin Wall** in 1989 may have helped to reduce the perceived political threat of 'Socialists' in the intervening years.   The impact of the **current economic recession** (2009 –) on the political standing of 'Capitalists' should prove an interesting finding in the next National Survey of social distance and rationalisation in 2026-27!

There has been a significant and substantial decrease in the politically negative rationalisation in relation to the **'Unionists'** (from **59.8%** in 1988-89 to **35.9%** in 2007-08) and in the case of **'Northern Irish'** (from **42.6%** in 1988-89 to **23.2%** in 2007-08).   This helps to explain the substantial improvement in the 'Unionists' rank-order of preference on the social-distance scale from **33rd** in 1988-89 to **26th** in 2007-08 and doubling of the percentage of those who would welcome 'Unionists' into the family from **33.4%** in 1988-89 to **66.2%** in 2007-08. Percentages welcoming 'Northern Irish' into the family went from **70.9%** in 1988-89 to **75.1%** in 2007-08 (while they slipped in the rank order of stimulus categories from **12th** in 1988-89 to **17th** in 2007-08).

The reductions in politicisation as the main reason for not admitting to kinship of **'Northern Irish' (42.6%** to **23.2%)**, **'English' (31.6%** to **18.0%)** and **'British' (35.6%** to **16.5%)** over the period 1988-89 to 2007-08 are indications of *normalisation* of the respondents' perception of these three neighbouring ethnic categories.   Such a change is to be welcomed and is conducive to the continued improvement in intergroup relations between the Republic of Ireland and Northern Ireland, England and Britain as parts of the **'archipelago'** of Ireland and Great Britain (England, Scotland and Wales).

2.4 Religious:
Twenty-one of the stimulus categories had a score of 5% or more for **religious beliefs or practices** as their main reason for not "welcoming members into the family".   The following extract from Table No. 5.1 lists the twenty-one stimulus categories in question.   Corresponding percentages for 1988-89 are listed in brackets.   It should be borne in mind that in the case of **'Roman Catholics'**, relatively few **(8.9%)** would not admit members into the family, and 53% of them would do so for 'way of life' and 'cultural/nationality' reasons (see Table No. 5.1, pages 86-87).

Table No. 5.5:   Religious Rationalisation

	Stimulus Category	Religious Rationalisation 2007-08	1988-89		Stimulus Category	Religious Rationalisation 2007-08	1988-89
1.	'Atheists'*	46.4%	(75.5%)	12.	'Israelis'	14.2%	(11.2%)
2.	'Agnostics'*	38.7%	(70.3%)	13.	'Roman Catholics'*	11.8%	(63.3%)
3.	'Muslims'*	37.9%	(63.3%)	14.	'Unionists	11.4%	(13.6%)
4.	'Protestants'*	32.0%	(83.9%)	15.	'Africans'	11.2%	(7.3%)
5.	'Jews'*	31.3%	(63.0%)	16.	'Indians'	10.0%	(8.3%)
6.	'Arabs'	22.3%	(15.2%)	17.	'Nigerians'	9.7%	(5.1%)
7.	'Pakistanis'	17.2%	(6.4%)	18.	'Romanians'	7.3%	---
8.	'Palestinians'	16.7%	---	19.5	'Russians' ⎱	6.8%	(7.3%)
9.	'Communists'	16.6%	(28.2%)	19.5	'Blacks' ⎰	6.8%	(2.9%)
10.	'Northern Irish'	15.3%	(12.1%)	21.	'Afro-Americans'	5.9%	(3.2%)
11.	'Iranians'	15.0%	---				

* Notionally classified as **Religious Stimulus Categories** (See Mac Gréil, Micheál, *Ibid.*)
   Note: 1988-89 percentages are in brackets.

The overall lesson from the above extract from Table No. 5.1 is the significant and **very substantial reduction** (between 1988-89 and 2007-08) in religion as the main negative reason for not welcoming members of the notionally classified religious stimulus categories to kinship, i.e. 'Atheists', 'Agnostics', 'Muslims', 'Protestants', 'Jews' and 'Roman Catholics'. What does this mean?   Is it because many respondents **feel indifferent** towards particular religious beliefs or the absence of such beliefs?   Or is it that they are **more ecumenical** in relation to different religious beliefs?   The evidence on changes in religious attitudes and beliefs (see Chapter XVII) will indicate that the more probable cause is *religious indifference*[3].

Despite the considerable reduction in the level of religious rationalisation in the case of religious categories, there remains a very substantial minority who seem to reject religious exogamy, i.e. marrying **outside** one's religious group or collectivity.

The presence of a significant level of religious rationalisation in the case of those who would not welcome Middle-Eastern Ethnic Categories into kinship is likely to be the result of the negative stereotypes of 'Muslims' and of 'Jews', associated with these categories.   The substantial drop in the percentage who gave religion as the main reason for not welcoming

---

[3] See Mac Gréil, Micheál, (2009), *The Challenge of Indifference: A Need for Religious Revival in Ireland*, Maynooth, Survey and Research Unit, Department of Sociology, NUI Maynooth.

'**Communists**' into the family shows a change in the people's definition of 'Communists' as more a secular category and with less negative religious connotations.   This may reinforce the presence of 'religious indifferentism' in a minority of the population?

2.5 'Not Socially Acceptable':

"Not Socially Acceptable" indicates a type of social stigma.   It has, in modern Western society, a strong link with social class prejudice and is a more severe level of disapproval of the minorities' lifestyle and potential influence.   Social Acceptability is particularly important when it comes to "welcoming into the family through marriage".   For instance, in most societies there is an implicitly agreed code of informal class-endogamy. People's leisure practices are important forms of informal class-reinforcing procedures.   The associational function of private schools, recreational and professional associations, sports' organisations (especially the more exclusive ones) is part of the informal class endogamous structure. Carefully controlled admissions to new and talented members with exceptional qualities permit an enriching renewal of the 'class pool'!   Even membership of certain religious groups is implicitly social-class determined.

The following extract from Table No. 5.1 lists stimulus categories with 5% or higher opting for the "not-socially-acceptable" rationalisation for not admitting their members to kinship.

Table No. 5.6: Categories "Not Socially Acceptable"

	Stimulus Category	"Not Socially Acceptable" 2007-08	1988-89		Stimulus Category	"Not Socially Acceptable" 2007-08	1988-89
1.	'Drug Addicts'	30.3%	(20.1%)	12.	'Unmarried Mothers'	7.0%	(28.9%)
2.	'Alcoholics'	24.9%	(19.4%)	13.	'People/Physical Dis.'	6.9%	(18.9%)
3.	'Heavy Drinkers'	24.5%	---	14.	'Italians'	6.5%	(1.2%)
4.	'Travellers'	17.8%	(20.3%)	15.	'Iranians'	6.1%	---
5.	'Gay People'	11.2%	(20.4%)	16.	'Nigerians'	6.0%	(1.6%)
6.	'People/Mental Dis.'	10.3%	(18.9%)	17.5	'Israelis'	5.6%	(1.5%)
7.	'Romanians'	8.7%	---	17.5	'Communists'	5.6%	(5.2%)
8.	'Unemployed'	7.2%	(6.8%)	19.	'Arabs'	5.2%	(2.0%)
10.	'Working Class'	7.1%	(12.1%)	20.	'Indians'	5.1%	(2.7%)
10.	'Socialists'	7.1%	(5.3%)	21.	'Muslims'	5.0%	(1.8%)
10.	'Capitalists'	7.1%	(4.9%)				

Note: Percentages in brackets are from the 1988-89 National Survey (See Mac Gréil, Micheál, *Ibid.*)

The first three categories were refused admission to kinship on the grounds that they were "not socially acceptable" by significant and substantial proportions of respondents. It is possible that their compulsive behaviours and addiction were what respondents found "not socially acceptable". It is sometimes difficult "to **love** the sinner while **hating** the sin"! The three categories in question (as do all addicted persons) need the positive support of their friends and the public in general, to assist them in their efforts at rehabilitation. The above findings are not conducive to these victims of addiction receiving the necessary social support.

'Travellers', 'Gay People' and 'People with Mental Disability' recorded moderately high percentages, i.e. over ten per cent, but experienced a reduction in "not-socially-acceptable" rationalisation, when compared with the scores of 1988-89. Of the remaining stimulus categories, three had significant decreases in this category of rationalisation between 1988-89 and 2007-08, i.e. 'Working Class' (from **12.1%** to **7.1%**), 'Unmarried Mothers' (from **28.9%** to **7.0%**) and 'People with Physical Disability' (from **18.9%** to **6.9%**). The stigma (which "not socially acceptable" indicates) against 'Unmarried Mothers' was substantially reduced. This must ensure greater support for the 'Unmarried Mother' in rearing their children than they would have received in 1988-89. This is to be welcomed in modern Irish society.

The relatively small minority of respondents (5.1% to 6.5%) who find 'Italians', 'Iranians', 'Nigerians', 'Israelis', 'Communists', 'Arabs', 'Indians' and 'Muslims' "not socially acceptable" is still significant. Apart from 'Communists', the other categories have recorded a significant increase in their scores since 1988-89. The causes of this change are likely to be mixed and probably due to media reports originating abroad. Because of the more global nature of the mass media, negative stereotypes are regularly diffused throughout many countries. International news media and news agents implicitly transmit or reinforce negative images of certain categories by their continuous and selective reporting of the negatively sensational. There is a real need **to monitor** international news media (with their ideological undertones) which are being 'forced' on guests and patrons in hotels and pubs throughout the country without critical comment. Some of the negative fruits of media stereotyping are reflected in many of the results of the survey reported in this book. At the same time, positive news presentation, with minimum ideological bias, has contributed to the growth in tolerance towards many stimulus categories measured in this survey.

2.6 Ethnic or Cultural:

Forty-seven of the fifty-one stimulus categories were above 5% in the "ethnic or cultural" rationalisation. The following thirty categories received over 19% giving "ethnic or cultural" as their main reason for not admitting their members into the family.

Table No. 5.7:
Ethnic or Cultural Rationalisation

	Stimulus Category	"Ethnic or Cultural" 2007-08	1988-89		Stimulus Category	"Ethnic or Cultural" 2007-08	1988-89
1.	'French'*	42.0%	(73.8%)	16.5	'Palestinians'*	32.3%	---
2.	'Dutch'*	41.6%	(72.1%)	16.5	'Scottish'*	32.3%	(66.4%)
3.5	'Indians'**	39.8%	(54.4%)	18.	'Pakistanis'**	32.2%	(51.6%)
3.5	'Lithuanians'*	39.8%	---	19.	'Blacks'***	31.8%	(37.5%)
5.	'Chinese'**	38.2%	(57.4%)	20.	'Romanians'*	31.3%	---
6.	'Polish'*	37.5%	(73.1%)	21.	'Euro-Americans'**	31.2%	(63.4%)
7.	'Canadians'*	37.2%	(65.0%)	22.	'English'*	29.7%	(42.1%)
8.	'Coloureds'***	37.0%	(35.1)	23.	'Welsh'*	29.6%	(74.1%)
9.	'Germans'*	36.2%	(72.1%)	24.	'Iranians'*	29.0%	---
10.5	'Italians'*	36.1%	(73.1%)	25.	'British'*	28.3%	(36.0%)
10.5	'Nigerians'**	36.1%	(47.3%)	26.	'Israelis'*	26.5%	(56.2%)
12.	'Russians'*	36.0%	(52.2%)	27.	'Arabs'*	25.5%	(50.0%)
13.	'Africans'**	35.8%	(39.7%)	28.	'Jews'****	25.1%	(17.7%)
14.	'Afro- Amer.'**	33.3%	(38.6%)	29.	'Northern Irish'*	21.0%	(17.4%)
15.	'Spaniards'*	32.4%	(76.0%)	30.	'Irish Speakers'*	19.2%	(29.8%)

Note: Percentages in brackets are from the 1988-89 National Survey (See Mac Gréil, Micheál, *Ibid.*)
*   Notionally Ethnic Categories.
**   Notionally Ethnico-Racial Categories.
***   Notionally Racial Categories.
****   Notionally Religious Category.

The substantial levels of ethnic/cultural rationalisation are considered to be a reflection of the degree of ethnic endogamy in the population. The fact that twenty-seven of the thirty categories could be classified notionally as 'ethnic' or 'ethnico-racial' categories points to the awareness of the respondents of the importance of cultural diversity. It could also be interpreted as an acknowledgement of cultural pluralism. "Ethnic/cultural" rationalisation is **more human** than "racial" as a reason for not welcoming a member of a stimulus category into kinship. **'Cultural differences' are**

human differences while 'racial differences' are but visible traits of humans and are not learned and are of no human/cultural significance in themselves. 'Racial' traits are genetically inherited. Therefore, it is a serious error to extend the concept *racialism* or *racism* to groups who are ethnically, culturally, or religiously different.

The very substantial change in the level of "Ethnic or Cultural" rationalisation for "not admitting members of categories into the family" between 1988-89 and 2007-08 was not anticipated. In effect, it means that the level of **ethnic endogamy**, i.e. Irish people wishing to marry *Irish spouses only*, seems to have weakened considerably. This would lead to a degree of 'amalgamation' of those ethnic categories **in-migrating** to Ireland and the *indigenous* population more easily than would have happened twenty years ago. Is this a product of membership of the European Union leading to intercultural assimilation or amalgamation?

In the case of the ten ethnic categories on the above Table (No. 5.7) who are members of the European Union, i.e. 'French', 'Dutch', 'Polish', 'Germans', 'Italians', 'Spaniards', 'Scottish', 'English', 'Welsh' and 'British', the average "ethnic or cultural" rationalisation percentage has dropped from 65.9% in 1988-89 to 34.5% in 2007-08, i.e. a decrease of **47.6%** (or a nominal average reduction of 31.4%). These figures are very significant and are likely to lead to an increase in **miscegenation** between the Irish and other ethnic groups in the future, because of the further reduction in Irish ethnic endogamy. What effect this will have on native Irish culture is a matter of anthropological interest. It will inevitably lead to a degree of **cultural diffusion**. The growing practice in recent years of Irish adolescents and young adults travelling abroad, as well as culturally diverse in-migration, coupled with the growing cosmopolitan ethos of university campuses, are likely to have caused this drop in cultural endogamy (at the attitudinal level, at least). The significance of the changes in ethnic/cultural rationalisation, however, should not be exaggerated because of the relatively high percentage already welcoming members of European nationalities into kinship. *Irish ethnic endogamy* (at the attitudinal level) was already weakened.

The above findings, at the same time, raise very interesting questions in relation to **cultural pluralism**. Perhaps, further research is required to examine the issues raised above! Will the 'global village' have just **one** **'global culture'**? Are there indications here that a significant and substantial percentage of Irish people are willing to move in this direction? One step to ensure the continuity of uniquely Irish culture would be to strengthen its own ethos so as to be able to absorb whatever degree of amalgamation with other cultures occurs, without losing our cultural identity.   Cultural diffusion can enrich the native culture as well as assimilate or absorb it.

2.7 Way of Life:

The rationalisation adopted by most respondents as to the main reason for not welcoming members of various categories into the family was their *"Way of Life"*.   It is clear from the results (See Table No. 5.1) that "Way of Life" includes a variety of meanings, i.e. cultural norms, lifestyle and unacceptable behaviour, to name but three possible meanings.   Some respondents may have chosen it, as already pointed out, as a 'hold-all' reason.

Despite the above qualifications, the results of this rationalisation response are very interesting and merit serious reflection in what they tell us about how a substantial proportion of respondents perceive (negatively) the "Way of Life" of various categories.   All fifty-one 'stimulus categories' received over 20% in the 'way of life' as a principal rationalisation for not "welcoming members into the family".   Table No. 5.8 lists the 29 stimulus categories with 'way of life' rationalisation of 30% plus.   What is meant by 'way of life' varies according to the stimulus category.   The changes in the percentages between the 1988-89 and 2007-08 national surveys raise interesting questions.   There was a nominal average increase (among the 27 categories with over 30% in the 2007-08 survey) of **9.6%**, i.e. from 36.5% in 1988-89 to 46.1% in 2007-08.   This is the equivalent of an increase of 26.3% over a period of nineteen years.

As already noted, the ambiguity of *"Way of Life"* as a main reason for not admitting a member of a particular 'stimulus category' into kinship, presents difficulty when interpreting the above scores.

Table No. 5.8:
"Way of Life" as Rationalisation

	Stimulus Category	"Way of Life" 2007-08	1988-89		Stimulus Category	"Way of Life" 2007-08	1988-89
1.	'Gay People'	74.5%	(74.5%)	16.	'Canadians'*	38.9%	(16.2%)
2.	'People/Physical Dis'*	68.0%	(56.0%)	17.	'Spaniards'	38.6%	(13.1%)
3.	'Heavy Drinkers'	65.1%	---	18.	'Italians'	38.4%	(14.4%)
4.	'Travellers'	63.7%	(74.2%)	19.	'Trade Unionists'	38.3%	(27.5%)
5.	'Working Class'*	62.2%	(68.1%)	20.5	'British'	37.2%	(14.2%)
6.	'Alcoholics'	61.0%	(67.4%)	20.5	'Socialists'	37.2%	(26.9%)
7.	'Unmarried Mothers'*	59.7%	(60.8%)	22.	'Capitalists'	36.6%	(38.9%)
8.	'Drug Addicts'	59.6%	(68.4%)	23.	'Scottish'*	35.3%	(17.6%)
9.	'People/Mental Dis.'	54.6%	(52.8%)	24.	'French'	34.2%	(15.7%)
10.	'Unemployed'*	53.7%	(62.0%)	25.	'Dutch'	33.8%	(14.7%)
11.	'Gardaí'*	50.5%	(64.0%)	26.	'Romanians'	33.7%	---
12.	'Welsh'*	47.1%	(14.1%)	27.	'English'*	33.5%	(12.0%)
13.	'Euro-Americans'*	45.8%	(24.3%)	28.	'Germans'	32.9%	(11.5%)
14.	'Irish Speakers'*	44.4%	(45.4%)	29.	'Agnostics'	30.7%	(14.5%)
15.	'Roman Catholics'*	41.8%	(16.7%)		**Average %**	**46.1%**	**36.5%**

* Stimulus Categories with 80% or over being 'welcomed into kinship'.
Note: Percentages in brackets are from the 1988-89 National Survey.

In the case of 'stimulus categories' who are different classifications of domestic-centred groups, i.e. 'Gay People', 'Unmarried Mothers' and 'People with Physical and Mental Disability', the majority of respondents not welcoming them into the family would appear to have some difficulty with the 'lifestyle' of these categories. With regard to 'Gay People' and 'Unmarried Mothers' there may be a perceived *ethical* dimension to their perceived lifestyle. In relation to "people with handicaps" it could be a fear of being unable to cope adequately with them. It could be a benevolent reluctance to welcome people with handicap into the family. This does not necessarily mean that if a person with a handicap was born into the family that he or she would not be *accepted* and treated well.

"Way of Life" in the case of 'Heavy Drinkers', 'Alcoholics' and 'Drug Addicts' more than likely refers to disapproval of their addicted behaviour and a fear of being unable to cope with possible disruptive behaviour. Table No. 5.6 (page 93) has shown that these three categories were the three with **the highest** rationalisation scores for being "not socially acceptable". This would reinforce the more negative interpretation of their "Way of Life" rationalisation.

For people addicted to alcohol and drugs, rehabilitation **is necessary** for social acceptance. This is very difficult to bring about without domestic and community support, which the above findings make problematic and difficult, therefore, the dilemma for the addicted person and for his or her friends or supporters. They have to transcend popular attitudes and opinions, which are negative and counterproductive!

Ethnic and cultural categories elicited significant and substantial rationalisation responses in the category of "Way of Life". This result was anticipated because of the cultural factors, i.e. languages, religious practices, ethical norms, dietary differences and lifestyles which are socio-culturally determined. Such differences are at the basis of ethnic and religious endogamy, i.e. marry a person from one's own religion and culture. This may also be defined as the "principle of religious and cultural propinquity". **Cultural Pluralism** facilitates a degree of religious and cultural endogamy on the basis of equality. The fact that such a high percentage of respondents would welcome members of most ethnic and religious groups into kinship confirms that they are not opposed to cultural and ethnic exogamy, i.e. marrying outside one's own religious and cultural/national group. Minority religious denominations in Ireland have, over the years, lost membership because of religious exogamy, even where both parties permit their children to select their preferred affiliation.

Part III – Conclusion

In the previous chapter (IV) the classification of the various groupings of stimulus categories was 'notional'. In Chapter V, the performance of the rationalisation scale, which measured the "main reason" the respondent gave for not admitting members of particular categories into kinship. The purpose of the rationalisation question was to discover how Irish respondents defined members of groups or categories they refused to admit to the closest level of social distance. A number of **multi-dimensional definitions** appeared in the replies to the rationalisation question (see Table No. 5.1, pages 86-87).

The following Table (No. 5.9) lists the twenty-eight categories with three or more rationalisations scoring 10% or more:

Table No. 5.9:
Stimulus Categories with Three or More Rationalisations of 10% or More

	R/O	Stimulus Category	Rationalisations (Three or More)			No.
1.	1st	'Roman Catholics'	Rel. (11.8%);	Eth./Cult. (11.2%);	Way of Life (41.8%).	77
2.	4th	'Irish Speakers'	Pol. (15.4%);	Eth./Cult. (19.2%);	Way of Life (44.4%)	137
3.	7th	'Gardaí'	Pol. (20.8%);	Eth./Cult. (9.9%);	Way of Life (50.5%)	166
4.	9th	'English'	Pol. (18.0%);	Eth./Cult. (29.7%);	Way of Life (33.5%)	173
5.	15th	'British'	Pol. (16.5%);	Eth./Cult. (28.3%);	Way of Life (37.2%)	209
6.	16th	'Trade Unionists'	Pol. (27.9%);	Eth./Cult. (10.2%);	Way of Life (38.5%)	199
7.	17th	'North. Irish' *	Rel. (15.3%); Pol. (23.2%); Eth./Cult. (21.0%); Way of Life (27.5%)			230
8.	21st	'Unionists' *	Rel. (11.4%); Pol. (35.9%); Eth./Cult. (12.5%); Way of Life (26.5%)			320
9.	27th	'Socialists'	Pol. (22.6%);	Eth./Cult. (14.5%);	Way of Life (37.2%)	312
10.	28th	'Lithuanians'	Eth./Cult. (39.8%);	Econ. (13.1%);	Way of Life (28.6%)	330
11.	29th	'Russians' *	Pol. (10.5%); Eth./Cult. (36.0%); Econ.(10.1%);Way of Life (26.1%)			344
12.	30th	'Coloureds'	Rac. (13.3%);	Eth./Cult. (37.0%);	Way of Life (26.8%)	390
13.	31st	'Jews'	Rel. (31.3%);	Eth./Cult. (25.1%);	Way of Life (25.3%)	381
14.	32nd	'Indians'	Rel. (10.0%);	Eth./Cult. (39.8%);	Way of Life (25.3%)	413
15.	33rd	'Capitalists' *	Pol. (21.7%); Eth./Cult.(13.0%); Econ.(13.2%); Way of Life (36.6%)			372
16.	34th	'Afro-Americans'	Rac. (14.9%);	Eth./Cult. (33.3%);	Way of Life (26.1%)	447
17.	35th	'Blacks'	Rac. (15.7%);	Eth./Cult. (31.8%);	Way of Life (23.8%)	456
18.	37th	'Africans'	Rel. (11.2%);	Eth./Cult. (35.8%);	Way of Life (26.6%)	455
19.	38th	'Agnostics' *	Rel. (38.7%); Pol. (9.7%); Eth./Cult. (10.1%); Way of Life (30.7%)			471
20.	39th	'Romanians'	Eth./Cult. (31.3%);	Econ. (9.7%);	Way of Life (33.7%)	432
21.	41st	'Pakistanis' *	Rel. (17.2%); Pol. (11.4%); Eth./Cult. (32.2%); Way of Life (25.0%)			494
22.	42nd	'Palestinians' *	Rel. (16.7%); Pol. (16.7%); Eth./Cult. (32.3%); Way of Life (21.0%)			487
23.	43rd	'Nigerians'	Rel. (9.7%);	Eth./Cult. (36.1%);	Way of Life (21.8%)	478
24.	44th	'Israelis' *	Rel. (14.2%); Pol. (20.8%); Eth./Cult. (26.5%); Way of Life (23.1%)			506
25.	45th	'Iranians' *	Rel. (15.0%); Pol. (17.4%); Eth./Cult. (29.0%); Way of Life (23.2%)			479
26.	46th	'Arabs' *	Rel. (22.3%); Pol. (13.7%); Eth./Cult. (25.5%); Way of Life (21.6%)			461
27.	47th	'Communists' **	Rel.(16.6%); Pol.(28.7%); Eth./Cult. (11.5%); Econ.(9.9%); WoL (22.2%)			462
28.	50th	'Muslims' *	Rel. (37.9%); Pol. (14.1%); Eth./Cult. (13.1%); Way of Life (23.0%)			559

    * = **four** rationalisations
   ** = **five** rationalisations

The above findings confirm the degree of complexity of intergroup definition. The information on Table No. 5.9 is crucial in order to understand the multiple reasons for our negative dispositions towards members of certain categories. The most complex of all are our attitudes toward 'Communists' with **five** rationalisations. It is interesting to compare the rationalisation of 'Communists' of 2007-08 with those of 1988-89.

Table No. 5.10:
Rationalisation for Not Admitting to Kinship of 'Communists'

Rationalisation	A. 2007-08	B. 1988-89	Nominal Change (A – B)
1. Religious	16.6%	28.2%	-11.6%
2. Political	28.7%	27.4%	+1.3%
3. Ethnic/Cultural	11.5%	7.1%	+4.4%
4. Economic	9.9%	11.7%	-1.8%
5. Way of Life	22.2%	18.7%	+3.5%
Number	462	737	---
Mean Social Distance	2.920	3.769	-0.849

The above change in rationalisations is a good example of current patterns of perception in relation to a controversial stimulus category, 'Communists', that experienced substantial improvements in mean-social-distance between 1988-89 and 2007-08, i.e. a drop of **22.5%** from 3.769 to 2.920. Likely causes of change may have been the weakening of the religious rationalisation and association of 'Communists' with nationality or cultures/ethnic categories in the mind of respondents. It is noteworthy that the **political** and **economic** rationalisations were maintained in 2007-08 more or less as they were in 1988-89.

It is interesting that eleven of the twenty-eight categories on Table No. 5.9 had **four** rationalisations, i.e. 'Northern Irish', 'Unionists', 'Russians', 'Capitalists', 'Agnostics', 'Pakistanis', 'Palestinians', 'Israelis', 'Iranians', 'Arabs' and 'Muslims', in addition to 'Communists' who elicited **five** reasons for not being admitted to kinship.

The five Middle-Eastern categories with four rationalisations, i.e. 'Pakistanis', 'Palestinians', 'Israelis', 'Iranians' and 'Arabs' had a similar pattern of intergroup definition. They were perceived as **religious-political-ethnic** stimulus categories with variations of emphasis. Any progress in improvement in intergroup relations with members of these minorities will need to address the religious, political and cultural traits which are perceived as negative. Of course, religious and ethnic endogamy can co-exist with **pluralist integration**.   The relatively low incidence of **racial** rationalisation among the ethnico-racial stimulus categories points to **a weakening of racial endogamy** in the Irish population.   Of course, it could also be indicative of the 'political incorrectness' of admitting racial bias!

***

CHAPTER VI
Ethnic, Ethnico-Racial and Racial Prejudices

Of the fifty-one 'stimulus categories' measured on the Social-Distance scale there were twenty notionally classified as **ethnic** (Table No. 4.4), two as **racial** (Table No. 4.5) and a further seven as **ethnico-racial** (Table No. 4.6). In Chapters VI to IX it is proposed to measure the ethnic and racial prejudices of the Irish people as represented by the responses of a national sample to these twenty-nine categories. In Chapter V when dealing with the findings of the **Rationalisation Scale**, it was clear that, with a number of notable exceptions, the main rationalisation, the principal reason for not admitting into kinship was **ethnic.** Therefore, it is but logical that all 'ethnic, racial and ethnico-racial' stimulus categories are brought together. The correlation tables (Tables Nos. 6.3, 4, 5, 6 and 7) will show that the racial dimension is still significant in the respondents' attitudes.

Part I – Social Distance Scores of Total Sample

1.1 Social Distance (Kinship, Denial of Citizenship and MSD):
Table No. 6.1 (extracted from Table No. 4.3, pages 68-69 above) gives the rank-order, admit-to-kinship, denial-of-citizenship and mean-social-distance scores of the twenty-nine ethnic, ethnico-racial and racial categories. The relative decline in the significance of 'race' as a negative intergroup rationalisation among the Irish people is very noteworthy. It shows a welcome and positive change in respondents' outlook. It is a sign of maturity and progress that the **myth of race** is so clearly on the decline (but by no means eradicated) in the Irish adult population. In Chapter IX it is proposed to examine the current state of racism and discern its influence in our attitudes to a number of ethnico-racial nationalities or cultural stimulus categories.

Once again, it needs to be repeated that the widespread use of **'racism'** by critics is inappropriate when addressing discrimination and prejudice in society in general. In effect, they are referring to other forms of prejudice, e.g. ethnocentrism, sexism, homophobia and political, religious and social prejudices. This is no more than being **scientifically correct**. By avoiding the term racism they can help to prevent a return of a form of prejudice based on genetic inheritance, which has been used to justify genocide, slavery and gross abuse of minorities in the past. Racism's origin owes much to the implicit elitism underpinning the rise of the so-called **'Enlightenment'** in Europe[1] which saw that 'white', male and, at times, Christian people, were inherently superior! Cartoonists should also avoid racist imagery, e.g. 'atavistic' facial expressions. In a real sense, the **'Enlightenment'** strengthened **'Euro-centrism'** as a form of prejudice!

Table No. 6.1: Ethnic and Ethnico-Racial Social Distance

Rank-Order	Stimulus Category	Welcome to Kinship	Denial of Citizenship	Mean-Social-Distance	Number
1.	'Irish Speakers' *	84.4%	1.5%	1.324	1,010
2.	'Welsh' *	82.4%	2.0%	1.388	1,012
3.	'Euro-Americans' **	81.3%	2.0%	1.416	1,010
4.	'English' *	81.0%	2.1%	1.422	1,012
5.	'Canadians' *	80.1%	2.2%	1.430	1,012
6.	'Scottish' *	81.7%	2.9%	1.436	1,011
7.	'French' *	78.5%	3.4%	1.4829	1,012
8.	'British' *	77.2%	2.8%	1.488	1,010
9.	'Northern Irish' *	75.1%	4.3%	1.603	1,009
10.	'Dutch' *	74.2%	3.7%	1.632	1,010
11.	'Germans' *	73.9%	4.6%	1.644	1,010
12.	'Spaniards' *	75.4%	5.9%	1.660	1,008
13.	'Italians' *	73.0%	5.1%	1.703	1,010
14.	'Polish' *	69.6%	5.3%	1.790	1,011
15.	'Chinese' **	63.0%	5.9%	1.924	1,011
16.	'Lithuanians' *	65.5%	9.5%	2.044	1,000
17.	'Russians' *	63.9%	10.2%	2.091	1,005
18.	'Coloureds' ***	58.7%	9.7%	2.164	1,010
19.	'Indians' **	57.2%	11.3%	2.276	1,011
20.	'Afro-Americans' **	52.7%	11.9%	2.342	1,013
21.	'Blacks' ***	52.6%	12.1%	2.348	1,011
22.	'Africans' **	52.3%	13.7%	2.440	1,013
23.	'Romanians' *	55.6%	16.7%	2.566	1,008
24.	'Pakistanis' **	49.4%	18.1%	2.682	1,010
25.	'Palestinians' *	49.4%	19.1%	2.709	1,010
26.	'Nigerians' **	50.5%	19.0%	2.726	1,010

[1] See Hesse, Barror and S. Soygid (eds), (2006), "Narrating the Post-Colonial Political and Immigrant Imaginary" in *A Post-Colonial People – South Asians in Britain*, London, Hurst and Company.

Rank-Order	Table No. 6.1 (Cont'd.) Stimulus Category	Welcome to Kinship	Denial of Citizenship	Mean-Social-Distance	Number
27.	'Israelis' *	47.9%	22.2%	2.842	1,007
28.	'Iranians' *	47.5%	22.1%	2.850	1,008
29.	'Arabs' *	45.6%	20.8%	2.908	1,011

Note: Notional Classification: * = Ethnic
         ** = Ethnico-Racial
       *** = Racial

A clear pattern of preferences emerges from Table No. 6.1 above. They are in line (more or less) with the *'principle of ethnic and racial propinquity'*. It is possible to identify four main 'groups' of stimulus categories, i.e. (in order of preference):

(a) *Irish, British and American Stimulus Categories*:-

     1. 'Irish Speakers';   6. 'Scottish';
     2. 'Welsh';   7. 'British';
     3. 'Euro-Americans'(White); 8. 'Northern Irish';
     4. 'English';   9. 'Afro-Americans'(Black);
     5. 'Canadians'.

(b) *Continental European Nationalities*:-

     1. 'French';   6. 'Polish People';
     2. 'Dutch';   7. 'Lithuanians';
     3. 'Germans';   8. 'Russians';
     4. 'Spaniards';   9. 'Romanians'.
     5. 'Italians';

(c) *African, Asian and Racial Stimulus Categories*:-

     1. 'Chinese';   5. 'Africans';
     2. 'Coloureds';   6. 'Pakistanis';
     3. 'Indians';   7. 'Nigerians'.
     4. 'Blacks';

(d) *Middle-East Stimulus Categories*:-

     1. 'Palestinians';   3. 'Iranians';
     2. 'Israelis';   4. 'Arabs'.

1.2 Irish, British and American Categories:
The Irish people's most preferred group of categories is the *"Irish, British and American Group"* (with the exception of *'Afro-Americans'*) with the *"Continental European Nationalities"* in second place. This would seem to confirm that *"we feel closer to Boston than to Brussels or Berlin"* (to paraphrase an eminent Irish politician). It is very interesting to see 'Euro-Americans' and 'Canadians' as part of the Irish-British group of nations in the dispositions of the sample.

Later in Chapter VI it is proposed to examine the social-distance scores of each of the above groups of categories and the various personal variables. This should enable the reader to get a detailed measure of ethnic and ethnico-racial social prejudice in the Republic of Ireland in the first decade of the 21st century.

In the 'Irish, British and American' group of stimulus categories the order of preference is interesting. The *Euro-Americans*, i.e. 'American Whites' and 'Canadians', are ahead of the 'Scottish, 'British' and 'Northern Irish'. In the case of the 'English', 'Euro-Americans' were ranked ahead of them.

The position of 'Northern Irish' is in breach of the *'principle of propinquity'*. As an Irish ethnic stimulus category it would be expected that 'Northern Irish' would rank second after 'Irish Speakers'. The above result is a negative social legacy of the division, resentment and hostility of a history of ethnic cleansing (plantations), post-Reformation inter-denominational religious and political conflict and the division of Ireland into the **Irish Free State** and **Northern Ireland** by Britain in 1922. With improved cross-border favourable contact in recent years, it is to be expected that the attitudes and preferences of the people in the Republic of Ireland for their fellow-Irish (men and women) will become closer in social-distance terms. As it stands at present (2007-08) it is 'out of kilter' and becoming less-preferred in rank-order terms. 'Northern Irish' went from **12th** in 1988-89 to **17th** in 2007-08 (see Table No. 4.2, pages 65-66 above). The improvement of intergroup attitudes and relationships between the citizens of the Republic of Ireland and those of Northern Ireland would seem to be a future priority from the above evidence. One of the most reliable ways to bring about an improvement in North-Republic relations would be through widespread **favourable contact**.

The improvement of the position of the **'Welsh'** as a 'stimulus category' is significant and substantial. In terms of rank order, they went from **13**[th] to **6**[th] on the overall scale (Table No. 4.2) and experienced a **9.6%** nominal increase in the percentage who would welcome 'Welsh' into their family, i.e. from **72.8%** in 1988-89 to **82.4%** in 2007-08. The 'Welsh' have replaced the 'English' as the more preferred ethnic group outside Ireland. This change of fortunes was not anticipated.

The highly preferred position of 'Euro-Americans', i.e. 'American Whites', contrasts with that of their fellow-Americans, the 'Afro-Americans', i.e. 'American Blacks'. The concepts 'Euro-Americans' and 'Afro-Americans' emphasise their **ethnic** designation. This shows how dominant the **racial factor** still is in Irish intergroup attitudes. The improvement of the standing of 'Afro-Americans' ('American Blacks') since 1988-89 have been very substantial, i.e. from **26.2%** (in 1988-89) to **52.7%** (in 2007-08) 'welcoming them into the family'. Their overall rank-order went from **39**[th] to **33**[rd] in the same period. The fact that **11.9%** would still deny 'Afro-Americans' Irish citizenship is not a very tolerant reflection on Irish adults! As stated already, the election of **Barack Obama** as President of the United States may influence further positive change!

1.3 Continental European Categories:
The spread of the "Continental European Nationalities" highlights the West-East divide. Within the Western European categories we prefer the 'French', 'Dutch' and 'Germans' to the 'Spaniards' and 'Italians' despite our stronger religious propinquity with the latter two stimulus categories. Here, we may have adopted the implicit affinities of the English. The proliferation of the English press and television in Ireland diffuses their preferences and prejudices in the Republic of Ireland. Also, there has been a long history of Irish migrant labourers to Britain where they induced some aspects of English culture and attitudes.

The overall improvement in Irish social-distance scores between 1988-89 and 2007-08 for "Ethnic, Ethnico-Racial and Racial" categories has been statistically significant and very substantial, i.e. an average drop of almost half a stage **(0.437)** on the social-distance continuum of 1 to 7 (see Table No. 6.2 below). It was even greater in the case of seven "Continental European Categories" measured in both surveys, where the average mean-social distance score dropped by **0.461**.

The relatively positive standing of the 'Polish People' and the 'Lithuanians' reflects favourably on the impact of migrant workers from both of these countries in recent years. It was a very great challenge to admit a significant percentage of migrant workers from Eastern Europe and elsewhere over a relatively short period of time. Apparently, from the findings of Table No. 6.2, this was a quite successful operation, especially for the 'Polish' migrant workers to Ireland. Their predominantly 'Roman Catholic' religious affiliation and reputation (known anecdotally by the author) for 'hard work', probably recommended them to the **69.6%** of the national sample who would welcome a Polish person into the family. The fact that the late **Pope John Paul II** was Polish was also probably relevant.

The relatively weaker position of 'Romanians' (with **55.6%** welcoming them into the family) may be due to the negative stereotype of **Romany People** associated with begging on the streets. It could also have an element of **social-class** prejudice. The relatively high percentage, i.e. **16.7%**, who would deny Romanians citizenship (as compared with only **5.3%** denying citizenship to 'Polish People') is a serious reflection on Irish attitudes towards members of a member-state of the European Union, i.e. the Romanians. Prejudice against Romany Gypsies has been quite widespread in Europe for many years with very negative consequences for members of this culturally colourful minority!

Table No. 6.2: Changes in Ethnic/Ethnico-Racial Social-Distance Scores Between 1988-89 and 2007-08

Rank Order	Stimulus Category	Welcome into Family 1988-89	2007-08	Nominal Change	Denial of Citizenship 1988-89	2007-08	Nominal Change	Mean-Social-Distance 1988-89	2007-08	Nominal Change
1.	'Irish Speakers'	84.4%	84.4%	**0.0%**	0.3%	1.5%	**+1.2%**	1.287	1.324	**+0.037**
2.	'Welsh'	72.8%	82.4%	**+9.6%**	3.8%	2.0%	**-1.8%**	1.641	1.388	**-0.253**
3.	'Euro-Americans'	78.6%	81.3%	**+2.7%**	3.4%	2.0%	**-1.4%**	1.514	1.416	**-0.098**
4.	'English'	77.9%	81.0%	**+3.1%**	2.8%	2.1%	**-0.7%**	1.475	1.422	**-0.053**
5.	'Canadians'	75.8%	80.1%	**+4.3%**	4.1%	2.2%	**-1.9%**	1.582	1.430	**-0.152**
6.	'Scottish'	74.2%	81.7%	**+7.5%**	3.8%	2.9%	**-0.9%**	1.592	1.436	**-0.156**
7.	'French'	66.2%	78.5%	**+12.3%**	7.3%	3.4%	**-3.9%**	1.883	1.483	**-0.400**
8.	'British'	76.7%	77.2%	**+0.5%**	3.5%	2.8%	**-0.7%**	1.521	1.488	**-0.033**
9.	'Northern Irish'	70.9%	75.1%	**+4.2%**	2.6%	4.3%	**+1.7%**	1.637	1.603	**-0.034**
10.	'Dutch'	63.9%	74.2%	**+10.3%**	7.9%	3.7%	**-4.2%**	1.946	1.632	**-0.314**
11.	'Germans'	62.0%	73.9%	**+11.9%**	8.7%	4.6%	**-4.1%**	1.994	1.644	**-0.350**

Rank Order	Table No. 6.2 cont. Stimulus Category	Welcome into Family 1988-89	2007-08	Nominal Change	Denial of Citizenship 1988-89	2007-08	Nominal Change	Mean-Social-Distance 1988-89	2007-08	Nominal Change
12.	'Spaniards'	58.3%	75.4%	**+17.1%**	12.0%	5.9%	**-6.1%**	2.252	1.660	**-0.592**
13.	'Italians'	55.1%	73.0%	**+17.9%**	12.7%	5.1%	**-7.6%**	2.339	1.703	**-0.636**
14.	'Polish'	54.6%	69.6%	**+15.0%**	12.3%	5.3%	**-7.0%**	2.315	1.790	**-0.525**
15.	'Chinese'	30.9%	63.0%	**+32.1%**	18.8%	5.9%	**-12.9%**	3.009	1.924	**-1.085**
16.	'Lithuanians'	---	65.5%	---	---	9.5%	---	---	2.044	---
17.	'Russians'	40.9%	63.9%	**+23.0%**	21.2%	10.2%	**-7.4%**	2.882	2.091	**-0.791**
18.	'Coloureds'	34.3%	58.7%	**+24.4%**	14.9%	9.7%	**-5.2%**	2.715	2.164	**-0.551**
19.	'Indians'	31.0%	57.2%	**+26.2%**	21.3%	11.3%	**-10.0%**	3.108	2.276	**-0.832**
20.	'Afro-Americans'	26.2%	52.7%	**+26.5%**	20.7%	11.9%	**-8.8%**	3.212	2.342	**-0.870**
21.	'Blacks'	29.7%	52.6%	**+22.9%**	18.4%	12.1%	**-6.3%**	3.019	2.348	**-0.671**
22.	'Africans'	30.1%	52.3%	**+22.2%**	16.0%	13.7%	**-2.3%**	2.916	2.440	**-0.476**
23.	'Romanians'	---	55.6%	---	---	16.7%	---	---	2.566	---
24.	'Pakistanis'	24.2%	49.4%	**+25.2%**	25.9%	18.1%	**-7.8%**	3.404	2.682	**-0.722**
25.	'Palestinians'	---	49.4%	---	---	19.1%	---	---	`2.709	---
26.	'Nigerians'	29.1%	50.5%	**+21.4%**	21.3%	19.0%	**-2.3%**	3.131	2.726	**-0.405**
27.	'Israelis'	32.4%	47.9%	**+15.5%**	22.6%	22.2%	**-0.4%**	3.117	2.842	**-0.275**
28.	'Iranians'	---	47.5%	---	---	22.1%	---	---	2.850	---
29.	'Arabs'	20.1%	45.6%	**+25.5%**	26.7%	20.8%	**-5.9%**	3.509	2.908	**-0.601**
	Average Scores*	52.0%	67.3%	+15.3%	12.4%	8.1%	-4.3%	2.360	1.923	-0.437

*Average Scores for the 25 Stimulus Categories measured in both national surveys.
Note: Nominal Changes in **bold.**

1.4 African, Asian and Racial Categories:

The 'racial factor', as well as 'social propinquity', is evident in the placement of the "African, Asian and Racial Categories" on Irish rank order of preferences (see Table No. 6.2). At the same time, it must be admitted that there has been a significant and very substantial improvement in the social-distance performance of the seven stimulus categories between 1988-89 and 2007-08 in this group of categories. On average, there was a drop of **0.691** in mean-social-distance score and a nominal increase of **21.8%** in those who would welcome members of these categories into the family. These results are significantly higher than the Table No. 6.2 average. This in turn may be explained by the relatively high MSD score these categories had in the 1988-89 National Survey.

The improvement of the standing of the '**Chinese**' (i.e.: **-1.085** MSD and **+32.1%** admit to family) represents an exceptionally positive change between 1988-89 and 2007-08. The reasons for this change are multiple. Among the causes, the following three may be stated, i.e. (1) Irish people's positive perception of the Chinese minority in the Republic of Ireland, (2) the change in the international status of the Chinese people, and (3) the overall reduction in racial and ethnic prejudice of the Irish people over the past two decades. What the latter is due to will be discussed later.

'**Indians**' were another Asian stimulus category to experience a very positive improvement in their social-distance scores since 1988-89, i.e. **-0.832** MSD and **+26.2%** admit to family. Again, this is likely to be due to the positive experience of respondents of Indians working and living in Ireland and of the international respect in Ireland for the people of India. The fact that the Bogardus Social Distance Scale places 'Coloureds' as a stimulus category between 'Chinese' and 'Indians' reflects the improvement in Irish racial attitudes and prejudices.

The relatively negative position of '**Nigerians**' on the social-distance scale is disappointing and points to the need to counter any negative stereotypes about 'Nigerians' among the Irish population. Considering the long association between Ireland and Nigeria through the foreign missions over the past one hundred years, it is surprising that respondents did not respond more positively. The **racial endogamy factor** is pretty strong in the case of the percentages admitting to family on Table No. 6.2, i.e.:

Stimulus Category		Admit to Kinship
'Afro-Americans'	-	52.7%
'Blacks'	-	52.6%
'Africans'	-	52.3%
'Nigerians'	-	50.5%

The range of difference between the above diverse categories is less than 3% (2.2%), which reiterates the role of the **racial-endogamy** factor.

1.5 Middle-East Stimulus Category:
The "Middle-East Stimulus Categories" come at the bottom of the rank-order scale of the twenty-nine 'Ethnic/Ethnico-Racial/Racial Social-Distance Scale' (Table No. 6.2). Not only do they rank low in our order of

preference, they also reveal a very severe level of negative dispositions towards them with **less than 50%** of the sample willing to welcome their members into the family and **over 19%** not willing to grant them citizenship in the Republic of Ireland.

The two categories that were measured in the 1988-89 national survey, i.e. **'Israelis'** and **'Arabs'**, have shown a substantial improvement in their individual social-distance levels, which reflects the overall increase in tolerance and reduction in social prejudice. The score for both stimulus categories were as follows (extract from Table No. 6.2):

Stimulus Category	Admit to Kinship			Deny Citizenship		
	1988-89	**2007-08**	**Change**	**1988-89**	**2007-08**	**Change**
'Israelis'	32.4%	47.9%	**+15.5%**	22.6%	22.2%	**-0.4%**
'Arabs'	20.1%	45.6%	**+25.5%**	26.7%	20.8%	**-5.9%**
Average Scores for 29 categories	52.0%	67.3%	+15.3%	12.4%	8.1%	-4.3%

It is very obvious from the findings on Table No. 6.2 that the enduring violent conflicts in the Middle-East and the partisan reporting on them in the Western mass media are giving these categories a negative image to the people of Ireland. The **polarisation** of the social-distance results, i.e. relatively strong support for kinship and high percentages willing to deny citizenship, indicates that the *"political factor"* is influencing the responses. In previous studies (1972-73 and 1988-89) a similar 'bi-modal' response pattern was recorded (see Mac Gréil, Micheál, *Prejudice in Ireland Revisited*, 1996, Figure No. 28, page 276).

1.6 Overall Changes in Ethnic, Ethnico-Racial and Racial Prejudice:
Table No. 6.2 gives the changes which have taken place in the social-distance scores of each of the twenty-nine Ethnic/Ethnico-Racial/Racial Stimulus Categories between the 1988-89 and 2007-08 national surveys. As noted already, there has been a significant and substantial increase in social tolerance and a consequent reduction in social prejudice. The increase in personal (economic) security brought about by a decade of economic growth and prosperity is a most likely contributing source of changes. The favourable contact between Irish people and those of different nationality, who arrived in Ireland as workers and new residents in recent years, is likely to have increased ethnic and racial tolerance and, thereby, reduced prejudice.

Part II – Inter-Category Correlations

The value of examining the *product moment correlation coefficients* between the social-distance responses of the various ethnic and ethnico-racial stimulus categories is to find out the level of consistency in respondents' replies. Scores above **0.20** would be considered **significant**, while those **0.50** or higher would be evidence of a *special factorial relation* between the categories reaching that figure. Those stimulus categories with 80% plus percentages admitting to family, i.e. in-groups, have a low variation potential and are, thereby, less discerning.

Categories with extra-ethnic associations, e.g. political, religious, etc. in the mind of the respondents will tend to register lower correlation coefficients. This, in itself, is valuable information for the better understanding of intergroup attitudes, loyalties and prejudices. The *principle of propinquity* is also confirmed in the correlation tables. (See Table No. 6.7, page 119 below.)

2.1 Irish, British and American Categories:
Table No. 6.3 gives the correlation coefficients between the nine Irish, British and American categories.

Table No. 6.3:
Irish, British and American Categories
– Pearson Correlation Coefficients

	Stimulus Categories	Irish Speakers 1	Welsh 2	Euro-Americans 3	English 4	Canadians 5	Scottish 6	British 7	Northern Irish 8	Afro-Americans 9
1.	'Irish Speakers'	1.00	**0.53**	0.40	0.46	0.45	**0.58**	0.38	**0.51**	0.27
2.	'Welsh'		1.00	**0.66**	**0.60**	**0.63**	**0.78**	0.47	0.47	0.34
3.	'Euro-Americans'			1.00	0.49	**0.63**	**0.60**	**0.50**	0.37	0.37
4.	'English'				1.00	**0.57**	**0.56**	**0.79**	0.44	0.37
5.	'Canadians'					1.00	**0.61**	**0.59**	0.41	0.39
6.	'Scottish'						1.00	0.45	**0.49**	0.35
7.	'British'							1.00	0.41	0.42
8.	'Northern Irish'								1.00	0.43
9.	'Afro-Americans'									1.00

Note: Scores 0.50 and higher in **bold**

The above Table (No. 6.3) shows that all scores are significant, i.e. **+0.20** of the **36** cells in the matrix, some **15** or 41.7% of them recorded a plus **0.50** score.   The variety of scores is quite revealing.   The **relatively low level** of correlation between **'Afro-Americans'** and the other eight categories is in contrast with that of **'Euro-Americans'**.   This confirms both the **ethnic** and the **racial** factors in relation to attitudes towards the 'Afro-Americans' stimulus category.   The absence of a +0.50 correlation coefficient between Euro- and Afro-Americans is most disappointing.   Irish people's long association with the United States and Canada failed to develop a strong interpersonal relationship with Afro-Americans.   Irish-Americans seemed to have absorbed the racial prejudices of the 'Euro-Americans' (White Americans) with whom they identified over the centuries.   With the advance of integration in the United States, it is to be expected that Afro-Americans, i.e. 'Black-Americans', will become more accepted as 'full Americans' on the basis of equality.   This, in turn, should have a more positive effect on Irish attitudes towards 'Afro-Americans'.

'Irish Speakers' registered a **plus 0.50** correlation coefficient with only three stimulus categories in Table No. 6.3, i.e. the 'Welsh', the 'Scottish' and 'Northern Irish'.   This result singles out the **Celtic factor**, which is to be expected as an ethnically relevant phenomenon.   The fact that the four 'Celtic' stimulus categories were pulled together by the Pearson Correlation Coefficients is most discerning and confirms a further common cultural trait with the 'Northern Irish', i.e. 'Gaelic and Scots-Irish'.   Such a finding, however tentative, may be something worth building on for the sake of *"pluralist coexistence in Ireland"*.

Stimulus categories numbers 2 to 7 show a very close social-distance pattern, i.e. 'Welsh' – 'Euro-Americans' – 'English' – 'Canadians' – 'Scottish' and 'British'.   The correlation coefficients range from **0.56** between responses between 'English' and 'Scottish' responses and **0.78** between 'Welsh' and 'Scottish'.   'Euro-Americans' scored moderately high in relation to 'Canadians' (**0.63**), 'Scottish' (**0.60**) and 'Welsh' (**0.66**).   The strong identity in the minds of the respondents between Euro-Americans and 'British' ethnic categories is noteworthy.   Is this a remnant of the *White Anglo-Saxon Protestant* (WASP) image of the former dominant elite in the United States?   The correlations between Anglo-American categories and Western European nationalities are also moderately high (in general).   This can be gauged from Table No. 6.7.

2.2 Continental European Ethnic Categories:

Continental European ethnic categories divide into two subgroupings, i.e. 'Western' and 'Eastern' Europeans nationalities. Table No. 6.4 gives the correlation coefficients between the various categories.

Table No. 6.4:
Continental European Nationalities
– Pearson Correlation Coefficients

Rank Order	Stimulus Categories	French 1	Dutch 2	Germans 3	Spaniards 4	Italians 5	Polish People 6	Lithu-anians 7	Russians 8	Roman-ians 9
1.	'French'	1.00	**0.71**	**0.66**	**0.62**	**0.66**	0.47	0.45	**0.53**	0.40
2.	'Dutch'		1.00	**0.70**	**0.65**	**0.66**	**0.58**	**0.57**	**0.56**	**0.50**
3.	'Germans'			1.00	**0.60**	**0.57**	**0.58**	**0.53**	**0.56**	0.48
4.	'Spaniards'				1.00	**0.65**	**0.64**	**0.60**	**0.61**	**0.50**
5.	'Italians'					1.00	0.47	**0.51**	**0.54**	0.45
6.	'Polish People'						1.00	**0.74**	**0.66**	**0.63**
7.	'Lithuanians'							1.00	**0.76**	**0.70**
8.	'Russians'								1.00	**0.69**
9.	'Romanians'									1.00

Note: Scores 0.50 and higher in **bold**

The above matrix once again confirms the validity of the *Bogardus Social Distance Scale* in that it groups the Continental European categories together with significant product-moment coefficient correlations. Within the nine stimulus categories, the 'Western European' group, i.e. numbers 1 to 5, and the 'Eastern European' group, i.e. numbers 6 to 9, recorded higher correlation numbers. This confirms the principle of European ethnic propinquity not only in their rank-order ratings but also in their common intergroup attitude patterns as manifested by the correlation groupings. The six highest correlations were:

(a) 'Lithuanians' with 'Russians' at $r = 0.76$

(b) 'Polish People' with 'Lithuanians' at $r = 0.74$

(c) 'French' and 'Dutch' at $r = 0.71$

(d) 'Dutch' with 'Germans' at $r = 0.70$ ⎤

(e) 'Romanians' with 'Lithuanians' at $r = 0.70$ ⎦

(f) 'Russians' and 'Romanians' at $r = 0.69$

2.3 African and Asian Racial Categories:

African and Asian racial categories registered relatively high correlation coefficient scores, as borne out on Table No. 6.5 below:

Table No. 6.5:
African, Asian and Racial Categories
– Pearson Correlation Coefficients

Rank Order	Stimulus Categories	Chinese 1	Coloureds 2	Indians 3	Blacks 4	Africans 5	Pakistanis 6	Nigerians 7
1.	'Chinese'	1.00	0.74	0.69	0.65	0.61	0.58	0.58
2.	'Coloureds'		1.00	0.66	0.82	0.75	0.63	0.70
3.	'Indians'			1.00	0.70	0.68	0.73	0.72
4.	'Blacks'				1.00	0.83	0.67	0.75
5.	'Africans'					1.00	0.70	0.77
6.	'Pakistanis'						1.00	0.75
7.	'Nigerians'							1.00

Note: Scores 0.50 and higher in **bold**

The above matrix of correlations is most revealing and (again) confirms the validity and reliability of the Bogardus Social Distance scale. The range of correlation scores were as follows:

1. 'Blacks' with 'Africans'at $r = 0.83$
2. 'Coloureds' with 'Blacks' at $r = 0.82$
4. 'Africans' with 'Coloureds' at $r = 0.75$
4. 'Nigerians' with 'Blacks' at $r = 0.75$
4. 'Pakistanis' with 'Nigerians' at $r = 0.75$
6. 'Chinese' with 'Coloureds' at $r = 0.74$
7. 'Indians' with 'Nigerians at $r = 0.72$
8. 'Pakistanis' with 'Indians' at $r = 0.71$
10. 'Blacks' with 'Indians' at $r = 0.70$
10. 'Coloureds' with 'Nigerians' at $r = 0.70$
10. 'Africans' with 'Pakistanis' at $r = 0.70$

12.5 'Chinese' with 'Indians' at $r = 0.69$
12.5 'Pakistanis' with 'Nigerians' at $r = 0.69$
14. 'Blacks' with 'Pakistanis' at $r = 0.67$
15. 'Coloureds' with 'Indians' at $r = 0.66$
16. 'Chinese' with 'Blacks' at $r = 0.65$
17. 'Coloureds' with 'Pakistanis' at $r = 0.63$
18. 'Africans' with 'Chinese' at $r = 0.61$
19.5 'Indians' with 'Africans' at $r = 0.58$
19.5 'Chinese' with 'Pakistanis' at $r = 0.58$
21. 'Nigerians' with 'Chinese' at $r = 0.55$

These correlations' pairings tell us about the patterns of responses between each of the categories paired. When they are perceived similarly, it is to be expected that the correlation will be higher, e.g. in the case of two categories perceived to have similar racial, ethnic, political, religious, or other traits.   For instance, the perceived **'racial' trait** in the case of the first two pairings, i.e. 'Blacks' and 'Africans' **and** 'Coloureds' and 'Blacks', was obviously the common factor determining the social-distance responses of the sample.

As is known from the rationalisation scale results (see Table No. 5.1, pages 86-87 above) most categories listed on Table No. 6.5 have mixed intergroup definition traits, i.e. classification/rationalisation.   The following sub-table is an extract from Table No. 5.1:

Rank Order	Stimulus Categories	Religious	Racial	Political	Cultural /Ethnic	Economic	Not Socially Acceptable	Way of Life
1.	'Chinese'	4.0%	4.9%	**7.9%**	**38.2%**	**7.7%**	1.3%	**29.6%**
2.	'Coloureds'	3.5%	**13.3%**	4.6%	**37.0%**	4.9%	3.2%	**26.8%**
3.	'Indians'	**10.0%**	4.7%	**5.8%**	**39.8%**	4.2%	**5.1%**	**25.3%**
4.	'Blacks'	**6.8%**	**15.7%**	**6.9%**	**31.8%**	3.9%	4.2%	**23.8%**
5.	'Africans'	**11.2%**	**7.9%**	4.2%	**35.8%**	**5.1%**	3.0%	**26.6%**
6.	'Pakistanis'	**17.2%**	3.7%	**11.4%**	**32.2%**	3.1%	2.8%	**25.0%**
7.	'Nigerians'	**9.7%**	**7.4%**	**6.8%**	**36.1%**	**7.0%**	**6.0%**	**21.8%**

Note: Rationalisations over 5% are in **bold.**

The above percentages represent the main reasons why respondents did not welcome members of the seven stimulus categories into the family through marriage.   The spread of reasons indicate how they saw the members of these categories as not being suitable for admission to kinship. It is assumed, therefore, that such intergroup perception would affect the degrees of closeness to which they were willing to admit members of the stimulus category (outside kinship) since the rationalisation scale's measures are **nominal** rather than **ordinal** it is not possible to correlate them with those of the social-distance scale (which is ordinal).   Nevertheless, the findings of Table No. 5.1 (The Rationalisation Scale) point to the complexity and irrationality of some, if not most, of our intergroup attitudes and prejudices and should make the reader aware of the danger of singular causality when trying to explain variations in the levels of social prejudice against different stimulus categories and by diverse personal variable sub-samples.

In the case of minorities who are the objects of severe prejudice, there is a tendency to classify the members as being *"all the same[2]"*.   Little, if any, serious effort is made to get to know members of such minorities in order to discern their variety of traits and qualities.   In these situations people resort to the *'lazy way out'* of negative stereotyping.   Classic examples have been the popular characterisation of Travellers in Ireland, and of Muslims and Jews in societies where they are the object of anti-Muslim and of anti-Semitic prejudice.

2.4 Middle-East Stimulus Categories:

The final sub-set of ethnic and ethnico-racial stimulus categories in Table No. 6.1 (see pages 104-105) are from the Middle-East Stimulus Categories.

Table No. 6.6:
Middle-East Stimulus Categories – Pearson Correlation Coefficients

Rank Order	Stimulus Categories	Palestinians 1	Israelis 2	Iranians 3	Arabs 4
1.	'Palestinians'	1.00	0.81	0.81	0.72
2.	'Israelis'		1.00	0.90	0.74
3.	'Iranians'			1.00	0.75
4.	'Arabs'				1.00

Note: Scores 0.50 and higher in **bold**

In the social-distance responses of the total national sample of the over eighteen-year-olds of the Republic of Ireland in 2007-08, there seems to be a significant and relatively high correlation between the patterns of attitudes toward each of the four stimulus categories on Table No. 6.6.   The six correlations in the above matrix are worth serious reflection.

Correlation Coefficients

1. 'Israelis' with 'Iranians' at   r = **0.90**
2.5 'Palestinians' with 'Israelis' at   r = **0.81** ⎤
2.5 'Palestinians' with 'Iranians' at   r = **0.81** ⎦
4. 'Iranians' with 'Arabs' at   r = **0.75**
5. 'Israelis' with 'Arabs' at   r = **0.74**
6. 'Palestinians' with 'Arabs' at   r = **0.72**

---

[2] This phenomenon may be referred to as **'Racial Essentialism'** (i.e. when measuring racial and ethnico-racial categories).   See Hirschfeld, Laurence (1997), "The Conceptual Politics of Race: Lessons from our Children" in *Ethos*, Vol.1, March 1997, pp. 63-92.

The relatively high *Pearson Product-Moment Correlation Coefficient* of **r = 0.81** between the social distance patterns in relation to 'Israelis' and 'Palestinians' reflects the very close mean-social-distance scores recorded in respect of both stimulus categories, i.e. **2.709** for 'Palestinians' and **2.842** for 'Israelis'.   Some **49.4%** of the sample would welcome 'Palestinians' into the family through marriage while **47.9%** would admit 'Israelis' into kinship.   It is interesting how similar Irish attitudes are to each category.

The denial-of-citizenship percentages are significantly (but not very substantially) more negative towards Israelis, i.e. **22.2%** would deny citizenship to 'Israelis' while **19%** would do in the case of 'Palestinians' (see Table No. 4.1, pages 62-64 above).   This polarisation of attitudes (i.e. relatively high percentages welcoming members into the family, on the one hand, while a substantial minority would deny citizenship) has not been unusual in past surveys using the Bogardus Scale in the case of stimulus categories associated with political or social conflict or agitation (see Mac Gréil, Micheál, *Prejudice in Ireland Revisited,* Maynooth, 1996, pages 276-7).

2.5 Overall Inter-Category (Ethnic, Ethnico-Racial and Racial) Correlations:

The pattern of correlation scores between the twenty-nine Ethnic, Ethnico-Racial and Racial Stimulus Categories is given on Table No. 6.7.   It confirms the patterns anticipated with a few exceptions.   Each of the four subclasses of categories' scores, i.e. (1) **Irish, British and American**, (2) **Continental European Nationalities**, (3) **African, Asian and Racial Categories**, and (4) **Middle-East Categories**, are repeated on Table No. 6.7. What is of special interest in this table is how categories correlate with ones outside their special 'triangles'.

Stimulus Categories Nos. 1 to 14 (excluding No. 9 'Afro-Americans') factored together (more or less) as did Nos. 15 to 29 (including No. 9), i.e. scores of *Rho=0.50 plus*.   In other words, Irish, British, Euro-Americans and Western European nationalities clustered together.   'Irish Speakers' clustered only with the Celtic Categories and the 'French'.

Table No 6.7: Pearson Product-Moment Correlation Coefficients between Ethnic, Ethnico-Racial and Racial Categories

			Irish Speak.	Welsh	Euro-Amer.	English	Canadians	Scottish	British	North. Irish	Afro-Amer.	French	Dutch	Germans	Spaniards	Italians	Polish	Lithuanians	Russians	Romanians	Chinese	Coloureds	Indians	Blacks	Africans	Pakistanis	Nigerians	Palestinians	Israelis	Iranians	Arabs
	R/O	Stimulus Categories	1	2	3	4	5	6	7	8	9	10	11	12	13	14	15	16	17	18	19	20	21	22	23	24	25	26	27	28	29
Irish British and American	1	Irish Speakers	1.0	**.53**	.40	.46	.45	**.58**	.38	**.51**	.27	**.60**	.48	.46	.41	.48	.38	.28	.34	.28	.27	.27	.27	NS	.31	.27	.25	.27	.24	.22	.30
	2	Welsh		1.0	**.66**	**.60**	**.63**	**.78**	.47	.47	.34	**.69**	**.69**	**.63**	**.60**	**.55**	.46	.40	.49	.40	.43	.31	.37	.26	.34	.34	.34	.39	.35	.34	.34
	3	EuroAmericans			1.0	.49	**.63**	**.60**	**.50**	.37	.37	**.50**	**.61**	**.56**	**.57**	**.55**	.47	.44	**.51**	.38	.38	.33	.42	.30	.36	.37	.34	.39	.38	.37	.32
	4	English				1.0	**.57**	**.56**	**.79**	.44	.37	**.60**	**.57**	.49	**.57**	.47	.48	.45	.45	.39	.46	.41	.41	.32	.35	.32	.31	.35	.32	.33	.32
	5	Canadians					1.0	**.61**	**.59**	.41	.39	**.69**	**.73**	**.61**	**.57**	**.58**	**.50**	.45	.49	.41	**.56**	.42	.45	.35	.38	.35	.33	.37	.36	.36	.35
	6	Scottish						1.0	.45	.49	.35	**.66**	**.60**	**.56**	**.65**	**.60**	.47	.38	.48	.40	.38	.29	.38	.25	.32	.32	.32	.37	.36	.35	.34
	7	British							1.0	.41	.42	.45	**.56**	.44	**.55**	.40	**.51**	.45	.42	.40	.44	.38	.40	.41	.36	.31	.32	.33	.30	.32	.35
	8	Northern Irish								1.0	.43	**.53**	.48	.44	.47	**.58**	.41	.41	.45	.44	.41	.36	.47	.42	.44	.40	.40	.40	.36	.38	.43
	9	Afro-Americans									1.0	.35	.48	.44	**.51**	.43	**.63**	**.70**	**.67**	**.71**	**.64**	**.80**	**.71**	**.89**	**.84**	**.65**	**.75**	**.66**	**.66**	**.67**	**.69**
Continental European Nationalities	10	French										1.0	**.71**	**.66**	**.62**	**.66**	.47	.45	**.53**	.40	.44	.34	.43	.25	.37	.35	.34	.37	.35	.34	.36
	11	Dutch											1.0	**.70**	**.65**	**.66**	**.58**	**.57**	**.56**	**.50**	**.56**	.44	**.50**	.40	.45	.45	.45	.48	.42	.43	.41
	12	Germans												1.0	**.60**	**.67**	**.58**	**.53**	**.56**	.48	.44	.41	.49	.36	.42	.42	.47	.46	.41	.39	.38
	13	Spaniards													1.0	**.65**	**.64**	**.60**	**.61**	**.50**	**.53**	.46	**.56**	.42	.45	.46	.44	.48	.46	.44	.42
	14	Italians														1.0	.47	**.51**	**.54**	.45	.47	.37	**.53**	.36	.41	.47	.39	.46	.45	.42	.39
	15	Polish People															1.0	**.74**	**.66**	**.63**	**.63**	**.59**	**.63**	**.57**	**.57**	**.55**	**.54**	**.54**	.47	.46	.48
	16	Lithuanians																1.0	**.76**	**.70**	**.63**	**.70**	**.70**	**.65**	**.66**	**.64**	**.66**	**.63**	**.59**	**.58**	**.55**
	17	Russians																	1.0	**.69**	**.62**	**.68**	**.73**	**.60**	**.64**	**.66**	**.67**	**.67**	**.62**	**.64**	**.58**
	18	Romanians																		1.0	**.58**	**.63**	**.70**	**.70**	**.70**	**.69**	**.76**	**.69**	.69	.69	.65
African, Asian & Racial Cat.	19	Chinese																			1.0	**.74**	**.69**	**.65**	**.61**	**.58**	**.58**	**.55**	**.55**	**.56**	**.55**
	20	Coloureds																				1.0	**.66**	**.82**	**.75**	**.63**	**.70**	**.62**	**.64**	**.66**	**.63**
	21	Indians																					1.0	**.70**	**.68**	**.73**	**.72**	**.71**	**.70**	**.74**	**.65**
	22	Blacks																						1.0	**.83**	**.67**	**.75**	**.64**	**.65**	**.68**	**.70**
	23	Africans																							1.0	**.70**	**.77**	**.69**	**.67**	**.70**	**.65**
	24	Pakistanis																								1.0	**.75**	**.89**	**.77**	**.79**	**.72**
	25	Nigerians																									1.0	**.76**	**.75**	**.77**	**.67**
Middle-East	26	Palestinians																										1.0	**.81**	**.81**	**.72**
	27	Israelis																											1.0	**.90**	**.74**
	28	Iranians																												1.0	**.75**
	29	Arabs																													1.0

Notes: Correlations *Rho=0.50* plus are in **bold.**
Correlations less than *Rho=0.20* are not significant (NS)

Categories Nos. 9 and 15 to 29, i.e. Afro-Americans, East-European nationalities, Asian, African and Racial categories and Middle-East categories have elicited mutual correlation scores of a most impressive nature. Only three of the 120 correlation coefficients were less than *Rho*=**0.54** and one hundred were over **0.60**. This points to the presence of the **racial and political** as well as the **ethnic** dimensions in the respondents' attitudes towards this wide range of categories. The *Rho scores* for the 'Afro-American', once again, emphasise the extent of the racial factor of respondents' prejudices towards this category.

The Irish seem to be viewing 'Afro-Americans' **more as Africans** than as Americans. Their moderately low correlation with 'Euro-Americans' (**0.37**) compared with their high correlation with 'Africans' (**0.84**) confirms this view. This is problematic for the Irish perception of Afro-Americans, despite all that black Americans have contributed to modern US culture!

In summary, therefore, the value of *Pearson Product-Moment Correlation Coefficient Matrixes* is their contribution to the patterns of social prejudice in society. They also help in the exercise of factor analysis of multiple sub-scales and responses to particular items. In addition, the grouping together of different stimulus categories helps to validate the *Bogardus Social Distance Scale*.

Part III – Conclusion

The findings presented in Part I and Part II of this chapter dealt with the responses of the *total sample* to twenty-nine **ethnic, ethnico-racial** and **racial stimulus categories**. A closer examination of these findings by personal variables will be reported on in subsequent chapters. In a society with ever-growing interaction with people from diverse ethnic and ethnico-racial categories (through in-migration, involvement in the European Union and other international bodies and the marked increase in Irish people travelling abroad for work and other reasons), the levels of ethnic and racial prejudice and tolerance are most important.

The social-distance findings show an overall reduction in ethnic and racial prejudice, i.e. a substantial reduction in MSD scores. The influx of migrant workers and other immigrants, due to the economic development of the late 1990s and the early 2000s, has improved social tolerance in Ireland.

This is indicative of **favourable contact** despite difficulties of language and differences of socio-cultural norms and values. The level of general economic security experienced in times of prosperity was also a factor in the reduction of ethnic and racial prejudice.

The twenty-nine ethnic, ethnico-racial and racial categories were sub-classified into four 'geographic' groupings, i.e. (a) Irish, British and American categories; (b) Continental European categories; (c) African, Asian and Racial categories; and (d) Middle-East categories. It was confirmed that the *'principle of propinquity'* operated with very few exceptions.

The position of relative prejudice and preference within the twenty-four (out of the twenty-nine) categories since 1988-89 remained more or less constant. The Ethnico-Racial (with the exception of 'Euro-Americans'), Racial and Middle-East categories occupied the lower range of preferences. The **polarisation of dispositions**, as expressed in relatively high 'denial of citizenship' percentages, is quite unacceptable in an integrated pluralist society!

The changes in social distance given on Table No. 6.2 are quite remarkable over a period of nineteen years, i.e. 1988-89 to 2007-08. Allowing for the limitations of improvement for in-group categories, the following nine stimulus categories experienced nominal **increases** in percentages 'welcomed into the family' of over 20%, i.e. extract from Table No. 6.2:

Category	Year of Survey		Increase in 'Admit to Family'	
	1988-89	**2007-08**	**Nominal %**	**Actual %**
1. 'Chinese'	30.9%	63.0%	*+32.1%*	**+103.9%**
2. 'Afro-Americans'	26.2%	52.7%	*+26.5%*	**+101.1%**
3. 'Indians'	31.0%	57.2%	*+26.2%*	**+84.5%**
4. 'Arabs'	20.1%	45.6%	*+25.5%*	**+126.9%**
5. 'Pakistanis'	24.2%	49.4%	*+25.2%*	**+104.1%**
6. 'Russians'	40.9%	63.9%	*+23.0%*	**+56.2%**
7. 'Blacks'	29.7%	52.6%	*+22.9%*	**+77.1%**
8. 'Africans'	30.1%	52.3%	*+22.2%*	**+73.8%**
9. 'Nigerians'	29.1%	50.5%	*+21.4%*	**+73.5%**

Note: Nominal Increases in *italics* and Actual Increases in **bold.**

The above extract speaks for itself and highlights the capacity of Irish society to change intergroup attitudes when prevailing conditions are conducive to more openness. It would also question the level of support in the population for certain **European Union restrictive immigration policies** from outside the Continent of Europe. Of course, anti-immigrant propaganda in the media can 'whip-up' fear of members of non-European minorities based on negative stereotyping. The above changes took place in a socio-economic setting conducive to establishing better intergroup relations! The above findings are good news!

While the findings of the above extract from Table No. 6.2 are optimistic, it must be realised that even after such substantial progress in replacing prejudice with positive dispositions, there is still much positive change to come before the Irish people relate to the new guests on an *integrated pluralist* basis. For most of the categories on the list of nine, **over 40%** would still *not welcome* them into their families as members!

The findings of Tables Nos. 6.3, 6.4, 6.5, 6.6 and 6.7 present a series of *'Pearson Product-Moment Correlation Matrices'* giving the patterned relations between each of the attitudes towards twenty-nine categories. These Tables confirm the stimulus categories that factor together in the dispositions of the respondents. The results are as anticipated. Tables Nos. 6.3, 6.4, 6.5 and 6.6 show the connection within the categories of each of the subgroupings. Table No. 6.7 runs all of the twenty-nine **ethnic, ethnico-racial and racial stimulus categories** together and provides much valuable information about Irish intergroup attitudes. The anomalous position of 'Afro-Americans' *vis-à-vis* their fellow-citizens, i.e. 'Euro-Americans', highlights the negative influence of the racial factor!

***

CHAPTER VII
Ethnic, Ethnico-Racial and Racial Social Distance
by Personal Variables

Part I – Introduction

One of the best ways to describe, discover and explain social attitudes and prejudices is to find out the variations within and between the sub-samples of the personal variables. The standard **personal variables** used in the current research include:

(a)	Age	(f)	Region of Residence
(b)	Gender	(g)	Education
(c)	Marital Status	(h)	Occupational Status
(d)	Area of Birth	(i)	Social Class Position
(e)	Place of Rearing		

Five of the above personal variables are **ordinal**, i.e. there is a 'more than' or 'less than' relationship between the subsamples. These five are age, area of birth (level of urbanisation), education, occupational status and social class position.

In addition to the personal variables listed above, there are other **independent** variables which are likely to be causally related to social prejudice, i.e. authoritarianism, social anomie, religious belief and practice, attitudes towards, competence in and use of the Irish language, ethnic self-identity, personal income and political-party preferences. It will be possible to include these additional 'independent variables' when seeking to explain the variations in the levels of the various forms of social prejudice.

Because of the large number of ethnic, ethnico-racial and racial 'stimulus categories' (i.e. twenty-nine) it was proposed to divide them into the four groupings in the previous chapter, i.e.:

(a) Irish, British and American Stimulus Categories;
(b) Continental European Nationalities;
(c) African, Asian and Racial Stimulus Categories [1];
(d) Middle-East Nationalities.

---

[1] The two 'racial categories' were included because of the relatively high level of 'ethnic/cultural' rationalisation. See Table No. 5.1, pages 86-7.

123

The mean social-distance score of **each group** of the individual stimulus categories (within the group) by the normal personal variables will be used to **indicate** the variations in the level of social prejudice against the different nationalities. It will also enable the researcher to identify the trends in relation to the levels of prejudice.

The main purpose of this chapter includes focusing on the performance of the different personal variables in order to identify the causes of prejudice. Commenting on the performance of the variables in relation to individual stimulus categories (the different nationalities) will be minimal. The information provided on the tables would make detailed commentary redundant at this stage.

Racial prejudice or racialism/racism, as distinct from ethnic prejudice, is a relatively recent form of social prejudice and seems to have become serious and widespread following European expansionism and colonisation in the 15th century and the white elitism outlook of the '**Enlightenment**'. The main function[2] (as distinct from 'purpose') of racialism was the justification of ethnic cleansing, enslavement and, at times, genocide of indigenous populations in Africa, Asia and the Americas. It facilitated the popular exploitation of indigenous people and undervalued and undermined their culture and religion. In fact, these peoples were denied their basic human rights by effectively defining them as less than human. In addition to the rationalisation of the mass exploitation of non-European (Non-White) cultures via colonisation, slavery, etc., *racism* was also implicitly (and benevolently) present as a justification of the propagation of the 'Western Way of Life', i.e. liberal capitalism, majority democracy, science and technology, forms of Western Christianity, etc.

From reading the popular literature of *the Black slavery period in the United States*, one gets the impression that Black People and even Native Americans (referred to as 'Indians') were treated only as **intelligent 'high primates'**, without even having the protection of animal rights, which today's liberal societies have enshrined in their legislation. This enabled scrupulous slave owners to treat their Black Slaves as **less than human**, while retaining their high 'moral' standards when dealing with their fellow-Whites! The European-based **great Enlightenment Movement** of the 17th and 18th centuries, despite its good work for liberation among European

---

[2] By **function** is meant "the objective consequence of racialism".

White People, failed to acknowledge the universal equality of all human beings, irrespective of their racial, ethnic or social-class position! This, in turn, appears to have affected the mentality of European expansionists outside the limits of the restricted European Continent and helped to sow the seed of centuries of colonisation, slavery, expulsion, segregation or even occasions of genocide. (See Part I of Chapter IX below, pages 193-200, for further discussion on the nature of 'racism'.) It could be argued that when some of the 'equality' principles of the Enlightenment were made universal, they helped to undo the human damage that they facilitated earlier!

Social Class Prejudice (which underpinned feudal society) and *Ethnocentrism* are probably the oldest forms of prejudice which have contributed to the most painful forms of persecution and international wars down the years of human history, and in prehistoric times. Social Class Prejudice has helped to rationalise and justify **feudal systems** at the expense of the vast majority of the people in the course of human history. It is reasonable to assume that social class prejudice is both a **cause** and an **effect** of most forms of social prejudice. Minorities who are the object of social prejudice usually end up in the lower social classes, i.e., the 'urban under-class' and the rural 'deprived peasantry'. This has been the case, notably in India, United States and South Africa, at times of feudal dominance and racial discrimination and segregation. Strictly speaking, feudal systems, which ascribe authority on the basis of **genetic inheritance**, are racist ideologies such as the myth of the superiority of *'blue blood'*!

Part II – Ethnic, Ethnico-Racial and Racial Social Distance by Personal Variables

The following Table measures ethnic and ethnico-racial social-distance scores by personal variables. The measure used for each group of stimulus categories is the collective mean-social-distance measures (1-7) of each group of categories.

Table No. 7.1 shows a number of personal variables, i.e., 'Marital Status', 'Area of Birth', and 'Place of Rearing', which were statistically **not significant** (N/S) in two or more groupings of categories. In the case of groupings recording **N/S** the chi-square measure is >0.05 (meaning that variations could be due to chance). In other words, there was **consensus** between the subsamples. **'Gender'** failed to elicit significant variations for any of the four groups of stimulus categories.

One would expect such an outcome in the case of 'in-groups', i.e. 1.500 (MSD), or under, because of the limited range of possible variation. The 'Irish, British and American Categories' collective MSD was as low as **1.539** (which includes the 'Afro-American' score of 2.342). The MSD for Continental European Nationalities was also relatively low at **1.692** and, thereby, had limited scope for significant variations.

Table No. 7.1:
Mean-Social-Distance for Ethnic/Ethnico-Racial and Racial Categories by Personal Variables

Variable	Irish, British, American Group	Continental European Group	African/Asian & Racial Group	Middle-East Group	No.
Total Sample	**1.539**	**1.692**	**2.362**	**2.821**	1,000
A. Age	P<.003	P<.03	P<.002	P<.002	
1. 18-25 years	**1.741**	**1.851**	2.632	**3.247**	167
2. 26-40 years	1.462	1.546	2.072	2.486	318
3. 41-55 years	**1.600**	**1.775**	2.387	2.836	244
4. 56-70 years	1.454	**1.712**	2.519	2.869	175
5. 71 years plus	1.450	1.649	2.499	3.057	96
Range of Variation	*0.291*	*0.305*	*0.560*	*0.761*	
B. Marital Status	P<.03	N/S	N/S	N/S	
1. Single/Never Married	**1.629**	---	---	---	357
2. Married	1.477	---	---	---	466
3. Separated/Divorced	1.477	---	---	---	44
4. Permanent Relationship	**1.687**	---	---	---	71
5. Widowed	1.383	---	---	---	68
Range of Variation	0.304	---	---	---	
C. Area of Birth	N/S	N/S	P<.001	P<.02	
1. City (100,000 plus)	---	---	2.264	2.782	415
2. Large Town (10,000+)	---	---	2.118	2.549	116
3. Town (1,500 plus)	---	---	1.929	2.514	129
4. Rural/Village	---	---	**2.733**	**3.083**	340
Range of Variation	---	---	*0.804*	*0.569*	
D. Place of Rearing in Ireland	N/S	N/S	N/S	P<.001	
1. Dublin (City & County)	---	---	---	**2.929**	265
2. Rest of Leinster	---	---	---	**3.366**	160
3. Munster	---	---	---	2.539	230
4. Connaught/Ulster	---	---	---	2.647	162
Range of Variation	---	---	---	*0.827*	

Table No. 7.1 Cont'd. Variable	Irish, British, American Group	Continental European Group	African/Asian & Racial Group	Middle-East Group	No.
E. Region of Residence	P<.001	P<.001	P<.001	P<.001	
1. B.M.W.	**1.574**	**1.756**	**2.628**	**3.147**	268
2. Dublin	**1.604**	**1.712**	2.336	**2.887**	283
3. Mid-East & South-E.	**1.645**	**1.885**	**2.529**	**3.053**	214
4. Mid-West & South-W.	1.325	1.420	1.937	2.163	236
Range of Variation	*0.320*	*0.465*	*0.691*	*0.890*	
F. Education	N/S	P<.02	P<.001	P<.001	
1. Primary or Less	---	**1.787**	**2.621**	**3.052**	117
2. Incomplete Second-Level	---	**1.721**	**2.602**	**3.036**	259
3. Complete Second-Level	---	**1.824**	**2.484**	**2.986**	251
4. Third-Level	---	1.556	2.036	2.494	376
Range of Variation	---	*0.268*	*0.585*	*0.558*	
G. Occupational Status	P<.001	P<.001	P<.001	P<.001	
1. Unskilled/Semi-Skilled	**1.690**	**1.893**	2.273	**3.393**	204
2. Skilled/Routine Non-M.	1.488	1.618	2.254	2.643	321
3. Inspectional/Supervisory	1.511	1.547	**2.368**	2.793	131
4. Professional/Executive	1.367	1.448	1.961	2.328	190
Range of Variation	*0.323*	*0.445*	*0.407*	*1.065*	

Notes: Score above sample average are in **bold**. Range of Variation in *italics*.

The performance of the **age variable** in the above Table was not as anticipated. The youngest age subsample (18 to 25 years) recorded the highest average mean-social-distance score in relation to each of the groupings. In other words, this subsample had the most severe level of 'ethnic prejudice', despite their on-average higher level of education. (See Table No. 7.8, page 158 below.) This, once again, raises serious questions in relation to the reasons for such relatively intolerant attitudes among the '18 to 25 year-olds' in a time of unprecedented educational and other material opportunities and job security.

A. Age (Extract from Table No. 7.1)

	Variation	Highest (Most prejudiced)	Between	Lowest (Least prejudiced)
1. Middle-East Group	0.751	18-25 yrs (3.247)	and	26-40 yrs (2.486)
2. African/Asian/Racial Group	0.560	18-25 yrs (2.632)	and	26-40 yrs (2.072)
3. Continental European Group	0.305	18-25 yrs (1.851)	and	26-40 yrs (1.546)
4. Irish, British, American Group	0.291	18-25 yrs (1.741)	and	71 years plus (1.450)

The **26 to 40 years' subsample** recorded the **most tolerant** result across the three groupings and was substantially below average 'mean-social- distance' in each case. This is a very significant 'age-cohort' and has 32% of the national sample. The respondents of this subsample are also likely to become young parents and influential members of the workforce. Their more tolerant attitudes are a source of optimism. The middle-age adult cohort, i.e. the 41 to 55 years subsample, is very close to the sample average across the board. Are we seeing here an effect of the age-process in the young middle-aged (26 to 40 years), i.e. growth in greater tolerance? It is noteworthy that the oldest age-group, i.e. '71 years plus', was the **least prejudiced** in the case of the 'Irish, British and American' ethnic categories.

In the case of the older age cohort, the '71 years plus' subsample shows mixed results. These respondents have lowest prejudiced scores in the case of the 'Irish, British, American Group' and were below average in relation to the 'Continental European Nationalities'. This means that older people, who were expected to have higher prejudice scores (because of the restrictive effects of old age and lower educational achievement), have shown that they are more tolerant in the case of the above two groupings of categories. This was not anticipated. The '56 to 70 years' subsample has recorded a below average MSD for the 'Irish, British and American Categories' and above average in the case of the other three groupings. The normal effects of old age can lead to a degree of frustration[3], which is a cause of prejudice.

B. Marital Status (Extract from Table No. 7.1)

	Variation	Highest (Most prejudiced)	Between	Lowest (Least prejudiced)
Irish, British, American Group	0.304	Permanent Rel'ship (1.687)	and	Widowed (1.383)

Marital Status elicited a statistically significant variation only in the case of the 'Irish/British/American' group of stimulus categories. The 'single/never married' and those living in 'permanent relationships' were the most intolerant subsamples. This is probably a reflection on the relatively young mean-age of both sub-variables.

C. Area of Birth (Extract from Table No. 7.1)

	Variation	Highest (Most prejudiced)	Between	Lowest (Least prejudiced)
1.. African/Asian/Racial Group	0.804	Rural/Village (2.733)	and	Town (1.929)
2.. Middle-East Group	0.569	Rural/Village (3.083)	and	Town (2.514)

---

[3] **Frustration** leads to **tension** which seeks relief in **aggression**. **Prejudice** is a form of **psychological aggression**.

Area of Birth, which is an ordinal variable, has recorded significant variations in relation to 'African/Asian/Racial Categories' and the 'Middle-East Nationalities'. The most tolerant subsample has been 'Towns' (1,500-9,999). The subsample least tolerant was the 'Rural/Village' one.

D. Place of Rearing (Extract from Table No. 7.1)

			Between		
	Variation	Highest (Most prejudiced)			Lowest (Least prejudiced)
Middle-East Group	0.827	Rest of Leinster (3.366)	And		Munster (2.539)

'Munster' and 'Connaught/Ulster'-reared respondents were *more tolerant* than average towards 'Middle-East Nationalities' than their fellow-respondents reared in 'Dublin' and the 'Rest of Leinster'.

E. Region of Residence (Extract from Table No. 7.1)

			Between	
	Variation	Highest (Most prejudiced)		Lowest (Least prejudiced)
1. Middle-East Group	0.890	BMW Regions (3.147)	and	Mid-W. & Sth-W. (2.163)
2. African/Asian/Racial Group	0.691	BMW Regions (2.628)	and	Mid-W. & Sth-W. (1.937)
3. Continental European Group	0.465	Mid -East & Sth-E. (1.885)	and	Mid-W. & Sth-W. (1.420)
4. Irish, British, American Group	0.320	Mid-East & Sth-E. (1.645)	and	Mid-W. & Sth- W. (1.325)

Region of Residence was a most discerning variable. It recorded a significant variation in relation to each of the four 'ethnic and ethnico-racial groupings'. Those living in the Mid-West and South-West (i.e. Munster regions) were the *most tolerant* in each of the four groupings. The Dublin (City and County) subsample was below average in the average mean social-distance score in the case of 'African, Asian and Racial Categories', i.e. lower than average prejudice.

F. Education (Extract from Table No. 7.1)

			Between	
	Variation	Highest (Most prejudiced)		Lowest (Least prejudiced)
1. African/Asian/Racial Group	0.585	Primary or Less (2.621)	and	Third Level (2.063)
2. Middle-East Group	0.558	Primary or Less (3.052)	and	Third Level (2.494)
3. Continental European Group	0.268	Complete Sec.Lev. (1.824)	and	Third Level (1.556)

Education recorded significant variations in relation to three of the four groupings. There was *consensus* in regard to the 'Irish, British, American Group'. Third-level respondents showed the highest level of tolerance in the case of all three groupings recording significant variations. This was as anticipated.

The performance of those with 'complete second-level education' was not as anticipated in that the subsample's average mean-social-distance score was higher than the sample average by significant numbers. This raises questions about the liberalising effect of second-level education on respondents!

G. Occupational Status (Extract from Table No. 7.1)

	Variation	Highest (Most prejudiced)	Between	Lowest (Least prejudiced)
1. Middle-East Group	1.065	Unsk. & SemiSk. (3.393)	and	Inspect./Super. (2.793)
2. Continental European Group	0.445	Unsk. & SemiSk. (1.893)	and	Prof./Exec. (1.448)
3. African/Asian/Racial Group	0.407	Inspect./Super. (2.368)	and	Sk./Routine NM (2.254)
4. Irish, British, American Group	0.323	Unsk. & SemiSk. (1.690)	and	Prof./Exec. (1.367)

Occupational Status' performance was as anticipated. A statistically significant variation was recorded in the case of each of the 'groupings'. Those with the 'highest occupational status' were the most tolerant in each case, while 'Unskilled/Semi-Skilled' were the least tolerant, i.e. with the highest average mean-social-distance scores, in the case of three of the four groupings.

The 'African, Asian Racial Groups' was the exception where the 'Inspectional/Supervisory Subsample' was the least tolerant. The fact that the 'highest occupational status subsample' records the lowest levels of social prejudice, as indicated by social distance, is to be welcomed in relation to fairer employment policies.

Part III – Anticipated Patterns of Variance by Personal Variables

Table Nos. 7.4, 7.5, 7.6 and 7.8 give the individual social-distance scores for each of the twenty-nine 'ethnic and ethnico-racial categories'. The standing of individual nationalities and ethnico-racial categories is likely to be determined by the *'principle of propinquity'*, i.e. the degree of perceived similarity between one's own category or group and that of each of the various categories in terms of culture, religion, class, racial characteristics, historical association, political ideology, economic policy, and so forth.

It was anticipated that there would be a higher level of ethnic and ethnico-racial tolerance among younger respondents, those with higher education, urban (more cosmopolitan) residents, people with greater economic security and higher jobs prestige. These anticipations or hypotheses were based on the findings of previous research and the expected impact of education and personal security and prestige. The period of interviewing, i.e. between November 2007 and March 2008, marked the final months of **relative economic prosperity**, despite some early signs of the global downturn abroad leading to an international **economic recession**. In the actual results, the performance of the '18 to 25 year-olds' meant that the **age** variable did not confirm the anticipated pattern of responses.

The following Table (No. 7.2) gives the fairly optimistic levels of satisfaction felt by respondents in 2007-08. These are compared with 1988-89 in Table No. 7.3. The importance of these findings is two-fold. In the first place, it is clear that the impact of the pending economic recession had not yet been felt by the vast majority **(87%)** of respondents. Secondly, this points to the relatively sudden arrival of the decline in economic growth and prosperity and the vulnerability of the Republic of Ireland to global trade, financial and commercial activity.

Table No. 7.2: Satisfaction with Family Income

Question: *"How about your material standard of living? Would you say that your (family's) income at present is: very satisfactory, fairly satisfactory, not very satisfactory, poor or very poor?"*

	Level of Satisfaction	Number	Actual	Cumulative
1.	Very satisfactory	261	25.8%	25.8%
2.	Fairly satisfactory	619	61.2%	87.0%
3.	Not very satisfactory	112	11.1%	
4.	Poor	18	1.8%	13.1%
5.	Very poor	2	0.2%	
		1,011	100.1%	100.1%

It is frequently said that people are reluctant to admit that their personal (material) standard of living is not satisfactory because they would see it as a reflection on their ability or success. This can lead to a degree of exaggeration in the answers to the above question. (See Mac Gréil, 1996, pages 386-7.)

Allowing for a possible degree of exaggeration[4], the findings of Table No. 7.2 are still most impressive. Seven out of every eight respondents (**87%**) said their 'level of satisfaction with their material standard of living' was either "very satisfactory" (**26%**) or "fairly satisfactory" (**61%**). Only 2% found the *family income* to be "poor" (**1.8%**) or "very poor". This reflects very positively on the felt effects of the so-called 'Celtic Tiger' period.

The extraordinary success of the renewal of domestic housing 1990-2007 (the greatest in the Republic of Ireland since the "removal of the thatch" campaign in the late 1930s) was an outstanding achievement for the Republic of Ireland (despite the negative aspects associated with it). This is reflected in the people's satisfaction with their material standards of living (in 2007-08) in the above table. It was unfortunate for the Republic of Ireland that this great achievement was to become a source of serious financial difficulties after the 'collapse' of banks – based on excessive lending policies. The self-regulated free-market 'neo-liberal' system let the people down badly!

The changes in level of satisfaction since 1988-89 are highlighted in Table No. 7.3.

Table No. 7.3:
Changes in Satisfaction with Family Income between 1988-89 and 2007-08.

	Level of Satisfaction	1988-89 A	2007-08 B	Change (B – A)
1.	Very satisfactory	11%	26%	+15%
2.	Fairly satisfactory	62%	61%	-1%
	(1 + 2)	**(73%)**	**(87%)**	**(+14%)**
3.	Not very satisfactory	**20%**	**11%**	**-9%**
4.	Poor	5%	2%	-3%
5.	Very poor	2%	0%	-2%
	(4 + 5)	**(7%)**	**(2%)**	**(-5%)**
	Number	1,001	1,011	---

---

[4] Survey research on perceived levels of satisfaction with personal/family standard of living seems to indicate that respondents may tend to exaggerate their level of satisfaction. It is thought that to admit dissatisfaction would reflect on one's self-esteem! People also tend to exaggerate their perceived social status! Biemer and Lyberg (2003) refer to "**social desirability response set**" which means that respondents tend to portray themselves well. (See Biemer, P. and Lyberg L., *Introduction to Survey Quality*, Wiley, New Jersey, 2003, page 144.

Table No. 7.3 shows a significant and fairly substantial increase in the level of satisfaction with a significant reduction in the three lower levels (between 1988-89 and 2007-08). This should lead to a reduction in prejudice in general and an increase in tolerance due to the improved sense of security. Such changes in prejudice and tolerance have been confirmed in Table No. 4.2, pages 65-66.

Of course, the impact of **the later economic recession** on intergroup attitudes is likely to be negative. Anecdotal evidence (in 2010) has reported an increase in more frequent expressions of hostility towards 'migrant workers' from foreign countries in Ireland, which were rare in the period up to the summer of 2008. Hopefully, such hostility will be short-lived and will be firmly dealt with by the enforcement of our minority-rights' legislation. In times of insecurity due to economic scarcity, the authorities need to be extra-vigilant to protect vulnerable members of minorities from irrational abuse and discrimination. They are liable to be scapegoated and become the objects of displaced aggression. It is possible for charismatic and demagogic leaders to manipulate public anger against scapegoated minorities in times of relative hardship following periods of comparative prosperity.

Part IV – Irish, British and American Stimulus Categories

There were nine ethnic and ethnico-racial categories [5] under this sub-groupings, (in order of preference), 'Irish Speakers', 'Welsh', 'Euro-Americans', 'English', 'Canadians', 'Scottish', 'British', 'Northern Irish' and 'Afro-Americans'. The mean-social-distance score is the measure of prejudice used to discover the variations. As stated elsewhere, this score ranges from **one** (including 100% of respondents "Welcoming members of the category into their families") to **seven** (showing that 100% would "debar or deport" members of the category). In-groups tend to have scores of around 1.500 and under. The higher the MSD score the higher the level of social prejudice against the particular group.

Table No. 7.4 gives the score for each personal variable in the case of the nine 'Irish, British and American Categories'.

---

[5] In the questionnaire **'Euro-Americans'** were described as 'White Americans' and **'Afro-Americans'** were presented as 'Black Americans'. The concepts 'Euro-American' and 'Afro-American' are more ethnic than racial in line with the rationalisation findings (see Table No. 5.1, pages 86-87.

Table No. 7.4:
Irish, British and American Categories' Mean-Social-Distance by Personal Variables

Variable	Irish Speakers	Welsh	Euro-Americans	English	Canadians	Scottish	British	Nth. Irish	Afro-Americans	Average Number
Total Sample	1.324	1.388	1.416	1.422	1.430	1.436	1.488	1.603	2.342	1,000
A. Age	P<.05	P<.05	N/S	N/S	P<.001	P<.05	P<.001	P<.03	P<.001	
1. 18-25 years	**1.476**	**1.648**	---	---	**1.681**	**1.703**	**1.662**	**1.669**	**2.859**	167
2. 26-40 years	1.285	1.342	---	---	1.355	1.362	**1.476**	1.538	**2.001**	318
3. 41-55 years	**1.397**	**1.468**	---	---	1.424	**1.592**	1.480	**1.785**	**2.392**	244
4. 56-70 years	1.169	1.248	---	---	1.295	1.254	1.396	1.464	**2.489**	175
5. 71 years plus	1.287	1.141	---	---	**1.503**	1.149	1.410	1.504	**2.541**	96
B. Marital Status	P<.02	P<.02	N/S	P<.03	P<.05	N/S	N/S	N/S	N/S	
1. Single/Never Mar'd	**1.461**	1.476	---	**1.457**	**1.511**	---	---	---	---	357
2. Married	1.209	1.329	---	1.407	1.315	---	---	---	---	466
3. Separated/Divorced	1.239	1.342	---	1.235	1.404	---	---	---	---	44
4. Permanent Rel'ship	**1.526**	**1.627**	---	**1.734**	**1.684**	---	---	---	---	71
5. Widowed	1.231	1.114	---	1.142	**1.544**	---	---	---	---	68
C. Area of Birth	P<.05	P<.05	N/S	N/S	P<.02	P<.04	P<.008	P<.003	P<.05	
1. City (100,000 +)	**1.438**	**1.506**	---	---	**1.537**	**1.550**	**1.516**	**1.604**	2.222	415
2. Lge.Town (10,000 +)	1.294	**1.391**	---	---	1.226	**1.499**	1.306	**1.702**	2.100	116
3. Town (1,500 +)	1.272	1.354	---	---	1.484	1.360	1.370	1.166	1.870	129
4. Rural/Village	1.216	1.258	---	---	1.350	1.305	**1.563**	**1.736**	**2.757**	340
D. Place of Rearing in Republic of Ireland	P<.03	P<.005	P<.02	N/S	P<.02	P<.03	N/S	P<.05	P<.001	
1. Dublin (City & Co.)	**1.395**	**1.550**	**1.551**	---	**1.533**	**1.525**	---	1.585	**2.401**	265
2. Rest of Leinster	1.219	1.279	1.338	---	1.431	1.420	---	**1.609**	**2.549**	160
3. Munster	1.208	1.203	1.261	---	1.253	1.231	---	1.424	2.318	230
4. Connaught/Ulster	**1.361**	**1.439**	1.395	---	**1.491**	1.366	---	**1.780**	2.367	162
E. Region of Residence	N/S	N/S	P<.02	P<.03	P<.04	P<.05	N/S	P<.002	P<.05	
1. B.M.W.	---	---	1.357	1.342	**1.502**	**1.421**	---	**1.809**	2.528	268
2. Dublin	---	---	**1.493**	**1.526**	**1.516**	1.504	---	**1.610**	2.300	283
3. Mid-East & Sth-East	---	---	**1.601**	**1.551**	1.402	**1.592**	---	**1.621**	**2.676**	214
4. Mid-West & Sth-Wst	---	---	1.221	1.270	1.267	1.226	---	1.341	1.891	236
F. Education	P<.05	P<.05	N/S	P<.05	N/S	P<.002	P<.001	P<.05	P<.05	
1. Primary or Less	1.177	1.144	---	1.244	---	1.208	1.269	1.433	**2.554**	117
2. Incomplete Sec-Level	1.189	1.366	---	1.479	---	1.407	**1.614**	**1.787**	**2.591**	259
3. Complete Sec-Level	**1.377**	**1.521**	---	**1.522**	---	**1.499**	**1.649**	**1.609**	**2.526**	251
4. Third-Level	**1.427**	**1.390**	---	1.377	---	**1.483**	1.360	1.525	1.982	376
G. Occupational Status	N/S	N/S	N/S	P<.05	N/S	N/S	P<.05	P<.001	P<.03	
1. Unskilled/Semi-Skill.	---	---	---	**1.586**	---	---	**1.765**	**1.788**	**2.843**	204
2. Skilled/R. Non-M.	---	---	---	1.334	---	---	1.371	**1.623**	2.207	321
3. Inspect./Supervisory	---	---	---	1.438	---	---	1.546	**1.711**	2.174	131
4. Professional/Exec.	---	---	---	1.294	---	---	1.264	1.278	2.020	190

Note: Scores above sample average are in **bold**.

4.1 Age:

The most surprising (and disappointing) finding of Table No. 7.4 is, once again, the relatively high mean-social-distance score of *the youth* (18 to 25 years), the city-born and those reared in Dublin and living there at present. The opposite was anticipated because of the better educational chances and participation of the young people and the more 'cosmopolitan' character of the city people.   These signs of 'ethnic prejudice' among a substantial minority of the youth should be a matter of concern for community leaders, educationalists and those striving to set up and maintain a tolerant pluralist society.

The educational participation of the '18 to 25 year-olds' is relatively high in the Republic of Ireland at present. The percentage of respondents of this age group with third-level education was substantially higher than the sample average, i.e. 42.0% as compared with 37.6% for the total sample (see Table No. 7.8, page 158).   Since education was expected to reduce prejudiced attitudes towards members of other ethnic categories, it was, therefore, anticipated that the '18 to 25 year-olds' would have a below-average level of social distance towards these categories.   The opposite has happened. This raises, among other issues, questions about the quality of education received by young people today in the Republic of Ireland.   The extent to which our child-rearing patterns at home affect prejudice not being challenged also needs to be examined.   The potentially negative impact of extended adolescence, exclusive peer-socialisation, cybernetics (i.e. information technology) and other developments likely to influence this age group's attitudes should be examined (see Part VIII, pages 156-160 below).

The most tolerant age group [according to the findings of Table No. 7.1 (pages 126-7) and Table No. 7.3 (page 132)] is the 26 to 40 year-olds. They scored under the sample average mean-social-distance score in the case of six of the seven categories, i.e. 'Irish Speakers', 'Welsh', 'Canadians', 'Scottish', 'Northern Irish' and 'Afro-Americans'.   The middle-aged subsample (41 to 55 year-olds) recorded above-average social-distance scores in six of the seven categories registering a significant variation. The exception was 'Canadians'.   This again was not expected since the two older subsamples, i.e. '56 to 70 years' and '71 years plus', showed significantly more tolerance than their younger fellow-respondents, i.e. 40 to 55 year-olds.   One would be tempted to ask the question: "Have some of the 41 to 56 year-olds been transmitting their prejudices to their 18 to 25 year-old children?"   This may be too speculative.   Of course, there are multiple factors at influence on the intergroup attitudes of the different age subsamples.

4.2 Marital Status:
This variable registered a statistically significant variation only in the case of four out of the nine 'Irish', British and American Categories, i.e. 'Irish Speakers', 'Welsh', 'English' and 'Canadians'. The 'Married', 'Separated/Divorced' and the 'Widowed' subsamples were the most tolerant while the 'Single/Never Married' and those living in 'permanent relationships' were the least tolerant, i.e. having above sample average social-distance scores. The age factor is present in the scores of the 'Single/Never Married'.

The fact that five of the stimulus categories, i.e. 'Euro-Americans', 'Scottish', 'British', 'Northern Irish' and 'Afro-Americans', failed to elicit significant variations between the marital status subsamples is, in itself, noteworthy. This high level of **consensus** would seem to indicate that the pattern of our ethnic attitudes (in the case of these categories) is quite universal.

4.3 Area of Birth:
This is an important ordinal variable in that it measures the influence of urbanisation on the attitudes to relatively close ethnic stimulus categories. It has been quite a discerning variable, i.e. it registered a statistically significant variation between the subsamples in the case of seven of the nine categories – 'Irish Speakers', 'Welsh', 'Canadian', 'Scottish', 'British', 'Northern Irish' and 'Afro-Americans'.

In regard to all categories, except 'Afro-Americans', there is a negative correlation between ethnic tolerance and the level of urbanisation of the area of the respondents' birth. In other words, those born in rural areas and small towns were more welcoming to members of the other six categories. This result was not anticipated as it was felt that city-rearing would be in a more cosmopolitan environment. The reasons for these results are difficult to explain. Here again we may see the negative influence of the younger respondents! Urban populations are, on average, younger than are those of rural and village areas. Those born in towns of 1,500 to 9,999 residents seem to be the most tolerant subsample.

The mean-social-distance score of the 'Town' subsample for **Northern Irish** is quite substantially lower than the other three subsamples. This is the **second lowest** MSD score of the whole Table (No. 7.4) at **1.166**. If this is representative of the populations throughout the State, our 'Northern Irish' fellow-citizens should feel very much at home in the towns (1,500-9,999) of the Republic of Ireland!

4.4 Place of Rearing:
This is very much a nominal variable. It shows the significance of the geographic place/province where respondents were reared in the Republic of Ireland. (Those reared abroad were not included because of smallness of the numbers reared in different countries.)

The pattern of responses is quite clear. Dublin (City and County) and Connaught/Ulster have the highest above-average mean-social-distance scores. The 'Munster' subsample is the most tolerant sub-sample, i.e. with the lowest mean-social-distance scores. Respondents reared in the 'Rest of Leinster' have also registered below-average mean-social-distance scores in the case of five categories and above-average for 'Northern Irish' and 'Afro-Americans'. The overall pattern for the 'Rest of Leinster' respondents is on the side of ethnic tolerance.

4.5 Region of Residence:
This is also a nominal variable in that there is not a "more than/less than" relationship between the subsamples, as in the case of 'ordinal variables'. Again, it measures the impact of geographic influences. In modern Irish society there is a degree of geographic mobility in the population which has been amplified because of imbalanced regional development over the years, i.e. **migration** from the rural west to the east coast of Ireland.

The pattern of responses of this variable is fairly clear from the findings of Table No. 7.4 (e). The 'Mid-West and South-West Regions' is the most tolerant subsample, i.e. with below-sample-average MSD scores in each of the six categories registering significant variations, i.e. 'Euro-Americans', 'English', 'Canadian', 'Scottish', 'Northern Irish' and 'Afro-Americans'. This result confirms the findings of the 'Place of Rearing variable' which showed that 'Munster-Reared' respondents were the most tolerant.

4.6 Education:
This is an important ordinal variable. The findings for 'education' were mixed and not as anticipated. It was expected that there would be a clearly positive correlation between ethnic tolerance and education in the case of all ethnic and ethnico-racial stimulus categories. This was based on the assumption that formal education, through the influence of the humanities, would counter prejudice and xenophobia. The mixed result questions the universal tolerance of the more highly educated! What was discovered in the 1988-89 National Survey was that there was a degree of *'selective liberalness'* in relation to certain minorities or stimulus categories[6]! Tolerance which is not universal is essentially biased! It was unexpected to see respondents with *'third-level education'* registering an above-average mean-social-distance score in the case of four of the seven categories with significant variations. This, again, raises the question about the quality of Irish education as a promotion of social tolerance.

4.7 Occupational Status:
The fact that only **four** of the **nine** stimulus categories elicited significant variations, i.e. a *chi-square* score of 0.05 or less, shows that there was a consensus in relation to 'Irish Speakers', 'Welsh', 'Euro-Americans', 'Canadians' and 'Scottish'. Such consensus may, in part, be owing to the relatively low MSD scores of these categories.

The 'unskilled/semi-skilled' subsample registered an above-average score for each of the four categories with significant variations, i.e. 'English', 'British', 'Northern Irish' and 'Afro-Americans'. The 'Inspectional/Supervisory' subsample also registered an above-average score in the case of the first three of the above named categories with British connections. The mixed results for 'occupational status' were not anticipated.

4.8 Conclusion:
The findings of Table No. 7.4 enable the reader to discover where the tendencies towards ethnic and other prejudices exist within the adult population of the Republic of Ireland. It should be noted the potential for variation in social-distance scores among the 'Irish', 'British' and 'American categories' is limited by the fact that all except one of these stimulus categories, i.e. 'Afro-Americans', fall within the 'in-group' categories. The

---

[6] See Mac Gréil, M. *Prejudice in Ireland Revisited*, Maynooth, Survey and Research Unit, 1996, pp.350f.

anomalous position of the **'Northern Irish'** being outside its expected place at the top of the rank order of ethnic preference (next to 'Irish Speakers') will be dealt with in a later chapter (see Chapter X below). Such a high placing would be in accordance with the *'principle of propinquity'*.

Part V – Continental European Nationalities

The **rank-ordering** of the nine stimulus categories within this grouping of ethnic categories is interesting from the point of view of the *principle of propinquity*, i.e. preferring categories with most in common with the Irish people. Going on that basis one would have expected 'Italians' and 'Spaniards' to be in second and third position because of the Irish people's religious and cultural similarities with these two 'Catholic Nations'. Instead, we seem to prefer the 'Protestant Nationalities' from central and northern Europe, i.e. 'Germans' and 'Dutch'. It could be argued that the relatively lower status of the 'Latin cultures' is due to our adopting the preferences and biases portrayed in the English media.

The juxtaposition of 'Russians' and 'Romanians' also seems to be another breach of the 'principle of propinquity', in that Romania is a fellow-member of the European Union with Russia not in the Union. The scores against 'Romanians' indicate a relatively high level of social prejudice, because of the association of Romanians with Romany Gypsies. This may be in part due to our bias against Gypsies and Travellers. The findings in relation to 'Romanians', i.e. MSD of 2.566, places them close to the 'out-group' classification and, thereby, may be in a precarious position in society from certain extremist groups such as militant neo-Nazis. The attack on, i.e. **roughing-up**, of 'Romanians' in Belfast in June 2009[7] should have raised the alarm (see pages 29f above).

Table No. 7.5 gives a breakdown to the nine 'Continental European Categories' by six personal variables, i.e. Age, Area of Birth, Place of Rearing, Region of Residence, Education and Occupation. Because of the higher mean-social-distance scores, the potential for significant differences in the variables in Table No. 7.5 is greater. This is reflected in some of the variables.

---

[7] A number of Romanian in-migrants were forced out of their homes by ethnocentric local extremists (see *The Irish Times*, 17th June, 2009).

Table No. 7.5: Continental European National Categories'
Mean-Social-Distance by Personal Variables

Variable	French 1	Dutch 2	Germans 3	Spanish 4	Italians 5	Polish 6	Lithuan. 7	Russians 8	Romanians 9
Total Sample	**1.483**	**1.632**	**1.644**	**1.660**	**1.703**	**1.790**	**2.044**	**2.091**	**2.566**
A. Age	P<.02	P<.004	P<.03	P<.04	P<.02	P<.009	P<.005	P<.005	P<.05
1. 18-25 years	**1.647**	**1.835**	**1.822**	**1.941**	1.693	**2.006**	**2.103**	**2.110**	**2.811**
2. 26-40 years	1.393	1.450	1.503	1.598	1.620	1.625	1.788	1.855	2.288
3. 41-55 years	**1.576**	**1.701**	**1.775**	1.659	**1.790**	**1.929**	**2.155**	**2.201**	2.640
4. 56-70 years	1.357	**1.661**	1.615	1.610	**1.716**	1.784	**2.327**	**2.210**	**2.801**
5. 71 years plus	**1.492**	**1.654**	1.527	1.468	**1.749**	1.617	1.994	**2.343**	2.451
B. Area of Birth	P<.005	N/S	N/S	N/S	N/S	P<.02	P<.005	P<.04	P<.005
1. City (100,000 plus)	**1.611**	---	---	---	---	1.789	1.916	1.987	2.507
2. Large Town (10,000 +)	1.394	---	---	---	---	1.624	1.735	2.071	2.269
3. Town (1,500 plus)	1.402	---	---	---	---	1.513	1.640	1.775	2.004
4. Rural/Village	1.389	---	---	---	---	**1.955**	**2.467**	**2.353**	**2.957**
C. Place of Rearing in Republic of Ireland	P<.001	P<.02	P<.03	P<.003	P<.002	P<.03	P<.005	P<.01	N/S
1. Dublin (City & Co.)	**1.571**	**1.814**	**1.798**	**1.695**	**1.771**	**1.842**	**2.112**	2.055	---
2. Rest of Leinster	1.371	1.522	1.508	1.649	**1.818**	**1.790**	**2.342**	**2.534**	---
3. Munster	1.339	1.436	1.547	1.599	1.457	**1.854**	**2.183**	2.061	---
4. Connaught/Ulster	1.457	**1.724**	**1.702**	1.609	**1.826**	1.744	1.915	1.890	---
D. Region of Residence	P<.02	N/S	P<.002	P<.005	P<.001	P<.002	P<.005	P<.005	N/S
1. B.M.W.	**1.520**	---	1.519	**1.709**	**1.900**	**1.824**	**2.180**	**2.237**	---
2. Dublin	**1.566**	---	**1.777**	1.632	**1.709**	1.783	2.010	1.963	---
3. Mid-East & South-East	**1.508**	---	**1.740**	2.037	**1.757**	**2.108**	**2.337**	**2.597**	---
4. Mid-West & Sth-West	1.317	---	1.481	1.292	1.421	1.466	1.665	1.620	---
E. Education	N/S	N/S	P<.005	P<.005	N/S	P<.02	P<.005	P<.005	N/S
1. Primary or Less	---	---	**1.656**	1.526	---	1.755	**2.312**	**2.526**	---
2. Incomplete Sec-Lev.	---	---	1.573	**1.891**	---	**1.872**	**2.145**	**2.230**	---
3. Complete Second-Lev.	---	---	**1.884**	**1.818**	---	**1.980**	**2.238**	2.157	---
4. Third-Level	---	---	1.527	1.437	---	1.617	1.763	1.812	---
F. Occupational Status	N/S	P<.05	P<.005	P<.005	N/S	P<.004	P<.008	P<.005	P<.05
1. Unskilled/Semi-Skilled	---	**1.709**	**1.861**	**2.024**	---	**2.106**	**2.415**	**2.419**	**2.889**
2. Skilled/R. Non-Manual	---	1.552	1.600	1.523	---	1.713	1.881	1.940	2.417
3. Inspect./Supervisory	---	1.550	1.361	1.501	---	1.675	1.769	1.937	**2.631**
4. Professional/Executive	---	1.364	1.481	1.370	---	1.476	1.776	1.735	2.295

Note: MSD scores above sample average are in **bold**.

5.1 Age:

This ordinal variable registered significant variations for **each** of the nine stimulus categories by age. The pattern of response is more or less similar to that of the "Irish, British and American Categories" (see Table No. 7.4, page 134).

The '26 to 40 years' subsample is clearly the *most tolerant* of all the age subsamples. It records a *below average* mean-social-distance score in the case of *all* nine "Continental European Categories"! At the same time, the '18 to 25 years' subsample is *above average* in eight of the nine categories, the 'Italians' being the only exception. The middle-age sub-sample (in 41 to 55 year-olds) has also got above average MSD scores towards eight of the nine categories. Older respondents showed a higher level of tolerance than did their younger and middle-aged fellow countrymen and countrywomen! This seems to confirm the findings of Table No. 7.4.

The problem of youth '18 to 25 years' intolerance is emerging, once again, as a serious one in the event of aggravating social situations. History gives us numerous instances of the involvement of youth in hostility against minorities who had been scapegoated in times of economic crisis. Some young people seem to be particularly vulnerable to simplistic interpretations and clichés about the passing crisis and attracted to demagogic leadership, i.e. the Hitler youth. The high level of tolerance of the young adults '26 to 40 years' is again, a source of relief in that members of this age group will become 'role models' for the younger respondents as they move on in years. This, however, does not remove the urgency of trying to reduce the age of tolerance within the population.

5.2 Area of Birth:
This variable has registered significant variations in regard to five of the nine categories, i.e. 'French', 'Polish', 'Lithuanians', 'Russians' and 'Romanians'. The level of consensus in the Irish people's attitudes towards 'Dutch', 'Germans', 'Spanish' and 'Italians', when measured by 'area of birth', was noteworthy. There has been no significant difference between the responses of the subsamples towards these four categories.

The pattern of response towards the 'French' was the opposite to that in the case of 'Polish', 'Lithuanians', 'Russians' and 'Romanians'. In the case of the latter four categories, respondents born in the rural/village areas were substantially above the average mean-social-distance scores, while all the urban subsamples were below the MSD average. The city-born respondents had the highest mean-social-distance score in relation to the 'French'. The highest MSD score of the whole Table was recorded by the rural/village-born against the 'Romanians', i.e. 2.957. The town-born were again the most tolerant subsample overall. The MSD score against 'Romanians' by the 'town-born' respondents was as low as **2.004**. The scores for the 'French' showed that the city-born were least tolerant.   It is difficult to explain this unanticipated result.

5.3 Place of Rearing:
This nominal variable registered significant variations in the case of eight of the nine "Continental European National Categories".   Dublin (City/County)-Reared had above average MSD scores in the case of seven of the eight categories.   The Dublin MSD score was less than average in regard to **'Russians'**.   This performance by Dublin-reared was out of line with the other categories.   Is it because of the impact of in-migration on the Dublin City and County?   Or to what extent is it reflecting the age-composition of the adult population as reflected in the sample?   Higher MSD scores mean greater prejudice!   The absence of a statistically significant variation against 'Romanians' reflects a high degree of consensus in prejudice against this stimulus category at a relatively high level.

The 'Rest of Leinster' (reared) was the second most prejudiced sub-sample in that it recorded above average mean-social-distance scores towards four of the nine categories, i.e. 'Italians', 'Polish', 'Lithuanians' and 'Russians'.   'Munster-reared' respondents are, once again, the most tolerant subsample, although they were above average in the case of 'Polish' and 'Lithuanians'.   The most friendly and tolerant towards the Eastern European nationalities were the 'Connaught/Ulster-reared'.   This is surprising because of the high proportion of 'rural/village-reared' in Connaught/Ulster.   The experience of Eastern Europeans in Connaught/Ulster must have been favourable.   'Place of rearing' was exclusively in the Republic of Ireland. The consensus in relation to **'Romanians'** was, again, a disappointing finding.

5.4 Region of Residence:
The difference between 'Area of Birth' and 'Place of Rearing' and 'Region of Residence' reflects the level and origin of geographic mobility between regions and the density of in-migration in the subvariables.   The relatively high level of tolerance reflected in the scores of those living in Dublin as contrasted with that of 'Dublin-reared' is interesting.   The former includes those who have migrated from rural/village Ireland and from abroad.   The combination of these two population shifts has resulted (it would seem) in Dublin's low level of mean-social-distance scores towards 'Polish', 'Lithuanians' and 'Russians'.   (The latter was already low in the Dublin-reared.)   The opposite has happened to respondents' scores from 'Mid-East

and North-East'. *Munster* residents are the *most tolerant* across the board for all seven Continental European Nationalities eliciting statistical significance, i.e. respondents living in the 'Mid-West and South-West' regions.

The significance of 'Romanians' not eliciting a significant variation in relatively high mean-social-distance scores among the residents of the Republic of Ireland's regions is fairly serious.   In effect, this means that there is consensus throughout the State in relation to relatively severe prejudice (MSD **2.566**) against 'Romanians'.   The consensus in relation to the 'Dutch' is not that serious in that the sample average is close to 'in-group status' at an MSD of **1.632**.   Prejudice against 'Romanians' reflects the widespread hostility toward 'Romany Gypsies', who faced the 'gaschamber' under the Nazis in the early 1940s in Germany.   There are danger signs in these findings!

5.5 Education:
Education has elicited a significant variation in five of the nine "Continental European National Categories".   'French', 'Dutch', 'Italians' and 'Romanians' registered consensus between the education subsamples, i.e. differences were not significant (N/S).   'Third-Level' respondents were the most tolerant in the five nationalities having significant variations.   The performance of the 'Complete Second-Level' respondents was quite disappointing, i.e. with an above-average mean-social-distance score for each of the seven nationalities.   It was again most disappointing and not anticipated that **'Romanians'** failed to register significant variation by education!

5.6 Occupational Status:
Two of the Continental European National categories failed to get a statistically significant variation by occupational status, i.e. 'French' and 'Italians'.   The 'unskilled/semi-skilled' subsample was the most prejudiced (highest MSD score) in the case of each of the seven categories with statistically significant variations.   The 'professional/senior executive' sub-sample was the most tolerant in each category.   This was as anticipated. The range of scores in the case of **'Romanians'** was disappointing.   All sub-variables were higher than **2.29**.   This category seems to be attracting a higher level of prejudice, and merits careful monitoring!

5.7 Conclusion:
Table No. 7.5 has been most useful in measuring the variations in Irish ethnic prejudice and tolerance towards nine "Continental European Nationalities". Eight of the nine are *de jure* 'fellow-European citizens' and full members of the European Union. There is a certain degree of British/English influence, reflected in the rank order of preference and, possibly, in the degree of prejudice or tolerance expressed. The impact of English media (popular and 'quality') on Irish social attitudes needs to be researched in order to quantify this level of influence.

The relatively negative attitudes towards **'Romanians'** should be of concern to those who wish a pluralist integration of ethnic minorities (on an equality basis). The seeds for discrimination against this ethnic category are present in the above findings. The fact that there was **consensus** in the MSD towards 'Romanians' by 'Place of Rearing', 'Region of Residence' and 'Education' is quite serious when one considers that the sample average was as high as **2.566**!

Part VI – African, Asian and Racial[8] Categories

The seven stimulus categories included in these paragraphs measure ethnico-racial and racial social distance. As a result of the significant and substantial decrease in the level of purely racial prejudice (i.e. based on genetically inherited physical and physiognomic traits) over the past thirty-five years in Ireland, it has become clear that the ethnic or cultural rather than the racial is the predominant influence in the categories tested in Table No. 7.6.

The stimulus categories measured in Table No. 7.6 are, in rank order of preference, the following: 'Chinese', 'Coloureds', 'Indians', 'Blacks', 'Africans', 'Pakistanis' and 'Nigerians'. The **1.3%** of the population of the Republic of Ireland of Asian origin is largely made up of migrants from China, India, Pakistan and the Philippines. Both the 'Chinese' and the 'Indians' have established good reputations in Ireland in the catering trade and as medical doctors and nurses. Nigerians make up a substantial proportion of the **1%** of the Irish population of African origin. Pakistanis have come to Ireland over a number of years, many of whom were already

---

[8] 'Black' and 'Coloured' Stimulus Categories are included because of their relatively high **ethnic and cultural** rationalisation scores (see Table No. 5.1, pages 86-87).

established in Great Britain. In all, the immigrants from Africa and Asia have been a great asset to Ireland through their work and service at all levels and their cultural and social contributions. The 'fortress Europe' policy of the European Union has resulted in fewer immigrants than would be expected from Africa and Asia.

Ireland's contact with African and Asian countries has also been very positive thanks to the missionary religious orders and congregations and through voluntary overseas services, including the United Nations' peace-keeping military personnel from Ireland. Through the positive influence of missionaries, volunteers and United Nations peacekeeping Defence Forces, the former patronising ('Black Babies') mentality towards the peoples of Africa and Asia is changing to one of mutual respect and equality. This change is confirmed in the findings of the 2007-08 national survey (see Table No. 4.2, pages 65-66).

Table No. 7.6:
African, Asian and Racial Categories' Mean-Social-Distance by Personal Variables

Variable	Chinese 1	Coloureds 2	Indians 3	Blacks 4	Africans 5	Pakistanis 6	Nigerians 7	Average Number
Total Sample	1.924	2.164	2.276	2.348	2.440	2.682	2.726	1,000
A. Age	N/S	P<.001	P<.005	P<.005	P<.005	P<.005	P<.005	
1. 18-25 years	---	2.412	2.468	2.667	2.892	2.912	2.948	167
2. 26-40 years	---	1.929	1.995	2.045	2.057	2.359	2.378	318
3. 41-55 years	---	2.104	2.393	2.355	2.499	2.660	2.805	244
4. 56-70 years	---	2.300	2.409	2.434	2.531	2.970	3.001	175
5. 71 years plus	---	2.418	2.340	2.631	2.625	2.882	2.796	96
B. Marital Status	N/S	N/S	P<.01	N/S	P<.01	P<.007	N/S	
1. Single/Never Married	---	---	2.428	---	2.629	2.913	---	357
2. Married	---	---	2.239	---	2.321	2.555	---	466
3. Separated/Divorced	---	---	2.060	---	2.444	2.400	---	44
4. Permanent Relationship	---	---	2.149	---	2.273	2.375	---	71
5. Widowed	---	---	2.010	---	2.443	2.845	---	68
C. Area of Birth	P<.003	P<.005	P<.003	P<.005	P<.007	P<.005	P<.001	
1. City (100,000 plus)	1.847	2.110	2.089	2.219	2.430	2.595	2.607	415
2. Large Town (10,000 +)	1.714	1.874	2.221	1.859	2.016	2.483	2.698	116
3. Town (1,500 plus)	1.643	1.677	1.804	1.850	1.943	2.273	2.321	129
4. Rural/Village	2.200	2.519	2.705	2.866	2.794	3.016	3.039	340
D. Place of Rearing in Republic of Ireland	P<.005	P<.005	P<.005	P<.005	P<.001	P<.005	P<.005	
1. Dublin (City & County)	1.883	2.286	2.218	2.320	2.550	2.662	2.810	265
2. Rest of Leinster	2.123	2.489	2.628	2.610	2.774	3.223	3.052	160
3. Munster	1.883	2.105	2.189	2.353	2.311	2.448	2.592	230
4. Connaught/Ulster	2.024	2.099	2.432	2.554	2.397	2.602	2.692	162

Table No. 7.6 (Cont'd.) Variable	Chinese 1	Coloureds 2	Indians 3	Blacks 4	Africans 5	Pakistanis 6	Nigerians 7	Average Number
E. Region of Residence	P<.005	P<.005	P<.005	P<.005	P<.005	P<.005	P<.005	
1. B.M.W.	**2.248**	**2.397**	**2.678**	**2.710**	**2.564**	**2.941**	**2.904**	268
2. Dublin	1.867	**2.292**	2.152	2.302	**2.485**	2.630	2.692	283
3. Mid-East & South-East	1.909	**2.217**	**2.469**	2.417	**2.661**	**2.963**	**2.991**	214
4. Mid-West & South-West	1.637	1.695	1.791	1.924	2.041	2.191	2.321	236
F. Education	P<.005	P<.005	P<.005	P<.005	P<.005	P<.005	P<.005	
1. Primary or Less	**2.000**	**2.412**	**2.570**	**2.590**	**2.770**	**3.045**	**3.029**	117
2. Incomplete Sec.-Level	**2.216**	**2.412**	**2.606**	**2.693**	**2.510**	**2.871**	**2.935**	259
3. Complete Second-Level	**1.950**	**2.198**	**2.391**	**2.564**	**2.593**	**2.832**	**2.930**	251
4. Third-Level	1.682	1.892	1.880	1.894	2.188	2.338	2.352	376
G. Occupational Status	P<.001	P<.003	P<.005	P<.005	P<.005	P<.005	P<.009	
1. Unskilled/Semi-Skilled	**2.171**	**2.477**	**2.759**	**2.751**	**2.769**	**3.101**	**3.105**	204
2. Skilled/Routine Non-M.	1.815	2.020	2.171	2.242	2.287	2.524	2.702	321
3. Inspectional/Supervisory	**2.007**	2.085	2.248	**2.379**	**2.510**	**2.876**	2.646	131
4. Professional/Executive	1.558	1.845	1.762	1.994	2.177	2.086	2.300	196
H. Social Class Position	P<.005	P<.005	P<.005	P<.005	P<.005	P<.005	P<.005	
Class I: "Upper Class"	1.683	**2.282**	1.683	2.134	**2.781**	2.052	2.474	39
Class II: "Upr-Mid. Class"	1.453	1.586	1.564	1.777	1.820	1.896	1.995	138
Class III: "Mid.-Mid. Class"	1.875	2.026	2.172	2.223	2.422	**2.704**	**2.791**	228
Class IV: "Working Class"	**2.028**	**2.293**	**2.566**	**2.590**	**2.594**	**2.892**	**2.937**	361
Class V: "Lower Class"	**2.026**	**2.308**	**2.377**	**2.587**	**2.496**	**2.749**	**2.790**	85

Note: Mean-Social-Distance scores above sample average are in **bold.**

According as the mean-social-distance scores increase, the range of possible variation also increases. This can be confirmed in the proportionately more variables eliciting significant variations between sub-samples of Table No. 7.6. Only **five** variable/category sub-tables out of a total **forty-nine** registered a non-significant (N/S) result. With the exception of the **'Chinese' (1.924)**, each of the other stimulus categories examined in Table No. 7.6 recorded a mean-social-distance score of **2.000 plus**. Scores over 2.000 reflect a substantial degree of social prejudice.

6.1 Age:

Once again the above-average prejudice scores for the 18 to 25 year-olds is true in the case of the six categories registering a significant variation between subsample scores. The 26 to 40 year-olds also re-affirm their status as the most tolerant age group right across the same six categories. The negative effects of older age on the levels of "ethnic and ethnico-racial" tolerance are also confirmed in the above findings.

The gap between the mean-social-distance scores of **'Nigerians'** and that of **'Africans'** raises questions about the reasons for the relatively higher level of social prejudice against 'Nigerians'.   This should be researched further in relation to the negative stereotypes against immigrants from Nigeria.   Anti-locution or ridicule against 'Nigerians' in Ireland should be countered more vigorously in the interests of intergroup justice!

6.2 Marital Status:

This variable failed to produce a statistically significant variation between subsamples in the case of four of the seven stimulus categories on Table No. 7.6.   This meant 'consensus' with regard to 'Chinese', 'Coloureds', 'Blacks' and 'Nigerians'.   Consensus at the relatively high level of social distance is indicative of a fairly established pattern of ethnic and ethnico-racial prejudice and provides less hope of likely positive change in the short-term!

The 'Single/Never Married' were the most prejudiced against each of the three categories with significant variations, i.e. 'Indians', 'Africans' and 'Pakistani'.   This probably reflects the influence of the younger respondents.

6.3 Area of Birth:

This ordinal variable was most discerning.   Respondents who were born in 'Rural/Village' areas were consistently and substantially less welcoming to members of each of the seven "African, Asian and Racial Categories", i.e. they were the only subsample to record above-average mean-social-distance scores.   Those born in 'Towns (1,500-9,999 inhabitants)' were the least prejudiced of the four subsamples in each of the seven categories.   Is this owing to the fact that small town populations tend to be more integrated because of their numbers and limited space for the build-up of ghettoes?

6.4 Place of Rearing in Ireland:

This is a nominal variable which lacks 'more than' or 'less than' quantitative measures between its subsamples.   Nevertheless, it is useful to note the impact of geographic area of rearing in the prejudices of the people.

'Munster' respondents, once again, register the lowest levels of social distance overall.   The 'Rest of Leinster' subsample is the only one with above-average social-distance scores across each of the seven categories, while 'Dublin City and County' and 'Connaught/Ulster' subsamples have mixed results.

147

The reasons for inter-provincial variations are likely to be influenced by the demographic make-up of the population, in terms of minority proportions, (see Table No. 2.3, page 19) and the level of **favourable contact** with members of the immigrant population in the area.

6.5 Region of Residence:
Comparison between 'Region of Residence' and 'Area of Rearing' reflects the level of inter-regional geographic mobility. The BMW regions are the most likely to have experienced out-migration of workers because of imbalanced regional development over the years. Also the BMW has regions of low-density population, i.e. with a higher than normal proportion living in 'Rural/Village' areas. This goes to explain the relatively high level of prejudice towards each of the seven categories, i.e. above-average social-distance scores.

The 'Mid-East and South-East' subsamples mirror the findings of the 'Rest of Leinster-reared' in Table No. 7.6 (d) above. The respondents living in the 'Mid-West and South-West' confirm the relatively low level of prejudice of the 'Munster-reared'. The socio-cultural factors favouring greater intergroup tolerance in these regions merit special research.

6.6 Education:
A clear pattern is discernible from the findings of Table No. 7.6 (f) showing a **negative correlation** between **education** and **prejudice** as measured by mean-social-distance scores. This is as anticipated. What is surprising is the limited impact of second-level education on the score in all seven categories. (See Table No. 7.8 for the distribution of education by age, page 157.) Of course, the most serious question emerging from the findings of Table No. 7.6 is the relatively high level of overall prejudice for a population with above-average participation in education and relative economic security!

6.7 Occupational Status:
The findings of this ordinal variable are, more or less, as anticipated with greater tolerance among the 'professional and high executive' sub-sample. There are, however, two anomalies in the results of Table No. 7.6 (g), namely, the relatively low level of prejudice in the 'skilled/routine non-manual' subsample. This is a very important subsample making up over 32% of the total sample. The 'inspectional/supervisory' subsample shows a

mixed result with four stimulus categories recording an above-average mean social-distance score.

6.8 Social Class Position:
The findings for social class position show a moderately positive correlation between social status and tolerance towards the seven categories, allowing for some anomalies. Those at the bottom of the social ladder had the higher mean-social-distance scores.

6.9 Conclusion:
The main emphasis of the above commentary has been more on the performance of the variables rather than on the individual stimulus categories. Table No. 7.6 has been a very significant one insofar as *it shows the level of ethnic and ethnico-racial prejudice, which is still much higher than it should be in a population with relative economic security and a high level of participation in education.* The racial factor is inevitably present in the attitudes towards each of the seven stimulus categories of Table No. 7.6. Many may convince themselves they are 'colour-blind' in their perception without being so in their outlook and behaviour!

Part VII – Middle-East Categories

The four stimulus categories, included in the questionnaire to measure Irish attitudes towards the Middle-East region of the world, are: 'Palestinians', 'Israelis', 'Iranians' and 'Arabs'. These four categories are likely to elicit very complex sets of attitudes.

The attitudes are primarily **ethnic,** since the four categories have strong association with nationalities and cultures. 'Palestinians' are an old nation emanating from the ancient civilisation of the Middle-East. 'Israelis' are a people rooted in Judaic Christian origins. 'Iranians' are heirs to the rich Persian nation and culture. 'Arabs' represent an ancient civilisation which embraces a number of nationalities and has roots in the beginning of human civilisation.

The second aspect associated with these four categories is **religious,** i.e. Islam, Judaism and Christianity, whose origins lie in the Middle-East. The history of the inter-religion relations between Christianity, Islam and Judaism has been turbulent over the centuries. This has an inevitable residue in the attitudes of Irish (predominantly Christian) respondents to the four stimulus categories listed.

A third element present may be **racial** because of the physiognomic differences perceived in members of the Middle-East countries in general. This would be a much weaker influence than the religious or ethnic attitudes.

The fourth dimension to the perceptions on which current attitudes may be based is the **political** dimension. This has been to the forefront since the end of World War II in 1945. Western powers have manipulated the peoples of the Middle-East for multiple reasons – economic as well as political, e.g. oil.

Table No. 7.7:
Social-Distance Scores of Middle-East Nationalities by Personal Variables

Variable	Palestinians	Israelis	Iranians	Arabs	Average Number
Total Sample	**2.709**	**2.842**	**2.850**	**2.908**	1,000
A. Age	P<.005	P<.005	P<.005	P<.001	
1. 18-25 years	**3.081**	**3.435**	**3.327**	**3.145**	167
2. 26-40 years	2.407	2.525	2.460	2.575	318
3. 41-55 years	**2.721**	2.731	**2.877**	**3.095**	244
4. 56-70 years	**2.893**	**2.849**	**2.896**	2.819	175
5. 71 years plus	2.695	**3.124**	**3.151**	**3.293**	96
B. Marital Status	N/S	P<.005	P<.02	P<.005	
1. Single/Never Married	---	**3.116**	**3.060**	**3.140**	357
2. Married	---	2.671	2.734	2.740	466
3. Separated/Divorced	---	2.600	2.615	2.856	44
4. Permanent Relationship	---	2.660	2.606	2.728	71
5. Widowed	---	**2.913**	**2.941**	**3.063**	68
C. Area of Birth	P<.004	P<.04	P<.002	P<.008	
1. City (100,000 plus)	**2.723**	2.790	2.802	2.809	415
2. Large Town (10,000 plus)	2.535	2.646	2.696	2.477	116
3. Town (1,500 plus)	2.346	2.629	2.430	2.646	129
4. Rural/Village	**2.897**	**3.059**	**3.125**	**3.280**	340
D. Place of Rearing in R.O.I.	P<.005	P<.005	P<.005	P<.005	
1. Dublin (City & County)	**2.782**	**2.975**	**2.988**	**2.975**	265
2. Rest of Leinster	**3.164**	**3.492**	**3.468**	**3.381**	160
3. Munster	2.479	2.394	2.515	2.795	230
4. Connaught/Ulster	2.493	2.620	2.655	2.817	162

Table No. 7.7 (Cont'd.) Variable	Palestinians	Israelis	Iranians	Arabs	Average Number
E. Region of Residence	P<.005	P<.005	P<.005	P<.005	
1. B.M.W.	**2.877**	**3.266**	**3.222**	**3.266**	268
2. Dublin	**2.756**	**2.924**	**2.944**	**2.911**	283
3. Mid-East & South-East	**3.041**	**3.079**	**3.076**	**3.062**	214
4. Mid-West & South-West	2.161	2.042	2.103	2.353	236
F. Education	P<.005	P<.005	P<.005	P<.001	
1. Primary or Less	**2.998**	**3.064**	**3.120**	**3.120**	117
2. Incomplete Second-Level	**2.872**	**3.018**	**3.117**	**3.131**	259
3. Complete Second-Level	**2.978**	**3.077**	**2.897**	**3.043**	251
4. Third-Level	2.331	2.496	2.550	2.597	376
G. Occupational Status	P<.005	P<.005	P<.005	P<.005	
1. Unskilled/Semi-Skilled	**3.301**	2.453	**3.287**	**3.530**	204
2. Skilled/Routine Non-M.	2.508	2.649	2.673	2.803	321
3. Inspectional/Supervisory	2.706	2.612	**2.945**	**2.949**	131
4. Professional/Executive	2.100	2.394	2.332	2.486	190
H. Social Class Position	P<.005	P<.005	P<.005	P<.005	
Class I: "Upper Class"	2.070	2.781	2.519	**3.134**	39
Class II: Upr-Mid. Class"	1.887	2.120	2.107	2.204	138
Class III: "Mid.-Mid. Class"	2.627	2.647	2.755	2.714	228
Class IV: "Working Class"	**2.932**	**3.029**	**3.092**	**3.286**	360
Class V: "Lower Class"	**2.990**	**3.232**	2.891	**3.195**	85

Note: Mean-Social-Distance scores above sample average are in **bold**.

Twenty-seven of the twenty-eight sub-scales reported in the above Table (No. 7.7) have registered significant variations between the sub-samples for each of the four stimulus categories. The **one case** recording **consensus** was 'Palestinians' by 'Marital Status'. The mean-social-distance score towards each of the four "Middle-East Categories" is over 2.700. This means that a wide range of inter-subsample variations of MSD scores was expected and confirmed by Table No. 7.7.

The patterns of variation confirm earlier findings in the Tables dealing with "Irish, British and Americans" (Table No. 7.4, page 134), "Continental European Nationalities" (Table No. 7.5, page 140) and "African, Asian and Racial Categories" (Table No. 7.6, pages 145-6). This also shows the universal nature of **Ethnic Prejudice** or **Ethnocentrism**, allowing for the presence of political, religious and racial features in individual stimulus categories.

7.1 Age:

The '26 to 40 year-olds' subsample has, once again, recorded the **lowest** mean-social-distance scores towards each of the four Middle-East categories, i.e. 'Palestinians', 'Israelis', 'Iranians' and 'Arabs'. The younger age group, i.e. '18 to 25 years', has scored the **highest** mean-social-distance in the case of all four categories. The range of difference between the mean-social-distance scores is **very substantial** in the case of each category as the following extract from Table No. 7.7 (a) will show:

Stimulus Category	Mean-Social-Distance Score		
	18 to 25 years	26 to 40 years	Difference
1. 'Palestinians'	3.081	2.407	+0.674
2. 'Israelis'	3.435	2.525	+0.910
3. 'Iranians'	3.327	2.460	+0.867
4. 'Arabs'	3.145	2.575	+0.570

The mean-social-distance range of scores is from 1 to 7, which means a **six-stage** continuum, i.e. from "welcome to kinship" (1) to "debar or deport" (7). In the case of the four categories, the range of differences between the MSD scores of the '18 to 25 years' subsample and the '26 to 40 years' subsample go from more than 'half a stage' **(57%)** to almost 'one full stage' **(91%)**. These are very substantial levels of difference. This is further confirmation of the problematic ethnic and ethnico-racial attitudes of the young people and the urgent need to find out the reasons for such relative intolerance. Further commentary on the age variable is given below. (See Part VIII - *Nota Bene*, pages 156-160.)

7.2 Marital Status:

The pattern of social-distance responses towards 'Palestinians' by 'Marital Status' is one of consensus. As stated already, this is the only sub-table not to record a statistically significant variation between the sub-samples on Table No. 7.7.

The failure of the four "Middle-Eastern Grouping of Stimulus Categories" to elicit a significant variation by Marital Status on Table No. 7.1 above (see pages 126-7) raises questions in the light of the performance of individual categories. Is this due to the complexity of respondents' perception of the four categories, i.e. 'Palestinians', 'Israelis', 'Iranians' and 'Arabs', i.e. ethnic, religious, political, historical and racial? Are these elements or perceptions neutralising each other in the collective sub-scale on Table No. 7.1?

The pattern of prejudice in relation to the three stimulus categories with significant variations is clear and consistent, i.e. the 'Single/Never

Married' and the 'Widowed' recorded mean-social-distance scores above the sample average, with the former substantially less tolerant than the latter. The obvious influence of 18 to 25 year-olds among the 'Single/Never Married' is contributing to the subsample's relatively high mean-social-distance scores. The widowed would be suffering from the frustrations sometimes associated with aspects of old age such as physical constraints. These frustrations would cause tension-seeking release in aggression. Social prejudice is a form of psychological aggression!

7.3 Area of Birth:
Once again, those born in 'Towns (1,500 to 9,999)' stand out as the *most tolerant* subsample. 'Rural/Village-born' respondents are above average in the mean-social-distance towards each of the four categories. The range of variations between the two subsamples is substantial as the following extract from Table No. 7.7 (c) shows:

Stimulus Category	Mean-Social-Distance Score		
	Town (1,500 to 9,999)	Rural/Village	Difference
1. 'Palestinians'	2.346	2.897	-0.533
2. 'Israelis'	2.629	3.059	-0.430
3. 'Iranians'	2.430	3.125	-0.695
4. 'Arabs'	2.646	3.280	-0.634

This range of difference of between 43% and 70% of a social-distance stage is quite substantial and shows the strong influence of urban-rural background on the attitudes of prejudices of people.

7.4 Place of Rearing (in the Republic of Ireland):
The results of the 'Place of Rearing' variables highlight the impact of **geographical** background on ethnocentrism. Factors other than the degree of urbanisation are at work here. The most tolerant 'Provinces of Rearing' are Munster and Connaught/Ulster while Dublin City and County and the Rest of Leinster record above-average mean-social-distance scores for each of the four Middle-East categories. If anything, these results tend to be out of line with the 'Area of Birth' findings, where 'rural/village' scored above-average. Factors such as experience of favourable social contact or regional (subcultural) ethos of tolerance or population distribution patterns could influence provincial attitudes. In practically every stimulus category 'Munster-Reared' respondents have been notably more ethnically tolerant than their fellow-respondents reared in the other provinces. Is there a Munster 'tolerant ethos'?

7.5 Region of Residence:
The 'Munster' factor is very much at work in the findings of Table No. 7.7 (e). Regions 'Mid-West and South-West' (which cover Munster) are below the sample average for each of the four stimulus categories; while the other three subsamples are above the sample average in the case of each of the categories, i.e. 'Palestinians', 'Israelis', 'Iranians' and 'Arabs'.

Once again, there is evidence here of **geographic influences** which are not wholly explained by the level of urbanisation within the regions. The degrees of tolerance can be influenced by the extent of pluralist integration in communities. Unfortunately, these measures have not been researched in the current survey. Such things as local media (print and electronic) can influence 'for better or for worse' the levels of prejudice and tolerance and create a 'pluralist ethos' in the locality. Churches and religious groups have a significant influence on intergroup tolerance. The Christian Churches in the United States, for instance, played a leading role in the *civil rights' movement,* e.g. **Rev. Martin Luther King** and others. Also, in South Africa we had the positive role of **Archbishops Hurley and Tutu** and others. Travellers, for instance, find certain communities or counties in Ireland to be friendlier than other areas throughout the country. This is often reflected in the parishes where Travellers seem to halt or to settle. The combination of these factors in Munster or in the 'Mid-West and South-West Regions' is likely to contribute to the relatively positive attitudes reflected in their social-distance scores towards 'Palestinians', 'Israelis', 'Iranians' and 'Arabs'!

7.6 Education:
The performance of this variable is most interesting in relation to each of the four categories. The most tolerant subsample was the 'Third-Level' one with substantially lower mean-social-distance scores toward each of the four categories. Each of the other subsamples, i.e. 'Primary or less', 'Incomplete Second-Level' and 'Complete Second-Level' all registered scores above the sample average. The performance of the 'Complete Second-Level' subsample was disappointing in that it was not that significantly different from that of respondents with 'Primary or Less' education. This raised questions about the impact of 'Second-Level Education' on the prejudices of the people! The relatively high percentage of '18 to 25 year-olds' with 'Complete Second-Level' education (41%) may have influenced this negative result! Or have they been influenced by the education they received (insofar as it made them more or less tolerant)?

The following extract from Table No. 7.7(f) highlights the difference between those with 'Third-Level' education and those with 'Complete Second-Level' participation. ('Admission to Kinship' percentages are also compared.)

Stimulus Category	Complete Second Level A			Third Level B			Difference (B – A)		
	Admit to Kinship	Deny Cit.	MSD	Admit to Kinship	Deny Cit.	MSD	Admit to Kinship	Deny Cit.	MSD
1. 'Palestinians'	46.6%	24.3%	2.978	50.4%	12.2%	2.331	+3.8%	-12.1%	-0.647
2. 'Israelis'	45.4%	27.5%	3.077	49.5%	15.9%	2.496	+4.1%	-11.6%	-0.581
3. 'Iranians'	48.6%	24.7%	2.897	46.9%	15.9%	2.550	-1.7%	-8.8%	-0.347
4. 'Arabs'	43.9%	24.1%	3.043	47.4%	14.0%	2.597	+3.5%	-10.1%	-0.446

The above extract shows the level of difference in attitudes between the third-level subsample and the complete second-level subsample. The mean-social-distance scores' differences are more substantial than those of percentages admitting to family. The area of real variation in the percentages 'denying citizenship' contributes most to the wider MSD variations. As noted when dealing with the significance of social-distance patterns, categories eliciting strong 'political or extremist' connotations tend to polarise responses, i.e. with a substantial proportion 'welcoming to kinship' and others 'denying citizenship'. This is particularly so in the case of 'Iranians' as is clear from the above sub-table.

7.7 Occupational Status:

Some may query the findings of Table No. 7.7 (g) in the relatively **few cases** of above-sample average mean-social-distance scores. This is owing to the fact that only **84.6%** gave their occupational status. The remaining **15.4%** with undeclared occupational status seem to have been more prejudiced (on average) than the 84.6% who gave their occupation to the interviewers. This explains why all occupational subsamples were below the average mean-social-distance score. The findings by 'occupational status' was as expected with respondents in the highest statused occupations least prejudiced in the case of each of the four categories. 'Inspectional/supervisory' respondents were more negative than was anticipated.

7.8 Social Class Position:

The five levels of social class position are arrived at by combining educational achievement and occupational status. The most tolerant sub-sample was Class II ("Upper-Middle-Class") for each of the four Middle-

East stimulus categories.   The least tolerant subsamples varied between Class V ("Lower-Class") and Class IV ("Working-Class").   The following extract from Table No. 7.7(h) gives the range of variation between the 'most tolerant' and 'least tolerant' for each category:

Category	Range of Variation	Highest MSD (Most tolerant)		Between Lowest MSD (Least tolerant)
1. 'Palestinians'	1.103	"Lower-Class" (2.990)	and	"Upper-Middle-Class" (1.887)
2. 'Israelis'	1.112	"Lower-Class" (3.232)	and	"Upper-Middle-Class" (2.120)
3. 'Iranians'	0.985	"Working-Class" (3.092)	and	"Upper-Middle-Class" (2.107)
4. 'Arabs'	1.082	"Working-Class" (3.286)	and	"Upper-Middle-Class" (2.204)

The above extract emphatically points to the significant and substantial importance of **social class position** in influencing social prejudice and tolerance.   Why this is so requires further research to arrive at the full explanation.   The security of those with higher social status in part explains the higher level of tolerance.   Their education is also a factor in determining their level of social tolerance.

7.9 Conclusion:
Table No. 7.7 deserves close reading and examination.   Its findings are revealing in two aspects, i.e. what they highlight in relation to the patterns of ethnic and ethnico-racial prejudice and the particular levels of prejudice towards Middle-East nationalities on different sides of the political and religious divides.   Since religious and political issues in the Middle-East are central to the serious crisis in that region of the world, these findings raise questions which merit further research and appropriate collective action conducive to mutual respect and tolerance.

The problems of the Middle-East are at the heart of a world trying to find a way of coexistence between peoples deeply rooted in the history of civilisation, including the three major world religions of Semitic origin.   In the modern world where pluralism and diversity are characteristic factors, a *modus vivendi* must be found which honours and respects different religions and facilitates social equality for all.   Hence, the importance of the above findings!

Part VIII – *Nota Bene*: The Age-Factor in Ethnic and Racial Prejudice

8.1 Extended Adolescence (Irish Youth):
The most surprising performances in social-distance scores so far have been in the *age sub-variables,* where the results were very mixed and not in

accordance with anticipations[9]. The real question is the performance of the 18 to 25 year-olds, who could be classified as occupying a transition phase in the modern phenomenon of extended adolescence, i.e. not yet enjoying full adult status. A substantial minority of this age group have expressed a serious level of ethnic and ethnico-racial intolerance.

A large percentage of this age group has not experienced the two most important "adult-incorporating rituals", namely, marriage and occupying a full-time job. This may create ambivalence in the 18 to 25 year-olds, which society has not clarified. On the one hand, they enjoy **dependence** as students, apprentices, etc., while, on the other hand, they do not have the **independence** or the **responsibility** for themselves and for others, as is the case of married couples and providers. This is likely to lead to frustration and deep personal tension arising from **delayed adulthood**. Does such tension seek expression in prejudice which is a form of psychological aggression?

The cause of **extended adolescence** is to be found in the requirements of modern industrial/post-industrial society and the decline of the role and importance of the family in favour of a more widespread individualism. It is an area worthy of very serious cultural, social and psychological research and attention by those who create the socio-cultural norms at national and international levels. The nature of child-rearing (socialisation) in modern Ireland needs to be re-appraised because of its failure to counter prejudice among 18 to 25 year-olds. Perhaps a break from fulltime education on completion of second-level to enable young people to work and get married in their early twenties would bring forward adult status to this age-group! It would also facilitate more real contact across the generations. Third-level education could then become an **adult** phenomenon, which it should be!

8.2 Age and Education:
On the specific question of the influence of education on the attitudes of respondents of different age subsamples, the following Table (No. 7.8) measures *Age by Education.*

---

[9] It will be shown in Chapter XVIII below that young respondents' level of **authoritarianism** was lower than that of older respondents. This is a welcome result in that it counters the young people's negative performance in the social-distance findings. (See Table No. 18.2, pages 492-3.)

Table No. 7.8: Age by Education

	Age Education	18 -25 yrs 1.	26-40 yrs 2.	41-55 yrs 3.	56-70 yrs 4.	71 yrs + 5.	No.
A.	1. Primary or Less	0.6%	0.9%	9.7%	**24.7%**	**47.4%**	118 **(11.6%)**
	2. Incomplete Sec-Lev.	16.0%	20.9%	**30.8%**	**36.0%**	27.8%	262 **(25.8%)**
	3. Complete Sec.-Lev.	**41.4%**	23.4%	**27.5%**	12.9%	17.5%	254 **(25.0%)**
	4. Third-Level	**42.0%**	**54.8%**	32.0%	26.4%	7.2%	381 **(37.6%)**
	Number	169	325	247	178	97	1,015
	Percent. of Total	(16.6%)	(32.0%)	(24.3%)	(17.5%)	(9.5%)	---
	Distribution of Third-Level						
B.	1. Cert. or Diploma	48.6%	52.2%	**72.2%**	**56.5%**	N/S	213 **(55.9%)**
	2. Primary Degree	**43.1%**	**35.4%**	17.7%	23.9%	N/S	122 **(32.0%)**
	3. Post-Grad. Degree	8.3%	**12.4%**	10.1%	**19.6%**	N/S	46 **(12.1%)**
		72	178	79	46	6*	381

Note: Percentages above the sample averages are in **bold**.
    * Because of the small number of cases, distribution percentages are not significant (statistically).

It is very clear from the above Table (No. 7.8) that **age** and **education** are negatively correlated.   If one were to score the education variable on a 0 to 3 scale, the results would be as follows, i.e. calculated from Table No. 7.8 (A):

Age Variable	Mean Education Score (0 – 3)
1. 18 to 25 years	<u>2.25</u>
2. 26 to 40 years	<u>2.32</u>
3. 41 to 55 years	1.82
4. 56 to 70 years	1.41
5. 71 years plus	0.84

Notes: Mean Education Score: Primary or Less = 0;   Incomplete Second-Level = 1;
Complete Second-Level = 2;   Third-Level   = 3.   Scores above sample means of <u>1.89</u> are underlined.

The above sub-table shows that the 26 to 40 year-olds are the most highly educated of the five age subsamples with the 18 to 25 year-olds in second place and above the total sample average to a substantial degree.   This shows that higher education performance has not been able to counter the relatively high level of prejudice for the latter age group.   Are we seeing in modern education the emergence of 'the dominance of practical intelligence' leading to 'instrumentalised reason'?   This results from the influence of the economic institution on public education leading to a more restricted curriculum.   *"The dominance of practical intelligence arises as a result of a general bias against comprehensive intelligence in charting the future of society"* (see Moloney, Raymond, 2010, pp30-33). Has Irish second- and third-level education become dominated by pragmatic and materialist issues such as science and technology without sufficient emphasis on the humanities, personal development and community awareness?

Table No. 7.8 (B) examines the breakdown of Third-Level participation by (a) Certificate or Diploma; (b) Primary Degree; and (c) Postgraduate Degree. Both the 18 to 25 year-olds and the 26 to 40 year-olds had a relatively high proportion of their subsamples with primary and graduate degrees. The 41 to 55 years and 56 to 70 years subsamples were ahead in the proportions participating in incomplete Second-Level education. In the overall, therefore, the relatively high level of participation in 'Third-Level' by the 26 to 40 years subsample must explain, in part, at least, its high level of ethnic tolerance. Also, having achieved full adult status in society reduces the level of frustration of the subsample. Of course, education and academic achievement are not necessarily the same as **wisdom**, which is the product of life experience and **informal socialisation** as well as formal education and training. Tolerance is as much a product of 'wisdom' as it is of 'education'. This is something which needs to be researched seriously.

8.3 Cybernetics and Peer-Association:
Yet another interesting feature of modern Irish society (which it shares with other 'Western', 'Developed' societies) is the predominance of **exclusive peer socialisation**, i.e. the campus, youth-club subcultures and fewer opportunities to relate to older or younger age groups. This is likely to impede the transmission of cultural beliefs, values and norms which have evolved over centuries of human experience. In other words, our youth seem to have lost much real contact with older generations at the informal level. The decline of the role of the **family** in socialisation has been replaced by extra-familial structured peer-environments such as schools, colleges, and commercialised leisure. The influence of various forms of mass media is also significant.

For the first time in the evolution of civilisation, there is a danger of a break in the transmission of the culture of parents to their children. Are we seeing signs of the fears of George Orwell (1903-1950)[10] in his futuristic

---

[10] See Orwell, George, (1945), *Animal Farm: A Fairy Story*, London, Secker & Warburg, (1949), *Nineteen Eighty-Four*, London, Secker & Warburg.

fiction being confirmed in the findings? Such **cultural de-radicalisation** can lead to a diminution of the role of parents in the education and socialisation of their families.

The advances in communications technology, the arrival of universal telephonisation (which, in itself, marks real human progress) and the **'virtual society'** are also very serious factors influencing peer socialisation today. The mass media (print and electronic) are also part of the formative influences on the socialisation of young people's intergroup attitudes. The impact of the recent affluence of young people on their attitudes and behaviour is worth researching! Television and laptop-viewing isolate the viewer from conversation, even on train journeys! Earplugs lead to isolation. The influence of the relatively small elite who control modern mass media should be appraised objectively in the interests of youth and society. Commercial interests can be limited in their socio-cultural understanding of the real needs of youth.

8.4 The Prejudiced Minority of Young People:
The above does not exhaust the factors which may have contributed to the negative attitudes of the substantial minority of 18 to 25 years respondents presented in the various Tables of this text on intergroup prejudices in the Republic of Ireland at the beginning of the 21st century. Serious research is called for to discover the causes of these findings and measures likely to liberate those locked in potentially destructive social prejudice. When such intolerance finds expression in negative behaviour, a more serious crisis has arrived!

8.5 Conclusion:
In conclusion, it is necessary **to caution against alarmism**. It is only a **substantial minority** of young people (18 to 25 years old) who are prejudiced, while the majority are very tolerant. What is necessary is to find out the **socio-cultural changes** needed to counter the negative causes of the intolerance of the minority of young people. The nature, causes and effects of social prejudice would provide an ideal subject for the senior cycle of the second-level curriculum and the third-level undergraduate curricula. The problem of extended adolescence appears to be the most serious one to be addressed by society.

***

CHAPTER VIII
Ethnic Prejudice and Irish Ethnic Self-Identity

Part I – Irish Ethnic Self-Identity

One's ethnic self-identity is part of one's own self-perception, which includes family, local community, religious affiliation, political ideology or party, occupational status, social-class position, etc. At various times in history the level of one's ethnic self-identity can become more explicit, e.g. during times of international conflict and of struggles for national independence. Also, the nature of this self-identity can vary between societies with *imperialist achievements or aspirations* and those who have been the *victims of such expansionist colonial ambitions*. At the recreational level, international group sports' and athletics' competitions provide occasions for the awareness of the people's ethnic self-identity. Flags, anthems, commemorative national ceremonies, national dress and rituals, as well as national languages and cultural events, all contribute to the strengthening of the people's national self-identity. While exaggerated emphasis on one's ethnic self-identity can lead to *xenophobia*, tolerant ethnic self-identity is a socially positive thing which helps to bind people together and create just social solidarity.

1.1 General Findings:
The following Table (No. 8.1) establishes the ethnic self-identity of the 2007-08 national sample. The original question was included in Richard Rose's survey of Northern Ireland in 1968[1]. In addition to asking the respondents which ethnic category they identified with, Rose also asked the respondents **how strongly** they identified with it. The assumption behind the follow-up question was that those who said they **strongly** identified with their category of choice were more **insecure** in their self-identity than those who thought themselves as being **just average**. At the time (1968) Rose found that Unionists were 'more strongly' in their perceived ethnic self-identity than were Nationalists in Northern Ireland. This pointed to a possible insecurity among those who over-emphasised their self-identity at the time of possible exaggerated expressions of ethnic/religious/national self-identity in Northern Ireland.

---

[1] Rose, Richard, *Governing Without Consent*, London, Faber, 1971, page 285.

Table No. 8.1:
Primary Ethnic Self-Identity of the Total Sample, Irish-Born and Non-Irish-Born

Question: *"Which of these terms best describes the way you usually think of yourself?"*

Category		Total Sample		Irish-Born*		Non-Irish-Born	
		1st Choice %	2nd Choice %	1st Choice %	2nd Choice %	1st Choice %	2nd Choice %
1.	Irish	78.4	12.8	**87.3**	11.5	22.4	**23.3**
2.	County/City where Grew-up	5.4	15.4	5.2	**15.7**	**7.0**	15.0
3.	Anglo-Irish	3.4	1.8	**3.7**	**1.9**	2.1	1.4
4.	European	3.0	34.0	0.5	**34.3**	**18.5**	28.0
5.	Southern Irish	2.2	29.0	2.5	**32.3**	0.3	9.5
6.	British	1.9	1.5	---	1.1	**13.6**	**3.8**
7.	Northern Irish	0.9	1.2	0.8	**1.4**	**2.1**	0.3
8.	Other	4.8	4.3	0.1	1.7	**34.1**	**18.6**
	Total Number	1,015	979	857	857	141	141

* Irish Born includes those born in Northern Ireland.
Note: Percentages above the sample averages are in **bold**.

The above findings are very interesting. They show the predominance of Irish as the primary ethnic self-identity for the sample **(78.4%)** and, particularly, for the **'Irish-Born'** **(87.3%)**. They confirm the relatively widespread nature of Irish **national** self-identity. The failure of 'European' to attract primary loyalty in the case of 'Irish-born' is noteworthy. One-third (34%) of the 'Irish-born' sample gave **'European'** as the second choice of ethnic self-identity. **'Non-Irish-Born'** had a wider range of ethnic-identity.

Table No. 8.2 highlights the numbers seeing themselves with **local or internal** (Irish) primary ethnic self-identities. In the 1972-73 Greater Dublin Survey, it was clear that respondents from the 'working class' saw themselves primarily as 'county or city' rather than 'Irish or national'. National primary self-identity was largely a middle-class phenomenon.

Table No. 8.2:
Ethnic Self-Identity Summary Table

Category		Total Sample		Irish-Born*		Non-Irish-Born	
		1st Choice	2nd Choice	1st Choice	2nd Choice	1st Choice	2nd Choice
1.	Irish	78.4%	12.8%	**87.3%**	11.5%	22.4%	**23.3%**
2.	Internal – City/County/Province	8.5%	45.6%	8.4%	**49.4%**	**9.3%**	24.9%
3.	Anglo-Irish/British	5.3%	3.3%	3.7%	3.0%	**15.7%**	**5.2%**
4.	European	3.0%	34.0%	0.5%	**34.3%**	**18.5%**	28.0%
5.	Other	4.8%	4.3%	0.1%	1.7%	**34.1%**	**18.6%**
	Total Number	1,015	979	857	857	141	141

* Irish Born includes those born in Northern Ireland.
Note: Percentages above the sample averages are in **bold**.

The Irish national ethnic self-identity of the 'Irish-Born' is very high, i.e. **98.8%** gave 'Irish' as either their *first or second* choice (87.3% + 11.5%), while **57.8%** put 'Internal Irish' as either their *first or second* choice (8.4% + 49.4%). As already noted, it is evident from the above findings that membership of the **European Union** has had very little effect so far on Irish people's primary ethnic self-identity. In the second choice of ethnic self-identity, one-third (34.3%) of the 'Irish Born' saw themselves as 'European', while almost half of the sample **(49.4%)** opted for an 'internal Irish' identity. The shift towards a broader primary national identity, i.e. from 'internal Irish' to 'Irish', could well indicate a weakening of the local community for many of contemporary Irish citizens (see Table No. 8.3). It also shows the *embourgeoisement* of the majority of the Irish people, i.e. their responses in relation to primary ethnic self-identity are more 'middle-class'! In the 1972-73 survey of Greater Dublin it was found that primary ethnic self-identity was divided between Irish and internal Irish and that working class respondents and those from small farms tended to see themselves primarily as **'Dubliners or County'**. The middle-class respondents saw themselves as **'Irish'** in the first place.

In the light of the relatively recent influx of non-Irish nationals into the Republic of Ireland, the relatively high proportion who opted for an Irish ethnic self-identity is encouraging. Some **31.7%** recorded an Irish (including internal Irish) primary ethnic self-identity, while 48.2% identified themselves as Irish as their second choice. This is indicative of a sensed positive reception and a favourable experience on coming to Ireland, which corroborates the improvement of overall ethnic social-distance measures recorded elsewhere in this text. (See Table No. 4.2, pages 65-6.)

Table No. 8.3 gives the responses to the primary ethnic self-identity in the three surveys, i.e. Greater Dublin 1972-73, National Sample 1988-89 and National Sample 2007-08. The Irish-born responses are probably a more realistic figure from which to measure changes between the national samples of 1988-89 and 2007-08.

Table No. 8.3:
Changes in Irish (Primary) Ethnic Self-Identity (1972-73, 1988-89, 2007-08)

	Irish 1	Internal City/Co. 2	Total Irish 1 & 2	Anglo- Irish/British 4	European 5	Other 6	No.
(A) 2007-08 Nat. Sample	78.4%	8.5%	**86.9%**	5.3%	3.0%	4.8%	1,015
(Irish-born)	(87.3%)	(8.4%)	**(95.7%)**	(3.7%)	(0.5%)	(0.1%)	(857)
(B) 1988-89* Nat. Sample	67.5%	28.5%	**96.0%**	2.0%	1.4%	0.6%	1,005
Change A - B	+10.9%	-20.0%	**-9.1%**	+3.3%	+1.6%	+4.2%	---
	(+19.8%)	(-20.1%)	**(-0.3%)**	(+1.7%)	(-0.9%)	(-0.3%)	
(C) Dublin 2007-08	85.0%	7.3%	**92.3%**	0.3%	3.1%	4.2%	286
(D) Dublin 1988-89	74.0%	22.0%	**96.0%**	3.0%	1.0%	1.0%	1,005
(E) Dublin 1972-73 **	48.0%	46.5%	**94.5%**	2.0%	2.0%	1.5%	2,311
Change C - D	+11.0%	-14.7%	**-3.7%**	-2.7%	+2.1%	+3.2%	---
Change C - E	+37.0%	-39.2%	**-2.3%**	-1.7%	+1.1%	+2.7%	---

Sources: * Mac Gréil (1996); ** Mac Gréil, (1977).

Note: Total Irish (Primary) Ethnic Self-Identity scores are in **bold.**
Irish-born scores are in brackets.

The overall **Irish** primary ethnic self-identity has remained constant between 1972-73 and 2007-08. The area of significant and substantial change is in **the decline** in primary identification in **'internal Irish'**, i.e. counties, cities, regions, etc. There was a nominal drop of **20.1%** in those who saw themselves as 'internal Irish' when 'Irish-Born' of 2007-08 and the total sample of 1988-89 are compared. In real percentage terms this indicates a decline of **70.5%,** i.e. from 28.5% in 1988-89 to 8.4% in 2007-08. There has been an increase of **29.3%** in those seeing themselves as 'Irish' first, i.e. from 67.5% in 1988-89 to 87.3% in 2007-08. If identifying first with 'Irish' rather than with one's county or province is seen as more a middle-class phenomenon then, there has been a strong degree of *'embourgeoisement'* among the Irish-born respondents in the intervening nineteen years! This trend had already been detected in the 1988-89 Dublin results when compared with those of 1972-73.

Slightly more than one-third (34.1%) of 'Non-Irish-Born' respondents (or 4.8% of the total sample) identified with nationalities outside Ireland. This adds to the richness of the cultural mix among contemporary Irish citizens. So long as there is **favourable contact** between the native Irish and those born outside the country, this influx of immigrants should add to the 'cultural mix' of inhabitants. *Pluralist coexistence* is no threat to Irish ethnic self-identity in the present time or in the near future.

The respondents were asked the following question after they had indicated "how they saw themselves", i.e. first choice:

Table No. 8.4:
How Strongly Respondents Identified with Their Ethnic Category
Question: *"Would you say you are strong or average in thinking of yourself in these terms?"*

	Level of Strength	Percentage	Number
1.	Strong	76.7%	765
2.	Don't Know	2.2%	22
3.	Average	21.0%	210
	Total:	99.9%	997

*The Non-Irish-born were the only respondents to opt for 'other' identity

Rose's hypothesis accepts that those who see themselves as **strong** members of their chosen ethnic category reflect a degree of uncertainty about their national identity. In the following quotation, Rose comments on the findings of his Northern Irish survey of 1968. (See Mac Gréil, M., 1977[2])

"Because of uncertainty about their national identity, Ulster Protestants are more likely to assert it; 45 per cent claim a 'strong' rather than 'average' sense of nationality. Among Protestants who think of themselves as Ulstermen, 59 per cent feel strongly about this loyalty. By contrast, only 28 per cent who think themselves as Irish identify strongly with the label, almost the same proportion as among Catholics. This further emphasises the extent to which an Irish identity is natural to Catholics. Because they perceive it as normal, it does not require special emphasis." (Rose, 1971[3])

---

[2] Mac Gréil, Micheál, *Prejudice and Tolerance in Ireland*, Dublin, C.I.R. 1977, page 126.
[3] Rose, Richard, *Governing without Consent*, London, Faber, 1971, pages 207-8.

Applying this interpretation to the findings of the 2007-08 national survey, it would appear that there is a widespread degree of **implicit uncertainty** about their ethnic self-identity among respondents. Changes in the levels of assertion in relation to respondents' nationality are given in Table No. 8.5.

Table No. 8.5:
Changes in Assertion of Ethnic Self-Identity (including 'Don't Knows')

	Levels of Assertion	National Samples		Dublin Samples			North. Irl.
		2007-08	1988-89	2007-08	1988-89*	1972-73**	1968***
1.	Strong	77%	41%	79%	43%	52%	38%
2.	Don't Know	2%	2%	5%	2%	1%	2%
3.	Average	21%	57%	16%	55%	47%	60%
	Number	997	960	281	265	2,287	1,291

* Mac Gréil, 1996, p.100
** Mac Gréil, 1977, p.125
*** Rose, 1971, p.285

The above figures show a significant and substantial change in the levels of assertion of ethnic self-identity between 1988-89 and 2007-08, i.e. a nominal increase of **36%** (from 41% in 1988-89 to 77% in 2007-08) in the percentage stating **'strong'**. There was a corresponding decrease in the 'average' scores. According to Richard Rose's interpretation we have a **growing ambiguity** in relation to how we see ourselves in the Republic of Ireland. This weakening in the proportion who would see it as "normal" or "natural" to be Irish or whatever, should raise further questions about the level of identity we have with our country! A more widespread use of the **Irish language** in the general population would give the people more security in their Irish self-identity! It would also remove the need to overemphasise our ethnic Irishness. One's national language is accepted by most cultural anthropologists as the principal symbolic meaningful system of a distinct people.

When examined by the assertion of ethnic identity of those born in Ireland and those born outside the country the situation of the native Irish is more emphatic than that of the others.

Table No. 8.6: Strength of Ethnic Self-Identification of Native Irish and of those Born outside Ireland

	Levels of Assertion	Irish-Born	Non-Irish-Born	Difference
1.	Strong	78%	65%	-13%
2.	Don't Know	2%	1%	-1%
3.	Average	20%	34%	+14%
		850	141	

The differences between the two subsamples are significant. The native Irish are substantially more assertive than the 'non-Irish-born'. One of the possible reasons for this might be an implicitly perceived threat to our national identity. Such phenomena as the weakening of religious culture and our failure to use our native language and the pressures from media and other sources to become more cosmopolitan and less rooted in the Irish culture could also put our people on the defensive. Many would argue that the most secure way to be **international** is to be at ease with, and secure in, our own **national** identity!

Part II – Primary Ethnic Self-Identity by Personal Variables

In this section it is proposed to examine the findings on primary ethnic self-identity by personal variables in order to find out the influence of age, gender, marital status, area of birth, place of rearing (in the Republic of Ireland), region of residence, education and occupation on how respondents see themselves. With the exception of 'place of rearing', all other variables are taken from the total sample which includes 14% plus respondents born outside of the Republic of Ireland. Table No. 8.2 (page 163) shows the difference between Irish-born and those born abroad.

Table No. 8.7 gives the "Primary Ethnic Self-Identity by Personal Variables" for the whole sample.

Because of the relatively high percentage of the total sample (86.9%) giving **Irish** (78.4%) or **internal Irish** (8.5%), as their "primary ethnic self-identity", it is not possible to get a wide range of variations between various subsamples. Nevertheless, each of the *eight personal variables* tested recorded a statistically significant variation; hence, the need to study the contents of Table No. 8.7.

Table No. 8.7: Primary Ethnic Self-Identity by Personal Variables

Personal Variables	Irish 1.	Local Irish 2.	(1+2) %	Anglo-Irish/British 3.	European 4.	Other 5.	Number
Total Sample	**78.4%**	**8.5%**	**(86.9)**	**5.3%**	**3.0%**	**4.8%**	1,014
A. Age	p<.001						
1. 18-25 years	72.4%	7.6%	(80.0)	2.9%	**5.9%**	**11.2%**	170
2. 26-40 years	72.4%	**9.5%**	(81.9)	**5.8%**	**4.0%**	**8.3%**	325
3. 41-55 years	**81.8%**	**9.3%**	**(91.1)**	**5.7%**	2.4%	0.8%	246
4. 56-70 years	**83.6%**	6.8%	**(90.4)**	**8.5%**	0.6%	0.6%	177
5. 71 years plus	**90.7%**	8.2%	**(98.9)**	1.0%	0.0%	0.0%	97
B. Gender	p<.001						
1. Males	74.9%	8.0%	(82.9)	**5.8%**	**4.8%**	**6.6%**	501
2. Females	**82.1%**	**9.2%**	**(91.3)**	4.7%	1.2%	2.9%	512
C. Marital Status	p<.002						
1. Single/Never Married	75.1%	**9.8%**	(84.9)	3.9%	**4.5%**	**6.7%**	358
2. Married	**79.2%**	**8.9%**	**(88.1)**	**7.0%**	1.1%	3.8%	472
3. Separated/Divorced	75.0%	**9.1%**	(84.1)	2.3%	**4.5%**	**9.1%**	44
4. Permanent Relationship	**79.2%**	4.2%	(83.4)	4.2%	**8.3%**	4.2%	72
5. Widowed	**92.6%**	2.9%	**(95.5)**	2.9%	1.5%	0.0%	68
D. Area of Birth	p<.001						
1. City (100,000 plus)	**79.9%**	**8.9%**	**(88.8)**	1.7%	**4.1%**	**5.5%**	418
2. Large Town (10,000 +)	69.7%	8.4%	(78.1)	**7.6%**	**6.7%**	**7.6%**	119
3. Town (1,500 plus)	**83.2%**	2.3%	(85.5)	1.5%	1.5%	**11.5%**	131
4. Rural/Village	78.3%	**10.4%**	**(88.7)**	**10.1%**	0.6%	0.6%	345
E. Place of Rearing in ROI.	p<.001						
1. Dublin (City & County)	**92.9%**	6.7%	**(99.6)**	0.0%	0.4%	0.0%	267
2. Rest of Leinster	**85.5%**	**13.9%**	**(99.4)**	0.0%	0.6%	0.0%	165
3. Munster	**85.7%**	5.7%	**(91.4)**	**8.7%**	0.0%	0.0%	230
4. Connaught/Ulster	**87.9%**	6.7%	**(94.6)**	4.8%	0.6%	0.0%	165
F. Region of Residence	p<.001						
1. B.M.W.	**80.1%**	6.3%	(86.4)	**6.3%**	1.8%	**5.5%**	271
2. Dublin	**85.0%**	7.3%	**(92.3)**	0.3%	**3.1%**	4.2%	286
3. Mid-East & South-East	72.7%	**17.7%**	**(90.4)**	3.2%	2.3%	4.1%	220
4. Mid-West & South-West	74.2%	3.8%	(78.0)	**12.3%**	**4.7%**	**5.1%**	236
G. Education	p<.002						
1. Primary or Less	**83.9%**	**10.2%**	**(94.1)**	2.5%	1.7%	1.7%	118
2. Incomplete Second-Level	**81.7%**	8.4%	**(90.1)**	**6.5%**	1.5%	1.9%	262
3. Complete Second-Level	**80.9%**	**8.6%**	**(89.5)**	3.9%	2.7%	3.9%	256
4. Third-Level	72.7%	7.9%	(80.6)	**6.3%**	**4.7%**	**8.4%**	381
H. Occupational Status	p<.02						
1. Unskilled/Semi-Skilled	76.8%	**9.7%**	(86.5)	**5.8%**	**4.3%**	3.4%	207
2. Skilled/Routine Non-M.	77.1%	8.0%	(85.1)	**5.8%**	2.1%	**7.0%**	327
3. Inspectional/Supervisory	**83.3%**	**12.9%**	**(96.2)**	2.3%	0.8%	0.8%	132
4. Professional/Executive	76.4%	7.9%	(84.3)	**9.4%**	**3.1%**	**3.1%**	191
Average Number	796	87	(883)	53	30	48	1,014

Note: Percentages above sample average are in **bold**.

The total sample is composed of two important subsamples, i.e. 'Irish-born' (**86%**) and 'Non-Irish-Born' (**14%**), which obviously influence primary ethnic self-identity. In the case of age, for instance, the following is the composition of each age group in the case of Irish-Born and Non-Irish-Born:

Table No. 8.8: Age Distribution of Irish-Born and Non-Irish-Born

Age Variable	Irish-Born	Non-Irish-Born	Total Sample
1. 18 to 25 years	15.3%	**27.0%**	**16.6%**
2. 26 to 40 years	29.4%	**47.3%**	**32.0%**
3. 41 to 55 years	**24.5%**	18.6%	**24.3%**
4. 56 to 70 years	**19.6%**	6.7%	**17.5%**
5. 71 years plus	**11.2%**	0.4%	**9.5%**
Sample Average	86.0%	14.0%	N=1,015

Note: Percentages above sample averages are in **bold**.

When one reflects on the findings of Table No. 8.2 and sees the contrast between the responses of **Irish-Born** and those of **Non-Irish-Born**, it is possible to explain some of the variations in Table No. 8.7(a). The mean and median age of the Non-Irish-Born is substantially lower than that of the Irish-Born as is clear from the above sub-table. The mean age of respondents who were Irish-Born is **45.4 years** while that of the Non-Irish-Born is **35.2 years**. In relation to ethnic self-identity, the presence of a significant minority of foreign-born in the national sample affects most variable findings, especially in the cases of **age** and **education**.

Table No. 8.9: Education Distribution of Irish-Born and Non-Irish-Born

Education Variable	Irish-Born	Non-Irish-Born	Total Sample Average
1. Primary or Less	**13.0%**	3.8%	**11.6%**
2. Incomplete Second-Level	**28.0%**	14.5%	**25.8%**
3. Complete Second-Level	**25.9%**	23.5%	**25.1%**
4. Third-Level	33.2%	**58.2%**	**37.5%**
Sample	(86.0%)	(14.0%)	N=1,015

Note: Percentages above sample averages are in **bold**.

The combination of age and education significantly affects the variations in practically all of the other personal variables, since the total sample reflects the current Irish population and this work is focused on the attitudes of the total population.

2.1 Age:
It is quite clear from Table No. 8.7(a) that the influence of 'Non-Irish-Born' respondents has strengthened the positive correlation between age and primary **Irish ethnic self-identity**. For the over-70 year-olds it is practically 100% Irish **(98.9%)**. It is over 90% for respondents over-40 years of age (see Table No. 8.8).

The relatively low primary ethnic self-identity with '**Anglo-Irish/British**' **(5.3%)** in a country which won its independence only 85 years before the date of the survey (2007-08) may appear surprising. The response of the sample, especially that of the older respondents seems to endorse the struggle for National Independence from Britain and 'going it alone' in 1922. Irish neutrality during the Second World War was also a very clear assertion of support for Irish Independence.

2.2 Gender:
Females were significantly more in favour of Irish primary ethnic self-identity than were males. This again reflects the influence of the 'Non-Irish-Born' in the sample who were more male than female (i.e. 61% Male and 39% Female). Also, the age difference of males and females differed, with the latter on average slightly older.

2.3 Marital Status:
'Married' and 'Widowed' respondents were above average in opting for Irish primary ethnic self-identity. This was as anticipated and reflects a stronger attachment to the country for respondents with 'a greater stake' in Irish society. The age and in-migration factors were also influential in the above variation in Table No. 8.6 (c).

2.4 Area of Birth:
This variable measures the influence of urban/rural rearing on the responses. It is quite interesting to note that both respondents born in 'cities' and those of 'rural/village' origins were above average in their percentages in favour of Irish primary ethnic self-identity with practically similar percentages. Again, the influence of non-Irish birth seems to have resulted in the significantly lower Irish scores for those born in 'larger towns' (10,000 to 99,999 citizens).

2.5 Place of Rearing (in Republic of Ireland):
This variable is made up exclusively of those reared in the Republic of Ireland.   All scores are above the sample average.   Dublin-reared respondents were highest in opting for 'Irish' (as distinct from 'local Irish') at 92.9%.   Those from the 'rest of Leinster' were significantly higher than average in identifying with 'internal Irish' identity.   'Munster' and 'Connaught/Ulster' had significant minorities i.e. **8.7%** and **4.8%** with 'Anglo-Irish/British' primary ethnic self-identities.   Are we seeing here a link with the old Anglo-Irish minority in Ireland?

2.6 Region of Residence:
The variation in the scores reflects the spread of the 'Non-Irish-Born' in the regions.   Compared with 'Place of Rearing' [Table No. 8.7 (e)], Dublin respondents show a drop of **7.3%** in 'Irish and Local Irish' percentages, i.e. between the 'reared' and the 'residents'.   The relatively high identity with 'local city or county' of the Mid-East and South-East **(17.7%)** repeats the relatively high score **(13.9%)** of the 'rest of Leinster-reared'.   The relatively high percentage **(12.3%)** primarily identifying with 'Anglo-Irish/British' in those resident in the Mid-West and South-West mirrors the relative scores of the Munster-reared (8.7%).

2.7 Educational Standard Reached:
The differences between the subsamples of education again reflect the influence of in-migration, especially in the case of 'third-level'.   The lower levels identify more with Irish ethnic self-identity whereas Third-Level and, to a degree, 'Complete-Second-Level' have higher non-Irish preferences. Since in-migrants have a substantially higher proportion of respondents with 'Third Level' than have native Irish, i.e. **58.2%** as compared with **33.2%**, this finding is to be expected (see Table No. 8.9).   For the Irish-born, **96.2%** saw themselves as Irish or local (i.e. their first choice).

2.8 Occupational Status:
There is a relatively strong degree of consensus between the occupational grades. The most Irish in their self-identity are the 'inspectional/ supervisory' respondents.   The subsample with the highest non-Irish primary ethnic self-identity is the 'professional/executive', followed closely by the 'supervisory/routine non-manual' category.   The former scored highest in Anglo-Irish/British **(9.4%)** while the latter were well above average in the non-European category of identity at **7%**.   Does this tell us

171

something about the ethnic origins of those who manage and those with skills and who work in clerical positions?

2.9 Conclusion:
Because of the overwhelming level of Irish (national and local) primary ethnic self-identity (**86.9%**) there has been limited scope for significant variations. Without the presence of the **'Non-Irish-Born'** in the sample there would be little or no significant variation. The weak performance of **European** in 'Irish-Born' respondents' primary ethnic self-identity shows the relatively weak ethnic appeal of the European Union in the personal ethnic self-identity of Irish citizens. Such weakness may be influenced by the survival of a national self-identity, on the one hand, and the growing pre-eminence of 'globalisation'. The disparate cultural make-up of the 27 states of the European may make it more difficult to see it as a basis for our primary ethnic self-identity.

Part III – Public Reaction to Immigration

3.1 Introduction:
The relatively recent in-migration of a substantial minority of people into the Republic of Ireland has been a new experience for the native population. Since the early 19th century, Ireland has been predominantly **an emigrant country**, i.e. vast numbers of Irish men and women left the country to find work and residence abroad. They emigrated largely to English-speaking countries. Until 1922 Ireland was officially part of the United Kingdom of Great Britain and Ireland. This made it easy for our surplus population to go to other countries of the British Empire and settle there.

The reasons for the emigration of Irish people were largely economic. Britain did not develop Ireland as an industrial society in the late 19th century and early 20th century. We were primarily an agricultural society operating under a quasi-feudal farm structure of large estates and poor peasant tenant farmers. The agrarian revolution during the latter part of the 19th century brought about the demise of the landlords and gave the Irish tenant farmers ownership of their small and not-so-small holdings in the first decade of the 20th century, thanks to the work of **the Land League** under the leadership of **Michael Davitt** and others. The Irish Great Famine of 1845-48 had earlier 'broken the back' of the Irish peasantry and forced many to seek refuge in emigration.

Forced emigration had been used as a penal sanction up to 1850 and was used by the British Government to help to colonise Australia and the other islands around it. After 1850, large prisons were built in Ireland to create a 'Van Diemen's Land' at home for Irish law-breakers and agrarian agitators, e.g. Mountjoy Jail.

Emigration played an important role in the creation of an Irish diaspora, who would send home remittances in times of scarcity. When the economy would develop in Ireland, the Irish abroad and their subsequent generations would be in a position to invest in the country of their ancestors and support its economic growth. The history of Ireland over the past two hundred and fifty years has been characterised by the out-migration of much of its native talent and in the recent decade by a new in-migration to fuel the engine of economic expansion.

The 2007-08 national survey was ideally situated just in time (at the end of the current so-called **'Celtic Tiger'**[4]) to find out the reactions to immigration of the native population and of those who came to Ireland for work and residence. The fieldwork was completed before the financial crisis became evident.

3.2 Overall Response:
Respondents were asked to indicate on a continuum of **0 to 10** the degree to which recent in-migration of people was: (1) **good for the economy**; (2) **enriching of cultural life**; and (3) made Ireland a **better place to live in**. Table No.8.10 gives the responses.

Table No. 8.10: Positive Impact of Immigration on Irish Society

	Opinion	Total Sample (0 – 10)	Irish-Born (0 – 10)	Non-Irish (0 – 10)
1.	"It is good for the economy that people come here from other countries."	6.67	6.46	8.02
2.	"Enriched the culture of Ireland to have people coming here from other countries."	6.44	6.18	7.97
3.	"People coming here make Ireland a better place to live in."	6.46	6.26	7.93
	Number	973	832	133

Source of Questions: The European Social Survey, Round Three, 2006-07
Note: The above scores are the average on a **continuum of from 0 to 10.**

---

[4] **'Celtic Tiger'** was a popular name given to the exceptional growth and development of the Irish economy from the mid-1990s until 2008.

The overall response of the sample has been **relatively positive** for each of the three statements. The position of the 'Irish-born' respondents was significantly **less enthusiastic** than that of those who were born outside Ireland and constituted the representatives of the **in-migrants**. The fact that those who came to Ireland felt so positive about the benefits of their coming is something to be welcomed and reveals a high level of self-confidence in their own personal worth and value to Irish society.

The immigrants rightly see themselves as (on balance) a beneficiary to the host society. There is always the danger of the in-migrant feeling a lack of self-worth and being a dependant rather than a net contributor to his or her host society. The compliment is always (on balance) on the side of the host society. This is not to deny that the immigrant benefits from the encounter with the host society. In-migrants who are willing to work are often among the least 'parasitic' (in the economic sense) in society. The 'leisure classes' would seem to be among the more 'parasitic' categories!

In times of relatively full employment and significant economic growth, the presence of migrant-workers does not present a threat to gainful employment for the native workforce. Such was the case in the Republic of Ireland at the time of the fieldwork for this research. The issue of job insecurity in the population was more or less absent – at least due to the competition from non-Irish. Therefore, the responses reported on Table No. 8.10 should be optimal. Had the fieldwork been held eighteen months later the results might have been less favourable!

3.3 Attitudes to In-Migrants by Personal Variables:
Since the average response is around a PQ^5 of around 60/40 there is a good possibility of a range of significant variations between subsamples. Table No. 8.11 gives a breakdown of responses by personal variables.

The difference between the opinions of the Irish-born respondents and those born outside Ireland in every subsample of the eight variables measured in Table No. 8.11 shows a significantly more positive appraisal of the effects of immigration to the Republic of Ireland by those born outside Ireland. The Irish-borns' moderately positive opinions were maintained. This is likely to be a factor in the overall improvement in tolerance towards

---

[5] $P = 100 – Q$ $(P+Q = 100)$

Table No. 8.11:
Respondents' Reaction to Immigration by Personal Variables

Variable	Bad-Good for Economy (0-10)			Undermine-Enrich the Culture (0-10)			Worse – Better Place to Live (0-10)		
	Total Sample	Irish-Born	Non-Irish -Born	Total Sample	Irish-Born	Non-Irish -Born	Total Sample	Irish-Born	Non-Irish -Born
Total Sample	**6.67**	**6.46**	**8.02**	**6.44**	**6.18**	**7.97**	**6.46**	**6.26**	**7.93**
A. Age									
1. 18-25 years	**6.94**	**6.62**	8.01	**6.81**	**6.52**	7.80	**6.71**	**6.40**	7.79
2. 26-40 years	**6.86**	**6.51**	8.13	**6.61**	**6.25**	8.00	**6.64**	**6.37**	7.91
3. 41-55 years	**6.76**	**6.65**	8.06	6.39	**6.19**	8.01	6.44	**6.30**	8.47
4. 56-70 years	6.12	6.07	---	6.07	5.93	---	6.19	6.14	---
5. 71 years plus	6.35	6.34	---	5.96	5.94	---	5.91	5.89	---
Range of Variation	*0.82*	*0.58*	*0.12*	*0.85*	*0.59*	*0.21*	*0.80*	*0.51*	*0.68*
B. Gender									
1. Males	6.64	6.31	**8.26**	6.31	5.93	**8.19**	6.36	6.01	**8.08**
2. Females	**6.71**	**6.59**	7.62	**6.56**	**6.41**	7.64	**6.55**	**6.49**	7.70
Range of Variation	*0.07*	*0.28*	*0.64*	*0.25*	*0.48*	*0.55*	*0.19*	*0.48*	*0.38*
C. Marital Status									
1. Single/Never Married	**6.71**	**6.55**	7.79	**6.47**	**6.26**	7.84	**6.57**	**6.42**	7.53
2. Married	**6.72**	**6.48**	8.36	6.44	6.16	**8.16**	6.45	**6.27**	8.23
3. Separated/Divorced	6.54	6.02	7.66	**6.55**	5.79	**8.08**	6.21	5.41	7.84
4. Permanent Relationship	**6.82**	**6.64**	7.57	**6.90**	**6.83**	7.42	**6.88**	**6.60**	8.13
5. Widowed	6.02	5.89	---	5.61	5.51	---	5.62	5.52	---
Range of Variation	*0.80*	*0.75*	*0.79*	*1.30*	*1.32*	*0.74*	*1.26*	*1.06*	*0.70*
D. Area of Birth									
1. City (100,000 plus)	**6.96**	**6.66**	8.13	**6.55**	6.15	8.03	**6.72**	**6.53**	7.94
2. Large Town (10,000 +)	**7.54**	**7.30**	8.63	**7.23**	**6.95**	8.26	**7.05**	**6.78**	8.06
3. Town (1,500 plus)	6.52	6.37	7.32	**6.53**	**6.35**	7.73	**6.48**	6.22	7.94
4. Rural/Village	6.08	6.06	6.80	5.97	5.94	6.82	5.90	5.86	7.27
Range of Variation	*1.46*	*1.24*	*1.31*	*1.26*	*1.01*	*0.55*	*1.15*	*0.92*	*0.79*
E. Place of Rearing in ROI.									
1. Dublin (City & County)	**6.90**	---	---	6.27	---	---	**6.52**	---	---
2. Rest of Leinster	6.51	---	---	6.39	---	---	6.26	---	---
3. Munster	6.08	---	---	5.99	---	---	6.10	---	---
4. Connaught/Ulster	6.01	---	---	6.08	---	---	5.83	---	---
Range of Variation	*0.89*	*---*	*---*	*0.40*	*---*	*---*	*0.69*	*---*	*---*
F. Region of Residence									
1. B.M.W.	6.37	6.12	7.62	**6.47**	**6.23**	7.68	6.29	6.03	7.64
2. Dublin	**6.96**	**6.69**	8.82	6.39	6.04	**8.68**	**6.60**	**6.47**	8.59
3. Mid-East & South-East	**6.91**	**6.83**	7.83	**6.49**	**6.31**	8.10	**6.51**	**6.41**	7.40
4. Mid-West & South-West	6.45	6.19	7.88	6.39	6.17	7.60	6.43	6.13	**8.05**
Range of Variation	*0.59*	*0.71*	*1.20*	*0.10*	*0.27*	*1.08*	*0.31*	*0.44*	*1.19*

Table No. 8.11 (Cont'd)	Bad-Good for Economy (0-10)			Undermine-Enrich the Culture (0-10)			Worse – Better Place to Live (0-10)		
Variable	Total Sample	Irish-Born	Non-Irish -Born	Total Sample	Irish-Born	Non-Irish -Born	Total Sample	Irish-Born	Non-Irish -Born
G. Education									
1. Primary or Less	6.29	6.19	---	6.15	6.04	---	5.94	5.81	---
2. Incomplete Second-Level	5.59	5.43	7.44	5.26	5.07	7.29	5.58	5.44	7.14
3. Complete Second-Level	**6.75**	**6.51**	**8.34**	**6.52**	**6.30**	**8.08**	6.44	**6.26**	7.70
4. Third-Level	**7.49**	**7.38**	7.98	**7.25**	**7.05**	**8.03**	**7.22**	**7.12**	8.17
Range of Variation	*1.88*	*1.95*	*0.90*	*1.99*	*1.98*	*0.79*	*1.64*	*1.68*	*0.91*
H. Occupational Status									
1. Unskilled/Semi-Skilled	5.57	5.15	7.95	5.51	5.06	7.88	5.61	5.37	7.63
2. Skilled/Routine Non-M.	**6.79**	**6.50**	**8.30**	**6.51**	**6.19**	**8.08**	6.46	6.23	7.81
3. Inspectional/Supervisory	**7.05**	**7.02**	7.30	**6.78**	**6.71**	7.51	**6.90**	**6.85**	7.42
4. Professional/Executive	**7.67**	**7.65**	7.99	**7.22**	**7.11**	7.97	**7.29**	**7.11**	8.52
Range of Variation	*2.10*	*2.50*	*0.35*	*1.71*	*2.05*	*0.57*	*1.68*	*1.74*	*1.10*

Note: Percentages above sample average are in **bold**. (Variations in *italics*)

different nationalities.   While welcoming the positivity of the responses of Irish-born respondents, there is, at the same time, a significant minority who are not that positive towards in-migrants.   Should the economic climate change and people revert to concern for their basic needs (*"primo vivere deinde philosifari"*), the challenge of a welcoming appreciation of immigrants becomes more difficult.

Political, community, religious and academic leaders would be advised to study these findings and commit themselves to countering any return to primitive hatred of and prejudice against the immigrant minorities who are so weak.   **Scapegoating** of immigrant minorities for the pain of unemployment and a lowering of the material standard of living in the mass media (print and electronic) and by populist political and community leaders, must be challenged and, where necessary, brought to court under the relevant minority rights' legislation.   During the current economic recession there is a real danger of anti-immigrant scapegoating for problems for which in-migrants are not even remotely responsible in fact.   The scapegoating of the 'Jews' in Germany during the economic depression of the 1930s was an extreme example of projection of blame on a relatively weak minority with appalling consequences!

Returning to Table No. 8.11, it is proposed to comment on the findings of each of the eight standard personal or independent variables. Scores are recorded for three samples, i.e. the *total sample*, the *Irish-born* and *those born outside Ireland.* The difference between the 'Irish-Born' and 'those born outside Ireland' are most interesting. The 'Irish-Born' sub-sample is probably the most important for the quality of intergroup relations. 'Irish-born' represents the **dominant group** while 'those born outside Ireland' represent the **minority groups**.

The level of positivity on the **0 to 10 continuum** in the case of each of the three areas of assessment is as follows:

	Total Sample	Irish-Born	Non-Irish-Born
(a) *Good or bad for the economy*	**6.67**	**6.46**	**8.02**
(b) *Enriching or undermining the culture*	**6.44**	**6.18**	**7.97**
(c) *Making Ireland a better or worse place to live in*	**6.46**	**6.26**	**7.93**

The above figures represent the 'total sample' / 'Irish-Born' / 'Non-Irish-Born', and show a relatively small variation between the sample's and sub-samples' scores for the three questions. This level of agreement confirms the broad consensus within the sample and the subsamples in relation to the three areas of 'economy', 'culture' and 'place to live'.

3.3.1 Age: It is quite clear from the findings of Table No. 8.11(a) that there is a link between age and appreciation of the contribution of immigrants to Ireland. This is especially true for 'Irish-Born' respondents. The three age groups under 55 years of age are significantly more positive in their replies to the three questions. The members of 'Non-Irish-Born' respondents over 55 years are not significant (statistically speaking). The variations in scores are only moderate.

These findings, especially for the 18 to 25 age group, are reassuring and help to modify the performance of this subsample in relation to relatively higher intolerance of ethnic and ethnico-racial stimulus categories reported on Table Nos. 7.4 (page 134), 7.5 (page 140), 7.6 (pages 145-6) and 7.7 (pages 150-1). The social-distance score of the 18 to 25 age group is one of the problematic findings of the 2007-08 survey which requires deeper analysis of the socialisation of Irish young adults and, possibly, the negative effects of extended adolescence. Their reactions to immigrants seem to be different. The difference between **social distance** and **reactions** to immigrants to Ireland is the difference between **attitudes** (social distance) and **opinions** (reaction to immigrants). The former is pre-reflectional while the latter allows for reflection and, maybe, partly rationalisation.

3.3.2 Gender: There is a relatively moderate level of consensus in the reactions of males and females, especially in the case of 'Irish-born' respondents. 'Non-Irish-Born' respondents differed in two regards – their range of variation was over 0.50 in the case of question one and two and males were more positive than females for all these questions. This was in contrast to the 'Irish-Born' where females were more welcoming than their male counterparts.

It has already been noted that there is a growing homogenisation between the attitudes of males and females. This is probably partly due to the results of the 'feminist' movement and greater shared experience in the workplace. The reduction of domestic or home and family experience, where male and female roles were different, may also have reduced the attitudinal and opinion differences of males and females. This shows the significance of socio-cultural norms on people's attitudes and opinions. The positive or negative impact of gender homogenisation is worthy of research.

3.3.3 Marital Status: This variable has elicited a more substantial range of variations. Among the 'Irish-Born' the 'Widowed' and the 'Separated /Divorced' seemed to be the least enthusiastic (although still positive) of the contributions of immigrants to the **economy** and the **culture** of their making Ireland a better place to live in. Those living in 'Permanent Relationships' had the highest scores among the 'Irish-Born' [see Table No. 8.11(c), page 175].

Among the 'Non-Irish-Born' respondents, the 'Married' were most enthusiastic in reaction to each of the three questions. This is an important result in that 'married' respondents are in a better position to evaluate the contributions to the economic, cultural and domestic scene. 'Married' respondents are also in a better position to discern local attitudes throughout the population through their contact with schools, etc. In a mixed local community the children are the first to integrate. They are generally 'colour-blind'. As one wise citizen remarked: "There are no 'blow-in' children"!

3.3.4 Area of Birth: The cosmopolitan and large urban environment is more likely to have contact with people of non-local ethnic backgrounds. People born and reared in such areas would have experienced the contributions of 'Non-Irish-Born' immigrants to the economic, cultural and domestic life of the people. People born and reared in rural and small town districts are less likely to have benefited from a mixed (ethnically) community and, thereby, would tend to be more sceptical (not necessarily hostile) towards ethnic **strangers**.

The findings reported in Table No. 8.11(d), (page 175), confirm the greater appreciation of immigrants among 'Irish-Born' and 'Non-Irish-Born' from **City** (100,000 plus) and **Large Towns** (10,000 plus). The 'large town' environment was the 'Area of Birth' most conducive to appreciating the contribution of immigrants to Ireland. It is very interesting to note that the Irish immigrants to Great Britain and the United States and elsewhere in the past centuries seemed to drift to cities and large towns and contribute to their economic, cultural and domestic development. Are we seeing here a similar appreciation of and attraction to the cities and large towns expressed in the attitudes of the 'Area of Birth' variable?

The range of variation between the urban and the rural is quite substantial for both the indigenous and the in-migrant respondents. This clearly establishes the importance of the urban ethos in welcoming the immigrant.

Of course, it should be noted that for people born in the recent past, the 'intrusion' of the mass media (print and electronic) into rural Ireland has begun to inculturate rural-born-and-reared with a largely urban and cosmopolitan (Anglo-American) culture and erode the uniquely Irish rural ethos. The difference between rural and urban ethos has been greatly reduced. The changing of the farming culture into that of mechanised agri-business has also diminished rural cultural differences. Add to these changes the proliferation of 'non-farming rural residents' and 'ex-urbanites', one gets a measure of the 'revolutionary' change in the Irish landscape. This will in time reduce the significance of rural-urban cultural diversity. That is, unless a fairly dramatic and pervasive change takes place, which seems unlikely at present. This is but one other area of 'cultural homogenisation' in the so-called *Western Developed World*! Cultural diversity provided the people with diverse and enriching nuances on social reality!

3.3.5 Place of Rearing (in the Republic of Ireland): This variable measures 'Irish-Born' respondents only. Its focus is geographic variation between the provincial backgrounds of respondents. 'Rearing' refers to the province where the person spent the first sixteen years of life (or the greater part of it). The findings confirm those of 'Area of Birth' with 'Dublin City and County' as the most appreciative subsample (reflecting its predominantly urban make-up).

3.3.6 Region of Residence: Because of the level of geographic mobility, region of current residence is different for a minority of residents, even those who were born and reared in the Republic of Ireland. The four sub-variables coincide with clusters of regions.

In the case of 'Irish-Born' respondents there seems to be quite a degree of consensus across the regions. Those with greater urban populations and a higher proportion of 'guest workers' living in the area (see Table No. 2.3, page 19) have a slightly **more** favourable reaction to immigrants, i.e. 'Dublin' and 'Mid-East and South-East'. This is further evidence of the constructive impact of 'favourable contact' on people's intergroup attitudes. This has been borne out in the current research in the Tables dealing with changes in social-distance towards ethnic and racial stimulus categories. The level of appreciation of the contribution of in-migrants could also be affected by the type of work local migrants were engaged in!

The range of variation in the case of respondents 'not born in Ireland' has been substantial. Those living in the Dublin region were most positive, while 'Non-Irish-Born' living in the 'BMW' cluster of regions were least positive in response to each of the three questions.

3.3.7 Educational Standard Reached: 'Irish-Born' respondents with higher levels of educational achievement had a greater appreciation of the contribution of immigrants to the Irish economy, culture and neighbourhood. The anomaly in the findings was the relatively low appreciation of those with 'Incomplete Second-Level' education, which was substantially lower than that of respondents with 'Primary or Less' (education). This sub-sample consists of one-quarter of the total sample. The result was not anticipated and requires further research.

The response of 'Non-Irish-Born' respondents by education was as anticipated. Because the numbers in 'Primary or Less' were so small, they were statistically not significant (see page 176 above). The range of variation in the case of 'Non-Irish-Born' respondents is **only half** of that of the 'Irish-Born' [see Table No. 8.11(g), page 176].   This is probably due to the narrower spread of educational standards of the foreign-born.

3.3.8 Occupational Status: It is quite clear from the findings of this variable that those 'Irish-Born' in positions of supervision and management have a *relatively high appreciation* of the positive contributions of guest workers and their families to Irish life – economy, culture and neighbourhood.   This is a very significant fact for the future of in-migration to Ireland.   Granted that in the current (2009-10) climate of economic down-turn, there will be fewer job opportunities for non-Irish (and for Irish-born).   Hopefully, the current position is the **exception** rather than the **norm** in the near future.   After all, we are an under-populated and relatively highly developed society living in an over-populated world!

In the case of the 'Non-Irish-Born' respondents, it is interesting to note that the most appreciative subsample was the 'Skilled/Routine Non-Manual' category.   The range of variation of the 'Non-Irish-Born' was fairly moderate.

The relatively negative scores of the 'Unskilled/Semi-Skilled' of the 'Irish-Born' mirror that of the 'Incomplete Second-Level' (in education).   Do these findings reflect a sense of insecurity among these subsamples in relation to migrant workers to Ireland?   This merits further research.

When the educational standards of 'Non-Irish-Born' respondents and their occupational status are compared with those of 'Irish-Born', there is evidence of over-qualification for 'Non-Irish-Born' workers as spelled out in Table No. 8.12.

Table No. 8.12:
Occupational Status and Educational Standard of Irish-Born and Non-Irish-Born

Occupational Status			Educational Achievement		
Occupation	Irish-Born	Non-Irish-Born	Education	Irish-Born	Non-Irish-Born
1. Unskilled/Semi-S.	23.7%	25.2%	1. Primary or Less	13.0%	3.8%
2. Skilled/Routine NM	36.9%	43.5%	2. Incomplete Sec.-Lev.	28.0%	14.5%
3. Inspec./Supervisory	16.9%	8.5%	3. Complete Sec.-Level	25.9%	23.5%
4. Prof./Executive	22.5%	22.8%	4. Third-Level	33.2%	58.2%

When one compares education with occupation distribution, it is quite clear that there is a serious level of relative over-qualification among foreign workers in Ireland at present. Hopefully, this is not leading to the exploitation of the 'migrant worker'! Or is this part of a universal pattern of the members of a minority having to be more highly qualified than those of the dominant group to get the same job?

3.3.9 Conclusion: The value of the above findings for Irish society is important. As we begin to experience in-migration, we must become aware of the contribution the migrant worker brings to our economy, since work is the main source of the wealth of the nation. Positive contact with other ethnic groups enriches Irish culture. This makes Ireland 'a better place to live in'. This can only happen when the migrant worker coming to Ireland is treated with total and comprehensive equality, i.e. in conditions of work, training, living accommodation, health services, protection of privacy, freedom of religion, recreational facilities, and access to the law, etc.

Part IV – Ethnic Social-Distance – Kinship and Denial of Citizenship

In this part (IV) of Chapter VIII it is proposed to examine more closely the variations in social distance by personal variables in relation to a sample of the *Ethnic Stimulus Categories*, i.e. 'English', 'Canadians', 'Dutch', 'Spaniards' and 'Poles'. The two measures used are:
> (a) *Percentage admitting to kinship, and*
> (b) *Percentage denying citizenship.*

The reason for selecting these two measures is to spell out for the reader in a more 'realistic' manner what variations in social-distance scores (mostly presented in mean-social-distance scores) mean for concrete intergroup relations, i.e. in the event of the attitudes underlying the responses being acted out in the community or society.

Admitting to kinship is seen as the closest to which a respondent can welcome a member of a stimulus category. What is measured here is the *a priori* disposition towards a member of the category. Of course, in the event of other issues impeding so close a relationship should the respondent become acquainted with a member, e.g. unfavourable experience or social pressure, the realisation of this positive disposition would be unlikely. Such a response would be based on the *person's judgement* of the situation and could not be seen as an expression of *personal prejudice* toward a member of the group or category.   What is measured in the tables of this and other chapters is the disposition before the encounter.

In the case of denial of citizenship, i.e. "admit as visitor only" or "debar or deport", this disposition is seen as the most negative (*a priori*) disposition.   As in the case of "admission to kinship", the behavioural expression of the attitude manifested in 'denial of citizenship' can be modified due to circumstances perceived to be more favourable or advantageous to the respondent, e.g. influence of friends or a member of the excluded category providing material, social or cultural benefits to one's group or to oneself.

The selection of the sample of five ethnic categories was based on the regions they represent, i.e. Britain, the Americas, Northern, Southern and Eastern Europe.   These ethnic stimulus categories lack significant 'racial' connotations.   This should be a sufficient range of ethnic categories to establish a pattern of responses from the personal variables.   Table No. 8.13 below analyses the findings primarily from the point of view of the variations of respondents.   One can gauge or estimate from these variations between the variable subsamples, i.e. the influence of age, education, urbanisation, etc. on social distance and intergroup ethnic prejudice.   The **range** of variations within each variable is also given in Table No. 8.13.

In addition to reporting the influence of variable inter-subsample variations, the two measures, i.e. 'kinship' and 'denial of citizenship', point to the severity of the prejudice and the comparative degree of polarisation. Percentages **above average** in 'admitting to kinship' and in 'denying citizenship' have been printed **in bold** in order to highlight such measures.

Table No. 8.13 gives the percentages 'admitting to kinship' and 'denying citizenship' by personal variables.   Variables not eliciting of $p<.05$ are considered not significant (N/S), i.e. variations could be due to chance in one in twenty cases or more often.

Table No. 8.13 recorded significant variations in the case of 27 of 35 sub-tables.   Age, place of rearing and education produced significant variations in all five of the stimulus categories.   Gender and marital status failed to elicit statistically significant variation in the case of **any** of the five categories.   Does this mean that there is domestic consensus in relation to

Table No. 8.13: 'Admission to Kinship' and 'Denial of Citizenship' of Ethnic Stimulus Categories by Personal Variables

Personal Variable	English		Canadians		Dutch		Spaniards		Poles		Av. No.
	Kinship	Denial	Kinship	Denial	Kinship	Denial	Kinship	Denial	Kinship	Denial	
Total Sample	**81.0%**	2.1%	**80.1%**	2.2%	**74.2%**	3.7%	**75.4%**	5.9%	**69.6%**	5.3%	1,015
A. Age	p<.001		p<.001		p<.004		p<.036		p<.009		
1. 18-25 years	71.6%	**3.0%**	69.0%	**3.6%**	64.5%	**7.1%**	63.9%	**9.5%**	61.5%	**6.5%**	169
2. 26-40 years	**82.4%**	2.5%	**83.6%**	0.9%	**81.3%**	1.6%	**79.6%**	5.0%	**77.3%**	4.3%	321
3. 41-55 years	**81.8%**	1.6%	**80.2%**	2.8%	72.0%	3.3%	**76.5%**	5.7%	66.3%	**6.9%**	246
4. 56-70 years	**82.6%**	1.7%	**82.7%**	0.6%	72.9%	**4.0%**	74.6%	5.6%	64.6%	**5.6%**	177
5. 71 years plus	**87.6%**	1.0%	**82.3%**	**5.2%**	**76.0%**	**5.2%**	**79.2%**	4.2%	**75.3%**	3.1%	96
Range of Variation	*16.0%*	*2.0%*	*14.6%*	*4.6%*	*16.8%*	*5.5%*	*14.7%*	*5.3%*	*15.8%*	*3.8%*	*1,009*
B. Area of Birth	N/S		p<.011		N/S		N/S		p<.019		
1. City (100,000 +)	---	---	75.6%	**2.9%**	---	---	---	---	68.2%	4.5%	417
2. Lge.Town (10,000 +)	---	---	**90.8%**	0.8%	---	---	---	---	**76.7%**	5.0%	119
3. Town (1,500 +)	---	---	79.8%	**3.1%**	---	---	---	---	**76.7%**	1.6%	129
4. Rural/Village	---	---	**82.3%**	1.2%	---	---	---	---	65.8%	**8.1%**	343
Range of Variation	*---*	*---*	*15.2%*	*2.3%*	*---*	*---*	*---*	*---*	*10.9%*	*6.5%*	*1,008*
C. Place of Rearing ROI	p<.05		p<.015		p<.011		p<.003		p<.023		
1. Dublin (City & Co.)	**81.0%**	**3.4%**	77.9%	**4.1%**	72.9%	**6.8%**	**76.6%**	**6.8%**	69.5%	**5.6%**	266
2. Rest of Leinster	**84.1%**	0.6%	79.9%	1.2%	**77.0%**	3.0%	**78.0%**	**6.1%**	68.9%	3.0%	165
3. Munster	80.2%	**3.9%**	**86.5%**	0.0%	**79.1%**	1.3%	**79.2%**	**6.5%**	**70.9%**	**8.7%**	230
4. Connaught/Ulster	78.7%	0.0%	76.8%	**2.4%**	67.5%	3.7%	68.9%	1.9%	65.2%	3.0%	163
Range of Variation	*5.4%*	*3.9%*	*9.7%*	*4.1%*	*11.6%*	*5.5%*	*10.3%*	*4.9%*	*5.7%*	*5.7%*	*824*
D. Region of Residence	p<.021		p<.033		N/S		p<.001		p<.002		
1. B.M.W.	**82.0%**	0.4%	77.9%	**3.0%**	---	---	69.9%	5.2%	65.8%	4.4%	271
2. Dublin	79.7%	**3.5%**	79.0%	**4.2%**	---	---	**78.6%**	**6.3%**	**71.2%**	4.6%	286
3. Mid-East & Sth-East	78.4%	**4.1%**	**81.2%**	0.5%	---	---	69.7%	**11.9%**	66.1%	**10.6%**	217
4. Mid-West & Sth-Wst	**83.5%**	0.4%	**83.1%**	0.4%	---	---	**82.8%**	0.8%	**75.1%**	2.5%	237
Range of Variation	*5.1%*	*3.7%*	*5.2%*	*3.8%*	*---*	*---*	*13.1%*	*11.1%*	*9.3%*	*8.1%*	*1,011*
E. Education	p<.001		p<.001		p<.011		p<.001		p<.05		
1. Primary or Less	**89.7%**	0.9%	**84.7%**	**5.1%**	**74.6%**	**7.6%**	**83.1%**	**6.8%**	**75.2%**	5.1%	118
2. Incomplete Sec-Lev.	**81.3%**	**3.4%**	**83.9%**	1.5%	**77.0%**	2.3%	71.4%	**10.0%**	69.3%	**6.1%**	261
3. Complete Sec-Level	79.2%	**4.3%**	78.8%	**3.9%**	71.3%	**6.3%**	72.8%	**9.1%**	66.4%	**8.7%**	254
4. Third-Level	79.4%	0.0%	77.0%	0.5%	**74.1%**	1.9%	**77.5%**	0.5%	**70.1%**	2.9%	378
Range of Variation	*10.3%*	*4.3%*	*7.7%*	*4.6%*	*5.7%*	*5.7%*	*11.7%*	*9.5%*	*8.8%*	*5.8%*	*1,011*
F. Occupational Status	p<.043		N/S		N/S		p<.001		p<.004		
1. Unskilled/Semi-Skil.	78.7%	**4.3%**	---	---	---	---	69.1%	**12.6%**	64.3%	**10.1%**	207
2. Skilled/R. Non-M.	**83.1%**	1.2%	---	---	---	---	**77.8%**	3.1%	**70.2%**	4.0%	325
3. Inspect./Supervisory	80.6%	**5.2%**	---	---	---	---	**80.0%**	4.6%	**73.3%**	4.6%	133
4. Professional/Exec.	**83.9%**	0.5%	---	---	---	---	**82.2%**	1.6%	**77.5%**	2.1%	190
Range of Variation	*5.2%*	*3.8%*	*---*	*---*	*---*	*---*	*13.1%*	*11.0%*	*13.2%*	*8.0%*	*855*
G. Social Class Position	p<.001		N/S		N/S		p<.001		p<.016		
Class I: "Upper Class"	68.8%	0.0%	---	---	---	---	76.3%	0.0%	73.7%	0.0%	38
Class II: "Upr-Mid. Cl."	**87.6%**	0.0%	---	---	---	---	**84.1%**	2.2%	**81.2%**	2.2%	137
Class III: "Mid-Mid Cl"	70.2%	**8.6%**	---	---	---	---	76.5%	1.8%	66.5%	**5.7%**	228
Class IV: "Working Cl"	**83.2%**	1.4%	---	---	---	---	74.4%	**8.4%**	68.0%	**5.8%**	361
Class V: "Lwr Class"	**82.5%**	0.6%	---	---	---	---	**77.4%**	**9.5%**	**75.3%**	**9.4%**	84
Range of Variation	*8.9%*	*8.6%*	*---*	*---*	*---*	*---*	*9.7%*	*9.5%*	*14.7%*	*9.4%*	*848*

Note: Percentages above sample average are **in bold**.   (Variations are in *italics*.)

social distance towards the five categories or is it that the other variables are combining to neutralise expected variations?   The unexpected and relatively high ethnic social distance of the 18 to 25 year-olds seems to have had an effect on the performance of the 'marital status' variations.   The growing **homogenisation** of variations between the attitudes of **males** and **females** has been noted elsewhere in this text.   This is likely to be a latent function of the feminist movement.   The interesting question would be to find out whether 'female attitudes' have moved towards those of 'males' or *vice versa*?

4.1 Age:

The performance of the age variable has confirmed, once again, the relatively high level of ethnic intolerance of the younger age group (18 to 25 year olds) in relation to **each** of the five ethnic variables.   It had been anticipated (prior to the research) that the opposite would be the case because of the trends in society and the relatively high level of educational participation[6] of this subsample, i.e. with **83.4%** with 'Complete Second-Level' or higher (**42%** with 'Third-Level' achievement).   The **range of variation** for each stimulus category is quite substantial.

The relative severity of the 18 to 25 year olds' intolerance is to be seen when one measures the range of percentages 'Admitting to Kinship' between this subsample and the 26 to 40 year olds, i.e. extract from Table No. 8.13(a):

Stimulus Category	Admitting to Kinship		Nominal % Difference
	A	B	
	18 to 25 year olds	26 to 40 year olds	(B – A)
1. 'English'	71.6%	82.4%	+10.8%
2. 'Canadians'	69.0%	83.6%	+14.6%
3. 'Dutch'	64.5%	81.3%	+16.8%
4. 'Spaniards'	63.9%	79.6%	+15.7%
5. 'Poles'	61.5%	77.3%	+15.8%

The above findings are very stark and consistent across the range of categories.   The pattern is clear and the validity of the findings is confirmed. This raises serious questions in relation to the future trends in tolerance, that

---

[6] See Table No. 7.8, page 158 above for full details of **Age by Education**.

is, unless this age cohort will change substantially *as they age and mature into a more open-minded disposition as a group.* The above percentages show the extent of the relative intolerance.

4.2 Area of Birth:

There was consensus in relation to social distance towards three of the five categories, i.e. 'English', 'Dutch' and 'Spaniards', in the case of the 'Area of Birth' personal variable. Respondents from 'larger towns' and 'rural/village' backgrounds were more tolerant toward 'Canadians', while 'city' and 'rural/village' subsamples were least tolerant of 'Poles'. 'City' respondents had a less-than-average welcome into 'kinship' for both stimulus categories.

4.3 Place of Rearing (in the Republic of Ireland):

Unlike the previous variable which classifies respondents by type of area they were born into, this variable explores the influence of province of rearing of the respondent. By 'Place of Rearing' is meant the place where the respondent spent the most of the first sixteen years of life. Each of the five stimulus categories elicited a (statistically) significant variation. 'Place of rearing' is **not** an ordinal variable, i.e. there is no 'more than'/ 'less than' *relationship* between the sub-variables, as in the case of 'area of birth', where the **degree of urbanisation** was the 'ordinal' factor.

Relatively speaking, 'Munster' respondents are the most tolerant sub-sample in relation to three of the five ethnic categories, i.e. 'Canadians', 'Dutch' and 'Spaniards', that is, they had the highest percentages 'admitting to kinship' and the lowest 'denying citizenship'. 'Munster' responses to 'English' and to 'Poles' were mixed.

Connaught/Ulster respondents recorded the lowest percentages 'welcoming into kinship' in the case of each of the five categories. They seem to be the most ethnically endogamous of the subsamples. That being noted, it must be stated that the percentages 'admitting to kinship' by 'Connaught/Ulster' respondents were quite high, ranging from **78.7%** in the case of 'English' to **65.2%** in relation to the 'Poles'.

4.4 Region of Residence:

Because of the degree of geographic mobility, the region of current residence is quite different from their 'Place of Rearing' or 'Area of Birth'. Again this variable is **nominal** rather than **ordinal.** The four subsamples of 'region of residence' are clusters of regions in the State. One of the 'stimulus categories', i.e. the 'Dutch', did not produce a statistically significant variation between subsamples.

The relatively high level of tolerance in the case of 'Munster-reared' is reflected in the percentages of the 'Mid-West/South-West' subsample, i.e. above average in 'admitting to kinship' and below average in 'denying citizenship' for the four categories – 'English', 'Canadians', 'Spaniards' and 'Poles'. The other subsamples are mixed but interesting [see Table No. 8.13(d)].

4.5 Education:

This ordinal variable has produced statistically significant variation in the case of each of the five ethnic stimulus categories. It was anticipated that there would be a clearly positive correlation between educational standard achieved and ethnic tolerance as indicated in the percentage 'admitting to kinship'. This has not been so as Table No. 8.13(e) shows. In fact, the **highest percentages** 'admitting to kinship' in each of the five stimulus categories were produced by the subsample with the lowest level of education. In the case of two ethnic categories, i.e. 'English' and 'Canadians', both 'Complete Second-Level' and 'Third-Level' respondents elicited percentages 'admitting to kinship' **lower** than the sample average! Further, those with 'Complete Second-Level' education registered a below-average percentage for 'admitting to kinship' in regard to **each** of the five ethnic categories. The following extract from Table No. 8.13(e) spells out the range of percentages in relation to "admit to kinship" by education.

Stimulus Category	Range of Variation	Highest % (Most tolerant)		Between	Lowest % (Least tolerant)		Mean
1. 'English'	10.5%	Primary or Less	(89.7%)	and	Complete 2nd Lev.	(79.2%)	81.0%
2. 'Canadians'	7.7%	Primary or Less	(84.7%)	and	Third Level	(77.0%)	80.1%
3. 'Dutch'	5.7%	Incomplete 2nd Lev	(77.0%)	and	Complete 2nd Lev.	(71.3%)	74.2%
4. 'Spaniards'	11.7%	Primary or Less	(83.1%)	and	Complete 2nd Lev.	(72.8%)	75.4%
5. 'Poles'	8.8%	Primary or Less	(75.2%)	and	Complete 2nd Lev.	(66.4%)	69.6%

It is difficult to explain these anomalous results. The unanticipated findings for the age variable will have an expected influence on the performance of the education variable. Since 83.4% of the '18 to 25 year-olds' have an educational achievement of 'Complete Second-Level' or higher, it was not expected that they would be **below average** in admitting the members of the five ethnic categories into kinship (see Table No. 7.8, page 158). This inevitably affects the education variable's performance! Or are we seeing here a failure in education to make graduates more open and tolerant?

We may be witnessing, once more, in these surprise replies evidence of the dysfunctional aspects of extended adolescence. Of course, there could be other age-related or education-related sources of frustration for the 18 to 25 year-olds (in 2007-08) and for some of the more highly educated which leads to tension. The latter, in turn, seeks release in aggression and social prejudice is a form of psychological aggression! The negative potential of these findings is the possibility of the young educated cohort moving through the population over time and leading to an increase in ethnic prejudice just when Ireland is beginning to welcome new citizens of diverse ethnic backgrounds (see pages 156-160 above). Hopefully their attitudes will become more tolerant as they increase in age and maturity!

4.6 Occupational Status:
This ordinal variable has performed more or less as anticipated. It failed to register a statistically significant variation in the case of 'Canadians' and 'Dutch'. In the case of the remaining three stimulus categories, i.e. 'English', 'Spaniards' and 'Poles', there was a positive correlation between 'occupational status' and percentage 'admitting to kinship'. The most highly statused were the least prejudiced as indicated by the findings of Table No. 8.13(f).

This result is quite positive especially for migrant workers coming to Ireland. Their managers and supervisors (as well as their employers) are likely to be well disposed to them and their families. Teachers, clergy and other community leaders are also likely to be more tolerant and supportive according to the findings.

4.7 Social Class Position[7]:

'Social Class Position' is an ordinal variable comprising of a combination of education and occupational status to measure on a five-step status scale. This scale was devised by **August de Belmont Hollingshead** (in 1949) to measure 'social class' (in the context of social status) in New York[8]. The present author has used the Hollingshead 'Social Class' scale in his previous publications, i.e. *Prejudice and Tolerance in Ireland* (1977) and *Prejudice in Ireland Revisited* (1996). It proved to be a valid and reliable method of gauging the respondent's social status. Hollingshead moved away from the tradition of classifying people according to their income and overall wealth.

It can be seen from Table No. 8.13(g) that the largest single sub-sample is Class IV ("Working Class"). It makes up 361 (**42.4%** of the total sample) while Class V ("Lower Class") is only 84 (**9.9%** of the sample). As will be shown later (see Table No. 9.6, page 209 below) the proportion of Irish residents in the "Lower Class" had contracted to **9.9%** from **21.2%** in 1988-'89 due to the decline in blue-collar work and the increase in participation in education.

Returning to the findings on Table No. 8.13(g), the consensus in the occupational status variable in the case of 'Canadians' and 'Dutch' has been repeated in the case of the 'Social Class Position' variable, i.e. both stimulus categories produced non-significant (N/S) variations.

The "Upper-Middle Class" (Class II) scored the overall most tolerant findings, i.e. in 'welcoming into kinship' and in 'denying citizenship' percentages for 'English', 'Spaniards' and 'Poles'. Otherwise the results have been quite mixed – largely due to the influence of the education

---

[7]

Table No. 8.14:
Hollingshead's Social Class Position (Occupation/Education)

Occupation	Education	Class Ratings (Combined Occupation & Education)	Popular Designations
1. High Professional, etc (7)	1. Postgraduate (4)	Class I = 11-17 points	"Upper Class"
2. Senior Executive, etc. (14)	2. Graduate (8)	Class II = 18-31 points	"Upper-Middle Class"
3. High Inspectional, etc. (21)	3. Incomplete U/Grad. (12)	Class III = 32-47 points	"Middle-Middle Class"
4. Supervisory, etc. (28)	4. Complete Sec.-Level (16)	Class IV = 48-63 points	"Working Class"
5. Sk. Man/Routine N-M (35)	5. Incomplete Sec.-Level (20)	Class V = 64-77 points	"Lower Class"
6. Semi-Sk. Manual, etc. (42)	6. Complete Primary (24)		
7. Unskilled Manual (49)	7. Incomplete Primary (28)		

One's position on the scale is arrived at by adding one's **education** and **occupation** scores (given in brackets). See Mac Gréil (1996), *Prejudice in Ireland Revisited*, pp.368ff. The classification of occupations is given in the appendix to Mac Gréil (1977), *Prejudice and Tolerance in Ireland*.
[8] See Hollingshead, AB, (1949), *Elmstown Youth: the Impact of Social Classes on Adolescents*, New York, Wiley.

variable (which, in turn, was affected by the anomaly in the age variable). In measures where there is a strong positive correlation between both **education** and **occupation** in relation to a finding, the 'social-class-position' finding will be very strongly correlated. As has been pointed out, this has not been the case in relation to ethnic social-distance scores.

4.8 Conclusion:

In Part IV of this chapter, the social-distance measures in relation to a sample of five ethnic stimulus categories, i.e. 'English', 'Canadians', 'Dutch', 'Spaniards' and 'Poles' were given by personal variables. *Explicit percentages* ('admitting to kinship' and 'denying of citizenship') were abstracted from the seven-point *Bogardus Social Distance Scale* in order to give the reader a more realistic report on what variations in mean-social-distance scores mean in the current intergroup relations situation in Irish society today. Very often statistically accurate measures are difficult to interpret. Not infrequently, presentation of the more explicit findings can add to the appreciation of the findings even for the 'statistical expert'. Table No. 8.13 is intended to "put flesh on the more abstract statistical bones" presented elsewhere. Hopefully, this aim has been achieved.

Part V – Conclusion

In this part it is proposed to summarise and conclude the ethnic prejudice and related findings which have been presented in Chapters VII and VIII above. Between the two chapters an attempt was made to spell out the nature of Irish ethnocentrism and its links with racism and with nationalism. Also, the connection with ethnic self-identity as well as the impact of intergroup definition in relation to ethnic prejudice has been teased out. *The principle of ethnic propinquity* was borne out in most cases.

The four subgroupings within the twenty-nine **ethnic, ethnico-racial and racial stimulus categories** made the analysis easier to present. The four subgroupings were:

1) *Irish-British-American*: 'Irish Speakers', 'Welsh', 'Euro-Americans', 'English', 'Canadians', 'Scottish', 'British', 'Northern Irish', 'Afro-Americans'.

2) *Continental European Nationalities*: 'French', 'Dutch', 'Germans', 'Spaniards', 'Italians', 'Polish People', 'Lithuanians', 'Russians', 'Romanians'.

3) *African, Asian and Racial Stimulus Categories*: 'Chinese', 'Coloureds', 'Indians', 'Blacks', 'Africans', 'Pakistanis', 'Nigerians'.

4) *Middle-East Ethnic Stimulus Categories*: 'Palestinians', 'Israelis', 'Iranians', 'Arabs'.

In Chapter VII, each of the four subgroupings were measured by personal variables as four factors, i.e. the combined mean-social-distance for each of the subgroupings was the measure tested (see Table No. 7.1). The unanticipated relatively high levels of ethnic, ethnico-racial and racial prejudice of the 18 to 25 year-olds was surprising and would need further research to find out why this age group was so negative. Part VIII of Chapter VII tried to address possible reasons for such a negative disposition among a sub-variable who were, relatively speaking, highly educated, fairly secure economically and enjoying the benefits of the so-called 'Celtic Tiger'. Questions were raised about the quality of higher education, changes in the socialisation process, the influence of modern cybernetics and the growing virtual society, exclusive peer-socialisation and the dysfunctional aspects of extended adolescence (see pages 156-160).

One of the clearest signs of the survival of 'race' as a factor in intergroup attitudes/prejudices [despite the very low level of 'racial' rationalisation (see Table No. 5.1, pages 86-7)] has been the stark difference between social distance towards *Euro (white)-Americans* and *Afro (black)-Americans*. This bears out some of the commentary at the beginning of Chapter IX about the nature of 'racism' itself (see pages 193-200 below). While most people tend not to admit to themselves that they are racists, their attitudes and behaviour belie their self-perception in this regard.

The changes in ethnic and related prejudices between 1988-89 and 2007-08 have been, on the whole, quite positive. Twenty-five of the twenty-nine stimulus categories measured in the 2007-08 survey were replicated from the 1988-89 national survey. The **increase** in 'admission to kinship' and **decrease** in 'denial of citizenship' were taken as valid indicators of reduction in social prejudice and increase in intergroup tolerance.

Finally, readers are encouraged to study the findings of Chapters VII and VIII carefully. The Tables of these two chapters show very clearly the level of relevant **intergroup prejudice** and the impact of recent in-migration on Irish society on ethnic self-identity and the social attitudes of Irish adults. Ambivalence of a high percentage of adults towards their **perceived (Irish) ethnic-self-identity** raises important questions for the success of the transmission of Irish culture to the young. Much of the popular media (print and electronic) being circulated and broadcast in the Republic of Ireland rarely gives due prominence to the Irish language and culture. Such obvious neglect is likely to contribute to the worrying findings of Table No. 8.5 (see page 166 above).

***

CHAPTER IX
Racial Prejudice

Part I – Reflection on Recent Commentary

1.1 Introduction:

Much has been written by human scientists[1] over the past two decades about the concept of **race**, **racism** and **racialism** and how intergroup relations have been affected by perceived differences based on physiological and physiognomic traits. Among the most noted human scientists have been anthropologists, sociologists, social psychologists, political scientists, human geographers, historians and philosophers. While it is generally accepted among the body of human scientists and by biologists, *the biological concept of race as representing a reality in the human population lacks scientific validity*. The **political and social concepts of race** are, however, serious factors in intergroup relations today. The 'myth of race' still results in the perpetuation of human inequality between groups perceived to be racially different to the dominant group(s). There is but **one human race** and all humans are fundamentally equal, objectively speaking. Nevertheless, subjectively for many, that is not so!

The present author agrees that there is but one human race and the biological and anthropological arguments for poly or multiple human races are void of a scientific basis. Humanly speaking, the colour of one's skin is not any more (humanly) important than the size of one's shoes, i.e. **objectively** speaking! Unfortunately the story can be different **subjectively**, when people ascribe or assign **human** significance to perceived differences in the colour, size, physiognomy and other genetically inherited visible body traits. The self-fulfilling prophecy begins to work when this false perception translates the perceived differences into prejudice (which is called 'racism' or 'racialism') and discrimination and the unfair distribution of power, standards of living and treatment before the law.

---

[1] The following is a selection of recent authors and researchers who have made worthwhile contributions to the current scientific literature on 'race' (full references given in Bibliography)**: Richard Adams** (Anthropologist, 2005); **Les Back** (Sociologist, 1994); **Eduardo Bonilla-Silva,** (Sociologist, 2003); **Markus Braur** (Psychologist, 1995); **Ashley Doane** (Sociologist, 2006); **Virginia R. Dominguez** (Anthropologist, 1997); **Sue E. Estroff** (Anthropologist, 1997); **Lawrence Hirschfeld** (Psychologist, 1997); **Charles M. Judd** (Psychologist, 1991, 1993 and 1995); **Susan Kraus** (Psychologist, 1995); **Patrick H. Miller** (Historian, 1998); **Keiichi Omoto** (Anthropologist, 1997); **Bernadette Park** (1991, 1993 and 1995); **Paul Paolucci** (Sociologist, 2006); **Carey S. Ryan** (Psychologist, 1991 and 1995); and **John Solomos** (Sociologist, 1994).

As already noted, problems arise when the widespread and misguided use of the term 'racism' or 'racialism' takes place to define prejudice towards groups or categories according to culture, political ideology, social-class, gender-orientation, religion, occupational status and so forth. This only adds to the 'myth of race', as was experienced in Nazi Germany, South Africa, the Deep South of the United States and elsewhere. It seems the term **"racism"** is also a more powerful provocative term to focus public attention on genuine social issues. In this text the use of the concept **race** is restricted to the influence of perceived genetically inherited physical appearances which are different to those of the dominant group in the Republic of Ireland.

1.2 'Colour Blindness':

Denying that 'race' plays a negative role in our intergroup attitudes and behaviour can be very deceptive. **Political correctness**, largely among middle-class 'white people', produces the 'colour-blind' syndrome. People will not admit to themselves that they have racist attitudes because this would reflect negatively on their own 'liberated self-image', while at the same time being prepared to justify negative predispositions against members of 'black' and other physiognomically-different categories, e.g. the difference between social-distance scores in this research in relation to *'Euro-Americans'* (i.e. 'White Americans') and *'Afro-Americans'* (i.e. 'Black Americans'). One of the most interesting discourses on the 'double-think' in relation to the current ideology of racism in the United States has been written by Ashley Doane of the University of Hartford, USA, in an article entitled "What is Racism? Racial Discourse and Racial Politics" in *Critical Sociology,* No. 32, 2006, pages 255-274. The following extract from the above article summarises the 'double-think'.

> "At the core of white racial reaction has been the recasting of racial ideologies or understandings to defend white advantages while simultaneously acknowledging the value of 'racial equality'. The dominant ideology in their endeavour has been 'colour-blindness' (Bonilla-Silva, 2001, 2003)...... This ideology of 'color-blindness' has enabled practitioners to claim the legacy of Martin Luther King, Jr., and the Civil Rights Movement ... while attacking race-based remedies such as affirmative action and political redistricting as violations of democratic principles (on 'abstract liberalism', see Bonilla-Silva, 2001, pp. 142-147) and deriding multiculturalism as 'identity politics' or 'political correctness'.
>
> (Doane, Ashley, 2006, p.259)

What is true of the United States at the beginning of the 21st century seems to be confirmed in the Irish findings of 2007-08. It is very interesting to observe that well-intentioned ('abstract liberals') can convince themselves to be free of 'racism' while at the same time supporting socio-cultural norms and structures which reinforce racial inequality and prevent racial emancipation.   This is probably also true of the dilemma of liberal-minded elites in relation to other minorities, i.e. ethnic, social-class, etc. **Individual colour blindness** seems to be able to co-exist with **institutional racism**, i.e. *"structural or systemic racism"* (Doane, Ashley, 2006, page 267).   The ideology behind current European Union 'fortress' immigration policies may smack of this 'colour-blind' illusion!

1.3 Racial Essentialism:
The psychologist, Lawrence Hirschfeld of the University of Michigan, Ann Arbor, has also written a most enlightening article in *Ethos*, Vol. 1, No.1 (March 1997, pages 63-92) entitled: "The Conceptual Politics of Race: Lessons from Our Children".   Hirschfeld makes a most valuable comment on the difference between children's and adults' perception of race, i.e.

> "... Race has a fundamentally different *meaning* for young children than it does for the adults around them (Abond 1988; Holmes 1995; Katz 1982).   According to this view young children conceive of race as a superficial quality of people, one that is literally skin-deep ....   For adults, race is about physical appearance, but it is also about racial *essence*; for children, race is only about physical appearance; never about essence."   (Hirschfeld 1997, p.82).

This attributing of **essence** to racial (physical) appearance is at the root of racism.   It makes members of racial groups innately different and places them on a hierarchical order of superiority-inferiority.   This is known as **racial essentialism**, which is not scientifically tenable.   Once race is 'essentialised', it is conceivable that racists can rationalise and justify to themselves, or accept as part of a particular political ideology, that certain 'racial groups' ('races' in their eyes) are 'less than human' and can be dealt with summarily, e.g. assigned the status of slave, outside the protection of the 'rule of law' and even annihilated with impunity!   Slavery of black people was justified by **the ideology of racial essentialism** in the Deep South of the United States, South Africa and elsewhere.

1.4 Biological Concept of Race:
Students of racism owe much to anthropologists like **Keiichi Omoto** (from the International Research Centre for Japanese Studies, Kyoto, Japan) for questioning and undermining the false 'biological concept of race', which resulted in the devaluing of so many millions of human beings over the

recent centuries. In his article "The Rise and Fall of the Biological Concept of Race", he traces the history of the rise of "racism or the ideology of inequality of the human groups defined as races" and its pseudo-scientific bases. The article is published in the *Japan Review*, No. 9, 1997, pages 65-73. The author has many other valuable publications. Omoto considers "race as a social concept like gender, as opposed to sex as a biological concept" (Omoto, Keiichi, page 70). "Race will remain as a social concept like gender, but it will never become an important concept again in biological anthropology" (*Ibid*, p.71). Hopefully, this optimistic proposition of Omoto will be true. At the same time, it is prudent to be on our guard against the resurrection of racial essentialism or 'biological racism'!

1.5 Cultural Racism:

With the demise of the credibility of "biological racism", which dominated societies such as **South Africa** during most of the second half of the 20th century, are we now seeing the rise of **"cultural racism"**? Or are we seeing the **"racialisation"** of ethnic minorities in order to lock them in at an inferior rung of the social ladder? **John Solomos** and **Les Back** in their informative article: "Conceptualising Racisms: Social Theory, Politics and Research", published in *Sociology*, Vol. 28, No. 1, 1994, pages 143-161, examine the changes of focus in the definition of racism in the final decades of the 20th century. They seem to have a less restricted use of the concept 'racism'. They quote from David Goldberg: "The presumption of a single monopolitic racism is being displaced by a mapping of the multifarious historical formulations of racisms" (Goldberg, 1988). Solomos and Back deal with the conceptualisation of the 'right' and of the 'left' in Britain. The development of an articulate 'right-wing' opposition towards Commonwealth and other in-migrants in Britain during the 1980s is seen by Solomos and Back as the origin of **'cultural racism'**:

> "… Its focus is the defence of the mythic 'British/English way of life' in face of attack from enemies *outside* ('Argies', 'Frogs', 'Krauts', 'Iraqi') and *within* ('black communities', 'Muslim fundamentalists'). Paul Gilroy points to an alarming consequence of new racism when blackness and Englishness are reproduced as "mutually exclusive categories" (Gilroy, Paul, *There Ain't No Black in the Union Jack*, London, Hutchinson, 1987, pages 55-56)
> (Solomos and Back, 1994, page 150).

The **politicising** of the concept 'race' is something to be most wary of in modern Ireland and elsewhere. In the end it could lead to the **'racialising'** of social, ethnic and political relations, with the obvious negative consequences; hence, the importance for spokespersons for ethnic, social and political minorities to desist from presenting the problem as **racist.** Call it what it is basically, i.e. **ethnic** discrimination, **social** discrimination and **political** discrimination, irrespective of the **apparent** 'racialist' behaviour of the 'dominant group' towards the particular minority. *By the defenders of the minority accepting the racialisation of the situation, they are but playing into the exploitative hands of those in the 'dominant group' who may be racist at heart!*

1.6 Marx and Racism:

The rise of 'racism' during European expansionism in the 15th century and its use to justify (to the expansionists or colonisers) the institution of **slavery** of people from the African Continent has been interpreted by serious socialist (Marxist) scholars as part of the ideology of early capitalism. Slavery in Western Europe pre-dated the rise of racism.

Sociologist **Paul Paolucci** examines the contribution of Marx's academic work to our understanding of "race and racism" in modern capitalist societies in his article entitled: "Race and Racism in Marx's Camera Obscura", published in *Critical Sociology*, Vol.32, No.1, 2006, pages 618-648. Marx saw "knowledge and reality" presented to society in bourgeois ideology in "an inverted form of historical relations" (Paolucci, 2006, page 619). The author quotes from Marx and Engels' *German Ideology* (1846) as follows: "If in all ideologies men and their relations appear upside-down as in a camera obscura, this phenomenon arises just as much from their historical life-process as the inversion of objects on the retina does from this physical life-process" (Marx and Engels, 1846/1976, p.36)" (Paolucci, *Ibid*).

Marx claimed that racism succeeded European and American slavery, thereby refuting the idea that racism was the motive for its institution. **Slavery** was an instrument of exploitation of labour at a worldwide level, e.g. the enslavement of the Irish and British peasants. The change to racial slavery made it normal. 'Racism' was seen by Marx as a rationalisation or justification of stratification of the workforce. Race was a 'sociological-historical phenomenon' (Paolucci, page 636).

One of the facts emerging from the effects of racial discrimination in societies where it is (was) widespread has been the hierarchisation of labour, i.e. via **slavery** in the 18th and 19th centuries in America (U.S.) and

apartheid in 20th century South Africa.   In both of these situations Marxist theory would see racism as the accepted justification of capitalist exploitation.   Paolucci concludes his article as follows:

> "... Race as a form of knowledge was an outcome, not a cause of this process[2]. Race and racism, then, are quintessentially *modern* forms of knowledge.   But this form of knowledge has outlasted its function in justifying slavery.   Capitalism, evidently, functions better with racism than it did with slavery.   The question pressing on us collectively today is why this is so." (Paolucci, *Ibid*, page 645).

The answer to the above question is not easy from a socio-cultural determinist epistemological point of view.   It has been pointed out by Hesse[3] and others that the 18th century **'Enlightenment'** contributed to the rise of racism because of its white, male, European elitist presumptions! The legacy of the 'Enlightenment' on the rise and continuation of racism merits very serious critical research.   It would seem not to have been universal in its ideal of equality!

1.7 Body-Mind Dichotomy:

Finally in this summary review of development in the perception of race and racism, a selection of recent authors on the subject of 'race and racism' was drawn on.   It is worthwhile to note the subtlety of the differences highlighted by racist commentators.   'White people' were often prepared to concede that 'Black people' excelled in areas of **physical achievement,** i.e. sport, dance (rhythm), vigour, expressive religion, energy, and so forth. They would even concede that their bodies were more beautiful, etc.   White people, however, excelled in achievement of the **mind**, i.e. science, literature, politics, theology, creative composition of music, and so forth. This division of compliments was highly racial and needs to be addressed today.

Patrick H. Miller, North-eastern Illinois University (Department of History), indirectly addressed this issue in his article "The Anatomy of Scientific Racism: Racialist Responses to Black Athletic Achievement" published in the *Journal of Sport History*, Vol.25, No.1, 1998, pages 119-151.   The physical prowess stereotype of the agile Black Person is an inverted compliment not that dissimilar to the body-beautiful stereotype of

---

[2] Race came into being after "industrial slavery, scientific biology and moral-religious-legal discourse about non-White, non-Christian, non-Western peoples of the world arose" (Paolucci, 2006, p. 645).
[3] See Hesse, Barror and B. Soygid (Editors) "Narrating the Post-Colonial and Immigrant Imagery" in *A Post-Colonial People – South Asians in Britain*, London, Hurst & Co., 2006.

the young woman frequently displayed in popular (sexist) newspapers. Whites are prepared to accept that Blacks excel in the **body** while Whites shine in the **mind**. Pornography is, for the most part, degrading and racist and should be outlawed on those grounds alone. It turns **subjects** into **objects** and, thereby, dehumanises human persons.

Returning to Patrick Miller's excellent article that summarises the findings of scholars of 'post-colonial ideology' thus:

"...As scholars of post-colonial ideology and experience have demonstrated, the ranking of 'racial' traits – especially as it has elaborated the age-old dichotomy between mind and body – continues to serve as a means of suppressing the claims of people around the world. What remains is the pseudoscience of racial difference and the pernicious social policies it both inspires and informs."

(Miller, 1998, page 121).

This all points to **racial essentialism** surviving after the post-colonial and so-called 'enlightened' times. **Academic racism** still survives when one reads sports commentators who see measures of athletic performance as indicators of "racial difference". The challenge facing America (and the world) today is to move beyond "racial essentialism" in sport, dance, intellectual achievement, scientific excellence, political and social leadership. The words of Patrick Miller are also worth noting in this regard, i.e.:

"...Yet it is... crucial that progressive, or expansive, thinkers on the subject – rather than institute- and foundation-based conservative ideologies – become the cartographers of the contemporary discussion of 'race'. Better still, though from a different interpretive position, we might start erasing 'racial' boundaries altogether." (Miller, 1998, page 140)

One of the positive latent functions of the election of **President Barack Obama** in the United States in 2008 has been his humanity and various talents rather than his race! The growing number of world and local leaders from 'minority racial groups' in every area of intellectual and athletic fields on a par with dominant group representatives must help to erase the racial factor. The contribution of **Tiger Woods** in 'the white man's game of golf' could also be seen as a positive integrationist stimulus. At the same time, the perceptive analysis of Patrick Miller merits serious reflection and shows the survival of 'racial essentialism' decades beyond the American Civil Rights' Movement!

If one may add a note on what might be called the *"mechanism of exceptionality"* which has frequently been used to preserve the norm of racial or cultural superiority: when a member of the minority racial group excels academically or otherwise, we are quick to note that he or she is **an exception**, while, when somebody in our racial group fails to reach our standards of excellence, he or she is also **an exception**.

In other words, **virtue** in the minority is exceptional while **weakness** in the dominant group is exceptional. Both are **deviant** and the norm of superiority of the dominant group survives!

1.8 Conclusion:

In the above reflections and commentary, key issues have been addressed which have been raised by a wide range of authors on the evolution of the concept of 'race' and 'racism' in society. The topics discussed have been approached from a number of academic perspectives. Hopefully, the discussion will help to draw the readers' attention to the complexity of the chameleon nature of the 'virus of racism' in human society with its socially destructive effects on the lives of countless people and institutions. The texts and articles chosen above are but a selective list of recent observations. They in no way exhaust the literature available on the topic of 'racism'.

The questions raised in the above paragraphs are very relevant for Irish society and the need to make every effort to erase or prevent 'racism' as a factor in our intergroup relations. The lessons of history in other heterogeneous societies should put us on our guard as we become a more pluralist and culturally diversified society.

Part II – Racial Prejudice in Ireland

2.1 Introduction:

It has already been noted in previous chapters and will be shown in the findings below that **racism** (as measured by social distance) has been on the decline in Ireland over the past thirty-five years. Considering that the level of 'racial prejudice' in 1972-73 (in the Greater Dublin survey) was not any greater than in other societies in the Western World at the time and that it was a more benevolent form of racial prejudice, i.e. 'Black Babies' (see Mac Gréil, 1977, page 246), the current findings are more hopeful still. Despite the welcome change that has been confirmed, it will also be shown that the level of **'racial prejudice' in Ireland is still far too high**. In fact, in the case of the special **Racialist Scale**, the overall prejudice score did not improve overall since 1988-89 (see Table No.9.2, page 202 below).

The **explicit awareness** of the specifically racial factor, i.e. prejudice due to genetically inherited physical and physiognomic traits, has also reduced over the past decades. The dramatic decline in the 'racial' **rationalisation** of failure to welcome members of ethnico-racial and racial categories "into the family" is clearly confirmed in Table No. 9.1 below.

Table No. 9.1: Changes in 'Racial' Rationalisation of Ethnico-Racial and Racial Categories between 1988-89 and 2007-08

Stimulus Category	Racial Rationalisation		Nominal Change
	2007-08 (A)	1988-89 (B)	(A – B)
1. Chinese	4.9%	17.0%	**-12.1%**
2. Coloureds	13.3%	49.6%	**-36.3%**
3. Indians	4.7%	19.3%	**-14.6%**
4. Afro-Americans	14.9%	39.4%	**-24.5%**
5. Blacks	15.7%	46.2%	**-30.5%**
6. Africans	7.9%	35.5%	**-27.6%**
7. Pakistanis	3.7%	24.8%	**-21.1%**
8. Nigerians	7.4%	32.5%	**-25.1%**

The above findings hardly need any further comment!

2.2 Special Racialist Scale:

The Racialist Scale reported in Table No. 9.2 was first used in the 1972-73 survey of Greater Dublin. One item has been dropped from the original scale of ten items because it failed to factor[4] with other items.

---

[4] The item dropped from the scale was: *"Do you believe that Black People are by nature more highly sexed than White People?"* Response to item dropped was (1988-89 percentages in brackets):

Sample	Yes	Don't Know	No	Number	P. Score
1. Total Sample 2007-08	13.2%	48.5%	38.3%		74.9
1988-89	(17.4%)	(50.0%)	(32.6%)	(990)	(84.7)
2. Irish-Born	12.2%	51.9%	35.9%		76.3

This item did not correlate significantly with the other items on the scale. The findings are interesting in that almost 50% 'did not know'. The plurality of the sample said 'no'. The change since 1988-89 has been in the positive direction. This item was intended to test the strength of the 'body-mind' myth discussed on pages 198-200 above.

Table No. 9.2: Racialist Scale (2007-08 and 1988-89)

Question: *"Now I would like to get your views in relation to Black People. Could I ask you a number of questions?"*

	Item	Yes	Don't Know	No	Number	Racial Score (0-200)	Change Since 1988/89
1.	"If you had a boarding house, would you refuse digs/accommodation to Black People?"	**13.2%** **(14.7%)**	6.6% (5.8%)	80.3% (79.6%)	1,015 (1,003)	**33.0** (35.2)	-2.1
2.	"Do you think that because of their basic make-up Black People could never be as good Irish people as others?"	**13.2%** **(16.7%)**	12.9% (10.0%)	73.9% (73.3%)	1,013 (1,000)	**39.3** (43.4)	-4.4
3.	"Do you believe that there should be a stricter control on Black People who enter this country than on Whites?"	**32.3%** **(26.8%)**	7.7% (8.7%)	60.1% (64.5%)	1,015 (999)	**72.3** (62.3)	+16.6
4.	"Do you believe that the Black Person is basically or inherently inferior than the White Person?"	**8.3%** **(10.8%)**	8.1% (5.9%)	83.6% (83.3%)	1,015 (999)	**24.7** (27.5)	-6.8
5.	"Would you stay in a hotel or guesthouse that had Black Guests also?"	86.3% (90.9%)	4.7% (2.9%)	**9.0%** **(6.2%)**	1,012 (1,001)	**22.7** (15.3)	+7.4
6.	"Do you believe that the Black Person deserves exactly the same social privileges as the White Person?"	84.4% (92.9%)	7.7% (3.5%)	**7.9%** **(3.6%)**	1,015 (1,001)	**23.5** (10.7)	+12.8
7.	"Do you hold that by nature the Black and the White Person are equal?"	85.4% (86.8%)	6.2% (5.7%)	**8.3%** **(7.5%)**	1,011 (1,000)	**22.8** (20.7)	+2.1
8.	"Would you hold that Black People should be sent back to Africa and Asia where they belong and kept there?"	**8.4%** **(8.9%)**	11.3% (6.8%)	80.2% (84.3%)	1,013 (1,000)	**28.1** (24.6)	+3.5
9.	"Do you agree that it is a good thing for Whites and Blacks to get married where there are no cultural or religious barriers?"	58.4% (52.4%)	19.8% (16.2%)	**21.8%** **(31.4%)**	1,012 (1,002)	**63.4** (79.0)	-16.6
	Scale Racialist Score (0-200) in 2007-08 =					**36.8**	+1.4
	Scale Racialist Score (0-200) in 1988-89 =					(35.4)	

Note: 1988-89 National Survey results are in brackets. Negative percentages are in **bold**.
Cronbach Alpha = 0.768

The overall level of racial prejudice measured in the above Table is **relatively low** and is not much different from 1988-89 figures. The Racial Prejudice score for the sample is **36.8** (on a 0 to 200 scale) which is just **1.4** higher than it was in 1988-89. This change is statistically not that significant.

It is interesting to note the items which elicited significantly negative changes since 1988-89, i.e. Nos. 3 and 6. No. 3 seems to mark an increase in the support for greater control of migrant workers from Africa and other non-European countries. Allowing for this increase, still **less than one-third (32.3%)** would endorse the EU 'fortress policy', which reflects well on the remainder of the sample (**7.7%** Didn't Know and **60.1%** Disagreed).

The relative change in relation to Item No. 6, although modest, is, nevertheless, disappointing. The 7.9% who did not agree with the 'Black Person' *"deserving exactly the same social privileges as the 'White Person'"* represents a small minority of respondents who appear severely racialist in their dispositions. This is an area where propaganda in the media and stereotyping immigrants as parasitic in their demands on social welfare can elicit popular support in times of economic scarcity. Nevertheless, the fact that **84.4%** agree to the question is very encouraging, although not as impressive as the 1988-89 score. The above findings are a small but significant measure of possible decline in support for **exact social equality** for 'Black People' in our society.

The item recording most significant improvement is No. 9 in *"that it is a good thing for Whites and Blacks to get married where there are no cultural or religious barriers"*. This confirms the findings of the *Bogardus Social Distance Scale*, i.e. where **52.6%** would welcome Blacks in kinship. The racial prejudice score on Item No. 9 dropped by 16.6 (from 79.0 in 1988-89 to 62.4 in 2007-08). This result is highly significant and marks a substantial *drop in racial endogamy* which is a key indicator of the welcome reduction in racism.

There is still room for further improvement before we reach the position when one's **'racial features'** will have no significance in choosing a partner in life with whom to raise a family. Ethnic rather than racial **pluralism** is the human basis of true integration. The path towards **erasing the 'racial factor'** in intergroup relations is a slow and gradual process.

The legacy of pseudoscientific rationalisation for the biological concept of 'race' seems to be deeply implanted in the belief of a small but significant minority of respondents. A similar residue is to be found in the 'bio-anthropological' theory of the **'criminal types'** propagated by **Cesare Lombroso**[5], which is still in the folk belief of people. A number of late 19th century and early 20th century criminologists seemed to accept that certain

---

[5] Lombroso, Cesare, *The Criminal Man*, 1876.

people were **physiologically and genetically determined** to be prone to criminal behaviour. Later scientific analysis refuted this erroneous criminal determinism. Lombroso created the concept of the **'atavistic types'** which he defined as conducive to crime. Police and Gardaí, who would be so foolish as to have such a 'racist' attitude to crime and deviance, could bias their objective pursuit of justice. Again, this approach has led to negative 'self-fulfilling prophecy'!

2.3 Factor Analysis of the Special Racialist Scale:

The inter-item **correlation matrix** between each of the nine items of the Special Racialist Scale has resulted in two different factors, namely, the 'exclusion' sub-scale and the 'pure racialist' sub-scale. Table No. 9.3 gives the correlation matrix as follows:

Table No. 9.3:
Racial Scale Inter-Item Correlation Matrix

	Item	No.1	No.2	No.3	No.4	No.5	No.6	No.7	No.8	No.9
1.	Refuse digs to Black People.	1.000	**0.273**	0.175	**0.250**	**0.243**	0.132	0.197	**0.215**	**0.249**
2.	Blacks could not become as good as Irish people as others		1.000	**0.350**	**0.342**	**0.354**	**0.208**	**0.236**	**0.287**	**0.347**
3.	Stricter control of Blacks than of Whites.			1.000	0.169	**0.347**	0.148	**0.247**	**0.360**	**0.295**
4.	Black People are inherently inferior to Whites.				1.000	**0.354**	**0.360**	**0.333**	**0.235**	**0.408**
5.	Blacks should be sent back to Africa and Asia where they belong.					1.000	**0.225**	**0.309**	**0.314**	**0.412**
6.	Would stay in the same hotel as with Blacks.						1.000	**0.355**	**0.213**	**0.263**
7.	Blacks deserve exactly the same privileges as Whites.							1.000	**0.218**	**0.418**
8.	A good thing for Whites and Blacks to marry where there are no religious or cultural barriers.								1.000	**0.321**
9.	Black and White persons are by nature equal.									1.000

Note: Items correlations 0.200 and over are in **bold**.

In the case of thirty-one of the thirty-six scores, there is a moderately significant (0.2 plus) level of 'inter-item correlation'. When the items are tested further to discover sub-scales or factors, two distinctive factors emerge, i.e. one emphasising **'pure racialist'** attitudes and the other referring to a **'racial exclusion'** factor.

The items in **factor one**, i.e. 'racial exclusion', included items nos. 1, 2, 3, 5 and 8, while **factor two**, i.e. 'pure racialist', included items nos. 4, 6, 7 and 9. The *Cronbach Alpha* test at 0.768 is quite satisfactory and re-validates the scale. The racial score for 'pure racialism' is at **23.6** (on a 0-200 prejudice scale). The 'racial exclusion' sub-scale was double that score at **47.2**. Both scores are relatively small with limited scope for significant variation. The 'exclusion' factors probably include a number of "fair-weather liberals"!

2.4 Racial Sub-Scales by Personal Variables:

Table No. 9.4 gives a breakdown of the variations in the racialist scale and the two sub-scales, i.e. the two factors.

Table No. 9.4:
Racial Scale Variations by Personal Variables[6]

Variable	Total Scale P. Score (0-200)	Factor I Exclusion Sub-scale (0-200)	Factor II Pure Racialist Sub-scale (0-200)	Number
Total Sample	36.8	47.2	23.6	1,004
(a) Age	p<.005	p<.005	p<.005	---
1. 18-25 years	34.3	42.9	23.0	167
2. 26-40 years	33.5	40.6	**24.5**	317
3. 41-55 years	31.1	43.1	16.2	247
4. 56-70 years	**43.5**	58.4	24.4	176
5. 71 years plus	**54.3**	66.5	**39.0**	96
Score Variation	*22.3*	*25.9*	*22.8*	*1,003*
(b) Gender	p<.004	p<.001	N/S	---
1. Males	**40.5**	**52.3**	---	498
2. Females	33.1	42.2	---	508
Score Variation	*7.4*	*10.1*	*---*	*1,006*

---

[6] **Clusters of Items:**
(a) Exclusion Factor: (1) *"If you had a boarding house would you refuse digs (accommodation) to Black people?"* (2) *"Would you think that because of their basic make-up, Black people could never become as good Irish people as others?"* (3) *"Do you believe that there should be stricter control of Black people who enter this country than on Whites?"* (4) *"Would you hold that Black people should be sent back to Africa or Asia where they belong and kept there?"* (5) *"Do you agree that it is a good idea for Whites and Blacks to get married where there are no cultural or religious barriers?"*
(b) Pure Racialist Factor: (1) *"Do you believe that the Black person is basically or inherently inferior to the White person?"* (2) *"Would you stay in a hotel or guesthouse that had Black guests also?"* (3) *"Do you believe that the Black person deserves exactly the same social privileges as the White person?"* (4) *"Do you hold that by nature the Black and White person are equal?"*

Table No. 9.4 (Cont'd) Variable	Total Scale P. Score (0-200)	Factor I Exclusion Sub-scale (0-200)	Factor II Pure Racialist Sub-scale (0-200)	Number
(c) Marital Status	p<.005	p<.005	p<.015	---
1. Single/Never Married	33.8	42.9	21.4	352
2. Married	**37.2**	**48.6**	23.2	469
3. Separated/Divorced	43.3	**53.8**	**30.2**	44
4. Permanent Relat'ship	27.7	35.3	18.2	71
5. Widowed	**55.2**	**68.1**	**39.1**	68
Score Variation	*275*	*32.8*	*20.9*	*1,004*
(d) Area of Birth	N/S	p<.005	N/S	---
1. City (100,000 plus)	---	44.4	---	417
2. Large Town (10,000 +)	---	40.1	---	115
3. Town (1,500 plus)	---	38.9	---	126
4. Rural/Village	---	**56.1**	---	344
Score Variation	---	*17.2*	---	*1,001*
(e) Region of Residence	p<.007	N/S	p<.005	---
1. B.M.W.	36.2	---	17.8	269
2. Dublin	36.5	---	**24.6**	285
3. Mid-East & Sth.-East	**44.3**	---	**38.0**	217
4. Mid-West & Sth.-W.	30.9	---	15.6	233
Score Variation	*13.4*	---	*22.4*	*1,004*
(f) Education	p<.005	p<.005	p<.005	---
1. Primary or Less	**50.2**	**63.0**	**34.1**	117
2. Incomplete Sec.-Lev.	**50.0**	**65.6**	**30.3**	261
3. Complete Sec.-Level	35.7	46.7	21.4	252
4. Third-Level	24.2	29.9	17.1	374
Score Variation	*26.0*	*33.1*	*17.0*	*1,004*
(g) Occupational Status	p<.005	p<.005	p<.026	---
1. Unskilled/Semi-Sk.	**45.9**	**62.3**	**25.3**	207
2. Skilled/Routine N-M.	35.0	42.9	**25.3**	323
3. Inspect./Supervisory	27.9	35.4	18.5	131
4. Professional/Exec.	26.0	33.7	15.5	166
Score Variation	*19.9*	*28.6*	*9.6*	*827*

Note: Scores above sample average are in **bold**.   (Variations in *italics*)

The findings of Table No. 9.4 are more or less as anticipated save for a number of surprises. There was a moderately positive correlation between **age** and racial prejudice in the case of the full scale and the two factors, apart from the slight aberration in the case of the 26 to 40 years' subsample eight points higher than the 41 to 55 year-olds in the Factor II scores. The latter age group was the **most tolerant** in the case of each of the three results.

The most tolerant age group was the middle-aged subsample, i.e. 41 to 55 year olds.

In the case of **gender,** females were significantly less prejudiced from the total scale with a variation of **7.4** and for the 'exclusion factor' the variation was 10.1. There was consensus in relation to the 'pure racialist' factor. This, once again, shows the decline of gender difference in relation to social attitudes – a possible latent function of the feminist movement. The interesting question would be: "Are male attitudes moving towards those of females?" In the earlier research into prejudice, differences were more marked although there were signs of their coming together more closely!

The 'Widowed' and the 'Separated/Divorced' had the highest p-score in the **'Marital Status'** variable in all three measures. The 'Married' were close to the sample and subsamples' averages. Those in 'Permanent Relationships' were least racist while the 'Single/Never Married' were below average in all three scores. The age and education of respondents is reflected in this subsample would tend to be an influence for tolerance.

'Area of Birth' elicited consensus in the case of the full scale and the 'Pure Racialist' factor. Responses to the 'Exclusion Factor' clearly shows that those born in 'the rural countryside and in small villages' were less open to Black people than their more unbiased compatriots. The ethos of unbiased people would tend to be more 'cosmopolitan' and likely to have more opportunities for favourable contact with Black people.

'Education' as a personal variable performed as was anticipated, i.e. the greater the respondents' education achievement the lower the level of racial prejudice. The findings of Table No. 9.4(f) confirm this trend and show a negative correlation between **prejudice** and **education**. The *range of variation* in this variable is exceptionally wide, i.e. total sample = **26.0**; Factor One 'Exclusion' = **33.1**; and 'Pure Racialist Factor' = **17.0**. The trend and range made it very clear that the education variable has performed positively in the case of racism, despite its mixed performance elsewhere, e.g. in the case of attitudes towards 'Irish Travellers'[7], where **class issues** possibly distort the liberal impulses of educational achievement.

---

[7] See Mac Gréil, Micheál (2010), *Emancipation of the Travelling People*, Maynooth, Survey and Research Unit, Dept. of Sociology, NUIM, pages 64ff.

Finally, **'Occupational Status'** performed quite tolerantly in relation to the "racialist scale".   There was a negative correlation between occupational status and racial score for the 'total sample' and the 'Exclusion' and 'Pure Racialist' factors.   This reflects a welcome reduction of racism among respondents with the higher professions and those likely to be in managerial and supervisory roles.   This is very important to prevent preferential treatment for White people at the expense of Black people.   If the attitudes expressed in Table No. 9.4(g) prevail in the Republic of Ireland, race could soon be weakened or erased as a source of discrimination at work or in business at the managerial levels.   Such a trend is of vital economic and social interest for the future of a more diverse workforce.

2.5 Special Racialist Scale by Social Class Position:
Social Class Position is the grading of respondents according to their general social status in society.   It was originally devised by August de Belmond Hollingshead (Hollingshead, 1949; Hollingshead and Redlick, 1958)   to measure social status by combining one's **occupational status** and one's **educational achievement**.   (See footnote, Chapter VIII, page 189.) Hollingshead divided society into **five classes** depending on the combined scores of education and occupation[8].

Table No. 9.5 gives the racialist scale score (0-200) by social-class-position.   The sub-scales' scores are also given on this Table.

Table No. 9.5:
Racial Scale's Prejudice Scores by Social Class Position (P. Score 0-200)

Social Class Position (p<.001)	Total Scale	Factor I Exclusion Sub-scale	Factor II Pure Racialist Sub-scale	Average Number
Class I ("Upper Class")	23.64	28.96	16.99	39 (4.6%)
Class II ("Upper-Middle Class")	23.47	30.92	13.09	136 (16.6%)
Class III ("Middle-Middle Class")	29.44	36.13	21.76	224 (26.6%)
Class IV ("Working Class")	**38.12**	**49.53**	**23.37**	360 (42.7%)
Class V ("Lower Class")	**57.24**	**75.13**	**34.88**	84 (10.0%)
Mean P. Score	34.68	44.52	22.14	843 (100.0%)
Range of Variation	*33.77*	*46.17*	*21.78*	---

Note: Scores above average are in **bold**.   Variations are in *italics*.

---

[8] See Mac Gréil, Micheál (1996), *Prejudice in Ireland Revisited*, Survey and Research Unit, St. Patrick's College, Maynooth, pages 368-370.

The findings of Table No. 9.5 clearly show that the levels of racial prejudice are negatively correlated to the level of the respondent position on the 'social-class ladder', i.e. the higher up the 'social ladder' the lower the level of one's prejudice (as measured by the *Racialist Scale)*. This is as was anticipated, because of the expected influence of education and occupational status. The people at the lower end of the 'social-class ladder' would tend to feel less secure economically and more open to frustration leading to prejudice as a form of psychological aggression.

The changes in social class position distribution in the Republic of Ireland since 1988-89 are interesting from the point of view of its influence on the levels of racial prejudice of the 2007-08 sample. Table No. 9.6 gives the changes recorded at each class level.

Table No. 9.6:
Changes in Social Class Position Distribution of Total National Sample
between 1988-89 and 2007-08

Social Class Position	1988-89 A	2007-08 B	Change (B – A) (Nominal %)
Class I ("Upper Class")	3.8%	4.5%	+ 0.7%
Class II ("Upper-Middle Class")	11.8%	16.3%	+ 4.5%
Class III ("Middle-Middle Class")	30.2%	26.9%	- 3.3%
Class IV ("Working Class")	33.0%	42.4%	+ 9.4%
Class V ("Lower Class")	21.2%	9.9%	- 11.3%

The changes in the configuration of the Irish Class (status) structure over the period 1988-89 to 2007-08 reflect the influx of migrant workers and the expansion in the construction-related occupations, i.e. skilled manual and routine non-manual. The "lower class" declined by over **52.8%** from 21.2% to 10.0%, i.e. -11.2% (nominally). The upward move is moderate and **within** the middle classes. The trends prior to the arrival of the migrant workers were from "working-class" to "middle-class" within the indigenous Irish population. What is measured in Table No. 9.6 is not necessarily a measure of upward or downward class mobility but, rather, changes in the social class position structure of the adult population as represented by the 2007-08 sample as compared with the findings of 1988-89. Are we seeing here a repeat of earlier patterns of social-class mobility, i.e. greater movement within the *'white-collar classes'* and the *'blue-collar classes'* with fewer crossing the collar-colour line?

With all of the above qualifications, it could have been expected that there would be little overall change in the level of racism as measured by the Racialist Scale. Table No. 9.2 confirms this absence of significant change in the overall level of the p-score, i.e. **36.8** in 2007-08 and **35.4** in 1988-89. The change in social-class position and its influence on the p-score would seem to help to explain the absence of substantial change.

Part III – Racial Prejudice as Measured by Social Distance

Before completing this chapter on Racial Prejudice it is proposed to re-examine the level and nature of social-distance scores towards **four of the eight** 'racial and ethnico-racial' stimulus categories, whose mean-social-distance scores by personal variables were presented on Table No. 7.6 on page 145-6 above. The focus on that Table was on the **ethnic dimension** of the eight stimulus categories. 'Afro-Americans' (from Table No. 7.4, pages 134) are added to the four categories from Table No. 7.6, since the focus here is in the 'racial' dimensions.

The five stimulus categories reported on Table No. 9.7 are: 'Coloureds', 'Afro-Americans', 'Blacks', 'Africans' and 'Nigerians'.

Table No. 9.7:
'Admission to Kinship' and 'Denial of Citizenship' of Racial and Ethnico-Racial Categories from Africa and to United States (by Personal Variables)

Variable	'Coloureds'		'Afro-Americans'		'Blacks'		'Africans'		'Nigerians'	
	Admit to Kinship	Denial of Citizen'p	Admit to Kinship	Denial of Citizen'p	Admit to Kinship	Denial of Citizen'p	Admit to Kinship	Denial of Citizen'p	Admit to Kinship	Denial of Citizen'p
Total Sample	57.8%	9.9%	52.7%	11.9%	52.6%	12.0%	52.3%	13.7%	50.5%	18.9%
A. Age	p<.001		p<.001		p<.005		p<.005		p<.005	
1. 18-25 years	44.6%	11.9%	41.9%	15.6%	41.4%	16.0%	38.5%	21.3%	41.7%	23.2%
2. 26-40 years	65.2%	6.9%	60.7%	8.0%	60.9%	8.1%	63.5%	9.5%	59.9%	14.6%
3. 41-55 years	58.1%	7.6%	51.4%	10.1%	51.2%	10.5%	49.2%	11.8%	46.3%	18.3%
4. 56-70 years	58.2%	13.0%	51.6%	14.2%	52.8%	14.8%	48.6%	14.2%	46.0%	21.6%
5. 71 years plus	60.4%	16.6%	52.6%	19.0%	48.0%	17.3%	53.1%	18.7%	52.6%	22.7%
Range of Variation	*20.6%*	*9.7%*	*18.8%*	*11.0%*	*19.5%*	*9.2%*	*25.0%*	*11.8%*	*18.2%*	*8.5%*

B. Marital Status	N/S		p<.042		N/S		p<.01		N/S	
1. Single/Never Mar'd	---	---	50.4%	**14.0%**	---	---	49.4%	**17.1%**	---	---
2. Married	---	---	**53.4%**	10.4%	---	---	**53.9%**	10.6%	---	---
3. Separated/Divorced	---	---	**53.5%**	16.3%	---	---	**55.8%**	18.6%	---	---
4. Permanent Rel'ship	---	---	**54.2%**	7.0%	---	---	52.1%	8.4%	---	---
5. Widowed	---	---	**54.4%**	14.4%	---	---	**54.4%**	16.2%	---	---
Range of Variation	---	---	*9.0%*	*9.3%*	---	---	*6.4%*	*8.7%*	---	---

C. Area of Birth	p<.005		p<.001		p<.005		p<.007		p<.001	
1. City (100,000+)	58.9%	8.1%	52.2%	**16.5%**	52.8%	9.1%	51.4%	12.9%	**54.8%**	18.2%
2. Large Town (10,000+)	**64.7%**	5.1%	**56.7%**	8.3%	**62.4%**	4.3%	**62.2%**	8.4%	**54.6%**	19.3%
3. Town (1,500 +)	**66.7%**	3.2%	**59.5%**	3.8%	**60.3%**	6.1%	**64.4%**	10.6%	52.7%	12.4%
4. Rural/Village	52.9%	16.1%	47.7%	18.3%	45.9%	20.7%	45.1%	18.0%	42.6%	22.4%
Range of Variation	*13.8%*	*12.9%*	*11.8%*	*14.5%*	*16.5%*	*16.4%*	*19.3%*	*9.6%*	*12.3%*	*10.0%*

D. Place of Rearing (in Rep. of Ireland)	p<.005		p<.001		p<.005		p<.001		p<.005	
1. Dublin (City & Co.)	59.4%	**12.0%**	54.3%	**12.5%**	54.0%	**11.3%**	49.8%	**14.6%**	52.1%	21.2%
2. Rest of Leinster	53.7%	**15.4%**	52.4%	**14.6%**	48.5%	15.3 %	49.7%	**18.2%**	46.3%	23.8%
3. Munster	65.8%	9.8%	59.5%	12.9%	60.2%	14.7%	58.4%	13.0%	56.7%	17.8%
4. Connaught/Ulster	50.0%	6.1%	39.6%	10.9%	38.7%	14.1%	43.8%	12.4%	36.2%	14.1%
Range of Variation	*7.9%*	*9.3%*	*19.9%*	*3.7%*	*21.5%*	*5.9%*	*15.0%*	*6.4%*	*20.5%*	*12.2%*

E. Region of Residence	p<.005		p<.001		p<.005		p<.005		p<.005	
1. B.M.W.	46.2%	**11.0%**	39.9%	**12.5%**	36.8%	**15.8%**	43.8%	**14.8%**	37.5%	**20.3%**
2. Dublin (City & Co.)	60.8%	**11.9%**	58.6%	**11.9%**	56.8%	10.9%	54.4%	**14.6%**	57.3%	19.5%
3. Mid-East & Sth-East	60.0%	**10.7%**	50.7%	**16.5%**	55.0%	**13.8%**	52.5%	**19.1%**	46.1%	21.2%
4. Mid-West & Sth-Wst	68.8%	5.1%	62.6%	6.7%	63.6%	7.6%	59.2%	6.7%	61.0%	14.4%
Range of Variation	*14.6%*	*6.8%*	*22.7%*	*9.8%*	*26.8%*	*8.2%*	*15.4%*	*12.4%*	*23.5%*	*7.8%*

F. Education	p<.005		p<.001		p<.005		p<.005		p<.005	
1. Primary or Less	**62.9%**	18.1%	**55.9%**	18.6%	**56.9%**	18.1%	**54.3%**	22.4%	52.5%	28.8%
2. Incomplete Sec-Lev.	55.0%	**13.7%**	49.0%	**15.3%**	45.9%	**17.7%**	51.3%	14.2%	47.1%	20.7%
3. Complete Sec-Level	58.0%	**11.8%**	50.6%	**14.9%**	50.8%	**15.0%**	50.8%	**16.5%**	48.8%	**22.9%**
4. Third-Level	**60.4%**	3.2%	**55.5%**	5.5%	**57.4%**	4.2%	**54.1%**	8.7%	**53.3%**	12.2%
Range of Variation	*7.9%*	*14.9%*	*6.9%*	*13.1%*	*11.5%*	*13.9%*	*3.5%*	*13.9%*	*6.2%*	*16.6%*

G. Occupational Status	p<.003		p<.001		p<.005		p<.005		p<.009	
1. Unskilled/Semi-Skill.	52.4%	**12.5%**	44.4%	**17.9%**	42.7%	**16.5%**	45.4%	**14.4%**	44.9%	**23.6%**
2. Skilled/R. Non-M.	59.4%	7.4%	**53.8%**	9.8%	**55.2%**	9.8%	**53.7%**	10.7%	**51.2%**	19.1%
3. Inspect./Supervisory	62.1%	**11.3%**	**53.4%**	12.8%	51.9%	**15.8%**	49.6%	**15.0%**	48.9%	17.3%
4. Professional/Exec.	68.2%	7.8%	**61.3%**	9.5%	**62.1%**	9.0%	**62.1%**	13.7%	**58.6%**	14.1%
Range of Variation	*15.8%*	*5.1%*	*16.9%*	*8.4%*	*19.4%*	*7.0%*	*16.7%*	*8.1%*	*9.0%*	*9.4%*

H. Social Class Position	p<.001		p<.001		p<.001		p<.001		p<.001	
1. Class I: "Upper Class"	57.9%	**13.2%**	56.4%	**12.8%**	56.4%	**12.8%**	55.3%	**26.3%**	55.0%	15.0%
2. Class II: "Upr-Mid Cl"	**72.7%**	2.8%	**65.7%**	4.2%	**66.9%**	5.0%	**66.9%**	6.4%	**62.6%**	8.6%
3. Class III: "Mid-M. Cl"	57.1%	6.7%	48.7%	10.0%	50.4%	8.3%	48.5%	12.6%	45.6%	**19.0%**
4. Class IV: "Work.Cl."	57.6%	**12.2%**	50.8%	**13.9%**	49.7%	**16.2%**	48.3%	**14.1%**	47.8%	**21.3%**
5. Class V: "Lower Cl."	57.6%	**12.9%**	49.4%	**18.8%**	50.0%	**17.9%**	56.5%	**16.5%**	57.1%	**26.2%**
Range of Variation	*15.1%*	*6.5%*	*17.0%*	*9.2%*	*16.7%*	*8.9%*	*18.6%*	*19.9%*	*17.0%*	*12.7%*

Notes: Percentages above sample average are in **bold**.   Range of variation percentages are in *italics*.

211

The findings of Table No. 9.7 replicate the overall findings reported in Table No. 7.6 (pages 145-6) where summary results (Mean-Social-Distance Scores) are given. The above Table, however, spells out in more descriptive terms the concrete areas of difference between the performance of eight personal variables, age, marital status, area of birth, place of rearing (in the Republic of Ireland), region of residence, education, occupational status and social class position. Gender failed to elicit a statistically significant variation for any of the five stimulus categories.

The two measures presented on Table No. 9.7 are 'admission to kinship' and 'denial of citizenship' for members of the various stimulus categories reported. Despite the relatively low percentage of respondents who gave **race** as their main reason for not admitting members to kinship (see Table No. 9.1), it is clear from the overall pattern of response that a level of 'implicit racism' is at work. The present author agrees with sociologist, Ashley Doane, when he states that it is possible to convince oneself of being *'colour-blind'*, while at the same time assenting to an ideology of racial inequality. This internal dissonance in our attitudes seems to be a characteristic of Western White People's racialist position[9].

Returning to Table No. 9.7, the level of the **positive** and **negative** dispositions or attitudes of respondents to 'racial and ethnico-racial' stimulus categories are spelled out. On the positive side, the percentages "Welcoming into the family" are, as already noted, encouraging and are beginning to challenge **racial endogamy**, which should be welcomed from a humanity point of view. The level of negativity in the percentages who would "debar/deport" or allow in as "visitors only", (i.e. would deny citizenship) has declined but is still far too high for social comfort. This evidence of polarisation is tending to dampen the positive significance of increases in numbers admitting to kinship.

3.1 Age:
The findings of the age variable are seriously problematic. The '18 to 25 year-olds' level of racism, i.e. relatively low percentages 'admitting to kinship' and relatively high percentages 'denying citizenship' is, once again, difficult to explain. Without being alarmist, this unanticipated finding

---

[9] See Doane, Ashley, "What is Racism? Racial Discourse and Racial Politics", in *Critical Sociology*, No. 32, 2006, pages 255-274.

needs further research before the negative attitudes displayed are translated into hostility towards and discrimination against members of the various ethnico-racial categories.

The range of variations between the subsamples in each of the five stimulus categories is quite substantial and following a clear pattern, i.e. between the '18 to 25 year-olds' and the '26 to 40 year-olds'.

Table No. 9.8:
Differences in Racial/Ethnico-Racial Social-Distance Scores of
18 to 25 year-olds and 26 to 40 year-olds

Stimulus Category		A 18 to 25 year-olds		B 26 to 40 year-olds		B – A Variation	
		Admit	Denial	Admit	Denial	Admit	Denial
1.	Coloureds	44.6%	11.9%	65.2%	6.9%	+ 20.6%	- 3.8%
2.	Afro-Americans	41.9%	15.6%	60.7%	8.0%	+18.8%	-7.6%
3.	Blacks	41.4%	16.0%	60.9%	8.1%	+ 19.5%	- 7.9%
4.	Africans	38.5%	21.3%	63.5%	9.5%	+ 25.0%	- 11.8%
5.	Nigerians	41.7%	23.2%	59.9%	14.6%	+ 18.2%	- 8.6%

Table No. 9.8 highlights, once again, in a clear and patterned way the contrast between the racial and ethnico-racial attitudes of the '18 to 25 year-olds' and the '26 to 40 year-olds'. The significant differences are not only in 'welcoming into kinship' of members of each of the stimulus categories but even more emphatically the differences in percentages who would be willing to 'deny citizenship' to such members. Compared with the '26 to 40 year-olds', the '18 to 25 year-olds' are quite **intolerant** in their attitudes. Again, serious research is required to find out the reasons for relatively highly-educated young people (25 years and younger) in a time of relative economic security (2007 to March 2008) producing the above figures! The socialisation and 'associational' pattern of late teenagers and young adults needs to be examined in order to find out what is obstructing their necessary development towards greater tolerance!

The responses of the older age groups, '56 to 70 years' and '71 years plus' were expected to be more prejudiced (relatively speaking) than the findings show. While 'denial of citizenship' percentages were above average, this was ameliorated somewhat by the number of above average 'welcome-to-kinship' percentages. This polarisation between the responses at each end of the continuum could be attributed not only to the frustrations of old age but also to a sense of fear or anxiety towards strangers!

3.2 Marital Status:

The most significant result in relation to marital status has been the lack of significant variation in relation to Coloureds, Blacks and Nigerians. This means that there is consensus between the different subsamples in relation to fairly substantial levels of social distance. This is probably due to the counterbalancing effects of age and education, area of birth, etc.

In the case of 'Africans' it is interesting to note that 'Married', 'Widowed' and 'Separated/Divorced' are above sample average in 'welcoming them into the family'. Since these three subsamples are most likely to be **parents**, it means that there would be greater support for inter-marriage between people with different physical and physiognomic (visible) traits. This is to be welcomed.

3.3 Area of Birth:

Respondents born in 'Rural/Village' areas are clearly the most reluctant to admit members of the five categories listed as citizens. Some **27.7%** of 'Rural/Village'-born respondents would deny citizenship to 'Nigerians'. This level or negative disposition in the 'Rural/Village'-born population towards 'Nigerians' is much higher than anticipated. The racial nature of the negativity is confirmed by the same subsamples 'denial of citizenship' to 'Blacks' by **20.7%**. This, once again, highlights the continuity of racism in a population which has explicitly underplayed it as in the case of the rationalisation scale (No. 5.1, page 5.4) where only **15.7%** gave 'race' as the main reason for not welcoming Blacks into kinship and an even lower percentage, i.e. **7.4%** gave 'race' in the case of 'Nigerians'. 'Colour blindness' (as expressed in the rationalisation scale) does not measure 'implicit racism'.

Large and Small Towns (sub-variables 2 and 3) are the least racist subsamples on Table No. 9.7(c). They score the highest percentages 'admitting to kinship' across the five stimulus categories and the lowest 'denial of citizenship' scores for each of the five, i.e. 'Coloureds', 'Blacks', 'Afro-Americans', 'Africans' and 'Nigerians'. The town social environment is less conducive to 'ghettoisation' and more suitable for regular favourable contact between members of different and ethnic groups. At the same time 'towns' can regulate and control more tightly those who may reside through the control of housing, and so forth.

3.4 Place of Rearing (in Rep. of Ireland):

This is a nominal variable, although concentration of large urban areas varies from province to province. The results are mixed. 'Munster' respondents elicit an above-average percentage 'admitting to kinship' for all five stimulus categories, while 'Connaught/Ulster' respondents are below average in their 'denial-of-citizenship' percentages in each of the five categories. The 'Rest-of-Leinster' attitudes seem the least positive of the 'Place-of-Rearing' sub-variables.

3.5 Region of Residence:

Again, the findings are fairly mixed in this nominal variable. It could be argued that the minority make-up of the regional population and the favourableness of the intergroup contact in the regions would affect the responses.

The BMW cluster of regions seems to have the most negative results, i.e. with **below average** percentages 'admitting to kinship' and **above average** percentages for 'denial of citizenship' in the case of **all** racial and ethnico-racial stimulus categories on Table No. 9.7(e). The reader may wish to examine the findings of the other three sub-variables to find out the profile of social distance in the different clusters of regions.

3.6 Educational Standard Achieved:

This is an ordinal variable which gives insight into the impact of education on the people's level of 'racism' as measured by social distance in relation to five 'Racial and Ethnico-Racial' categories. The results are not as anticipated. In the case of 'admitting to kinship', the **least** educated and the **highest** educated were the two subsamples most in favour in every case. The 'middle subsamples', i.e. those with 'Incomplete Second Level' and 'Complete Second Level' were the most prejudiced.

It is difficult to explain this unexpected result. The anomaly in the age variable would obviously affect the education variables' results. The effect of education on tolerance is quite disappointing. Perhaps it is time to question the predominant influence of economic pragmatism on education policy in Ireland since the 1960s (following the publication of *Investment in Education*[10]). The anomaly of the age and education findings in relation to social distance is discussed in pages 156-160 above.

3.7 Occupational Status:

The findings of the 'Occupational Status' variable were somewhat as predicted. The top professionals and executives were the most tolerant in relation to the 'racial and ethnico-racial' categories examined. The least tolerant subsample was in the 'Unskilled/Semi-Skilled' classification. The other two subsamples performed relatively positively.

It is interesting to note from the history of the **racial desegregation of South Africa** the positive role played by industrial leaders in challenging the economic folly of *apartheid*. Racism interfered with the priority of "talent for the job" in the case of the 'colour barrier' to promotion in the farm, factory, mine or office. The pragmatic industrialists saw that talent was not determined by colour, etc. There is evidence of such positive realism in the Republic of Ireland in the findings of Table No. 9.7(g). Insecurity is possibly a factor in the relatively negative score of the 'Unskilled/Semi-Skilled' subsample.

3.8 Social Class Position:

Some of the findings of this independent variable were mixed and not as anticipated. "Upper Class" were above average in 'admitting to kinship' in each of the five stimulus categories as in line with expectations. They were also above average in the percentages 'denying citizenship' which was not expected.

Above-average percentages 'denying citizenship' to each of the five categories by the "Lower Class" and "Working Class" sub-variables was anticipated. The findings of the five subscales, however, point to the "Upper-Middle Class" and "Middle-Middle Class" as the most tolerant sub-sample in the case of all categories.

---

[10] Lynch, Patrick, *Investment in Education*, Dublin, OECD, 1966.

Part IV – Conclusion

In the course of Chapter IX the level of **'racism'** in the Republic of Ireland between November 2007 and March 2008 has been presented and discussed in some detail. Earlier in the text the general findings on racism have been referred to on a number of occasions (see Chapter VI above). In previous discussion the main emphasis was more on **ethnocentrism rather than racism**. In the current chapter, the emphasis is in reverse, i.e. primarily on **racism**, which is quite a complex phenomenon in Irish society today.

There were two major measures of racism used in the current chapter, i.e. the *"Special Racialist Scale"* and the *"Bogardus Social Distance Scale"*. With regard to the latter, a selection of five stimulus categories, i.e. 'Coloureds', 'Blacks', 'Afro-Americans', 'Africans' and 'Nigerians' were measured in relation to the percentages 'admitting them to kinship' and the proportions 'denying them citizenship'. This examination, as in the case of the *'Special Racialist Scale'*, was carried out in detail, i.e. by personal variables.

Overall the findings were both positive and disappointing. Social-distance levels improved, while in the case of the *Special Racialist Scale*, findings showed more or less the same results as in 1988-89. The **average improvement** in (nominal) percentages 'admitting to kinship' for the five categories between 1988-89 and 2007-08 was **+23%**, i.e. from 30% to 53%, while the average **decrease** in percentages 'denying citizenship' was -5%, i.e. from 18% to 13%. Both percentages show room for further improvement.

The analysis of the findings of the *'Special Racialist Scale'* and the *'Bogardus Social Distance Scale'* showed a difference in the responses of age and education. The former scale was as anticipated, i.e. positive correlation between 'age' and 'prejudice' and a negative correlation in the case of 'education', while social distance findings were in the opposite direction. The reasons for such differences would need further research to explain them. Is the Special Scale measuring more the respondents' 'colour blindness' while social distance is unearthing implicit racialism?

While the level of racialism, as measured by social distance, has reduced substantially and racial tolerance has improved correspondingly, it would be irresponsible to ignore the unacceptable remaining degree of prejudice. 'Denial of citizenship' percentages are still too high, i.e. **10% or higher** in the case of the total sample. When the findings of Table No. 9.7 (pages 210-11) are gauged, some issues of concern emerge, e.g. the *range of variation* within the variables. Also, the geographic factor seemed to play a substantial and significant role in the case of each of the five stimulus categories tested, i.e. 'Coloureds', 'Afro-Americans', 'Blacks', 'Africans' and 'Nigerians'. The findings for social-class position and occupational status were interesting and more or less as expected. Unlike the performance of the *Special Racialist Scales* in the case of **age**, the *Bogardus Social Distance* results were contrary to expectation with the youngest age-cohort (18 to 25 year-olds) being among the most prejudiced. The Bogardus findings are likely to be closer to the pre-reflective dispositions of respondents as they measure their "first-feeling responses".

Finally, the brief scan of current views of human scientists on the phenomenon of 'race' and 'racism/racialism' given in Part I of this chapter (see pages 193-200) raises very important questions about the nature of racism and its continued presence in the attitudes and dispositions of a substantial proportion of the adult population. The failure of the **18ᵗʰ century** *'Enlightenment'* to perceive the basic equality of all racial groupings and categories is a serious limitation of post-Renaissance European culture. The evidence of history bears this out with the acceptance of **'racial slavery'** during the centuries of European colonial expansionism (and the failure to outlaw sexism and anti-Semitism)!

It would be unfair to the evidence to end on a negative note in face of the positive advances in the substantial reduction of racial prejudice between 1988-89 and 2007-08. Hopefully, the downturn in the Irish economy since the summer of 2008 will not reverse such welcome progress towards the elimination of the 'myth of race'!

***

CHAPTER X
Attitudes towards Northern Ireland

Part I – Introduction

1.1: In the course of the thirty-five years, i.e. 1972 until 2007, the situation in Northern Ireland has changed radically. The violent conflict had, for all practical purposes, ceased within the Northern Ireland community since 1994. Successful negotiations have been achieved between the Unionists and the Nationalists and between the Irish and British Governments. The 1998 *Good Friday Agreement* marked a major step forward towards community integration in Northern Ireland and was given overwhelming public support in the Republic of Ireland. The setting-up of a devolved Northern Ireland Administration has taken a number of years to settle in since 1998. The *St Andrew's Agreement* (2006) paved the way for **Sinn Féin** and the **Democratic Unionist Part**y to lead a joint administration from **a largely working-class background** and provide a *modus vivendi* for the republicans and more committed loyalists to share power. The long-term effect of this arrangement will be the de-radicalisation of the more revolutionary loyalist and republican leaderships. Paramilitary strife has made way for political negotiation and democratic compromise! Such a development can be explained theoretically by the "momentum model of society" (see pages 49-51 above). The recent **Saville Enquiry Report (2010)** acknowledged the innocence of those killed by the British Army in Derry on 'Bloody Sunday'. This will contribute further to the reconciliation of nationalists within the Northern Ireland community. The positive work for reconciliation between Loyalists and Republicans in Northern Ireland supported by **President Mary McAleese** and her husband **Dr Martin McAleese** since 1997 has been significant.

1.2: The developments in Northern Ireland since 1972-73 have been indirectly monitored by the present author in his three major social surveys, i.e. 1972-73 (Greater Dublin)[1], 1988-89 (National Sample)[2] and 2007-08 (the current National Survey). In the *Bogardus Social Distance Scale* three stimulus categories are of special interest, i.e. **'Northern Irish'**, **'Protestants'** and **'Unionists'**. An examination of variations and changes in social-distance scores towards the three selected categories will give an

---

[1] Mac Gréil, Micheál, (1977), *Prejudice and Tolerance in Ireland*, Dublin, C.I.R.
[2] Mac Gréil, Micheál, (1996), *Prejudice in Ireland Revisited*, Maynooth, St Patrick's College.

insight into the changes in attitudes towards significant categories in Northern Ireland by a representative national sample (overwhelmingly Roman Catholic).

1.3: The *Special Northern Ireland Scale* is made up of twelve items which measure **opinions** concerning issues of relevance to the development of intergroup relations on the 'Island of Ireland'. It will be possible to measure changes in the responses to the questions/statements on this scale since 1972-73 when the scale was first devised by the present author. The items in the Northern Irish Scale cover a number of areas of interest, i.e. *(a) Catholic-Protestant Identity; (b) National and Community Unity*; and *(c) Cooperation and Violence.* The impact of the political progress since 1994 is expected to have had a positive effect on the replies to most items.

1.4: **Attitudes towards Britain** are closely linked to the 'Northern Ireland Problem'. The latter has had a negative effect on Irish-British relations since the 1920s and, for that matter, ever since the Reformation in the 16th century. The positive role played by the British Government under the leadership of Prime Minister, **Mr Tony Blair, MP**, in facilitating the negotiations leading up to the *Good Friday Agreement*[3] is generally recognised. The leadership of *An Taoiseach*, **Mr Bertie Ahern, TD**, was also crucial in the final negotiations. Other British and Irish political leaders had helped earlier to prepare the way for the final agreement, especially **Mr John Hume, MP, Mr Gerry Adams, MP, Mr Martin McGuinness, MP**, and **Rev Dr Ian Paisley, MP.** The *Anglo-Irish Agreement of 1985* negotiated between the then *Taoiseach*, **Dr Garret Fitzgerald, TD** and the British Prime Minister, **Mrs Margaret Thatcher, MP**, was an important precursor to later agreements, as was the initiative of **Mr Albert Reynolds, TD**, during his time as *Taoiseach.* **Fr Alex Reid, Fr Denis Faul** and other members of the clergy on all sides worked constantly for peace and justice in Northern Ireland over the years.

In measuring attitudes towards the British it is proposed to examine the social-distance scores towards 'British', 'English', Scottish and 'Welsh' and to evaluate the findings of the Anti-British Special Scale. Irish attitudes towards the British are measured in the next chapter, Chapter XI.

---

[3] The important contribution of the U.S. Government under the leadership of **President Bill Clinton** and his envoy, **Senator George Mitchell**, was also crucial.

1.5: The *Anti-British Scale* will be tested in relation to the survival of the phenomenon of *post-colonial attitudinal schizophrenia*. It is anticipated that it will be substantially reduced according as the Irish people gain self-confidence *vis-à-vis* their former 'colonial masters'! The historical effects of past perceived grievances against Britain also incorporate 'social-class' injustices which have survived, despite political independence. The class-structure in Ireland has survived post-independence republicanism. Membership of the European Union has not successfully promoted an effective policy of social egalitarianism so far. The real threat may well be that Brussels will replace London as the source of a new master class! This, in turn, could lead to a sense of powerlessness (alienation) which was at the root of 'post-colonial attitudinal schizophrenia' reported in the 1972-73 and 1988-89 surveys[4].

Part II – Northern Ireland Stimulus Categories

2.1 Social Distance of Total Sample:

The three stimulus categories, i.e. Northern Irish, Protestants and Unionists, tested in Table No. 10.1 are likely to provide a glimpse of attitudes in the Republic of Ireland towards Northern Ireland. The findings are compared with those of 1972-73 and 1988-89.

Table No. 10.1:
'Admit to Kinship' and 'Deny Citizenship' Responses for 2007-08, 1988-89 and 1972-73 for Northern Stimulus Categories

Year of Survey	'Northern Irish'		'Protestants'		'Unionists'		Av. No.
	Admit to Kinship	Deny Citizenship	Admit to Kinship	Deny Citizenship	Admit to Kinship	Deny Citizenship	
(a) National Sample							
1. 2007-08	75.1%	4.3%	78.4%	2.6%	66.2%	8.0%	1,010
2. 1988-89	70.9%	2.6%	62.2%	1.6%	33.4%	18.6%	1,002
Change (1-2)	+4.2%	+1.7%	+16.2%	+1.0%	+32.8%	-10.6%	---
(b) Dublin Subsample							
3. 2007-08	76.8%	4.3 %	80.1%	1.8%	74.0%	3.5%	285
4. 1988-89	79.7%	---	79.0%	1.0%	---	---	265
5. 1972-73 (sample)	79.5%	2.8%	73.0%	1.0%	---	---	2,269
Change (3-4)	-2.9%	---	+1.1%	+0.8%	---	---	---
Change (3-5)	-2.7%	+1.5%	+7.1%	+0.8%	---	---	---
Change (4-5)	+0.2%	---	+6.0%	0.0%	---	---	---

---

[4] See Mac Gréil, Micheál, (1996), *Prejudice in Ireland Revisited*, Má Nuad, St Patrick's College, pp. 262ff.

The two measures of social distance chosen for analysis are from the **positive** and **negative** extremes of the *Bogardus Social Distance Scale*. The significance is self-explanatory to the reader. The measures in question are:
- (a) *"Admit to Kinship";* and
- (b) *"Deny Citizenship".*

These two measures are compared (in Table No. 10.1) with the previous findings in the 1972-73 and 1988-89 surveys, which were carried out at times when paramilitary violence was very severe in Northern Ireland. In addition, the responses are examined (in Table No. 10.2) by personal variables, i.e., age, gender, marital status, area of birth, place of rearing, region of residence, education, occupation and social-class position (i.e. social status). From this analysis certain patterns will be established which will help to explain variations and predict trends.

2.1.1 Northern Irish: Overall the changes in attitudes towards the three categories have been positive and show a welcome increase in tolerance and mutual respect [see Table No. 10.1(a)]. The category to change least was 'Northern Irish', largely because its original rating both nationally and in the case of the Dublin subsample was relatively high (at over 70% 'admitting to kinship'). With the changes in the Dublin subsample there was a slight drop in percentages 'admitting to kinship' between each of the surveys.

The above findings show a definite improvement in Social Distance in relation to the three categories, i.e. 'Northern Irish', 'Protestants' and 'Unionists'. While 'Northern Irish' 'admission to kinship' improved by a nominal **4.2%** between 1988-89 and 2007-08, their 'denial of citizenship' scores rose by **1.7%**, which was not expected. On the overall *rank-ordering of 51 categories* on Table No. 4.1 (pages 62-4 above), 'Northern Irish' rank 17th out of 51 categories, less favoured than 'Welsh' (6th), 'English' (9th), 'Scottish' (11th), 'Protestants' (13th) and 'British' (15th).

The relatively lower ranking of 'Northern Irish' raises serious questions for communities both sides of the Border. Favourable contact needs to be promoted between people in the Republic of Ireland and those living in Northern Ireland. Also highly publicised **manifestations of hostility** between loyalist and nationalist communities are most likely to contribute to the anomalous position of 'Northern Irish' in the rank order of preference reported on Table No. 4.1 (pages 62-4 above). The legacy of generations of violence, hostility and resentment may take some time to heal. Special efforts will be required to bring about the still much-needed improvement in mutual respect and even preference for fellow-Irish brothers and sisters north of the Border!

2.1.2 Unionists: The very substantial improvement in the standing of 'Unionists' between 1988-89 and 2007-08 (national samples) has already been commented on (see page 76 above). The doubling of the percentages (from **33.4%** in 1988-89 to **66.2%** in 2007-08) who would welcome 'Unionists' into kinship is very noteworthy and bodes well for the future of relations between Northern Ireland and the Republic of Ireland. The coming closer of 'Unionists'/'Loyalists' and 'Nationalists/'Republicans' through pragmatic and realistic negotiations and cooperation is affirmed in these findings. The *post-bellum* situation is a big advance of the *ante bellum* social distance[5]. What makes this finding more significant still is the greater than halving of the percentage who would deny citizenship to 'Unionists', i.e. from **18.6%** in 1988-89 to **7.9%** in 2007-08. Readers should remember that these findings reflect the current **popular** views of a random sample of adults (18 years and over) in the Republic of Ireland in 2007-08. Leaders, advisers and others who worked for a peaceful solution to the Northern Irish problem should feel reassured by these findings. At the same time, there is little room for complacency because the residue of negativity from the past can always ignite passions and promote prejudice (i.e. hatred) if the momentum for peace and justice is not maintained and the authorities lower their vigilance in the restoration of inclusive social justice.

In terms of rank-order position, the 'Unionists' went from **33rd** (in 1988-89) to **26th** (in 2007-08) among the 46 categories measured in both surveys. These results give a convincing mark of approval to the developments in the political arrangements in Northern Ireland from a representative sample of the adult population in the Republic of Ireland.

2.1.3 Protestants: The partition of Ireland in the 1920s into the **Irish Free State** (26 Counties) and Northern Ireland (6 Counties) was on religious and political lines, i.e. the Irish Free State overwhelmingly Roman Catholic (**92.6%**) and Northern Ireland predominantly Protestant (**62.2%**). For that reason current attitudes in the Republic of Ireland towards Protestants are very significant. Table No. 10.1 shows a *substantial improvement* in the standing of 'Protestants'. Their MSD score is under 1.500 thereby putting

---

[5] See: Coulter, Colin and Murray, Michael, (2008) *Northern Ireland after the Troubles, a Society in Transition*, Manchester, Manchester University Press.

them in the in-group class. The significant (nominal) improvement in percentage of 16.2% admitting Protestants to kinship, i.e. from **62.2%** in 1988-89 to **78.4%** in 2007-08, is most noteworthy. This clearly shows that *the last vestiges of significant anti-Protestantism* in the Republic of Ireland are being removed at present.

The changes in attitudes towards Protestants by a predominantly Roman Catholic national sample [reflecting the denominational (demographic) distribution in the Republic] is also to be welcomed and is quite substantial. Interdenominational animosity in Northern Ireland in modern times and throughout the whole island of Ireland in early modern (post-Reformation) times had fuelled political and social strife throughout the land. The finding reflects preparedness for a higher degree of **ecumenical pluralism**. While some of the decline in interdenominational conflict or prejudice may be due to a growth in **religious indifference**[6], nevertheless, it will be seen in Table No. 10.3 below that the older and more devout people are among those strongest in support of Christian Unity (see Chapter XVII below).

2.1.4 Conclusion: In conclusion, the three Northern Ireland related stimulus categories have performed quite positively in the 2007-08 survey, when compared with previous findings. These findings reflect changes in attitudes which are central to the continued progress towards **pluralist integration** in Northern Ireland and throughout the island of Ireland. The challenge facing Irish people is to keep up the momentum and continue to maintain tolerance and reduce interdenominational and inter-political prejudice. The promotion of occasions of **favourable contact**, including increased cross-border holidaying, is very important. The above findings constitute evidence of positive 'peace dividends'!

2.2 Social Distance to Northern Categories by Personal Variables:
Table No. 10.2 measures percentages 'admitting to kinship' and 'denying citizenship' in relation to the three categories, i.e. 'Northern Irish', 'Protestants' and 'Unionists' by personal variables. The findings reported on Table No. 10.2 below are quite mixed and do not perform as anticipated in the majority of variables. This is owing to the complex set of attitudes

---

[6] See: MacGréil, Micheál (2009) *The Challenge of Indifference: A Need for Religious Revival in Ireland*, Maynooth, Survey and Research Unit, pp. 17/18 and Chapter XVII below.

which Irish people (in the Republic) have towards Northern Ireland, as shown in the Northern Ireland Scale (Table No. 10.3, page 231) below.

Table No. 10.2:
Percentages 'Admitting to Kinship' and 'Denying Citizenship'
to 'Northern Irish', 'Protestants' and 'Unionists' by Personal Variables

Personal Variable	'Northern Irish'		'Protestants'		'Unionists'		Average No.
	Admit to Kinship	Deny Citz'ship	Admit to Kinship	Deny Citz'ship	Admit to Kinship	Deny Citz'ship	
Total Sample	**75.1%**	**4.3%**	**78.4%**	**2.6%**	**66.2%**	**7.9%**	1,010
A. Age	P<.001		P<.004		P<.001		
1. 18-25 years	69.5%	**5.4%**	67.5%	**6.5%**	57.4%	**16.0%**	167
2. 26-40 years	**79.2%**	3.1%	**79.8%**	1.8%	**69.2%**	7.1%	318
3. 41-55 years	71.5%	**6.9%**	78.9%	2.4%	67.9%	4.5%	244
4. 56-70 years	**75.7%**	1.1%	**83.1%**	1.1%	64.6%	6.6%	175
5. 71 years plus	**80.2%**	5.2%	**83.5%**	1.0%	**70.1%**	**9.3%**	96
Range of Variation	*10.7%*	*5.8%*	*16.0%*	*5.5%*	*12.7%*	*11.5%*	*1,000*
B. Gender	N/S		P<.005		P<.001		
1. Males	---	---	78.4%	2.2%	**66.7%**	**9.4%**	498
2. Females	---	---	78.2%	**2.9%**	65.8%	6.4%	512
Range of Variation	*---*	*---*	*0.2%*	*0.9%*	*0.9%*	*3.0%*	*1,010*
C. Marital Status	P<.001		P<.001		P<.001		
1. Single/Never Married	72.9%	**6.7%**	73.5%	**3.6%**	64.4%	**11.5%**	357
2. Married	**76.6%**	2.6%	**82.6%**	1.7%	**66.7%**	5.3%	471
3. Separated/Divorced	**82.2%**	2.2%	**84.1%**	2.3%	**72.7%**	6.8%	44
4. Permanent Relation'p	69.0%	4.2%	66.7%	**2.8%**	60.6%	**8.4%**	71
5. Widowed	**80.6%**	4.5%	**82.9%**	1.4%	**73.9%**	**8.6%**	69
Range of Variation	*11.6%*	*4.5%*	*17.4%*	*2.2%*	*13.3%*	*6.2%*	*1,012*
D. Area of Birth	P<.001		P<.011		P<.001		
1. City (100,000+)	73.1%	3.3%	**79.6%**	1.2%	**68.6%**	4.6%	416
2. Large Town (10,000+)	75.6%	**5.8%**	**82.4%**	**5.0%**	**68.9%**	4.2%	119
3. Town (1,500+)	**88.4%**	0.8%	78.3%	0.8%	**68.2%**	**9.3%**	129
4. Rural/Village	72.3%	**6.4%**	75.7%	**3.8%**	61.5%	**12.8%**	343
Range of Variation	*16.1%*	*5.6%*	*6.7%*	*4.2%*	*7.4%*	*8.6%*	*1,007*
E. Place of Rearing (ROI)	P<.001		P<.018		P<.001		
1. Dublin (City & Co.)	74.4%	**3.0%**	**79.9%**	1.1%	**71.4%**	3.8%	246
2. Rest of Leinster	76.2%	**5.5%**	79.4%	1.2%	63.8%	**16.0%**	159
3. Munster	**79.7%**	1.3%	78.9%	**3.9%**	**69.0%**	8.2%	231
4. Connaught/Ulster	68.3%	**6.7%**	73.0%	3.1%	56.4%	5.5%	159
Range of Variation	*11.4%*	*5.4%*	*6.9%*	*2.1%*	*15.0%*	*10.5%*	*795*
F. Region of Residence	P<.001		P<.001		P<.001		
1. B.M.W.	66.8%	**7.4%**	74.4%	2.2%	53.3%	**11.9%**	273
2. Dublin	**76.6%**	**4.5%**	**80.4%**	1.8%	**73.9%**	3.6%	285
3. Mid-East & South-East	**76.9%**	4.2%	74.8%	**6.9%**	64.1%	**14.8%**	218
4. Mid-West & Sth-West	**81.3%**	0.9%	**84.0%**	0.4%	**73.8%**	2.1%	237
Range of Variation	*14.5%*	*6.5%*	*9.6%*	*6.5%*	*20.6%*	*12.7%*	*1,013*

Table No. 10.2 cont'd. **Personal Variable**	'Northern Irish'		'Protestants'		'Unionists'		**Average No.**
	Admit to Kinship	Deny Citz'ship	Admit to Kinship	Deny Citz'ship	Admit to Kinship	Deny Citz'ship	
G. Education	P<.001		P<.007		P<.02		
1. Primary or Less	**84.6%**	**5.2%**	**88.9%**	0.0%	**76.8%**	7.6%	117
2. Incomplete Sec.-Level	72.8%	**5.4%**	**80.8%**	2.3%	64.0%	**8.0%**	261
3. Complete Sec.-Level	**75.8%**	**4.8%**	71.8%	**4.7%**	62.6%	**9.5%**	255
4. Third-Level	73.5%	3.5%	78.0%	1.9%	**66.3%**	6.9%	378
Range of Variation	*11.8%*	*1.9%*	*17.1%*	*4.7%*	*14.2%*	*2.6%*	*1,011*
H. Occupational Status	P<.001		P<.005		P<.039		
1. Unskilled/Semi-Sk.	70.5%	3.3%	75.7%	**4.9%**	65.4%	**9.7%**	205
2. Skilled/R. Non-Man.	74.5%	**6.6%**	**78.8%**	3.0%	65.2%	7.4%	325
3. Inspect./Supervisory	73.7%	**6.1%**	**81.2%**	0.0%	64.1%	**9.2%**	131
4. Professional/Exec.	**85.3%**	0.5%	**83.2%**	0.0%	**73.8%**	4.1%	191
Range of Variation	*14.8%*	*6.1%*	*7.5%*	*4.9%*	*9.5%*	*5.6%*	*852*
I. Social Class Position	P<.001		P<.001		P<.001		
1. Class I "Upper Class"	**86.8%**	0.0%	**79.5%**	0.0%	**69.2%**	**12.8%**	38
2. Class II "Upper-Middle"	**87.1%**	0.0%	**87.1%**	0.0%	**77.3%**	2.1%	140
3. Class III "Middle-Middle"	70.4%	**4.9%**	76.2%	2.2%	60.2%	**9.7%**	226
4. Class IV "Working Class"	72.6%	**6.4%**	76.3%	**3.3%**	65.7%	**8.3%**	361
5. Class V "Lower Class"	**79.8%**	3.6%	**87.1%**	**3.6%**	**71.1%**	6.0%	83
Range of Variation	*16.7%*	*6.4%*	*10.9%*	*3.6%*	*17.1%*	*10.7%*	*848*

Note: Percentages above sample average are **in bold**. Range of Variation in *italics*.

2.2.1 Age: Age as a variable for most social distance findings has been quite problematic. The youngest age group, 18 to 25 years, has recorded the highest level of intolerance towards the three categories. This group recorded the lowest percentages 'admitting to kinship' in the case of each of the three and the highest percentages 'denying citizenship' to 'Northern Irish' and to 'Unionists'. It was anticipated that the younger, highly educated, would be more tolerant and less prejudiced. The findings reject this and leave the 'researcher' in search of an adequate explanation.

Because the younger cohort 18 to 25 years vary so much from the middle-age and older respondents, it raises the question of the level and depth of inter-generational contact in modern Ireland for a substantial percentage of young people. It also raised the question of the quality of our youth culture. Is its **ethos** more open to prejudice than it was in the past, i.e. that of previous generations? **Serious research** into its impact on young people and their ability to become citizens with minimum bias and prejudice is needed. There does not seem to be an adequate substitute for person-to-person relationships in community! See the special commentary on the relative intolerance of the 18 to 25 year-olds, i.e. pages 156-160 above.

2.2.2 Gender: This variable produced significant variation only in the case of 'Unionists'. There was inter-gender consensus in relation to 'Northern Irish' and 'Protestants'. Males were marginally but not significantly more in favour of admitting 'Unionists' to kinship than females, i.e. only **1.1%.** The margin in the percentages 'denying citizenship' to 'Unionists' was significantly higher between males and females.

2.2.3 Marital Status: The responses of the 18 to 25 year-olds have (obviously) influenced the relatively negative scores of the 'Single/Never Married' sub-sample. The 'Married', 'Widowed' and 'Separated/Divorced' subsamples have scored above average in 'admitting to kinship' members of the three stimulus categories. The 'Widowed' repeated the tolerance of the old age group (71 years plus).

The significance of the findings of the Marital Status variable is evidence of the growing acceptance of the Northern categories and the implicit affirmation of the new peace arrangement, i.e. the *Good Friday Agreement* (1998) and the subsequent agreement which resulted in the joint administration. The above-average of the subsample's scores is most likely to reflect parents' tolerance which is important. The only disappointing finding is the relatively negative performance of the 'Single/Never Married'.

2.2.4 Area of Birth and Place of Rearing: Area of Birth means the influence of the degree of urbanisation on the attitudes of respondents towards the Northern Categories. 'Rural/Village' respondents are the least welcoming subsample in the case of each of the three stimulus categories, i.e. 'Northern Irish', 'Protestants' and 'Unionists'. The urban-born findings varied between 'Town', 'Large Town' and 'City'.

Place of Rearing refers to the province in which respondents spent the first sixteen years or the greater part of that time. The findings are quite mixed. The 'Connaught/Ulster' respondents 'admitting Unionists into kinship' is 10% below the sample average at **56.4%.** In this subsample there are respondents from the Border Counties!

2.2.5 Region of Residence: The subsample with the most negative score has been respondents from the BMW cluster of regions [see Table No.10.2 (f)]. Again, this subsample has a proportion of respondents from the Border Counties. The most positively disposed towards members of each of the three Northern Stimulus Categories were the respondents from the Mid-

227

West/South West, i.e. the Munster cluster of regions. This is in line with the findings of other measures of social distance. The relatively high percentage of 'BMW' and 'Mid-East/South East' subsamples who would deny citizenship to Unionists (**11.9%** and **14.8%** respectively) is disappointing and is not easy to explain.

2.2.6 Education: The performance of education was **not** as anticipated, which expected those with highest educational achievement to register the most tolerant results. Once again, these findings raise questions about the 'quality' of Irish education as a source of greater tolerance and self-therapeutic in relation to prejudice and narrow-mindedness. Since there is no correlation between intelligence and authoritarianism[7], we are dependent on socialisation to challenge the latter[8].

The relatively negative performance by respondents with 'Third-Level' education in the percentage 'admitting to kinship' in the case of 'Northern Irish' and 'Protestants' is more than significant when compared with those with 'Primary or Less', i.e.

'Admit to Kinship'

Education	'Northern Irish'	'Protestants'	'Unionists'
1. Primary or Less	84.6%	88.9%	76.8%
2. Third Level	73.5%	78.0%	66.3%
Difference (1-2)	+11.1%	+10.9%	+10.5%

This is difficult to explain and goes against the anticipated findings which expected the results to be in the opposite direction. Of course, the unanticipated findings in the **age** variable probably contributed to the mixed results in education (or *vice versa*). What may be problematic about these results is their significance for the direction of future trends in public attitudes. When age and education are not producing expected correlations with prejudice, regress rather than progress can follow; hence, the necessity to reappraise the quality of Irish education at the second and third levels.

2.2.7 Occupational Status: The findings for Occupational Status are far healthier than those for 'Education' or 'Age'. It would seem necessary to

---

[7] See: Adorno, T.W. *et al*, *The Authoritarian Personality*, New York, Harper, 1950.
[8] Mac Gréil, Micheál (1977) *Prejudice and Tolerance in Ireland*, Dublin, CIF.
        (1996) *Prejudice in Ireland Revisited*.

focus attention on age as a serious cause of the proportionate negativity (and the failure of current second-level and third-level education in making a higher proportion of young graduates more tolerant).   Also, it could point to the superiority of education in earlier decades in liberating graduates from prejudice.   Of course, the wisdom and maturity of experience of life, as well as the security of senior occupations, contribute to a lower level of social prejudice.

The 'Professional/Executive' subsample has the highest percentage 'admitting to kinship' and the lowest 'denying citizenship' in the case of each of the three Northern stimulus categories.   The largest subsample, 'Skilled Manual and Routine Non-Manual', were very close to the average scores in the responses for each of the three categories, i.e. 'Northern Irish', 'Protestants' and 'Unionists'.

2.2.8 Social Class Position: As already noted, respondents' social class position is a compound variable measuring social status.   Education and occupational status are divided into seven grades and then weighted by factor of **four** and **seven** respectively.   The combined scores of 11 to 77 are divided into five classes as outlined on Table No. 10.2(i).   This method of discovering social class position was originally devised by A.B. Hollingshead.

The findings are mixed and out of line with what was anticipated, i.e. that there would be a positive correlation between social class position and 'admission to kinship', the higher the respondents' social class position the greater the percentage 'admitting to kinship'.   But this has not been confirmed in the findings.   The "lower class" (Class V) and the two highest classes ("Upper Class" and "Upper-Middle Class") were above the sample average.   It is encouraging that the two highest 'classes' have relatively **high scores** for kinship in all three categories and **zero** 'denial-of-citizenship' percentages in regard to 'Northern Irish' and 'Protestants'.   The above average 'denial of citizenship' for 'Unionists' by Class I ("Upper Class") was not anticipated!

2.2.9 Conclusion: The findings of Table No.10.2 merit close examination by the reader.   The findings reflect the dispositions of the Irish adult population.   They are fluctuations on a basically positive sample score. The counter-balancing of the age and other variables seems to have contributed to intra-variable anomalies.   The relatively high range of variations in a large proportion of subscales would seem to point to the dynamic state of attitudes towards the three stimulus categories, i.e. 'Northern Irish', 'Protestants' and 'Unionists'.

Part III – Special Northern Ireland Scale

3.1 Introduction:

This scale was devised originally for inclusion in the 1972-73 survey of intergroup attitudes in the Greater Urban-Suburban area of Dublin.   As stated in *Prejudice and Tolerance in Ireland* (1977): This scale was "designed especially to measure attitudes and opinions toward Northern Ireland" and was not a prejudice scale, as such[9].

The special Northern Ireland Scale can be divided into three factors:
>   (a) *Catholic-Protestant Identity* (1, 2 & 3)
>   (b) *National and Community Unity* (4, 5, 6, 7 & 8)
>   (c) *Cooperation and Violence* (9, 10, 11 & 12)

The perception of Catholic-Protestant common identity *versus* common cross-community identity is measured in Item Nos. 1, 2 and 3.   In other words, are people seen to have more in common with their fellow-coreligionists than with their fellow-citizens in Northern Ireland and in the Republic of Ireland?   The fluctuations in the responses since 1972-73 will be duly noted.

National and Community Unity have been major issues at the root of the integration of Northern Ireland and its relations with the Republic of Ireland.   In a relatively small area the **'unity'** and **'loyalty'** issues have led to strife, misery and disunity for generations.   Movement towards agreement on these issues has been quite slow and tedious to date.

Attitudes/opinions towards cooperation and violence in regard to Northern Ireland have not been straightforward and reflect the tragic history of mistrust and intransigence for generations.   The findings of Table No. 10.3 will record that there is still an uncomfortable degree of ambivalence in the Republic of Ireland towards the goal of mutual cooperation and social integration, despite significant improvements.

---

[9] Mac Gréil, Micheál, (1977), *Prejudice and Tolerance in Ireland*, Dublin, C.I.R., p.375.

It is proposed to reflect on the items of each of the sub-scales separately. One aspect of most of the responses has been the substantial increase in the percentages opting for the **'don't know'** answer. Generally speaking, an increase in 'don't know' replies is indicative of a mood of change in relation to the particular attitudes or opinions.

Table No. 10.3: Northern Ireland Scale – 2007-08 and 1988-89

Question: *"Northern Ireland is a topic of interest and concern for many people; I would like to get your views on some aspects relating to the Northern problems. Would you agree or disagree with each of the following statements?"*

	Item	Agree	Neither/ Don't Know	Disagree	Number
1.	"Catholics in Northern Ireland have more in common with Northern Protestants than they have with Catholics in the Republic."	26.6% (45.0%)	43.6% (21.0%)	29.9% (34.0)	1,011 (998)
2.	"Protestants in the Republic have more in common with Catholics here than they have with Protestants in Northern Ireland."	40.1% (67.0%)	41.9% (16.0%)	18.0% (16.0%)	1,011 (998)
3.	"Northern Irish Protestants have more in common with the rest of the Irish people than they have with the British."	26.8% (36.0%)	43.9% (20.0%)	29.2% (44.0%)	1,008 (997)
4.	"Northern Ireland and the Republic of Ireland are two separate nations."	38.5% (49.0%)	22.3% (9.0%)	39.1% (42.0%)	1,010 (999)
5.	"Having separate Catholic and Protestant schools (Primary and Secondary Schools) has been a major cause of division in the Northern community."	65.8% (74.0%)	27.6% (13.0%)	6.6% (13.0%)	1,010 (1,000)
6.	"A return to the Irish language and culture could provide a good basis for Irish unity in the long-term (even though it might present difficulties in the short term)."	30.0% (24.0%)	37.5% (19.0%)	32.5% 57.0%)	1,011 (1,000)
7.	"The position and influence of the Catholic Church in the Republic is a real obstacle to Irish unity."	29.0% (36.0%)	37.7% (20.0%)	33.3% (45.0%)	1,011 (997)
8.	"National unity is an essential condition for the just solution of the present Northern problems."	42.0% (50.0%)	38.0% (25.0%)	20.0% (25.0%)	1,010 (999)
9.	"There should be increased cooperation across the Border with people in Northern Ireland."	72.6% (90.0%)	25.0% (7.0%)	2.4% (3.0%)	1,011 (999)
10.	"The *'Good Friday Agreement'* (1998) provides a good basis for community cooperation."	75.4% ---	22.3% ---	3.2% ---	1,010 ---
11.	"Northerners on all sides tend to be extreme and unreasonable."	13.4% (35.0%)	31.0% (19.0%)	55.6% (46.0%)	1,006 (997)
12.	"The use of violence, while regrettable, has been necessary."	13.6% (16.0%)	24.6% (8.0%)	61.8% (76.0%)	1,010 (1,000)

Note: 1988-89 scores are in brackets.

3.2 Perceived Catholic-Protestant Identity:

The three questions answered in Item Nos. 1, 2 and 3 on Table No.10.3 are:

(1) "Catholics in Northern Ireland have more in common with Northern Protestants than they have with Catholics in the Republic."

(2) "Protestants in the Republic have more in common with Catholics here than they have with Protestants in Northern Ireland."

(3) "Northern Protestants have more in common with the rest of the Irish people than they have with the British."

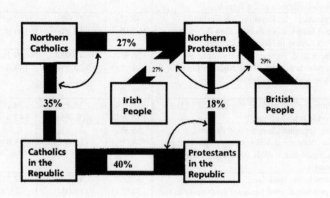

Figure No.10.1:
Cross-Border/Cross-Nation/Cross-Denomination Perceptions

The findings of Table No. 10.3 show a very significant increase in relation to the direction of perceived *'intra-denominational (Cross-Border) identity'* in the case of Items Nos. 1 and 2. The 1988-89 responses saw that **the internal**, i.e. Northern Ireland and Republic of Ireland, inter-denominational identity was stronger than it was in the 2007-08 replies. The decline in internal interdenominational percentages was **45.0% - 26.6% = 18.4%** in Item No. 1 and **67.0% - 40.1% = 26.9%** for Item No. 2. In other words, Protestants and Roman Catholics have been seen by respondents to have increased these intra-denominational cross-border similarities and reduced their interdenominational common traits *vis-à-vis* the former (Northern Ireland or the Republic)!   This is in line with the formal **all-Ireland structures** of the Protestant and Roman Catholic Churches.   These opinions reflect the experience of a representative sample of adults in the Republic.   If one adds to these changes in the 'agree' percentages, the actual more than doubling of the **'don't know'** replies, i.e. from **21.0% to 43.6%** (Item No. 1) and from **16.0% to 41.9%** (Item No. 2), these opinions are likely to continue changing in the direction indicated.   Of course, a reversal of this trend could occur in the event of negative cross-border developments.

Item No. 3 addresses the perceived common identity of Northern Protestants.   The sample were quite evenly divided on this question, i.e. **26.8%** "more in common with the rest of the Irish people" and **29.2%** "more in common with the British" with a quite substantial increase in the percentage of **'don't knows'** (from 20.0% to 43.9%).   The perceived national identity of Northern Protestants (by adults in the Republic) is more equally poised than it was in 1988-89.   It would be interesting to find out how true this result is to the actual **self-perception** of Northern Protestants?

One of the possible lessons from the above findings is the level of sensitivity of adults in the Republic of Ireland to the complexity of the self-identity (religion and nationality) of the inhabitants of Northern Ireland and the resultant need to be patient in facilitating a **pluralism of identities** co-existing in Northern Ireland in the future.

3.3 National and Community Unity:
The five questions relating to national and community unity address a number of aspects of unity:

(4) "Northern Ireland and the Republic of Ireland are two separate nations."

(5) "Having separate Catholic and Protestant schools has been a major cause of division in the Northern community."

(6) "A return to the Irish language and culture could provide a good basis for Irish unity in the long term (even though it might present difficulties in the short term)."

(7) "The position and influence of the Catholic Church in the Republic is a real obstacle to Irish unity."

(8) "National unity is an essential condition for a just solution to the present Northern problems."

There was less support for the view of *the two-nation Ireland* than in 1988-89. The sample is evenly divided on the view expressed in Item No. 4 as distinct from the plurality in favour of it in 1988-89. There was more than a doubling of the **'don't know'** percentages (from 9.0% to 22.3%). This slight move away from the *two-nation opinion* (although still 38.5% agree with it) may be due to the growing success of the *Good Friday Agreement* and its impact on the All-Ireland population!

If Item Nos. 5 and 7 are taken together, the perceived potentially **divisive role** of separate Catholic and Protestant schools in Northern Ireland and the role of the Roman Catholic Church in the Republic have been modified somewhat since the previous national survey in 1988-89. The shifts from 'agreement' and 'disagreement' to 'don't knows' are noteworthy. The "jury is still out" on these two questions. The fact that the change has not been more marked may be due to a slowing-down in the desire for Christian-Church unity[10].

The potential role of the Irish language as a "good basis of Irish unity" has seen a nominal increase of **6%** in agreement and a very substantial nominal decrease (-24.5%) in disagreement with the view, i.e. from **57.0%** in 1988-89 to **32.5%** in 2007-08. This indicates a move towards wider support for the view expressed in the item. Many of the idealists who have promoted the restoration of the Irish language wished it to be the common inheritance of all religions, political persuasions and social classes. The findings of Item No. 6 show decreased opposition and increased support for it as an inclusive cultural symbol of Irish unity.

The change which has taken place in the view expressed in Item No. 8 has experienced a drop in support and a corresponding drop in opposition to "national unity as essential". Still there is a strong plurality in favour of the view, i.e. **42.0%** for and **20.0%** against, with **38.0%** not knowing. The

---

[10] Mac Gréil, Micheál, (2009), *The Challenge of Indifference – a Need for Religious Revival in Ireland*, Maynooth, Survey and Research Unit, pp 125ff.

Good Friday Agreement may have modified the urgency of unity. Is this an indication that a more **federal** integration of the Republic of Ireland and Northern Ireland will emerge in the medium term?

Taking Item Nos. 5, 6, 7 and 8 together, it is possible to see evidence of some moderation of views and a more qualified answering. There are signs of the country moving towards the acceptance of a more inclusive and pluralist type of Irish unity.

3.4 Cooperation and Violence:
Item Nos. 9 and 10 deal with issues concerning cooperation across the Border and internally in Northern Ireland. Item No. 11 addresses the negative disposition in the Republic towards "all Northerners" while Item No. 12 measures support for the armed struggle as necessary.

(9)   *"There should be increased cooperation across the Border with*
         people in Northern Ireland"

(10)   *"The Good Friday Agreement (1998) provides a good basis for*
         community cooperation."

(11)   *"Northerners on all sides tend to be extreme and unreasonable."*

(12)   *"The use of violence, while regrettable, has been necessary."*

Support for increased *Cross-Border Cooperation* is still strong after decreasing significantly from the very high percentage (90.0%) in favour in 1988-89 to the moderately high percentage (72.6%) in 2007-08. The increase in the '**don't knows**' (from **7.0%** to **25.0%**) again shows a degree of hesitancy. Had the experience of cross-border trading after the decline in the value of sterling been experienced, there might have been a further reduction in support. Different currencies and V.A.T. rates resulted in one-way traffic, which could hardly be defined as cooperation on an egalitarian scale!

The endorsement of the *Good Friday Agreement* in Item No. 10 was hardly surprising. In fact, a higher figure than the **75.4%** in favour was anticipated. What is most hopeful is the low level of disagreement to the statement at **3.2%**!

Item No. 11 has recorded a substantial and positive change since 1988-89.   Agreement with this 'plague-on-all-your-houses' statement decreased from **35.0%** to **13.4%** over the nineteen years from 1988-'89 to 2007-08.   This is to be welcomed and shows a warming of the dispositions and evaluations of adults in the Republic towards their fellow-Irish brothers and sisters north of the Border, be they Republicans or Loyalists!   Both **'disagreement'** (at **55.6%**) and **'don't-knows'** (at **31.0%**) are indicative of the trend towards further improvement in the esteem for "Northerners on both sides".   This is but a further confirmation of the positive results of the negotiated *Good Friday* and *St. Andrew's Agreements*.   It is, once again, a measure of the real 'peace dividend'!

Finally, the replies to the statement on the **justification of the use of violence** to bring about change or, for some, perhaps to prevent change. **Agreement** with the statement dropped from **16.0%** to **13.6%** which was quite moderate.   When coupled with the nominal drop of **14.2%** (from **76.0%**) in 1988-89 to **61.8%** in 2007-08 of respondents who **disagreed** with the "justification-of-violence" statement, it shows a significant minority who still agree with or are ambivalent towards what has often been referred to as the justification of the "**armed struggle**" in the liberation of the Irish people. The more democratic approach by Britain, the former imperial coloniser, as has been evidenced in the mid- to late-1990s and since the year 2000AD, is probably the most effective way of reducing support for armed struggle and paramilitary insurgency at present or in the future.   This process of change should also be true of other regions of the world where people's independence and equality are perceived to be coercively denied.

The change in attitudes can take place in people who may be ambivalent towards the need for "armed struggle" to win what they believe to be legitimate goals.   The **"armed struggle" tradition** has been deeply-rooted even in modern Irish history, i.e. 1798, 1848, 1867, 1916 and 1918-21.   Further resort to violence in Northern Ireland since 1921 has been seen by those involved as a continuity of the 'armed struggle' tradition.   The majority of Irish political leaders disagreed with the efficacy of such claims. Some questioned their legitimacy.

Part IV – Conclusion

Northern Ireland has ceased to preoccupy the political, security, economic, media and religious establishments in the Republic of Ireland since the relatively successful outcome of the **Peace Process**, which intensified during the 1990s and has taken place in the early 2000s.   Thanks to wise and courageous initiatives and commitments within Northern Ireland and outside of it, especially in Great Britain, the Republic of Ireland, the United States of America and elsewhere, the net effect was a **ceasefire** and an **agreement** between the parties in Northern Ireland to operate a system of democracy based on a **consensus model**.   The sharing of power between Republicans and Loyalists, Nationalists and Unionists and the Alliance Party has meant the possibilities for relative peace within Northern Ireland and better relations between the Republic of Ireland, Northern Ireland and Great Britain.   The positive endorsement of these improved relations has been evident in the findings reported in this chapter.

The removal of the **political institution** from the pivotal position has facilitated a greater focus on the **economic institution** on both sides of the Border.   Unfortunately, the international financial crisis (and the failure of self-regulation) of summer 2008 have prevented the best efforts of both societies to reap sustainable benefits from such a focus in the current economic atmosphere.   Since the fieldwork of this survey ended in March 2008 (prior to **the recession in the US** which triggered the world economic downturn), the evidence presented in this text was collected in a time of relative economic success.

Two sources of data examined in this chapter were the *Special Northern Ireland Scale* and the *Bogardus Social Distance Scale* in relation to three Northern Ireland stimulus categories ('Northern Irish', 'Protestants' and 'Unionists').   When compared with 1988-89 (national survey), there was **a very substantial** improvement in the social distance towards 'Unionists', i.e. from **33.4%** 'admitting to kinship' in 1988-89 to **66.2%** willing to do so in 2007-08.   There was a **substantial** improvement for 'Protestants' and a *moderate* advance for 'Northern Irish'.   **Age** and **education** as variables failed to perform as expected, which had occurred in the case of most of the stimulus categories.   Further research would be necessary to discover these anomalies in intergroup attitudes and prejudices.

The *Special Northern Ireland Scale* dealt with 'Catholic-Protestant Identity', 'National and Community Unity' and 'Cooperation and Violence'. The scale was not treated as a normal attitudes' scale but, rather, as a testing of **opinions** in relation to the Northern Ireland 'problem'.   Comparison was made between the response of the 1988-89 national survey and that of 2007-08.

The overall message from the changes in opinions tested in the scale has been positive for North-Republic relations. There is an implicit improvement in the case for greater pluralism. The substantial increases in the **"don't know"** percentages in the case of all of the opinions would indicate a continuity of opinion change in the direction of the findings. If that be so, any future unity of Ireland would be more likely as a **Federal (pluralist) Republic of Ireland**! This would be in line with 'integrated pluralism'. Also, the final goal of the unity of Christian Churches would need to be **a pluralist unity of the Christian Churches.**

***

CHAPTER XI
Irish Attitudes towards the British

Part I – Socio-Historical Background

As already noted, one of the real success stories since 1988-89 has been the dramatic change in Irish-British relations which led to and followed the *Good Friday Agreement* **in 1998**. This agreement followed a period of 25 years (1969-1994) of paramilitary strife in Northern Ireland between Republicans and the Forces of the Crown. The latter were supported by the Ulster Loyalists. This twenty-five years of 'armed struggle' resulted in very serious casualties among members of the Crown Forces as well as others on both sides within Northern Ireland. Casualties were also experienced within the Republic of Ireland and on the British 'mainland'. Inevitably Irish-British relations were affected negatively at times during the 'Troubles'. The current survey 2007-08 gives the reader an opportunity to gauge the impact of the positive and negative developments on Irish attitudes and opinions towards the British.

The history of Ireland has been dominated by the relation with Great Britain for almost one thousand years. As a former colony of Britain, the Irish people resisted various attempts to deny them their freedom of political, religious and cultural expression. During feudal times (prior to the Reformation) the conflict between native Irish Chieftains and Anglo/Norman Lords weakened the rule of the former in certain regions of the country. During the 16th century, the **religious factor** aggravated the situation when the King of England, Henry VIII, broke with Roman Catholicism and suppressed Irish monasteries and initiated a campaign against the Catholic Church in Ireland. Irish Chieftains were replaced by feudal Lords loyal to the English Crown, and their lands were confiscated at the beginning of the seventeenth century.

The Treaty of Westphalia in 1648, which marked the end of the Thirty Years' War, declared that the religion of the King would be that of the people. This meant that all citizens of Ireland were formally (*de jure*) Protestant, despite the fact that the vast majority of the Irish people were (*de facto*) Roman Catholic. The rise of Oliver Cromwell in England, who had revolted against and executed the King of England in 1649, did not emancipate the Roman Catholics and proceeded to impose **Puritanism** on them and, to a lesser extent, on Anglicans.   In 1654, the Act of Settlement was passed in Cromwell's Parliament and a large part of Ulster was planted with Presbyterians from Scotland.   Roman Catholics were 'ethnically cleansed' and sent to Connaught and elsewhere.

The Restoration of the Monarchy in 1660 and the arrival of a Roman Catholic King, James II, in 1685 failed to reverse the deprivation of those removed from their lands to any great extent.   King James' Protestant son-in-law, William of Orange, waged a war against him in 1690 and deposed him from the throne.   This had a traumatic effect on Irish Catholics and was followed by a systematic persecution of Irish Roman Catholics (the vast majority of the people) in 1691 by a series of **Penal Laws** enacted and enforced by the Irish 'Protestant' Parliament in College Green in Dublin. By the time these (religious) 'apartheid' laws began to be modified by the 1770s, Irish Roman Catholics were deprived of their material and spiritual rights and could be defined, in modern terms, as **Ireland's underclass**, not dissimilar to the Black population in South Africa at the height of the Apartheid Regime.   It was a classic example of a suppressed people – the victims of social class, religious and political oppression.

The failed attempt in **1798** to follow the example of the American Revolution of 1775 and that of the French Republic in 1789, led to the Act of Union with Britain and the loss of the Irish Parliament (which was exclusively Protestant).   This left Ireland with strong landlords and weak peasants.   The success of Daniel O'Connell's campaign to win Catholic Emancipation (i.e. the right of Catholics to be elected to Westminster) in 1829 was a sign of hope – although the franchise was exclusively male and based on property.   **'The Tithe's War'**, i.e. against Roman Catholics paying Church taxes for non-Catholic Churches, continued.   **The Great Famine** of 1845-48 reduced the population by one-quarter through death from hunger and forced emigration.   The inhuman restrictions of *liberal capitalism* (which dominated Westminster) prevented the British Government from intervening adequately to alleviate the plight of Irish peasant (Catholic) people starving as a result of a disastrous **potato blight** – despite the fact that food was being exported from Ireland while its people were dying from hunger.   It was considered more important to protect the "freedom of the market" than the lives of the people! Mass emigration from Ireland to North America gained momentum during the latter part of the 19th century.

After the Famine, **the Landlords** and the **strong farmers** (including a minority of Roman Catholic farmers) consolidated their position and stretched their boundary fences to include the smallholdings of the evicted Roman Catholic tenant peasants. The reaction to this appalling inequity led in time to a most successful **Land War**, which, eventually, forced the Landlords to sell-out, resulting in their land being divided among the tenant farmers in the early years of the twentieth century (see Wyndham Act, 1905). This was seen as a victory at the time but the later outcome did not prove it to be so. It may have been more lasting had the estates been given to the tenants in a *cooperative rather than an individual* manner! The net outcome at the perceived 'success' of the Land War was a growing self-confidence of the peasant farmer.

During the second-half of the 19th century, Ireland was to experience a severe decline in its **native language**.   The newly established National School system failed to help the people to transmit their own Irish language to their children.   In fact, it assimilated the children into the Anglicised culture and discouraged children from speaking their native tongue[1].

The **disestablishment of the Church of Ireland in 1869** was good for both the Church of Ireland and the Roman Catholic Church.   During the 19th century there was a growth in Roman Catholic education (following the establishment of St Patrick's Catholic Seminary in Maynooth in 1795), largely due to the Religious Sisters, Brothers and Priests.   This led to Catholics qualifying for the 'professions' of law, medicine, engineering, etc. (professions which were practically exclusively Protestant in the 17th and 18th centuries).   The growth of Catholic education led to a Roman Catholic elite *bourgeoisie* by the end of the 19th century but it failed to correct the process of the Anglicisation of the Irish people.   The movement towards **Irish Independence** gained pace on the success of the Land War.   The **Trade Union Movement** tried, and eventually succeeded, in winning workers' rights among the waged workers. **Voluntary movements** such as the **Cooperative Movement**, the **Gaelic Athletic Association**, the **Gaelic League**, the **Pioneer Total Abstinence Association**, etc. had also helped to restore a degree of self-confidence and national self-respect in the people as the 19th century was coming to a close.   Irish politicians in the British Parliament were supporting a case for the restoration of an Irish Parliament. In the early years of the 20th century, **Sinn Féin** was set up to add to the

---

[1] See: DeFréine, Seán, (1965), *The Great Silence*, Dublin, Foilseacháin Náisiúnta Teo.

campaign for **self-reliance**. By 1914 the **Home Rule Bill** was passed in Westminster but its application was postponed because of World War I. The resistance to Home Rule from **Ulster Unionists** was trenchant and led to a threat of armed opposition (**the Ulster Volunteers**). As a result, a group of supporters for Home Rule constituted themselves as the **Irish Volunteers**. Among the latter were former members of the **Fenians** and the **Irish Republican Brotherhood**. By 1916 a leadership group in the Irish Volunteers (together with the Irish Citizen Army) decided to declare a Republic and defend it with arms (rifles). They occupied the General Post Office in Dublin and a number of other symbolically important buildings on **Easter Monday 1916**. The British Army easily defeated them within a week and had the leaders executed. This counter-violent reaction raised the ire of the people and when the **promised enforcement of Home Rule in 1918** did not take place, a widespread **'War of Independence'** was waged. This led to a truce in 1921 and a Peace Treaty which established the current Border between **Northern Ireland** and the new **Irish Free State** in 1922.

This was followed by a cruel **Civil War** between those *'pro'* and *'con'* the Treaty. Having been defeated in the civil war the majority of Republicans (under **Éamon deValera**) agreed to give up the fight in 1923 and enter the Dáil (parliament). A minority refused to recognise the new system and, on a number of occasions, resorted to **paramilitary action** against the Northern Irish system. The most serious paramilitary campaign was waged between 1969 and the 1994 ceasefire. The *Good Friday Agreement* in 1998 led to the current devolved government in Northern Ireland which is organised on a **democratic consensus** basis and ultimately led to the decommissioning of the IRA and other paramilitary organisations.

The above concise and 'over-generalised' history of British/English-Irish relations has emphasised the negative aspects from the point of view of Ireland which are still lingering in the folk-memory and make the material of ballad, song and story-telling. During the centuries of British/English occupation of Ireland there were obvious benefits accruing to the Irish in social and economic areas of life. By being part of the British Empire and later, Commonwealth (until 1949), our people had relatively easy access to a large part of the so-called 'developed Western world'. We were to benefit from our association with the British education system – despite the Irish cultural deficit, i.e. in terms of the Irish language and all that went with it. One of the reasons for Irish Independence was the restoration of the Irish language and culture. The success of Irish emigrants in Britain, the United

States, Canada, Australia and New Zealand was to create quite a strong 'lobby' in favour of Irish Independence and socio-economic development. The positive roles played by the United States and Great Britain in facilitating the *Good Friday Agreement* could be seen as one of the positive outcomes of our colonisation. The extraordinary level of U.S. investment in Irish industry in recent years can also be related to our otherwise unfortunate history as a colonised people.

Despite the negative aspects of Anglo-Irish history, the English, Welsh and Scottish people have been very popular in the three surveys of social distance, i.e. 1972-73, 1988-89 and 2007-08[2]. This shows a degree of maturity in the respondents in that they appreciate their ethnic neighbours despite the behaviour of former British establishments in their negative policy and behaviour towards the Irish. Of course, some of the persecution suffered by the peasant Irish in the 19th century was equally endured by poorer English, Welsh and Scottish people under the liberal elites who controlled the British Empire. One has but to read Charles Dickens[3] and other social commentators of 19th/20th century Britain to bear this out. The Irish did not have the monopoly on suffering under their colonial masters!

Part II – Social Distance towards 'Great Britain' Categories

The four main 'Great Britain' stimulus categories measured in the 2007-08 national survey are: 'British', 'English', 'Scottish' and 'Welsh'. When dealing with ethnic prejudice in general in Chapters VI and VII above, these four stimulus categories were included among the nine "Irish, British and American Stimulus Categories"[4]. In the above chapters the measures used were *mean-social-distance scores* in order to analyse the overall levels of social prejudice. The 'Great Britain' categories were presented as part of the broader set of stimulus categories.

2.1 Changes in Social-Distance Scores (between 1988-89 to 2007-08):

In Table No. 11.2 below it is proposed to examine variations in attitudes /prejudices as expressed in percentages 'admitting to kinship' and

---

[2] See Table No. 4.1, pages 62-4 above; See also Mac Gréil, Micheál (1996), *Prejudice in Ireland Revisited*, Maynooth, St Patrick's College, Table No.5, page 65 and Table No. 7.4, pages 134 above.
[3] Dickens, Charles, (1850) *David Copperfield*, Penguin; (1861) *Great Expectations*, Penguin.
[4] 'Irish Speakers', 'Welsh', 'Euro-Americans (White)', 'English', 'Canadians', 'Scottish', 'British', 'Northern Irish' and 'Afro-Americans (Black)'. See pages: 106-7, 112-3, and 133-9.

proportions 'denying citizenship' by personal variables.   These indicators are more descriptive of the social-distance scores and should prove more meaningful to the reader.   The changes which have taken place in social-distance responses since 1988-89 are given in the following Table No. 11.1:

Table No. 11.1:
Changes in Social Distance towards 'Great Britain' Categories (1988-89 to 2007-08)

Stimulus Category	1988-89		2007-08		Change	
	Admit to Kinship	Deny Citizenship	Admit to Kinship	Deny Citizenship	Admit to Kinship	Deny Citizenship
1. 'Welsh'	72.8%	3.8%	82.4%	2.0%	+9.6%	-1.8%
2. 'English'	77.9%	2.8%	81.0%	2.1%	+3.1%	-0.7%
3. 'Scottish'	74.2%	3.8%	81.7%	2.9%	+7.5%	-0.9%
4. 'British'	76.7%	3.5%	77.2%	2.8%	+0.5%	-0.7%

Source: Table No. 6.2 (pages 108-9)

The change in each of the four 'Great Britain' categories' percentages in relation to 'admitting to kinship' and 'denial of citizenship' are all in the direction of tolerance since 1988-89.   The category with least movement has been 'British', which is interesting.   In the rank order of categories on Table No. 4.2 above (pages 65-6) the 'British' dropped seven places from **8**[th] in 1988-89 to **15**[th] in 2007-08 while the 'Welsh' went up six places from **13**[th] to **6**[th] over the same period of time.   Despite this slippage in rank order of preference, it should not be forgotten that the 'British' are an **in-group** in the Republic of Ireland with a mean-social-distance score of less than **1.500** (i.e. **1.488**).   The other three categories, i.e. 'Welsh', 'English' and 'Scottish' are also in-groups at **1.388, 1.422** and **1.436** respectively.

2.2 Social Distance of 'Great Britain' Categories by Personal Variables:
The value of examining the findings by personal variables is the insight it gives readers about the personal, regional, social class, etc. influences on Irish attitudes towards the 'Great Britain' categories.   It also enables them to detect and predict possible trends in the attitudes in the near future. Table No. 11.2 shows the absence of statistically significant differences (N/S) in the case of four variables out of a total of thirty-two sub-scales. This means that the *chi-square* score was more than 0.05, i.e. variation could be due to chance in more than one-in-twenty cases.   For all practical purposes there would be consensus between the sub-variables in such cases. Cases where the *chi- square* score is higher than 0.05 are marked N/S (not significant).

Table No. 11.2:
Percentages 'Admitting to Kinship' and 'Denying Citizenship' for 'Great Britain'
Stimulus Categories by Personal Variables

Personal Variable	'Welsh' Admit to Kinship	Deny Citizen'p	'English' Admit to Kinship	Deny Citizen'p	'Scottish' Admit to Kinship	Deny Citizen'p	'British' Admit to Kinship	Deny Citizen'p	Av. No.
Total Sample	**82.5%**	**2.0%**	**80.9%**	**2.1%**	**81.8%**	**2.9%**	**77.3%**	**2.8%**	1,000
A. Age	P<.05		P<.02		P<.001		P<.001		
1. 18-25 years	70.6%	**5.9%**	71.6%	**3.0%**	69.2%	**5.3%**	65.5%	**3.6%**	167
2. 26-40 years	86.3%	0.9%	82.1%	2.5%	84.2%	1.2%	77.8%	1.8%	318
3. 41-55 years	79.8%	1.6%	**81.5%**	1.6%	80.2%	**5.3%**	**80.9%**	2.8%	244
4. 56-70 years	86.9%	1.1%	82.1%	2.3%	86.0%	1.7%	**84.7%**	**3.9%**	175
5. 71 years plus	**89.6%**	0.0%	**87.6%**	1.0%	**91.7%**	0.0%	75.0%	1.0%	96
B. Marital Status	P<.02		N/S		P<.05		P<.02		
1. Single/Never Married	79.9%	**3.4%**	---	---	80.2%	**3.3%**	74.4%	**3.9%**	357
2. Married	**84.9%**	1.5%	---	---	83.2%	2.8%	80.4%	1.9%	466
3. Separated/Divorced	81.8%	0.0%	---	---	79.5%	2.3%	81.8%	**4.5%**	44
4. Permanent Relation'p	71.8%	1.4%	---	---	70.4%	2.8%	**85.3%**	**4.2%**	71
5. Widowed	**91.2%**	0.0%	---	---	**92.6%**	0.0%	77.9%	0.0%	68
C. Area of Birth	P<.05		P<.001		P<.001		P<.002		
1. City (100,000 +)	77.6%	**2.6%**	79.7%	1.9%	77.0%	**3.1%**	73.9%	2.1%	415
2. Lge.Town (10,000 +)	84.2%	2.5%	**87.3%**	1.7%	84.0%	**5.9%**	**89.1%**	1.7%	116
3. Town (1,500 +)	85.2%	**3.1%**	81.5%	1.6%	84.4%	2.3%	81.7%	**3.1%**	129
4. Rural/Village	**86.0%**	0.9%	80.2%	**2.6%**	**86.0%**	1.5%	75.6%	**3.8%**	340
D. Place of Rearing (in Republic of Ireland)	P<.005		P<.002		P<.001		N/S		
1. Dublin (City & Co.)	77.5%	**3.4%**	81.0%	**3.3%**	79.2%	**4.2%**	---	---	265
2. Rest of Leinster	87.3%	1.8%	**83.6%**	1.2%	85.3%	3.1%	---	---	160
3. Munster	**87.9%**	0.0%	80.5%	**3.9%**	**87.0%**	0.9%	---	---	230
4. Connaught/Ulster	80.4%	1.8%	79.1%	0.0%	82.2%	0.0%	---	---	162
E. Region of Residence	P<.001		P<.001		P<.001		N/S		
1. B.M.W.	**83.5%**	1.8%	**82.0%**	0.4%	79.4%	1.5%	---	---	268
2. Dublin	79.0%	**3.5%**	79.7%	**3.5%**	79.9%	3.2%	---	---	283
3. Mid-East & Sth-East	81.2%	2.3%	78.8%	**4.1%**	82.0%	**7.0%**	---	---	214
4. Mid-West & Sth-W.	**85.7%**	0.4%	83.5%	1.7%	**86.4%**	0.4%	---	---	236
F. Education	P<.05		P<.001		P<.012		P<.002		
1. Primary or Less	**91.5%**	0.0%	**89.0%**	0.8%	**94.0%**	0.9%	**86.3%**	0.0%	117
2. Incomplete Sec-Lev.	87.0%	2.7%	81.6%	3.4%	83.5%	3.1%	75.9%	**4.5%**	259
3. Complete Sec-Level	78.7%	**4.7%**	79.2%	**4.3%**	79.6%	**4.7%**	73.6%	**5.1%**	251
4. Third-Level	78.8%	0.3%	79.2%	0.0%	78.2%	2.1%	78.0%	0.5%	376
G. Occupational Status	P<.03		P<.012		N/S		P<.001		
1. Unskilled/Semi-Skil.	81.2%	0.5%	78.7%	**4.4%**	---	---	65.7%	**3.9%**	204
2. Skilled/R. Non-M.	84.0%	2.4%	83.1%	1.2%	---	---	81.8%	2.4%	321
3. Inspect./Supervisory	85.0%	**3.0%**	80.6%	**5.2%**	---	---	80.3%	**6.8%**	131
4. Professional/Exec.	**87.4%**	0.0%	**84.3%**	0.5%	---	---	**83.9%**	0.5%	190

Table No. 11.2 (Cont'd) Personal Variable	'Welsh'		'English'		'Scottish'		'British'		Av. No.
	Admit to Kinship	Deny Citizen'p	Admit to Kinship	Deny Citizen'p	Admit to Kinship	Deny Citizen'p	Admit to Kinship	Deny Citizen'p	
H. Social Class Position	P<.001		P<.001		P<.001		P<.035		
1. Class I: Upper Class	76.9%	0.0%	73.7%	0.0%	76.9%	0.0%	73.7%	0.0%	39
2. Class II: Upper-Mid. Cl.	**89.1%**	0.0%	**88.6%**	0.7%	**87.7%**	2.2%	**85.6%**	0.7%	138
3. Class III: Mid-Mid. Cl.	81.9%	1.8%	77.3%	**2.6%**	80.2%	**4.0%**	**81.3%**	**3.1%**	226
4. Class IV: Working Cl.	**83.4%**	**2.5%**	**81.2%**	**3.0%**	**82.3%**	**2.8%**	73.8%	**4.1%**	362
5. Class V: Lower Class	**90.5%**	0.0%	**89.4%**	**3.6%**	**86.9%**	0.0%	77.4%	**3.6%**	84

Note: Percentages above sample average are **in bold**.

The findings of Table No. 11.2 merit serious reflection. In most variables there is a strong degree of consistency between the sub-variable differences for each of the four stimulus categories. Such consistency confirms the validity and reliability of the findings and the establishment of patterns to responses throughout the Table. It should be noted that there is a limit to the scope of variation because of the relatively low social-distance score of each category, i.e. each of the four are in-groups'.

2.2.1 Age: For each of the three 'Great Britain' categories with significant variations, the youngest age group, i.e. 18 to 25 years, has produced the most intolerant results. The percentages 'admitting to kinship' are more than 10% lower than the sample average, while the percentages 'denying citizenship' are well above the average score. This was not anticipated. What is more serious is that it confirms a pattern already found in the social-distance percentages of a wide range of other stimulus categories (already reported in this text).

It seems there is a significant and substantial minority within the '18 to 25 years-olds' who are quite intolerant in their dispositions towards most stimulus categories. Members of this age group were born between 1983 and 1990, and, since the age of 15 years, have experienced a prolonged period of economic prosperity. Few would have had the insecurity of high unemployment in their earlier years and would not have seen serious deprivation around them. They had reasonably easy access to disposable income. Of course, there are exceptions. In other words, they witnessed a relatively high material standard of living. Some older residents would be inclined to see them as the "spoiled generation". This judgement may be too harsh! For a more detailed discussion of this unexpected finding of relative intolerance among a minority of 18 to 25 year-olds, see pages 156-160 above.

If this evidence of relative intolerance is to continue in this age-cohort as they become older and assume more authority in Irish society, we might experience a serious regression in the growth towards greater tolerance. Of course, it could be but a phase in 'growing up' which will change to be like the more tolerant standards of the 26 to 40 year-olds and, even the older sub-samples! A review of the quality of education at the second and third level is necessary. The over-emphasis on 'pragmatism' in education does not seem to have had a liberating effect on a significant minority of students.

2.2.2 Marital Status: This variable elicited significant variations in the case of 'Welsh', 'Scottish' and 'British'. The cross-variable influence of age on marital status is evident in the findings, i.e. the relatively low 'admission to kinship' percentages for 'Single/Never Married' and 'Permanent Relationships' and the very positive scores of 'Widowed' and the 'Married' respondents. This is a mixed result.

Returning to the influences on the minority of young respondents (18 to 25 year-olds) who are negative, it is quite clear from the performance of 'Married' and 'Widowed' that the 'illiberal tendencies' are unlikely to be coming from the home. The 'Married' and 'Widowed' respondents are above average in 'admission to kinship' and below average in 'denial of citizenship'.

2.2.3 Area of Birth: The four 'Great Britain' categories registered statistically significant variations. Those born in cities were the least welcoming into kinship in all four cases. Normally, it is expected that those born in the more cosmopolitan environment in cities would be more open than those reared in *Rural/Village* areas. This has not been the case in relation to 'Welsh' and 'Scottish' categories. The responses of the 'Rural/Village' subsample in relation to the 'British' category are significantly less welcoming when compared with the other categories, i.e. 'Welsh' and 'Scottish', i.e. **75.6%** would admit 'British' to kinship as compared with **86.0%** admitting 'Welsh' and 'Scottish'. The age factor could also be influencing these results!

2.2.4 Place of Rearing and Region of Residence: The 'Dublin' sub-sample was the **least** in favour of 'admitting to kinship', two of the three categories registering significant variations, i.e. those reared in Dublin City and County for 'Welsh' and 'Scottish'. Respondents reared in 'Munster' and living in the 'Mid-West/South-West' regions' cluster were the most tolerant subsamples. This has been consistent with findings in relation to most categories measured. Does this mean that Munster-reared enjoy a particularly tolerant outlook towards 'Great Britain' and other groups? It would appear so. The Munster ethos seems to be special!

2.2.5 Education: The findings of the 'Education' variable are almost the opposite to what was anticipated. It was expected that the higher the education standard reached, the higher the percentage 'admitting to kinship'. The following extract from Table No. 11.2(f) traces the difference between the responses of the **lowest** and the **highest** education subsamples:

"Admission to Kinship"

Category	Lower Education	Higher Education		Nominal Range of Difference
	Primary or Lower	Complete 2nd Level	Third Level	
	(A)	(B)	(C)	(A – C)
1. 'Welsh'	91.5%	78.7%	78.8%	+12.2%
2. 'English'	89.0%	79.2%	78.2%	+9.8%
3. 'Scottish'	94.0%	79.6%	78.2%	+15.8%
4. 'British'	86.3%	73.6%	78.0%	+8.3%

The impact of the age (variable) on the above is an obvious partial cause of such an extraordinary result. It raises, once again, the issue of the quality of education and its impact on intolerance. If education in intergroup prejudice is shown to be self-therapeutic for the learner, it may be time to introduce serious courses in intergroup attitudes (including prejudices) at the senior cycle in the second-level curriculum and in that of all degree and diploma third-level courses! The above findings and those of other categories (reported elsewhere in this text) provide a *prima facie* case for such an addition to the general education curriculum.

2.2.6 Occupational Status: This variable produced a significant variation for two of the four stimulus categories, i.e. 'English' and 'British'. The results were more or less as anticipated. Respondents with higher occupational status were more tolerant than those at the lower end of the occupational scale. The 'professional/executive' were among the highest subsamples in all the variables to welcome 'English' and 'British' into kinship and the lowest to deny them citizenship [see Table No. 11.2(g)]. It is reassuring to see a high level of tolerance among those with socio-economic authority!

2.2.7 Social Class Position: This is a variable of **social status** based on a hierarchical scale determined by a combination of education and occupation and devised by A.B. Hollingshead[5]. The findings are mixed. The "Upper Class" scored zero in 'denying citizenship', while they were also **lowest** in 'admitting to kinship' in each of the four 'Great Britain' categories. The "Upper-Middle Class" respondents were the most tolerant overall. This is likely to be owing to the neutralising effects of education and occupation.

2.2.8 Conclusion: The above information gives the reader an insight into variations by age, marital status, area of birth, place of rearing, region of residence, education, occupation and social class position in the social-distance indicators, i.e. 'admission to kinship' and 'denial of citizenship'. Again, it must be pointed out that, of necessity, there is a limited range of variation because of the low mean-social-distance scores of each of the stimulus categories, 'Welsh', 'English', 'Scottish' and 'British', i.e. 'Great Britain' categories. It is hoped that this information will give the reader a better understanding of contemporary Irish attitudes toward our former 'colonial neighbours'. The four variable cells showing 'not significant' (N/S) is indicative of a relatively low degree of attitudinal consensus in relation to these in-group categories, i.e. with a mean-social-distance score of less than **1.500** in a one-to-seven continuum. The areas where variations were significant were duly noted.

Part III – The Special Anti-British Scale

It is quite clear from the findings of Table Nos. 11.1 and 11.2 above that the social-distance position of the 'British', 'English', 'Scottish' and 'Welsh' is quite close and they fall within the **in-group categories**, i.e. with mean-social-distance scores of **less than 1.500.** Table No. 11.1 shows the extent of improvement in the social-distance scores between 1988-89 and 2007-08. This information is greatly to be welcomed in Irish (Republic of Ireland) attitudes toward their nearest neighbours.

The *Special Anti-British Scale* was devised (by the present author) for inclusion in the 1972-73 social survey of the Greater Dublin population and replicated in the national social surveys of 1988-89 and 2007-08. Table No.

---

[5] Hollingshead, August de Belmont, (1949), *Elmstown Youth: the Impact of Social Class*, New York, Wiley. See Footnote 7, (Table No. 8.14) page 189 above.

11.3 gives the responses of the three social surveys, i.e. 1972-73, 1988-89 and 2007-08. The items are arranged into the two factors, i.e. (1) **Political/Hostility Factor** and (2) **Low Esteem Factor**, as in the case of the previous surveys[6]. One of the 'discoveries' from the 1972-73 survey in relation to the Anti-British Scale was *"post-colonial attitudinal schizophrenia"*[7]. This meant that low esteem of British people failed to have correlated positively with anti-British hostility; in fact it was the opposite. When "we looked-up to the British", we were really "looking-down on ourselves"!

The findings of Table No. 11.3 below show a consistency (with modifications) in response-patterns in three major social surveys over a period of thirty-five years, i.e. 1972-73, 1988-89 and 2007-08. This confirms the **reliability** of the scale. The *Cronbach Alpha* for the scale is **0.774**, which is quite satisfactory. The overall prejudice score decreased by **14.9%**, i.e. from **73.7** in 1988-89 to **62.7** in 2007-08[8]. While this is still significant, it is, at the same time, quite moderate.

The positive percentage in each item is **in bold**. This makes it easier to note the changes in attitude or opinion. Changes in the negative scores also affect differences in prejudice scores. Negative scores include agreement with anti-British statements and disagreement with *pro-British* items. In all there are six pro-British items, i.e. nos. 1, 2, 3, 4, 5 and 10 and seven anti-British items, i.e. 6, 7, 8, 9, 11, 12 and 13. The order in which these statements were in the questionnaire was quite random to prevent the possibility of uni-directionality, which could have distorted the responses.

The two factors, i.e. low esteem of the British and political hostility towards the British, are important. In previous surveys, especially the 1972-73 one, their comparative performance had been contrary to the normal expectation of low esteem correlating positively with anti-British feelings of hostility. The present author interpreted this apparent contradiction to mean a proportion of those "who looked up to the British" were really "looking down on themselves". Low self-esteem *vis-à-vis* the British was the legacy

---

[6] See: Mac Gréil, Micheál, (1996), *Prejudice in Ireland Revisited*, Maynooth, St Patrick's College, pp. 262-269.
[7] See: Mac Gréil, Micheál, (1977), *Prejudice and Tolerance in Ireland*, Dublin, CIR, pp. 374-5.
[8] Prejudice score is on a continuum from 0 to 200.

Table No. 11.3: Special Anti-British Scale (1972-73, 1988-89 and 2007-08) *

Item	2007-08			1988-89			1972-73		
	Agree	Don't Know	Disagree	Agree	Don't Know	Disagree	Agree	Don't Know	Disagree
A. Esteem Factor:	%	%	%	%	%	%	%	%	%
No.1. If Ireland did not have its own team in the Olympic Games or international sports, I would cheer for the British.	46.7	22.2	*31.1*	41.8	10.2	*48.0*	54.3	4.3	*41.4*
No.2. I would rather live in Britain than any other place abroad.	19.1	19.6	*61.3*	27.0	12.0	*61.0*	39.7	5.7	*61.0*
No.3. The world owes a lot to Britain.	28.3	26.7	*45.0*	29.1	19.2	*51.7*	30.6	7.7	*61.8*
No.4 The British have been even-handed when dealing with Northern Ireland since 1969.	19.8	41.9	*38.2*	22.4	21.1	*56.5*	---	---	---
B. Political/Hostility Factor:									
No.5 The British are a pretty decent people.	79.1	14.5	*6.4*	84.7	10.2	*5.1*	88.8	3.5	*7.5*
No.6 Some British qualities are admirable but on the whole I don't like them (the British).	*14.5*	20.5	**64.9**	*24.1*	14.4	**61.5**	*22.1*	3.5	**74.5**
No.7 The British are inferior in every way.	*3.9*	14.1	**82.0**	*6.1*	7.4	**86.5**	*5.2*	1.3	**93.5**
No.8 British people are slow and unimaginative.	*4.7*	13.6	**81.7**	*8.5*	11.5	**79.9**	*14.2*	5.3	**80.5**
No.9 I don't object to the British people but I don't like the British Government.	*19.2*	29.6	**51.3**	*49.4*	20.6	**30.0**	*36.2*	9.1	**54.7**
No.10 I am happy to see British people get on in Ireland.	**78.2**	17.1	4.8	**83.7**	9.9	*6.3*	**73.9**	5.7	*20.3*
No.11 I would never marry a British person.	*12.2*	22.3	**65.5**	*15.9*	11.5	**72.5**	*14.5*	2.4	**83.3**
No.12 I would be happy if Britain were brought to her knees.	*3.9*	12.8	**83.2**	*9.2*	10.6	**80.2**	*17.1*	3.6	**79.3**
No.13 The British have little respect for the Irish people.	*18.9*	31.7	**49.4**	*48.1*	18.9	**33.0**	---	---	---
Sample Number		1,015			1,005			2,311	

Note: Positive percentages (pro-British) are in **bold** and negative (anti-British) responses are in ***bold italics***.
Cronbach Alpha = 0.774
* The 1972-73 results are from a random sample of the Greater Dublin urban and suburban population, while the 1988-89 and 2007-08 findings are from a survey of national samples in the Republic of Ireland.

of centuries of colonial-induced submissiveness, which created a deep resentment expressed in their hostility toward the former colonial masters! The unexpected result was termed *'post-colonial attitudinal schizophrenia'*. This phenomenon is to be found in the early generation of emancipated and decolonised peoples.

The following Table gives the changes (by item) in the findings of 1988-89 and 2007-08 as measured by the (prejudice) anti-British score on a 0 to 200 continuum.

Table No. 11.4:
Changes in the Anti-British Scale between 1988-89 and 2007-08

Item (abbreviated)	Anti-British Score (0-200)		Change (B – A)
	1988-89 (A)	2007-08 (B)	
A. Esteem Factor:	(124.2)	(115.4)	**(-8.8)**
1. Cheer for the British.	106.2	84.4	**-21.8**
2. Rather live in Britain.	134.0	142.2	+8.4
3. World owes Britain a lot.	122.6	116.7	**-5.9**
4. British even-handed in Nth. Ireland.	134.0	118.4	**-15.6**
B. Political/Hostility Factor:	(51.2)	(39.2)	**(-12.0)**
5. British a decent people.	20.4	27.3	+6.9
6. Admirable but don't like British people.	62.7	49.6	**-13.1**
7. British are inferior.	19.6	21.8	+2.2
8. British slow/unimaginative.	28.6	22.9	**-5.7**
9. Don't like British Government.	119.4	67.9	**-51.5**
10. Happy for British to get on in Ireland.	22.6	26.6	+4.0
11. Would never marry a British person.	43.4	46.6	+3.2
12. Happy at Britain brought to its knees.	29.0	20.7	**-8.3**
13. British have little respect for the Irish.	115.1	69.5	**-45.6**
Scale Mean Score (0-200)	73.7	62.7	-11.0

Note: Items recording a decrease in anti-British scores are in **bold**.

Viewing the above items as 'opinions' in their own right, it is very interesting to note the five issues which experienced greatest positive change in the intervening 19 years, i.e.:

Item	Change in A-B Score
No. 9 – "I don't object to the British people but I don't like the British Government."	-51.5 (-43.3%)
No.13 – "The British have little respect for the Irish people."	-45.6 (-39.6%)
No.1 – "If Ireland did not have its own team in the Olympic Games or international sports, I would cheer for the British."	-21.8 (-20.5%)
No.4 – "The British were even-handed when dealing with Nth. Ireland since 1969."	-15.6 (-11.6%)
No.6 – "Some British qualities are admirable but, on the whole, I don't like them (the British)."	-13.1 (-20.9%)

We already know the high esteem in which respondents hold the 'British people', i.e. 77.2% 'welcoming into kinship' with mean-social-distance score of **1.483** (i.e. in-group).   This is confirmed in No.6 above which represents only **14.5%** agreeing with the statement (see Table No. 11.3).   That having been said, the meaning of the decrease in the 'anti-British score' of Item No. 9 from **119.4** in 1988-89 to **67.9** in 2007-08 on a continuum of **0 to 200** is the very substantial decline in Irish people's disdain for the British Government over the period of nineteen years.   This could be legitimately interpreted as a positive recognition of the role played by the British Government in the Northern Irish Peace Process under the leadership of **Prime Minister, Tony Blair, MP**, Minister **Mo Mowlam, MP**, Minister **Peter Brooke, MP**, and others.

Item No.13 shows a very substantial decrease in Irish people's hostility towards the British people.   This also shows a more favourable view of the British as people to be trusted in relation to Ireland and prepares the way for still more friendly relations, which in turn will lead to further growth in mutual respect.   As neighbouring states this will lead to the material and cultural advantage of both societies[9].   Again, the success of the Northern Peace Process is likely to have contributed substantially to this change in attitude.

The *principle of propinquity* would predict that the Irish would be more supportive of their neighbour's team (in sport) than other international

---

[9] See Table No. 4.1, pages 62-4 above.

teams.   Of course, issues other than proximity can affect sports' loyalties. For example, Ireland is a, relatively speaking, small country while Britain is a large one.   The tendency to support the weaker side may play a role.

While Item No. 1 above shows a significant and substantial increase in support for British teams in the event of Ireland not participating, there is still a substantial minority of respondents (**31.1%**) who would not support the British team (and **22.2%** were undecided).   In this regard, the anti-British score has dropped from **106.2** to **84.4** in the nineteen years between 1988-89 and 2007-08.   This is an important popular confirmation of the improvements in Anglo-Irish relations over the period.

The modest change in Item No. 4 (i.e. from **134.0** to **118.4**) over the nineteen years shows how deeply held is the opinion of the unfairness of the handling of the Northern problem over the 25 years of violence.   This has been the Irish people's perception of the situation.

On the negative side, probably the most disappointing result on Table No. 11.4 has been the moderate increase (since 1988-89) of +**8.4** in relation to the statement: *"I would rather live in Britain than any other place abroad."*   This could be a reflection on the portrayal of living conditions in Britain or the popular print and electronic media.   It is more surprising still in the light of so many people of Irish descent living in Great Britain. Perhaps those responsible for the promotion of the British image in Ireland could take this negative finding on board and seek to correct the obvious distortion of living in Great Britain, which lies behind the opinion expressed in Item No. 2 of Table Nos. 11.3 and 11.4 above.

Other changes recorded were as anticipated and, for the most part, reflect the improving Anglo-Irish relations in the first decade of the 21st century.   These findings must be welcome news for everyone involved in the Northern Irish Peace and Justice Process to date.   Nevertheless, it would be irresponsible to become complacent at this stage as the Anti-British score is still too high in a number of cases.   Additional inter-community, cross-border and Anglo-Irish positive action is required, not only to heal wounds from the past but also to improve perceptions and relations at each of the three levels.   On the ground, there are still too many so-called 'peace-lines' within Northern Ireland, which will require constant effort in Anglo-Irish cooperative action to make redundant.

Part IV – Anti-British Scale by Personal Variables

The examination and analysis of the anti-British scale and its sub-scales by personal variables give the reader a better understanding of the current state of Anglo-Irish attitudes (in the Republic of Ireland). The measure used will be the scale and sub-scales' **anti-British scores** which are calculated on a zero-to-two-hundred (0-200) continuum (see Table No. 11.4 above). The personal variables used are: age, gender, marital status, area of birth, place of rearing (in the Republic), region of residence, education, occupation and social-class position. From an analysis of the variable findings it should be possible to explain the levels of anti-British prejudice and predict changes in the short to medium term.

Table No. 11.5 reports the variation of anti-British scores in each variable. All scores above the sample average are in bold, i.e. scores **above** average indicate **higher** levels of social prejudice against the British.

Table No. 11.5:
Anti-British Scale and Sub-Scales by Personal Variables (P-Scores)

Personal Variable	Full Scale	Political/ Hostility Sub-scale	Low-Esteem Sub-scale	Number
National Sample	62.7	39.2	115.4	992
A. Age	P<.001	P<.002	P<.001	
1. 18-25 years	**69.6**	**46.4**	**122.6**	165
2. 26-40 years	**68.1**	**43.7**	**125.1**	313
3. 41-55 years	58.5	33.2	115.7	242
4. 56-70 years	54.1	34.7	100.0	175
5. 71 years plus	60.0	**41.7**	115.8	96
Score Variation	*15.5*	*13.2*	*25.1*	*(992)*
B. Gender	P<.011	P<.008	N/S	
1. Males	**65.7**	**43.3**	---	493
2. Females	59.9	36.5	---	499
Score Variation	*5.8*	*6.8*	*---*	*(992)*
C. Marital Status	N/S	N/S	P<.001	
1. Single/Never Married	---	---	**116.4**	345
2. Married	---	---	112.8	468
3. Separated/Divorced	---	---	**137.7**	43
4. Permanent Relationship	---	---	**136.5**	70
5. Widowed	---	---	96.9	66
Score Variation	*---*	*---*	*40.8*	*(992)*

255

Table No. 11.5 cont'd. Personal Variable	Full Scale	Political/ Hostility Sub-scale	Low-Esteem Sub-scale	Number
D. Area of Birth	P<.021	P<.047	P<.001	
1. City (100,000 plus)	**64.7**	39.3	**122.7**	415
2. Large Town (10,000 +)	**69.7**	**48.4**	**119.9**	113
3. Town (1,500 plus)	58.2	33.9	115.5	123
4. Rural/Village	59.8	**40.0**	106.2	340
Score Variation	*11.5*	*14.5*	*16.5*	*(991)*
E. Place of Rearing in ROI.	N/S	N/S	P<.004	
1. Dublin (City & County)	---	---	**122.9**	263
2. Rest of Leinster	---	---	**116.4**	158
3. Munster	---	---	105.7	229
4. Connaught/Ulster	---	---	**118.1**	157
Score Variation	---	---	*17.2*	*(808)*
F. Education	P<.001	P<.001	P<.002	
1. Primary or Less	59.0	**41.4**	100.4	115
2. Incomplete Second-Level	**70.2**	**51.1**	113.7	257
3. Complete Second-Level	62.7	38.7	**118.5**	249
4. Third-Level	58.8	32.5	**120.3**	371
Score Variation	*11.4*	*18.6*	*19.9*	*(992)*
G. Occupational Status	N/S	P<.014	P<.019	
1. Unskilled/Semi-Skilled	---	**44.6**	**116.2**	198
2. Skilled/Routine Non-Man.	---	37.0	**121.0**	325
3. Inspectional/Supervisory	---	38.3	107.6	130
4. Professional/Executive	---	31.8	108.9	186
Score Variation	---	*12.8*	*13.4*	*(838)*
H. Social Class Position	N/S	P<.001	N/S	
1. Class I: "Upper Class"	---	38.4	---	39
2. Class II: "Upper-Middle Class"	---	29.7	---	133
3. Class III: "Middle-Mid. Class"	---	35.3	---	226
4. Class IV: "Working Class"	---	39.6	---	354
5. Class V: "Lower Class"	---	**51.8**	---	82
Score Variation	---	*16.5*	---	*(834)*

*Hostility has 9 items. ** Esteem has 4 items
Note: Scores above sample average are in **bold**.   Score variations are in *italics*.

This Table merits serious analysis.   It not only examines the actual findings of the anti-British scale's variations, but it will also be possible to determine the extent to which *post-colonial attitudinal schizophrenia* still survives in our attitudes towards the British, i.e. is low esteem for the British failing to correlate positively with feelings of hostility toward them (the British).

The four items, which combine to produce the average *low-esteem sub-scale* score of **115.4**, are the following (in summary form):

1. Cheer for the British.	**(84.4)**
2. Rather live in Britain.	**(142.2)**
3. World owes Britain a lot.	**(116.7)**
4. British even-handed in Nth. Ireland.	**(118.4)**

The score **115.4** (out of 200) is very useful statistically as it represents a P x Q[10] of 58 x 42 = **2,436**, which is ideal for the production of significant variations. It is close to the maximum P x Q score which is **2,500**.

The nine items, which make up the *Political/Hostility sub-scale* and produced a lower mean score of **39.2** out of 200, are the following (again in summary form):

5. British a decent people.	**(27.3)**
6. Admirable but don't like them.	**(49.6)**
7. British are inferior.	**(21.8)**
8. British slow and unimaginative.	**(22.9)**
9. Don't like British Government.	**(67.9)**
10. Happy for British to get on in Ireland.	**(26.6)**
11. Would never marry a British person.	**(46.6)**
12. Happy at British brought to their knees.	**(20.7)**
13. British have little respect for the Irish.	**(69.5)**

The score of **39.2** represents a much smaller PQ score, i.e. 20 x 80 = **1600**, which is more limited in its potential range of variations between the variable subsamples.

4.1 Age:
The performance of the age variable is, once again, contrary to expectations. The younger age groups have higher anti-British scores than the middle-aged and older. There is hardly any significance between the scores of the 18 to 25 year-olds and the 26 to 40 year-olds.

What is also quite interesting is the consistency between the scoring of the two factors, **low esteem** and **hostility**, which points to a decline in *'post-colonial attitudinal schizophrenia'*. This was to be expected and is an indication that the Irish no longer "look down on themselves while looking up to the British", as was evident in the 1972-73 findings (and to a lesser

---

[10] P = 100-Q. The maximum P x Q is 50 x 50 = **2,500**.

extent in the 1988-89 findings). The absence of signs of 'post-colonial schizophrenia' in the **age variable** has not been confirmed that clearly in other variables in Table No. 11.5 (see **Education**).

The question remains as to the reasons causing younger respondents to be more anti-British than their older fellow-respondents. Both young age groups, i.e. 18 to 25 years and 26 to 40 years, have relatively high levels of educational achievement[11]. This pattern in the case of the 18 to 25 year-olds repeats their response to the social-distance scores in relation to the four 'Great Britain' categories, i.e. 'Welsh', 'English', 'Scottish, and 'British' (see Table No. 11.2, pages 245-6 above). The relatively high anti-British scores of the 26 to 40 year-olds in Table No. 11.5(a) is surprising since this age group has been the most tolerant in other scales. Would this be due to the presence of a political or socio-economic association with the British? It is something that needs to be monitored!

4.2 Gender:
Males have responded more negatively than females in two measures on Table No. 11.5(b) i.e. total scale and 'political/hostility sub-scale'. The differences are not very substantial and are just within the statistical margin of error. This trend towards consensus between male and female attitudes has been borne out many times in the various findings of the 2007-08 survey, i.e. males have been slightly more prejudiced than were females. The 'low esteem' sub-scale failed to elicit a statistically significant variation between the sub-variables.

4.3 Marital Status:
The findings in relation to 'marital status' have been quite mixed. Two scales, i.e. 'full scale' and 'political/hostility sub-scale' produced consensus between the sub-variables. The least negative scores on the 'low-esteem sub-scale' have been the 'Married' and the 'Widowed'. The score variations here have been among the highest of all the variables. This has been largely due to the relatively low level of negativity among the widowed respondents. Obviously, this reflects the findings of the 'age' variable which found that the older respondents were more appreciative and tolerant of the British than were their younger fellow-respondents.

---

[11] See: Table No. 7.8, page 158 above.

4.4 Area of Birth:

This variable measures the influence of urbanisation on the 'anti-British' attitudes of respondents. The findings of Table No. 11.5(d) show that the more urbanised the area of birth of the respondents, the more negative their attitudes towards the British. Small-town-born respondents were the most tolerant subsample and the rural-village-born were also below average in the negativity towards the British. The score-variations of the area of birth variable were substantial in the case of the 'total scale' and the two sub-scales.

It was anticipated (but not confirmed) that the more urbanised would be more positive towards the British than would be the rural/village respondents. The reasons for this anticipation included the more cosmopolitan nature of populations in cities and large towns and the possibility of more favourable contact with the British coming to Ireland. It is possible that the positive experience of Irish workers in Britain down the years and, particularly in recent times, by emigrants from rural and small-town backgrounds (from which areas a large proportion of the population emigrated) has created a better perception of the British people by less urbanised respondents.

4.5 Place of Rearing and Region of Residence:

The negative effect of urban background on the score is evident in the findings of both variables. 'Region of residence' failed to get significant variations in any of the three scales. This represents a very high level of consensus between geographically different places and regions, which is very significant in itself.

4.6 Education:

The following extract from Table No. 11.5(a) and (f) highlights the performance of these two key ordinal variables:

Variable	Range of Variation	Highest Anti-British Score		Between	Lowest Anti-British Score		Mean Sample Score (0-200)
1. Age:							
(a) Total Scale	15.5	18-25 years	**(69.6)**	and	56-70 years	**(54.1)**	62.7
(b) Hostility S-Scale	13.2	18-25 years	**(46.4)**	and	41-55 years	**(33.2)**	39.2
(c) Low Esteem S-S	25.1	26-40 years	**(125.1)**	and	56-70 years	**(100.0)**	115.4
2. Education:							
(a) Total Scale	11.4	Incomplete Sec.	**(70.2)**	and	Third Level	**(58.8)**	62.7
(b) Hostility S-Scale	18.6	Incomplete Sec.	**(51.1)**	and	Third Level	**(32.5)**	39.2
(c) Low Esteem S-S	19.9	Third Level	**(120.3)**	and	Primary or Less	**(100.4)**	115.4

The findings of this ordinal variable show the strongest evidence of the survival of (if reduced) absence of a positive correlation between the performances of the two sub-scales. On the contrary, their trends seem to be going in the opposite direction, i.e. the higher the education the lower their esteem while, at the same time, the lower the education the higher the hostility, when normally low esteem should correlate positively with higher hostility! These are the conditions of *"post-colonial attitudinal schizophrenia"*. The range of variation is quite substantial between education subsamples.

4.7 Occupational Status:

Occupational status performed more or less as anticipated. The high-statused respondents had lower anti-British scores than those lower down on the scale and this was true of all three scales, i.e. full scale and the two sub-scales. This also confirms the absence, so far in the Republic of Ireland, of a high positive correlation between education and occupational status.

In Ireland over the past two decades, there has been an increase in educational participation. At the same time, there has appeared to be an inflation in educational qualifications for most occupations, thereby reducing the correlation between educational standard achieved and occupational status. The anomaly of the absence of a more positive correlation between **education** and **occupation** in the above and other scales merits attention. At times of high unemployment and of high in-migration, the degree of educational inflation is likely to increase. This may have serious consequences for job satisfaction arising from the creative challenge of a person's occupation. Are we seeing here a deskilling of people's work through technology and automation, and at the same time an increased emphasis on education focused towards greater skilling, without adequate attention to the humanities? The emphasis on pragmatism in modern (post-1960s) education needs to be reappraised!

4.8 Social Class Position:

The "Upper Class" and the "Upper-Middle Class" respondents have been the most favourably disposed to the British according to Table No. 11.5(i). There was inconsistency between the findings of the **'Low-esteem'** and **'Hostility'** sub-scales in the case of "Middle-Middle Class", "Working Class" and "Lower Class" respondents. This again points to a degree of the *"post-colonial attitudinal schizophrenia"* present in the population at these levels. See footnote below[12].

Part V – Conclusion

5.1:

The findings of Table No. 11.5 provide a valuable insight into the current state of Irish attitudes towards the British. The complexity of these attitudes is fascinating from the point of view of research into prejudice and tolerance. Despite an appalling history of socio-politico-religious relations which involved colonisation, religious persecution, non-violent and paramilitary conflict over almost one thousand years, the Irish are quite close to the British in more than territorial proximity. The above findings bear this out. What is most noteworthy about recent changes is the reduction in political hostility since 1988-89. In the opinion of the present author, the arrival at an acceptable settlement to the problems of Northern Ireland, as confirmed in the *Good Friday Agreement of 1998*, has had a most positive influence on Irish people's appreciation of the British political establishment's role in facilitating such progress (see Item No. 9 of the scale on pages 251 and 252). The nurturing of this new situation, despite inevitable difficulties from time to time, deserves maximum support from the political and economic establishments of Great Britain and the Republic of Ireland. The change in Irish attitudes towards the British because of the acceptable solution to the Northern Irish 'Troubles' could well provide a model for other areas of deeply engrained conflict in the world. If this change can happen in Ireland, surely it can happen elsewhere!

---

[12] The difference between respondents' perceived social status and their actual position on the five-step scale worked out according to the Hollingshead Method which is most interesting, i.e.:

Table No. 11.6:
Perceived Self-(Social) Status of Irish-Born Respondents by Calculated Social Status

Social Status	Perceived A	Calculated B	Nominal % Difference (A – B)
Class I: "Upper Class"	0.7%	4.5%	-3.8%
Class II: "Upper-Middle Class"	7.9%	16.3%	-8.4%
Class III: "Middle-Middle Class"	49.2%	26.9%	+22.3%
Class IV: "Working Class"	39.8%	42.4%	-2.6%
Class V: "Lower Class"	2.4%	9.9%	-7.5%
Number	819	855	---

The above findings show that almost half of the respondents (**49.2%**) thought of themselves as **"Middle-Middle Class"**, while only **26.9%** fitted into that status according to Hollingshead social class position rating. There was an underrating by respondents of their perceived social status of **12.2%** in the upper two "Classes" and of **10.2%** in the lower two "Classes".

5.2:

When the anti-British scale is examined by personal variables, there is evidence of a reduction in the level of *post-colonial attitudinal schizophrenia*, which reflects not only a decline in Irish hostility toward the British but also a growth in Irish people's acceptance of themselves as **an independent people**.   In relation to our esteem for the British, it is now much less a 'slavish' **looking up** to our 'former masters' and **looking down** on our 'former colonised selves'.   Most emancipated minorities need time to believe they are equal and do not have to exaggerate their equal status.   This is a welcome maturing of Irish-British inter-perception which is reflected in the above findings.

5.3:

Having agreed with and welcomed the evidence of the maturing of Irish-British intergroup perception and overall improvement in mutual respect (on the basis of adult equality), there are still residues of negativity in the Irish attitudes towards the British.   There is little room for complacency.   The **low esteem factor anti-British score** is still too high (at 115.4 out of 200) for the preferred status one expects between independent 'national' neighbours.

Also there is the question of the relatively **higher anti-British scores** among the 18 to 40 year-olds on Table No. 11.5(a) on page 255 above.   It would be regrettable if this were indicative of a negative trend in the near-future.   The performance of education, i.e. 'Complete Second-Level' and 'Third-Level', with above-average anti-British low-esteem scores, is disappointing and contrary to expectations.   **Northern Ireland**, which for decades was the source of much anti-British sentiment and hostility, has now become the occasion of improving tolerance of, and respect for, Britain.   In a sense, Northern Ireland has become a *felix culpa* for Irish-British attitudes and relations!   The task facing both peoples is to keep up the positive momentum and avoid retreating into past animosities of perceiving 'each other' in unfriendly terms.   Because of our history, Irish-British relations cannot be taken for granted!

In the light of the above findings, serious research into the attitudes of the citizens of Great Britain towards Ireland and the Irish people would be most interesting.

***

CHAPTER XII
Prejudice towards Social Categories

Under the general heading "Prejudice towards Social Categories" it is proposed to examine the Irish people's attitudes towards nine stimulus categories, i.e. (in alphabetical order):

1. 'Alcoholics'
2. 'Drug Addicts'
3. 'Gay People'
4. 'Heavy Drinkers'
5. 'People with Mental Disability'
6. 'People with Physical Disability'
7. 'Unemployed'
8. 'Unmarried Mothers'
9. 'Working Class'

It is possible to divide the above nine categories into three particular groups, namely,

(a) *Personal/Domestic*, i.e. 'Gay People', 'People with Mental Disability', 'People with Physical Disability' and 'Unmarried Mothers';

(b) *Compulsive Behaviour*, i.e. 'Alcoholics', 'Drug Addicts' and 'Heavy Drinkers;

(c) *Socio-Economic*, i.e. 'Unemployed' and 'Working Class'.

In the case of most of the 'social categories', the attitudes of the public towards them are especially important because of their dependence on public support for their well-being. With regard to people with **mental or physical disability**, their special needs require public as well as domestic support. For those with problems arising out of compulsive behaviour or addiction, positive public attitudes are essential for their rehabilitation while negative dispositions towards them tend to aggravate their situation. Social prejudice impedes the personal and social development and fulfilment of members of all categories. Prejudice leads to negative behaviour and discrimination. 'Gay bashing' is a classic expression of anti-gay prejudices.

Part I – General Findings

Table No. 12.1 gives the social-distance score for the nine social (stimulus) categories for 2007-08 and 1988-89. Two measures are highlighted, i.e.

percentages willing to "admit members of each category to kinship" and prepared to "deny them citizenship". The 'mean-social-distance' scores are also recorded in each case. The nominal differences in each of the three measures between 1988-89 and 2007-08 are given in each category. This gives the degree of change in prejudice and tolerance for the intervening nineteen years.

In addition to changes in actual scores, the **rank-order** position of each stimulus category is reported on Table No. 12.1 for both national surveys, i.e. 1988-89 and 2007-08. It should be noted that 'Heavy Drinkers' (as a category) were introduced for the first time in the 2007-08 survey and thereby are not available for comparative performance.

As pointed out in earlier Tables, categories with low mean-social-distance scores, i.e. numbers one to four on the Table, would have limited capacity for change. Each of the four, 'Working class', 'People with Physical Disability', 'Unmarried Mothers' and 'Unemployed', are within the **in-group classification** (MSD less than 1.500).

Table No. 12.1:
Social Distance towards the Social Categories (2007-08 and 1988-89)

Stimulus Category (In order of prejudice)	Rank Order 2007-08 (1988-89)	A. 2007-08			B. 1988-89			Nominal Difference (A – B)		
		Kinship	Deny C'ship	MSD	Kinship	Deny C'ship	MSD	Kinship	Deny C'ship	MSD
1. Working Class	2nd (2nd)	85.6%	0.2%	1.228	86.8%	0.0%	1.210	**-1.2%**	**+0.2%**	**+0.028**
2. People with Physical Disability	3rd (8th)	83.0%	0.3%	1.268	57.8%	0.3%	1.581	**+25.2%**	**0.0%**	**-0.313**
3. Unmarried Mothers	5th (16th)	82.4%	0.7%	1.339	61.1%	1.0%	1.684	**+21.3%**	**-0.3%**	**-0.345**
4. Unemployed	12th (5th)	80.9%	2.2%	1.446	78.1%	0.2%	1.345	**+2.8%**	**+2.0%**	**+0.101**
5. People with Mental Disability	18th (21st)	74.4%	3.1%	1.612	34.6%	0.8%	2.010	**+39.8%**	**+2.3%**	**-0.398**
6. Gay People	24th (54th)	62.8%	5.3%	1.923	12.5%	25.8%	3.793	**+50.3%**	**-20.5%**	**-1.870**
7. Heavy Drinkers	40th (---)	41.9%	13.6%	2.626	---	---	---	---	---	---
8. Alcoholics	48th (42nd)	32.7%	14.5%	2.937	13.8%	8.4%	3.105	**+18.9%**	**+6.1%**	**-0.168**
9. Drug Addicts	51st (58th)	19.7%	33.7%	4.194	5.3%	43.7%	4.798	**+14.4%**	**-10.0%**	**-0.604**

Notes: (1) The rank-order for **2007-08** is out of a range of **51 Stimulus Categories**.
The range of categories for **1988-89** was **59 Stimulus Categories**.
(2) The rank-order places for **1988-89** are given (in brackets).

The findings of the above Table are, for the most part, quite optimistic, with still much progress necessary. Changes in 'Working Class' score were not significant, i.e. within the normal margin of error. All other changes were statistically significant. The relatively high level of hostility towards 'Drug Addicts' is likely to militate against their rehabilitation in society. In fact, the current level of prejudice (which is a hate attitude) is likely to have the opposite effect on 'Drug Addicts' behaviour and lead to the inclination to indulge more in this self-destructive compulsive behaviour.

Commentary on the present state of attitudes towards the nine social categories will be given in Parts II, III and IV of this chapter. In Part II it is proposed to examine 'Personal and Domestic Categories' (i.e. 'People with Physical Disability', 'Unmarried Mothers', 'People with Mental Disability' and 'Gay People') by personal variables. Part III examines 'Compulsive Behaviour Categories', (i.e. 'Alcoholics', 'Drug Addicts' and 'Heavy Drinkers') while Part IV analyses the 'Socio-Economic Categories' (i.e. 'Unemployed' and 'Working Class'). 'Travelling People' as a 'social category' is dealt with separately in this text in Chapter XIII below[1].

Part II – Personal and Domestic Social Categories by Personal Variables

The four stimulus categories experienced a substantial nominal increase in the percentage admitting to family of over 20% between 1988-89 and 2007-08, i.e. 'Gay People' (+50.3%), 'People with Mental Disability' (+39.8%), 'People with Physical Disability' (+25.2%) and 'Unmarried Mothers' (+21.3%). These are very significant measures of improvement in social tolerance and are very welcome results. 'Gay People', for instance, dropped by almost two stages (1.866) in the *Bogardus Social Distance Scale* within the relatively short time span of nineteen years. This must be unique in social-distance measurement! It indicates a very substantial decrease in **homophobia** in the Republic of Ireland.

Table No. 12.2 gives the social distance scores (i.e. 'Admission to Kinship' and 'Denial of Citizenship') by personal variables.

---

[1] See Mac Gréil, Micheál, (2010), *Emancipation of the Travelling People*, Maynooth, Survey and Research Unit, Department of Sociology, NUI Maynooth.

Table No. 12.2:
'Personal' and 'Domestic Social' Categories by Personal Variables

Personal Variable	People with Physical Disability		Unmarried Mothers		People with Mental Disability		Gay People		No.
	Admit to Kinship	Deny Citizen'p	Admit to Kinship	Deny Citizen'p	Admit to Kinship	Deny Citizen'p	Admit to Kinship	Deny Citizen'p	
Total Sample	83.0%	0.4%	82.4%	0.7%	74.4%	3.1%	62.8%	5.3%	1,015
A. Age	P<.001		P<.001		P<.005		P<.001		
1. 18-25 years	75.1%	**0.6%**	81.7%	**1.8%**	**74.4%**	1.8%	56.0%	**6.6%**	168
2. 26-40 years	**84.8%**	0.0%	**86.3%**	0.3%	**78.3%**	2.4%	**72.1%**	4.9%	325
3. 41-55 years	79.7%	0.0%	80.2%	**0.8%**	66.8%	**4.0%**	57.7%	1.6%	245
4. 56-70 years	**89.3%**	0.6%	79.5%	0.6%	**75.7%**	1.7%	61.2%	4.4%	178
5. 71 years plus	87.6%	1.0%	82.3%	0.0%	**77.9%**	6.3%	59.4%	**15.6%**	96
Score Variation	*14.2%*	*1.0%*	*6.8%*	*1.8%*	*11.1%*	*4.6%*	*16.1%*	*14.0%*	*1,012*
B. Marital Status	P<.001		P<.001		P<.001		P<.001		
1. Single/Never Married	79.8%	0.0%	**83.0%**	**0.9%**	73.7%	**5.3%**	62.0%	**7.3%**	356
2. Married	**86.0%**	2.0%	82.7%	0.4%	74.6%	1.2%	61.8%	2.3%	468
3. Separated/Divorced	**86.0%**	2.3%	**84.1%**	0.0%	**86.0%**	0.0%	76.7%	9.3%	44
4. Permanent Relation'p	74.6%	0.0%	73.2%	**4.2%**	62.5%	4.2%	71.4%	0.0%	72
5. Widowed	**89.7%**	0.0%	**85.3%**	0.0%	83.3%	4.5%	58.8%	17.7%	69
Score Variation	*15.1%*	*2.3%*	*12.1%*	*4.2%*	*23.5%*	*5.3%*	*17.9%*	*17.7%*	*1,009*
C. Area of Birth	P<.001		P<.001		P<.001		P<.001		
1. City (100,000 +)	78.9%	**0.4%**	80.3%	0.4%	70.2%	2.7%	**68.4%**	2.4%	419
2. Lge.Town (10,000 +)	**83.3%**	**0.8%**	**83.2%**	**0.8%**	**78.3%**	1.6%	67.2%	3.4%	119
3. Town (1,500 +)	**87.6%**	0.0%	**84.6%**	**0.8%**	**79.1%**	3.9%	60.5%	4.7%	132
4. Rural/Village	**86.0%**	0.0%	**83.2%**	1.5%	75.7%	3.5%	55.2%	9.9%	345
Score Variation	*8.7%*	*0.8%*	*4.3%*	*1.1%*	*8.9%*	*2.3%*	*13.2%*	*7.5%*	*1,015*
D. Place of Rearing (in Republic of Ireland)	P<.003		P<.001		P<.001		P<.001		
1. Dublin (City & Co.)	79.0%	**0.4%**	79.2%	0.4%	73.5%	2.3%	**69.2%**	1.6%	243
2. Rest of Leinster	**89.6%**	0.0%	81.7%	**1.2%**	**81.5%**	3.8%	65.9%	6.7%	157
3. Munster	**88.7%**	0.0%	**88.3%**	0.4%	**77.8%**	2.6%	65.1%	7.3%	219
4. Connaught/Ulster	77.9%	0.0%	**81.6%**	0.0%	67.7%	3.6%	48.2%	7.9%	154
Score Variation	*11.7%*	*0.4%*	*9.1%*	*1.2%*	*13.6%*	*1.5%*	*21.0%*	*6.3%*	*773*
E. Region of Residence	N/S		P<.001		P<.015		P<.001		
1. B.M.W.	---	---	**83.4%**	**1.8%**	70.1%	**4.4%**	48.5%	**7.7%**	269
2. Dublin	---	---	**82.2%**	0.3%	**74.0%**	3.2%	**70.3%**	1.7%	284
3. Mid-East & Sth-East	---	---	76.1%	0.5%	**80.1%**	2.4%	64.2%	**9.1%**	218
4. Mid-West & Sth-W.	---	---	**86.9%**	0.4%	**74.3%**	2.1%	68.5%	3.0%	234
Score Variation	*---*	*---*	*10.8%*	*1.5%*	*10.0%*	*2.3%*	*21.8%*	*7.4%*	*1,005*
F. Education	P<.001		N/S		P<.001		P<.001		
1. Primary or Less	**94.0%**	0.0%	---	---	**84.7%**	2.5%	65.0%	**12.0%**	117
2. Incomplete Sec-Lev.	**89.2%**	0.0%	---	---	**82.1%**	3.0%	63.6%	5.0%	262
3. Complete Sec-Level	**83.9%**	0.4%	---	---	75.1%	**5.6%**	58.8%	7.0%	255
4. Third-Level	75.0%	**0.6%**	---	---	64.9%	1.6%	**64.3%**	2.4%	381
Score Variation	*19.0%*	*0.6%*	*---*	*---*	*19.8%*	*4.0%*	*6.2%*	*9.6%*	*1,015*

Table No. 12.2 cont'd. Personal Variable	People with Physical Disability		Unmarried Mothers		People with Mental Disability		Gay People		No.
	Admit to Kinship	Deny Citizen'p	Admit to Kinship	Deny Citizen'p	Admit to Kinship	Deny Citizen'p	Admit to Kinship	Deny Citizen'p	
G. Occupational Status	N/S		N/S		P<.001		P<.001		
1. Unskilled/Semi-Skil.	---	---	---	---	**77.9%**	1.5%	58.5%	**7.3%**	207
2. Skilled/R. Non-M.	---	---	---	---	71.4%	**4.0%**	**65.1%**	4.4%	328
3. Inspect./Supervisory	---	---	---	---	74.0%	**7.7%**	61.7%	**6.8%**	133
4. Professional/Exec.	---	---	---	---	72.3%	0.5%	**71.9%**	1.0%	191
Score Variation	*---*	*---*	*---*	*---*	*6.5%*	*7.2%*	*13.4%*	*5.8%*	*859*
H. Social Class Position	P<.001		P<.001		P<.001		P<.001		
1. Class I: Upper Class	79.5%	0.0%	79.5%	0.0%	64.1%	2.6%	**74.4%**	0.0%	38
2. Class II: Upper-Mid. Cl.	82.7%	**0.7%**	**83.6%**	**1.4%**	73.4%	0.0%	**75.4%**	1.4%	140
3. Class III: Mid-Mid. Cl.	78.0%	**0.4%**	78.4%	0.9%	65.8%	**4.4%**	57.0%	2.7%	226
4. Class IV: Working Cl.	**84.5%**	0.3%	**84.3%**	**1.2%**	**76.5%**	**4.2%**	64.6%	**7.4%**	361
5. Class V: Lower Class	**92.9%**	0.0%	**92.9%**	0.0%	**87.1%**	2.4%	58.3%	**8.3%**	83
Score Variation	*14.9%*	*0.7%*	*14.5%*	*1.4%*	*23.0%*	*4.4%*	*18.4%*	*8.3%*	*848*

Note: Percentages above sample average are **in bold**.   Variations are *in italics*.

At first glance, it is noteworthy that only four of the thirty-two variable sub-scales failed to register a significant variation in scores, i.e. 'People with Physical Disability' by 'Region of Residence' and by 'Occupation', and 'Unmarried Mothers' by 'Education' and 'Occupational Status'. In the case of each of the three sub-scales, there was statistical consensus between the responses of the sub-variables.

It is proposed to examine/analyse the findings of the above Table (No. 12.2) under three headings, namely, 'People with Disabilities', 'Unmarried Mothers' and 'Gay People'. The two 'disability' categories will be taken together.

2.1 People with Disabilities (by Personal Variables):

Table No. 12.1 has shown that both categories' social-distance scores improved substantially between 1988-89 and 2007-08. 'Admission to Kinship' improved from **57.8%** to **83.0%** (nominal +25.2%) for 'People with Physical Disability' and from **34.6%** to **74.4%** (nominal +39.8%) for 'People with Mental Disability' over the nineteen years' interval. When calculated by percentage improvement the extent of favourable changes stands out, i.e. 43.6% and 115.0% respectively. 'People with Physical Disability' have moved into the 'in-group' categories (less than 1.500) with their MSD of **1.268**, while 'People with Mental Disability' are very close to 'in-group' status with their MSD of **1.612**. This is very positive news for people with disabilities in Irish society today and reflects well on the dispositions of the adult population.

An examination of the attitudes of the various subsamples within the personal variables (on Table No. 12.2) for each of the 'Disability' stimulus categories is interesting. '**Age**' groups most favourably disposed in 'Admitting to Kinship' were the older subsamples, i.e. those 56 years and older and the 26 to 40 year-olds. The relatively high percentage (13.6%) of the 71 years plus, who would 'Deny Citizenship' to 'People with Mental Disability' was disappointing and reveals a degree of polarisation in their response.

'**Marital Status**' recorded relatively favourable results for 'Married', 'Separated/Divorced' and 'Widowed' in relation to both categories. These are encouraging results in that they are the main family subsamples. The performance of respondents living in 'Permanent Relationships' was disappointing.

In the case of '**Area of Birth**', which measures the influence of the degree of urbanisation of the respondents' background, those born in cities *(100,000 plus)* were the least welcoming of 'People with Disabilities' into kinship, whereas the more rural and townspeople were above average in their 'Admission to Kinship' scores.

'**Place of Rearing**' and '**Region of Residence**' produced mixed results. The latter variable failed to elicit a statistically significant variation in relation to 'People with Physical Disability' which means there was a consensus between the subsamples.

'**Education**' findings were not as anticipated for both categories. Those with lower educational achievement were more tolerant towards 'People with Disabilities' than were those with 'Third Level'. This is difficult to explain. It raises questions about the link between the higher educated and social tolerance! Is it an example of 'meritocratic' prejudice and a bias against perceived weakness and in favour of the "survival of the fittest"?

There was consensus in relation to 'People with Physical Disability' in the case of '**Occupational Status**'. In the findings for 'People with Mental Disability', the 'Unskilled/Semi-Skilled' subsample was the most tolerant, while the **other grades'** respondents were not as welcoming. It should be pointed out that the **score variations** were quite moderate.

'**Social Class Position**' results were not as expected. The "Lower Class" and the "Working Class" were more supportive towards both categories of 'People with Disabilities' than were the "Upper and Middle Classes". This points to an element of 'social class' as well as a 'meritocratic' prejudice at work. This is all the more surprising when one realises that physical or mental disability is not social-class determined. It can be the product of accidents, illness or genetic inheritance. This level of solidarity between those at the lower end of the social ladder with people suffering from disability is both noteworthy and praiseworthy!

It should be noted that all of the above variations are within a relatively high level of tolerance towards 'People with Disabilities'. The value of the information about the performance of the different variables is to discover parts of the population whose support could be improved. This is particularly true for 'People with Disabilities' since many of them need public support for a good quality of life.

2.2 Unmarried Mothers:

The improvement in the status of 'Unmarried Mothers' in the Republic of Ireland since 1988-89 has been substantial and significant. They now rank *5th in rank-order* preference out of a list of 51 stimulus categories (see Table No. 4.1, pages 62-4 above). The percentage admitting 'Unmarried Mothers' to kinship went from **61.3%** in 1988-89 to **82.4%** in 2007-08 (nominal increase of 21.3%) or a proportionate increase of **34.9%**. 'Unmarried Mothers' are very much an in-group in the Republic of Ireland with an MSD of **1.339**. This result is most reassuring for a category of citizens who needs public support to enable them to carry out the onerous and responsible maternal role.

The range of score variations in relation to most personal variables in the case of 'Unmarried Mothers' has been relatively moderate. 'Marital Status', 'Region of Residence' and 'Social Class Position' were exceptions in producing a score variation of over 10% between the subsamples.

'**Marital Status**' had three subsamples over the sample average in the percentages 'Admitting to Kinship' of 'Unmarried Mothers', i.e. 'Married', 'Separated/Divorced' and 'Widowed' – all the 'parental' variables. This shows solidarity between married and unmarried mothers and must be very reassuring for women who become pregnant outside of marriage. It is also an indication of potential domestic support for their 'children' and their acceptance within the unmarried mother's family of origin, thereby making the extended family an ally to them!

'**Education**' failed to produce statistically significant variations between its subsamples. In other words, there was consensus between the responses of the different educational levels *vis-à-vis* social distance towards 'Unmarried Mothers' along the sample's average scores.

'**Occupational Status**' failed to register a statistically significant variation, while '**Social Class Position**' findings show that "Lower" and "Working Class" respondents were more for welcoming 'Unmarried Mothers' into kinship. The "Upper-Middle Class" was also above average in welcoming them into kinship. The least welcoming were the "Upper Class" and the "Middle-Middle Class". Of course, even those subsamples with lowest scores were still over 78% in welcoming 'Unmarried Mothers' into kinship.

2.3 Homophobia or Prejudice against Gay People:
Tables Nos. 4.1 and 4.2 (pages 62-6 above) have recorded the very substantial improvement in the social-distance score of 'Gay People' between 1988-89 and 2007-08. Of the 46 stimulus categories tested in both surveys, 'Gay People' improved most. Within the nineteen years, the mean-social distance score reduced by **1.870**, which is almost two stages on a one-to-seven scale. 'Gay People's' rank-order of preference position went from **45th** in 1988-89 to **24th** in 2007-08, (i.e. an improvement of 21 places on the 46-place scale). This must be one of the highest levels of improvement of the standing of a minority group over such a relatively short period of time. That being said, there is still room for further improvement in the social-distance scores of 'Gay People'. Because of the history of segregation and persecution of 'Gay People' throughout the world, it is very important to counter any signs of homophobic expression in Irish society.

'Gay People' registered a statistically significant variation in each of the eight personal variables on Table No. 12.2. The response of '**Age**' was **mixed** and against expectations. Both of the youngest and oldest age-groups were the least positive, i.e. 18 to 25 year-olds and the 71 years plus. These two subsamples had below-sample-average percentages admitting

'Gay People' to kinship and above-average 'denying them citizenship'. The response of the young respondents was not expected while the 71 years plus registered the highest percentage (15.6%) 'denying citizenship'!

'**Marital Status**' produced an interesting result which shows 'Single/Never Married' and 'Married' within the 'margins of error' of the mean in admitting to kinship. The 'Separated/Divorced' and those in 'Permanent Relationships' being most in favour of welcoming 'Gay People' into kinship, although the former subsample had an above-average percentage denying citizenship. The 'Widowed' were least tolerant of the subsamples, with over three times the sample average (5.3%) 'denying citizenship', i.e. **17.7%**. The age factor influenced this result.

The responses of subsamples of the variable '**Area of Birth**' were as anticipated with the more urbanised being more tolerant. 'Rural/Village' respondents were substantially more intolerant of 'Gay People' than were those from an urbanised background. This again was reflected in the 'Place of Rearing' and 'Region of Residence' variables.

'**Education**' produced a mixed result, which was not as anticipated. The 'Complete Second-Level' was the subsample that was least welcoming into kinship. The score variation of 'Education' was relatively low. '**Occupational Status**' was as anticipated with the 'Professional/Executive' most tolerant and the 'Unskilled/Semi-Skilled' least so.

Social Class Position subsamples' results were mixed. The least well-disposed to 'Gay People' were respondents from the "Lower Class" and the "Middle-Middle Class". The two highest classes were most in favour, i.e. the highest percentages 'Admitting to Kinship' (74.4% and 75.4%) and the lowest percentages 'Denying Citizenship' (0.0% and 1.4%). The "Working Class" subsample had a mixed result, i.e. above-average 'Admitting to Kinship' (64.6%) and above-average 'Denying Citizenship' (7.4%).

In summary, the position of 'Gay People' in the attitudes of the adults of the Republic of Ireland has improved very substantially between 1988-89 and 2007-08. Having acknowledged this welcome result, there is still a need for further improvement, i.e. increase the percentage 'welcoming into the family' from **62.8%** and reduce the **5.3%** who would 'deny citizenship'. 'Denying Citizenship' to a person on the basis of perceived sexual orientation is repugnant to the Irish Constitution and contrary to basic human rights. Of course, this is also true for other minorities, many of whom have had much higher negative percentages, e.g. 'Travelling People' with **18.2%** of respondents denying them citizenship.

Part III – Compulsive-Behaviour Categories

The special importance of public attitudes towards people with 'compulsive-behaviour' problems is the effect of such attitudes on the rehabilitation or moderation of their compulsive behaviour. The three stimulus categories selected for inclusion in the 2007-08 national survey do not include all forms of compulsive behaviour.

The following **extract** from Table No. 12.1 (page 264) gives the overall performance of the three compulsive-behaviour categories.

Stimulus Category	Year of Survey	Admission to Kinship	Denial of Citizenship	MSD
1. 'Heavy Drinkers'	2007-08	41.9%	13.6%	2.626
	1988-89	---	---	---
	Change	---	---	---
2. 'Alcoholics'	2007-08	32.7%	14.5%	2.937
	1988-89	13.8%	8.4%	3.105
	Change	+18.9%	+6.1%	-0.168
3. 'Drug Addicts'	2007-08	19.7%	33.7%	4.174
	1988-89	5.3%	43.7%	4.798
	Change	+14.4%	-10.0%	-0.604

'Heavy Drinkers', as a stimulus category, was introduced in the 2007-08 survey thereby not making it possible to measure change since the previous surveys. The findings for 2007-08 are much more negative than anticipated. In a society that has become fairly notorious for its heavy drinking, the above findings must be quite surprising. Irish people are often said to be too tolerant of over-indulgence in alcoholic liquor. This general impression does not match with these findings.

Only two-fifths of the adult population (41.9%) would be happy to welcome a 'Heavy Drinker' into kinship. Worse still, one-in-seven (13.6%) would 'deny citizenship' to those seen as heavy drinkers. These are serious indicators of **widespread public disapproval of heavy drinking in Ireland**! In this context, it is difficult to understand how the aggressive promotion of alcohol and its very wide availability (in off-licences and supermarkets) is tolerated in Irish society. Is it owing to the fact that the production and distribution of alcohol is a macro-commercial interest and young people are inducted (unwittingly) into the over-dependence on alcohol for their normal indoor recreational pastime for commercial and vested interests?

The above figures should strengthen the hands of those who are engaged in promoting the moderate use of alcohol and the prevention of excessive drinking. They also implicitly support the implementation of **statutory control of heavy drinking** and the **curtailment of unregulated outlets** for the easy access to alcoholic drink.

The position of **'Alcoholics'** has both improved and disimproved over the intervening nineteen years. The percentage 'admitting to kinship' more than doubled, i.e. it went from 13.8% in 1988-89 to 32.7% in 2007-08. This is very good in that it indicates a greater level of sensed-support for the rehabilitation of 'Alcoholics' in the Republic of Ireland, despite the fact that two-thirds would still not welcome 'Alcoholics' into kinship.

On the negative side, two-in-thirteen (14.5%) would deny 'Alcoholics' citizenship, which is nearly double what it was in 1988-89, i.e. percentage 'denying citizenship' to 'Alcoholics' went from **8.4%** in 1988-89 to **14.5%** in 2007-08. This is further evidence of a growing intolerant minority in Irish society (Republic of Ireland) which is large enough to be socially dysfunctional and, possibly, disruptive of public support for the rehabilitation of 'Alcoholics'. It can also become a cause of the 'Alcoholic's' even greater indulgence in alcoholic liquor!

The position of 'Drug Addicts' is still very negative and totally counterproductive. It should be remembered that 'Drug Addicts' are not 'Drug Pushers'. Like 'Alcoholics' they are most likely to be **victims** of exploitation by pushers and commercial interests and the failure of society to provide protective norms and socialise the young to enjoy life without dependence on addictive substances to provide escape from boredom by exotic experience! Drug addiction in modern society is quite common and is being promoted by a 'super-rich underworld'.

The change in 'admission to kinship' improved by a factor of four, i.e. from **5.3%** in 1988-89 to **19.7%** in 2007-08 is greatly to be welcomed. It is, however, still dangerously low for the successful rehabilitation of the 'Drug Addict'. The percentage willing to deny citizenship to 'Drug

Addicts' has remained very high at **33.7%** over the nineteen years' gap between the two national surveys.

This result is typical of the public's negative attitudes to what it considers **deviant**, i.e. **"insulate the deviant"** or remove him or her from social circulation.   Hence, the desire to incarcerate all deviants in prisons: "Lock them up and throw away the key".   In Ireland, it had been the practice to **deport** our deviants to Van Diemen's Land and elsewhere in the early 19th century.   Our prisons and asylums became "Van Diemen's Lands at home" since the 1850s (because of the closure of deportation opportunities).   Of course, this approach to social deviance is counter-productive especially for people who become defined as compulsive behaviour 'deviants'.   When addiction is seen as **an illness**, the public reaction is **"to cure"** or **"to rehabilitate"** the ailing victim of the habit. Hence, the importance of redefining alcoholism or drug addiction as **diseases** rather than **deviant behaviour**!

Table No. 12.3 gives a breakdown of the key social-distance scores of 'Compulsive-Behaviour Categories' by personal variables.

Table No. 12.3:   Compulsive-Behaviour Stimulus Categories by Personal Variables

Personal Variable	Heavy Drinkers		Alcoholics		Drug Addicts		No.
	Admit to Kinship	Deny Citz'ship	Admit to Kinship	Deny Citz'ship	Admit to Kinship	Deny Citz'ship	
Total Sample	41.9%	13.6%	32.7%	15.5%	19.7%	33.7%	1,015
A. Age	P<.020		P<.012		P<.002		
1. 18-25 years	41.1%	**16.0%**	25.9%	**18.8%**	17.8%	**36.7%**	168
2. 26-40 years	**47.5%**	14.8%	**38.0%**	12.8%	**25.7%**	28.5%	325
3. 41-55 years	36.5%	10.6%	30.9%	13.0%	15.6%	32.8%	245
4. 56-70 years	39.9%	9.6%	**34.3%**	12.3%	16.9%	**33.9%**	178
5. 71 years plus	41.2%	**21.6%**	27.6%	**21.6%**	18.6%	**48.5%**	96
Score Variation	*11.0%*	*12.0%*	*10.4%*	*9.3%*	*10.1%*	*20.0%*	*1,012*
B. Gender	P<.001		N/S		N/S		
1. Males	**46.1%**	12.0%	---	---	---	---	499
2. Females	37.9%	**15.0%**	---	---	---	---	516
Score Variation	*8.2%*	*3.0%*	*---*	*---*	*---*	*---*	*1,015*
C. Marital Status	P<.011		N/S		N/S		
1. Single/Never Married	41.3%	**16.1%**	---	---	---	---	356
2. Married	41.2%	10.4%	---	---	---	---	468
3. Separated/Divorced	**41.9%**	9.3%	---	---	---	---	44
4. Permanent Relation'p	**43.7%**	25.4%	---	---	---	---	72
5. Widowed	**49.3%**	14.4%	---	---	---	---	69
Score Variation	*8.2%*	*16.1%*	*---*	*---*	*---*	*---*	*1,009*

Table No.12.3 (Cont'd.) Personal Variable	Heavy Drinkers		Alcoholics		Drug Addicts		No.
	Admit to Kinship	Deny Citz'ship	Admit to Kinship	Deny Citz'ship	Admit to Kinship	Deny Citz'ship	
D. Area of Birth	N/S		N/S		P<.002		
1. City (100,000+)	---	---	---	---	17.9%	30.0%	419
2. Large Town (10,000+)	---	---	---	---	**22.7%**	29.4%	119
3. Town (1,500+)	---	---	---	---	18.0%	31.2%	132
4. Rural/Village	---	---	---	---	**21.6%**	**40.2%**	345
Score Variation	*---*	*---*	*---*	*---*	*4.8%*	*10.8%*	*1,015*
E. Place of Rearing (ROI)	P<.001		P<.001		P<.001		
1. Dublin (City & Co.)	**44.6%**	**16.1%**	29.7%	**17.3%**	21.5%	30.6%	243
2. Rest of Leinster	39.9%	**20.2%**	31.5%	**19.1%**	17.9%	**51.9%**	157
3. Munster	**50.4%**	6.8%	**46.5%**	7.0%	**23.6%**	26.7%	219
4. Connaught/Ulster	26.2%	10.4%	23.2%	12.8%	12.1%	**34.5%**	154
Score Variation	*24.2%*	*13.4%*	*23.3%*	*12.1%*	*11.5%*	*26.2%*	*773*
F. Region of Residence	P<.001		P<.001		P<.001		
1. B.M.W.	30.1%	**19.5%**	23.9%	**19.1%**	12.3%	**43.9%**	269
2. Dublin	**50.9%**	12.3%	30.4%	**16.6%**	**23.4%**	26.6%	284
3. Mid-East & South-East	42.4%	**14.8%**	**35.2%**	11.8%	**21.7%**	**44.3%**	218
4. Mid-West & Sth-West	**44.1%**	7.2%	**43.2%**	8.9%	**21.6%**	21.2%	234
Score Variation	*20.8%*	*12.3%*	*12.8%*	*10.2%*	*11.1%*	*23.1%*	*1,005*
G. Education	P<.001		P<.001		P<.001		
1. Primary or Less	**50.4%**	18.8%	41.5%	**18.7%**	**26.7%**	**40.5%**	117
2. Incomplete Sec-Level	**48.1%**	13.0%	**34.9%**	12.7%	19.2%	**35.8%**	262
3. Complete Sec.-Level	**44.7%**	13.0%	31.5%	**16.8%**	18.5%	**39.9%**	255
4. Third-Level	32.8%	12.5%	29.5%	12.9%	18.8%	26.2%	381
Score Variation	*17.6%*	*6.3%*	*11.0%*	*6.0%*	*8.2%*	*16.3%*	*1,015*
H. Occupational Status	P<.001		P<.004		N/S		
1. Unskilled/Semi-Sk.	41.5%	**14.0%**	28.2%	14.1%	---	---	207
2. Skilled/R. Non-Man.	**43.8%**	12.3%	32.1%	13.8%	---	---	328
3. Inspect./Supervisory	39.1%	**15.8%**	34.8%	**21.2%**	---	---	133
4. Professional/Exec.	40.3%	10.0%	**36.1%**	11.0%	---	---	191
Score Variation	*4.7%*	*5.8%*	*7.9%*	*10.2%*	*---*	*---*	*859*
I. Social Class Position	P<.001		P<.001		P<.005		
1. Class I "Upper Class"	**59.0%**	7.7%	**42.1%**	**21.1%**	**25.6%**	**35.9%**	38
2. Class II "Upper-Middle C."	37.7%	9.4%	35.0%	8.6%	17.9%	26.4%	140
3. Class III "Mid.-Mid. Cl"	34.4%	12.4%	30.6%	12.7%	18.9%	28.1%	326
4. Class IV "Working Class"	**42.9%**	**15.3%**	30.0%	**16.7%**	19.7%	**36.2%**	361
5. Class V "Lower Class"	**56.0%**	9.6%	**36.5%**	15.3%	**20.2%**	32.1%	83
Score Variation	*24.6%*	*7.6%*	*12.1%*	*12.5%*	*7.7%*	*9.5%*	*848*

Note: Percentages above sample average are **in bold**.   Variations are *in italics*.

The findings of Table No. 12.3 deserve serious examination not only for what they say in relation to the people's attitudes towards members of the different stimulus categories, but what they mean in relation to the level of enlightenment in society towards addiction and compulsive behaviour.

The continuity of substantial minorities willing to deny citizenship to members of these compulsive-behaviour categories is likely to add to the overindulgence of the addicted and prevent or impede their rehabilitation. Charity towards or support for victims of addiction to drugs and alcohol is fairly limited right across the subsamples of the different variables, should the findings be acted out in society. Members are seen more as *deviant* than as *victims of addiction* (greatly aggravated by easy access to alcohol and drugs in modern Irish society).

3.1 Age:

Once again, the age variable repeats the finding of other scales, i.e. the *lower* level of tolerance by the '18 to 25 year-olds' and the *consistently higher* tolerance of the '26 to 40 year-olds'. Considering the constant image being portrayed in the print media of young people overindulging in alcohol and drugs, the findings of Table No. 12.3(a) show how relatively unpopular 'Heavy Drinkers', 'Alcoholics' and 'Drug Addicts' are for the youngest age group. This should, in part, dispel the myth that **heavy drinking** is being idealised by the majority of young people. Many commentators would say that *"Drinking to get drunk"* is a minority ideal for the 18 to 25 year-olds!

Going on percentages denying citizenship, the oldest age group are the most severely negative. Almost half **(48.5%)** of the 71 years plus age-group would 'deny citizenship' to 'Drug Addicts', while over one-fifth **(21.6%)** would not offer citizenship to 'Heavy Drinkers' and 'Alcoholics'. For many in this age group overindulgence in alcohol and drugs is seen as **deviant** and possibly **'threatening'** behaviour. Such findings provide a *prima facie* case for serious research into the impact of excessive drinking and drug addiction on the lives of older people in the Republic of Ireland. The tendency to treat the behavioural practices as matters of jest and as trivial aberrations underrates the seriousness of the social problem of abuse of alcoholic drink and drug addiction in Ireland and elsewhere.

3.2 Gender:

Only one of the three compulsive-behaviour stimulus categories, i.e. 'Heavy Drinkers', elicited a statistically significant variation. In the case of the other two, namely, 'Alcoholics' and 'Drug Addicts', there was consensus between males and females around the sample averages. As in the case of other categories, the coming together of 'male' and 'female' attitudes has become a feature of the 2007-08 national survey. As stated elsewhere, this merging of attitudes is probably due (in part at least) to the influence of the *'Feminist Movement'* over the past forty years!

With regard to 'Heavy Drinkers', female scores were more negative than male scores, i.e. lower percentage 'admitting to kinship' (-8.2%) and higher percentage 'denying citizenship' (+3.0%). Women are more conscious probably of the negative consequences of heavy drinking than are men and the above findings would reflect such speculation. This reaction may reflect awareness of domestic conflict arising from abuse of alcohol by males!

3.3 Marital Status:
As in the case of '**Gender**', 'Heavy Drinkers' was the only stimulus category to record a statistically significant variation by 'marital status'. The other two categories, 'Alcoholics' and 'Drug Addicts' recorded a consensus among the five subsamples.

In relation to 'Heavy Drinkers' the relatively low tolerance of the 'Single/Never Married' towards them was obviously affected by the attitudes of the '18 to 25 year-olds' or *vice versa*. 'Widows' were highest in welcoming 'Heavy Drinkers' into kinship, while respondents living in 'Permanent Relationships' were most severe in denying them citizenship **(25.4%).**

3.4 Area of Birth:
This variable registered a significant variation only in the case of 'Drug Addicts' and was 'non-significant' for 'Heavy Drinkers' and 'Alcoholics'. The most tolerant subsample towards 'Drug Addicts' was the 'Large Town' (10,000-99,000) one. Consensus at such a relatively high level of social distance was disappointing in itself, i.e. toward 'Heavy Drinkers' and 'Alcoholics'.

Overall the findings in relation to 'Drug Addicts' showed a serious degree of polarisation. The 'Rural/Village' manifested this with an above-average **(21.6%)** 'admitting to kinship' and an above-average **(40.2%)** also 'denying citizenship'. The influence of degree of urbanisation of the respondents' area of birth on their attitude towards 'Drug Addicts' varies according to the above findings.

3.5 Place of Rearing and Region of Residence:

These two **non-ordinal or nominal variables** produced relatively high score variations and had statistically significant variations in the case of all three of the 'compulsive-behaviour' stimulus categories.   Readers should examine for themselves the performance of each sub-variable.

Factors affecting variations in scores are both quantitative and qualitative, i.e. demographic make-up, educational achievement, cultural and religious ethos, etc.   Munster-respondents are among the most tolerant overall.   Dublin respondents are also relatively tolerant.   Connaught /Ulster-reared and those living in the BMW regions seem to be the most negative in their attitudes toward all three categories, i.e. 'Heavy Drinkers', 'Alcoholics' and 'Drug Addicts'.

3.6 Education:

The results of the education variable are quite mixed and not in line with anticipations which expected those with higher education to be more tolerant.   In fact, respondents with **lowest** educational qualifications have been more welcoming of the members of the three categories into kinship than were those with **highest** achievement.   The following extract from Table No. 12.3(g) highlights the difference:

Stimulus Category	A. Primary or Less		B. Third Level		(A – B) Difference	
	Kinship	Deny C'ship	Kinship	Deny C'ship	Kinship	Deny C'ship
1. 'Heavy Drinkers'	50.4%	18.8%	32.8%	12.5%	+12.2%	-6.3%
2. 'Alcoholics'	41.5%	18.7%	29.5%	12.9%	+12.0%	+5.8%
3. 'Drug Addicts'	26.7%	40.5%	18.8%	26.2%	+7.9%	+14.3%

The mixed nature of the performance of the **education** variable is evident from the above extract from Table No. 12.3(g).   The lower education subsample is more generous in welcoming members of each of the three stimulus categories and lower in 'denial of citizenship' for one of the three, i.e. 'Heavy Drinkers'.   In the case of 'Alcoholics' and 'Drug Addicts', Third-Level respondents are less severe in denying them citizenship.   The performance of respondents in the two middle subsamples, i.e. 'Incomplete Second-Level' and 'Complete Second-Level' are quite negative in relation to 'Drug Addicts', i.e. with relatively low percentages 'admitting to kinship' and above-average percentages 'denying citizenship'.

It is quite clear from these findings that those with better education (and, thereby, likely to be influential in society) define **drug addiction** more as **deviant** behaviour rather than **an illness**, i.e. the effect of compulsive craving. As already stated, deviant behaviour elicits a response of social exclusion and insulation in the mind of the public, i.e. denial of citizenship or incarceration. *A definition of illness would be conducive to social support and rehabilitation.* These findings show the importance of social attitudes for remedial and preventive action in relation to personally and socially destructive practices like alcoholism and drug addiction – especially when there are commercial and deviant interests promoting such behaviour. The latter creates the various forms of addiction and feeds them!

3.7 Occupational Status:

There was consensus within the occupation variable in the social-distance responses to 'Drug Addicts', i.e. along the sample mean, which is quite disappointing for such negative scores. The performance in the other two categories, i.e. 'Heavy Drinkers' and 'Alcoholics' is mixed and lacks a discernible pattern as would have been anticipated (with higher occupations showing more tolerance). In regard to 'Alcoholics' the response was more **in line** with expectations. A consensus response should not be equated with a tolerant one in the case of highly prejudiced mean scores!

3.8 Social Class Position:

The performance of this variable was very interesting. It was anticipated that those with higher social status would be more tolerant towards each of the three stimulus categories than those with lower status. This has not happened. Class I ("Upper Class") and Class V ("Lower Class") had above-average percentages in favour of 'admitting to kinship' for each of the three categories [see Table No. 12.3(i)]. The middle grades were most intolerant. There was a degree of polarisation in the 'social-class-position' responses, i.e. above-average 'admitting to kinship' and above-average 'denying citizenship' at the same time, e.g. 'Working Class' and 'Lower Class' towards 'Heavy Drinkers' and 'Upper Class' and 'Working Class' towards 'Drug Addicts'. The responses of the different 'class grades' towards the addicted minorities is most important. The **solidarity** of the "Working Class" and "Lower Class" in support of those suffering from addiction is a *sine qua non* for the rehabilitation of 'Alcoholics' and 'Drug Addicts'. The support of the "Middle and Upper Classes" is necessary to restrict the abuse of alcoholic liquor by suppliers etc. and for the endorsement of **anti-drug dealer** legislation.

3.9 Conclusion:

The findings of Table No. 12.3 dealing with social-distance towards 'Heavy Drinkers', 'Alcoholics' and 'Drug Addicts' present a challenge to Irish society. They clearly point out that each of these three categories ranks very low in the respondents' *rank order of preference*, i.e. 40th, 48th and 51st out of a total of **fifty-one** varied stimulus categories. In other words, they are at the bottom of Irish choice of preferences, despite the overall improvement in social distance scores since 1988-89. Such improvement was likely to be due to the improvement in social-economic security during the 'Celtic Tiger' years up to the late summer of 2008 and a growing enlightenment in the population.

The following extract from Table No. 12.3(a), (g) and (i) highlights the response of the three ordinal variables, i.e. 'Age', 'Education', and 'Social Class Position' in *denying citizenship*:

Variable	Range of Variation	Highest % (least favourable)	Between	Lowest % (most favourable)		Mean %
1. Age:						
(a) Heavy Drinkers	12.0%	71 years plus **(21.6%)**	and	56-70 years	**(9.6%)**	13.6%
(b) Alcoholics	9.3%	71 years plus **(21.6%)**	and	56-70 years	**(12.3%)**	15.5%
(c) Drug Addicts	20.0%	71 years plus **(48.5%)**	and	26-40 years	**(28.5%)**	33.7%
2. Education:						
(a) Heavy Drinkers	6.0%	Third Level **(16.2%)**	and	Primary or Less	**(10.2%)**	13.6%
(b) Alcoholics	6.0%	Primary or Less **(18.7%)**	and	Incomplete Sec. Lev. **(12.7%)**		15.5%
(c) Drug Addicts	16.3%	Primary or Less **(40.5%)**	and	Third Level	**(26.2%)**	33.7%
3. Social Class Position						
(a) Heavy Drinkers	7.6%	Working Class **(15.3%)**	and	Upper Class	**(7.7%)**	13.6%
(b) Alcoholics	12.5%	Upper Class **(21.1%)**	and	Upper-Mid. Class	**(8.6%)**	15.5%
(c) Drug Addicts	9.5%	Working Class **(36.2%)**	and	Upper-Mid. Class	**(28.1%)**	33.7%

At the core of the attitudes reflected in the above findings has been the underlying public definition of people with compulsive behaviour problems relating to alcohol and drugs. If they are defined solely as deviant behaviour, the public reaction tends to be penal, whereas, if these problems were seen as illness (due more to weakness than malice) the response would be one of cure, rehabilitation and support. It would appear from the findings that the 'deviant' definition is still quite strong in the Irish population. The net effect of this is the further aggravation of the compulsive-behaviour condition rather than help towards its rehabilitation. When addiction is viewed as a disease, there will be support for necessary

preventative measures in relation to the promotion and supply of "mood-changing substances".

The **rationalisation scale**[2] had already revealed something special about the three 'compulsive-behaviour' stimulus categories, i.e. the exceptionally high levels of "not socially acceptable" as a main reason for not 'admitting to kinship'.   Table No. 5.6 (page 93 above) shows that the three categories headed the list and there was a substantial increase in the "not socially acceptable" rationalisation in the case of 'Drug Addicts' and 'Alcoholics' between 1988-89 and 2007-08, i.e. for 'Drug Addicts' from **20.1%** to **30.3%** and for 'Alcoholics' from **19.4%** to **24.9%**.   This is the most negative form of rationalisation, which has greatly reduced in the case of most of the other social stimulus categories (see Table No. 5.6, page 93 above).   This 'exclusion definition' finds best expression in 'denial of citizenship'.   It is indicative of a negative stigma!

The challenges presented by the above findings are very serious.   It is to be expected that society's acceptable aims are to facilitate the avoidance of compulsive behaviour likely to be socially and personally destructive, and the promotion of rehabilitation for those already entrapped by the condition (as is evident in 'Heavy Drinkers', 'Alcoholics' and 'Drug Addicts'). Hopefully, the above findings and discussion will contribute to the achievement of 'society's acceptable social aims'!   The role of the media (print and electronic) in relation to the presentation of the "drink and drugs problem" is very important in relation to the public definition of 'compulsive-behaviour' categories.   To date in Ireland the media have not been successful in presenting the addict as an **ill victim** of highly commercialised and skilfully promoted intoxicating substances.

Part IV – Socio-Economic Social Categories

Two of the nine social categories reported on in Table No. 12.1 (page 264 above) were classified as 'Socio-Economic Social Categories', i.e. 'Unemployed' and "Working Class".   Both categories have been given relatively favourable social distance scores.   The following is an extract from Table No. 12.1 giving a breakdown of the 'admission to kinship', 'denial of citizenship' and mean social-distance scores.

---

[2] See: Table No. 5.1, pages 86-7 above and Table No. 5.6, page 93 above.

Stimulus Category	A. 2007-08			B. 1988-89			Change (A – B)		
	Kinship	Deny Citiz'p	MSD	Kinship	Deny Citiz'p	MSD	Kinship	Deny Citiz'p	MSD
1. 'Working Class'	85.6%	0.2%	1.228	86.8%	0.0%	1.210	-1.2%	+0.2%	+0.028
2. 'Unemployed'	80.9%	2.2%	1.446	78.1%	0.2%	1.345	+2.8%	+2.0%	+0.101

It is quite clear that both stimulus categories have retained their in-group status, i.e. mean-social-distance scores of under **1.500**. Within these limits the categories' MSDs increased very moderately, i.e. by 0.028 and 0.101. The former change is not statistically significant. It must be remembered that an increase in MSD scores indicated a downward shift in desired social closeness. Unemployment was very low at the time of interviewing in 2007-08 and this may be the cause of the disimprovement in mean-social-distance. At the time of writing (2009/2011) the levels of unemployment have increased due to the global and national economic downturn. The 'new unemployed' represent the *white-collar* as well as the *blue-collar* workers. In these circumstances it is likely that the status of the 'Unemployed' would be restored to its 1988-89 level!

Table No. 12.4 gives a breakdown of the social-distance scores ('admission to kinship' and 'denial of citizenship') by personal variables.

Table No. 12.4:
Socio-Economic Categories by Personal Variables

Personal Variable	"Working Class"		"Unemployed"		No.
	Admit to Kinship	Deny Citizenship	Admit to Kinship	Deny Citizenship	
Total Sample	85.6%	0.2%	80.9%	2.1%	1,015
A. Age	N/S		P<.001		
1. 18-25 years	---	---	75.7%	**3.6%**	168
2. 26-40 years	---	---	**83.2%**	2.8%	325
3. 41-55 years	---	---	79.4%	2.0%	245
4. 56-70 years	---	---	**82.0%**	0.6%	178
5. 71 years plus	---	---	**84.4%**	1.0%	96
Score Variation	---	---	*8.7%*	*3.0%*	*1,012*
B. Marital Status	P<.005		P<.001		
1. Single/Never Married	84.7%	0.0%	80.8%	**2.5%**	356
2. Married	**87.2%**	**0.2%**	81.5%	1.5%	468
3. Separated/Divorced	**86.0%**	0.0%	**86.0%**	0.0%	44
4. Permanent Relation'p	77.5%	0.0%	69.4%	**6.9%**	72
5. Widowed	**88.2%**	0.0%	**84.1%**	1.4%	69
Score Variation	*3.5%*	*0.2%*	*16.6%*	*6.9%*	*1,009*

Table No. 12.4 (Cont'd.) Personal Variable	"Working Class"		"Unemployed"		No.
	Admit to Kinship	Deny Citizenship	Admit to Kinship	Deny Citizenship	
C. Area of Birth	P<.001		N/S		
1. City (100,000+)	80.6%	0.0%	---	---	419
2. Large Town (10,000+)	**89.1%**	**0.8%**	---	---	119
3. Town (1,500+)	**90.7%**	**0.8%**	---	---	132
4. Rural/Village	**89.0%**	0.0%	---	---	345
Score Variation	*10.1%*	*0.8%*	*---*	*---*	*1,015*
D. Place of Rearing (ROI)	P<.001		P<.005		
1. Dublin (City & Co.)	81.6%	**0.4%**	81.6%	1.9%	243
2. Rest of Leinster	**89.1%**	**0.6%**	78.5%	**3.0%**	157
3. Munster	**90.5%**	0.0%	**84.5%**	2.6%	219
4. Connaught/Ulster	**86.6%**	0.0%	78.0%	0.6%	154
Score Variation	*8.9%*	*0.6%*	*6.5%*	*2.4%*	*773*
E. Region of Residence	N/S		P<.001		
1. B.M.W.	---	---	77.8%	**2.6%**	269
2. Dublin	---	---	**82.5%**	2.4%	284
3. Mid-East & South-East	---	---	76.7%	**3.7%**	218
4. Mid-West & Sth-West	---	---	**86.1%**	0.4%	234
Score Variation	*---*	*---*	*9.4%*	*3.3%*	*1,005*
F. Education	N/S		P<0.012		
1. Primary or Less	---	---	**92.3%**	0.0%	117
2. Incomplete Sec-Level	---	---	**83.1%**	3.5%	262
3. Complete Sec.-Level	---	---	80.2%	3.2%	255
4. Third-Level	---	---	76.7%	1.3%	381
Score Variation	*---*	*---*	*15.6%*	*3.5%*	*1,015*
G. Occupational Status	N/S		P<.001		
1. Unskilled/Semi-Skilled	---	---	**83.0%**	**3.9%**	207
2. Skilled/R. Non-Manual	---	---	80.4%	1.5%	328
3. Inspect./Supervisory	---	---	**80.9%**	1.5%	133
4. Professional/Exec.	---	---	**83.2%**	3.1%	191
Score Variation	*---*	*---*	*2.8%*	*2.4%*	*859*
H. Social Class Position	N/S		P<.001		
1. Class I "Upper Class"	---	---	76.9%	**2.6%**	38
2. Class II "Upper-Mid. Class"	---	---	**84.2%**	**3.6%**	140
3. Class III "Middle-Mid. Class"	---	---	76.1%	0.9%	326
4. Class IV "Working Class"	---	---	**82.4%**	**3.3%**	361
5. Class V "Lower Class"	---	---	**90.5%**	1.2%	83
Score Variation	*---*	*---*	*14.4%*	*2.7%*	*848*

Note: Percentages above sample average are **in bold**.   Variations are in *italics*.

As would be expected, there has been a high proportion of non-significant variable scores in the case of "Working Class" because of the category's low MSD score of 1.228, which leaves little room for statistically significant (P<.050) variations. In the case of 'Unemployed' there is slightly more room for significant variation (as Table No. 12.4 shows).

4.1 Age:

This variable returned a consensus result between the age subsamples in the case of "Working Class". This makes the "Working Class" an 'in-group' for each of the age groups. In relation to the 'Unemployed', the age variable results are quite mixed and not in line with expectations. The '18 to 25 year-olds' have a lower-than-average percentage 'admitting to kinship' and an above-average 'denying citizenship', whereas the 71 years plus group have an above-average 'welcoming into kinship' for members of the 'Unemployed' and a below-average percentage 'denying citizenship'. This reversal of anticipated findings shows a relatively high level of tolerance among the older citizens of the Republic of Ireland and a relatively low level among the young.

4.2 Marital Status:

Before commenting on 'Marital Status' it is necessary to record that 'Gender' failed to produce statistically significant variations for either stimulus category, i.e. "Working Class" or 'Unemployed'. This consensus along the sample mean scores between the attitudes towards the two categories is yet another confirmation of the homogenisation of male and female attitudes.

The performance of 'Marital Status' elicited statistically significant variations in relation to "Working Class" and 'Unemployed'. The differences between the percentages of the subsamples have been minimal in regard to "Working Class". The score variation for 'admission to kinship' in the case of the 'Unemployed' is substantial at 16.6%. 'Single/Never Married' and people in 'Permanent Relationships' are the least tolerant of the five subsamples. Respondents most likely to have children and/or grandchildren, i.e. 'Married', 'Separated/Divorced' and 'Widowed' recorded an above-average welcome for the 'Unemployed' into kinship. This support for the 'Unemployed' by the parental categories is reassuring in times of high rates of joblessness!

4.3 Area of Birth:

This variable measures the impact of urban/rural background on attitudes to the "Working Class". There was consensus between the subsamples in relation to the 'Unemployed' at the sample-average level.

There was a negative correlation between urbanisation and tolerance of the "Working Class" (within a relatively narrow range of variation because of the very low MSD score of variable). This rejects the anticipation of the researcher in relation to the 'Area of Birth' background. Some readers may be surprised to discover that **city-born** respondents were the least welcoming as a sub-variable of the "Working Class" into kinship (by a relatively small percentage). Cities today are predominantly middle-class in Ireland!

4.4 Place of Rearing and Region of Residence:
Place of Rearing (in the Republic of Ireland) has registered a statistically significant variation for the stimulus categories, "Working Class" and 'Unemployed'. Those reared in Munster has been **most** 'welcoming into kinship' for both categories. Otherwise the results are quite mixed. This, once again, confirms the tolerant ethos of Munster-reared respondents.

Region of Residence returned a consensus result for 'Working Class'. The attitudes toward the 'Unemployed' reflected the findings for 'place of rearing' with 'Mid-West and South-West' regions showing most tolerant dispositions as was the case for 'Munster-reared' respondents. As the 'Connaught/Ulster-reared' were surprisingly (in the light of their experience of high unemployment in the past) least welcoming to the unemployed – at a still relatively high percentage of **78.0%,** so also were those living in the 'BMW regions' below average in their percentage 'admitting to kinship' and above average in 'denying citizenship'.

4.5 Education:
Once again, education has been the opposite to what was anticipated. The score variation was relatively high and those with highest education were the least sympathetic to both categories, i.e. "Working Class" and 'Unemployed', while respondents with lowest educational achievement were most tolerant towards both categories. Are we seeing here expressions of class prejudice or social snobbery? The results raise questions in relation to the 'liberating' impact of higher education on respondents. Both 'Complete Second-level' and 'Third-Level' subsamples returned disappointing results.

4.6 Occupational Status:
This variable shows consensus in regard to the "Working Class" which, in itself, is interesting. The findings in the case of the 'Unemployed' are mixed and not as anticipated. Those with lowest and highest occupational

status are above average in 'admitting to kinship' and in 'denying citizenship'. The score variations are quite small.

4.7 Social Class Position:
This variable is based on a combination of educational and occupational status (see footnote 7, page 189 above). It was anticipated that there would be a positive correlation between 'Social Class Position' and the levels of tolerance, i.e. **higher** percentages 'admitting to kinship' and **lower** percentages 'denying citizenship'.

The findings on Table No. 12.4(h) do not confirm the above anticipation or hypothesis. There was consensus in relation to "Working Class". The score variation for 'Unemployed' was substantial. Those with lowest status were most welcoming into kinship, while "Upper Class" and "Middle-Middle Class" were least welcoming.

This reflects the perception (during 2007-08) of unemployment as a lower-statused workers' lot, while in 2009-10 this condition (unemployment) is spread throughout the 'social classes'. Would their responses be different if the survey were carried out during a period of economic depression? Also, during periods of relatively full employment, there was a popular tendency to blame the 'Unemployed' for not being willing to work, despite the fact that the range of occupation available to the unemployed might not suit the qualifications or satisfaction of the potential worker.

Because of the history of unbalanced socio-economic development in Ireland, there are wide areas of the West and Midlands where workers were forced to migrate to get gainful employment which was socially useful and personally satisfying. The tens of thousands who opted to stay at home in these 'deprived' areas were forced to go *"on the dole"* in order to raise their families[3]. Without such 'dolers' many local communities would be so depopulated as to make them unviable. Ireland owes much to the *'patriotic dolers'* who resisted the attraction of out-migration and kept communities alive for better days. This aspect of the positive contribution of the unemployed in deprived areas (rural or urban) has rarely been acknowledged by socially superficial commentators.

---

[3] See: Mac Gréil, Micheál, *Quo Vadimus: Report on the Pastoral Needs and Resources of the Archdiocese of Tuam*, Tuam, 1998.

4.8 Conclusion:
Because of the low level of social distance of each of the two stimulus categories, i.e. 'working class' (**1.228**) and 'unemployed' (**1.446**), (which meant that each category was in the "in-group" classification), it was to be expected that there would be limited room for variations between the variable subsamples.   This was borne out in the relatively low score variation and the five sub-scales registering non-significant (N/S) differences.

Where statistical significance was achieved, variations were contrary to expectations in the case of age, area of birth, education and social-class position.   There was an element of social class prejudice as well as above-average intolerance among 'young' and more 'highly educated' respondents. These unexpected results were found in the case of social distance towards the majority of stimulus categories already reported in this text!   Unless there is a change towards greater tolerance among the 'young' and the 'more highly educated', there is a limit to the optimism of the Republic of Ireland reaching the level of tolerance towards minorities that an ethnically and socially-diverse society should strive for in the years ahead!

Part V – Correlation Matrix of Political, Religious and Social Categories

Before completing the presentation of the findings of the *Bogardus Social Distance Scale*, it would be fruitful to bring together the twenty-two stimulus categories [not included in the twenty-nine ethnic, ethnico-racial and racial categories (see Table No. 6.7, page 119)] to test their *Pearson Product-Moment Correlation Coefficients*.   These categories include:

(a) Political Categories: 'Gardaí', 'Trade Unionists', 'Unionists',
         'Socialists', 'Capitalists' and 'Communists';

(b) Religious Categories: 'Roman Catholics', 'Protestants', 'Jews',
         'Atheists', 'Agnostics' and 'Muslims';

(c) Social Categories: 'Working Class', 'People with Physical Disability',
         'Unmarried Mothers', 'Unemployed', 'People with Mental
         Disability', 'Gay People', 'Heavy Drinkers', 'Alcoholics',
         'Travellers' and 'Drug Addicts'.

The above stimulus categories are listed according to their 'Rank Order of Preference' within each of the three groupings.

The overall findings of Table No. 12.5 show a number of interesting features about the prejudice or intergroup-attitude patterns of the national sample, allowing for the different impact of relatively high or low mean-social-distance scores on correlations. The disparate range of stimulus categories classified as **Social Categories** has been confirmed by the relatively low incidence of *Rho = 0.50 plus* scores, i.e. 9 out of a possible 45 correlations (20%). The **Religious and Political Categories** registered 7 *Rho = 0.50 plus* scores each out of a possible 15 correlations (46.7%).

The relatively high percentage of 'Roman Catholic' correlations not reaching a statistically significant correlation (NS), with three of the six 'Religious Categories', i.e. 'Atheists', 'Agnostics' and 'Muslims', once again points out the unique position of this stimulus category in the Irish attitude-syndrome which merits further research.

Looking at the relatively high frequency of *Rho = 0.50 plus* scores (15 out of 36 correlations with only one NS) between **Political and Religious Categories**, it appears that the political relevance of religion is still quite real for the Irish people. This questions the assumption of 'secularisation', which is a prevalent view being asserted by commentators in the Irish media. From the above findings it is reasonable to assume that religion is still relevant in relation to Irish social and political life.

The lack of relatively high correlations between most categories among the ten social stimulus categories points out the diversity and unrelatedness of them. 'Travellers' failed to establish a *Rho = 0.50 plus* with any other of the 21 stimulus categories on Table No. 12.5. The Compulsive Behaviour Categories, i.e. 'Heavy Drinkers', 'Alcoholics' and 'Drug Addicts', produced *0.50 plus* only between themselves! This information is important for those wishing to understand the nature of prejudice against compulsive behaviour categories and 'Travellers'.

Table No. 12.5: Pearson Product-Moment Correlation Coefficients between Political, Religious and Social Categories

	Stimulus Category	1	2	3	4	5	6	7	8	9	10	11	12	13	14	15	16	17	18	19	20	21	22	No.
Political Categories	'Gardaí'	1.0	.49	.46	.29	.38	.20	.49	**.51**	.35	.27	.25	.22	**.50**	**.57**	.40	.44	.38	.29	.21	.22	.20	NS	1
	'Trade Unionists'		1.0	**.59**	**.51**	.45	.36	.30	.48	.44	.33	.31	.28	**.52**	.44	.46	**.60**	.37	.30	.20	NS	.21	NS	2
	'Unionists'			1.0	**.67**	.49	**.52**	.32	**.60**	**.61**	**.52**	.45	.44	.40	.35	.46	**.53**	.37	**.51**	.30	.29	.36	.24	3
	'Socialists'				1.0	**.61**	**.56**	.23	.47	**.64**	**.51**	.49	**.50**	.37	.24	.34	.40	.23	.44	.31	.42	.33	.26	4
	'Capitalists'					1.0	**.60**	.22	.43	**.56**	**.60**	**.59**	**.57**	.30	.29	.34	.37	.43	.37	.31	.31	.31	.24	5
	'Communists'						1.0	NS	.34	**.54**	**.66**	**.61**	**.65**	.21	NS	.24	.30	.26	.39	.27	.36	.39	.31	6
Religious Categories	'Roman Catholics'							1.0	.43	.23	NS	NS	NS	.46	.38	.36	.35	.34	.23	NS	NS	NS	NS	7
	'Protestants'								1.0	**.52**	.44	.39	.35	**.51**	.49	.43	**.51**	.42	**.57**	.23	.25	.30	NS	8
	'Jews'									1.0	**.67**	**.55**	**.60**	.32	.28	.36	.42	.31	.48	.27	.27	.39	NS	9
	'Atheists'										1.0	**.81**	**.59**	.23	.24	.25	.30	.28	**.50**	.25	.38	.35	.26	10
	'Agnostics'											1.0	**.59**	.23	.21	.27	.31	.25	.44	.25	.37	.29	.24	11
	'Muslims'												1.0	NS	NS	.23	.26	.29	.38	.30	.39	.43	.33	12
Social Categories	'Working Class'													1.0	**.65**	**.62**	**.58**	.43	.31	.22	.21	NS	NS	13
	'People with Physical Disability'														1.0	**.55**	**.51**	.47	.32	.20	.20	NS	NS	14
	'Unmarried Mothers'															1.0	**.65**	.45	.34	.29	.26	.28	NS	15
	'Unemployed'																1.0	**.51**	.28	.27	.24	.24	NS	16
	'People with Mental Disability'																	1.0	.28	.32	.34	.27	.22	17
	'Gay People'																		1.0	.26	.27	.36	.25	18
	'Heavy Drinkers'																			1.0	**.65**	.35	.22	19
	'Alcoholics'																				1.0	.32	**.50**	20
	'Travellers'																					1.0	.38	21
	'Drug Addicts'																						1.0	22

Notes: (1) *Rho* Scores **0.50 plus** are in **bold**; (2) Score under *Rho* = 0.20 are marked NS.

289

Part VI – Overall Conclusion

In the course of this chapter, the social-distance scores were examined towards nine social stimulus categories, i.e. (in alphabetical order) *'Alcoholics', 'Drug Addicts', 'Gay People', 'Heavy Drinkers', 'People with Physical Disability', 'People with Mental Disability', 'Unemployed', 'Unmarried Mothers'* and *'Working Class'*. These categories were classified into three groups, i.e. Personal/Domestic, Compulsive-Behaviour and Socio-Economic, for the purpose of detailed examination.

The general findings were interesting and quite optimistic for some categories. There was a substantial increase in the percentages 'admitting to kinship' since 1988-89 for **six** of the eight categories measured in both national surveys – 1988-89 and 2007-08. One stimulus category, 'Heavy Drinkers' was included for the first time in 2007-08.

The two measures of 'admit to kinship' and 'deny citizenship' were selected to report attitudes (social distance) by personal variables. Because of the very high rank-order correlation coefficient between 'admission to kinship' and 'mean-social-distance' (*Rho* = 0.99), (see Table No. 4.3 above), the findings of Tables Nos. 12.2, 12.3 and 12.4 above validly and reliably represent the overall social-distance measures towards the different stimulus categories.

6.1:
In the case of the Personal and Domestic Social Categories, i.e. 'People with Physical or Mental Disability', 'Unmarried Mothers' and 'Gay People', there has been a substantial decrease in social prejudice (with room for improvement still to come). *'Unmarried Mothers' are now held in very high regard throughout Irish society.* Where variation between the sub-samples occurred, it was against anticipation, i.e. in the case of 'age, 'area of birth', 'occupation' and 'social-class position'.

The level of **homophobia** in the Republic of Ireland has greatly decreased since 1988-89. Variations between subsamples were mixed or as expected. Score variations in the different variables have been quite substantial which is indicative of the growing discussion among members of the subsamples. If current trends continue, homosexuals will become even more acceptable as members of the general population and cease to be victims of prejudice and discrimination.

Attitudes toward 'People with Disabilities' are very healthy according to the findings of Table No. 12.2. Traces of social stigma are practically removed in the case of 'People with Physical and Mental Disability'. This facilitates greater public support for members of these categories. The differences in variable subsamples were not in line with anticipations especially in the case of 'education', 'occupation' (for 'People with Mental Disability') and 'social class position'. These variations are disappointing.

6.2:
The responses towards 'People with Compulsive-Behaviour' problems were analysed by personal variables on Table No. 12.3, i.e. the three stimulus categories, 'Heavy Drinkers', 'Alcoholics' and 'Drug Addicts'. The severity of the hostility towards these stimulus categories is still far too high to facilitate their rehabilitation. It is quite clear that 'compulsive behaviour' in Irish society is defined more as **deviant behaviour** than as **illness**, hence, the response was one of **'exclusion'** rather than **rehabilitation** from a large proportion of respondents. The variations for the most part were against anticipation and otherwise mixed.

6.3:
The two **socio-economic** stimulus categories, i.e. "Working Class" and 'Unemployed', retained their **in-group status** in the national population. The performance of the 'Unemployed' has slightly disimproved since the previous survey in 1988-89. Unemployment was minimal in the Republic of Ireland during the time of the fieldwork (November 2007 until March 2008), while it was a social problem in 1988-89. Should the survey be carried out after 2009, the status of the unemployed would, in all probability, be restored to that of the 1988-89 level of popularity, because of its spread into the "Middle Class" white-collar workers!

6.4:
Table No. 12.5 presents the *Pearson Product-Moment Correlation Coefficients* of the twenty-two non-ethnic/racial stimulus categories in one table/matrix. This shows the broader correlations between political, religious and social categories. The most interesting finding is the obvious relatively high correlations between **political and religious** categories, which prove that religion has not lost its political relevance in the Republic of Ireland. Other interesting results are to be found on Table No. 12.5.

The careful monitoring of social attitudes towards **social minorities** within Irish society is both valuable and necessary. The quality of life of members of our social minorities is quite dependent on such attitudes, since most behaviour is socio-culturally determined.

***

CHAPTER XIII
The Travelling People – Ireland's Apartheid

Part I – Introduction

The Travelling People is Ireland's biggest indigenous ethnic minority who, until the 1960s was largely nomadic in lifestyle and moved throughout the country along recognised circuits. Their domestic accommodation consisted of tents, horse-drawn 'barrel-wagons' and trailers drawn by cars, vans and pick-ups. Encampments along the primary and secondary roads were the normal places where families would live. The introduction of temporary halting sites in the 1960s was followed by more permanent serviced sites and a policy of housing Traveller families in urban areas. The decline of the horse and the arrival of the popular family car and van enabled Travellers to travel and return to base. Roadside camping on public grounds gradually reduced over the years until it was 'criminalised' or 'outlawed' by the *Miscellaneous Housing Act of 2002 A.D.*

Over the past fifty years Travellers became more and more 'urbanised', i.e. by **2006**[1]: 25.9% lived in Rural/Village, 8.9% in Small Towns (1,500-4,999), 12.3% in Towns (5,000-9,999), 21.8% in Large Towns (10,000-39,999), 11.8% in Cities (over 40,000) and 19.4% lived in the Greater Dublin area. This urbanisation of Travellers was not necessarily voluntary but as a result of the pressures of social change in Ireland which had implications for the nomadic lifestyle. Travellers tended to move to 'settle' at the periphery of towns and cities, in districts experiencing relative deprivation already. The pressure for a permanent address in order to draw unemployment benefit and other welfare payments was a constant counter-nomadic requirement.

This chapter is dealing with the findings of the 2007-08 survey measuring the attitudes of the national sample in relation to the Irish Travelling People and the demographic profile of this minority of Irish citizens as reported in the *2006 Census Reports*. A more detailed account of the current position of Irish Travellers has been published in a special Report

---

[1] *Census 2006: Ethnic and Cultural Background*, Dublin, CSO, 2007.

entitled *Emancipation of the Travelling People* in April 2010[2]. In addition to reporting on the findings of the 2007-08 survey, this chapter also monitors the changes which have taken place in public attitudes towards Travellers since 1972-73. The 1977 Anti-Traveller Scale (ESRI) was replicated in the 1988-89 and 2007-08 national surveys. **Social Distance** towards 'Travellers' was also monitored between 1972-73, 1988-89 and 2007-08[3].

The Travelling People are Ireland's largest and oldest indigenous **ethnic minority** whose nomadic lifestyle has been seriously disrupted by socio-cultural forces outside its control and the failure of the establishment to acknowledge the uniquely ethnic character of this collectivity. **The Settled Community**, i.e. the 'dominant group', has so far failed to integrate the Travelling People into Irish society in an egalitarian and pluralist manner. The Travellers have had to face interference with their own socio-cultural norms and control, which in the past were governed by an accepted *extended-family social structure* and facilitated by a more detached Settled Community.

Travellers, with the help of statutory and voluntary bodies sympathetic towards them, have tried to adjust to the new 'modern' industrial and post-industrial society, which, on the whole, has not been supportive of Travellers. As a result of society's hostility, as expressed in social prejudice, the plight of Travellers has failed to improve as it could have done over the past decade of prosperity in Ireland.

Indications of **relative deprivation**, which will be outlined below, are: *shorter life expectancy, relatively poor standards of accommodation, grossly higher levels of unemployment, relatively poor levels of participation and achievement in education, restricted access to normal outlets of commercialised indoor recreation and other forms of discrimination*. The reaction to this widespread level of 'relative deprivation' has included unacceptable deviant behaviour from a minority of Travellers and a negative public image of the whole group.

---

[2] Mac Gréil, Micheál, *Emancipation of the Travelling People*, Maynooth, Survey and Research Unit, Department of Sociology, NUI Maynooth, 2010. *Note:* The findings of this chapter are reproduced in the special Report.
[3] Mac Gréil, Micheál, (a) *Prejudice and Tolerance in Ireland*, Dublin, College of Industrial Relations, 1977 and 1978, and New York, Praeger, 1980. (b) *Prejudice in Ireland Revisited*, Má Nuad, St Patrick's College, 1996 and 1997.

The findings of the Greater Dublin Survey in 1972-73 pointed to the position of the **Travelling Community** as being one of *lower caste*. The prejudice toward Travellers tended to be more benevolent. In 1988-89, the National Survey produced 'a real shock' in that the level of *social distance* towards Travellers increased dramatically and the level of prejudice was becoming less benevolent. This led to the suggestion that Travellers were fast becoming classified as *'outcasts'* in their own society. This inevitably led to deviant reactions from some of the Travelling Community who felt they were given little or no stake in their own society. Since that time (1988-89) certain regrettable incidents attributed to a small minority of Travellers looked like the deviant response of people defined as 'outcasts' in their own society!

It will be shown in this chapter that the current attitudes and opinions of the public *vis-à-vis* the Travellers are mixed. In some areas there has been much improvement, while in other aspects there is little or no progress to report. In the pattern of responses in relation to social distance (i.e. how close respondents would be prepared to admit Travellers), *a more polarised response emerges* with a twofold increase in the percentages admitting Travellers to family through marriage while, at the other end of the scale, there has been a substantial increase in the minority who would deny Travellers citizenship. This is indicative of a response to a minority that is beginning to assert itself and its rights. On the scale of preferences, Travellers are still an **'out-group'** but no longer **'lower caste'**.

The Travelling People constitute a relatively small minority in the national population, i.e. 22,369 Travellers or 0.5% of the National Population at the time of the 2006 Census. It should be well within the capacity of the Irish people to integrate this *native ethnic minority* and give them their proper stake in Irish society. The model of integration strongly proposed by the author is that of *integrated pluralism* which means support for the *genuine and valuable cultural traits* of the Travelling Community which have been learned and handed on during centuries of nomadic living in Ireland. At the same time, Travellers are guaranteed access to all amenities and services of modern Irish society on the basis of total equality. These amenities and services include: living accommodation, education, work, health services, religious services, protection of the law, participation in local and national public life, recreational facilities (indoor and outdoor), freedom of movement, etc. The causes of *'the culture of poverty and deprivation'* should be removed. **Institutional duplication** should be provided where the continuity of the Traveller's culture requires it. Such an approach by society to its indigenous minority will enable Travellers to get their 'stake in Irish society' and enable them to become positive contributors to the welfare of all the people!

Part II – Demographic Profile of the Irish Travelling People

The origin of the Irish Travelling People is not that well documented. They have been the product of a long series of acts of **ethnic cleansing** in Ireland which have been referred to in our 'history books' as **'plantations'** by the colonial authorities. The Travellers were part of the 'fallout' of these population shifts in the sixteenth, seventeenth and eighteenth centuries. In addition to these acts of dispossession in favour of those close to the colonial authorities at the time, there have been periods of widespread evictions of small farmers (tenants) by the landlord class, which resulted in many poor peasants being forced to live on the roadside under canvas. This was particularly severe after the Great Famine. Travelling trades- people and horse-dealers seemed to have joined the Travelling Community down the years.

The Irish Travelling Community is almost totally an Irish ethnic subgroup with very few ties with Romany Gypsies or 'New Age Travellers'. Their cultural traits seem to be akin to those of an Irish dispossessed peasantry at its roots. Despite the changes in the Settled Community due to industrialisation and modernisation, Travellers have maintained a strong extended-family structure. In recent years this may have been weakened with their being forced to live 'on the edges' of urban society.

The demographic make-up of the current Travelling Community is published by the *Central Statistics Office* in its Report: *Census 2006 – Ethnic and Cultural Background*. One of the difficulties in analysing the Irish Travellers' position in Irish society has been the mistaken use of the terms **'race'** or **'racial'** by commentators when referring to the treatment of this minority by the dominant society. This is **very unhelpful** and makes analysis very difficult. In this text Travellers will be treated as an **'ethnic'** group or subgroup and not as a **'racial'** group or subgroup, i.e. a group distinctive because of their cultural or 'way of life' rather than the biological and genetically inherited physical or physiological traits, which are racial-group traits. It is unscientific to use concepts which are **not precise,** thereby contributing to our inability to arrive at the true causes of discrimination against the Travelling Community. The term 'racial' is sometimes used because of its 'political' or 'ideological' and emotive quality in popular parlance! The ethnic composition of the population of the Republic of Ireland is given on Table No. 2.1 above (page 17).

As noted already, the number of people who declared themselves to be Travellers, i.e. **22,369** or **0.5%** of the population, was lower than the projected population of 27,000 in the 1990s. The reduction could be due to emigration to Britain or a number of Travellers joining the Settled Community, i.e. 'passed' into the dominant group and no longer declared themselves as Travellers in the 2006 Census of the population.

The following Table No. 13.1 gives a breakdown of the Travelling population in the Republic of Ireland by age, gender, marital status, urban/rural place of residence, province of residence, country of birth, religious affiliation, employment status, education and involvement in voluntary work. The comparative percentages for the national population are also given on Table No. 13.1. The figures are taken from the *2006 Census Report*. This is essential information for a clear understanding of the *Profile of the Irish Travelling Community*.

By examining the different variables of this Table it is possible to get a fairly detailed demographic profile of the Irish Travelling Community. The facts and patterns emerging are not very positive and reflect poorly on the policies and programmes aimed at the pluralist integration of this minority into Irish society on the basis of social equality.

(a) Age Variable:
The clearest message coming from the Census findings by age is the relatively low life expectancy of the Travellers. Only **4%** of Travellers have reached an age beyond 60 years, while **15.3%** of the Total Population lived to an age older than 'the three score' target.

Low life expectancy is one of the strongest indicators of social deprivation and the presence of unnecessary health hazards, normally caused by socio-economic conditions and material quality of life, i.e. living accommodation, health care, education, etc. Action is **urgently** called for to reverse the vicious circle causing the appalling result presented in Table No. 13.1(a) below.

Table No. 13.1:
Travellers by Personal Variables (from the *2006 Census Report*)

Personal Variable	Number	Percentage of Travellers	Percentage of Total Irish Population
(a) Age			
1. 0 - 19 years	11,800	52.9%	27.5%
2. 20 – 39 years	6,633	29.7%	32.5%
3. 40 – 59 years	3,021	13.5%	24.7%
4. 60 – 79 years	838	3.7%	12.6%
5. 80 years plus	77	0.3%	2.7%
Number	22,369	100.0%	4,172,013
(b) Gender			
1. Male	10,990	49.1%	50.0%
2. Female	11,379	50.9%	50.0%
Number	22,369	100.0%	4,172,013
(c) Marital Status			
1. Single	14,351	64.2%	54.7%
2. Married	6,518	29.1%	36.9%
3. Separated (incl. Divorced)	1,004	4.5%	3.9%
4. Widowed	496	2.2%	4.5%
Number	22,369	100.0%	4,172,013
(d) Urban/Rural Place of Residence			
1. Greater Dublin Area	4,253	19.4%	24.5%
2. Other Cities over 40,000	2,578	11.8%	9.3%
3. Large Towns over 10,000	4,771	21.8%	14.5%
4. Towns over 5,000	2,701	12.3%	6.5%
5. Small Towns over 1,500	1,959	8.9%	5.6%
6. Rural / Village	5,673	25.9%	39.6%
Number	21,935	100.1%	4,067,755
(e) Province of Residence			
1. Leinster	11,315	50.6%	54.2%
2. Munster	5,382	24.1%	27.6%
3. Connaught	4,908	21.9%	11.8%
4. Part of Ulster (Cavan Donegal Monaghan)	764	3.4%	6.3%
Number	22,369	100.0%	4,172,013

Table No. 13.1 (Cont'd) Personal Variable	Number	Percentage of Travellers	Percentage of Total Irish Population
(f) Country of Birth			
1. Ireland (Republic)	20,564	91.9%	85.3%
2. Northern Ireland	195	0.9%	1.2%
3. England and Wales	1,542	6.9%	4.9%
4. Scotland	59	0.3%	0.4%
5. Elsewhere Abroad	9	0.04%	8.2%
Number	22,369	100.0%	4,172,013
(g) Religious Affiliation			
1. Roman Catholic	21,277	95.1%	87.4%
2. Church of Ireland	528	2.4%	2.9%
3. Presbyterian	8	0.04%	0.5%
4. Methodist	---	---	0.3%
5. Orthodox	---	---	0.5%
6. Other Christian Religions	40	0.2%	0.7%
7. Muslims	9	0.04%	0.8%
8. Other Stated Religions	10	0.04%	1.3%
9. No Religion	67	0.3%	4.2%
10. Not Stated	430	1.9%	1.6%
Number	22,369	99.8%	4,172,013
(h) Employment Status			
(1) Labour Force:			
1. At Work	1,806	25.1%	91.5%
2. Seeking First Job	800	11.1%	1.3%
3. Unemployed	4,594	63.8%	7.1%
Total Labour Force	7,200 (55.0%)	100.0%	2,068,329 (62.5%)
(2) Not in the Workforce:			
1. Student	1,215	20.6%	27.5%
2. Looking after Home/Family	2,915	49.4%	30.8%
3. Retired	379	6.4%	29.7%
4. Sick or Disabled	1,164	19.7%	11.1%
5. Other	225	3.8%	1.0%
Total Not in Labour Force	5,898 (45.0%)	99.9%	1,243,178 (37.5%)
Total Aged 15 and Over	13,098	---	3,311,517

Table No. 13.1 (Cont'd) Personal Variable	Number	Percentage of Travellers	Percentage of Total Irish Population
(i) Education			
1. Primary or Less	6,905	52.7%	15.4%
2. Lower Second Level	1,621	12.4%	17.8%
3. Higher Second Level	369	2.8%	23.2%
4. Non-Degree Third Level	42	0.3%	9.0%
5. Degree or Higher	33	0.3%	15.4%
6. Not Stated	1,008	7.7%	3.7%
7. Full-time Education Not Ceased	3,120	23.8%	15.4%
Total 15 Years Plus	13,098	100.0%	3,311,517
(j) Involvement in Voluntary Work			
1. Social & Charitable Work	262	2.0%	5.7%
2. Religious Work	221	1.7%	4.2%
3. Sporting Organisations	194	1.5%	5.4%
4. Political or Cultural	128	1.0%	1.4%
5. Any Other	218	1.7%	4.2%
Total in One or More Activities	587	4.5%	16.4%
Total Not Involved	12,511	95.5%	83.6%
Total 15 Years Plus	13,098	100.0%	3,311,517

Source: *Census 2006 Ethnic and Cultural Background (2007)*

Some **52.8%** of Travellers are **under the age of twenty years** as compared with **27.5%** of the national population in the same age-bracket. This reflects the very **healthy level of fertility** among Travellers who seem to get married earlier and do not have to endure prolonged adolescence before settling down. The **age pyramid** of the national population does not look that healthy with the 0-19 years **lower** at 27.5% than the second age group of 20-39 years at 32.5%. Of course, in-migration has affected the national population pyramid.

300

Figure No. 13.1: Age Pyramids of Travellers and of the National Population

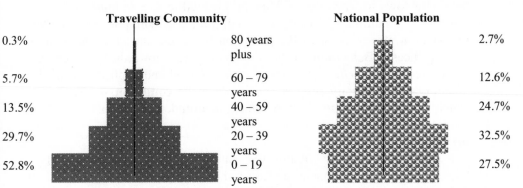

Travelling Community		National Population
0.3%	80 years plus	2.7%
5.7%	60 – 79 years	12.6%
13.5%	40 – 59 years	24.7%
29.7%	20 – 39 years	32.5%
52.8%	0 – 19 years	27.5%

From the above pyramids it is clear that Travellers need to live longer and the national population is displaying too low a level of fertility to maintain a labour force necessary to meet the needs of the population. The 0 to 19 year-olds are proportionately too low and are in marked contrast with that of the Travelling Community with high fertility, who are in a position to provide a potentially valuable asset to society as a whole if they are equitably integrated and given a stake in Irish society, which has been denied to them to date [as will be seen in Table No. 13.1(h) above].

The relative size of the Traveller minority at 22,369, or 0.5% of the population, should not present such a difficult problem for society to address and correct in terms of resources, despite the negative attitudes which will be discussed in subsequent paragraphs. Such improvements should be inserted into 'the vicious circle' at each of the three points, i.e. **attitudes, behaviour** and **conditions**.

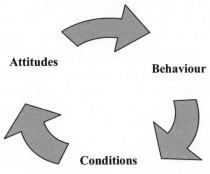

Attitudes   **Behaviour**

Conditions

Figure No. 13.2: The Vicious-Circle Model

An improvement in **attitudes** will lead to an improvement in behaviour towards Travellers. This, in turn, will cause an improvement in Travellers' conditions of living which will reinforce more positive attitudes. Intervention at any or all of the points on the circle can generate positive consequences. **Behaviour** of the 'dominant group' towards Travellers can be ensured by *minority rights' legislation* enforced and applied effectively. Statutory and voluntary support can improve the **conditions** of Travellers which will be reflected in an improvement in attitudes and so on.

(b) Gender:

The demographic census figures for males and females show a slightly higher proportion of females (+1.8%) than that of males. The 50/50 distribution in the general population has been influenced by the higher proportion of males among the migrant workers into Ireland in the late 1990s and early 2000s[4].

(c) Marital Status:

The age variation due to shorter life expectancy and the relatively high proportion of the Traveller population under twenty years of age result in the proportion of single people being ten per cent higher than that of the Settled Community (even allowing for Travellers' earlier marriage age). The 4.5% separated (including divorced) is slightly higher than the percentage for the National Population (3.9%). The proportion widowed is only half of that in the National Sample, i.e. 2.2% as compared with 4.5%. This reflects the relatively shorter life-expectancy of the Irish Traveller which, in turn, is due to the deprivations of their socio-economic conditions of living.

(d) Urban/Rural Place of Residence:

The progressive urbanisation of the Travelling people is clearly reflected in Table No. 13.1(d) above. In earlier times when Travellers were mostly nomadic, their area of residence was in the countryside within various 'circuits'. This facilitated extended family control and helped to develop informal relations with local residents. Their tinsmith skills and their expertise with horses were appreciated by local farmers. A number of families regularly camped on the outskirts of local towns.

---

[4] **Gender Distribution of 2007-08 sample:**

	Total Sample	Travellers *
Males	49.4%	49.1%
Females	50.6%	50.9%

* Census 2006

In recent years Travellers have been forced to move towards the urban areas. This has been a serious impediment to the extended family control and has created problems for unemployed Traveller youth who are often camped or housed in areas of towns and cities with serious delinquency and other problems caused in large part by the deprived (settled) social and cultural environment. There are notable and positive exceptions where Travellers have been accommodated successfully in urban environments.

(e) Province of Residence:
Travellers were always attracted to towns and villages where people were generally *kind, charitable and welcoming.* According to the findings on Table No. 13.1(e), Connaught has the most Travellers (proportionately) at 21.9% in a province with only 11.8% of the National Population. Half of the Irish Travellers live in Leinster (50.6%) with 19.4% resident in the Greater Dublin Area. The area least represented is the 'Part of Ulster' (Cavan, Donegal and Monaghan) which has 6.3% of the National Population and only 3.4% of the Travellers. About a quarter (24.1%) of Irish Travellers live in Munster.

(f) Country of Birth:
Travellers are overwhelmingly Irish Born, i.e. 92.8%. A further 7.2% were born in the United Kingdom (of Irish Traveller parents, barring the case of rare exceptions). This clearly proves that Irish Travellers are completely distinct from Romany Gypsies. A friend of Travellers and a promoter of their rights once put up a **public sign** in a Halting Site in Dublin which read: *"Don't despise us we are your ancestors!"* The above finding bears out the truth of the protestor's notice.

Travellers, as an Irish ethnic subgroup, have been endogamous (married within the Travellers with only rare exceptions). For some time they were viewed as a **lower caste** and, at times, as **'outcasts'** in Irish society.

(g) Religion:
The findings on Table No. 13.1(g) show that Irish Travellers are 95.1% **Roman Catholic** which is 7.7% more than the national population at 87.4% Roman Catholic. Some 2.4% (528 members) are **Church of Ireland.** The percentage declaring themselves as subscribing to 'No Religion' was as low as 0.3%.

One of the characteristics of Travellers' religious practice has been the high participation in pilgrimages at the traditional shrines, i.e. *Cnoc Mhuire*, Croagh Patrick, Lough Derg, Our Lady's Island (in County Wexford) and elsewhere. They are very genuine pilgrims.

(h) Employment Status[5]:
Table No. 13.1(h) confirms the appalling plight of this native Irish minority. Only **25.1%**, i.e. a quarter, of the **7,200 strong workforce** of Irish Travellers have gainful employment, in contrast to the **91.5%** of the National Population.   A further **11.1%** are seeking their first job as compared with **1.3%** in the national workforce!   This means that **63.8% are unemployed,** in contrast to the **7.1%** of the National Population.   These figures speak for themselves.

The cause of such negative figures is multiple and deserves very serious research.   The tradition of factory and office work was never part of the Traveller norms in the case of those over thirty years.   The new demands on education for gainful employment and the discrimination against Travellers getting normal work would be a fairly widespread expression of anti-Traveller prejudice.   Travellers are a most talented group of people. All they need is a structured work environment which will enable them to exercise their talents for the benefit of society.   The issue of Traveller employment needs to be addressed seriously in consultation with the elders of the Traveller Community.   There is no reason, for instance, why Travellers could not be employed in the building of their own fully-serviced Halting Sites, to give but one example. There are many other examples of potentially valuable work in which young Travellers could be gainfully employed.   There appears to be a need for **positive discrimination** in favour of Travellers' employment to compensate for their having to overcome the effects of **negative discrimination** over the years!

(i) Education:
Allowing for one quarter of the Travellers of 15 years and over to be still at school, the level of education achieved by those who have left the system is still very low.   More than half of Travellers (52.7% of the 15 years plus) ended with **Primary or Less** which is more than three times that of the National Population, i.e. **15.4%** of those who went beyond Primary.   Some **2,065** went beyond Primary education, with **78.5%** of them ending school at

---

[5] *Note:* All percentages in this Variable refer to the 15 year-olds and over.

Lower Second-Level. A further 2.8% of all Travellers completed their Second-Level. Less than 1% of Travellers achieved a Third-Level accreditation, while 24.4% of the National Population reached the same level.

It appears that there is some movement in education for a small proportion of the Travellers' 15-years-and-over population. There is yet another factor which needs to be kept in mind when trying to improve the chances of all the Travellers, namely, to prevent 'passing' out of the Traveller subculture while at the same time improving the standards of the students. What is authentic in the Travellers' culture should be handed on to the young while the **'culture of poverty'** is removed. This requires the maximum participation of the Travellers themselves in the education processes. The aim should be to train **Traveller teachers** to teach the young children and communicate to them the music, song, dance, folklore, traditions and history and geography of the Irish Travelling People. Audio-visual and other aids to good learning should be provided to stimulate the young to learn. Also, the parents and other Travellers should be given the opportunities to engage in adult education likely to help them. Otherwise, there is a real danger that an increase in educational participation will result in *cultural de-radicalisation*, i.e. remove them from the distinctive culture of their parents and families. In other words, the young will be assimilated into the Settled Community's culture and removed from their own. This will be an anti-pluralist form of socialisation and may create serious psychological problems for those educated out of their own human roots!

The transmission of technical skills appropriate to those required for the jobs necessary for the young people is essential. For some these skills will be in the areas of skilled trades, clerical work and the services' skills. For Travellers with the aptitude to go on to teaching, nursing and medicine, etc. opportunities should be open to those with the motivation and ability to do so. It is very important that further educational specialisation should be encouraged for Travellers leading to qualifications in law, religious studies, creative arts and whatever level of advance in psychology, arts, human sciences, chemistry, physics, engineering and other areas. This should not result in graduates being pressurised to leave their Traveller Community. The wide range of opportunities is now possible with commitment to their *Travelling Community* and improved standards of living and job-opportunities. Raising the current level of education and training demands **a whole new approach** from Travellers themselves. The maximum cooperation of those who are committed to lend a hand and respect their unique culture is also required.

ꞏ (j) Participation in Voluntary Work:

To preserve the policy of *integrated pluralism*, the contribution of Travellers in voluntary work by committed members of the *Travelling Community* is a very valuable guarantee to the emancipation of this ancient Irish minority. Table No. 13.1(j) lists the level of participation of Irish Travellers in the various areas of voluntary social, religious, sporting, political and cultural activity to be less than one-third of the level of active involvement of the National Population, i.e. **4.5%** as compared with 16.4%, at a time when volunteerism is in decline in Irish society.

The Travellers' area of voluntary support is still mainly within **the extended family's** informal structure. As time moves on, there will be greater need for more involvement of committed Travellers in the various areas of social activity. This will attract the young to focus more on constructive activity and avoid being drawn into certain destructive practices, and the tendency to deal with difficulties outside the rule of law in Irish society. It will also help to keep young Travellers away from the excessive use of alcohol.

Travellers will need to become part of the Gardaí, the judiciary and the legislature. Travellers should be members of juries in cases required to deal with internal conflict and cases between **Travellers** and members of the **Settled Community**. This is a necessary dimension of participative pluralist integration within Irish society. Otherwise, Travellers will feel alienated from the Irish legal and justice system!

(k) Conclusion:

The above findings of the *2006 Census Report* of the ethnic and cultural background of the Irish National Population and the Irish Travelling Community should give the reader a fairly comprehensive profile of this ancient socio-cultural minority. Travellers represent a most distinguished minority, which has been treated as a 'lower caste' and, at times, as an 'outcast' minority, (with an appalling level of neglect and discrimination in a relatively wealthy Irish society), the results of which on such a small and culturally rich minority have been spelled out in the Report of the 2006 Census of Population. The biggest human tragedy has been the **relatively short life expectancy** in the middle of a society with a sophisticated and comfortable material and social standard of living. This is akin to the state of the Black People in South Africa during the Apartheid era!

Nothing short of a radical change of policy with the initially necessary social and economic support to reverse the vicious circle which has been perpetuating the misery of one of Ireland's most valuable young and potentially energetic minorities will be required. It is time to call an end to **the informal apartheid**! It is also time to give the Travellers **a stake in this society,** the result of which will be their willingness to conform to the general norms of society and develop as a valuable partner of the Settled Community and other ethnically different and religiously pluralist groups in our increasingly diverse society.

Part III – Social Distance towards Travellers

3.1 Introduction:
As noted elsewhere, social distance is the principal measure of social prejudice against numerous stimulus categories in this text. The results can be assessed under three general headings, i.e.

(1) Actual mean-social-distance (MSD);
(2) Pattern of social distance responses;
(3) Rank order of preference of the category.

Examined under **actual mean-social-distance**, 'Travellers' record an improvement of their overall position when the findings of the 1988-89 national survey are compared with those of the 2007-08, i.e. from **3.681** to **3.030**. It has been an improvement from a relatively negative base at **3.681**.

The pattern of social distance responses in the case of the Traveller is becoming more polarised, i.e. an increase in 'admission to kinship' percentages accompanied by a rise in the proportion of respondents prepared to 'deny Travellers citizenship'. This polarisation is indicative of a reaction of members of the minority beginning to assert its basic human rights.

The **rank order** of 'Irish Travellers' out of 46 categories replicated in the questionnaire for the 1988-89 survey, shows they went from **44th** in 1988-89 to **45th** in 2007-08, i.e. second from last on the list. This rating reflects a most serious position for Travellers and is totally contrary to the *principle of propinquity*, which in the normal course of events would expect to find an indigenous Irish minority close to the in-groups (**1.500 MSD or under**) rather than their approaching out-group status (at **3.030** MSD).   If no other evidence were available, the mean-social-distance scores would be sufficient to alert the people of Ireland to the intolerable status of Travelling People in the dispositions of their fellow citizens.   The country's commendable concern for deprived and discriminated-against overseas would gain consistency and credibility if the problem of equality and social justice for the Travelling People were successfully responded to by Irish society.   The Report, *Emancipation of the Travelling People,* proposed recommendations aimed at achieving such a resolution as a matter of priority (see pages 93-97).

3.2 Overall Social Distance towards Travellers:

Table No. 13.2 records the social-distance scores of the total sample towards 'Travellers':

Table No. 13.2: Social Distance towards Travellers (Total Sample)

Social Distance	Actual Percentage	Cumulative Percentage	Number
1. Kinship	39.6%	(39.6%)	400
2. Friendship	13.8%	(53.4%)	139
3. Next-Door Neighbour	8.3%	(61.7%)	84
4. Co-Worker	8.0%	(69.8%)	81
5. Citizenship	12.1%	(81.8%)	122
6. Citizen Only	8.9%		89
7. Debar / Deport	9.3%	(18.2%)	94
Number	100.0%	(100.0%)	1,009

The above findings, while recording a very substantial improvement in the case of welcoming to **kinship**, when compared to the findings of 1988-89, are in the overall quite disappointing.   It is difficult to understand why so many respondents would not be willing to admit to kinship or even to **friendship** to fellow Irish men and women.   It reflects badly on our sense of universal openness, and reveals quite a level of social prejudice towards our 'native minority'.   The above findings are an embarrassment to the tolerant Irish citizen.   Nevertheless, when compared with the two previous

Irish surveys of 1972-73 and 1988-89, they show a ray of hope that a breakthrough might be happening.

Table No. 13.3:
Changes in Social Distance towards Travellers from 1972-73 to 2007-08

Survey	Kinship	Friendship or Closer	Next-door neighbour or closer	Co-Worker or Closer	Citizen or Closer	Visitor Only	Debar or Deport	No.
1. Nat. Sample 2007-08	39.6%	53.4%	61.7%	69.8%	81.8%	8.9%	9.3%	1,009
2. Nat. Sample 1988-89	13.5%	26.7%	41.0%	63.7%	90.0%	7.0%	3.0%	1,000
Change (1-2)	**+26.1%**	**+26.7%**	**+20.7%**	**+6.1%**	**-8.2%**	**+1.9%**	**+6.3%**	---
3. Dublin SS 2007-08	48.6%	59.9%	69.8%	81.8%	88.8%	7.7%	3.5%	284
4. Dublin SS 1988-89	16.4%	29.2%	42.3%	70.8%	90.5%	5.1%	4.4%	274
5. Dublin S. 1972-73	29.0%	51.1%	64.3%	75.5%	93.4%	2.8%	3.8%	2,302
Change (3-4)	**+32.2%**	**+30.7%**	**+27.5%**	**+11.0%**	**-1.7%**	**+2.6%**	**-0.9%**	---
Change (3-5)	**+19.6%**	**+8.8%**	**+5.5%**	**+6.3%**	**-4.6%**	**+4.9%**	**-0.3%**	---

The changes reported in Table No. 13.3 are both very optimistic and somewhat pessimistic. The very substantial increase in the percentages of the National Sample who would *welcome members of the Travelling Community into the family* almost trebled since 1988-89 **from 13.5% to 39.6%**. Such a large change in national attitudes was not anticipated in the light of the perpetual negative reporting and stereotyping of Travellers in the national print and electronic media over the past nineteen years. It is reassuring that there are so many in the country who have a more balanced view and are prepared to give everyone a fair chance, which is what these figures represent. The findings have certainly lifted the cloud of 'lower caste' from this native Irish minority. With such support, even the classification of 'lower caste' has been challenged.

When it comes to Dublin people, the improvement in the welcome to kinship at 48.6% has been even greater than the change in the National Sample. The Dublin figures also moved positively by a factor of three, i.e. **from 16.4% to 48.6%**. It must be very satisfying for the members of the Travelling Community and, especially, for their leaders who have worked tirelessly for Travellers' Rights in the face of media and other opposition, to realise that practically half of the Dublin representative sample would welcome Travellers into their family through marriage.

The pessimistic aspect of the above findings has been the increase in the percentages who would 'deny citizenship' to Travellers, i.e. **18.2%** of the sample – 8.9% as 'visitors only' and 9.3% who would 'debar' or 'deport'. This is quite serious.   There is an increasing polarisation in the population with growing support as both ends of the behavioural-tendency continuum. The probable causes of this reaction are the assertion by the minority of their rights and the publicity of negative behaviour associated with a minority of Travellers being highlighted, often in an unbalanced manner.   In the cycle of emancipation of a minority in various societies, such a polarisation occurs.   It was most clearly manifested in Northern Ireland once the Nationalist minority became assertive about their rights.   If this be true of the Irish Travellers' move towards their civil and human rights, the best route for the dominant (establishment) group is to make haste to satisfy these rights.

Sociologists of intergroup relations have noted the Park Cycle[6] which refers to a "patterned-sequence cycle" which follows a certain order in dominant-minority relations, i.e.:

(1) The *1ˢᵗ Stage* is the **initial contact stage**, which can last for an appreciable period of time, if the minority group does not come into competition with the dominant group;

(2) The *2ⁿᵈ Stage* is when the two groups enter **competition** for goods and services, e.g. housing, work, education, etc. **Conflict** can take place during this stage;

(3) **Accommodation** marks the *3ʳᵈ Stage* when 'space' is given to the minority and some moves are made to satisfy their basic needs. Such accommodation may be stratified, i.e. the minority are given menial jobs, minimal education and basic housing (sometimes in prescribed areas or locations);

(4) The *4ᵗʰ Stage* is **integration** often leading to **assimilation.** Park saw the fourth stage as leading to assimilation. Since Park's time (when he identified the four stages in 1926) many sociologists of intergroup relations seem to favour 'pluralism'[7] as the most equitable form of social integration of minorities. The 'integrated pluralist' solution is the most dignified one, culturally speaking.

---

[6] Park, Robert E., 1926 "Our Racial Frontier on the Pacific" in *Survey Geography Race and Culture*, New York, McGraw-Hill, 1950.
[7] Mac Gréil, Micheál, *Prejudice in Ireland Revisited*, Maynooth, St. Patrick's College, 1996, pp324.

The position of the Irish Travellers could be located **between Stage Two and Stage Three** at present, where attempts to accommodate their needs are a less-than-equitable form of 'accommodation'. Irish society is required to think again and address all the needs of this relatively small [in terms of proportion (0.5%) of the population] native Irish minority. The emergence of such a substantial minority (18.2%) of respondents who were prepared to 'deny citizenship' to Travellers heralds negative intergroup conflict if the problem is not addressed. The growing number of respondents who were favourably disposed to Travellers should make the task of equitable integration more feasible.

3.3 Intergroup Definition:

Intergroup Definition is a very important factor in explaining intergroup relations. In the current survey, interviewed respondents who did not welcome members of the Travelling Community into the family were asked the following question:

"Looking over your answer to this question (i.e. the social-distance question), there are a number of categories which you would not welcome into kinship. Which of the following would you say was your main reason for placing them at the distance indicated?"

The purpose of this question was to discover how those not admitting Travellers to kinship defined them. The **reasons** listed on the 'prompt card' were as given in column one of Table No. 13.4.

Table No. 13.4:
Main Reasons Why Travellers Were Not Welcomed Into the Family

Reasons	National Sample 2007-08	National Sample 1988-89	Dublin Sample 1972-73
1. Religious	0.3%	0.6%	0.3%
2. Racial	0.3%	0.0%	0.2%
3. Political	2.3%	0.0%	0.1%
4. National/Cultural	**9.6%**	2.3%	-
5. Economic	2.1%	1.8%	3.4%
6. Not Socially Acceptable	**17.8%**	**20.3%**	**62.1%**
7. Way of Life	**63.7%**	**74.2%**	**32.3%**
8. Other	3.9%	1.9%	1.6%
Number	586	844	1,592

Note: Percentages above 5% are in **bold**.

It is clear from the findings of Table No. 13.4 that the reasons why those not willing to welcome Travellers into the family in the 2007-08 survey are still predominantly their 'Way of Life' **(63.7%)**. Many of the unattractive aspects of this 'way of life' are likely to be due to the **culture of poverty** which has been forced on the Travellers for years. This has been a **seriously deprived minority** in terms of living accommodation, education, work opportunities and others. Some of the deviant behaviour associated with a minority of Travellers derives from this deprivation.

Respondents who would define Travellers as being 'not socially acceptable' were still too high a proportion for comfort, i.e. at **17.8%**. There has always been an element of this definition with regard to minorities whose perceived social standing was incompatible with that of the dominant group. This leads to avoidance and 'ghettoisation' of members of so-defined minorities. The challenge facing those who would wish to remove such intergroup definitions is to examine the **causes** of social unacceptability of the Travelling Community. Is it lifestyle, lack of favourable contact, lack of gainful employment, negative reporting in the media, poor social and economic conditions of Travellers, deviance of a minority of Travellers, and so forth, which causes the perception of "not socially acceptable"?

The national/cultural reason is an indication of the special cultural traits of the Travellers as distinct from those of the Settled Community. Those who would advocate a more pluralist form of integration for Travellers (which recognised their culture) rather than assimilation could take some modicum of hope from the **9.6%** who gave culture as a reason. Also, it should be noted that the 'cultural' factor may also be present in the minds of some of those who gave 'Way of Life' as a reason. The true identity of Travellers' positive cultural identity will not be possible until the **'culture of poverty'** has been removed.

Table No. 13.4 also gives the findings of the two previous studies which used the *Bogardus Social Distance Scale* to measure attitudes towards 'Travellers' in 1972-73 and 1988-89. The latter was a National Survey, while the former was a Survey of Greater Dublin Urban and Suburban society. The principal **change** in the 'rationalisation for not admitting Travellers into the family' was between them 'not being socially acceptable' in 1972-73 (62.1%) and their 'Way of Life' in 1988-89 (74.2%). This was a very substantial shift in the samples' definition of Travellers. In 1988-89 'not socially acceptable' dropped by over two-fifths to 41.8%, i.e. from 62.1% to 20.3% since 1972-73.

The changes between 1988-89 and 2007-08 were less dramatic. The patterns were more or less maintained. There were decreases in 'Way of Life' (from 74.2% to 63.7% = -10.5%) and in 'Not Socially Acceptable' (from 20.3% to 17.8% = -2.5%). The most significant change was in relation to the **cultural** reason which went from **2.3%** in 1988-89 to **9.6%** in 2007-08, i.e. a nominal change of +7.3%.

3.4 Social Distance towards Travellers by Personal Variables:

Table No. 13.5 gives a breakdown of social distance towards Travellers by personal variables which recorded a statistically significant variation, i.e. age, gender, marital status, area of birth, region of residence, education and occupational status. Percentages above the sample average are underlined. Three measures of social distance are abstracted from the full seven-point scale, i.e. admit to kinship, have as next-door neighbour or closer and denial of Irish citizenship ('visitor only' and/or 'debar or deport'). The responses to the item *"Would be reluctant to buy a house next door to a Traveller"* are much more negative than the findings of Column No. 3 (see Item No. 3, Table No. 13.6, page 321 below). Does this imply that a proportion of respondents who would welcome Travellers into kinship or friendship would not like to have them as "next-door neighbours"?

Table No. 13.5:
Social Distance towards Travellers by Personal Variables

Personal Variable	Kinship	Next-Door Neighbour or Closer	Denial of Irish Citizenship	MSD (1-7)	Number
Total Sample	39.6%	61.7%	18.2%	3.03	1,008
(a) Age	(p<.02)				
1. 18-25 Years	38.1%	**63.7%**	**19.6%**	3.10	168
2. 26-40 Years	**42.4%**	**63.5%**	**18.6%**	2.91	323
3. 41-55 Years	35.4%	60.2%	16.2%	3.10	246
4. 56-70 Years	39.4%	53.6%	**21.2%**	3.26	175
5. 71 Years plus	**43.8%**	**69.8%**	14.6%	2.70	96
Number	399	621	184		1,008
(b) Gender	(p<.002)				
Male	38.6%	57.1%	**20.4%**	3.16	495
Female	**40.6%**	**66.0%**	16.0%	2.91	512
Number	399	621	183		1,007

Table No. 13.5 Cont'd. Personal Variable	Kinship	Next-Door Neighbour or Closer	Denial of Irish Citizenship	MSD	Number
(c) Marital Status	(p<.006)				
1. Single/Never Married	**41.6%**	66.1%	19.4%	2.94	356
2. Married	38.9%	57.7%	16.9%	3.09	468
3. Separated/Divorced	27.9%	60.5%	**25.6%**	3.40	43
4. Permanent Relation'p	37.5%	61.1%	13.9%	3.03	72
5. Widowed	**44.9%**	**69.5%**	20.3%	2.97	69
Number	400	623	183		1,008
(d) Area of Birth	(p<.001)				
1. City (100,000+)	36.8%	61.4%	13.6%	2.86	418
2. Large Town (10,000+)	**47.1%**	**63.9%**	**22.7%**	2.89	119
3. Town (1,500+)	**49.6%**	**70.5%**	11.7%	2.56	129
4. Rural/ Village	36.4%	57.8%	**24.9%**	3.35	341
Number	398	621	184		1,007
(e) Region of Residence	(p<.001)				
1. BMW*	28.6%	60.6%	**19.4%**	3.25	269
2. Dublin	**48.6%**	**69.8%**	11.2%	2.55	284
3. Mid-East & South-E.	**46.3%**	60.5%	**22.9%**	3.09	218
4. Mid-West & Sth-West	35.5%	54.7%	**21.4%**	3.31	234
Number	399	621	184		1,005
(f) Education	(p<.007)				
1. Primary or less	**52.1%**	**65.7%**	13.6%	2.67	117
2. Incomplete Sec.-Lev	36.8%	**63.2%**	16.9%	3.02	261
3. Complete Second-Lev.	39.1%	61.2%	**23.3%**	3.14	253
4. Third-Level	37.8%	59.3%	17.1%	3.07	378
Number	399	621	184		1,009
(g) Occupational Status	(p<.001)				
1 Unskilled /Semi	30.4%	**64.7%**	17.9%	3.07	207
2. Skilled/ Routine n-m	**43.0%**	59.7%	**22.9%**	3.11	323
3.Inspectional/Supervis'y	**45.0%**	**65.6%**	11.4%	2.79	131
4. Professional /Execut.	38.5%	57.3%	15.1%	3.06	192
Number	335	523	155		853

Note: Percentages above sample average are **bold**.

* (Border, Midlands and West)

The direction of variations between the different subsamples is not always as anticipated. It is generally held that those whose cultural and economic resources make them more secure tend to be more tolerant, i.e. insecurity, and the frustration resulting from it, is recognised as one of the main psychological causes of social prejudice. This has not been confirmed in a number of the personal variables analysed in Table No. 13.5. The presence of a **social class factor** may be more dominant than anticipated.

(a) Age:

The variations within the age-variable are highlighted in the following extract from Table No. 13.5(a):

Age	Welcome into Family	Deny Citizenship	Number
1. 18 to 25 years	38.1%	**19.6%**	168
2. 26 to 40 years	**42.4%**	**18.6%**	323
3. 41 to 55 years	35.4%	16.2%	246
4. 56 to 70 years	39.4%	**21.2%**	175
5. 71 years plus	**43.8%**	14.6%	96
Number	399	184	1,008
Sample Average	39.6%	18.2%	---

Note: *Percentages above sample average are underlined in **bold**.*

Age has produced a chi-square of $p<.02$, which means that the variations for this personal variable are due to chance in less than one-in-fifty cases. The most tolerant age group is the 71 years plus group, i.e. highest score in 'admission to kinship' (43.8%) and lowest willing to deny Travellers citizenship (14.6%). The age-cohort least welcoming to Travellers was the 56 to 70 year-olds, i.e. lowest welcoming as 'next-door neighbours' (53.6%) and highest 'denying citizenship' at **21.2%**. The latter figure is quite disturbing in the light of the leadership role this age-group plays in society.

(b) Gender:

Males are significantly, if moderately, less tolerant of Travellers than are females. The range of difference is highest (-11%) in the case of welcoming Travellers as 'next-door neighbours or closer'. Females were more in favour of welcoming Travellers into the family through marriage (40.6% as compared with 38.6%) and less in favour of denying them citizenship of Ireland, i.e. 16.0% as compared with 20.4%.

(c) Marital Status:

The polarisation of responses is clear in the case of 'Single/Never Married' and 'Widowed' in the following extract:

Marital Status	Welcome into Family	Deny Citizenship	Number
1. Single/Never Married	**41.6%**	**19.4%**	356
2. Married	38.9%	16.9%	468
3. Separated/Divorced	27.9%	**25.6%**	43
4. Permanent Relationship	37.5%	13.9%	72
5. Widowed	**44.9%**	**20.3%**	69
Number	400	183	1,008
Sample Average	39.6%	18.2%	---

Note: *Percentages above sample average are underlined in **bold**.*

The pattern of replies from the 'Marital Status' variable is interesting. The 'Widowed' and the 'Single/Never Married' were the most welcoming to Travellers into the family and into the neighbourhood or closer, while barely significantly higher than the sample average in denying citizenship to members of the minority. The 'Married' (which represents 46.4% of the Total Sample) were slightly below average in each of the three measures recorded of Table No. 13.5(c).

(d) Area of Birth:

The range of scores is significant and relatively substantial in the case of 'Denial of Citizenship' in the following sub-table:

Area of Birth	Welcome into Family	Deny Citizenship	Number
1. City (100,000 plus)	36.8%	13.6%	418
2. Large Town (10,000-99,999)	**47.1%**	**22.7%**	119
3. Town (1,500 – 9,999)	**49.6%**	11.7%	129
4. Rural/Village	36.4%	**24.9%**	341
Number	398	184	1,007
Sample Average	39.6%	18.2%	---

Note: *Percentages above sample average are underlined in **bold**.*

Respondents born in large (10,000+) and smaller Towns (1,500+) were the most welcoming into the family through marriage of members of the Travelling People at **47.1%** and **49.6%** respectively. Smaller town respondents had the lowest percentage 'denying citizenship' at **11.7%**. There was evidence of polarisation in respondents from large towns whose denial of citizenship percentage was as high as **22.7%**, i.e. almost twice that of the smaller town area of birth. Those born in 'Rural/Village' areas were least welcoming into the family and most in favour of denying citizenship (at **24.9%**). Respondents born in 'Large Cities' (100,000+) were close to the sample-average in the case of welcoming into the family and in having a next-door neighbour.   They were also significantly below average in their denial-of-citizenship scores.

(e) Region of Residence:
The relative tolerance of those living in the east of Ireland towards Travellers is highlighted below:

Region of Residence	Welcome into Family	Deny Citizenship	Number
1. B.M.W.	28.6%	**19.4%**	269
2. Dublin	**48.6%**	11.2%	284
3. Mid-East & South-East	**46.3%**	**22.9%**	218
4. Mid-West & South-West	35.5%	**21.4%**	234
Number	399	184	1,005
Sample Average	39.6%	18.2%	---

Note: *Percentages above sample average are underlined in **bold**.*

The part of the country in which respondents lived had quite a significant influence on their attitudes towards the Travelling People. Dublin residents were by far the most tolerant respondents towards Traveller fellow citizens.   Almost half **(48.6%)** would welcome Travellers into their families through marriage, while **69.8%** would have them as next-door-neighbours or closer.   Only **11.2%** (when compared with other regions) would deny Travellers citizenship.   Although this percentage is unacceptable, it is relatively low in the findings of this survey.   The BMW and the Mid-West / South-West regions were quite negative in their social distance scores.   The BMW respondents' percentage welcoming into the family was the lowest recorded on Table No. 13.5 at **28.6%.**   The range of scores in the columns measuring admission to kinship and denial of citizenship are substantial.

(f) Education:
The responses in Table No. 13.5(f) are not as anticipated, i.e. in that it was expected that tolerance would increase according as the educational achievement increased.   In fact, this has **not** happened as the following extract from Table No. 13.5(f) underlined:

Education	Welcome into Family	Deny Citizenship	Number
1. Primary or Less	**52.1%**	13.6%	117
2. Incomplete Second-Level	36.8%	16.9%	261
3. Complete Second-Level	39.1%	**23.3%**	253
4. Third-Level	37.8%	17.1%	278
Number	399	184	1,009
Sample Average	39.6%	18.2%	---

Note: *Percentages above sample average are underlined in **bold.***

In society, certain 'liberal attitudes' are inclined to be towards minorities who enjoy "politically correct" categories. The **'all-weather liberal'** is quite rare (see Robert Merton[8]). Among the 'outside' categories for otherwise liberal respondents are 'Travellers', or so it would seem from the above findings, since the majority of liberal respondents would tend to be more highly educated and younger. Certain conservative categories would also seem to rate lower among some more 'liberal' respondents[9]. They seem to practise 'selected liberalness'!

The least educated subsample, i.e. those with 'primary education *or less*' were the most welcoming of all the subsamples on Table No. 13.5 at **52.1%** welcoming Travellers into their family through marriage. This reflects an exceptional level of potential social solidarity among the relatively poorly educated and those near the bottom of the social-class ladder, i.e. the Travellers. The open-mindedness of so many of those with a lower level of education, a large proportion of whom would be in the older age bracket, reflects a commendable level of wisdom and genuine charity. Unfortunately, this educational category would not have the power in society to establish institutions that would raise the conditions of living for Travellers. The 'Primary or Less' subsample recorded the lowest percentage prepared to deny citizenship to Travellers.

What seems to be emerging from the unanticipated findings of the education variable has been the resilience of the social-class prejudice factor among the more educated, many of whom would themselves be the first or second generation with a high formal achievement in education!

---

[8] Merton, Robert K., *Social Theory and Social Structure*, New York, Collier Macmillan, 1957.
[9] Mac Gréil, Micheál, *Prejudice in Ireland Revisited*, Má Nuad, 1996/1997, pp 177-8.

(g) Occupational Status:

The findings of Table No. 13.5(g) test the level of social-distance toward Travellers by occupational status. While the variations are very significant statistically, the correlation is not as anticipated, i.e. with the most secure being the most tolerant. The social-class-prejudice factor is again probably at work. The most tolerant subsample was the Inspectional/Supervisory with **45.0%** welcoming the Travellers into the family and two-thirds accepting Travellers as next-door neighbours. This is an interesting but mixed result. It shows that this significant group from the middle class is open to the members of the minority, and shows a higher level of tolerance than the Professional/Executive subsample.

(h) Conclusion:

The findings of Table No. 13.5 have revealed some interesting surprises, some optimistic in relation to the future improvement of the conditions of Irish Travellers. The most disappointing aspect that emerged has been a degree of social-class prejudice in the case of some of those with better education and higher occupational status. Their security and so-called 'liberal' attitudes have not made them more tolerant than their more deprived and older fellow-citizens. In a society where great emphasis is put on competitiveness and individual success, the popular role models and positive reference groups tend to be those who 'get on' in terms of wealth and power. This is part of the ideology of individualism. In a society where cooperation and social solidarity are prized, groups like Travellers have a much better chance of integration on the basis of social justice[10].

Part IV – The Special 'Anti-Traveller Scale': Attitudes and Opinions

4.1 Introduction:

This scale was devised by the late Professor Earl Davis and ESRI colleagues to measure social attitudes towards members of deprived groups/categories in Ireland in the mid-1970s. It was tested in relation to Travellers in their study published in 1977[11]. This scale has been most useful in that it has repeated a high *Cronbach Alpha* test of **0.83** in 1988-89 and 0.83 in 2007-

---

[10] *Note*: At this stage in the Report, *Emancipation of the Travelling People*, an examination of the rationalisation scale by personal variables in relation to 'Travellers' is made. Space does not permit its inclusion in this chapter.

[11] Davis, E.E., Grube, J.W., and Morgan, M., *Attitudes towards Poverty and Related Issues in Ireland*, Dublin, ESRI (No.117), 1984.

08.   Individual items are excellent measures of **opinions** relevant to the Travellers' position in society and highlight a number of areas of importance.

4.2 Overall Results of Anti-Traveller Scale:
Two factors emerge from the scale, i.e. **social** and **interpersonal** factor. The following are the items in each of the factors:

Social Factors: (Items Nos. 1, 4, 6 and 7 on the Scale)
1.   *"I would Respect a Traveller"*
2.   *"I would Be Willing to Employ a Traveller"*
3.   *"I would Consider a Traveller Competent to Serve on a Jury"*
4.   *"I would Avoid a Traveller on Social Occasions"*

Interpersonal Factors: (Items Nos. 2, 3 and 5)
1.   *"I would Be Reluctant to Buy a House Next Door to a Traveller"*
2.   *"I would Be Hesitant to Seek a Traveller's Company"*
3.   *"I would Exclude a Traveller from My Close Set of Friends"*

It will be seen from the results of the scale given on Table No. 13.6 that there is a more positive response to items in the 'Social Factor' than in the 'Interpersonal' ones.   It could be argued that there is a conflict between the more positive findings of the *Social Distance Scale* than is to be found in the interpersonal items of the *Anti-Traveller Scale*.   This is probably due to the difference between **attitudes** (which are pre-reflective) and **opinions** (which are post-reflective).   Respondents were urged to respond briskly to the *Bogardus Social Distance Scale* in order to get the "first-feeling response", which is closest to the disposition or attitude.   In the case of the Anti-Traveller Scale, there was no such pressure, which enabled the respondent to reflect on his or her answer and weigh up the broader consequences of the reply.   Opinions are behavioural expressions of multiple, and even contradictory, attitudes.

The negative scores for the interpersonal factor items have been more severe than were the items indicating social trust and respect.   This result should not be surprising in the case of Travellers as a group who have been perceived and defined as 'lower caste' or even as 'outcasts'.   As noted already, there are positive signs of a change in this negative exclusion.

Table No. 13.6: Travellers' Scale (Including Don't Knows)

Statements	Agree Strongly	Agree Moderately	Agree Slightly	Don't Know	Disagree Slightly	Disagree Moderately	Disagree Strongly	Number	Mean Negative Scores (1-6)	Factor
1. I would respect a Traveller.	29.4%	25.4% ↓ **76.4%**	21.6%	5.0%	8.0%	4.5% ↓ 18.6%	6.1%	1,015	2.75	1
2. I would be reluctant to buy a house next door to a Traveller.	37.7%	17.9% ↓ 75.3%	19.7%	5.4%	7.4%	6.3% ↓ **19.4%**	5.7%	1,015	5.32	2
3. I would be hesitant to seek a Traveller's company.	29.0%	21.5% ↓ 72.3%	21.8%	5.7%	8.4%	7.9% ↓ **21.9%**	5.6%	1,014	5.10	2
4. I would be willing to employ a Traveller.	21.0%	17.4% ↓ **53.9%**	15.5%	8.5%	13.4%	8.8% ↓ 37.6%	15.4%	1,015	2.10	1
5. I would exclude a Traveller from my close set of friends.	22.9%	16.5% ↓ 56.7%	17.3%	7.1%	15.7%	10.9% ↓ **36.1%**	9.5%	1,014	4.53	2
6. I would consider a Traveller competent to serve on a jury.	28.3%	18.9% ↓ **63.8%**	16.6%	12.8%	9.4%	5.0% ↓ 23.4%	9.0%	1,015	3.07	1
7. I would avoid a Traveller in social situations.	23.7%	16.3% ↓ 60.0%	20.1%	6.2%	14.3%	9.4% ↓ **33.7%**	10.1%	1,015	4.80	1

Notes: Positive attitudes are **bold**.
 Cronbach Test = 0.83

Hopefully, it will not take as long for Travellers to be accepted as it has taken the 'Native Americans' to emerge from lower caste / outcast status in the United States and parts of Central and Southern Americas, to be treated and respected as equals by their fellow-citizens. The findings of the above Table (No. 13.6) show that there is 'a mountain to climb', especially in the interpersonal evaluations. Even the one item with a high negative score in the social factor sub-scale, i.e. Item No. 7, i.e. "I would avoid a Traveller in Social Situations", has an element of personal social contact.

4.3 Changes in Findings between 1977 and 2007-08:

Table No. 13.7 records the changes over a period of thirty years for each item of opinion:

Table No. 13.7: Changes in the Findings of the Traveller Scale
(excluding Don't Knows) (1977 / 1988-89 / 2007-08)

Scale Item			Agreement				Disagreement				Mean Negative Score
			Strong	Mod.	Slight	Total	Slight	Mod.	Strong	Total	
			%	%	%	%	%	%	%	%	(1-6)
1. Respect a Traveller	A	1977	21.2	29.3	26.7	77.2	9.1	6.3	6.8	22.2	2.69
	B	1988-89	22.6	39.4	24.8	86.8	5.3	5.7	2.2	13.2	2.39
	C	2007-08	30.9	26.7	22.7	80.3	8.4	4.7	6.4	19.5	2.48
	C – B	-	+8.3	-12.7	-2.1	-6.3	+3.4	-1.0	+4.2	+6.3	+0.09
2. Reluctant to buy a house next door to a Traveller	A	1977	35.4	17.8	16.9	70.1	10.6	8.8	9.9	29.3	4.18
	B	1988-89	32.1	26.4	16.1	74.6	8.1	9.3	8.0	25.4	4.40
	C	2007-08	39.9	18.9	20.8	79.6	7.8	6.7	6.0	20.5	4.60
	C - B	-	+7.8	-7.5	+4.1	+3.0	-0.3	-2.6	-2.0	-4.9	+0.20
3. Hesitant to seek the company of a Traveller	A	1977	34.3	20.6	21.6	76.5	10.4	6.2	6.2	22.8	4.45
	B	1988-89	23.4	31.5	21.5	76.4	8.0	9.0	6.5	23.5	4.32
	C	2007-08	30.8	22.8	23.1	76.7	8.9	8.4	5.9	23.2	4.41
	C - B	-	+7.4	-8.7	+1.6	+0.3	+0.9	-0.6	-0.6	-0.3	+0.09
4. Willing to employ a Traveller	A	1977	11.9	17.3	25.6	54.8	15.0	11.4	18.0	44.4	3.48
	B	1988-89	10.4	25.5	21.0	56.9	12.1	17.3	13.7	43.1	3.42
	C	2007-08	23.0	19.0	17.0	59.0	14.7	9.6	16.8	41.1	3.20
	C - B	-	+12.6	-3.5	-6.0	+2.1	+2.6	-7.7	+3.1	-2.0	-0.22
5. Exclude a Traveller from close set of friends	A	1977	28.0	17.4	22.1	67.5	14.8	8.3	8.5	31.6	4.13
	B	1988-89	17.0	27.5	18.4	62.9	12.9	15.8	8.3	37.0	3.92
	C	2007-08	24.7	17.8	18.6	61.1	16.9	11.7	10.2	38.8	3.96
	C - B	-	+7.7	-9.7	+0.2	-1.8	+4.0	-4.1	+1.9	+1.8	+0.04
6. Competent to serve on a jury	A	1977	7.5	9.4	14.5	31.4	16.5	15.0	36.1	67.6	4.27
	B	1988-89	11.9	21.1	18.7	51.7	13.9	19.1	15.2	48.2	3.53
	C	2007-08	32.5	21.7	19.0	73.2	10.8	5.7	10.3	26.8	2.26
	C - B	-	+20.6	+0.6	+0.3	+21.5	-3.1	-13.4	-4.9	-21.4	-1.37
7. Avoid a Traveller in social situations	A	1977	25.1	18.3	21.9	65.3	16.2	9.2	8.6	34.0	4.05
	B	1988-89	13.5	24.1	18.3	55.9	14.5	18.6	11.1	44.2	3.27
	C	2007-08	25.2	17.3	21.4	63.9	15.2	10.0	10.8	36.0	4.00
	C - B	-	+11.7	-6.8	+3.1	+8.0	+0.7	-8.6	-0.3	-8.2	+0.73
Scale Mean Negative Score	A	1977	---	---	---	---	---	---	---	---	3.89
	B	1988-89	---	---	---	---	---	---	---	---	3.61
	C	2007-08	---	---	---	---	---	---	---	---	3.56
	C - B	-	---	---	---	---	---	---	---	---	-0.05

There has been a moderate improvement in the findings of the overall scale over the past thirty years. In a one-to-six scale, negative attitudes, as measured by the *Davis Scale*, have dropped from **3.89** in 1977 to **3.61** in 1988-89 to **3.56** in 2007-08. This indicates a **very slight** increase in tolerance overall. The significant improvement has taken place in Items Nos. 4 and 6.

The absence of improvement in the case of a number of negative responses must be a matter of concern for those who have worked for better personal relations between the Settled and the Travelling Community. There is evidence of a level of desired avoidance which perpetuated ostracisation of Travellers in Irish society. Unlike the findings of the social-distance measures in Part III above which reflected progress in more passive dispositions, the results of Table No. 13.7 records a lack of progress in responses which would seek (actively) greater personal contact. Co-existence, without friendly contact based on good mutual evaluations, is not likely to result in 'true pluralist integration'.

Although Travellers are **a** *distinctive cultural group* within the broad Irish Culture, they need the intercultural solidarity of their neighbours in the Settled Community throughout the country. They are too small a demographic minority, i.e. 0.5% or 22,369 persons, to survive in a meaningful and fulfilling manner without ongoing and supportive personal contact with their fellow-citizens in the Settled Community. The above negative dispositions do not provide such support, and are likely to lead to 'ghettoisation' of the Travellers and an absence of an understanding of their needs. They can become, or continue to be, *Ireland's strangers within their own native society!*

On the ground, some would see that Settled People's privileges taking precedence over Travellers' rights. It seems to be a psychological fact that privileges become perceived rights once we acquire them. This leads to the perpetuation of social injustice in Irish society and other societies as well. Karl Mannheim, the distinguished social analyst, pointed out that social welfare for all the people was not possible without a curtailment of the consumer's choice of the privileged[12]. In other words, the emancipation of the Travellers or any other deprived minority can only come about when the privileged are prepared to make concessions. The exceptionally negative

---

[12] See: Mannheim, Karl, *Man and Society in an Age of Reconstruction*, New York, 1942.

reply to Item No. 2, on Table No. 13.7, i.e. *"reluctance to buy a home next door to a Traveller"* (to which 79.6% agreed) is likely to be influenced by the threat to the value of houses and the privilege of having a home in a community with commercially valuable homes.

The *area of optimism* in the findings of Table No. 13.7 refers to the significant improvement in Items Nos. 4 and 6, i.e. *"willingness to employ a Traveller"* and the substantial increase in support for Travellers *"to serve on a jury"*. These items refer to **contractual** rather than **personal** relationships between the Settled and Travelling Communities. Serious research is necessary at this stage to find out the basic psycho-socio-cultural causes behind the *positive changes* in 'contractual relationships' at a time when there is *negative or no change* in the findings relating to 'personal relationships'.

4.4 Items of Opinion with Significant and Substantial Change in the Positive Direction:

The following extract from Table No. 13.7 highlights the changes in opinions of respondents in relation to 'willingness to employ Travellers' and agreeing that 'Travellers were competent to serve on a jury'. The importance of the progress in the opinions below should be a source of encouragement which could lead to the employment opportunities for Travellers in the near future.

Item		Year	Agreement	Disagreement
(4) *" I would be willing to*	(a)	1977	54.8%	44.4%
employ a Traveller"	(b)	1988-89	56.9%	43.1%
	(c)	2007-08	59.0%	41.1%
		b – a	+2.1%	-1.3%
Changes		c – a	+4.2%	-3.3%
		c – b	+2.1%	-2.0%
(6) *"I consider a Traveller*	(a)	1977	31.4%	67.6%
competent to serve on a jury"	(b)	1988-89	51.7%	48.2%
	(c)	2007-08	73.2%	26.8%
		b – a	+20.3%	-19.4%
Changes		c – a	+41.8%	-40.8%
		c – b	+21.5%	-21.4%

Progress in the findings of Item No. 4 has been slower than that recorded for Item No. 6, largely because of the fact that the two items begin from different bases. Also, negative stereotypes about the honesty of Travellers have been informally circulated because of the highly publicised deviance and delinquency of a minority of Travellers in the media and in public places. When a theft takes place in a district, the tendency to "round up the usual suspects" has a negative effect on all Travellers (who may be as honest as any other group) and on the suspicions of the Settled Community. The danger of the 'self-fulfilling prophecy' influencing the deviant and delinquent behaviour of a minority of Travellers is very real. Also, one has to consider the effects of the 'self-fulfilling prophesy' on the suspected minority.

Despite the reservations listed above, there is a source of optimism in the findings of Item No. 4, which means that **59%** of the respondents are willing to employ Travellers. The **41%** who are not willing to do so presents a serious challenge. This issue should be addressed as a specific project. Access to gainful employment is not a social luxury. It is an essential need to enable Travellers to serve society in jobs that are personally satisfying and socially useful. It also gives members of the Traveller Workforce a source of regular income which removes their need to **beg** or the temptation **to steal** (for a minority of Travellers who may have deviant tendencies). Being almost totally dependent on social welfare and charitable handouts is not likely to give the Traveller a sense of self-worth in a society that expects the able-bodied to earn their living and contribute to society.

The *2006 Census Report* points out that only **25.1%** of the 7,200 Travellers in the workforce had gainful employment, in contrast to the **91.5%** of the 2,068,329 workforce throughout the Republic of Ireland. Hence the importance of support in the population for the Traveller's right to *gainful employment*. When the numbers of Travellers seeking their first job (11.1% of the Traveller workforce) are taken into account, **63.8%** of the workforce are classified as unemployed in the *2006 Census Report* (published in 2007). What an extraordinary waste of human talent in a society that was forced to seek migrant workers from far and wide!

'Competence to serve on a jury' was one of the most optimistic findings indicative of public esteem for Travellers. With almost three quarters (**73.2%**) of the sample (excluding 'don't knows') considering Travellers to be competent to serve on a jury, and slightly more than one quarter (26.8%) not agreeing with that view, the overall result is quite convincing.

When the three National Surveys, i.e. 1977, 1988-89 and 2007-08, are compared, a very significant and substantial change has taken place over the thirty-one years, i.e. from **31.4%** in agreement in **1977** to **73.2%** in **2007-08**. This positive trend was continuous, rising to **51.7%** in favour in **1988-89**. What is probably most important about the fact that nearly three-quarters of the people agreed with Item No. 6 was the manifestation of **trust** in the Traveller to be competent to carry out a most responsible civic duty. Hopefully, in the not-too-distant future, the remaining quarter of respondents will be able to express similar trust in the integrity of the Traveller.

4.5 Live Traveller's Way of Life Decently:
One of the key questions for the Irish people to address is their willingness to facilitate the Travellers to continue living their lives as a separate ethnic group within Irish society. Irish official policy towards Travellers on the issue of recognition of their ethnic identity has been quite ambivalent and, at times, negative.

Table No. 13.8 measures the degree to which respondents agreed to "facilitating Travellers to live their own way of life decently", i.e. not trapped in a culture of poverty and deprivation as may have been forced to do to date. It also monitors the change which has taken place between 1972-73 and 2007-08.

Table No. 13.8:
"Travellers should be Facilitated to Live their own Way of Life Decently"
(1972-73, 1988-89 and 2007-08)

	Agree	Neither Agree nor Disagree	Disagree	Number
1. 2007-08 National Survey	72.3%	16.9%	10.8%	958
2. 1988-89 National Survey	93.0%	5.1%	1.9%	998
Change (1 – 2)	**-20.7%**	**+11.8%**	**+8.9%**	---
3. 2007-08 Dublin Subsample	77.4%	11.9%	8.0%	286
4. 1988-89 Dublin Subsample	90.9%	8.0%	1.1%	277
5. 1972-73 Dublin Subsample	87.5%	2.0%	10.5%	2,280
Change (3 – 4)	**-13.5%**	**+3.9%**	**+6.9%**	---
Change (3 – 5)	**-10.1%**	**+9.9%**	**-2.5%**	---
Change (4 – 5)	**+3.4%**	**+6.0%**	**-9.4%**	---

Note: Changes in percentages in **bold**.

While still very much in favour of the Travellers' right to live their own way of life decently (at **72.3%** in favour), the fact that **10.8%** disagreed with this very reasonable statement reveals an anti-pluralist minority.

The change in the opinions of the National Sample over a period of nineteen years has seen a nominal drop of **20.7%** in agreement with the statement, i.e. from **93.0%** in 1988-89 to **72.3%** in 2007-08.   This is a substantial change and could well reflect in part the hard core noted in the responses to the Social Distance Scale (**18.2%** who would deny Travellers citizenship, i.e. 8.9% visitor only plus 9.3% debar/deport – see Table No. 4.1 above, page 62-4).   The significant rise in the 'neither agree nor disagree' column shows a move towards 'disagreement' by a nominal **11.8%**, thereby reducing the increase in the percentage 'disagreeing' (between 1988-89 and 2007-08) to **8.9%**.   In monitoring social change, the rise in the middle column, e.g. 'neither agree nor disagree' is a useful 'parking place' for the attitudes or opinions in the process of change.

Changes in the opinions of Dubliners towards the Travellers are especially interesting.   Of all the variables the Dublin subsample is the best disposed to Travellers, e.g. social distance, etc.   This is good news for the Travellers because of the substantial percentage living in the Greater Dublin area **(19.4%)** according to the *Census 2006 Report* [See Table No. 13.1(d) above, page 298].

Between 1988-89 and 2007-08, however,   the percentage of the Dublin subsample agreeing with the Travellers' right to live their own 'way of life' decently has **dropped** from the very high 90.9% to nearer the national average at 77.4%, i.e. **-13.5%** or **-10.1%** since the 1972-73 Dublin Survey.   These are significant changes, the causes of which should be researched.

The special importance of the findings in relation to the opinion expressed in the statement *"Travellers should be facilitated to live their own way of life decently"* is its information on the willingness of the public to enable Travellers to retain their cultural differences, i.e. enjoy a status of integrated pluralism.   The opinion expresses more than an agreement in principle.   The verb "facilitated" has implications for society which include resources for institutional duplication when required.   The opinion also favours a **decent** standard of living, i.e. removing the 'culture of poverty' which may have been in large part responsible for the lack of progress among Travellers and attractiveness to the members of the Settled Community.

4.6 Buying a House Next Door to a Traveller:

The following Table (No. 13.9) measures the level of **reluctance** to buy a house next door to a Traveller and, in so doing, highlights the level of difficulty facing Local Authorities and Travellers in the provision of accommodation for members of the minority. The level of **avoidance**[13] indicated in the responses is quite challenging and very disappointing. It is generally accepted that a citizen has the **right** to decent accommodation at a location of his or her choice without hindrance.

Table No. 13.9:
Reluctance to Buy a House Next Door to a Traveller
(Excluding Don't Knows) 1977, 1988-89 and 2007-08

Year	Agree	Disagree
(a) 1977	70.1%	29.3%
(b) 1988-89	74.6%	25.4%
(c) 2007-08	79.4%	20.6%
(b – a)	+4.5%	-3.9%
(c – a)	+9.3%	-8.7%
(c – b)	+4.8%	-4.8%

The above findings are quite negative and reflect the growing deterioration over the thirty years since the first ESRI survey. The trend is quite clear and 'in the negative direction'. More people do not wish to settle near Travellers. More favourable contact between Travellers and Settled People is necessary. Also, it may be necessary to identify and correct any irritating aspects of the Travellers' way of life which may be unwittingly causing the dominant group's posture of avoidance!

The opinion expressed in responses to this item is fairly central to the satisfactory resolution to the challenge of the integration of the Travelling Community. The problem of providing decent living accommodation for Travellers is a top priority, be it in the settled towns and villages as permanent residents, as occupants of serviced sites, or as nomadic (mobile) homes with safe parking and amenities without intrusion on the family. So far, the combined efforts of Travellers, voluntary supporters, local communities, local authorities and central Government have failed to a large extent to respond to the need of decent accommodation for this small native

---

[13] **Avoidance or shunning** of members of a minority is the second-stage expression of social prejudice according to Social Psychologist, Gordon Allport (1954). See Chapter II, pp.25ff.

minority in a large number of cases.   While we lack some of the more extremely appalling deprivations of some developing countries, the conditions in which some parents are forced to rear their families are on the verge of Third-World conditions for a substantial percentage of Travellers. A further cause of misery is the inclemency of the weather and the amount of time young people have to spend in congested wagons, caravans, cars or vans.

The findings of the above Table (No. 13.9) are less than optimistic and reflect the current opinion of the national sample and how reluctant people are to buy a home next door to Travellers.   The social-distance finding was much more positive in that **61.7%** were willing *to accept* a Traveller as a 'next-door neighbour' or closer in contrast to **20.6%** who *would not be reluctant to buy a house next door*.   The social distance response is relatively *passive* when compared with the *initiative* implied in the opinion discussed in Table No. 13.9.   Also, the social distance scale elicits the pre-reflective dispositions of respondents, while the item analysed here is a measure of a post-reflective opinion, which includes perceived social pressure.

The reputation of Travellers as householders and their willingness to be sensitive to the external standards of the neighbourhood needs to be improved.   Some of the public criticisms of Traveller householders is exaggerated,   and   has   become   stereotypical   and,   thereby,   unfair. Nevertheless, there is need to address this problem.   Travellers themselves should do everything possible to allay the reluctance of people from living close to them by their attention to local external norms.

An examination of the responses to the item on reluctance "to buy a house next door to a Traveller by personal variables" is given in the special Report: *Emancipation of the Travelling People*[14].   It provides very interesting reading on the influence of gender, area of birth, place of rearing, education and occupational status.

The above findings on their own are not that optimistic in relation to the **pluralist integration** of Travellers in Irish society.   They tell us more about Irish Society than they do about the Travellers.   The alternative for the

---

[14] Mac Gréil, Micheál, *Emancipation of the Travelling People*, Maynooth, Survey and Research Unit, Department of Sociology, NUIM, 2010, pages 66-72.

Travellers seems to be a **stratified** form of integration, which would be unacceptable in a democratic republic.

Because of the higher level of passive acceptance of Travellers as next-door neighbours in the *Bogardus Scale* (see Table No. 13.2 above) by 61.7% of the total sample, there is a certain leeway for progress within limits. Once **favourable contact** has been established, changes in negative attitudes are likely to happen. The housing of Travellers needs adroit, yet firm, handling by local authorities and community leaders. With favourable contact within the community, negative stereotypes will be demythologised and the true attractiveness of Travelling People will become more manifest to neighbours and visitors alike. Travellers themselves will begin to realise that they have *'a stake in society'* and will respond constructively to the positive norms of the community, which they will transmit to their children. In this way, they will feel an integral part of the neighbourhood.

Part V – Anti-Traveller Scale by Personal Variables

It is possible to discuss two factors in the *Anti-Traveller Scale*, i.e. a **'social factor'** and a **'personal factor'**. As commented on above, the level of negativity in the personal factor (**389** out of 600) is very substantially higher than the social factor (**215** out of 600). This in itself is indicative of the lack of 'favourable contact' between members of the Settled Community and the Travellers. This has been reinforced by the visual impact of the culture of poverty and deprivation (which has nothing to do with the true cultural/ethnic character of this native minority) and the incidents of deviant behaviour of a minority of Travellers not infrequently highlighted in the public media. The following is a breakdown of the items by factor:

Social Factor
Item No. 1 *"Would respect a Traveller";*
Item No. 4 *"Would be willing to employ a Traveller";*
Item No. 6 *"Would consider a Traveller competent to serve on a jury".*
Personal Factor
Item No. 2 *"Would be reluctant to buy a house next door to a Traveller";*
Item No. 3 *"Would be hesitant to seek the company of a Traveller";*
Item No. 5 *"Would exclude a Traveller from close set of friends";*
Item No. 7 *"Would avoid a Traveller in social situations".*

Table No. 13.10 gives a breakdown of the Anti-Traveller Scale and its two factor sub-scales by personal variables, i.e. age, gender, marital status, area of birth, place of rearing (in the Republic of Ireland) and region of residence. The incidences of consensus, i.e. seven sub-tables eliciting a non-significant statistical variation, have been substantial which indicates a strong degree of **stability of prejudice against Travellers** in the population. The levels of variation between sub-variables registering statistical significance is also relatively moderate in most cases!

Table No. 13.10: Anti-Traveller Scale by Personal Variables

Personal Variable	Total Scale	Factor One Social Sub-Scale	Factor Two Personal Sub-Scale	Number
Sample Average	(0 – 600) 315 (52.5%)	(0 – 600) 215 (35.8%)	(0 – 600) 389 (64.8%)	1,011
A. Age	N/S	N/S	P<.006	
1. 18-25 years	---	---	348	169
2. 26-40 years	---	---	392	325
3. 41-55 years	---	---	398	247
4. 56-70 years	---	---	409	178
5. 71 years plus	---	---	386	97
Range of Variation	---	---	*61*	---
B. Gender	N/S	N/S	P<.019	
1. Males	---	---	401	501
2. Females	---	---	377	510
Range of Variation	---	---	*24*	---
C. Marital Status	N/S	N/S	P<.014	
1. Single/Never Married	---	---	384	357
2. Married	---	---	404	472
3. Separated/Divorced	---	---	397	44
4. Permanent Relationship	---	---	341	71
5. Widowed	---	---	372	67
Range of Variation	---	---	*63*	---
D. Area of Birth	P<.001	P<.001	P<.001	
1. City (100,000 plus)	306	193	390	418
2. Large Town (10,000 +)	301	212	369	117
3. Town (1,500 plus)	275	179	348	131
4. Rural/Village	345	257	410	343
Range of Variation	*30*	*64*	*62*	---
E. Place of Rearing in ROI.	P<.001	P<.001	N/S	
1. Dublin (City & County)	286	157	---	267
2. Rest of Leinster	338	255	---	163
3. Munster	339	237	---	229
4. Connaught/Ulster	314	217	---	164
Range of Variation	*53*	*98*	---	---

Table No. 13.10 cont'd. Personal Variable	Total Scale	Factor One Social Sub-Scale	Factor Two Personal Sub-Scale	Number
F. Region of Residence	P<.001	P<.001	P<.001	
1. BMW (Border Midlands West)	299	214	363	270
2. Dublin	291	158	392	286
3. Mid-East & South-East	**325**	**255**	378	220
4. Mid-West & South-West	**349**	**248**	**425**	235
Range of Variation	*58*	*97*	*62*	---

Note: Scores above sample average are **in bold**.

5.1 Age:

This variable registered statistical significance only in the case of one of the sub-tables, i.e. 'Factor Two' (personal sub-scale). The youngest age group (18 to 25 year-olds) and the eldest group (71 years plus) had below-average anti-Traveller scores. The **youth** were substantially more tolerant than they were elsewhere in the text. This is to be welcomed (in the light of other evidence).

The influence of age on the prejudice scores of the five age sub-variables failed to record statistically significant variations in relation to the whole scale and the 'social factor'. This means, in effect, a higher degree of consensus among the age groups. This is disappointing in relation to attitudes which need to change if Travelling People are to be in a position to improve themselves in Irish society.

5.2 Gender:

Again, the 'total scale' and the 'social factor' elicit consensus by gender. This is hardly surprising in the evidence of widespread homogenisation of gender attitudes in many scales in this text.

When a statistically significant variation was recorded, **men** were moderately more negative than **women** towards Travellers, i.e. in the case of the 'personal factor'. This is an interesting finding!

5.3 Marital Status:

This variable failed to elicit a statistically significant variation in the case of the 'total scale' and the 'social factor'! Persons living in permanent relationships were the most tolerant subsample on Table No. 13.10(c). Married respondents were those with the highest (above average) anti-

Traveller score, which was not anticipated.   The tolerance of the *widowed* was in line with that of the older age group.

Since parents are particularly significant in transmitting social prejudice and tolerance towards particular groups in society, the 'married' and 'separated/divorced' are likely to be especially influential in transmitting attitudes towards Travellers.   Attitudes are generally transmitted through primary socialisation to the young, hence the need to find ways of addressing the attitudes of parents towards Travellers.   The influence of such groups as the Irish Countrywomen's Association, *Na Teaghlaigh Gaelacha* and others could be invited to mediate for greater tolerance among married and separated/divorced parents.

5.4 Area of Birth:

This variable elicited statistically significant variations in all three variable scales, i.e. 'whole table', 'factor one' and 'factor two'.   The following extract from Table No. 13.10(d) gives the range of variation for each scale:

Scale	Range of Variation	Between		Mean Score
		Highest Score (Least Tolerant)	Lowest Score (Most Tolerant)	
1. Whole Scale	30	'Rural/Village' (345) and	'Town' (275)	315
2. Social Factor	64	'Rural/Village' (257) and	'Town' (179)	215
3. Personal Factor	62	'Rural/Village' (410) and	'Town' (348)	389

Note: All scores are out of **600**.

The above pattern is quite clear with the 'town' (1,500-9,999) the most tolerant sub-variable for all three scales and 'rural/village' respondents least tolerant.   In the light of the demographic distribution of Travellers in Ireland (see *2006 Census* distribution, Table No. 13.1(d), page 298) these findings ameliorate the situation somewhat because of the fact that three-quarters of Irish Travellers are urbanised and one-quarter in rural village neighbourhoods.

5.5 Place of Rearing and Region of Residence:

The levels of range-variations clearly show the significance of geographic location in relation to attitudes towards Travellers in Irish society (Republic of Ireland).   In the case of 'place of rearing', i.e. where the respondent spent the greater part of the first sixteen years of his or her life, one of the scales failed to register a statistically significant variation, i.e. Factor Two –

personal factor. All three sub-scales elicited significant variation for 'region of residence'.

Scale	Range of Variation	Between			Mean Score
		Highest Score (Least Tolerant)		Lowest Score (Most Tolerant)	
E. Place of Rearing					
1. Whole Scale	53	Munster	(339) and	Dublin (286)	315
2. Social Factor	98	Rest of Leinster	(255) and	Dublin (157)	215
F. Region of Residence					
1. Whole Scale	58	Mid-West & Sth.-W	(349) and	Dublin (291)	315
2. Social Factor	97	Mid-E & Sth.-East	(255) and	Dublin (158)	215
3. Personal Factor	62	Mid-West & Sth.-W	(425) and	BMW (363)	389

Note: Range of score = **0 - 600**

In the majority of scales in this current survey, Munster (place of rearing) and Mid-West & South West (region of residence) were the most tolerant subsamples. This has been practically reversed in Table No. 13.10(e) and (f). The factors causing such a reversal would require further research.

It is quite clear from the extracts that Dublin respondents record the most tolerant results. The performance of the BMW regions in relation to the personal factor is worth noting. Local issues such as publicity given to the deviance of a minority of Travellers and the degree of voluntary pro-Traveller support over the years probably affects the above results. The geographic aspect is, therefore, an important consideration for leaders of the Travelling Community and voluntary and statutory groups working for the pluralist integration of this native minority in the years ahead.

5.6 Conclusion:

The performance of personal variables as given in Table No. 13.10 shows a high degree of consensus among the ordinal variables. This points to the **more stagnant state** of **current prejudice** against Travellers in Ireland, which, in part explains its longevity as an area of bias. This would seem to indicate the need for a more radical and effective review of current policy and treatment of Travellers by the dominant group in Irish society, i.e. the Settled Community. This would create the necessary dialectic in the people's opinions and attitudes.

An area of hope has been the performance of the Dublin subsample in the geographic variables, i.e. 'place of rearing' and 'region of residence'.

Irish Travellers are becoming more urbanised and seem to be resident at the edges of towns and cities. In this context the above 'trends' give some modest relief!

Part VI – Concluding Remarks

The support for the employment of Travellers is positive with the trend in the direction of greater help (see Table No. 4.7 in the special Report: *Emancipation of the Travelling People[15]*). The barriers against the employment of Travellers are lowering at least at the level of disposition or opinion. It is to be hoped that a similar support is in the population for the education and training of Travellers to enable them to take up gainful employment that will be personally satisfying and socially useful. Despite the encouraging results presented above, there is need for further change in attitudes before our Travelling Community operates on a level playing ground. It may be necessary to adopt a policy of **'positive discrimination'** for a period in order to correct the centuries of 'negative discrimination' against Travellers in Ireland.

The analysis of single items (in addition to their inclusion as part of a scale) was considered useful because they expressed relevant points of **view** or **opinions**. This is especially true in the case of *"reluctance to buy a house next door to a Traveller"* and the *"willingness to employ a Traveller"*. Community and Traveller leaders should study the above findings when designing policy, plans and strategies deemed to help the promotion of the **integration** of Travellers on a **pluralist** and **egalitarian** basis.

For the Traveller who studies these findings, it would be understandable for him or her to feel disappointed with some of the negative opinions expressed. The fact that the findings also contain positive opinions (often from the same respondents) should give Travellers courage and enable them to address the causes of the negative attitudes, and take satisfaction from the growing support among a substantial proportion of the current Irish adult population. Working with community leaders in the local communities who are positively disposed towards Travellers, it should be possible to challenge negative stereotypes and remove irritants which may add to such stereotypes.

---

[15] Mac Gréil, Mícheál, *Ibid*, pages 73-74.

The 'dominant group' should also address the issues raised in this chapter. At the end of the day, the 'dominant group', i.e. the Settled Community, is the group with the power and resources to enable the **emancipation** of the Travelling Community from the current 'culture of poverty and deprivation' (as manifest in the relatively short life expectancy) to a position of **integrated pluralism** rather than that of **integrated stratification** or total **assimilation**. Society has much to gain from the unique contribution of the Irish Travelling Community, once it is freed from the culture of poverty and deprivation.

The demographic profile presented (in Part II) from an examination of the *2006 Census Report* provides, in itself, evidence of the failure of Irish society to emancipate its indigenous minority. Hopefully, the evidence presented in this chapter will encourage the Travellers themselves, the State and voluntary groups working with Travellers, to take a radical look at the current situation and devise policies, strategies and working programmes geared at achieving a status of 'integrated pluralism' and the elimination of the culture of poverty and deprivation. Current problems of **deviance** and **alienation** among a minority of young Travellers need to be approached by the Travelling Community, in cooperation with Gardaí, the Courts and the social services. Recognition of the extended family, as the accepted system of domestic and social support and of social control for many Travellers, is a *sine qua non*. This has implications for accommodation, work opportunities, etc. The preservation, recognition and support for the genuine cultural values and norms of the Travelling Community must be enshrined in the laws and customs of the people.

The emancipation of the Travelling People stands to benefit Travellers and Settled alike. Reconciliation of the two groups is very necessary to ensure mutual respect and cooperation in the task of building a more equitable pluralist solution to the current crisis. Travellers deserve their stake in Irish society and **they deserve it now** for the sake of social justice. Hopefully, the findings of this chapter will help to get rid of the current negative apartheid situation. Should Ireland succeed in resolving the current crisis in relation to the Travelling People (in an equitable and pluralist manner), the country could well provide a model for other countries to address their problem in relation to their own indigenous nomadic minorities!

***

CHAPTER XIV
The Irish Family and Attitudes towards Women

Part I – Demographic Aspects of the Family

1.1 Introduction:

This chapter examines selected facts about **the family** in the Republic of Ireland. Some of the findings are based on the *2006 Census of the Population*[1] and on data from the 2007-08 and 1988-89 national surveys. **Attitudes towards women** will be presented from the special *'Feminist Scale'* and other data found in the survey. Sexism against women has been a serious form of social prejudice which rationalised (erroneously) perceived inequalities between men and women over the centuries of **patriarchy** in Western and other societies. Sexist inequalities have been expressed in a number of ways, e.g. devaluing of particular female roles, refusal of access to prestige occupations for women, male dominance in marriage and in the family, exclusion of females from socio-political power and lower status in religious and other institutions.

Sexism against men has not been included specifically in the 2007-08 national survey. This is not to mean that it does not exist in society. It is possible to find evidence of anti-male prejudice in particular social groups, i.e. men in the 'underclass' and seriously deprived groups. The phenomenal disparity between the male-female distribution in the adult prison population (where men constitute the overwhelming majority) raises very serious questions in relation to the norms and expectations of Irish society which may be biased against men! The prevalence of men in Irish and other prisons could also point to inadequacies in the socialisation of males which ill-equips men to cope emotionally with frustration and anger in a non-aggressive manner.

According as **feminism** makes progress beyond the point of equality it will become necessary to monitor its development into incipient **matriarchy**, i.e. the dominance of females in society. Ideally, inclusive gender equality is the goal to be reached. This inclusive goal admits the possibility of role diversity and complementarity rather than uniformity. The latent functions of the women's movement's success have not, so far, been fully assessed. Its impact on the socialisation of youth and its

---

[1] See: *2006 Census Report on the Family*, Dublin Central Statistics Office, 2007.

influence on the role and functions of the **family** and **neighbourhood**, are areas worth serious research.   In a free-market (neo-liberal) society, for instance, the growing numbers of households with double incomes affected the inflation of house prices – to the detriment of the single-income household.   The individualisation of income tax on parental incomes has reinforced the economic pressures on single-income households and could be seen as anti-family.   In fact, it could have penalised parents who stay at home to raise their children!

The family as a social institution has, over the past forty years, lost its pivotal position in Irish society.   It is now, to some extent, in a subordinate role to the economic institution which, under neo-liberal ideology is more in favour of individual earners rather than the collective needs of the family units.   The consequences of this change on the family have not been researched to any great extent.   Questions have already arisen in this text as a result of the relatively intolerant attitudes of the 18 to 25 year-olds which could in part be due to the new child-rearing practices in the absence of parents for prolonged periods. The dominance of the economic institution and the apparent reduction of the priority of the family needs over those of greater economic productivity, etc., could well be part of the reason why a minority of youth are less tolerant when compared with older generations. Many have had less time with their parents in the formative years of childhood.   Crèches, playschools and childminders seem to have replaced the home and parents as primary agents of rearing for much of the time in the early formative years.

Of necessity, the data of the 2007-08 survey on the family is limited. It deals mainly with some key demographic findings with regard to marital status, family size and intergenerational changes.   These findings will be compared with those of the 1988-89 national sample.   Special information from the *2006 Census Report* on the family is reported in 1.2 below.

1.2 Demographic Profile of Fifteen Years and Over by Marital Status:
The following Table (No. 14.1) presents findings from the *2006 Census Report* dealing with "family units".

Table No.14.1: Population Fifteen Years Plus by Marital Status

Marital Status	Number (15 years plus)	Percentage
1. Single	1,015,078	32.6%
2. Married	1,529,036	49.0%
3. Separated/Divorced	159,489	5.1%
4. Permanent Relationship	243,526	7.8%
5. Widowed	171,007	5.5%
Total	3,118,136	100.0%

Source: *2006 Census Report on the Family* (Part IV).

The demographic profile of national sample is given on Table No. 14.2. It should be noted that the sample is based on persons 18 years and over in 2007-08. The range of difference is well within 3% either way.

Table No. 14.2: Marital Status of Total Sample (18 years plus)

Marital Status	Total Sample (18 yrs and over)	Irish Born	Non-Irish Born
1. Single/Never Married	35.3%	35.7%	36.1%
2. Married	46.6%	46.8%	42.9%
3. Separated or Divorced	4.3%	3.5%	9.9%
4. Living in Permanent Relationship	7.0%	6.4%	9.0%
5. Widowed	6.7%	7.6%	2.1%
Number	1,015	857	141

In both Tables, Nos. 14.1 and 14.2, it is interesting to note that the proportions *cohabitating* (and not married) at **7.8%** and **7.0%** respectively, are greater than the percentage *Widowed* at **5.5%** and **6.7%**. This is part of the weakening of the institution of marriage in contemporary Ireland. The proportions *Separated/Divorced* are still relatively low at **5.1%** and **4.3%** respectively. The relative similarity between the distribution of *Irish-Born* and *Non-Irish-Born* is significant[2].

The *2006 Census* figures on Married, Cohabiting Couples (with and without children) and Lone Parents are also very interesting. Table No. 14.3 gives the percentage of *Married* and *Cohabiting Couples* with and without children.

---

[2] Any differences are largely due to different age profiles, i.e. Irish-Born are older. See Table No. 8.8, page 169.

Table No. 14.3:   Married and Cohabiting Couples with and without Children

Couples	Number	%	With Children	Without Children	%
1. Married Couples	742,177	85.9%	69.6%	30.5%	100.0%
2. Cohabiting Couples	121,763	14.1%	36.1%	63.9%	100.0%
Total Couples	863,940	100.0%	---	---	---

Source: *2006 Census of the Population.*

It is interesting to note that **14.1%** of couples in the Republic of Ireland were classified as *cohabiting*. The relatively low fertility of this category, i.e. with **36.1%** *with children*, as compared with *Married Couples* with **69.6%** having children, may point to the comparative youth of 'cohabiting couples' in Ireland. A significant proportion of young cohabiting couples go on to get married.

The average family size of own family and family of origin of the 2007-08 national sample is given on Table No. 14.4:

Table No. 14.4:   Average Family Size of Sample (excluding Single/Never Married)

Sample	Mean No. of Children (incl. Adopted)	Mean No. of Children in Family of Origin	Number
1. Total Sample	1.89	4.85	1,015
2. Aged 44 years and younger	0.84	4.18	565
3. Aged 45 years and older	3.21	5.67	450

The above findings show an intergenerational drop of 2.46 between the generations of respondents 45 years and over. It is assumed that respondents over 45 years of age had completed their own family (with rare exceptions). This raises serious questions concerning fertility and population distribution by age (see Figure No. 13.1, page 301).

The question of *lone parents with children* is a cause of much concern in modern Ireland. The following extract from the *2006 Census* information shows the magnitude of the problem. The very positive standing of *'Unmarried Mothers'* should result in more support for them in Irish society (see pages 266-7 above).

Table No. 14.5: Lone Mothers and Lone Fathers (*2006 Census*)

Category of Parents	Number	%	Age of Children				%
			0-4 yrs	5-9 yrs	10-14 yrs	15 yrs +	
1. Lone Mothers	162,551	85.9%	25.2%	17.9%	12.7%	44.1%	99.9%
2. Lone Fathers	26,689	14.1%	7.4%	9.2%	11.6%	71.8%	100.0%
Total Lone Parents	189,240	100.0%	---	---	---	---	---

Source: *Census 2006 Report*

Of the total number of lone parents in Ireland in 2006, **14.1%** are lone fathers. The range of ages of the children are quite different (between lone-mothers and lone-fathers) with the average age of children substantially lower for women. The proportion of pre-marriage births for lone mothers influences the above numbers. The fact that over seventy per cent of the children of **lone fathers** are fifteen years or older, would indicate that they are survivors of marital break-up and widowhood.

1.3 Greater Female Participation in the Workforce:
The impact of *greater female participation* in the workforce has had a significant and substantial impact on the family and suffers from a degree of *culture-lag*, i.e. the failure of institutional consolidation between the greater participation (in the workforce) and the delay in the provision of institutional support in the changed culture. Areas such as childminding facilities, flexitime to accommodate parents at work, protection of family needs and tax equity, are only in the process of adapting Irish family norms to the new situation.

The period 1997 to 2007 has witnessed a decade of very substantial economic growth in the Republic of Ireland. Because of the successful peace accord in Northern Ireland in 1998, i.e. the *Belfast Agreement*, popularly referred to as the *Good Friday Agreement*, the **political institution** conceded its pivotal position to the **economic institution**. This enabled a concentration of socio-economic and political resources to focus on economic recovery in the Republic and in Northern Ireland, the net result of which was the unprecedented economic and commercial boom, i.e. the so-called *Celtic Tiger*. Unfortunately, the momentum of growth and the expectation of continuous inflow of migrant labour were 'rudely' checked by an almost instant collapse of global and local credit facilities in the summer of 2008.   This resulted in a **recession** which is likely to have serious effects on the family and on male and female employment in the short term, at least.

An important report[3] was published in 2009 by the Equality Authority and the ESRI examines the social, economic and cultural effects of the growth of female participation in the Irish workforce.   It gives one perspective, largely from the female participation point of view, which is worth studying.   It lacks a complete assessment of the impact on children. Space in this text does not allow a proper analysis of the 2009 Report referred to here.

Part II – The Feminist Scale
2.1 Introduction:
Substantial progress in **gender equality** was one of the most significant achievements in Ireland and elsewhere during the 20th century.   The *Enlightenment* at the end of the 18th century *had failed* to address the challenge of gender inequality in many aspects of human life.   It could be argued that it reinforced the sexism of post-Enlightenment Europe.   The patriarchal structures were maintained, despite other radical socio-political changes.   In effect, *patriarchy was democratised* in the new political arrangements after the French Revolution and the weakening of monarchies and feudal structures.

The *suffragist campaign* (derisively named the "suffragettes" by the reactionary English media) was a key movement in the promotion of women's legitimate political rights as adult human beings.   It is difficult to realise that prior to 1918 women were denied their right to vote for members of parliament.   It was fortunate for modern Ireland that women had the right to vote for the first *Dáil Éireann* in 1918.   In some European countries, female suffrage was first permitted after World War II (1939-45).   The current status of women is still evolving in Ireland and throughout most parts of the world.

Human society can be viewed (abstractly) as a series of interrelated **social institutions**[4].   The major institutions include: economy, education,

---

[3] See: Russell, Helen; Frances McGinnity, Tim Callan and Claire Keane (2009), *A Woman's Place: Female Participation in the Irish Labour Market*, Dublin, The Equality Authority and the Economic and Social Research Institute.

[4] See: Parson, Talcott, *The Social System*, Glencoe, Illinois, Free Press, 1951.
    Merton, Robert, *Social Theory and Social Structure*, New York, Collier-Macmillan, 1957.

family, law, polity and religion. Institutions are *sets of norms which enable the people to satisfy their day-to-day needs around the clock.* There is a *normative interdependence* between the social institutions. Changes in one institution will create pressure for related changes in other institutions. For instance, the achievement of *democracy* in the political institutions has had the effect of increasing discursive and democratic procedures in all the other institutions to a greater or lesser degree. There can be very strong resistance to serious social change in institutions and it can take long periods of time to bring about change. This reciprocal inter-institutional pressure is a major factor determining social change in society as a whole.

The changes in the status and role of women in political and economic institutions have had echoes in the family and elsewhere. Resistance to these changes was to be inevitable. But it was impossible to reverse the progress of change. The **feminist movement** became the main driving force for the promotion of the rights of women in all the institutions in the post-World War II Western society. The *'liberation of women'* became a goal for many and received fairly widespread support during the 1960s and 1970s. Progress in the advance of women's rights has not been even across the institutions and the conservative forces have slowed the pace of change from time to time. The unpublished comment by the late Professor John Jackson (Professor of Sociology in Trinity College Dublin) is confirmed in the difficulty experienced by women, i.e. "the conservative dynamism of social institutions"!

2.2 The Feminist Scale:
The 1988-89 survey included the (new) Feminist Scale to measure the current public attitudes towards women's liberation and monitor the level of anti-female sexism in the Republic of Ireland. The following Table (No. 14.6) replicates the 'Feminist Scale' and reports on the changes in attitudes and opinions which had taken place over the period from 1988-89 to 2007-08. As in the case of a number of other scales it is possible to examine the findings in two ways, namely, as individual items of opinion and as a collective expression of pro- or anti-feminist attitudes. Anti-feminism could be termed 'sexism'. The 1988-89 percentages are given in brackets on Table No. 14.6.

Table No. 14.6:
The New Feminist Scale (1988-89 and 2007-08)

	Item	Survey	Agree	Don't Know	Disagree	Mean Negative Score 0-200	Number
1.	A woman's place is in her home.	2007-08	**13.6%**	12.2%	74.2%	39.4	1,015
		1988-89	**(40.5%)**	(13.6%)	(46.0%)	(94.5)	(1,003)
	Change		*-26.9%*	*-1.4%*	*+28.2%*	*-55.1*	
2.	It is bad that there are so few women in Government in this country.	2007-08	63.8%	24.6%	**11.7%**	48.0	1,009
		1988-89	(75.4%)	(12.5%)	**(12.1%)**	(36.7)	(992)
	Change		*-11.6%*	*+12.1%*	*-0.4%*	*+11.3*	
3.	Generally speaking, women think less clearly than men.	2007-08	**10.0%**	16.5%	73.4%	36.7	1,006
		1988-89	**(12.0%)**	(6.3%)	(81.7%)	(30.3)	(990)
	Change		*-2.0%*	*+10.1%*	*-8.3%*	*+6.4*	
4.	Women work better than men in the caring professions.	2007-08	57.4%	21.6%	**21.0%**	63.6	1,013
		1988-89	(70.5%)	(11.3%)	**(18.2%)**	(47.7)	(996)
	Change		*-13.1%*	*+10.3%*	*-2.8%*	*+15.9*	
5.	People should be employed and promoted strictly on the basis of ability regardless of sex or gender.	2007-08	82.7%	8.6%	**8.8%**	26.2	1,015
		1988-89	(96.3%)	(2.7%)	**(1.0%)**	(4.7)	(996)
	Change		*-13.6%*	*+5.9%*	*+7.8%*	*+21.5*	
6.	The feminist movement is very necessary in Ireland.	2007-08	42.1%	38.5%	**19.4%**	77.3	1,011
		1988-89	(64.1%)	(21.2%)	**(14.6%)**	(50.5)	(998)
	Change		*-23.0%*	*+17.3%*	*+4.8%*	*+26.8*	
7.	Some equality in marriage is a good thing but by and large the husband ought to have the main say in family matters.	2007-08	**19.5%**	14.8%	65.7%	53.8	1,014
		1988-89	**(29.6%)**	(9.6%)	(60.8%)	(68.9)	(1,002)
	Change		*-10.1%*	*+5.2%*	*+4.9%*	*-15.1*	
8.	Education and vocational training are less important for girls than for boys.	2007-08	**6.2%**	10.7%	83.1%	23.1	1,012
		1988-89	**(9.9%)**	(3.7%)	(86.4%)	(23.6)	(997)
	Change		*-3.7%*	*+7.0%*	*-3.3%*	*-0.5*	
9.	A woman should be as free as a man to propose marriage.	2007-08	76.9%	12.7%	**10.4%**	33.5	1,011
		1988-89	(76.3%)	(10.1%)	**(13.6%)**	(37.3)	(1,000)
	Change		*+0.6%*	*+2.6%*	*-3.2%*	*-3.8*	
10.	Husbands and wives should have equal say in how to spend family money, irrespective of who earns it.	2007-08	86.2%	9.4%	**4.4%**	18.2	1,015
		1988-89	(96.3%)	(1.7%)	**(2.0%)**	(5.7)	(1,003)
	Change		*-10.1%*	*+7.7%*	*+2.4%*	*+12.5*	
11.	Women should be allowed to become Priests in the Roman Catholic Church.	2007-08	64.4%	20.7%	**14.9%**	50.5	1,015
		1988-89	(34.8%)	(14.6%)	**(51.4%)**	(117.4)	(1,002)
	Change		*+29.6%*	*+6.1%*	*-36.5%*	*-66.9*	
12.	The emigration of young women is less serious for the country than that of young men.	2007-08	**10.5%**	24.8%	64.7%	45.8	1,013
		1988-89	**(14.4%)**	(9.4%)	(76.3%)	(38.1)	(1,003)
	Change		*-3.9%*	*+15.4%*	*-11.6%*	*+7.7*	
	Scale Anti-Feminist Score	2007-08				43.0	1,015
	Scale Anti-Feminist Score	1988-89	---	---	---	(46.3)	(1,005)
	Change					*-3.3*	

Notes: Percentages indicating negative (anti-feminist) replies are **in bold**.
Changes are in *italics*. *Cronbach Alpha Score* = 0.702

344

While there are some variations in the above scores between the 1988-89 and the 2007-08 findings, there is a comparatively similar pattern of replies. The overall anti-feminist score reduced by **3.3** (i.e. a drop of 7.1%) over the nineteen years, i.e. from **46.3** in 1988-89 to **43.0** in 2007-08. This change was less than what was anticipated. When examined by items, this reduction may be over-influenced by the two items with over 50% change, i.e. Items Nos. 11 and 1.

	Item	2007-08 (0-200)	1988-89 (0-200)	Change in Anti-Feminist Score (0-200)
1.	No.11 "Ordination of Women"	50.5	117.4	-66.9 **(-57.0%)**
2.	No.1 "Women's Place is in the Home"	39.4	94.5	-55.1 **(-52.36%)**

Almost two-thirds of the respondents are in favour of the ordination of women in the Roman Catholic Church, while fewer than 15% are opposed to it. These figures speak for themselves!

In all, only **four** of the twelve items recorded a significant **decrease** in anti-feminist score, i.e. Nos. 1, 7, 9 and 11. Of the remaining **eight** items, seven registered a significant **increase** in anti-feminist attitudes or opinions. Item No. 8 had not produced a significant change. The four items to elicit an increase of over 10 in the 0-200 continuum were:

			2007-08 (0-200)	1988-89 (0-200)	Change in Anti-Feminist Score (0-200)
1.	No.6	"Necessity for Feminist Movement"	77.3	50.5	+26.8 **(+53.1%)**
2.	No.5	"Employment on Ability"	26.2	4.7	+21.5 **(+457.4%)**
3.	No.4	"Women Better in Caring Professions"	63.6	47.7	+15.9 **(+32.9%)**
4.	No.10	"Equal Say in Spending Money"	18.2	5.7	+12.5 **(+219.3%)**

The remaining items recording increases in anti-feminist scores were relatively small, i.e. Nos. 2, 3 and 12.

A more detailed analysis of the various items will be carried out in Table No. 14.7 which examines each item as an expression of opinion by personal variables. In Table No. 14.8 the scale scores and those of the sub-scales discerned by the process of factor analysis will be presented. Again it should be underlined that the modest reduction in anti-feminist scores was less than anticipated and shows a slowing down of pro-feminist dispositions. At the same time, the relatively low level of anti-feminist scores is to be welcomed.   Anti-feminism has stabilised at a relatively **low level** which should be a source of optimism.   To improve the situation further will require a reappraisal of the ways and means of promoting gender equality.

Part III – The Feminist Scale by Personal Variables

The measures selected for the next Table, i.e. Table No. 14.7, are the *mean anti-feminist scores* for each item.   In the 1988-89 study the anti-feminist percentage response, namely, the percentage agreeing with 'anti-feminist items' and disagreeing with 'pro-feminist items' was chosen as the measure for each sub-variable[5].   It was not possible to use the 1988-89 measure because of the overall increase in the 'don't know' responses, which are an integral part of the mean anti-feminist score.

On Table No. 14.7 there are **108** sub-tables.   Some thirty-five recorded a non-significant (N/S) result, i.e. in each of the **35** sub-tables the *chi-square* score was more than **0.050** which means that variation could be due to chance in less than one-in-twenty cases.   This means that there is a high degree of **consensus** in each of the N/S sub-tables.   Significant statistical variations were achieved in **73** or **67.7%** of the sub-tables.   Item No.7 registered a significant statistical variation in each of the nine variables.   This item also had high score-variations.

Score variations indicate the degree to which the topic expressed in the item is a **live issue** among the respondents.   This appears to be very much the case of opinions in each of the nine personal variables, i.e. on whether *"the husband should have the main say in family matters"*.   Score variations also show the variables with wide diversity of opinions between the subsamples.

The findings of Table No. 14.7 (below) deserve careful study by the readers and, especially, by those with a special (academic, pastoral or political) interest in women's liberation and equality.   From the findings it should be possible to get a better explanation of the levels of **sexism** in relation to females and to predict likely changes in the near future.

---

[5] See: Mac Gréil, Micheál, *Prejudice in Ireland Revisited*, Maynooth, St Patrick's College, 1996, pages 300-1.

3.1 Age:

There were significant variations in the case of **eight** of the twelve items on the 'feminist scale'. There was consensus across the age groups for Items Nos. 5, 6 and 8. In regard to **four** of the other items (2, 3, 10 and 12) the youngest age group (18 to 25 years) had above-average anti-feminist scores.

Items Nos. 1, 7 and 10 performed as expected, i.e. with a positive correlation between age and anti-feminist scores. The other five items (Nos. 2, 4, 9, 10 and 12) were not as predicted. Once again, **age** seems to have failed to confirm the anticipation or hypothesis of the researcher.

The range of score variations by age was higher than expected. In the case of **five** of the eight items, the score variation was **30.0 plus** between subsamples' scores.

	Item	Score Variation	Between Most Anti-Feminist	Least Anti-Feminist	Mean Score (0-200)
1.	"Women's Place is in the Home"	58.3	71 years+ **(84.3)** and	18-25 years **(26.0)**	39.4
2.	"Women Best Carers"	46.3	18-25 years **(83.8)** and	71 years+ **(37.5)**	63.6
3.	"Women's Ordination"	40.5	71 years+ **(79.3)** and	41-55 years **(38.8)**	33.5
4.	"Husbands Should Have Main Say"	38.6	71 years plus **(83.6)** and	26-40 years **(45.0)**	53.8
5.	"Female Emigration Less Important"	31.1	18 to 25 years **(64.0)** and	41-55 years **(32.9)**	45.8

The above figures point to a **dynamic range of difference** between the age subsamples. This is indicative that the issues represented by these items are likely to experience ongoing changes in their scores!

3.2 Gender:

In the case of each item registering a statistically significant variation, **males** had higher anti-feminist scores than **females.** For four items the score variations were more than **23.0.**

	Item	Score Variation	Between Most Anti-Feminist	Least Anti-Feminist	Mean Score (0-200)
1	"Feminist Movement Necessary"	34.2	Males **(94.7)** and	Females **(60.5)**	77.3
2	"Husbands Have Main Say"	33.1	Males **(70.5)** and	Females **(37.4)**	53.8
3	"Women in Government"	31.4	Males **(63.8)** and	Females **(32.4)**	48.0
4	"Women Think Less Clearly"	23.4	Males **(48.4)** and	Females **(25.0)**	36.7

Pluralism and Diversity in Ireland

Table No. 14.7: Feminist Scale by Personal Variables (by Mean Anti-Feminist Scores – 0 to 200)

Personal Variable	1. Women's Place in Home	2. Women in Govt.	3. Women think less Clearly	4. Women best Carers	5. Women should be Employed on Ability	6. Feminist Movement Necessary	7. Husbands have Main Say	8. Women's Education Less Important	9. Women to Propose Marriage	10. Husbands & Wives Equal in spending family Income	11. Women's Ordination in R.C. Church	12. Female Emigration less Serious	No.
Total Sample (A-F Scores)	39.4	48.0	36.7	63.6	26.2	77.3	53.8	23.1	33.5	18.2	50.5	45.8	1,015
A. Age	P<.001	P<.001	P<.050	P<.001	N/S	N/S	P<.001	N/S	P<.020	P<.004	P<.001	P<.001	
1. 18-25 years	26.0	55.5	46.3	83.8	---	---	48.5	---	30.9	26.7	47.9	64.0	168
2. 26-40 years	31.2	50.8	32.7	63.3	---	---	45.0	---	36.1	21.4	47.1	41.4	325
3. 41-55 years	30.0	44.9	33.9	65.1	---	---	50.5	---	21.1	12.5	38.8	32.9	245
4. 56-70 years	57.1	35.7	31.3	56.9	---	---	63.2	---	43.0	13.0	59.4	50.5	178
5. 71 years plus	84.3	55.3	49.9	37.5	---	---	83.6	---	43.7	16.7	79.3	51.5	96
Score Variation	*58.3*	*19.8*	*18.6*	*46.3*	---	---	*38.6*	---	*22.6*	*14.2*	*40.5*	*31.1*	*1,012*
B. Gender	N/S	P<.001	P<.001	N/S	P<.002	P<.001	P<.001	P<.002	N/S	P<.001	N/S	N/S	
1. Males	---	63.8	48.4	---	32.7	94.7	70.5	29.4	---	26.5	---	---	499
2. Females	---	32.4	25.0	---	19.6	60.5	37.4	17.0	---	10.1	---	---	516
Score Variation	---	*31.4*	*23.4*	---	*13.1*	*34.2*	*33.1*	*12.4*	---	*16.4*	---	---	*1,015*
C. Marital Status	P<.001	N/S	N/S	P<.037	N/S	N/S	P<.001	N/S	N/S	P<.003	P<.001	N/S	
1. Single/Never Married	32.5	---	---	74.7	---	---	52.8	---	---	19.4	43.5	---	356
2. Married	41.7	---	---	57.6	---	---	51.8	---	---	14.6	47.7	---	468
3. Separated/Divorced	37.9	---	---	70.4	---	---	46.2	---	---	41.0	70.4	---	44
4. Permanent Relation'p	22.9	---	---	59.3	---	---	38.0	---	---	14.4	56.6	---	72
5. Widowed	78.1	---	---	45.6	---	---	93.8	---	---	25.9	87.4	---	69
Score Variation	*56.7*	---	---	*29.1*	---	---	*55.8*	---	---	*26.6*	*43.9*	---	*1,009*
D. Area of Birth	N/S	P<.001	N/S	P<.006	P<.001	P<.030	P<.001	N/S	N/S	P<.050	P<.002	N/S	
1. City (100,000+)	---	54.8	---	73.6	36.3	80.1	48.8	---	---	23.3	48.0	---	419
2. Large Town (10,000+)	---	52.2	---	52.9	19.0	91.7	37.6	---	---	12.5	33.2	---	119
3. Town (1,500+)	---	29.3	---	65.8	8.1	62.4	47.9	---	---	16.2	49.6	---	132
4. Rural/Village	---	44.4	---	53.6	23.2	74.6	67.1	---	---	14.0	59.7	---	345
Score Variation	---	*22.9*	---	*20.7*	*28.2*	*17.7*	*29.5*	---	---	*10.8*	*26.5*	---	*1,015*
E. Place of Rearing ROI	N/S	N/S	N/S	P<.001	P<.001	N/S	N/S	P<.031	P<.001	P<.050	P<.040	N/S	
1. Dublin (City & Co.)	---	---	---	74.8	38.0	---	---	26.5	17.9	17.6	38.0	---	243
2. Rest of Leinster	---	---	---	66.1	12.6	---	---	7.8	23.4	7.0	53.9	---	157
3. Munster	---	---	---	44.2	21.1	---	---	21.0	42.7	14.6	49.9	---	219
4. Connaught/Ulster	---	---	---	63.4	27.5	---	---	19.0	41.3	19.5	57.2	---	154
Score Variation	---	---	---	*30.6*	*25.4*	---	---	*18.7*	*24.8*	*12.5*	*19.2*	---	*773*

Table No.14.7 (Cont'd.)

Personal Variable	1. Women's Place in Home	2. Women in Govt.	3. Women think less Clearly	4. Women best Carers	5. Women should be Employed on Ability	6. Feminist Movement Necessary	7. Husband have Main Say	8. Women's Education Less Important	9. Women to Propose Marriage	10. Husbands & Wives Equal in spending family Income	11. Women's Ordination in R.C. Church	12. Female Emigration less Serious	No.
F. Region of Residence	N/S	N/S	P<.050	P<.002	P<.001	N/S	N/S	P<.001	P<.001	N/S	N/S	P<.001	
1. B.M.W.	---	---	30.8	**67.9**	24.8	---	---	18.2	33.1	---	---	42.1	269
2. Dublin	---	---	**44.6**	63.9	**39.5**	---	---	**30.8**	21.4	---	---	**52.5**	284
3. Mid-East & South-E.	---	---	**39.0**	**74.0**	23.5	---	---	**31.3**	**34.7**	---	---	**53.9**	218
4. Mid-West & Sth-West	---	---	31.5	48.2	13.9	---	---	12.2	**47.4**	---	---	34.4	234
Score Variation			*13.8*	*25.8*	*25.6*			*19.1*	*26.0*			*19.5*	*1,005*
G. Education	P<.001	N/S	P<.001	P<.001	P<.001	N/S	P<.001	P<.001	N/S	P<.001	N/S	P<.001	
1. Primary or Less	**82.3**	---	**54.5**	50.0	**31.3**	---	**80.0**	**32.4**	---	**25.9**	---	**55.8**	117
2. Incomplete Sec-Level	**63.3**	---	**41.8**	59.6	**36.1**	---	**71.5**	**38.8**	---	**24.7**	---	**57.7**	262
3. Complete Sec.-Level	28.9	---	32.5	58.1	26.1	---	**57.8**	22.2	---	**18.2**	---	**47.3**	255
4. Third-Level	16.9	---	30.3	**74.1**	17.7	---	30.7	10.2	---	11.3	---	33.5	381
Score Variation	*65.4*		*24.2*	*24.1*	*18.4*		*49.3*	*28.6*		*14.6*		*23.2*	*1,015*
H. Occupational Status	P<.001	P<.001	P<.045	P<.001	P<.001	N/S	P<.001	P<.001	N/S	P<.001	N/S	P<.002	
1. Unskilled/Semi-Skill.	**49.6**	**59.9**	**43.0**	**75.0**	**34.8**	---	**74.8**	**37.5**	---	**25.8**	---	**57.4**	207
2. Skilled/R. Non-Man.	32.0	**54.6**	36.4	55.8	**28.5**	---	49.7	20.5	---	**21.7**	---	45.6	328
3. Inspect./Supervisory	35.6	36.3	22.7	**82.9**	**27.4**	---	34.6	19.6	---	6.6	---	33.5	133
4. Professional/Exec.	21.6	27.9	35.5	52.9	7.7	---	42.9	10.1	---	10.1	---	38.1	191
Score Variation	*28.0*	*32.0*	*20.3*	*30.0*	*27.1*		*40.2*	*27.4*		*19.2*		*23.9*	*859*
I. Social Class Position	P<.001	P<.002	P<.001	P<.001	P<.001	P<.001	P<.001	P<.001	N/S	P<.002	P<.001	P<.001	
1. Class I "Upper Class"	36.9	26.6	**58.0**	**97.5**	7.8	**85.9**	54.0	17.3	---	7.0	46.4	**70.7**	38
2. Class II "Upr-Middle Cls"	13.4	27.4	28.8	45.3	5.0	66.6	32.3	5.3	---	9.2	34.7	31.5	140
3. Class III "Mid-Middle Cl"	24.0	47.6	26.2	68.3	23.5	**88.1**	38.7	15.2	---	14.6	**55.8**	27.6	226
4. Class IV "Working Class"	**40.0**	**53.5**	38.8	64.2	**32.9**	72.3	**57.7**	**28.0**	---	**20.7**	46.4	**56.6**	361
5. Class V "Lower Class"	**73.8**	**60.3**	**41.8**	**69.0**	**39.2**	73.5	**95.2**	**47.0**	---	**33.4**	**63.1**	**53.2**	83
Score Variation	*60.4*	*33.7*	*31.8*	*52.2*	*34.2*	*21.5*	*62.9*	*41.7*		*26.4*	*28.4*	*43.1*	*848*

*Note: Scores above the sample average are in **bold**. (Variations are in italics.)*

349

The relatively wide score variations in the above four items (page 347) show the residue of patriarchal aspirations in a minority of the male population. The four items express opinions in relation to female power and the threat to *male power*. The optimist might well interpret the finding as quite favourable in that the relatively small minority of the male scores represent in absolute terms. The fact that there was consensus between males and females in the case of **five** of the **twelve** items showing non-significant (N/S) results may also be interpreted as positive, i.e. mutual recognition of women's equality in society.

The fourth item in the above extract from Table No. 14.7(b) is quite a severe expression of **fundamentalist sexism**, i.e. *"Women think less clearly than men"*. An anti-feminist score of **48.4** (0-200) for males is serious and pre-scientific. There is no foundation in science for such an erroneous opinion!

3.3 Marital Status:
This variable failed to elicit statistically significant variations between the subsamples in seven of the items tested, i.e. *"Women in Government"*, *"Women thinking less clearly"*, *"Women employed on ability"*, *"Feminist Movement necessary"*, *"Women's education less important"*, *"Women to propose marriage"* and *"Female emigration less serious"*. These items express a diverse range of opinions. Among the five items achieving significant variations between the subsamples, four registered a score variation of over **29.0**, i.e.

	Item	Score Variation	Between Most Anti-Feminist			Least Anti-Feminist		Mean Score (0-200)
1.	"Husbands Have Main Say"	55.8	Widowed	**(93.8)**	and	Perm.Rel'p	**(38.0)**	53.8
2.	"Woman's Place is in the Home"	55.2	Widowed	**(78.1)**	and	Perm.Rel'p	**(22.9)**	39.4
3.	"Women's Ordination"	43.9	Widowed	**(87.4)**	and	Single	**(43.5)**	50.5
4.	"Women Best Carers"	29.1	Single	**(74.7)**	and	Widowed	**(45.6)**	63.8

Some would see the subsamples with highest score as the most 'conservative' groups! The fact that the score variations are relatively substantial indicates that the opinions are determined (to some extent) by the marital status of the respondent and are prone to change one way or the other! The opinions of *"Women being the best carers"* elicited a very dynamic response and failed to factor with other items in the **Feminist**

Scale. These are divided views of this item, i.e. for some agreeing with it is seen as **a tolerant** thing to do and for **others** the item expressed a sexist opinion. In the full scale it was coded as a positive pro-woman item! The domestic role of women and men may have been biased by the pressures of the **economic institution** to increase the status of women working outside the home at the expense of mothers/women working at home! Because of the confusion about the item, it was decided to drop it from the scale, when examining the collective scores.

3.4 Area of Birth:

This variable seeks to find out the influence of the urban-rural background of respondents on the opinions. Five items, i.e. *"Women's place is in the home"*, *"Women think less clearly"*, *"Women's education is less important"*, *"Women to propose marriage"*, and *"Female emigration less serious"*, produced a consensus result. This, in itself is significant.

The score variations for the seven items showing statistically significant variations between the subsamples were less than in the case of 'Age', 'Gender' and 'Marital Status'. At the same time three items recorded a **26.0 plus** 'score variation' (although none exceeded **30.0**).

	Item	Score Variation	Between Most Anti-Feminist		Least Anti-Feminist	Mean Score (0-200)
1	"Husbands Have Main Say"	29.5	Rural/Village (**67.1**)	and	Large Town (**37.6**)	53.8
2	"Women Employed on Ability"	28.2	City (**36.3**)	and	Town (**8.1**)	26.2
3	"Women's Ordination"	26.5	Rural/Village (**59.7**)	and	Large Town (**33.2**)	50.5

Numbers 1 and 3 on the above extract from Table No. 14.7(d) are according to expectations in the sense that respondents from 'Large Town' backgrounds are more tolerant than those for Rural/Urban 'Area of Birth'. The opinions of city-born being more negative than (small) town-born was not expected.

3.5 Place of Rearing and Region of Residents:

'Place of Rearing' refers to where (within the Republic of Ireland) respondents spent the most part of the first sixteen years of their life. 'Region of Residence' indicates where they now live. Because of the frequency of internal migration within the State, a significant minority would have moved. Both are 'nominal variables' because of the absence of a 'more than/less than' relationship between the sub-variables, as is the case of 'Age', 'Education', etc. The latter are known as 'ordinal variables'.

'Place of Rearing' returned consensus (or N/S) in respect of five items, *"Women in Government", "Women think less clearly", "Feminist Movement necessary", "Husbands and Wives equal in spending family income"* and *"Women's Ordination"*. Of the remaining seven items that registered statistically significant variations between subsamples, three had score variations over **24.0**, i.e.:

Item	Score Variation	Between Most Anti-Feminist	Least Anti-Feminist	Mean Score (0-200)
1. "Women Best Carers"	30.6	Dublin City/Co. (**74.8**) and	Munster (**44.2**)	63.6
2. "Women Employed on Ability"	25.4	Dublin City/Co. (**38.0**) and	Rest of Leinster (**12.6**)	26.2
3. "Women to Propose Marriage"	24.8	Munster (**42.7**) and	Dublin City/Co. (**17.9**)	33.5

'Dublin City and County' respondents were most 'conservative' in the case of Nos.1 and 2 on the above extract from Table No. 14.7(e) and respondents from 'Munster' and 'Rest of Leinster' were the most tolerant (respectively). In response to *"Women's equal right to propose Marriage"*, 'Dublin City and County' respondents were most tolerant while 'Munster' respondents were most conservative. Otherwise the results were quite mixed, as expected.

'Region of Residence' recorded statistically significant variations in **six** of the twelve items. The six items providing consensus were: *"Women in Government", "Feminist Movement necessary", "Women's place is in the home", "Husbands and Wives have equal say", "Husbands and Wives have equal pay"* and *"Women's ordination"*. Five items recorded a score variation of over **19.0**, i.e.:

Item	Score Variation	Between Most Anti-Feminist	Least Anti-Feminist	Mean Score (0-200)
1. "Women Propose Marriage"	26.0	Mid-W. & Sth.W. (**47.4**) and	Dublin (**21.4**)	33.5
2. "Women Best Carers"	25.8	Mid-East & Sth.E. (**74.0**) and	Mid-W. & Sth.W. (**48.2**)	63.6
3. "Women Employed on Ability"	25.6	Dublin (**39.5**) and	Mid-W. & Sth.W. (**13.9**)	26.2
4. "Female Emigration Less Important"	19.5	Mid-E. & Sth.E. (**53.9**) and	Mid-W. & Sth.W. (**34.4**)	45.8
5. "Women's Education Less Important"	19.1	Mid-E. & Sth.E. (**31.3**) and	Mid-W. & Sth.W. (**12.2**)	23.1

The tolerant ethos of the respondents living in the 'Mid-West & South-West' Regions (covering the province of Munster) has, once again, been borne out in the above extract from Table No. 14.7(f). Respondents living in 'Dublin' and in the 'Mid-East & South-East' Regions appear to be less tolerant on the items listed above. It was expected that Dublin residents would have been more tolerant!

3.6 Education:

Educational achievement is an important ordinal variable in measuring social attitudes towards minorities. The *Feminist Scale* by 'Education' elicited statistically significant variations in eight of the twelve items. The four items which reported consensus between the education sub-samples were: *"Women in Government", "Feminist Movement necessary", "Women to propose marriage"* and *"Women's ordination"*.

There was a relatively high *score variation* in all the eight items recording significance. This indicates the link between educational standard and *feminist tolerance*. The responses were for the most part as anticipated, i.e. a positive correlation between educational achievement and feminist tolerance. Six of the eight items registered a score variation higher than **23.0**, i.e.:

Item	Score Variation	Between Most Anti-Feminist		Least Anti-Feminist	Mean Score (0-200)
1. "Women's Place is in the Home"	65.4	Primary or Less	(**82.3**) and	Third Level (**16.9**)	39.4
2. "Husband has Main Say"	49.3	Primary or Less	(**80.0**) and	Third Level (**30.7**)	53.8
3. "Women's Education Less Important"	28.6	Incomplete Sec.Lev.(**38.8**) and		Third Level (**10.2**)	23.1
4. "Women Think Less Clearly"	24.2	Primary or Less	(**54.5**) and	Third Level (**30.3**)	36.7
5. "Women are Best Carers"	24.1	Third Level	(**74.1**) and	Prim. or Less (**50.0**)	63.6
6. "Female Emigration Less Serious"	23.2	Incomplete Sec.Lev.(**57.7**) and		Third Level (**33.5**)	45.8

The above extract from Table No. 14.7(g) is quite revealing. The range of variation of the responses by education sub-variables is substantial in half of the items. This points to the absence of consensus in a number of key issues in relation to the goal of male-female equality.

With the exception of *"Women are best carers"*, the highest level of educational achievement, i.e. 'Third Level', was the most tolerant sub-sample. 'Primary or Less' and 'Incomplete Second Level' shared the least tolerant scores. The positive relation between education and greater tolerance towards women was anticipated.

The pattern of responses to the item: *"Women work better than men in the caring professions"* by education was the opposite to the response to the other five items. What it tells is that a higher percentage of those with Third-level education than respondents in the other education sub-samples **disagree** with this opinion which is intended to be complimentary to women. In other words, are we seeing here an implicit devaluation of the caring professions as recommended careers for women by a minority of third-level respondents?

3.7 Occupational Status:

When tested by 'Occupational Status' only three of the twelve items, i.e. *"Feminist movement necessary"*, *"Women to propose marriage"* and *"Women's Ordination"* had consensus between the subsamples. Since occupational and career status is one of the criteria by which feminist commentators assess the success of their movement, the responses of the four subsamples are of particular interest and could have some bearing on the roles and status of women in the labour force. The replies on Table No. 14.7(h) show that there is a positive correlation between occupational status and pro-feminist scores.

The range of difference between the scores of the subsamples is quite high. Only two of the nine items registering a statistically significant variation had score variations of less than **20.0**, i.e. *"Husbands and wives equal in spending income"* (**19.2**) and *"Women's ordination"* (**15.3**). The following extract from Table No. 14.7(h) gives a breakdown of the other eight items:

Item	Score Variation	Between		Mean Score (0-200)
		Most Anti-Feminist	Least Anti-Feminist	
1. "Husbands have Main Say"	40.2	Unskilled/Semi-Sk. (**74.8**) and	Inspect./Super. (**34.6**)	53.8
2. "Women in Government"	32.0	Unskilled/Semi-Sk. (**59.9**) and	Profess./Exec. (**27.9**)	48.0
3. "Women Best Carers"	30.0	Inspect./Supervis. (**82.9**) and	Profess./Exec. (**52.9**)	63.6
4. "Women's Place is in the Home"	28.0	Unskilled/Semi-Sk. (**49.6**) and	Profess./Exec. (**21.6**)	39.4
5. "Women's Education Less Important"	27.4	Unskilled/Semi-Sk. (**37.5**) and	Profess./Exec. (**10.1**)	23.1
6. "Women should be Employed on Ability"	27.1	Unskilled/Semi-Sk. (**34.8**) and	Profess./Exec. (**7.7**)	26.2
7. "Female Emigration Less Serious"	23.9	Unskilled/Semi-Sk. (**57.4**) and	Inspect./Super. (**33.5**)	45.8
8. "Women Think Less Clearly"	20.3	Unskilled/Semi-Sk. (**43.0**) and	Inspect./Super. (**22.7**)	36.7

A close examination of the findings summarised in the above extract tells much about the current level of attitudes towards women in the workplace by respondents from the different grades. The 'Unskilled/Semi-Skilled' subsample returned the least tolerant scores in seven (of the eight) items while the 'Professional/Executive' was the most tolerant in five of the eight items. The 'Inspectional/Supervisory' subsample was least tolerant in the case of *"Women as best carers"* while 'Professional/Executive' was the most tolerant. This anomaly reflects the unexpected response to the same item by education.

3.8 Social Class Position:

Only **one** out of the twelve items failed to register a statistically significant variation, i.e. *"Women to propose marriage"*, by 'Social Class Position'. This variable measures social status and the five classes are arrived at by combining respondents' educational achievement and their occupational status (see page 189, footnote 7). It is interesting that it achieved consensus in the case of only one of the opinion items, i.e. the right of women to propose marriage.

In each of the **eleven** items with significant variations, there has been a substantial range of variation between the subsamples. In the following extract from Table No. 14.7(i) a breakdown is given, i.e.:

Item	Score Variation	Between Most Anti-Feminist	Least Anti-Feminist	Mean Score (0-200)
"Husbands have Main Say"	62.9	"Lower Class" (**95.2**) and	"Upr.Mid. Class" (**32.3**)	53.8
"Women's Place is in the Home"	60.4	"Lower Class" (**73.8**) and	"Upr.Mid. Class" (**13.4**)	39.4
"Women Best Carers"	52.2	"Upper Class" (**97.5**) and	"Upr.Mid. Class" (**45.3**)	63.6
"Female Emigration Less Serious"	43.1	"Upper Class" (**70.7**) and	"Mid.Mid. Class" (**27.6**)	45.8
"Women's Education Less Important"	41.7	"Lower Class" (**47.0**) and	"Upr. Mid. Class" (**5.3**)	23.1
"Women Employed on Ability"	34.2	"Lower Class" (**39.2**) and	"Upr.Mid. Class" (**5.0**)	26.2
"Women in Government"	33.7	"Lower Class" (**60..3**) and	"Upr.Mid. Class" (**27.4**)	48.0
"Women Think Less Clearly"	31.8	"Upper Class" (**58.0**) and	"Mid.Mid. Class" (**26.2**)	36.7
"Women's Ordination"	28.4	"Lower Class" (**63.1**) and	"Upr.Mid. Class" (**34.7**)	50.5
"Husbands/ Wives Equal Say Spending"	26.4	"Lower Class" (**33.4**) and	"Upper Class" (**7.0**)	18.2
"Feminist Movement Necessary"	21.5	"Mid.-Mid. Cl." (**88.1**) and	"Upr.Mid.Class" (**66.6**)	77.3

The above extract from Table No. 14.7(i) points to class/status in relation to pro- and anti-feminist attitudes. The "Upper-Middle Class" seems to be the most favourably disposed to the feminist ideal while the "Lower Class" is least pro-feminist. These findings (i.e. score variations) must raise questions about the **class inclusiveness** of the **feminist movement** (*de facto* on the ground). Has it left behind the "Lower Class", the unskilled workers, the poorly educated and focused more on the white-collar, middle-class categories? In Table No. 14.7 each item is being examined also as an **opinion** (as well as an indicator of an attitude).

Without an "inclusive class dimension", women's liberation would be in danger of perpetuating a socially stratified society with a middle-class gender equality leading to an alienated (i.e. powerless) lower or underclass. Such a society would enjoy equality of privilege rather than equality of rights! The findings of the social class position variable raise serious questions about the impact of the feminist movement across the whole of Irish society. These findings will be confirmed when examining the scale collective scores on Table No. 14.8 below.

3.9 Conclusion:
Table No. 14.7 presents the performance (by personal variables) of each of the twelve items used in the *Feminist Scale* taken as statements of opinion. Tables Nos. 14.7 and 14.8 will examine the findings of the scale and its sub-scales (arrived at by factor-analysis). The value of analysing the various statements of opinion separately is to learn more about different views on specific issues (which collectively enable the reader to understand the level of anti-feminism in society).

The commentary on the different variables' findings was intended to delve a little deeper than mere description into the meaning of the patterns of variation. There was an interesting mix between consensus and significant variation (between the subsamples of the different variables). The absence of statistically significant variation, i.e. consensus, is in itself most meaningful in explaining the current state of attitudes, just as significant variation is in relation to items or scales.

Part IV – Feminist Scale and Sub-Scale Scores by Personal Variables

In this part, (IV) **anti-feminism** or **sexism** is measured (as distinct from separate opinions given in the replies to individual items which were examined in Part III above). One item: *"Women are better than men in the caring professions"* has been dropped from the *Feminist Scale* on Table No. 14.8 because it failed to correlate significantly with any of the other items. The reason for this is the difference of views in relation to the substance of the item, i.e. some see it as complimentary to women, while others view it as limiting the caring professions to women or denying men's aptitude to the caring professions. **The author of the Feminist Scale intended the item to be in praise of women and their liberation**. The exclusion of the item on the "caring professions" has raised the *Cronbach Alpha* Score from **0.702** to **0.737**. In the light of the above it was decided to exclude it from the scale in order to examine anti-feminism more accurately.

On completion of the factor analysis of the **eleven-item scale** three distinct factors emerged as follows:

Factor One: **Fundamentalist Sexism**: *"Women think less clearly"*, *"The husband should have the main say"*, *"Education for women is less important"*, *"It is less serious if women emigrate"* and *"Women should have equal say in spending income"*;

Factor Two: **Domestic and Religious**: *"Women's place is in the home"*, *"Women are able to propose marriage"* and *"Ordination of women"*;

Factor Three: **Political and Equality**: *"So few Women in Government"*, *"Women employed on ability"*, *"Feminist Movement is necessary"* and *"Women should have equal say in spending income"*.

The following Table (No. 14.8) gives the result of the correlations using the *'Principal Component Analysis'* **extraction method** and *'Varimax with Kaiser Normalisation'*[6] **rotation method**. Summary statements are used to indicate the eleven items used. The complete statements are given on Table No. 14.6 above.

---

[6] A rotation converged in six iterations.

Table No. 14.8:
Rotated Component Matrix (Eleven-Item Feminist Scale)

	Item (Summary Statements)	Factor One	Factor Two	Factor Three
1	"Woman's Place in the Home"	(0.399)	**0.575**	
2.	"Women Think Less Clearly"	**0.590**		
3.	"The Husband Should Have Main Say"	**0.529**	(0.498)	
4.	"Education for Women is Less Important"	**0.739**		
5.	"It is Less Serious if Women Emigrate"	**0.726**	(0.389)	
6.	"So Few Women in Government"			**0.536**
7.	"Women Should be Employed on Ability"			**0.663**
8.	"Feminist Movement is Necessary"		(0.386)	**0.714**
9.	"Women Should be Able to Propose Marriage"		**0.594**	
10.	"Women Should Have Equal Say in Spending"	(0.483)		**0.523**
11.	"Women Should be Eligible for Ordination"		**0.742**	

Note: Component variations in **bold** determine factors.

The following Table (No. 14.9) examines the *Feminist Scale* (eleven items) average/mean anti-feminist (total scale) scores (0-200) and the average/mean scores of each of the Factor sub-scales by personal variables. The findings measure the comparative levels of anti-feminism or sexism between the sub-variables.

Table No. 14.9:
Feminist Scale and Sub-Scales' Scores by Personal Variables
(Excluding "Caring Profession" Item) – Scores are 0 – 200

Personal Variable	Scale Score (0-200)	Sub-Scales			No.
		Fundamentalist Sexism (0-200)	Domestic & Religious (0-200)	Political & Equality (0-200)	
Total Samples' Anti-Feminist Scores	41.1	40.0	41.2	42.5	1,015
A. Age	P<.001	P<.004	P<.001	P<.025	
1. 18-25 years	42.6	44.4	35.0	47.6	168
2. 26-40 years	40.0	36.3	38.1	45.5	325
3. 41-55 years	35.3	34.9	29.9	39.7	245
4. 56-70 years	42.4	41.9	53.2	35.1	178
5. 71 years plus	54.5	54.6	68.9	44.7	96
Score Variation	*19.2*	*19.7*	*33.9*	*12.5*	*1,012*
B. Gender	P<.001	P<.001	P<.046	P<.001	
1. Males	49.6	49.2	44.3	54.4	499
2. Females	32.7	30.9	38.1	30.9	516
Score Variation	*16.9*	*18.3*	*6.2*	*25.5*	*1,015*

C. Marital Status	P<.001	P<.013	P<.001	P<.024	
1. Single/Never Married	40.8	**41.1**	37.2	**43.5**	356
2. Married	39.7	39.1	39.7	40.0	468
3. Separated/Divorced	**48.0**	35.4	**50.7**	**60.0**	44
4. Permanent Relationship	33.8	28.8	36.0	38.4	72
5. Widowed	**56.3**	**56.4**	**71.0**	**48.1**	69
Score Variation	*22.5*	*27.6*	*35.0*	*21.6*	*1,009*
D. Area of Birth	N/S	N/S	P<.044	P<.001	
1. City (100,000 plus)	---	---	38.9	**48.6**	419
2. Large Town (10,000 +)	---	---	33.3	**43.8**	119
3. Town (1,500 plus)	---	---	40.0	29.5	132
4. Rural/Village	---	---	**46.6**	39.2	345
Score Variation	*---*	*---*	*13.3*	*19.1*	*1,015*
E. Place of Rearing in ROI.	N/S	N/S	P<.001	N/S	
1. Dublin (City & County)	---	---	28.1	---	243
2. Rest of Leinster	---	---	40.1	---	157
3. Munster	---	---	44.3	---	219
4. Connaught/Ulster	---	---	46.6	---	154
Score Variation	*---*	*---*	*18.5*	*---*	*773*
F. Region of Residence	N/S	P<.001	P<.004	N/S	
1. B.M.W. (Border Midlands West)	---	36.3	**43.3**	---	269
2. Dublin	---	**45.5**	33.0	---	284
3. Mid-East & South-East	---	**46.6**	**41.4**	---	218
4. Mid-West & South-West	---	31.6	**48.3**	---	234
Score Variation	*---*	*15.0*	*15.3*	*---*	*1,005*
G. Education	P<.001	P<.001	P<.001	N/S	
1. Primary or Less	**52.9**	**56.1**	**61.1**	---	117
2. Incomplete Second-Level	**49.8**	**52.5**	**49.5**	---	262
3. Complete Second-Level	39.7	**40.2**	36.3	---	255
4. Third-Level	32.3	29.3	32.5	---	381
Score Variation	*20.2*	*26.8*	*28.6*	*---*	*1,015*
H. Occupational Status	P<.001	P<.001	P<.002	P<.001	
1. Unskilled/Semi-Skilled	**49.4**	**53.1**	**48.0**	**48.2**	207
2. Skilled/Routine Non-Manual	40.8	38.3	37.2	**45.8**	328
3. Inspectional/Supervisory	33.5	27.4	35.1	38.6	133
4. Professional/Executive	30.8	32.2	30.7	29.5	191
Score Variation	*18.6*	*25.7*	*17.3*	*18.7*	*859*
I. Social Class Position	P<.001	P<.001	P<.001	P<.001	
1. Class I: "Upper Class"	38.7	**50.0**	32.9	31.8	38
2. Class II: "Upper-Mid. Class"	26.7	25.1	27.6	27.8	140
3. Class III: "Middle-Mid. Class"	35.8	26.8	38.1	**43.5**	226
4. Class IV: "Working Class"	**43.1**	**45.4**	38.0	**44.9**	361
5. Class V: "Lower Class"	**55.8**	**59.2**	**58.8**	**51.8**	83
Score Variation	*29.1*	*34.1*	*31.2*	*24.0*	*848*

Note: Scores above the sample average are **in bold**.　(Variations are in *italics*.)

Eight of the **thirty-six** (**22.2%**) sub-scales on Table No. 14.9 failed to register a statistically significant variation. In other words, there was a **consensus** within eight variables with no significance (N/S). The fact that **77.8%** of the sub-scales did produce a significant variation on a topic with a relatively low Anti-Feminist sample and subsample average scores, i.e. **41.1**, **40.0**, **41.2** and **42.5** (out of a possible 200) is, in itself, interesting. The score variations are relatively higher than expected. In the light of the little or no change since 1988-89, it is difficult to predict how the level of anti-feminism is likely to move in the short term. It would be imprudent for the feminist movement or for citizens interested in the maintenance and promotion of true gender equality to be complacent with regard to future changes!

It may also be an opportune time to reappraise current pro-feminist policies in the direction of a more social-class inclusive approach. It will be shown that the findings of Table No. 14.9 indicate a strong 'social-class position' positive correlation between pro-feminist scores and social status. In other words, has feminism become identified with middle-class, 'individualist' equality? A more collectivist and class-inclusive approach could well counter tendencies to become an 'institutionalised', middle-class movement! Has the time arrived when the movement should change its focus from *women's rights* to the broader goal of *gender equality*, i.e. male and female rights?

4.1 Age:
The performance of the age variable has been most interesting and produced a statistically significant variation in each of the four sub-scales. The least sexist or anti-feminist age group overall is the 41 to 55 year-olds (born between 1952 and 1967), i.e. post-World War II babies! They grew-up (teenage years) in the heady 1970s. The score-variations for the four sub-scales probably tell their own story. It was not expected that the youngest age group, i.e. 18 to 25 year-olds, would have above-average anti-feminist scores in three of the four sub-scales! The following extract from Table No. 14.9(a) tells its own story.

	Sub-Scale	Score Variation	Between		Mean Score (0-200)
			Most Anti-Feminist	**Least Anti-Feminist**	
1.	"Domestic and Religious"	33.9	71 years+ **(68.9)** and	41 to 55 years **(29.9)**	41.2
2.	"Fundamentalist Sexism"	19.7	71 years+ **(54.6)** and	41 to 55 years **(34.9)**	40.0
3.	"Full Scale"	19.2	71 years+ **(54.5)** and	41 to 55 years **(35.3)**	41.1
4.	"Political and Equality"	12.5	18 to 25 yrs **(47.6)** and	56 to 70 years **(35.1)**	42.5

It is difficult to interpret the above figures, which are not in line with the expected positive correlation between age and sexism. It is as if the Feminist Movement has peaked and is in need of a revival. Has its success de-radicalised it? Or has it failed to adapt to the changing situation?

4.2 Gender:

The gap between the scores of males and females has been quite substantial except in the case of Factor Two: *"Domestic and Religious"*. The Factor with widest score variation is No.3: *"Political and Equality"* at **25.5**. In each of the four sub-scales, **males** were significantly more sexist than were the **females**. [See Table No. 14.9(b) above.]

These findings are unwelcome. It would be too simplistic to dismiss them as a manifestation of male chauvinism in men's reaction to the perceived threat to their status. The overall figures show that *women's liberation* is socially acceptable. This again raises the question: has the time come for a more 'inclusive' gender equality movement, which emphasises men's rights as well as women's rights? The findings of the gender variable provide a *prima facie* case for further research into a more inclusive movement for gender equality in Ireland! Women's rights and men's rights are (by definition) compatible!

4.3 Marital Status:

This non-ordinal variable has elicited statistically significant variations in each of the four sub-scales. The score variations in each of the four sub-scales are quite substantial. Because of the domestic implications of feminism, the findings are even more interesting. The following extract from Table No. 14.9(c) highlights the dynamic performance of the sub-variables.

Sub-Scale	Score Variation	Between Most Anti-Feminist			Least Anti-Feminist	Mean Score (0-200)
1. "Domestic and Religious"	35.0	Widowed	**(71.0)**	and	Perm. Rel'ships **(36.0)**	41.2
2. "Fundamentalist Sexism"	27.6	Widowed	**(56.4)**	and	Perm. Rel'ships **(28.8)**	40.0
3. "Full Scale"	22.5	Widowed	**(56.3)**	and	Perm. Rel'ships **(33.8)**	41.1
4. "Political and Equality"	21.6	Separated/Div. **(60.0)**		and	Perm. Rel'ships **(38.4)**	42.5

The influence of age is evident in the case of the relatively high scores of the 'Widowed'. Also, the possibility of a perceived threat to the primacy of family life and the rearing of children in contemporary Ireland being associated with the feminist movement could have influenced 'Widowed' respondents' scores. The strong 'pro-feminist performance' of respondents living in 'Permanent Relationships' in the above extract from Table No. 14.9 merits further research.

The findings for the 'Married' and the 'Single/Never Married' (who together represent 82% of the sample) were quite similar and close to the mean total sample scores which is very interesting. These results reflect a widespread consensus in relation to the current state of attitudes towards feminism (be they positive or negative) among the two largest subsamples.

4.4 Area of Birth:

This variable measures the influence of urbanisation on respondents' sexist or anti-feminist attitudes. In the case of the *"Full Scale"* and the *"Fundamentalist Sexism"* sub-scale there was consensus between the sub-samples. This, in itself, is significant indicating the relatively small influence of one's urban or rural background on attitudes toward sexist issues. It probably points to the homogenisation of people's values and attitudes by the common, predominantly urbanised and globalised electronic and print media in a population with English as a spoken language.

Sub-Scale	Score Variation	Between Most Anti-Feminist			Least Anti-Feminist		Mean Score (0-200)
1 "Political and Equality"	19.1	City	**(48.6)**	and	Town	**(29.5)**	42.5
2 "Domestic and Religious"	13.3	Rural/Village **(46.6)**		and	Large Town **(33.3)**		41.2

In the two sub-scales recording statistical significance, i.e. "Domestic and Religious" and "Political and Equality", the trends are in the opposite direction.   The **former** shows the more urbanised to be more tolerant and the **latter** records the more tolerant scores among the "Small Town" and "Rural/Village" respondents. [See Table No. 14.9(d).]

4.5 Place of Rearing (Republic of Ireland) and Region of Residence:

Only one sub-scale shows significant variation, i.e. "Domestic and Religious".   Dublin (City and County)-reared respondents were most tolerant, while Connaught /Ulster were most anti-feminist. This reflects the findings of 'Area of Birth' where the more urbanised had the lowest anti-feminist scores.

Region of Residence elicited a significant variation for the "Fundamentalist Sexism" and "Domestic and Religious" factors.

Sub-Scale	Score Variation	Between Most Anti-Feminist	Least Anti-Feminist	Mean Score (0-200)
1. "Domestic and Religious"	15.3	Mid-West & Sth.W. (**48.3**) and	Dublin (**33.0**)	41.2
2. "Fundamentalist Sexism"	15.0	Mid-East & Sth.E. (**46.6**) and Mid.W & Sth.W.(**31.6**)		40.0

In the case of the former, 'Dublin' and 'Mid-East and South-East' residents were most sexist, while those living in the 'BMW' and 'Mid-West and South-West' regions were least anti-feminist.   In the case of the "Domestic and Religious" factor, the most favourable score was among the Dublin residents.   Again, the lack of consistency between the two variables is noteworthy.   [See Table No. 14.9 (e) and (f).]

4.6 Education:

The performance of education was as anticipated, i.e. those with lowest educational achievement having higher anti-feminist or sexist scores.   This has been consistent across the three sub-scales recording statistically significant variations.   The factor failing to register significant variations was "Political and Equality", which was not anticipated.

The score variations in the following extract from Table No. 14.9(g) are noteworthy.

Sub-Scale	Score Variation	Between Most Anti-Feminist	Least Anti-Feminist	Mean Score (0-200)
1. "Domestic and Religious"	28.6	Primary or Less (**61.1**) and	Third Level (**32.5**)	41.2
2. "Fundamentalist Sexism"	26.8	Primary or Less (**56.1**) and	Third Level (**29.3**)	40.0
3. "Full Scale"	20.2	Primary or Less (**52.9**) and	Third Level (**32.3**)	41.1

The above findings confirm the anticipated correlation between 'education' and pro-feminist attitudes. The very substantial increase of female participation in second and third-level education over the past forty years in Ireland is also reflected in the above scores.

4.7 Occupational Status:
This variable elicited statistically significant inter-sub-variable differences. The direction of the variations was as anticipated. The score variations were substantial.

Sub-Scale	Score Variation	Between Most Anti-Feminist	Least Anti-Feminist	Mean Score (0-200)
1. "Fundamentalist Sexism"	25.7	Unskilled/Semi-Sk. (**53.1**) and	Insp./Super. (**27.4**)	40.0
2. "Political and Equality"	18.7	Unskilled/Semi-Sk. (**48.2**) and	Prof./Exec. (**29.5**)	42.5
3. "Full Scale"	18.6	Unskilled/Semi-Sk. (**49.4**) and	Prof./Exec. (**30.8**)	41.1
4. "Domestic and Religious"	17.3	Unskilled/Semi-Sk. (**48.0**) and	Prof./Exec. (**30.7**)	41.2

The pattern of responses is very clear. There is a negative correlation between anti-feminist scores and the occupational status of the respondent. This was anticipated and shows that bias against women in the higher profession is relatively low, thereby, facilitating equal access to job opportunities and promotion.

But there is a "sting in the tail" in the above results in that those most likely to experience socio-economic deprivation, i.e. the 'Unskilled and Semi-Skilled' returned a relatively high anti-feminist response for every sub-scale. There seems to be a perceived lack of solidarity between the lower status respondents and those pursuing the "liberation of women". Could this be interpreted as reflecting a lack of a social-class dimension in the feminist movement from the perspective of the underprivileged?

4.8 Social Class Position:

This variable's findings confirm what was reported in the previous variables of Education and Occupational Status as would be expected since the 'social class position' grades are determined by education and occupation (see Table No. 8.14, page 189). The most important result of the variable findings is its clear social status character. The "Upper-Middle Class" or Class II is the most favourable subsample to the feminist cause in each of the four sub-scales, while Class V was clearly the least pro-feminist subsample.

The score variations in Table No. 14.9(i) were very substantial in each of the sub-scales. The following extract from Table No. 14.9 shows the dynamic diversity within the "steps of the social-status ladder" in pro-and anti-feminist attitudes:

Sub-Scale	Score Variation	Between Most Anti-Feminist	Least Anti-Feminist	Mean Score (0-200)
1. "Fundamentalist Sexism"	34.1	Class V "Lower Cl." (**59.2**) and	Class II "Upr.Mid.Cl" (**25.1**)	40.0
2. "Domestic and Religious"	31.2	Class V "Lower Cl." (**58.8**) and	Class II "Upr.Mid.Cl" (**27.6**)	41.2
3. "Full Scale"	29.1	Class V "Lower Cl." (**55.8**) and	Class II "Upr.Mid.Cl" (**26.7**)	41.1
4. "Political and Equality"	24.0	Class V "Lower Cl." (**51.8**) and	Class II "Upr.Mid.Cl" (**27.8**)	42.5

These findings clearly show the very strong "Middle Class" support for the *feminist movement* and what it stands for. The weaker support of the "Lower and Working Classes" not only reflects overall intolerance but also the failure of the feminist movement to establish solidarity with those at the bottom of the social ladder. Liberation movements generally succeed in getting the support of the most underprivileged and are perceived as a threat to the more privileged. Of course, it could be argued that the results have more to do with the frustrations caused by the insecurity of the causes of the respondent's "Lower-Class position" than any rational reaction to the feminist movement. Others would argue that the findings portray the conservative attitudes of the respondents with higher-than-average scores. The conservative attitudes of respondents from the "Upper-Middle Class" would seem to contradict the general trends. The present author accepts that the findings are the product of **multiple causality** of which the middle-class public identity of the successful feminist movement and its apparent failure to be "class inclusive" are **among** the causes of the markedly social-status determined diversity in the findings of Table No. 14.9(i) above. Other readers are free to interpret the findings differently!

4.9 Conclusion:

Table No. 14.9 is an important Table measuring a most important issue affecting over half of the population, namely, sexism or anti-feminism (insofar that the latter expresses the form of social prejudice known as 'sexism'). Anti-feminism findings may be interpreted differently from other social prejudices in that they are measuring attitudes towards a movement whose aim is social and personal liberation in society at large. In such circumstances one would expect a sense of solidarity between respondents with relatively more deprived statuses to be most favourably disposed! The findings do not confirm this expectation! The strongest support comes from the middle-class and middle-age sub-variables!

Part V – Conclusion

Public attitudes and opinions in relation to **gender equality** in society today are central to social justice. After centuries, even millennia, of **patriarchy**, the struggle for **female equality** (with males) has been a necessary and noble struggle, which has been relatively successful in Western societies like the Republic of Ireland when compared with some non-Western societies. The *Women's Liberation Movement* has been essential. Its effect to date has been more successful in some institutions than in others, which means it has much work still to do, especially, in institutions resistant to change in the direction of gender equality.

The *feminist movement* has been active in Ireland (as elsewhere in the Western World). It promotes its own ideology which is known as **feminism**. In the above pages of this chapter a *special feminist scale* has been used to elicit pro- and anti-feminist attitudes and opinions. The overall anti-feminist scores remained relatively low at **43** (on a 0 to 200 range) which indicate that the majority of the respondents were favourably disposed to women's liberation. This is to be welcomed. What was not expected was the very small improvement between 1988-89 and 2007-08, i.e. a nominal drop of **3** points from **46** in 1988-89 to **43** in 2007-08 (see Table No. 14.6, page 344).

When each item was examined reflecting a public opinion, the changes were more spectacular (see the two extracts on page 345). Table No. 14.7 examined each of the twelve items by personal variables (pages 348-9). The results were quite interesting and mixed. A feature which emerged from the results was the **class** variations. "Lower class" respondents' scores were more negative, while "middle-middle" and "upper-middle class" respondents were least anti-feminist across the board (see extract on page 355).

When the items were examined collectively as a scale, three **factors** emerged from the findings, i.e. 'Fundamentalist Sexism Factor', 'Domestic and Religious Factor' and 'Political and Equality Factor'. An interesting finding was the failure of one item to align with any of the three factors, i.e. *"Women are better than men in the caring professions"*. It appeared that there was disagreement on whether such an opinion was complimentary or derogatory of women. The item was included in the scale as complimentary, based on the view of the **primacy of maternal caring** in the life of the people, which resulted in the greater capacity of women as carers, as complementary to the primary roles of men. Is the failure of a significant number of pro-feminist respondents to acknowledge the positive quality of this item reflective of the **current status of caring as a profession**? If so, there may be some degree of distortion in current social values!

Table No. 14.9 gives the findings of the *Feminist Scale* (of eleven items) and its three factor sub-scales, by personal variables. The range of score variations was substantial in most of the cases with 'statistically significant variations'. Eight of the thirty-six sub-tables on Table No. 14.9 recorded **consensus**, i.e. did not have 'statistically significant variation' of **P<.05**. The highest degree of consensus was in the geographic/territorial variables, i.e. 'Area of Birth', 'Place of Rearing' and 'Region of Residence'.

'Age' was mixed in its results. 'Gender' revealed that 'males' were substantially more anti-feminist than 'females'. 'Education' and 'Occupation' were more or less as anticipated, while 'Social Class Position' seemed to confirm the class bias of feminism. The latter result points to the perception of the feminist movement in society as a largely middle-class campaign.   Perhaps, the time has come to establish **a more inclusive gender-equality movement** which embraces men and women who are being discriminated against (because of their gender).   Such a movement would also have to include the needs and support of men and women in the "Working and Lower Classes".

***

CHAPTER XV
Irish Political Attitudes

Part I – Ideological Context

1.1:

The political institution constitutes *the set of norms which centres around society's goal-orientation, the control of power, the maintenance of social order, and the provision of social welfare.*   Over the course of history, the legitimation of society's political system has changed from tribal hierarchy to military authority to theocracy to feudal-cum-monarchist authority to dictatorship to popular democracy.   The above list of systems of government is not necessarily sequential.   Most political systems operate on an accepted system of social stratification which can be formally determined or informally operated[1].   The transition from one system to another often carries residues of the past, e.g. the House of Lords.   One might also see the United States' system as an elected monarchy based on the powers of George III of Great Britain (in the late 18th century) with elected members of the 'Commons' (House of Representatives) and the 'Lords' (newly named the Senate)!   It may have modified its Constitution over the years.

At the basis of political systems and parties there is a range of **ideologies** which rationalise and justify the direction of particular goal-orientations and operating procedures.   They are popularly expressed in political **sets of policies**.   Some political systems tolerate a diversity of political ideologies, while others outlaw ideological deviations from that of the ruling group or class.   The former is frequently referred to as a **liberal democracy** despite its almost intolerant defence of the ideology of 'liberal capitalism' in a number of Western societies for over two hundred years.

1.2:

Changes in political ideologies are ongoing.   Following the decline of feudalism-cum-monarchism in the eighteenth century, **the ideology of**

---

[1] See: Worsley, Peter, *et al.*, *Introducing Sociology*, Harmondsworth (England), Penguin, 1970, pp 283-336.

republicanism, on which the **nation state**[2] was based, led to the de-colonisation of populations (including the Republic of Ireland) over the twentieth century[3].   Imperial ambitions of certain strong nation-states interrupted the progress towards democracy and republicanism during the two wars of 1914-1918 and 1939-1945. The latter disastrous experience led to political developments in Europe, i.e. the **U.S.S.R.** and its Eastern European (occupied) block of nations, on the one hand, and the formation of the *Common Market* (later to become the **European Union**) in Western Europe, on the other hand.   The two developments were responses to the expansionist tyranny of **Nazi Fascism** (under Adolf Hitler) and **Soviet Centralism** (under Joseph Stalin).   Another political structure which emanated from the 1939-45 War was the establishment of the **United Nations** which recognised the autonomy of the nation state and promoted a system which would protect nations from the aggressive ambitions of other nations and develop greater international solidarity.   The ideological basis for the above international development is not yet fully developed.   The current crises in the Middle East and elsewhere are examples of such failure (so far) to arrive at an agreed international political ideology and the failure to honour state boundaries.

The role of religious and economic institutions in framing political ideologies is often underestimated by both Western and Eastern leaders, e.g. the influence of global religions and of economic globalisation on political structures and procedures.   The collapse of the 'Berlin Wall' in 1989 and the crash of the Banking System in 2008 presented serious challenges to the political viability of the ideologies of communism and capitalism respectively!   Perhaps some collectivist ideology with tolerance of pluralist systems will emerge to regulate avarice and ambition and, at the same time, promote social justice and encourage worthwhile incentives?

1.3:   The findings of the 2007-08 survey of political attitudes in the Republic of Ireland should be interpreted in the context of a serious fluidity

---

[2] Herbert C. Kelman's description/definition of the ideology of **Nationalism** is informative: "One can describe nationalism as an ideology that views the nation as the unit in which paramount political power is vested. The nation state, being the embodiment of the nation, is placed at the pinnacle of power and entitled to overrule both smaller and larger political units. The modern nation state derives its legitimacy and cohesiveness from the fact that it is seen as representing the nation – in other words, from the correspondence of the political entity with an ethnic, cultural and historical entity with which at least a large portion of the population identify." Kelman, Herbert C. (Editor), *International Behaviour: A Social-Psychological Analysis*, New York, Holt, Rinehart and Winston, 1965, page 576.

[3] Katz, David, "Nationalism and Strategies of International Conflict Resolution" in *International Behaviour*, (Editor, Herbert C. Kelman), New York, Holt, Rinehart and Winston, 1965, pp 350-391.

in the major schools of political ideology popularly referred to as the **'right'** (i.e. Capitalist) and **'left'** (i.e. Socialist). The dominance of the **economic institution** in so-called 'Western Societies' and of the **religious institution** in the Middle-East and Northern Africa and elsewhere require much more attention than political and academic leaders and 'authorities' seem to give them and the integration of the legitimate concerns or functions of each institution and their harnessing cooperation in the best interest of the common good. Popular media (political) commentators seem to be preoccupied with *immediate and personality issues* rather than with the underpinning structural and ideological issues

The decline of the pivotal place of **the family** as a social institution in Western capitalist/socialist societies also requires attention from political leaders. It would appear that the 'family' should be an integral part of progressive political ideologies. Neglect of the family inevitably leads to the decline of community, i.e. the territorial area within which people live their normal daily lives, and social dysfunction in the medium and long term. The socialisation of the young, for instance, requires viable and stable familial structures. We should not forget that human beings are the longest nesting animals! Evidence already reported in this text, i.e. the unanticipated levels of relative intolerance among a minority of the 18 to 25 year-old respondents towards ethnic, racial and social stimulus categories, points to possible *deficiencies in their socialisation* probably due (in part) to a decline of the perceived importance of the family over the past quarter of a century! This in turn may be due to the failure of support for the family by the Irish political institution in its concessions to the requirements of an increasingly dominant economic institution. Neglect of the family by the State inevitably leads to socio-political dysfunction.

Part II – Political Social Distance

2.1:
Six stimulus categories were included in the 2007-08 national survey to measure political social distance, i.e. 'Gardaí', 'Trade Unionists', 'Unionists', 'Socialists', 'Capitalists' and 'Communists'. Table No. 15.1 gives their level of social distance and compares the findings of the 2007-08 and those of 1988-89 surveys. The political classification of the above categories was based, in part, on the rationalisations by respondents not 'admitting them to kinship' in previous surveys.

Table No. 15.1:
Social Distance towards Political Categories in 2007-08 and in 1988-89

Category	A 2007-08			B 1988-89*			Change (A – B)		
	Admit to Kinship	Deny Citizen'p	MSD	Admit to Kinship	Deny Citizen'p	MSD	Admit to Kinship	Deny Citizen'p	MSD
1. 'Gardaí'	81.4%	1.8%	1.392	84.0%	0.2%	1.267	-2.6%	+1.6%	+0.125
2. 'Trade Unionists'	77.8%	2.8%	1.552	63.7%	4.2%	2.022	+14.1%	-1.4%	-0.047
3. 'Unionists'	66.2%	7.9%	1.944	33.4%	18.6%	3.084	+32.8%	-10.7%	-1.140
4. 'Socialists'	67.0%	9.1%	1.990	44.9%	13.4%	2.650	+22.1%	-4.3%	-0.660
5. 'Capitalists'	60.8%	11.8%	2.297	47.8%	13.6%	2.587	+13.0%	-1.8%	-0.290
6. 'Communists'	45.9%	19.7%	2.920	24.4%	34.3%	3.769	+21.5%	-14.6%	-0.849

* *Source of 1988-89*: Mac Gréil, Micheál, *Prejudice in Ireland Revisited*, Maynooth, St Patrick's College, 1996, pages 65-7.

2.2 'Gardaí':

The above findings show that the overall level of political tolerance has improved significantly between 1988-89 and 2007-08. The position of the 'Gardaí' disimproved slightly over the nineteen years but they still have retained their in-group status (i.e. MSD of under 1.500). It is very important that the 'Gardaí' maintain their very good standing within the community. Otherwise, the effectiveness of the force would be greatly reduced in their task of defending the citizens from injury and various forms of crime. It is generally accepted that a civil police force is as good as its ability to maintain the trust and confidence of the citizens it serves and protects. Even a relatively small decline in their standing as reported above is worth noting by those responsible for the community relations with the 'Gardaí'.

2.3 'Trade Unionists':

The social standing of 'Trade Unionists' has improved significantly. They are now on the border of the 'in-group' categories, i.e. just 0.052 outside the mean-social-distance score of **1.500**. Why this is so may be owing to a number of developments. It could be seen as a public endorsement of the value of trade-unions membership to ensure fair and just working conditions. Also, it could be interpreted as public confirmation of **'social partnership'**, which was in operation over almost thirty years in the Republic of Ireland – resulting in an unprecedented period of industrial peace and considerable social progress in times of economic difficulties and of relative success. It is also interesting to observe that the social status of unionised workers in Ireland has changed with the decline of the *blue-collar workers* and the predominance of *white-collar workers* (in the public services). Within the white-collar workforce, the majority of union members are employed in the public services. To what extent this affects the standing of 'Trade Unionists' is worth further research. These findings may appear surprisingly positive, if not problematic, to those managements who seem to operate a ban on trade unions organising within their workforces. Analysis by personal variables produces very interesting results (see Table No. 15.2 below).

2.4 'Unionists':
The category to experience greatest improvement in standing among the respondents (in Table No. 15.1) has been the 'Unionists'. The percentage willing to admit 'Unionists' into kinship went from **33.4%** in 1988-89 to **66.2%** in 2007-08. For all practical purposes it doubled! Over the same period the percentage denying 'Unionists' citizenship dropped from **18.6%** to **7.9%**. As stated earlier (see Chapter IV, page 76) the improvement in the status of 'Unionists' among a representative sample of adults in the Republic of Ireland is very positive and significant. The 'psychological' Border is being removed and mutual respect is replacing formerly hostile attitudes. It is also a clear endorsement of the *Good Friday Agreement* (1998) by the respondents. Such change in social distance indicates that we have crossed the 'Rubicon' *en route* to the normalisation of Northern Ireland/Republic relations which make a pluralist coexistence between 'Unionists' and 'Nationalists' feasible, as well as desirable. This is not to say that there is no need for continued efforts to remove the remaining degree of intolerance in the years ahead. The evidence presented here should be an incentive to continue the pursuit of such a socio-political goal.

2.5 'Socialists' and 'Capitalists':
The response to 'Socialists' and 'Capitalists' has recorded significant improvements in tolerance. The level of improvement for 'Socialists' is almost twice that for 'Capitalists'. In relative terms, 'Socialists' have passed out 'Capitalists' in popularity between 1988-89 and 2007-08, i.e. in 1988-89 'Socialists' were **26**[th] and in 2007-08 they were **27**[th] (out of 46 categories), while 'Capitalists' move from **24**[th] in 1988-89 to **32**[nd] in 2007-08. This marks a significant drop in the popularity of 'Capitalists' at a time when the country was still enjoying the benefits of the so-called **Celtic**

Tiger! Does this mean that Irish opinion was "moving to the left" or were the people beginning to question 'neo-liberal capitalism' and international corporations in advance of the banking and lending problems which were to cause the crisis in the summer of 2008?

2.6 'Communists':

There was a very substantial improvement in the percentage of respondents who were prepared to admit 'Communists' into kinship and a considerable drop in the percentage denying them citizenship:

Survey	Social Distance towards 'Communists'	
	Admit to Kinship	**Deny Citizenship**
1. 2007-08	45.9%	19.7%
2. 1988-89	24.4%	34.3%
Change (1 – 2)	+21.5% (**+88.1%**)	-14.6% (**-42.6%**)

The above extract from Table No. 15.1 shows the extent of change in the adults' attitudes towards 'Communists' over the nineteen years measured. To what extent has this been due to the collapse of the **Berlin Wall** in 1989 (just after the completion of the 1988-89 national survey) or is it due to disillusionment with **'Capitalism'** or a general momentum of change in Ireland to the 'left' as already seen in the case of social distance towards **'Socialists'**? Despite the noteworthy changes given above, the relative position of 'Communists' is second-last in a range of **51** categories. The residue of reports of cases where coercive force was used to impose 'totalitarian communist rule' may also be a factor in the relative unpopularity of this stimulus category among the respondents. The percentages of respondents 'admitting Communists to kinship' and 'denying citizenship' to them are still very negative! Communists had been 'demonised' by Church and State in most 'Liberal/Capitalist' Western States for almost one hundred years!

2.7 Conclusion:

The overall response to the six 'political stimulus categories' seems to place the respondents (as a group) **"left of centre"** as regards ideological outlook. Of course, the findings of Table No. 15.1 might also point to a level of political pragmatism, i.e. **"a-ideological"**. Does this mean that the Irish people (Republic of Ireland) are more adaptable to change than would be expected? The improvement in the attitudes of respondents towards

'**Unionists**' confirms the positive impact of the *Good Friday Agreement.* A successful broadly-based political party is said to change its ideological emphasis to suit the prevailing popular mood, e.g. the 'greening' of political parties in recent times!

The social-distance scores towards 'Socialists' and 'Capitalists' and the greater improvement between 1988-89 and 2007-08 in the case of the 'Socialist' position seem to place the Republic of Ireland in a **centrist ideological position**, with a slight leaning towards the "left". Does this reflect a degree of dissatisfaction with the **equality of the distribution** of the benefits of the very substantial improvement in the 'Gross National Product' during the 'heady' Celtic Tiger years? The examination of the findings by personal variables (Table No. 15.2) will provide some insight into possible trends in these attitudes. Since **the economic downturn** had not become evident at the time the survey took place, i.e. between November 2007 and March 2008, it would be necessary to exercise caution about short-term changes! Economic insecurity generates frustration and tension which seeks expression in aggression. Social prejudice is a form of psychological aggression!

Part III – Political Social Distance by Personal Variables

3.1 Introduction:
Table No. 15.2 presents political social distance towards 'Gardaí', 'Trade Unionists', 'Unionists', 'Socialists', 'Capitalists' and 'Communists' by personal variables. The two measures examined by personal variables are 'admission to kinship' and 'denial of citizenship'. In all, there are ten personal variables which registered statistically significant variation in the case of one or more stimulus category, i.e. Age, Gender, Marital Status, Area of Birth, Place of Rearing, Region of Residence, Education, Occupational Status, Social Class Position and Political Party Preference.

Of the **sixty** sub-scales on Table No. 15.2, forty-nine (81.7%) recorded a *chi-square* of p<.050. Of the eleven sub-scales not to return statistically significant variations, five were in the case of 'Gender'. It is possible to analyse the findings from two perspectives, i.e. by the performance of each of the ten personal variables or by focussing on each of the stimulus categories. In Section 3.2 below (pages 378-81) it is proposed to comment on the former while Section 3.3 (pages 381-8) will deal with the latter.

Pluralism and Diversity in Ireland

Table No. 15.2: Social Distance towards Political Categories by Personal Variables (Admit to Kinship and Deny Citizenship)

Personal Variable	'Gardai'		'Trade Unionists'		'Unionists'		'Socialists'		'Capitalists'		'Communists'		Number
	Admit Kinship	Deny Citiz.	Admit Kinship	Deny Citiz.	Admit Kinship	Deny Citiz.	Admit Kinship	Deny Citiz.	Admit Kinship	Deny Citiz.	Admit Kinship	Deny Citiz.	
Total Sample	**81.1%**	**1.8%**	**77.7%**	**2.8%**	**66.2%**	**7.9%**	**66.8%**	**9.2%**	**60.7%**	**11.7%**	**45.9%**	**19.7%**	**1,015**
A. Age	P<.001		P<.003		P<.001		N/S		P<.001		P<.001		
1. 18-25 years	71.0%	4.2%	70.6%	1.8%	57.4%	16.0%	---	---	51.8%	16.7%	44.6%	23.8%	168
2. 26-40 years	83.3%	2.1%	81.6%	2.5%	69.2%	7.1%	---	---	65.5%	9.3%	53.4%	14.9%	325
3. 41-55 years	79.7%	0.4%	74.1%	4.4%	67.9%	4.5%	---	---	57.7%	11.8%	42.7%	17.1%	245
4. 56-70 years	83.7%	0.6%	80.4%	1.7%	64.6%	5.7%	---	---	67.2%	10.2%	45.4%	25.8%	178
5. 71 years plus	90.6%	2.1%	81.2%	3.1%	70.1%	9.3%	---	---	55.5%	14.5%	35.1%	23.4%	96
Score Variation	*19.6%*	*3.8%*	*11.0%*	*2.7%*	*12.7%*	*11.5%*	---	---	*15.4%*	*7.4%*	*18.3%*	*10.9%*	*1,012*
B. Gender	N/S		N/S		P<.001		N/S		N/S		N/S		
1. Males	---	---	---	---	66.7%	9.4%	---	---	---	---	---	---	
2. Females	---	---	---	---	65.8%	6.4%	---	---	---	---	---	---	
Score Variation	---	---	---	---	*1.9%*	*3.0%*	---	---	---	---	---	---	
C. Marital Status	P<.001		P<.022		P<.001		N/S		P<.001		N/S		
1. Single/Never Married	77.8%	2.8%	79.3%	2.2%	64.4%	11.5%	---	---	58.5%	17.4%	---	---	356
2. Married	84.6%	0.4%	77.6%	3.0%	66.7%	5.3%	---	---	63.3%	7.7%	---	---	468
3. Separated/Divorced	84.1%	0.0%	75.0%	0.0%	72.7%	6.8%	---	---	56.8%	15.9%	---	---	44
4. Permanent Relation'p	70.4%	4.2%	70.8%	2.8%	60.6%	8.4%	---	---	56.9%	7.0%	---	---	72
5. Widowed	88.2%	2.9%	82.6%	5.8%	73.9%	8.6%	---	---	58.0%	15.9%	---	---	69
Score Variation	*18.2%*	*4.2%*	*11.8%*	*5.8%*	*13.3%*	*6.2%*	---	---	*6.5%*	*10.4%*	---	---	*1,009*
D. Area of Birth	P<.001		N/S		P<.001		N/S		P<.001		P<.001		
1. City (100,000+)	75.9%	1.5%	---	---	68.6%	4.6%	---	---	60.9%	9.9%	47.2%	18.1%	419
2. Large Town (10,000+)	86.7%	2.5%	---	---	68.9%	4.2%	---	---	62.7%	12.7%	55.1%	22.0%	119
3. Town (1,500+)	84.6%	2.3%	---	---	68.2%	9.3%	---	---	68.0%	10.9%	58.3%	13.4%	132
4. Rural/Village	84.5%	1.5%	---	---	61.5%	12.8%	---	---	57.0%	14.0%	36.8%	23.1%	345
Score Variation	*10.8%*	*1.0%*	---	---	*7.4%*	*8.1%*	---	---	*11.0%*	*4.1%*	*21.5%*	*9.7%*	*1,015*
E. Place of Rearing ROI	P<.005		N/S		P<.001		P<.001		P<.001		P<.001		
1. Dublin (City & Co.)	78.7%	0.4%	---	---	71.4%	3.8%	72.0%	8.3%	62.1%	13.3%	49.4%	19.5%	243
2. Rest of Leinster	85.3%	0.6%	---	---	63.8%	16.0%	63.0%	18.6%	59.1%	16.5%	41.5%	28.0%	157
3. Munster	87.9%	1.3%	---	---	69.0%	8.2%	67.5%	7.0%	66.4%	7.8%	50.7%	18.4%	219
4. Connaught/Ulster	79.9%	2.4%	---	---	56.4%	5.5%	62.0%	5.5%	54.0%	11.2%	29.3%	13.4%	154
Score Variation	*9.2%*	*2.0%*	---	---	*15.0%*	*12.2%*	*10.0%*	*13.1%*	*12.4%*	*8.7%*	*21.4%*	*14.6%*	*773*

Table No.15.2 (Cont'd)	'Gardaí'		'Trade Unionists'		'Unionists'		'Socialists'		'Capitalists'		'Communists'		Number
F. Region of Residence	P<.001		P<.001		P<.001		P<.001		P<.001		P<.001		
1. B.M.W.	77.2%	3.8%	73.8%	2.5%	53.3%	11.9%	57.8%	13.7%	49.8%	18.2%	29.8%	23.9%	269
2. Dublin	79.4%	1.0%	81.1%	3.2%	73.9%	3.6%	74.3%	5.3%	64.9%	9.8%	51.6%	17.3%	284
3. Mid-East & South-E.	85.8%	0.0%	71.6%	4.2%	64.1%	14.8%	63.1%	15.4%	58.8%	15.8%	53.0%	20.1%	218
4. Mid-West & Sth-West	84.4%	2.1%	84.4%	1.3%	73.8%	2.1%	72.6%	2.5%	70.3%	3.3%	51.1%	17.9%	234
Score Variation	*8.6%*	*2.1%*	*12.8%*	*2.9%*	*9.8%*	*12.7%*	*16.5%*	*12.9%*	*20.5%*	*14.9%*	*23.2%*	*6.6%*	*1,005*
G. Education	P<.001		P<.002		P<.020		P<.001		P<.001		P<.001		
1. Primary or Less	91.4%	1.7%	88.1%	3.4%	78.8%	7.6%	73.5%	12.8%	62.9%	15.5%	47.0%	27.3%	117
2. Incomplete Sec-Level	85.1%	1.9%	75.7%	4.5%	64.0%	8.0%	63.7%	9.6%	55.0%	15.1%	40.7%	19.0%	262
3. Complete Sec.-Level	80.9%	1.6%	77.2%	4.3%	62.6%	9.5%	69.0%	11.5%	62.1%	14.0%	44.9%	24.1%	255
4. Third-Level	75.9%	1.9%	76.3%	0.3%	66.3%	6.9%	66.1%	5.8%	62.9%	6.9%	49.9%	14.8%	381
Score Variation	*15.5%*	*0.3%*	*12.4%*	*4.2%*	*16.2%*	*2.6%*	*9.8%*	*7.0%*	*7.9%*	*8.6%*	*9.2%*	*12.5%*	*1,015*
H. Occupational Status	P<.001		P<.020		P<.039		P<.001		P<.002		P<.001		
1. Unskilled/Semi-Skill.	77.9%	6.0%	80.0%	5.9%	65.4%	9.7%	62.6%	14.5%	54.1%	16.4%	38.5%	19.5%	207
2. Skilled/R. Non-Man.	81.5%	4.2%	76.2%	1.2%	65.2%	7.4%	67.2%	8.3%	62.6%	10.3%	47.1%	18.0%	328
3. Inspect./Supervisory	87.2%	0.0%	77.4%	4.6%	64.1%	9.2%	65.1%	9.3%	63.2%	15.0%	42.4%	28.8%	133
4. Professional/Exec.	83.8%	2.6%	82.7%	0.5%	73.8%	4.1%	75.3%	2.6%	67.0%	4.7%	54.7%	15.2%	191
Score Variation	*9.6%*	*6.0%*	*6.5^*	*5.4%*	*9.7%*	*5.6%*	*12.7%*	*11.9%*	*12.9%*	*11.7%*	*16.2%*	*13.6%*	*859*
I. Social Class Position	P<.001		P<.001		P<.001		P<.001		P<.001		P<.001		
1. Class I "Upper Class"	76.3%	0.0%	78.9%	0.0%	69.2%	12.8%	74.4%	0.0%	68.4%	0.0%	63.2%	23.7%	38
2. Class II "Upr-Middle Cls"	84.9%	2.9%	84.8%	0.7%	77.3%	2.1%	76.8%	2.9%	67.6%	4.3%	55.4%	8.6%	140
3. Class III "Mid-Middle Cl"	79.8%	0.4%	71.8%	2.6%	60.2%	9.7%	62.5%	7.2%	62.3%	9.2%	43.9%	23.7%	226
4. Class IV "Working Class"	82.9%	1.4%	78.9%	3.3%	65.7%	8.3%	65.9%	11.4%	57.5%	17.1%	42.3%	19.0%	361
5. Class V "Lower Class"	83.3%	1.2%	84.7%	5.9%	71.1%	6.0%	69.4%	13.0%	62.4%	9.4%	42.9%	25.0%	83
Score Variation	*8.6%*	*2.9%*	*13.0%*	*5.9%*	*17.1%*	*10.7%*	*14.3%*	*13.0%*	*11.0%*	*17.1%*	*20.9%*	*16.4%*	*848*
J. Political Party Prefer.	P<.001		P<.001		P<.001		P<.003		P<.001		P<.001		
1. Fianna Fáil	86.8%	0.7%	78.7%	1.7%	68.8%	7.2%	67.1%	7.2%	58.6%	12.5%	45.4%	22.0%	304
2. Fine Gael	84.5%	1.6%	74.3%	4.7%	61.5%	11.4%	61.3%	12.0%	59.2%	11.0%	42.2%	22.4%	192
3. Labour	79.7%	0.0%	79.4%	0.0%	59.4%	4.7%	71.4%	4.8%	67.7%	3.1%	44.3%	11.5%	64
4. Greens	57.6%	0.0%	57.6%	6.8%	52.5%	6.8%	45.8%	6.8%	43.3%	11.7%	39.3%	14.8%	60
5. Sinn Féin	75.6%	6.7%	82.2%	4.4%	61.4%	13.6%	75.6%	4.4%	65.9%	13.7%	47.8%	24.0%	46
6. PDs/Independents	82.2%	6.6%	81.8%	2.3%	70.5%	15.9%	68.2%	13.6%	64.4%	15.5%	36.4%	15.9%	44
Score Variations	*29.6%*	*6.7%*	*24.6%*	*6.8%*	*18.0%*	*11.2%*	*22.4%*	*9.2%*	*24.4%*	*12.4%*	*23.8%*	*12.8%*	*710*

Note: Scores above the sample average are **in bold.** (Variations are in *italics*.)

3.2 Variable Performance:
The value of examining the performances of the different personal variables is to detect if there are clues as to the causes of the variations. It is also possible to see the extent to which the variations are similar to those recorded in relation to other stimulus categories, i.e. ethnic, racial, religious, class, etc. Deviations from the 'normal' patterns of variation will be interpreted below.

3.2.1 Age: The results in the case of 'age' are, once again, contrary to the expectation that social distance and age would be correlated positively. In each of the five categories with significant variations by age, the youngest age group were **below** the sample average in 'admission to kinship' and **above** average in four of the five categories when it came to the 'denial of citizenship'. With the exception of 'Capitalists' and 'Communists', the oldest age-group, '71 years plus', were well above average in welcoming 'Gardaí', 'Trade Unionists' and 'Unionists' into kinship. This age group was also above average in denying members of these categories citizenship. The **26 to 40 year-olds** were also once again among the most tolerant age group towards all categories. Otherwise, the results are quite mixed by age.

3.2.2 Gender: The only stimulus category to elicit a statistically significant variation by gender was 'Unionists'. The other five categories had consensus between males and females which is further evidence of the homogenisation of male-female attitudes. This finding points to a degree of gender homogenisation in relation to 'Socialists', 'Capitalists', 'Communists' and 'Gardaí'.

In the case of social distance towards 'Unionists', males have above-average scores in 'admission to kinship' and 'denial of citizenship'. The score variations are minimal.

3.2.3 Marital Status: Two stimulus categories, 'Socialists' and 'Communists', failed to register a statistically significant variation, i.e. there was consensus between the sub-variables. Respondents living in 'permanent relationships' were the least tolerant of the subsamples in relation to the four categories with significant variations, i.e. 'Gardaí, 'Trade Unionists', 'Unionists' and 'Capitalists'.

The influence of the age-factor affects the relatively low tolerance of the 'single/never married' in relation to the 'Gardaí', 'Unionists' and

'Capitalists'.   'Married', 'widowed' and 'separated/divorced', i.e. sub-variables likely to have children, returned relatively tolerant scores for 'Gardaí' and 'Unionists'.

3.2.4 Area of Birth: This variable measured the influence of the urban-rural background of respondents on their attitudes towards the different political categories.   With the exception of the 'Gardaí', those born in 'Rural/Village' areas were least tolerant.   In the case of 'Unionists', 'Capitalists' and 'Communists', the 'Rural/Village' respondents were below average in 'admission to kinship', and above average in 'denying citizenship'.   Those with an urban background were more tolerant.   There was a consensus in social distance towards 'Trade Unionists' and 'Socialists'.

3.2.5 Place of Rearing and Region of Residence: These two variables are nominal and they focus on the influence of the regions where respondents were reared and now live.   Both variables are influenced by the proportions of population of urban and rural backgrounds and variations in the age structure of the sub-variables.

'Place of Rearing' is restricted to those reared in the Republic of Ireland.   One of the six stimulus categories, 'Trade Unionists', produced a consensus response.   The response-pattern for the 'Gardaí' is different to that for the other four categories, i.e. 'Unionists', 'Socialists', 'Capitalists' and 'Communists'.   'Connaught/Ulster'-reared respondents were least tolerant towards all five categories, while 'Munster'-reared were overall the most tolerant sub-variables.   The 'Dublin'-reared had above-average percentages 'admitting to kinship' in the case of the four categories.

The patterns in regard to **'Region of Residence'** are quite varied. Respondents from the BMW regions seem to be the least tolerant of five of the six categories, 'Trade Unionists' being the exception.   'Mid-West and South West' respondents follow the pattern of the 'Munster'-reared and display an ethos of greater tolerance across the board.   Score variations (between the subsamples) have been exceptionally high in relation to 'denial of citizenship' for 'Unionists', 'Socialists' and 'Capitalists, i.e. 12.7%, 12.9% and 14.9% respectively.   These figures confirm the influence of region of residence on people's political attitudes.   The higher average level of polarisation (between those 'admitting to kinship' and respondents 'denying citizenship') is characteristic of social-distance responses to less favoured stimulus categories[4].   This is particularly true for the social distance patterns of 'Communists' where almost one-quarter (**23.9%**) of the 'BMW' respondents would 'deny them citizenship'.

3.2.6 Educational Standard Reached: This ordinal variable has elicited statistically significant variations in the case of all six political categories. The patterns are not as anticipated.   The lesser educated seem to be more tolerant than better-schooled respondents in their social distance towards 'Gardaí', 'Trade Unionists', 'Unionists' and 'Socialists'.   Attitudes towards 'Capitalists' and 'Communists' are mixed.

The explanation of the failure of 'educational standard reached' to return a positive correlation with measures of social tolerance is (as has been noted earlier in this text) not easy to explain.   It must challenge the liberating effects of education on social attitudes in the Republic of Ireland over the past thirty years or more.   This is also related to the socialisation **practices** of the youth in general, who performed (18 to 25 year-olds) more negatively than expected.   Because of the relatively high proportion of young people in the third-level subsample, the youth factor would inevitably affect the findings of that group and *vice versa* (see Table No. 7.8, page 158 above).

3.2.7 Occupational Status: The six political stimulus categories have registered statistically significant variations between the occupational sub-samples.   In the case of 'Unionists', 'Socialists', 'Capitalists' and 'Communists', the response patterns were as anticipated.   The 'Gardaí' responses were contrary to expectations, i.e. the lower statuses were more tolerant.   In regard to 'Trade Unionists', the results were mixed with the 'Unskilled/Semi-Skilled' and the 'Professional/Executive' being the most tolerant subsamples.

3.2.8 Social Class Position: This variable measures the impact of social status on respondents' social-distance scores towards the six political categories.   As already stated, the five classes were based on the Hollingshead system of combining educational achievement and occupational status (see Chapter VIII, Table No. 8.14).

---

[4] See: Mac Gréil, Micheál, *Prejudice and Tolerance in Ireland*, Dublin, C.I.R. 1977, page 248.

The findings of Table No. 15.2(i) are quite mixed across the range of the six categories. The clearest pattern appears in the case of 'Communists', i.e. there is a positive correlation between social-class position and tolerance towards 'Communists'. The "Middle-Middle Class" had relatively lower tolerance scores towards 'Gardaí', 'Trade Unionists', 'Unionists', 'Socialists' and 'Communists', i.e. the subsample had below-average percentages admitting members of the five categories into kinship.

3.2.9 Political Party Preference (Irish Born): Table No. 15.2(j) gives a breakdown of the responses by political party preference at the time of surveying between November 2007 and March 2008. Political party preference polls during 2009 and late 2008 (after the downturn in the Irish economy) report a fairly radical change in the popularity of the main Government party, *Fianna Fáil*. Some 30% of respondents (in 2007-08) stated that "they would not vote" or they "did not know".

Fianna Fáil supporters were above average in 'admitting to kinship' in the case of five of the six categories and were slightly below average (-2.1%) for one political category, i.e. 'Capitalists'. *Fine Gael* supporters were above average in admitting two categories to kinship, i.e. 'Gardaí' and 'Capitalists'. *Labour Party* supporters were above average in admitting to family in regard to 'Trade Unionists', 'Socialists', 'Capitalists' and 'Communists'. *Sinn Féin* supporters showed tolerant dispositions towards 'Trade Unionists', 'Socialists', 'Capitalists' and 'Communists'. The *Green Party* supporters were the least tolerant towards any of the political stimulus categories.

Since political party preference is not an ordinal variable, there is not much of a theoretical nature that can be deduced from the above findings. The differences between the dispositions of the parties' supporters may be of interest to the political scientist.

3.3 Individual Political Categories by Personal Variables:
In Section 3.2 above, the emphasis was on the performance of each personal variable by the six stimulus political categories. The measures used were 'admission to kinship' and 'denial of citizenship'. In the case of this section, the emphasis will be on each of the six political categories. The measure used will be the mean-social-distance scores (involving Kinship, Friendship, Next-door Neighbour, Co-worker, Citizenship, Visitor Only and Debar or Deport levels of closeness). The mean-social-distance score is

within a range of one to seven.   It is noted that there is a higher incidence of N/S (non-significant) variations in Table No. 15.3 than was the case in Table No.15.2 when only two measures, i.e. kinship and denial of citizenship were considered.

It will be clear from the findings of Table No. 15.3 that a high proportion of the sub-scales returned a non-significant (N/S) result, meaning the *chi-square* p-score was more than 0.050.   This indicates a high level of consensus in the case of the sub-scales in question.   It should be noted that the **higher** the MSD scores, the **lower** the level of tolerance.

Table No. 15.3:
Social Distance towards Political Categories (Mean-Social-Distance)
by Personal Variables

Personal Variable	Gardaí	Trade Un.	Unionists	Socialists	Capitalists	Communists	No.
Total Sample	**1.392**	**1.552**	**1.944**	**1.990**	**2.297**	**2.920**	**1,015**
A. Age	P<.001	N/S	P<.025	N/S	P<.011	P<.001	
1. 18-25 years	**1.648**	---	**2.316**	---	**2.685**	2.983	168
2. 26-40 years	1.385	---	1.916	---	2.109	2.559	325
3. 41-55 years	**1.412**	---	**1.787**	---	**2.394**	2.935	245
4. 56-70 years	1.225	---	1.919	---	2.067	**3.185**	178
5. 71 years plus	1.225	---	1.837	---	**2.420**	**3.506**	96
Score Variation	*0.423*	---	*0.529*	---	*0.618*	*0.946*	*1,012*
B. Marital Status	P<.001	N/S	N/S	N/S	P<.012	N/S	
1. Single/Never Married	**1.554**	---	---	---	**2.558**	---	356
2. Married	1.239	---	---	---	2.075	---	468
3. Separated/Divorced	1.329	---	---	---	**2.448**	---	44
4. Permanent Relationship	**1.702**	---	---	---	2.311	---	72
5. Widowed	1.320	---	---	---	2.342	---	69
Score Variation	*0.463*	---	---	---	*0.483*	---	*1,009*
C. Area of Birth	P<.028	N/S	P<.004	N/S	N/S	P<.001	
1. City (100,000 plus)	**1.506**	---	1.783	---	---	2.824	419
2. Large Town (10,000 +)	1.295	---	1.842	---	---	2.762	119
3. Town (1,500 plus)	1.360	---	1.857	---	---	2.252	132
4. Rural/Village	1.301	---	**2.209**	---	---	**3.349**	345
Score Variation	*0.211*	---	*0.426*	---	---	*1.097*	*1,015*
D. Place of Rearing (ROI)	N/S	N/S	P<.008	P<.015	N/S	N/S	
1. Dublin (City & County)	---	---	1.741	1.893	---	---	243
2. Rest of Leinster	---	---	**2.309**	**2.390**	---	---	157
3. Munster	---	---	1.936	1.915	---	---	219
4. Connaught/Ulster	---	---	**1.987**	1.870	---	---	154
Score Variation	---	---	*0.568*	*0.520*	---	---	*773*

Table No. 15.3 Cont'd. Personal Variable	Gardaí	Trade Un.	Unionists	Socialists	Capitalists	Communists	No.
E. Region of Residence	P<.031	P<.003	P<.001	P<.001	P<.001	P<.002	
1. BMW (Border Mids. West)	**1.494**	**1.648**	**2.281**	**2.308**	**2.696**	**3.347**	269
2. Dublin	**1.452**	1.513	1.658	1.734	2.126	2.703	284
3. Mid-East & South-East	1.246	**1.726**	**2.286**	**2.356**	**2.633**	2.866	218
4. Mid-West & Sth-West	1.337	1.329	1.587	1.603	1.739	2.737	234
Score Variation	*0.157*	*0.397*	*0.699*	*0.755*	*0.957*	*0.644*	*1,005*
F. Education	N/S	N/S	N/S	N/S	P<.008	P<.001	
1. Primary or Less	---	---	---	---	2.474	**3.263**	117
2. Incomplete Sec.-Level	---	---	---	---	**2.583**	**3.153**	262
3. Complete Second-Level	---	---	---	---	2.265	**3.082**	255
4. Third-Level	---	---	---	---	2.068	2.544	381
Score Variation	---	---	---	---	*0.515*	*0.719*	*1,015*
G. Occupational Status	N/S	N/S	N/S	P<.001	P<.001	P<.002	
1. Unskilled/Semi-Skilled	---	---	---	**2.350**	**2.676**	**3.277**	207
2. Skilled/Routine Non-M.	---	---	---	1.948	2.209	2.894	328
3. Inspectional/Supervisory	---	---	---	1.900	2.215	**3.166**	133
4. Professional/Executive	---	---	---	1.601	1.926	2.466	191
Score Variation	---	---	---	*0.749*	*0.750*	*0.811*	*859*
H. Social Class Position	N/S	N/S	P<.010	P<.002	P<.001	P<.001	
1. Class I: "Upper Class"	---	---	**2.025**	1.570	1.888	2.511	38
2. Class II: "Upr-Mid Class"	---	---	1.510	1.514	1.807	2.210	140
3. Class III: "Mid.-Mid. Cl"	---	---	**2.060**	1.951	2.110	**3.009**	226
4. Class IV: "Working Class"	---	---	**2.033**	**2.169**	**2.595**	**3.154**	361
5. Class V: "Lower Class"	---	---	1.736	**2.041**	2.206	**3.261**	83
Score Variation	---	---	*0.550*	*0.655*	*0.788*	*1.051*	*848*

Note: Scores above the sample average are **in bold**.　(Variations are in *italics*.)

It is noteworthy that **'Gender'** as a variable failed to elicit a statistically significant variation in any of the political stimulus categories. This is a further confirmation of the homogenisation of male and female attitudes.

3.3.1 'Gardaí':　The 'Gardaí' elicited a consensus response for 'place of rearing', 'education', 'occupational status' and 'social-class position'. This is in part due to the relatively low level of social distance (**1.392**) and to generally positive attitudes towards 'Gardaí' in the Republic of Ireland. They are one of the country's 'in-groups'.

'Age' and 'Marital Status' had the largest 'score-variations', i.e. over 0.400.　The following extract spells out the poles of the variation:

Variable	Score Variation	Highest (Least Tolerant)		Between	Lowest (Most Tolerant)		MSD
1. **Marital Status**	0.463	Perm.Relationships	**(1.702)**	and	Married	**(1.239)**	1.392
2. **Age**	0.423	18 to 25 yrs	**(1.648)**	and 41-55 yrs & 71 yrs+	**(1.025)**		1.392

Sub-variables with the highest score are the least tolerant, i.e. people living in permanent relationships and the 18 to 25 year-olds, while married and the age groups 56-70 year-olds and the 71 years-plus, were the most tolerant and welcoming towards the 'Gardaí'. It is important for the Gardaí to have the 'married subsample' so strongly on their side. The married constitute 46.4% of the sample.

The relatively higher level of social-distance between the young people ('18 to 25 year-olds') is part of a pattern in the overall social distance results. The score of **1.648**, although outside the 'in-group' range, is still indicative of a potentially good disposition between the young age group and the 'Gardaí'. Table No. 15.2(a) reported that **71.0%** would welcome 'Gardaí' into the family while **4.2%** would deny them citizenship. Better liaison between Gardaí and the under '18 to 25 year-olds' might reduce the hostility of the minority within that subsample!

3.3.2 'Trade Unionists': Only one of eight personal variables registered a statistically significant variation in relation to this stimulus category. This reflects a unique level of consensus towards 'Trade Unionists' which is most significant in itself. This is indicative of the cross-class representation of 'Trade Unions' in Irish society. The high participation of the middle-class white-collar workers in the unions has removed the "working class" and "lower class" image. Years of 'Social Partnership' had eroded the spectacle of strikes and public demonstrations (prior to the collapse of the financial system). In their participation with the political and economic establishments, they may appear to have **de-radicalised** and ceased to be the campaigning advocates for the lowly paid and underclass of society! Their prophetic voice may have been quietened! Such consensus points in that direction or else the whole population is now firmly on the radical left – which is hard to substantiate!

'Region of Residence' was the only variable to elicit a significant (statistically) variation for all political stimulus categories. The residents of Munster, i.e. 'Mid-West and South West', were the most tolerant (**MSD**

1.329), while the 'Mid-East and South East' regions registered the least welcoming score, i.e. **1.726**. This result is in line with most other findings, namely, the ethos of greatest tolerance among Munster-reared and those residing in Munster regions. The significance of 'Region of Residence' in relation to statistically significant variations in MSD scores is quite clear from Table No. 15.3(e) where each of the six political categories registered *chi-square* p-scores of **<.050**.

3.3.3 'Unionists': This stimulus category elicited significant variations in five of the eight personal variables. 'Marital Status', 'Education' and 'Occupational Status' returned a consensus result, which was not anticipated. 'Age', 'Area of Birth', 'Place of Rearing', 'Region of Residence' and 'Social Class Position' all produced substantial 'score variations' within the variables listed. The following extract from Table No. 15.3 gives the details of these variations:

Variable (in order of variation)	Score Variation	Highest (Least Tolerant)		Between	Lowest (Most Tolerant)		MSD
1. **Region of Residence**	0.699	Mid-East & Sth.E	(**2.286**)	and	Mid-W. & Sth. W	(**1.587**)	1.944
2. **Place of Rearing**	0.568	Rest of Leinster	(**2.309**)	and	Dublin (City &Co.)	(**1.741**)	1.944
3. **Social Class Position**	0.550	"Mid-Mid Class"	(**2.060**)	and	"Upr-Mid. Class"	(**1.510**)	1.944
4. **Age**	0.479	18 to 25 yr-olds	(**2.316**)	and	71 yrs plus	(**1.837**)	1.944
5. **Area of Birth**	0.426	Rural/Village	(**2.209**)	and	City (100,000+)	(**1.783**)	1.944

The subsamples expressing greatest tolerance have the **lowest** Mean-Social-Distance scores while the **highest** MSD score represent the sub-samples with the least tolerance. 'Area of Birth', which tests the influence of urbanisation, performed according to expectations in that those for the least urbanised area of birth were least tolerant while respondents born in the city were most tolerant of 'Unionists'. The performance of 'Age' was the opposite of what was anticipated. It is interesting to note the extreme scores between the 'Social Class Position' subsamples were within the middle-class range. The performance of 'Region of Residence' and 'Place of Rearing' shows a high degree of internal consistency and the significance of the geographic factor.

385

3.3.4 Socialists: Four personal variables registered statistically significant variations between variable subsamples for their stimulus category. Each had a substantial 'score-variation' i.e. 'Place of Rearing', 'Region of Residence', 'Occupational Status' and 'Social Class Position'. The three variables recording consensus in relation to 'Socialists' were 'Age', 'Marital Status', 'Area of Birth' and 'Education'. The following extract from Table No. 15.3 spells out the difference between the five variables with significant variations:

Variable	Score Variation	Highest (Least Tolerant)	Between	Lowest (Most Tolerant)	MSD
1. **Region of Residence**	0.755	Mid-East & Sth.East (**2.358**)	and	Mid-W. & Sth.W (**1.603**)	1.990
2. **Occupational Status**	0.749	Unskill/Semi-Skil. (**2.350**)	and	Profess./Exec. (**1.601**)	1.990
3. **Social Class Position**	0.655	"Working Class" (**2.169**)	and	"Upr.Mid.Class" (**1.514**)	1.990
4. **Place of Rearing**	0.568	Rest of Leinster (**2.309**)	and	Dublin City (**1.741**)	1.990

The above findings may surprise some readers and leaders of socialist movements. The "Working class", 'lower skilled' and 'lower educated' were least attracted toward 'Socialists', while 'Professional/Executive', "Upper Middle Class" and 'Third Level' respondents were the most tolerant towards them. 'Region of Residence' repeated the results of the 'Unionists' scores. 'Place of Rearing' saw 'Connaught/Ulster' as the least prejudiced against 'Socialists'!

3.3.5 'Capitalists': Six variables returned statistically significant variations toward 'Capitalists'. The two variables with consensus were 'Area of Birth' and 'Place of Rearing'. The score variations in the case of the six significantly different variables were very substantial. The following extract from Table No. 15.3 shows the pattern of variation between the subsamples:

Variable	Score Variation	Highest (Least Tolerant)	Between	Lowest (Most Tolerant)	MSD
1. **Region of Residence**	0.957	BMW Regions (**2.696**)	and	Mid-W. & Sth.W. (**1.739**)	2.297
2. **Social Class Position**	0.788	"Working Class" (**2.595**)	and	"Upr Mid.Class" (**1.807**)	2.297
3. **Occupational Status**	0.750	Unskilled/Semi-Sk. (**2.676**)	and	Prof. /Exec. (**1.926**)	2.297
4. **Age**	0.618	18-25 yr. olds (**2.685**)	and	56-70 yr. olds (**2.067**)	2.297
5. **Education**	0.515	Incomplete 2nd Lev. (**2.583**)	and	Third Level (**2.068**)	2.297
6. **Marital Status**	0.483	Single/Never Married (**2.558**)	and	Married (**2.075**)	2.297

'Education', 'Occupational Status' and 'Social Class Position' have responded to 'Capitalists' more or less as anticipated. The performance of 'Age' has, once again, gone against expectations in that the younger age group was the least tolerant. It is interesting to compare the responses to 'Capitalists' and 'Socialists' and discover a similar pattern, especially in the case of 'Social-Class Position', 'Occupational Status' and 'Education'. This would reinforce the basic centrist ideological position of Irish political opinion, with a moderate 'left' tendency! The relatively high MSD (**2.696**) of respondents from the 'BMW Regions' which represents a low-level of tolerance towards 'Capitalists' among respondents is an interesting result and is in line with this subsample's above-average MSD scores for each of the six categories [see Table No. 15.3(e)].

3.3.6 'Communists': Six variables registered a statistically significant variation in relation to 'Communists'. As expected, this category recorded some of the highest score variations which points to the wide range of attitudes. Two of the personal variables, i.e. Marital Status and Place of Rearing failed to elicit a statistically significant variation between the scores of their sub-variables. The six personal variables to register significant variations were: Age, Area of Birth, Region of Residence, Education, Occupational Status and Social Class Position. The following extract from Table No. 15.3 shows the pattern of variable score-variations:

Variable	Score Variation	Highest (Least Tolerant)		Between	Lowest (Most Tolerant)		MSD
1. **Area of Birth**	1.097	Rural Village	(**3.349**)	and	Town	(**2.252**)	2.920
2. **Social Class Position**	1.051	"Lower Class"	(**3.261**)	and	"Upr.Mid.Class"	(**2.210**)	2.920
3. **Age**	0.946	71 Years Plus	(**3.506**)	and	26 to 40 Years	(**2.559**)	2.920
4. **Occupational Status**	0.874	Unskilled/Semi-Sk..	(**3.277**)	and	Prof. /Exec.	(**2.466**)	2.920
5. **Education**	0.719	Primary or Less	(**3.263**)	and	Third Level	(**2.544**)	2.920
6. **Region of Residence**	0.644	BMW Regions	(**3.347**)	and	Dublin	(**2.703**)	2.920

The above extract (from Table No. 15.3, pages 382-3) highlights the very wide diversity of dispositions that exist in the adult population in the Republic of Ireland towards 'Communists' in six of the eight personal variables showing statistically significant variations on Table No. 15.3. Three of the variations were greater than one stage on the Bogardus one-to-seven scale. 'Social Class Position', 'Age' and 'Urban-Rural' Background performed more or less as expected. 'Education' and 'Occupational Status' were quite mixed.

For many people 'Communists' are still an **out-group** in the Republic of Ireland, i.e. with MSD score of 3.000 or over. The total sample's mean-social-distance (MSD) score is just under 3.000 at **2.920**. While this marks a substantial reduction between 1988-89 when it was **3.769** and 2007-08 (at **2.920**), it is still quite intolerant.

3.3.7 Conclusion: The level of consensus on Table No. 15.3 (in twenty-two of the forty-eight sub-tables) was more than anticipated, because of the substantial levels of social distance in four of the categories, i.e. 'Unionists', 'Socialists', 'Capitalists' and 'Communists'. Consensus would have been expected in the case of 'Gardaí' and 'Trade Unionists' because of their relatively low MSD scores. The score variations for 'Gardaí' in the 'Age' and 'Marital Status' variables were higher than expected and merit reflection. The influence of geographic 'Place of Rearing' and 'Region of Residence' is significant as is the 'Urban/Rural' background.

Overall, it is difficult to conclude the extent to which Irish adults are ideologically 'right' or 'left'. In Part IV the party political preferences of the sample of Irish-born will be examined in order to gauge further where they stand on the political spectrum. From the above findings it seems that respondents are **centrist** with a tendency towards the **'left'** ideological wing!

Part IV – Political Party Preference

4.1 Political Parties in Republic of Ireland:

In 2007-08 in Ireland, i.e. the Republic of Ireland as distinct from Northern Ireland, there were six political parties with a number of seats in the Houses of the *Oireachtas*, namely, *Dáil Éireann* and *Seanad Éireann*. At the time of the survey a new coalition Government was formed from *Fianna Fáil*, the *Green Party* and *Progressive Democrats* with the promised support of a number of non-party members. The leader of the Government changed in 2008, when *An Taoiseach*, **Bertie Ahern, T.D.** retired and **Brian Cowen, T.D.** was appointed leader in his place, i.e. became *An Taoiseach*.

It should also be noted that the two previous Governments since the General Election of 1997 until the time of the survey were led by *Fianna Fáil* (**1997 to 2002**: *Fianna Fáil* and *Progressive Democrats,* and **2002 to 2007**: *Fianna Fáil* and *Progressive Democrats*). The *Progressive Democrat Party* decided to 'wind-up' its operations as a political party in 2008 with elected members continuing as Independent/Non-Party members of the *Oireachtas.* In March 2011, *Fine Gael* and the *Labour Party* formed a Government, following a General Election. **Mr Enda Kenny**, T.D. was elected *Taoiseach.*

Anthony Giddens[5] in his celebrated text, *Sociology*, points to the significant role played by political parties in modern societies.

> "Party defines a group of individuals who work together because they have common backgrounds, aims or interests". [Giddens (2006), p.303]

Political Parties may be class-based, religion-based or cover a wide spectrum of social class and social status. Centrist parties tend to be multi-class in their base. Table No. 15.4 gives political party preference by social class position.

Table No. 15.4:
Political Party Preference by Social Class Position
(Excluding "Would Not Vote" and "Don't Know")

Social Class Position	Fianna Fáil	Fine Gael	Labour	Greens	Sinn Féin	PD & Ind.	Total Sample
1. Class I: "Upper Class"	3.9%	**8.6%**	4.1%	**7.1%**	2.5%	0.0%	**5.2%**
2. Class II: "Upr-Mid. Class"	**24.1%**	14.2%	14.3%	**32.1%**	0.0%	21.6%	**19.6%**
3. Class III: "Mid.-Mid.Class"	24.1%	**35.2%**	14.3%	**28.6%**	12.5%	13.5%	**25.3%**
4. Class IV: "Working Class"	40.1%	38.3%	**55.1%**	26.8%	**52.5%**	**54.1%**	**41.3%**
5. Class V: "Lower Class"	7.8%	3.7%	**12.2%**	5.4%	**32.5%**	**10.8%**	**8.7%**
Totals:	257	162	49	56	40	37	601

Note: Percentages above the total sample average are **in bold.**

---

[5] Giddens, Anthony, *Sociology,* (Fifth Edition), Cambridge, Polity Press, 2006

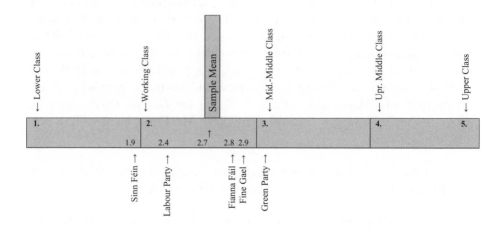

Figure No. 15.1: Mean Social Class Position of Political Party Preferences[6]

The above Table and Figure give a good picture of the make-up of support for Irish Political Parties in the Republic between November 2007 and March 2008.   The class-base of each party is very interesting.   *Fianna Fáil* is the most representative across the board and closest to the **sample mean** (of **2.7**) at **2.8**.   Support for *Sinn Féin* at **1.9** and *Labour* at **2.4** comes mainly from the "Working Class" and the "Lower Class".   *Fine Gael* at **2.9** and the *Greens* at **3.0** are based slightly higher on the social ladder.

4.2 Party Loyalty:
It is frequently said that Irish people have tended to be loyal to their political party of choice down the years, because of nationalist or social-class allegiances.   The late British Prime Minister, Harold Wilson, M.P., was reported to have noted that Governments were defeated more as a result of party supporters' abstention (which he called "selective abstention") rather than changing party allegiances.   If this is true then the Political Party who can persuade its followers to vote wins!

---

[6] *Sinn Féin* = **1.9**; *Labour* = **2.4**; *Fianna Fáil* = **2.8**; *Fine Gael* = **2.9**; *Greens* = **3.0**;
  Sample Mean = 2.7

Table No. 15.5 gives the response of the sample to the question on their previous voting patterns. The responses showed a fairly 'loyal' support for their party of preference in the case of the three main parties in the *Oireachtas*.

Table No. 15.5:
Previous Voting Patterns for Party of Preference of Irish-Born
(excluding "Would Not Vote" and "Don't Know")

Political Party of Preference	Regularly	Occasionally	Never	Number
1. Fianna Fáil	**82.6%**	14.6%	2.8%	288
2. Fine Gael	74.7%	**23.0%**	2.2%	178
3. Labour	71.7%	**22.6%**	**5.7%**	53
4. Green Party	59.2%	**30.6%**	**10.2%**	49
5. Sinn Féin	55.0%	**35.0%**	**10.0%**	40
6. PDs & Independents	65.0%	**22.5%**	**12.5%**	40
Sample Average	**75.0%**	20.5%	4.5%	648

Note: Percentages above the total sample average are **in bold.**

When interpreting the findings of Table No. 15.5, it must be remembered that these are the views of respondents (Irish-born) **who intended to vote** at the time of interview. The following is a breakdown of the voting intentions in Irish-born respondents.

Voting Intentions[7]	Irish-Born Respondents	
	Number	Percentage
1. "Intended to Vote"	656	79.2%
2. "Would Not Vote"	124	15.0%
3. "Don't Know"	48	5.7%
Total	828	100.1%

From the above figures it is possible to gauge the likely level of **voter volatility** in the Republic of Ireland. It would appear that Harold Wilson's **selective abstentionism** is the likely cause of change of Governments in regard to main party shifts in the Irish population. The opinion polls during 2009-11 as published in the newspapers would indicate a deeper change.

---

[7] Voting Intentions of the 79.2% of the sample were as follows:
Fianna Fáil = 44.1%; *Fine Gael* = 27.3%; *Labour* = 8.4%;
Green Party = 7.5%; *Sinn Féin* = 6.3%; *PDs & Independents* = 6.4%.

That change is still within the **20.7%** of those who said they "would not vote" or "didn't know". Also, the opinions recorded here are from within the Irish-born respondents. The influence of the 15% non-Irish-born citizens showed there would be less opportunity to establish traditional party loyalties. The results of the General Election held on the 25th February 2011 (which confirmed opinion polls conducted in the lead-up to the election) would seem to indicate a deeper change in political party preferences in the Republic of Ireland than heretofore experienced. It would be interesting to analyse the party preferences of those who did not vote in order to test the 'selective abstentionism' hypothesis.

The stability or change of Irish Party preference between the 1988-89 survey and that of 2007-08 is quite interesting.

Political Party	A 1988-89	B 2007-08	Change (A – B)
1. Fianna Fáil	52%	44%	-8%
2. Fine Gael	29%	27%	-2%
3. Labour	8%	8%	±0%

Despite the changes, the above movements in political party support show how relatively stable the pattern of political allegiance has been in the Republic. The two main political parties, i.e. *Fianna Fáil* and *Fine Gael,* owe their origin in the political divisions resulting from disagreement over the *Anglo-Irish Agreement of 1922.* The reasons for the division included the Partition of Ireland into what later became **Northern Ireland** (or "The Six Counties") and **The Irish Free State** (or "The Twenty-Six Counties"). Each of the two parties represented the interests of a wide social-status spectrum (as is still evident in Table No. 15.4). This, in turn, may have hindered the rotation of Left-Right Governments, as was the case in Great Britain.

The political divisions in Northern Ireland were between Unionists and Nationalists – each representing a wide social-status spectrum. Also, the net effect of these political party divisions in the Republic of Ireland and in Northern Ireland was to have changes of Governments without greatly upsetting the left-right ideological balance. In other words, most, if not all, of Irish administrations were more or less rotations of **centrist** political parties!

Taking the long-term view it is possible to note that the State has been able to cope with changes of fortune and come through periods of political crisis for almost ninety years without conceding to extreme anti-democratic methods or structures. This is not to say that there were not inadequacies in the quality of Governments from time to time. The **rule of law** has survived periods of emergency (external and internal), i.e. the Civil War of the early 1920s, the Economic War of the 1930s, the Rise of Fascism in Continental Europe, the 1939-46 Emergency, the Northern Ireland Troubles and a number of economic recessions. Of course, there have been occasions of dissatisfaction with political measures at times but the resource of the Supreme Court to test the constitutionality of such procedures has always been available.

The future of the 'Nation State' is at present being challenged by measures to increase the role of the *European Union's Central Administration*. The Irish people have by their recent voting patterns in EU Referenda expressed a desire to protect their freedom and independence while, at the same time, being willing to support the European project as an **interdependent system**. The findings of this survey show that there is a broad welcome for people of other nations who come and work in the Republic of Ireland.

4.3 Conclusion:

The aim of the above information and commentary on the political party preferences of the sample has been to provide the reader with an important dimension of Irish society. Political parties are essential for the successful operation of parliamentary democracies. With the growing power and influence of commercially owned (often multinationally based) public media, whose interests may not coincide with those of the citizens or with their culture, it is important to maintain the democratic power of the State and the right of the Irish people to protect their independence in order to pursue their needs and the 'common good'.

The socio-economic base of the political parties on Table No. 15.4 points to the concentration on the 'centre' for the *Green Party, Fine Gael* and *Fianna Fáil*. The *Labour Party's* base was left of centre while *Sinn Féin* was mainly "Working Class" and "Lower Class". *Fianna Fáil* is closest to the class spread of the general population! The strength of traditional party loyalty is measured in Table No. 15.5, i.e. by party preference.   The opinion that *'selective abstentionism'* rather than change of party allegiance can result in the loss of power for a particular party can be the case in societies like the Republic of Ireland.   This is unless extraordinary socio-political circumstances prevail from time to time!

Part V – Conclusion

In the course of this chapter an effort has been made to measure and comment on Irish political attitudes as indicated by the results of the social distance of the sample towards six 'political' categories, i.e. 'Gardaí', 'Trade Unionists', 'Unionists', 'Socialists', 'Capitalists' and 'Communists'.   The social distance of the 1988-89 and that of 2007-08 towards each of the categories was compared in order to point out changes which had taken place in the intervening nineteen years.   Political party allegiance and preference were also discussed.

There was an overall reduction in social distance (indicating a rise in tolerance) across the board except for the 'Gardaí', where there was a very moderate drop in closeness, while still remaining among Ireland's in-groups. The very substantial improvement in attitudes towards 'Unionists' indicated a positive move towards **integrated political pluralism**.   It also was a further endorsement of the peace and integration process in Northern Ireland and the acceptance of the *Good Friday Agreement* in 1998.

'Trade Unionists' were fast approaching 'in-group status' in the Republic of Ireland at the time of the interviews between November 2007 and March 2008.   This could be seen as an endorsement of 'social partnership' and the growth of the 'middle class' white-collar unions.   This *embourgeoisement* of the Trade Union Movement had, apparently, made it more acceptable to all classes!   Of course, these attitudes can change if socio-economic difficulties arise due to the downturn in the Irish economy.

This also reflects a shift in the nature of the employers.   The change over time from owner-manager to the employee-manager has also been accompanied by a parallel development of the Public Service (professional) manager in a wide range of public services.   The Public Service white-collar worker is a dominant part of the current Trade Union Movement, with the proportionate decline in private sector blue-collar worker membership.

Also, the younger Irish (native) workforce is more and more in pursuit of white-collar professions, partly because of the change in participation in education and training. Hence, the recent demand (prior to summer 2008) for blue-collar migrant workers "to hew the wood and draw the water"! This may change with the current downturn in the economy and Irish employee elitism would be forced to face a temporary reversal!

On the ideological front, Irish adults have become more tolerant towards 'Socialists', 'Capitalists' and 'Communists'. In terms of social preference, 'Capitalists' have become less preferred than 'Socialists' since 1988-89, while 'Communists' have maintained their low position at 50th out of 51 categories. Does this mean an ideological move to the 'left' – nineteen years after the fall of the 'Berlin Wall'? Or does it mean that 'socialism' has lost its threat to the current social order? It could also mean that Irish political attitudes have become 'pragmatic' and a-ideological!

The sliding in their position in the rank order (despite the increase in tolerance towards them) of 'Capitalists', at a time when the **'Celtic Tiger'** was still delivering the goods, raises a number of interesting questions. Unlike the original 'captains of industry', who lived relatively austerely, the new capitalists (super-managers and heavy investors) were distant from the work and the workers. In a real sense during the recent overdevelopment of some societies, work and wealth were divorced! This had been evident for some time and the image of 'the capitalist' in the mind of many people (even those who would support capitalism) seemed to have lost favour, relatively speaking. The rise of 'globalisation of capital', with the transferring of jobs from Ireland to countries with cheaper labour costs at the expense of the local workers, has hit Ireland badly in recent years and disrupted many communities. Speculation on the world's **stock markets** was seen to be 'playing or gambling' with people's livelihood. The anonymous 'Capitalist' and the risky pursuit of money by Banks and 'Financial Institutions' have, it would seem, contributed to the loss of status of the **'Capitalist'** in Irish society!

If Irish attitudes reflect those of other societies, the Western World could be at an **'ideological crossroads'** in the wake of the failure of **State Communism in 1989** and **Neo-Liberal Capitalism in 2008**. There may be more to read in the attitudes analysed in this chapter than appears on first glance at the findings. There is certainly a good case for serious economic, political and social research into the deeper causes of the failure of both systems, i.e. state communism and neo-liberal capitalism. Temporary patching-up of the current crisis should only "enable us to keep the trains running while we set about changing the station and the track"![8]

The fortunes of the political parties in the Republic of Ireland were changed radically in the General Election of 25th February 2011 when compared with the preferences indicated by the respondents reported above (see footnote number 7, page 391). The main governing party (*Fianna Fáil*) gained only 17.5% of the first preference vote in contrast to the 44.1% support in this survey carried out between November 2007 and March 2008 which was prior to the economic crisis leading to a severe recession. Opposition parties and independent candidates were to benefit from the collapse of government support (see *The Irish Times*, 28th February 2011). It would be interesting to find out the degree to which this drastic decline in support for *Fianna Fáil* was due to 'selective abstentionism' or to a change in party loyalty.

***

---

[8] Yinger, J. Milton, *The Scientific Study of Religion*, New York, Schocken Books, 1970.

CHAPTER XVI
The Irish Language

Part I – Introduction

1.1 The Nature of Culture:

The principal symbolic meaningful system of a people's culture is their language. By culture in this context is meant:

An interrelated set of beliefs/convictions, values, norms and symbolic meaningful systems, which characterise and influence the behaviour and the priorities of the people in their day-to-day living.

The above definition is derived from a whole series of definitions of culture by various cultural anthropologists and others[1] since the mid-19th century. The native language of a people incorporates the people's cultural memory and reflects their unique nuance on reality. Culture (and language) is a uniquely human trait. Not even the high primates have a culture. The symbol is at the core of culture. What is cultural in our lives is learned and is not instinctive, since instinct is the unlearned response to a particular need.

Culture is transmitted to the young, mostly informally, through primary socialisation, in the family, neighbourhood and other personal relations. Cultural diffusion happens through inter- or cross-cultural contact. The latter is caused by intercultural migration and visitation. The globalisation of the mass media has contributed to much cultural diffusion, often at the expense of the smaller cultures. Bureaucracy as a process tends to seek cultural uniformity and is a pressure for the assimilation or absorption of smaller cultures into one of the macro-cultures. In recent decades, there has been a timely reaction to this process and a move away from cultural assimilation towards a more culturally pluralist approach. This was evident in the case of the Travelling People, who are resisting their assimilation into mainstream Irish culture (see Chapter XIII above).

A special report, *The Irish Language and the Irish People*, based mainly on the findings of the 2007-08 national survey was published in

---

[1] See: Tylor (1871), Malinowski (1930), Benedict (1935), Kroeber (1948), Kluckhohn (1949), White (1949), Parsons (1954), Smelser (1962), Harris (1988)

2009[2]. The findings reported in this chapter do not exhaust those of the special report. Readers with a special interest in the Irish language are recommended to read the special report, which is published online. In a text dealing with **prejudice** and **tolerance** in Ireland, the people's attitudes towards the native language, their competence in and use of, Irish are relevant as independent and dependent variables. **The national language is a central ethnic trait**. It also influences the people's ethnic self-identity (see Chapter VIII, Part II, pages 167-172).

1.2 Preview of Findings:
The overall positive message emerging from the findings of the 2007-08 survey has been the continued increase in the support for the Irish language and competence in it by respondents with higher education and the more highly prestigious occupations. This trend had been identified in the findings of the 1988-89 national survey. It means that the crucially important 'social status' of Irish is on the increase in the Republic.

The reasons for the change in the social standing of the native language are multiple, and further research would be required to verify the causes. This has not been possible in this text because of constraints of time and resources. Hopefully, others will probe the causes in future surveys. Among the possible or probable causes of improvement in the social standing of Irish in the immediate past would be the raising of public awareness of Irish resulting from the public debate around the passing of *Acht na dTeangacha Oifigiula 2003* (*Official Languages Act 2003*) and the successful campaign for official status for Irish within the **European Union** in recent years. Previous research had already pointed to the growing status for the language for decades.

It will also be clear from the findings of the National Survey 2007-08 that the **most disappointing result** in the overall is the difference between **'reasonable' competence in (47%)** and **'regular' use of (23%) Irish**, i.e. for Irish-born respondents. The filling of this gap is a matter of priority. The high support for the **revival** and **preservation** of Irish should enable the State and others to take action to encourage popular changes in the patterns and occasions of use. The support of the State and of the voluntary

---

[2] Mac Gréil, Micheál, *The Irish Language and the Irish People*, Maynooth, Survey and Research Unit, Department of Sociology, NUI Maynooth, 2009. (Published online by *An Roinn Pobail Comhionannais agus Gaeltachta.*)

language movements are necessary to arrive at a joint strategy in favour of a substantial increase in the regular use of Irish in the life of the people.

It is proposed to present the findings as follows:

(a)   Aspirations of the People for the Future of Irish;
(b)   Attitudes towards Irish while in School and Now;
(c)   Self-perceived Competence in the Irish Language;
(d)   Frequency and the Use of Irish;
(e)   Irish as a Basis of Common National Identity;
(f)   Attitudes towards 'Irish Speakers'.

Most of the detailed analysis by personal variables has been done in relation to the **Irish-born**, i.e. 85% of the Total Sample. Respondents who were not born in Ireland (with some exceptions) have not had the opportunity of learning Irish when young, and come from a different socio-cultural background in the recent past, except in the case of a number of respondents born to Irish parents abroad. During previous studies in the 1970s and in the 1980s, the level of in-migration to the Republic of Ireland was hardly significant because the country was predominantly **an emigrant society**. This has changed considerably since the late 1990s.

Part II – Aspirations for the Irish Language

2.1 Response of Total Sample:
The aspirations of the Irish people for the future of the Irish language are an indication of the potential support in the population for revival and preservation of the native language. They also point to the place of the language in the ethnic self-identity of Irish adults, i.e. within the Republic of Ireland.

Table No. 16.1 below reports the aspirations for the Irish language of the total sample in 2007-08. One of the most interesting findings in this table (No. 16.1) is the complete consensus between the total sample and the Irish-born subsample. This confirms the amazing agreement between those who were born outside Ireland and the Irish-born.

Table No. 16.1: Aspirations for the Irish Language of the Total Sample and of Those Born in Ireland

Aspirations for Irish	Total Sample A		Irish-Born B	
	Actual	Cumulative	Actual	Cumulative
1. Irish as Main Language	3.7%	3.7%	3.4%	3.4%
2. Bilingual – Mainly Irish	4.7%	8.4%	4.9%	8.3%
3. Bilingual – Mainly English	32.5%	40.9%	32.1%	40.4%
4. In Gaeltacht & for Cultural Reasons	52.5%	93.4%	52.8%	93.2%
5. Discarded and Forgotten	6.6%	--	6.7%	--
Number	100.0%	973	100.0%	839

The level of support for the native language is very impressive at 93%. A little over half of the sample agrees that the Irish language should be **preserved** for its cultural value and spoken in the *Gaeltacht*. Forty per cent of respondents would wish to see the language **revived** throughout Irish society. Bilingualism with English as the principal language is the preference of four-fifths of those in favour of revival throughout the population. Of course, bilingualism in society can take many forms.

The level of change in aspirations since 1988-89 has been insignificant statistically, which means the pattern has been maintained. One rarely finds such a consistency of variation in survey research of a national population, i.e. in the case of two national samples with a gap of eighteen/nineteen years between them. Table No. 16.2 traces the changes in public aspirations between 1972-73 and 2007-08.

Table No. 16.2: Changes in Aspirations for the Irish Language since 1972-73

Aspirations for the Irish Language	National Sample 2007-08	National Sample 1988-89	Change (A-B)	Dublin Sub-Sample 2007-08	Dublin Sub-Sample 1988-89	Dublin Sample 1972-73	Change (C-E)
	A	B		C	D	E	
1. Irish as the Main Language	4%	4%	0.0%	6%	3%	8%	-2%
2. Bilingual: Irish as Principal Language	5%	5%	0.0%	8%	3%	10%	-2%
3. Bilingual: English as Principal Language	33%	34%	-1.0%	28%	31%	33%	-5%
4. Preserved in the *Gaeltacht* and Revived for its Cultural Value as in Music and Arts	53%	52%	+1.0%	45%	61%	34%	+11%
5. The Irish Language Should Be Discarded and Forgotten	7%	6%	+1.0%	13%	4%	15%	-2%
Number	1,015	1,000	--	246	274	2,282	--

The positive attitudes towards the Irish language have been 'maintained' nationwide since 1988-89 and have not been reduced by the influx of so many immigrants coming to Ireland as a result of the success of the so-called 'Celtic Tiger' and the advance of the economic institution into a pivotal position in Irish society.

The role of changes in public policy in *Dáil Éireann* (supported by all parties) and of the Irish Government seems to be bearing some fruit in maintaining for the Irish language a degree of viability in face of the sudden rise of materialism and globalisation.   Increases in the social status of Irish such as the establishment of TG4, ***Acht na dTeangacha Oifigiúla 2003***, together with the operation of the provisions of that Act, the achievement of official status for Irish in the ***European Union*** and the success of the Irish-medium sector in education are likely to have had a positive influence on aspirations, and prevented serious negative changes in the people's attitudes. The voluntary language and cultural movements have continued to encourage new leaders and reinforced those already committed to the revival of the language and the support of art and culture.   Specific research would be necessary to get an accurate estimate of the various influences which have combined to counter the growing and prevailing materialist culture of the currently pivotal 'economic institution' in the Republic of Ireland.

The changes in the percentages in the National Sample between 1988-89 and 2007-08 are not statistically significant.   Changes in the attitudes of Dublin people between **1972-73** and **2007-08** are significant but quite moderate, and less than the changes between 1972-73 and 1988-89. Support for the revival of Irish in Dublin in 1972-73 was actually higher than that recorded in 1988-89.

2.2 Aspirations of Irish-born Respondents by Personal Variables:

Table No. 16.3 gives a breakdown of the general findings by the personal variables of age, gender, area of birth, place of rearing, region of residence, education, occupational status and personal 'take-home' income.   This breakdown is restricted to the respondents who were born in Ireland, because it would not be reasonable to expect first-generation Irish inhabitants to have become involved with, or shared the experience of, being Irish throughout most of their lives.

**Table No. 16.3: Aspirations for the Future of the Irish Language
of Irish-Born Respondents by Personal Variables**

Variable	Irish as Main Language	Bilingual with Irish as Principal Language	Bilingual with English as Principal Language	Revived (1+2+3)	Preserved for Cultural and Gaeltacht reason	Discarded and Forgotten	Number
	(1)	(2)	(3)		(4)	(5)	
Total Sample	3.3%	4.9%	32.1%	**(40.3%)**	**52.9%**	**6.7%**	840
(a) Age	(p<.002)						
1. 18-25 Years	6.5%	5.6%	29.8%	**(41.9%)**	52.4%	5.6%	124
2. 26-40 Years	5.7%	6.1%	38.2%	**(50.0%)**	45.9%	4.1%	246
3. 41-55 Years	0.5%	4.2%	33.0%	**(37.7%)**	53.8%	8.5%	212
4. 56-70 Years	1.8%	4.2%	28.5%	**(34.5%)**	60.0%	5.5%	165
5. 71 Years plus	2.2%	4.3%	23.7%	**(30.2%)**	55.9%	14.0%	93
Number	28	42	270	**(340)**	443	57	840
(b) Gender	(p<.04)						
Male	3.3%	5.6%	34.3%	**(43.2%)**	48.0%	8.9%	394
Female	3.4%	4.3%	30.2%	**(37.9%)**	57.3%	4.7%	443
Number	28	41	269	**(339)**	443	56	837
(c) Area of Birth	(p<.001)						
1. City (100,000+)	4.4%	5.9%	34.1%	**(44.4%)**	46.6%	9.1%	320
2. Large Town (10,000+)	3.6%	9.5%	32.1%	**(45.2%)**	52.4%	2.4%	84
3. Town (1,500+)	0.9%	4.5%	35.7%	**(41.1%)**	55.4%	3.6%	112
4. Rural/ Village	3.4%	2.8%	28.9%	**(35.1%)**	58.4%	6.5%	322
Number	29	41	269	**(339)**	443	56	838
(d) Place of Rearing	(p<.001)						
1. Dublin (City / Co)	6.4%	8.0%	31.5%	**(45.9%**	43.4%	10.8%	251
2. Rest of Leinster	1.2%	3.1%	30.4%	**(34.7%)**	63.4%	1.9%	161
3. Munster	3.0%	3.5%	34.8%	**(41.3%)**	53.0%	5.7%	230
4. Connaught / Ulster	2.6%	5.8%	27.1%	**(35.5%)**	56.8%	7.7%	155
Number	29	42	250	**(341)**	421	55	797
(e) Region of Residence	(p<.001)						
1. BMW*	2.3%	2.8%	29.0%	**(34.1%)**	61.8%	4.1%	217
2. Dublin	6.6%	7.8%	27.5%	**(41.9%)**	45.5%	12.7%	244
3. Mid-East & South-East	4.3%	6.4%	37.8%	**(48.5%)**	51.1%	0.5%	188
4. Mid-West & Sth-West	0.0%	2.1%	36.3%	**(38.4%)**	53.7%	7.9%	190
Number	29	41	270	**(340)**	443	56	839
(f) Education	(p<.001)						
1. Primary or less	1.9%	4.7%	25.2%	**(31.8%)**	51.4%	16.8%	107
2. Incomplete Second-L.	5.1%	5.1%	29.5%	**(39.7%)**	53.2%	7.2%	237
3. Complete Second-Lev.	3.8%	1.9%	30.8%	**(36.5%)**	55.9%	7.6%	211
4. Third-Level	2.4%	7.3%	37.8%	**(47.5%)**	50.3%	2.1%	286
Number	29	42	270	**(341)**	443	57	841

Table No. 16.3 (Cont'd.) Variable	Irish as Main Language	Bilingual with Irish as Principal Language	Bilingual with English as Principal Language	Revived (1+2+3)	Preserved for Cultural and Gaeltacht reason	Discarded and Forgotten	Number
	(1)	(2)	(3)		(4)	(5)	
(g) Occupational Status	(p<.02)						
1 Unskilled / Semi	5.3%	4.7%	28.1%	**(38.1%)**	**56.1%**	**5.8%**	171
2. Skilled/ Routine non-m	2.7%	4.3%	28.9%	**(35.9%)**	**58.2%**	**5.9%**	256
3. Inspect. / Supervisory	1.7%	2.5%	27.3%	**(31.5%)**	**62.0%**	**6.6%**	121
4. Professional /Executive	3.8%	5.6%	45.6%	**(55.0%)**	**40.6%**	**4.4%**	160
Number	24	31	228	**(283)**	385	40	708
(h) Take-Home Income	(p<.001)						
1. Under €6,000 p.a.	3.3%	3.3%	55.0%	**(61.6%)**	**35.0%**	**3.3 %**	60
2. Under €24,000 p.a.	1.5%	5.1%	29.7%	**(36.3%)**	**55.9%**	**7.7%**	195
3. Under €60,000 p.a.	7.1%	7.7%	20.2%	**(35.0%)**	**59.6%**	**5.5%**	183
4. €60,000 plus p.a.	0.0%	3.3%	41.1%	**(44.4%)**	**51.1%**	**4.4%**	90
Number	18	29	165	**(212)**	285	31	528

* (Border, Midlands and West)

Note: The percentages in brackets indicate the proportion of each subsample who wishes to see Irish **revived.** Those in Column 4 wish to have the language **preserved,** while the percentages in Column 5 would have the language **discarded.**

The findings of the **total sample** of Irish-born respondents are given in the first row, i.e.

(a)	**Revived**	=	**40.3%**
(b)	**Preserved**	=	**52.9%**
(c)	**Discarded**	=	**6.7%**

A good guide to evaluating the findings of subsamples is to see how they fluctuate from the sample average as given above.   All variables except Marital Status recorded a significant variation between the subsamples.

(a) Age and the Future of Irish:
The results of this variable are quite favourable from the point of view of aspirations for the language.   The following summary Table is an extract from Table No. 16.3:

Variable — Age	Irish should be:		
	Revived	Preserved	Discarded
1. 18 to 25 years	41.9%	52.4%	5.6%
2. 26 to 40 years	50.0%	45.9%	4.1%
3. 41 to 55 years	37.7%	53.8%	8.5%
4. 56 to 70 years	34.5%	60.0%	5.5%
5. 71 years plus	30.2%	55.9%	14.0%
(Sample Average)	(40.3%)	(52.9%)	(6.7%)

Note: *Percentages above sample average are underlined.*

The two younger subsamples are the most positively disposed to the future of the Irish language. In the case of the 26 to 40 year-olds more were in favour of 'revival' (50%) than were for 'preservation' (45.9%). Both subsamples' percentages for 'discarding and forgetting' Irish were below the sample averages.

The most pessimistic subsamples were the 'middle-middle-aged', i.e. 41 to 55 year-olds and the older age group, 71 years plus. They were below sample averages in 'revival'. The middle-middle-age group is an important cohort whose support is important in society as parents and as leaders. Overall, the responses of the age subsamples are quite positive, especially in the case of the under-forties. This may reflect a new optimism and confidence which bodes well for future support for Irish if the appropriate policies and strategies are put forward. Without the latter, all the optimism in the world will achieve little.

(b) Gender and the Future of Irish:
The variation between the scores of males and females in relation to their aspirations for the Irish language in the future are interesting, if moderate. The range of difference between the percentages is quite low.

Variable – Gender	Irish should be:		
	Revived	Preserved	Discarded
1. Male	43.2%	48.0%	8.9%
2. Female	37.9%	57.3%	4.7%
(Sample Average)	(40.3%)	(52.9%)	(6.7%)

Note: Percentages above sample average are underlined.

The patterns of support by males and females are interesting. 'Males' are stronger for '**revival**' and for '**discarding**' while 'females' are stronger for the **preservation** (as in culture, arts and *Gaeltacht*) and least in favour of discarding the language. They were also weaker for **revival** than their male counterparts by 5.3%, i.e. 43.2% - 37.9%.

Research in several countries[3] and diverse cultures has shown that women tend to play a leadership role in language shift. Any tendency towards negative attitudes to the revival of Irish among women would therefore be of concern, given the role played by many women in language socialisation, i.e. intergenerational transmission of language. At the same time, one should not exaggerate the significance of the above variations in the light of other findings which show the very positive attitudes of females towards Irish and their competence in and use of the language.

(c) Area of Birth and Urban Status and the Future of the Irish Language:
'Area of Birth' is classified by the urbanised status of the area, i.e. City, Large Town, Town and Rural/Village. The socio-cultural significance of the rural-urban divide on the culture and social norms of the people has been greatly reduced by the intrusion of television and other forms of electronic media on the values and norms of the people. Broadcasting, printed mass media and, more recently, the Internet, have been agents of cultural homogenisation, which is largely urban and Anglo-American in its cultural base.

Nevertheless, there are differences of lifestyle affected by the density of population, the level of geographic mobility, the relative impact of extended family, and local neighbourhood and the stability of residence. The rise of non-farming rural residents and 'ex-urbans' has had an impact on the cohesion of rural/neighbour networks. The proliferation of the motor car has also had a traumatic impact on the culture of rural life as has the commercialisation of leisure and the arrival of universal telephonisation in the whole rural-urban population. All these changes have a considerable impact (positive and negative) on the aspirations and opinions of the people in both rural and urban environments in relation to the future of the Irish language.

---

[3] Gal, S. Language Shift, *Social Determinism of Linguistic Change in Bilingual Austria*, New York Academic Press, 1979.

Variable — Area of Birth	Irish should be:		
	Revived	Preserved	Discarded
1. City (100,000 +)	<u>44.4%</u>	46.6%	<u>9.1%</u>
2. Large Town (10,000 +)	<u>45.2%</u>	52.4%	2.4%
3. Town (1,500 +)	<u>41.1%</u>	<u>55.4%</u>	3.6%
4. Rural /Village	35.1%	<u>58.4%</u>	6.5%
(Sample Average)	(40.3%)	(52.9%)	(6.7%)

Note: Percentages above sample average are underlined.

The above extract from Table No. 16.3(c), shows a very interesting pattern which indicates that the 'Rural/Village' subsample is less in favour of the **revival** and more for the **preservation** of Irish for its cultural and *Gaeltacht* use and value. Since the trend in Irish society is towards greater urbanisation, increasing support for revival of Irish (subject to adequate programmes and strategies) into the future is likely. Rural Ireland is an area of great challenge for the revival. Still, the move from preservation to revival in the rural/village should be less difficult, because of the survival of community and family links.

(d) Place of Rearing and the Future of the Irish Language:

By 'place of rearing' is meant where one spent the first 16 years of life – or the most part of it. The subsamples are from Dublin City and County, Rest of Leinster, Munster and Connaught/Ulster. Since language is a cultural phenomenon, it has to be transmitted to the young and 'handed-on' from one generation to the next. What happened in the second half of the 19th century was the failure of one or two generations of Irish speakers to transmit or 'hand-on' their language to their children. The Irish language will never be revived or restored fully until parents pass it on to the children at a young and tender age as part of primary informal socialisation.

The following extract from Table No. 16.3(d) gives a breakdown of the impact of 'place of rearing' on aspirations for the future of Irish:

Variable — Place of Rearing	Irish should be:		
	Revived	Preserved	Discarded
1. Dublin City & County	<u>45.9%</u>	43.4%	<u>10.8%</u>
2. Rest of Leinster	34.7%	<u>63.4%</u>	1.9%
3. Munster	<u>41.3%</u>	<u>53.0%</u>	5.7%
4. Connaught /Ulster	35.5%	<u>56.8%</u>	<u>7.7%</u>
(Sample Average)	(40.3%)	(52.9%)	(6.7%)

Note: Percentages above sample average are underlined.

The results by 'place of rearing' show that 'Connaught/Ulster'-reared respondents were the most pessimistic with regard to revival, while those from Munster were the most optimistic overall. The pattern of 'Dublin City and County' was strongest in favour of revival and also of the Irish language being discarded. An almost similar response-pattern was recorded for those born in a city of more than one hundred thousand citizens. This makes sense and emphasises the urban factor. The very positive score of respondents reared in Munster is noteworthy.

(e) Region of Residence and the Irish Language:

The following extract from Table No. 16.3(e) shows the influence of where respondents were actually living.

Variable — Region of Residence	Irish should be:		
	Revived	Preserved	Discarded
1. BMW (Border, Midlands & West)	34.1%	61.8%	4.1%
2. Dublin	41.9%	45.5%	12.7%
3. Mid-East & South-East	48.5%	51.1%	0.5%
4. Mid-West & South-West	38.4%	53.7%	7.9%
(Sample Average)	(40.3%)	(52.9%)	(6.7%)

Note: Percentages above sample average are underlined.

When one compares the findings of the above sub-table with the previous one dealing with where respondents were reared, it is possible to detect the impact of geographic mobility. For example, the Dublin-reared were more positively disposed to the future of Irish than were those resident in Dublin.

Irish Should Be:	Dublin-Reared A	Resident in Dublin B	Difference (A – B)
1. Revived	45.9%	41.9%	+4.0%
2. Preserved	43.4%	45.5%	-2.1%
3. Discarded	10.8%	12.7%	-1.9%

The difference between the Dublin-Reared and those Resident in Dublin is significant. The former are more optimistic with regard to the future of Irish. We must remember that all respondents considered here are exclusively Irish-Born. The increase in pessimism among the current residents' subsample is probably due to the influence of the non-Dublin-reared who had come to live in Dublin from the provinces.   Respondents living in the 'Mid-East and South-East' regions were the most positively disposed to Irish.   It is very interesting that residents of **the Pale** are ahead of the rest of Ireland in their ambitions for the language!

(f) Education and the Irish Language:
This is an area in need of serious research because of the critical role being played by the schools and colleges in the transmission of competence in, and commitment to, the Irish language.   Since the late 1960s, largely owing to voluntary organisations, a parallel system of Irish-medium schools has existed, i.e. pre-school and primary, in response to a 'playing down' of the teaching of the language in the mainstream schools, where Irish is being taught **only** as a subject.

The following extract from Table No. 16.3(f) gives the findings of the respondents' aspirations in relation to the future of Irish by education.

Variable — Level of Education Reached	Irish should be:		
	Revived	Preserved	Discarded
1. Primary or Less	31.8%	51.4%	16.8%
2. Incomplete Second-Level	39.7%	53.2%	7.2%
3. Complete Second-Level	36.5%	55.9%	7.6%
4. Third-Level	47.5%	50.3%	2.1%
(Sample Average)	(40.3%)	(52.9%)	(6.7%)

Note: *Percentages above sample average are underlined.*

The above findings are very interesting.   Third-Level respondents who constitute 34% of the 'Irish-Born' sample are substantially more optimistic than the other grades.   Those with 'Primary or Less' constitute 12.7% of the sample and are the most pessimistic, with relatively low 'Revival' scores and high 'Discarded' percentages.   The differences between the scores of the two Second-Level subsamples are hardly significant statistically.   They are just half-way between those of 'Third-Level' and 'Primary or Less' subsamples.

When it is realised that current trends in educational participation and achievement in Ireland are heading for **over two-thirds** with participation in Third-Level for the relevant age-cohort, the importance of the above sub-table for the future of the Irish language becomes very significant. It also marks the fruit of much work for the Irish language by teachers and leaders of the community down the years.

(g) Occupational Status and the Irish Language:
Occupational status in Ireland today reflects many changes in agriculture, industry and the services. The trends revealed in the 1988-89 survey which recorded the acute decline in the 'Blue-Collar Workers' have continued over the past two decades.

The following extract from Table No. 16.3(g) shows a significant but moderate variation between the four subsamples:

Variable — Occupational Status	Irish should be:		
	Revived	**Preserved**	**Discarded**
1. Unskilled/ Semi-skilled	38.1%	56.1%	5.8%
2. Skilled / Routine Non-manual	35.9%	58.2%	5.9%
3. Inspectional / Supervisory	31.5%	62.0%	6.6%
4. Professional / Executive	55.0%	40.6%	4.4%
(Sample Average)	(40.3%)	(52.9%)	(6.7%)

Note: Percentages above sample average are underlined.

The above pattern is similar to that of the education variable in that the higher occupational status is significantly and substantially stronger in favour of **revival**. This is the first time that the majority **(55%)** of a sub-sample opted in favour of the revival of the Irish language. This once again confirms the pattern that support for the language has become very strong among the 'occupational elite'! Should this category become a positive role model for others aspiring to get top professions, the Irish language's status will continue to increase. A very important element of the social status of a language is the social status of its speakers and supporters[4].

(h) Take-Home Income and the Future of Irish:
When examined by 'Take-Home Income', i.e. income after tax, the variations are not as anticipated in all cases because of the mixed positive

---

[4] The remarkable revival of the *Me'phaa Language* in Mexico, ongoing from the nineteen seventies, was spearheaded by *Me'phaa* leaders (see Anoby, Stan J. *"Reversing Language Shift: Can Kwak'wala Be Revived"*, in Cantoni, St Clair and Yazzie, eds. *Revitalising Indigenous Languages*, Northern Arizona University, 1999). Website source: http://jan.ucc.nau.edu/~jar/RIL_4.html (Date accessed 12.02.2009.)

correlation between income and occupational status. The following sub-table also shows a mixed result:

Variable - Personal Income After Tax	Irish should be:		
	Revived	Preserved	Discarded
1. Under €6,000 p.a.	<u>61.6%</u>	35.0%	3.3%
2. Under €24,000 p.a.	36.3%	55.9%	<u>7.7%</u>
3. Under €60,000 p.a.	35.0%	<u>59.6%</u>	5.5%
4. €60,000 plus p.a.	<u>44.4%</u>	51.1%	4.4%
(Sample Average)	(40.3%)	(52.9%)	(6.7%)

Note: Percentages above sample average are underlined.

The highest support for revival has been evinced by those with the lowest take-home income. In fact, this category of persons is likely to be dependent on others, e.g. part-time workers, etc. or totally poor materially. The second highest support for the **revival** of the Irish language is in sub-sample No. 4, i.e. the highest paid respondents.

(i) Conclusion:
The above findings in relation to the aspirations of Irish-born adults (as represented in the respondents' replies) have been very optimistic. The **overwhelming support for the Irish language**, as expressed in the 1988-89 national survey, with less than **7%** wishing that the *"Irish language be discarded and forgotten"*, was maintained. Over **40%** of the Irish-born wished to **revive** the language, while **52%** would wish to see it **preserved** "in the *Gaeltacht* and for its cultural value as in music and the arts". Considering the highly materialistic and consumerist culture at the time of interview during the final year of the so-called **Celtic Tiger**, this result was very favourable.

The pattern of support for Irish in the personal variables saw greater positivity towards the language among younger, male, urbanised, people living in Dublin and the rest of Leinster, more highly educated and people with high occupational status. *Take-home income* gave a mixed result with the lowest and highest most favourably disposed. These results indicate that the trends are favourable and dispositions towards the Irish language are likely to improve further in the years ahead, barring negative policies and serious neglect in the teaching of Irish in the mainstream schools and colleges.

Part III – Attitudes towards Irish While in School and Now

The need to find out if adults had changed their attitudes towards Irish since they were at school is important from the point of view of comparing the impact of the school environment and that of the world since leaving school. Apart from environmental influences, there are also personality factors, such as the impact of adult maturity and growth in understanding in relation to the importance of the language and ethnic self-identity.

Respondents (Irish-born) were asked: *"Which of the following best describe the way you felt about Irish when in school and the way you feel now?"* The answers were pre-coded – "strongly in favour, somewhat in favour, no particular feelings, somewhat opposed, strongly opposed". The purpose of the question was to discover if there was any change in attitude, and in which direction it moved. Table No. 16.4 gives the overall findings for the Irish-born sample.

Table No. 16.4:
Attitudes of Irish-Born towards Irish in School and Now

Attitude Towards Irish	While in School A	Now B	Net Change (B – A)
1. Strongly in Favour	21.8%	25.5%	+3.7%
2. Somewhat in Favour	20.8%	31.2%	+10.4%
Total (1 + 2)	**(42.6%)**	**(56.7%)**	**(+14.1%)**
3. No Particular Feelings	**35.5%**	**31.8%**	**-3.7%**
4. Somewhat Opposed	11.6%	5.8%	-5.8%
5. Strongly Opposed	10.3%	5.7%	-4.6%
Total (4 + 5)	**(21.9%)**	**(11.5%)**	**(-10.4%)**
Number	848	842	--

There is clear evidence in the above that the net change, i.e. by subtracting the positive and negative changes, has been significant and fairly substantial. The change has been in the positive direction. In other words, the outcome of post-school experience and reflection has raised the level of commitment by **33.1%**, i.e. from 42.6% while in school to 56.7%. This is a very important finding.

What are the causes of such a change in attitudes towards Irish? The most favourable explanation would be the **wisdom of age**, i.e. a sign of maturity. A less favourable explanation would be the unattractive way Irish was taught and the failure of the teachers to make the language attractive and worthwhile, i.e. few occasions of favourable image for Irish and poor stimulation of motivation. Also, there may have been a negative attitude towards Irish at home and among peers when in school. Some of it would have stemmed from the previously very low social status of Irish. Even the curriculum could be off-putting. The lack of adequate Irish-language school texts, and the failure to present Irish as a living language which could be used as a medium for teaching other subjects in school also may have contributed to the negative attitudes.

There is quite a range of possible causes to explain the relative unpopularity of Irish while at school as compared to later in adult life. It has been known for a very long time (UNESCO 1958) that acquiring only a nodding acquaintance with a language can lead to frustration. Frustration, of course, can lead to aggression. It is possible that schools which provide a lesser standard of Irish teaching could have built up (unwittingly) a degree of resentment against the language.

The results of Table No. 16.4(a) are not all negative. Twice as many respondents (42.6%) were in favour of Irish as were opposed to it (21.9%). This is not a bad result for the school experience and is a credit to those who had the task of teaching Irish down the years.

The changes in the 2007-08 National Survey and the 1988-89 one are spelled out in Table No. 16.5 below:

Table No. 16.5: Changes of Attitudes towards Irish (1988-89 and 2007-08)

Attitude towards Irish	When in School			Now			Now – Then Other Changes	
	1988-89 Sample A	2007-08 Sample B	B – A	1988-89 Sample C	2007-08 Sample D	Change D — C	C – A	D – B
1. Strongly in Favour	18%	22%	+4%	19%	26%	+7%	+1%	+4%
2. Somewhat in Favour	26%	21%	-5%	38%	31%	-7%	+12%	+10%
Total (1 + 2)	(44%)	(43%)	(-1%)	(57%)	(57%)	(0%)	(+13%)	(+14%)
3. No Particular Feelings	33%	36%	+3%	29%	32%	+3%	-4%	-4%
4. Somewhat Opposed	13%	12%	-1%	9%	6%	-3%	-4%	-6%
5. Strongly Opposed	10%	10%	0%	6%	6%	0.0%	-4%	-4%
Total (4 + 5)	(23%)	(22%)	(-1%)	(15%)	(12%)	(-3%)	(-8%)	(-10%)
Number	973	848	--	973	840	--	--	--

There has been little change in the percentages of the various sub-samples of the findings of the 2007-08 Irish-born Sample and those of the1988-89 Total Sample.   There was a slight increase in the percentages who were 'Strongly in Favour', while in school, i.e. +4% and in those who were 'Strongly in Favour' now, i.e. +7%.   The total numbers in favour (1+2) were practically identical in both cases, 'While in School' and 'Now'.

The fact that the distribution remained more or less constant confirms the **positive pattern** of 33.3%, i.e. from a 43% to 57% increase between positive attitudes 'While in School' and positive attitudes towards the language later in life.   The changes within the two favourable answers, i.e. rows one and two in Table No. 16.5, show a significant strengthening of the favourable attitude, change from 'Somewhat in Favour' to 'Strongly in Favour' over the nineteen/twenty years between the two National Surveys. This means that the post-school attitudes have been improving steadily.   A firm pattern has been established.   The challenge facing those with responsibility for the promotion of Irish would be to bring about a further strengthening of positive attitudes in favour of Irish in the students/pupils while at school.   In other words, there is a need to make Irish more attractive in our schools and colleges!

Programmes of information integrated with plans of activity leading to increasing the use of Irish are necessary to avoid the possible build-up of frustration which could occur as a result of being highly motivated to learn the language and then not being able to use it.   The link between the positivity of post-school attitudes and those while at school is in part due to mutually supportive parents and teachers.

The responses to the question on changes in attitudes between being in school or college and now are examined by personal variables in Table No. 2.6 of the special report *The Irish Language and the Irish People*[5] (pages 26-35).

The measuring of perceived **attitudes** toward Irish while **at school** and **now** has confirmed the positive trends in relation to the **aspiration** questions. The school experiences were quite mixed for the respondents. One could speculate why the range of responses was given by the

---

[5] See: Mac Gréil, Micheál, *The Irish Language and the Irish People*, Maynooth, Survey and Research Unit, Department of Sociology, 2009.

respondents. Motivation to learn Irish was unevenly stimulated by the homes and the schools. It takes a post-colonial society a few generations to rediscover and identify with its own cultural base of which the language is a central symbolic system. The improvements in attitudes between *'when at school'* and *'now'* showed a marked maturing of acceptance of Irish in a favourable light. This is an important change which will have a further significant bearing on the strengthening of support for Irish in future generations.

Part IV – Declared Competence in the Irish Language

4.1 Introduction:

Ever since the 1840s, the Irish language had ceased to be the spoken language of the majority of ordinary people due to the decimation of the native Irish population as a result of the ***Gorta Mór*** (the Great Famine) and a negative disposition towards Irish by the colonial British Government and the local Irish and Anglo-Irish dominant classes. A deliberate strategy of language replacement was promoted through **the national schools' system,** and this was aided and abetted by the prestigious Church-run secondary schools which existed (with notable exceptions). The language was practically replaced by English within a space of two generations.

The arrival of a native Government in 1922 marked a very significant and substantial advance in the effort to restore and revive Irish. Fortunately, Irish had remained the communal language in a number of areas (now known as the *'Gaeltacht'*) which, during the heyday of the language movement had become sources of inspiration and language acquisition. Today's positive results are largely due to the State's effort to bring Irish back to the people through the education system and support for 'the *Gaeltacht* communities', as well as the efforts of the various Irish language voluntary movements, and allied associations and organisations. With the rise of economic pragmatism since the late 1960s, the State's commitment to Irish in the schools' curriculum had abated somewhat, and there are indications of this to be detected in the detailed findings below.

According as the State's commitment to Irish through the normal education system declined, the voluntary language movement sought to fill the gap created by promoting the ***naíoscoileanna*** (later known as *naíonraí*) and **Irish medium schools** (i.e. *Gaelscoileanna)[6]* Unfortunately, these excellent education organisations do not reach the vast majority of pupils – owing to limited resources or lack of commitment. Nevertheless, there is evidence to indicate that the results of this voluntarily inspired campaign (with measured State support) have helped to raise the social status of the Irish language in Irish society. It has certainly increased the level of competence in 'upper' sections of the current adult population. It also helped to neutralise the decline experienced in the mainstream schools in recent decades.

Table No. 16.6 measures the self-perceived competence in the Irish language by the total national sample and by the Irish-born respondents.

Table No. 16.6: Self-Perceived Competence in the Irish Language by Total Sample and Those Born in Ireland

Level of Competence *	Total Sample A		Irish-Born B		Difference (B – A)	
	Actual	**Cum.**	**Actual**	**Cum.**	**Actual**	**Cum.**
1. Very Fluent / Fluent	7.8%	7.8%	9.1%	9.1%	+1.3%	+1.3%
2. Middling	19.5%	27.3%	22.1%	31.2%	+2.6%	+3.9%
3. Not So Fluent	14.2%	**41.5%**	15.9%	**47.1%**	+1.7%	+5.6%
4. Only a Little	32.5%	74.0%	36.9%	84.0%	+4.4%	+10.0%
5. None	26.0%	---	16.0%	---	-10.0%	---
Number	100%	1,015	100%	855	---	---

* Respondents reporting their self-perceived competence to be 'not so fluent' or 'higher' will be judged to have 'reasonable competence' in the language.

The findings of Table No. 16.6, while a little lower than what was anticipated (due to the continued rise in educational participation since the 1980s), are, nevertheless, quite reassuring. Over two-fifths (41.5%) of the total sample and slightly less than half of the Irish-born adult respondents have sufficient competence to understand and engage in Irish conversation (with relatively little assistance). At no time since the *Gorta Mór* (the Great Famine) and *the Great Language Shift* has there been such a level of

---

[6] In 2006, within the State but outside the *Gaeltacht* there were 171 Irish-medium primary schools and 43 post-primary schools providing education through Irish for 35,500 children. (A further 32 Irish-medium primary schools and 4 post-primary were in Northern Ireland.) - website, *Gaelscoileanna Teoranta*. About 1,000 children are attending over seventy *naíonra* sessions in the *Gaeltacht* – website, *Comhar Naíonraí Teoranta*. There are about 170 *naíonra* sessions in the part of the State which is outside the *Gaeltacht*. The number of children has not been made available but may be approaching 3,000.

'reasonable competence' in Irish in the adult population outside the *Gaeltacht*. This has been achieved despite the noted withdrawal of some of the official support for Irish in the educational system. The fact that the level of competence is not higher is probably a reflection of this reduced official support, especially in mainstream primary and second-level schools. Obviously, the maximum and active support of the **Department of Education and Science** and of the schools' system is necessary for the fullest realisation of the restoration of the Irish language as a viable national language and central **symbolic meaningful system** in our culture. Anthropologists see the native language as the unique cultural nuance of reality of a people. It also contains our cultural memory. It is based on human beings' capacity **to symbol**.

At the same time, there is evidence in Table No. 16.6 to confirm that competence in the Irish language has survived sufficiently strongly in the population to provide a basis from which to make further advances in bringing it from the **minority,** who now benefit from it, to the **broader population**. This could be greatly helped by a change of policy in the ordinary schools' system and by extending the Irish-medium pre-schools, *Na Naíonraí* and **Irish-medium schools** more widely in the population.

There will be implications arising from this for the whole standard of teacher-training in the Irish language and the promotion of Irish-medium, third-level education. The degree of **institutional duplication**, i.e. separate Irish-medium schools, required for the development and restoration of Irish in society will be determined by the extent of support for the successful teaching of the Irish language in the mainstream schools. *The more these schools fail to teach the language adequately, the greater the need for 'institutional duplication' facilitating Irish-medium schools.*

The difference between the level of competence of the total sample and that of the Irish-born in the sample is quite substantial, and is also a source of optimism for the future of the language. Having already established that those not born in Ireland have the same level of positive aspirations as the Irish-born (see Table No. 16.6 above), it can be hoped that their children will be given the support of the parents in learning the Irish language. As new citizens of the State, they are entitled to learn the native language of the Irish people in order to enable them to relate to the culture and tradition of their adopted country. The percentage of Irish-born who stated they knew no Irish was as low as **16%**, which is explained (probably) by the age factor.   The rules and practices governing dispensations from learning Irish in the schools may well be already depriving the children of immigrants of the opportunity to acquire Irish.

Changes in self-reported levels of competence in the Irish language are given on Table No. 16.7.   The changes refer to the National Samples of 2007-08 and 1988-89 and the Dublin sub-samples of 2007-08 and 1988-89 and the Dublin sample of 1972-73.

Table No. 16.7:
Changes in Competence in the Irish Language since 1972-73

Level of Competence	National Samples				Dublin Samples				
	Total 2007-08	Irish Born 2007-08	Total 1988-89	Change (B-C)	Irish Born 2007-08	Sub-Sample 1988-'89	Sample 1972-73	D – E	D — F
	A	B	C		D	E	F		
1.Very Fluent/Fluent	8%	9%	8%	+1%	9%	11%	7%	-2%	+2%
2. Middling	20%	22%	19%	+3%	23%	22%	18%	+1%	+20%
3. Not So Fluent	14%	16%	14%	+2%	15%	16%		-1%	
(1 + 2 + 3)	(42%)	(47%)	(41%)	(+6%)	(47%)	(49%)	(25%)	(-2%)	(+22%)
4. Only a Little	33%	37%	40%	-3%	37%	32%	50%	+5%	-13%
5. None	26%	16%	19%	-3%	17%	20%	25%	-3%	-8%
Number	1,015	855	920	---	246	274	2,282	---	---

The changes between the findings of the National Samples of 1988-89 and 2007-08 are barely significant in the positive direction.   When compared with the Irish-born, the increase is significant at **+6%**.   This is quite disappointing and again raises some serious questions about the **success** of our mainstream schools in **transmitting** a working knowledge and ability to speak in Irish.   Also, the family and the school have important roles in giving young people the necessary **motivation** to **use** their Irish.

The changes in perceived self-competence in Irish between 2007-08 and 1988-89 in the Dublin subsamples are within the margins of error. While both mark a significant and substantial advance on the standards reported in the 1972-73 survey of Greater Dublin, progress was not continued between 1988-89 and 2007-08.   This certainly provides a *prima facie* case for a serious examination of the factors which have slowed down (to a halt) progress made over the previous sixteen years.   The author's hunch is that this is due to a reduction of the status of Irish **within** the education system and disimprovements in the efficacy of teaching the Irish language to the young!

Education today seems to put greater emphasis on serving the needs of the **economic institution** than on the socio-cultural development of the person in society.   Should this situation continue, a new intervention on behalf of the Irish language and culture from voluntary sources would be necessary, e.g. the Irish language movement, to restore the progress recorded between 1972-73 and 1988-89.   However, voluntary movements cannot take the place, or exercise the influence, of a Government organisation. The role of the European Union's influence on Irish Education, and the prevailing official approach in respect to bilingualism in education and the future of the national language all need to be assessed in the interest of future progress at every level.

Perceived self-competence in the Irish-born by personal variables is published in the special report: *The Irish Language and the Irish People* (see Mac Gréil 2009A) pages 43-55.   As in the case of aspirations for the future of the Irish language, the young, the more highly educated and those with the more prestigious occupations were the most competent in Irish. Education, as expected, seemed to be a most important positive independent variable when it came to ability to speak Irish.   When each of these three ordinal variables is returning positive results, it can be anticipated that the level of competence is likely to improve in the years ahead.   The factor which could impede further improvement would be a greater level of non-usage of Irish and a serious reduction in the teaching of Irish at school.   The former would lead to a deterioration of the standard of Irish because "if one does not use Irish, one inevitably loses the capacity to do so".   As the Irish proverb states: *"Beatha teanga í a labhairt"* (the life of a language is its constant use).

With regard to the **teaching of Irish**, a number of comments are relevant.   Firstly, it is necessary that the teaching of Irish to the young be **universal**, which requires a minimum standard of Irish of the **teachers in every school**.   Secondly, Irish needs to be taught as a **spoken language**.

The rapid increase in numbers of exemptions from Irish being dispensed under the rules of the Department of Education & Science on the basis of **certificates of inability** to learn Irish issued by professional consultants needs to be queried.   Seven thousand of the exemptees go on to take one or more continental languages (in addition to English) in their *Leaving Certificate,* and this raises many questions as to why they are deemed unable to learn Irish as a language[7].

Language is basically **aural** and **oral** and is, therefore, 'listened to' and 'spoken'[8]. Irish as a written symbolic system is an additional **visual** form, which was developed very early in European terms but long after the aural and oral stage. In the modern *Gaeltacht* Irish remained mostly 'aural' and 'oral' until relatively recently. In fact, most people used only the 'visual' form of language in its English form, e.g. English versions of names on the tombstones in the *Gaeltachtaí.* Communities with 'oral' and 'aural' language only (ignorantly referred to as 'illiterate') contribute to its development with greater freedom in response to socio-cultural change.

This is very relevant for the promotion of competence in the Irish language. In modern literate societies it would be unrealistic to neglect the 'visual' language. Reason would indicate that the 'oral' and 'aural' should precede the 'visual' if it is the intention of society to revive and preserve Irish. Without competence in 'oral' and 'aural' Irish, and focusing on literature alone, Irish would be presented as are the classics, i.e. for its literary value alone. Therefore, the first emphasis needs to be on the spoken word, *An Teanga Gaeilge* (the Irish Tongue).

Part V – Frequency and Occasions of Use of Irish

5.1 Frequency of Use:
Because of the relatively recent change from a country characterised as an **emigrant people** to becoming an **immigrant society**, i.e. since the mid-1990s, it was decided to focus on the 'Irish-born' respondents when measuring frequency of use of Irish. The percentages for the total sample will also be given but the changes in frequency will be calculated between that of the Irish-born in 2007-08 and the total samples in 1988-89 and in 1972-73. At the times of the latter two surveys, Ireland (Republic) was very much an 'emigrant society'.

---

[7] See: Delap, Brendán, *"Mí-Ionracas Daltaí agus a dTuismuitheoirí"*, ar www.beo.ie, Eagrán 84, Aibreán 2008.
[8] See: Edward Sapir in Mandelbaum, David S., *Selected Writings of Edward Sapir on Language, Culture and Personality*, University of California Press, 1949 and 1958.

As reported on Table No. 16.6 above, some **47%** of Irish-born respondents declared they had a **reasonable competence** in Irish, i.e. they were 'fluent/very fluent' (9%), 'middling' (22%) or 'not so fluent' (16%). Those who said they had 'only a little' (37%) or 'none' (16%) were excluded from the reasonably competent. Likewise in the case of use of the language, the category of **regular use** of Irish was restricted to those who reported using it 'weekly or more often' (11%) and 'occasionally' (12%), i.e. **23%**. The main challenge facing those who wish to promote the Irish language is to narrow the gap between **reasonable competence** (47%) and **regular use** (23%). The harnessing of the 'favourable attitudes' to stimulate those with 'reasonable competence' to use Irish more frequently should not be that difficult. Because of the gap between competence and use of Irish in the 1988-89 findings, it was necessary to be more cautious when anticipating the levels of use in this (2007-08) national survey. Among the obstacles are **social constraints on speaking Irish**, which have to be acknowledged and effective strategies devised to enable those with the necessary competence in Irish to overcome them.

Table No. 16.8 gives the reported frequency of use of Irish by the total sample and those born in the Republic of Ireland:

Table No. 16.8:
Frequency of Use of Irish by Total Sample and Those Born in Ireland

Frequency of Use	Total Sample A		Irish-Born B		Difference (B – A)	
	Actual	Cum.	Actual	Cum.	Actual	Cum.
1. Weekly or More Often	9.3%	9.3%	10.8%	10.8%	+1.5%	+1.5%
2. Occasionally	10.8%	**20.0%**	11.8%	**22.6%**	+1.0%	**+2.6%**
3. Rarely	20.1%	40.1%	22.8%	45.3%	+2.8%	+5.1%
4. Never	59.9%	---	54.7%	---	-5.2%	---
Number	100.1%	1,015	100.0%	855	---	---

The most striking aspect of the above findings is the gap between **competence** in Irish and **occasional use** or more often[9]. In the case of the Irish-born, almost half of respondents are capable of using Irish, while **less than one quarter,** reported that they use it occasionally or more often. Previous surveys, including that of the *Committee on Irish Language Attitudes Research CLÁR* (Report 1975) found similar gaps between ability

[9] Respondents who use **Irish occasionally or more often** will be classified as **Regular Users**.

420

or competence and usage[10]. Still, the fact that 20% of the National Sample and 22.6% of the Irish-born respondents do use the Irish language occasionally or more often is significant as a foundation on which to build greater use which, in itself, will result in improved competence. It will be shown that occasions of use are more informal than formal. It might be useful, therefore, for families or groups to identify special times and places set aside for the 'normal' use of Irish, e.g. informal conversation at table/meals, family prayers, etc. Earlier research has noted the popularity of Irish for informal and personal communication rather than use in formal contractual relations.

Table No. 16.9 compares frequency of use of Irish in the country over the period 1972-73 to 2007-08. Again the level of advance in the use of the language has not been commensurate with the potential opportunities. The results of this table may reflect other changes in home and communication patterns between people, including the rise of 'the virtual community' on mobile phones and the internet. The urgent need to 'Gaelicise' this form of interpersonal communication is probably more serious than some educators and leaders of the Irish language movement may realise. A manufacturer of mobile phones recently (January 2009) took the initiative by introducing a mobile phone with an Irish-language predictive-text capability.

Table No. 16.9: Changes in the Frequency of Use of Irish from 1972-73 to 2007-08

Frequency of Use	National Samples				Dublin Samples				
	Total Sample 2007-08	Irish Born 2007-08	Total Sample 1988-89	Change (B-C)	Irish Born 2007-08	Sub-Sample 1988-89	Dublin Sample 1972-73	Changes D – E	D — F
	A	**B**	**C**		**D**	**E**	**F**		
1. Weekly or More Often	9%	11%	10%	+1%	9%	6%	16%	+3%	-7%
2. Occasionally	11%	12%	18%	-6%	15%	20%	9%	-5%	+6%
(1 + 2)	(20%)	(23%)	(28%)	(-5%)	(24%)	(26%)	(25%)	(-2%)	(-1%)
3. Rarely	20%	23%	23%	0%	18%	23%	23%	-5%	-5%
4. Never	60%	55%	50%	+5%	58%	52%	52%	+6%	+6%
Number	1,015	855	975	---	246	274	2,282	---	---

The consistency in the frequency of usage of the Irish language over thirty-five years is remarkable. This is all the more amazing when it is considered that three separate surveys were involved. It gives a high level of reliability and validity to the patterns of frequency reported in each category.

---

[10] Committee on Irish Language Research Report, 1975, *Oifig Dhíolta Foilseachán Rialtais*, Dublin, 1975.

The slight increase in the percentage in the 'Never' row between 2007-08 and 1988-89 and 1972-73 must be seen as disappointing to those who would have expected improvements because of the rise in participation and achievement in education. It is very disappointing for those who had hoped that membership of the *European Union* would result in greater use of Irish in the Republic. (The period covered embraces Ireland's membership of the European Union.)

The optimist could respond to the above figures by expressing satisfaction in the fact that the 1972-73 figures for Dublin and the 1988-89 figures for the Irish-born sample were more or less maintained. At least, these findings should result in a greater priority in the promotion of the use of the Irish language in order to strengthen the language's restoration or revival.

5.2 Occasions of Use of Irish:

As already noted, Irish is used for the most parts **on informal occasions**. Its use in administrative and work situations appears to be quite minimal. Table No.16.10 reports on the occasions of the use of Irish by the total Irish-born sample and by those who use Irish rarely or more often.

Table No. 16.10:   Occasions when Irish is Used by Irish-Born Respondents' Total Sample and Those Using it Rarely or More Often

Occasion of Use (Order of Frequency)	Percentage of Respondents	
	Irish-Born Respondents Total Sample	Of Those who Use the Language Rarely or More Often*
1. Programmes on TV/Radio	23.9%	52.7%
2. At Home	19.1%	42.1%
3. With Irish-Speaking Friends	19.0%	41.8%
4. At Work	8.0%	17.7%
5. All Possible Opportunities	7.7%	16.9%
6. Reading Irish	6.5%	14.4%
7. Communicating with Officials	5.1%	11.2%
Number	855	388

* Excluding those who Never Use Irish

The above occasions of the use of Irish are more or less as anticipated. It is very clear from these findings that, among those who use Irish, it has been almost confined to the informal and domestic environments where there are fewer social constraints to use the language. The proportion who use the language in their work and when communicating with officials is relatively small, but significant in the light of how few civil servants and commercial employees (outside the *Gaeltacht*) would be at ease doing their business through Irish.

In the future this is an area of possible expansion in the use of Irish. Under *Acht na dTeangacha Oifigiúla 2003*, Government Departments and Semi-State Organisations are encouraged to promote the use of the Irish language. The recent introduction of bi-lingual announcements on the Dublin *Luas* and on *Iarnród Éireann's* new trains is a welcome sign of such a normal extension of the use of Irish.

Table No. 16.11 compares the findings of Table No. 16.10 with those of 1988-89:

Table No. 16.11: Comparison between Patterns of Use in 1988-89 and 2007-08

Occasion of Use	Percentage of Respondents (Excluding Those Who Never Use Irish)		
	Total Sample (1988-89) A	Irish Born (2007-08) B	Change (B — A)
1. Listening (Radio/TV)	50%	53%	+3%
2. At Home	45%	42%	-3%
3. With Irish-Speaking Friends	39%	42%	+3%
4. At Work	18%	18%	0%
5. All Possible Opportunities	13%	17%	+4%
6. Reading Irish	14%	14%	0%
7. Communicating with Officials	11%	11%	0%
Number	484	388	---

The repetition of practically the same pattern of using Irish by the two samples after a gap of nineteen years is almost uncanny. The three areas where there was minimum meaningful increase of plus three and four per cent reflect, in all probability, the arrival of *TG4* and a growth in competence and commitment. A challenge facing those who wish to make a dramatic breakthrough[11] in the use of Irish would be to find among the above seven occasions (which have been chosen by Irish speakers

---

[11] In this context, the recently published Government draft document: *Straitéis Fiche Bliain don Ghaeilge 2010-2020 / Twenty Year Strategy for the Irish Language 2010-2020*, the State seems to be addressing this challenge.

themselves in which to practise their Irish) opportunities to speak the language. Other occasions not mentioned could include: prayer and religious liturgies, recreational opportunities, sport, holidays, visits to the *Gaeltacht*, attending cultural events, etc. This may help to fill the gap between ability to use Irish and using it, as commented on already. The drop in the use of Irish at home may be due in part to changes which have taken place in the patterns of relations at home, due to the commercialisation of leisure and other alterations.

5.3 Findings by Personal Variables:
The measuring of frequency and occasions of use of the Irish language (with quite detailed commentary) is given in the report: *The Irish Language and the Irish People* on pages 62 to 81. The findings are most interesting and confirm the growth.

With regard to frequency of use, younger, more educated and those with more prestigious occupations were the respondents who reported the highest frequency of use with their respective variables. In the case of geographic influence, persons reared in 'Munster' and living in the 'Mid-West and South-West' regions were the sub-variables with the most frequent use of Irish. Gender failed to produce a statistically significant variation between the frequencies of use of Irish by 'males and 'females'. Because of 'women's' special influence in 'language shift', their support is crucial as mothers (see page 405 above, i.e. footnote 3).

A number of questions were asked of respondents in order to discover the extent to which there were informal structures in the people's socio-cultural norms which acted as impediments to their more frequent use of Irish. The following three statements were read out to Irish-born respondents for their response, i.e.

Statement	Response (Yes)
1. "Committed to using Irish as much as one can."	59.2%
2. "Reluctant to converse in Irish when unsure of the person's ability to speak Irish."	65.5%
3. "Reluctant to speak Irish when others who don't know Irish are present."	63.0%

Despite almost **60%** of respondents committed to use Irish as much as they could, almost two-thirds expressed reluctance to do so when not sure of the other's competence, or when a person is without Irish. In the concrete reality of Irish society, this means there are relatively few opportunities to use the language!   How to change these norms which discourage Irish speakers to take the **initiative** to speak Irish and only switch to English when others present refuse to engage in Irish conversation is another challenge. Also, persons without competence in Irish should be willing to indicate that they would be happy if others present continued to speak in Irish.   Such expressions of linguistic tolerance would be likely to result in a significant increase in the frequency of Irish speaking in normal social situations. Also, the possibility of **multi-language conversations** among groups where people understand Irish, but may not feel sufficiently competent to speak it, instead they respond in English!   This could be a transition phase in the process of Irish revival!

The responses to the "norms restricting the use of Irish" by personal variables are reported on in the special Irish language report[12].   Further research into the informal structural impediments to the use of Irish is necessary.

Part VI – Irish as a Basis of Common National Identity

6.1 Introduction:
The discussion and debate on what characterises the Irish people as a distinctive ethnic or cultural group has been central to the case for Irish National Independence and for Irish Ethnic Identity.   Most **anthropologists**, i.e. academics and writers who study human culture and ethnology, agree that the **people's language** is the most important symbolic meaningful system which characterises a people.   The language contains the cultural deposit of centuries of a people living together in good times and bad. It also contains their prayers, songs and poetry.   It is considered invaluable, totally unique and irreplaceable.   It also provides a unique nuance on the world the people live in and a link between past, present and future generations[13].

---

[12] See: Mac Gréil, Mícheál, *The Irish Language and the Irish People*, Maynooth, Survey and Research Unit, Department of Sociology, NUI Maynooth, 2009, pages 81 to 84.
[13] It is not only a means of communication.   In the words of the 1967 Canadian Royal Commission on Bilingualism and Biculturalism "Language itself is fundamental to activities which are distinctively human. It is through language that the individual fulfils his capacity for expression.   It is through language that man not only communicates but achieves communion with others.   It is language which, by its structures, shapes the very way in which men order their thoughts coherently.   It is language which makes possible social organisation.   Thus a common language is the expression of a community of interests among a group of people." (See Book 1, *The Official Languages, General Introduction, Report of the Royal Commission on Bilingualism and Biculturalism*, Queen's Printer, Ottawa, Canada, 1967).

Seeing the Irish language as a *symbolic basis of common identity* for the whole population of the island of Ireland (Republic of Ireland and Northern Ireland) has been a wish of many leaders over the years. It would be non-sectarian and capable of embracing diverse political ideologies and world views.

The question of "the Irish language and culture" providing "a good basis for Irish Unity" was first introduced in the 1972-73 Survey of Greater Dublin and repeated in the National Survey of 1988-89. In the 2007-08 National Survey the question was replicated.

A question on the people's Primary Ethnic Self-Identity was first introduced by Richard Rose of Strathclyde University in his survey of Northern Ireland in 1968[14] and replicated by the present author in the Greater Dublin Survey (1972-73) and in the National Surveys of 1988-89 and of 2007-08. The general findings of responses to both questions, i.e. Irish as the basis of Irish unity and the people's ethnic self-identity, will be presented and discussed here.

Table No. 16.12:
Irish as an Acceptable Symbolic Basis of Irish Unity
Question Asked: *"Would you agree or disagree that a return to the Irish Language and Culture could provide a good basis for Irish Unity in the Long Term (even though it might present difficulties in the Short Term?"*

Level of Agreement (2007-08)	Total Sample A		Irish-Born B		Difference (B – A)	
	Actual	Cum.	Actual	Cum.	Actual	Cum.
1. Agree	30.0%	30.0%	31.0%	31.0%	+1.0%	+1.0%
2. Neither Agree nor Disagree	21.4%	51.4%	22.5%	53.5%	+1.1%	+2.1%
3. Don't Know	16.1%	67.4%	11.3%	64.8%	-4.8%	-2.6%
4. Disagree	32.5%	---	35.2%	---	+2.7%	---
Number	100.0%	1,011	100.0%	855	---	---

The main result of the above Table is the fact that a slight plurality would not agree with the statement, i.e. 32.5% disagreeing and 30.0% agreeing. The Irish-born among the respondents do not differ that much from the Total Sample. The relatively high proportion in the 'neither agree nor disagree' and 'don't know' would seem to indicate around one-third are

[14] See Richard Rose, *Governing Without Consensus*, London, Faber, 1971.

indecisive, which could mean that their opinions are susceptible to change. Comparisons with the findings of earlier surveys would indicate a move towards agreement.

Table No. 16.13:
Changes in Attitudes towards Irish as a Symbolic Basis of Irish Unity

Level of Agreement	National Sample				Dublin Sub-Samples				
	Total Sample 2007-08	Total Irish Born 2007-08	Total Sample 1988-89	(A-C)	Sub-Sample Irish Born 2007-08	Sub-Sample 1988-89	Sample 1972-73	(C–D)	(C–E)
	A	B	C		C	D	E		
1. Agree	30%	31.0%	24%	+6%	24%	20%	18%	+4%	+6%
2. Don't Know/ Neither Agree nor Disagree	38%	34.0%	19%	+19%	40%	22%	4%	+18%	+36%
3. Disagree	33%	35.0%	57%	-24%	37%	58%	79%	-21%	-42%
Number	1,011	855	1,000	---	246	274	2,279	---	---

The findings of Table No. 16.13 show evidence of a significant and substantial change in the opinions of the people in relation to the potential of the Irish language as a symbolic basis of common identity for all Irish people. The biggest sign of change is the **reduction** of those who **disagree** (-24%) with the statement/question (see Table No. 16.12 above). The increase in the 'Don't Know/Neither Agree or Disagree' row, as already stated, is indicative of the transitional stage of change of opinion.

While the change is significant and substantial, there is much room for improvement. The achievement of the *Good Friday Agreement* in 1998 and efforts to promote Irish as the language for all people living in Ireland are noteworthy. These achievements for the improvement of **cultural solidarity** between people from diverse cultural, political and religious traditions may be beginning to have a positive effect on the people's opinions. This does not mean that the country is heading for a monolingual (Irish only) popular language. The increase of cultural diversity in Ireland today will result in many becoming **multilingual**, as is the case of citizens of Belgium, where a large number of citizens have a command of Flemish, French, English and German. The prominent languages in Ireland for some time will be Irish and English. The linguistic make-up of our population may add other languages. According as this diversity develops, the ethnic self-identity of many of our citizens will be mixed, hence the greater importance of Irish as a powerful symbolic system with the potential of promoting cultural solidarity which respects the cultural (or subcultural) pluralism of Ireland of the 21st century.

Despite the rational case in favour of the return to the Irish language and culture as symbols of common identity (giving some depth to the concept and reality of **being Irish**), there is need for caution and patience in the exercise of persuasion of others who have a different view.   The common use of Irish does not exclude the common use of English.   **Irish** and **English** are source partners of **Scots Irish**.   There is no reason why every Irish person should not respect the **three** traditions.

The link between the people's ethnic self-identity and the Irish language and culture is important as can be seen from the findings of Table No. 16.14, which gives the Pearson product-moment correlation coefficients between the three main findings of Irish Ethnic Self-Identity, Competence, Frequency of Use and Attitudes towards the Irish Language (now).

Table No. 16.14:
Pearson Correlations between Irish Ethnic Self-Identity, Competence in Irish, Frequency of Use and Attitudes towards Irish Now

	Ethnic self-Identity	How Frequently use Irish	Competency in Irish	How felt about Irish-now
Ethnic Self-Identity	1.000 n=1015	**0.243** n=1015	**0.384** n=1015	0.116 n=883
How Frequently use Irish		1.000 n=1015	**0.696** n=1015	**0.452** n=883
Competency in Irish			1.000 n=1015	**0.482** n=883
How felt about Irish-now				1.000 n=883

Note: Correlations over **0.200** are in **bold**.

This is a relatively strong correlation between 'competency' in Irish and 'frequency of use', i.e. **+0.696**.   'Ethnic self-identity' is moderately related to 'competency' in Irish, i.e. **+0.384** and 'frequency of use' i.e. = **+0.243**.   The non-significant link between 'attitudes towards the language now' and 'ethnic self-identity' is explained by the two different samples involved i.e. Irish-born and total sample respectively.   The moderately high correlation between 'attitudes towards the language now' and 'competency' **(+.482)** and 'use' **(+.452)** is as was expected.

Again, the measuring of respondents' attitudes/opinions in relation to the proposition that the Irish language would provide a basis for Irish unity by personal variables is published in the special Irish language report: *The Irish Language and the Irish People* (2009) pages 93-99. The progress since 1972-73 would indicate that according as competence in and use of Irish increases and support for the language grows, the appreciation of Irish as a good basis of (cultural) Irish unity will gain more approval.

Part VII – Attitudes towards Irish Speakers

The standing of the **'Irish speaker'** in Irish society is yet another test of the public status of Irish among the people. With the disappointingly low percentage of the sample regularly using the language, it would not be surprising if this were reflected in the attitudes towards the 'Irish speaker', which is measured below by means of a social-distance scale.

7.1 General Social Distance:

"Irish Speakers" were one of the fifty-one stimulus categories whose social distance was measured in the 2007-08 National Social Survey. Table No. 16.15 gives the responses of the Total Sample:

Table No. 16.15:
Social Distance towards 'Irish Speakers' by Total Sample

Levels of Social Distance	Percentages	
	Actual	Cumulative
1. Kinship	84.4%	84.4%
2. Friendship	8.6%	93.0%
3. Next-Door Neighbour	1.4%	94.4%
4. Co-Worker	3.0%	97.4%
5. Citizen of Ireland	1.2%	98.6%
6. Visitor Only	1.4%	1.5%
7. Debar / Deport	0.1%	
Number	1,010	---
Mean-Social-Distance (MSD)	1.324	

The above findings are extremely favourable and places 'Irish Speakers' as an in-group in the Republic of Ireland. They rank 4th in the rank order of 51 stimulus categories, i.e.

1st	Roman Catholics	-	**1.17**
2nd	Working Class	-	**1.23**
3rd	People with Physical Disability	-	**1.27**
4th	Irish Speakers	-	**1.32**

Table No. 16.16 traces the changes in social distance scores of the national samples between 1988-89 and 2007-08.

Table No. 16.16:
Changes in Social Distance towards 'Irish Speakers' Since 1988-89

Samples	Kinship 1.	Friend-ship or Closer 2.	Next Door Neighbour or Closer 3.	Co-Worker or Closer 4.	Citizen or Closer 5.	Visitor Only 6.	Debar or Deport 7.	MSD	No.
1. Total Sample 2007-08	84.4%	92.9%	94.4%	97.4%	98.6%	1.4%	0.1%	1.324	1,015
2. Irish-born 2007-08	84.8%	92.8%	94.3%	97.7%	98.9%	1.1%	0.1%	1.316	855
3. Nat. Sample 1988-89	84.1%	92.5%	96.6%	98.4%	99.8%	0.3%	0.0%	1.287	1,004
(1 – 2)	-0.4%	+0.2%	+0.1%	-0.3%	-0.3%	+0.3%	0.0%	+0.008	---
(1 – 3)	-0.3%	+0.5%	-2.2%	-1.0%	-1.2%	+1.1%	+0.1%	+0.028	---
(2 – 3)	+0.7%	+0.3%	-2.3%	-0.7%	-0.9%	+0.8%	+0.1%	+0.029	---

The most amazing result of Table No. 16.16 is the absence of any significant variation between the Social Distance Scores of the Total Sample of 1988-89 and the Irish-born of 2007-08. This is yet another example of the **stability** and **consistency** of the pattern of attitudes in the population towards matters Irish. Some would argue that, since the level of social closeness is so high, i.e. members of the in-group, there is little room for change. But that is not the issue. Rather, what has remained constant is the maintenance of such a high level of social preference. Does this finding reveal another fact about the level of the people's perception of Irish as part of their own implicit self-definition? Therefore, when we show such positive attitudes toward 'Irish Speakers' over such a long period (marked by all kinds of socio-cultural changes), are we in reality showing a healthy love for ourselves? Are we recovering from the imposed sense of inferiority which resulted from the long period of colonial cultural and social supremacy or dominance?

Despite this relatively high esteem for the 'Irish Speaker', there are only 22.7% of the Irish-born reporting that they speak/use Irish regularly, even though 47.2% of the sample see themselves as being reasonably competent in the Irish Language. Does this not confirm that the main obstacles to a greater use of Irish are **structural** and outside the personal scope of most people? Have the State and the voluntary organisations failed to generate a socio-cultural environment (at the formal or informal levels) which would be conducive to greater use of Irish?

On the positive side of the above findings, there are encouraging lessons to be learned about the attitudes towards the Irish language in Ireland. The fact that 'Irish Speakers' are a positive reference group should reassure those who are keen on speaking the language that they are admired for doing so. It also could be seen as a mandate to the State to provide structured changes which facilitate greater use of Irish. The findings confirm the other expressions of support (reported in Chapter II).

7.2 Social Distance towards 'Irish Speakers' by Personal Variables:

Again, because of the exceptionally high percentage of respondents opting for 'admission to kinship', i.e. **84.4%**, (which means a relatively low PD[15] of 84.4 x 15.6 = 1317) the room for variation is quite restricted.

---

[15] P = 100 - D. The maximum PD is 50 x 50 = 2,500 and the minimum is 99 x 1 = 99.

Table No. 16.17:
Extracts from Social Distance towards 'Irish Speakers' by Personal Variables

Personal Variable	Welcome into the Family	Deny Citizenship	Mean-Social-Distance
Total Sample	84.4%	1.5%	1..324
(a) Age (p=<.001)			
1. 18-25 Years	75.4%	1.2%	1.476 *
2. 26-40 Years	**86.4%**	0.3%	1.285
3. 41-55 Years	83.9%	**3.6%**	1.397
4. 56-70 Years	87.1%	0.0%	**1.169**
5. 71 Years plus	**88.5%**	**3.1%**	1.287
Number	853	15	---
(b) Gender (p=<.005)			
1. Male	**87.5%**	1.2%	**1.287**
2. Female	81.3%	**1.8%**	1.360 *
Number	852	15	---
(c) Marital Status (p=<.001)			
1. Single / Never married	79.9%	**1.7%**	1.461
2. Married	**88.2%**	1.3%	**1.209**
3. Separated / Divorced	82.2%	0.0%	1.239
4. Permanent relationship	76.4%	1.4%	1.526 *
5. Widowed	**89.7%**	**2.9%**	1.231
Number	852	15	---
(d) Area of Birth (p=<.001)			
1. City (100,000+)	77.9%	1.4%	1.438 *
2. Large Town (10,000+)	**88.3%**	**4.2%**	1.294
3. Town (1,500+)	**88.4%**	0.0%	1.272
4. Rural/ Village	**88.4%**	1.2%	**1.216**
Number	850	15	---
(e) Region of Residence (p=<.03)			
1. BMW- Border Midlands West	83.9%	**1.5%**	1.319
2. Dublin	81.8%	**1.7%**	1.394 *
3. Mid-East & South-East	**86.6%**	**3.2%**	1.362
4. Mid-West & South-West	**85.2%**	0.0%	**1.209**
Number	852	16	---
(f) Education (p=<.001)			
1. Primary or less	**92.4%**	**1.7%**	**1.177**
2. Incomplete Second-Level	**90.5%**	0.4%	1.189
3. Complete Second-Level	84.0%	**2.0%**	1.377
4. Third-level	77.4%	**1.9%**	1.427 *
Number	852	15	---

Table No. 16.17 (Cont'd.) Personal Variable	Welcome into the Family	Deny Citizenship	Mean-Social-Distance
(g) Occupational Status (p=<.03)			
1 Unskilled / Semi	**85.0%**	0.0%	**1.323**
2. Skilled/ Routine Non-Manual	**84.6%**	2.8%	1.347 *
3.Inspectional / Supervisory	83.5%	3.0%	1.335
4. Professional / Executive	**85.3%**	0.0%	1.324
Number	723	13	---

Notes: Lowest Mean-Social-Distance is in **bold** while the highest has an asterisk*.
　　　Percentages above sample average also in **bold.**

As is clear from the above Table, the range of percentages within each variable is moderate.　　Still, each of the variables recorded a statistically significant variation (on the range of replies to each level).　　The most reliable measure is the Mean-Social-Distance (on a 1 to 7 continuum).　　It must be emphasised that all subsamples vary very little and their MSD were under 1.500 which is the limit for a category to become an 'in-group'.

In the case of **age,** the two oldest age-cohorts were the **most** favourably disposed to 'Irish speakers', i.e. the '56 to 70 year-olds' and those '71 years and older'. The youngest age group was **least** welcoming to 'Irish speakers', i.e. with **75.4%** welcoming them into the family.　　This repeats a pattern in the 2007-08 MSD scores!

The percentages for **gender** subsamples have shown that 'males' were slightly more welcoming to 'Irish speakers' than were 'females'.　　Their range of difference when welcoming into the **family** was 6.2%, i.e. **87.5%** of 'males' would admit 'Irish speakers' to their family as compared with **81.3%** of 'females'.

There was a 13.3% difference of scores between the **marital status** subsamples admitting 'Irish speakers' to the family, i.e. **89.7%** of widowed as compared with **76.4%** for respondents in 'permanent relationships'. The difference between the 'married' and the 'widowed' in the welcoming to kinship percentages was less than the 'margin of error'.

'Rural/Village'-born respondents had the lowest MSD **(1.216)** and the highest percentage in **area of birth** subsamples for 'admitting to family' **(88.4%).**　It should be noted, however, that the three non-city subsamples had practically the same percentage 'welcoming to family', i.e. Large Town **88.3%,** Town 88.4% and Rural/Village 88.4%. Such **consensus** is very rare! The city-born was the subsample with the lowest percentage 'welcoming to the family' **(77.9%)** and the highest MSD **(1.438).**

The range of difference between the subsamples in the **region of residence** variable is minimal for significance statistically, which points to a high level of consensus across the State in esteem for 'Irish speakers'.

Education produced the highest percentage of all in the Table (No. 16.17), welcoming 'Irish speakers' into the family at **92.4%**, and the second-lowest Mean-Social-Distance score at **1.177**. The subsample to achieve this record is the respondents of the 'primary or less' level of achievement. Respondents with 'third-level' education were the **least** welcoming subsample within the variable, i.e. **77.4%** admitting 'Irish speakers' to the family and the highest MSD score at **1.427**.

'Unskilled/Semi-skilled' and 'professional/executive', the bottom and top **occupational status** subsamples, share the highest percentage admitting to family at **85.0%** and **85.3%** and the lowest MSD scores at **1.323** and **1.324** respectively. These findings show the high level of **consensus** between the social-distance scores of the occupational grades.

7.3 Conclusion:
The second question measured the standing of the **'Irish speaker'** as measured by the *Bogardus Social Distance Scale*. Not so long ago the *'Gaeilgeoir'* or the *'Tá sé'* was a category of benevolent comedy in the pubs and parlours of the 'chattering classes'. While relatively few **(22.7%** of Irish-born) use Irish regularly, it is reassuring to learn that the standing of 'Irish speakers' is very high, and falls within the 'in-group' set of categories, i.e. those with a mean-social-distance score of 1,500 or under on a continuum of 1 to 7. The percentage of respondents who 'would welcome Irish speakers into their family through marriage' was as high as **84.4%.**

Part VIII – Overall Conclusion of Chapter

In the course of Chapter XVI above, a report on the findings based on the 2007-08 national survey has been presented under seven main headings, i.e. introduction, aspiration of the people for the Irish language; attitudes towards Irish while in school and now; declared competence in the Irish language; frequency and occasion of use of Irish; Irish as a basis of common national identity; and attitudes to 'Irish Speakers' as a stimulus category.

The findings of, and commentary on, each of the above topics are covered in greater detail in a special report entitled: *The Irish Language and the Irish People*.   The central questions were addressed in relation to the Irish language, i.e. **attitudes** towards Irish, **competence** in the language and its **regular use**.   In the overall, the position of the Irish language in 2007-08 is seen to be positive and quite encouraging for those interested in its promotion.

The general level of **reasonable competence** among the Irish-born of the national sample is **47.2%** and the **attitudes** towards the future of Irish is very positive at **93.2%** in favour of its preservation and revival.   Only **6.7%** would wish to see the language **discarded**.   Some **40.2%** wish to see it **revived** in everyday life, while **52.9%** wanted Irish **preserved** for its cultural value and spoken in the *Gaeltacht.*

The **regular use** of Irish is **disappointing** at **22.7%** using it 'occasionally or more often'.   In other words, slightly less than half of those with reasonable competence in Irish use it on a regular basis.   Because of the high correlation between use and competence ($r = 0.696$), any **improvement in use** would generate a dynamic development which would enhance further improvement in competence in, and goodwill toward, Irish in the population.   The reverse does not seem to happen to date, i.e. increase in competence leading to increase in use!

The evidence of the 2007-08 and previous surveys shows that the conditions are now in place for a very significant breakthrough for the native language should the structural changes take place to translate competence into use!   Public education policy towards Irish is crucial for a major breakthrough.   Socio-cultural norms which impede the regular use of Irish should be identified and changed.

A major finding has been the relatively **high standing** of Irish in the community. The better educated, those in the higher professions, and the more urbanised, and young citizens are more competent in Irish and use it more often. The recognition of Irish as an official language in the European Union recently, as well as the status of Irish in *The Official Languages Act of 2003,* should improve the motivation of Irish people to know and use their native language more in the years ahead.

***

CHAPTER XVII
Religious Attitudes and Practices[1]

Part I – Historical Background of Religious Profile

The importance of religion in relation to prejudice and tolerance in the Republic of Ireland and in Northern Ireland is self-evident. Religious affiliation has been a central badge of identity and a source of social and political strife in Ireland since the mid-sixteenth century when the English establishment became Protestant and the vast majority of Irish people maintained their loyalty to the Roman Catholic Church. Ireland as an **emigrant society** continued with its historically-based religious minorities until very recently.

Following the Protestant Reformation, Roman Catholics were persecuted and ethnically cleansed from their lands in the Province of Ulster and elsewhere and transferred to the poorer parts of Connaught and to other areas of less fertile soil. They were replaced by Protestants, especially Presbyterians, in Ulster. The situation was further worsened in the 1690s following the Williamite victory over King James of England. For most of the 18th century, Roman Catholics were continuously being persecuted by the Irish Parliament in Dublin, which was exclusively Protestant. This was known as the period of the infamous 'Penal Laws'. Presbyterians were also to suffer under the Established Church's influence.

Throughout the 19th century, things began to improve for Roman Catholics and Presbyterians in Ireland. The granting of Roman Catholics' right to stand for Parliament under the *Act of Catholic Emancipation 1829* and the Disestablishment of the Church of Ireland in 1869 marked two important steps for the status and rights of Roman Catholics. The Penal Laws were gradually being ignored and annulled. The establishment of St Patrick's College, Maynooth, in 1795 was a very significant event for the re-legitimisation of Roman Catholic clergy. The involvement of Religious, Brothers, Priests and Sisters, provided second-level education for Roman Catholics and, thereby, enabled them to enter the professions. The Catholic University set up originally by John Henry Newman in Dublin in 1854 was

---

[1] A more comprehensive Report on religious attitudes and practices, based on the findings of the 2007-08 survey was published in June 2009 under the title: *The Challenge of Indifference: A Need for Religious Revival in Ireland.* It was published by the Survey and Research Unit, Department of Sociology, NUI Maynooth.

part of the emancipation of the Roman Catholic depressed population throughout the second half of the 19th century. Since denial of ownership of land was part of the segregating issues for Roman Catholics, the success of the Land War and the eventual buying-out of the Landlords in the early years of the 20th century, restored **land ownership** to the "peasant Irish farmers". This gave greater self-worth to the Roman Catholic population.

In the North-Eastern region of Ireland, the dominant Protestant group resisted Home Rule for the Island of Ireland and was successful in the creation of **Northern Ireland** and the Border around the six North-Eastern counties. Within this territory, Protestant Unionists had the majority and ruled the area more or less as a 'Protestant State' until the fall of Stormont in 1972 during a time of intensive paramilitary violence which broke out in 1969 and did not end until the ceasefire of 1994. In 1998, an Agreement was signed, i.e. *The Good Friday Agreement*, which provided a form of devolved power-sharing administration. This enabled **Nationalists**, who were predominantly Roman Catholic, and **Unionists**, who were for the most part Protestant, to cooperate on a consensus basis. At the time of the 2007-08 survey, this new arrangement was almost ten years in existence.

Part II – Demographic Profile of Religious Affiliation

With the creation of Northern Ireland, which was composed of the six north-eastern counties, the whole **island of Ireland** was divided into two areas, i.e. the Twenty-Six Counties with a 90% plus Roman Catholic population and the Six Counties with a 60% Protestant population. The impact on the Republic was to give a statistically predominant position to the Roman Catholic Church. Apart from the politico-religious effects of such an 'unnatural division' of the island of Ireland, which had been administratively one unit until 1922, it created a difficulty for the social researcher measuring the details of a 'random' sample. The numbers of respondents from denominations and religious groupings other than Roman Catholics are so small in a sample of 1,015 that they cannot be further divided into subsamples. The latter would be necessary to analyse the attitudes and practices of such non-Catholic respondents.

Table No. 17.1:
Demographic Distribution (by Religious Affiliation) in the Republic of Ireland 1861-2006

Year	Population	Roman Catholic %	C.of I. %	Presby. %	Method. %	Jewish %	Other Religion %	No Religion %	Not Stated %
1861	4,402,111	89.4	8.5	1.5	0.4	0.008	0.2	-	-
1871	4,043,189	89.2	8.4	1.5	0.4	0.006	0.4	-	-
1881	3,870,020	89.5	8.2	1.5	0.5	0.001	0.3	-	-
1891	3,468,694	89.3	8.3	1.5	0.5	0.004	0.3	-	-
1901	3,221,823	89.3	8.2	1.5	0.6	0.1	0.4	-	-
1911	3,139,688	89.6	7.9	1.4	0.5	0.1	0.4	-	-
1926	2,971,992	92.6	5.5	1.1	0.4	0.1	0.4	-	-
1936	2,968,420	93.4	4.9	0.9	0.3	0.1	0.3	-	-
1946	2,955,107	94.3	4.2	0.8	0.3	0.1	0.3	-	-
1961	2,818,341	94.9	3.7	0.7	0.2	0.1	0.2	0.04	0.2
1971	2,978,248	92.4	3.3	0.5	0.2	0.1	0.2	0.3	1.6
1981	3,443,405	93.1	2.8	0.4	0.2	0.1	0.3	1.2	2.1
1991	3,525,719	91.6	2.5	0.4	0.1	0.04	1.1	1.9	2.4
2002	3,917,202	88.4	3.0	0.5	0.3	0.05	2.3	3.5	2.0
2006	4,239,848	86.8	3.0	0.6	0.3	0.05	3.3	4.4	1.7

Sources: *Statistical Abstract (Ireland) 1950, 1966, 1980, Census 2006, Vol.13-Religion: 2007*

One of the features of the religious profile of the population of the Republic of Ireland has been its relative stability over one hundred and forty years. The recent influx of migrants to the Republic has not so far made a substantial difference due to the high proportion of Roman Catholics and other Christian denominations among those coming here. The EU policy resulting in limitations on migrants from outside Europe has inevitably slowed down the numbers of Muslims, Hindus and other non-Christians from coming to live in the Republic.

Table No. 17.2:
Demographic Distribution (by Religious Affiliation) of Sample

Affiliation	Respondents	Spouses	Parents		Number (Total Sample)
			Fathers	Mothers	
1.Roman Catholic	89.6%	91.8%	90.9%	91.0%	908
2. Protestants and Other Christians	4.4%	4.4%	5.4%	5.3%	45
3. Other Religion	2.7%	1.4%	2.5%	2.5%	27
4. No Religion	3.3%	2.5%	1.2%	1.1%	33
Number	1,013	584	1,002	1,003	1,013

When compared with the above distribution, the variations from the 2006 Census are quite minimal and within the margin of error. The survey had only two cases of "Not Stated". It is important to note that the sample represents the population aged eighteen years and older, while the census figures refer to the total population (including under-eighteen year olds). Allowing for this difference, the above distribution is close enough to the census. Table No. 17.2 also points to the extremely high level of denominational endogamy, i.e. marrying a person of one's own religion, for Roman Catholics and 'Protestants and other Christians'. The principle of 'denominational propinquity', i.e. endogamy, would be likely to broaden in the event of an advance in Christian ecumenism.

The intergenerational lack of change in religious affiliation would indicate a relatively low level of leakage from the Roman Catholic Church in the adult population. This is more surprising in the light of the level of criticism in the media of the Roman Catholic Church, and the significant and substantial decrease in formal religious practice over the past two decades, as will be shown below. Does this mean that religious affiliation can weather the storms of Church criticism and scandals? Other evidence reported below would seem to support a positive answer to this question. Of course, it could also be argued that disaffiliation takes place only *a generation after* practice weakens or ceases. This is something Church and religious leaders must be keenly aware of in Ireland today. Withdrawal from affiliation is the most serious threat to the future viability of any organisation or category of organisation.

The level of 'no religion' at 3.3% (or 4.4% in the 2006 Census) has been repeated later in the findings, i.e. in the reasons given for not feeling 'Close to God' at 3.9% who did not believe in God (see Table No. 17.17 below, for 'Perceived Closeness to God'). This confirms the overall findings that the vast majority of respondents have held on to a level of belief, however tenuous, which could be revived and find expression in prayer and worship, in the event of successful pastoral programmes, etc., and a change of religious outlook in society.

The following Table (No. 17.3) gives a breakdown of the population of Northern Ireland by Religious Denomination between 1911 and 2001:

Table No. 17.3:
Religious Denominations in Northern Ireland (1911-2001)

Year	Roman Catholics	Presbyter- ians	Church of Ireland	Methodists	Other Religion	No Religion Not Stated	Number
1. 1911	34.1%	31.6%	26.1%	3.7%	2.6%	1.6%	1,250,531
2. 1926	33.5%	31.3%	27.0%	3.9%	2.9%	1.4%	1,256,579
3. 1991	40.6%	23.5%	19.5%	4.2%	8.4%	3.9%	1,578,000
4. 2001	40.3%	20.7%	15.3%	3.5%	6.4%	13.9%	1,685,267

Source: *Census Reports.*

While the Roman Catholic proportion of the Northern Ireland population grew by **6%** during the ninety years from 1911 to 2001, the combined Protestant denominations, i.e. Presbyterians, Church of Ireland and Methodists, decreased from **61.4%** in 1911 to **39.5%** in 2001, i.e. - **21.9%**. The following extract (from Table No. 17.3) traces the years of decline:

Year	A Roman Catholic	B Combined Protestant Denominations	Nominal Difference (A – B)
1911	34.1%	61.4%	-27.3%
1926	33.5%	62.2%	-28.7%
1991	40.6%	47.2%	-6.6%
2001	40.3%	39.5%	+0.8%

The above extract from Table No. 17.3 records a situation in 2001 when the Roman Catholic has passed out the combined numbers of the three main Protestant denominations. Of course, a percentage of **Other Religions** probably represent members of smaller Protestant denominations. The nominal drop in the Protestant denomination over the ninety years (1911 to 2001) of **21.9%** is the equivalent of a percentage decline of **-35.7%**, which is more than one-third. This must be a matter of serious concern for the major Protestant denominations. The situation is likely to improve once normal relations aimed at **pluralist ecumenism** between the Christian Churches in Northern Ireland have begun to bear results.

Part III – Religious Practice over the Years

If one accepts that religion is based on faith in a **Transcendent God**, the expression of such belief is to be found in public worship, private prayer, and charitable behaviour. **Christian faith** may be defined as **a radical commitment to God's existence and a willingness to living one's life according to God's will as taught by Jesus Christ.** Since religion is basically a metaphysical reality, which has meaning only within the context of faith, it is not adequately explained by an empirical or positivist methodology. What can be measured in relation to religion by the sociologist are patterns of behavioural norms and dispositions open to empirical measurement and research. The "bifurcation of religion and spirituality" in some literature seems to be overstated (see Hill, Peter C. and Kenneth I. Pargament, 2003).

Table No. 17.4:
Formal Worship of Total Sample, Roman Catholics and Irish Roman Catholics

Frequency	Total Sample	Cum	Roman Catholics	Cum	Irish Roman Catholics	Cum
1. Daily	3.7 %	--	4.1 %	--	4.5 %	--
2. Several Times a Week	3.9 %	(7.6)	3.7 %	(7.7)	3.9 %	(8.3)
3. Once a Week	34.5 %	**(42.1)**	36.1 %	**(43.8)**	36.2 %	**(44.5)**
4. 1 to 3 times a Month	12.3 %	(54.4)	13.4 %	(57.2)	13.0 %	(57.5)
5. Several Times a Year	13.2 %	(67.7)	14.0 %	(71.2)	14.4 %	(71.9)
6. Less Frequently	19.3 %	(86.9)	19.4 %	(90.6)	19.1 %	(91.0)
7. Never	11.6 %		8.9 %		8.4 %	
8. No Answer / Not applicable	1.4 %		0.5 %		0.5 %	
Number	1,013		908		823	

The above figures reflect a significant and substantial *decline* in weekly worship since the previous survey (carried out by the present author) in 1988-89 when 79.3% reported worshipping formally once a week or more often. The difference between the weekly collective worship of Roman Catholics in general, and Irish Catholics in particular, is not that significant, and falls within a plus-minus 3% margin of error. This decline in weekly worship may have been influenced by an apparent change in the expected norm which seems to indicate monthly collective worship to be the new norm. This is implicit in Eoin O'Mahony's article in *Studies* (Dublin, Spring 2008).

Table No. 17.5:
Changes in Religious Practice of Total Population in the
Republic of Ireland since 1981

Frequency	1981 (EVS) * %	1988-89 (Mac Gr) *** %	1990 (EVS) * %	1999 (EVS) * %	2002 (ESS) ** %	2004 (ESS) ** %	2006 (ESS) ** %	2007-08 (Current Survey) %
1. Weekly or more often	82.2	79.3	80.8	65.4	53.8	55.6	46.7	42.1
2. Monthly or more often	87.9	85.1	87.7	74.7	67.1	69.5	60.5	54.4
3. Less frequently or more often	95.4	96.1	96.3	92.2	89.1	91.5	85.9	86.9
4. Never	4.6	3.9	3.7	7.8	10.9	8.5	14.2	11.6
Number	1,217	1,001	1,000	1,012	2,046	2,086	1,800	1,013

Sources: * *European Values Survey (EVS) 1981, 1990, 1999*   ** *European Social Survey (ESS) 2002, 2004, 2006*
*** Mac Gréil *Prejudice in Ireland Revisited, 1996*

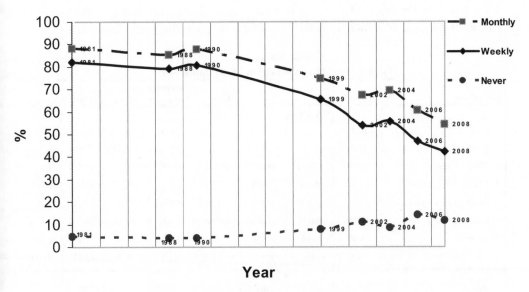

Figure No. 17.1:
Changes in Religious Practice of Total Population 1981 – 2008

The above findings of Table No. 17.5 and Figure No.17.1 clearly show an acute decline in formal religious practice over a period of twenty-seven years. Attendance at weekly worship declined by 40.1% between 1981 and 2008, and the trend is still negative and will not be corrected unless effective measures are taken to attract the absent faithful to return to weekly formal worship.

The intrusion of more commercialised activity into the Sabbath, i.e. recreational and trading, has also had an effect on weekly participation. 'Working' was given as a reason for 10.3% of Roman Catholics and 4.8% of Protestants (who did not attend weekly worship) for not participating.

With regard to those attending 'several times a year', it should be noted that these include a substantial number of believers who attend funeral and marriage liturgical services. It would not be unreasonable to speculate that a significant proportion of the adult population (who do not go to Mass every Sunday) would attend a funeral Mass or Service three to four times a month on average, i.e. forty-two Masses or Services a year, and five weddings. Add to that attendance at Mass or Service for Christmas and Easter and St Patrick's Day or some other great Church feast day. When one adds all these together it means fifty-one Masses in the year.

Table No. 17.6:
Formal Worship by Religion / Denomination

Frequency	Total Sample		Roman Catholics		Protestants and Other Christians		Other Believers	
		Cum		Cum		Cum		Cum
1. Daily	3.7%	–	4.1%	–	2.3%	–	0.0%	–
2. Several Times a week	3.9%	(7.6)	3.7%	(7.7)	9.1%	(11.4)	7.1%	(7.1)
3. Once a Week	34.5%	**(42.1)**	36.1%	**(43.8)**	22.7%	**(34.1)**	42.9%	**(50.0)**
4. 1 to 3 times a month	12.3%	(54.4)	13.4%	(57.2)	9.1%	(43.2)	0.0%	(50.0)
5. Several times a year	13.2%	(67.7)	14.0%	(71.2)	6.8%	(50.0)	10.7%	(60.7)
6. Less frequently	19.3%	(86.9)	19.4%	(90.6)	31.8%	(81.8)	10.7%	(71.4)
7. Never	11.6%	(98.6)	8.9%	(99.5)	18.2%	(100.0)	17.9%	(89.3)
8. No Answer / Not applicable	1.4%	(100.0)	0.5%	(100.0)	0.0%	(100.0)	10.7%	(100)
Number	1,013		908		44		28	

Formal Worship by Religion/Denomination in Table No. 17.6 shows a pattern which reflects the expected frequency norms of the various

categories.   The statistical predominance of Roman Catholics in the
population is also reflected in the level of practice overall.   Roman
Catholics have a marginally higher attendance rate and a significantly lower
percentage who stated they never attended formal religious worship.   The
low numbers of 'Protestant and other Christians' and of 'Other Religious'
prevents significant analysis of subsamples with these categories.

Table No. 17.7:
Participation in Mass, Holy Communion and Confession
(i.e. the Sacrament of Penance) of Roman Catholics

Frequency	All Catholics		
	Mass	Holy Communion	Confession
1. Daily	3.7%	3.5%	`0.2%
2. Several times a week (or more often)	7.5%	6.2%	0.3%
3. Once a week (or more often)	**42.8%**	33.3%	3.3%
4. One to three times a month (or more often)	54.9%	**43.1%**	9.0%
5. Several times a year (or more often)	69.8%	58.0%	**27.3%**
6. Less frequently (or more often)	88.8%	81.8%	64.8%
7. Never	9.1%	16.6%	32.9%
8. No answer / Not applicable	2.1%	1.6%	2.3%
Number	906	904	904

Participation in **Mass** by Roman Catholics is very close to the
percentages for Formal Worship, which points to the attachment of Catholic
Churchgoers to the Eucharist.

Participation in **Holy Communion** represents a very high proportion
of those Roman Catholics who take part in the Mass, i.e. 77.8% of weekly
(or more often) Mass-goers, 78.5% of monthly or more often, 83% of
'several times a year or more often' and 92.1% of the 'less frequently or
more often'.   Buried in these high percentages is the indication that those
who do not go to Mass weekly do not view it as an impediment to receiving
Holy Communion, i.e. missing Mass on Sunday is not seen by many as a
'mortal' or 'serious' sin.   (Figures for Confession confirm this
interpretation.   Or does it mean that receiving Holy Communion is seen as
an integral part of the *reconciliation process*?)

The level of taking part in the **Sacrament of Penance** has greatly
reduced over the past number of decades.   At present one-third of Roman

Catholics in the sample (32.9%) stated they never go to Confession at present. Does this mean that the 'sense of sin' is dying for many, or are they happy to confess to God privately when they realise they have sinned? For Christians, the loss of the sense of sin could be seen as a loss of faith in God. To believe in God for Christians is accompanied by a commitment to following his will as revealed in the teaching of Jesus Christ.

Table No. 17.8 gives the reasons put forward by respondents who did not attend weekly worship:

Table No. 17.8:
Reasons for Not Attending Weekly Worship

Reason	Total Sample	Roman Catholics	Protestants
1. Just Don't Bother	64.8%	68.1%	14.3%
2. Working	10.0%	10.3%	4.8%
3. Illness	4.5%	3.4%	28.6%
4. Other Reason	20.7%	18.2%	52.4%
Number	447	417	21

Figure No. 17.2:
Reasons for Not Attending Weekly Worship (Roman Catholics)

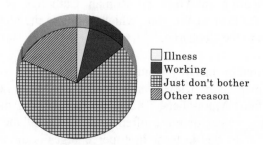

The three main reasons listed were 'just don't bother' (reflecting indifference), 'working' (on the Sabbath) and 'illness'. Over two-thirds of Roman Catholics who did not go to Church once a week (or more often) *'just did not bother'*. This level of indifference tells the reader much about the nature of the problem of Church attendance and the irrelevant standing of formal weekly Christian worship to so many of the total subsample of Roman Catholics. It tells something about the failure of 'handing on' the importance of formal weekly worship and the weakening of personal commitment to living out the faith by previously committed Roman Catholics.

It has been commented on already that **work** was given as a reason for not attending weekly worship by Roman Catholics. This was an inevitable consequence of the demise of the Sabbath as a day of worship and rest. The impact of this change is far wider than the 10% prevented from going to Church on Sunday. In societies where the Sabbath is honoured, there is likely to be more solidarity in weekly worship. The irony of this change is that it has happened, largely for commercial gain, at a time of more automation in work, shorter working hours and higher standards of living. A return to a work-free Sabbath could have wide-ranging personal and social, as well as religious, benefits for society. Family life would also benefit from the leisure and relaxation of a renewed Sabbath day of rest.

Frequency of Church attendance is largely dependent on the availability of believers to attend. From the above findings it could be assumed that **13.7%** of Roman Catholics (not attending weekly worship) were **not free** to attend worship. For instance, **43%** attending Mass each Sunday is really **50%** of the **86%** free to attend!

The following Table (No. 17.9) traces the changes in the practice of the Sacraments (Eucharist and Confession) and in Mass attendance since 1974:

Table No. 17.9:
Changes in Mass, Holy Communion and Confession Attendance of
Roman Catholics since 1974

Frequency of Attendance	A 1974 *	B 1984 **	C 1988-89	D 2007-08	Change D - C
1. Weekly Mass Attendance	91%	87%	82%	43%	-39%
2. Monthly Holy Communion	66%	64%	63%	43%	-20%
3. (a) Monthly Confession	47%	26%	18%	9%	-9%
3. (b) Confession Several Times a Year	---	---	80%	27%	-53%
Number	2,499	1,006	1,005	906	---

*   Nic Ghiolla Phádraig, Máire - R & D Report, 1974.
** Breslin A and John A. Weafer, - R & D Report, 1984.

The substantial decline in religious worship, i.e. Mass and the Sacraments of Holy Communion and Confession has taken place between 1988-89 and 2007-08, although there was a serious decrease in the practice of Confession during the 1970s and 1980s. Incidentally, this decline had predated the publicity on the clerical child-abuse scandals of the 1990s. The latter could have added to the reduction of practice in the period between 1988-89 and 2007-08.

Monthly Holy Communion practice has not declined as acutely as did weekly Mass attendance, i.e. a drop of 20% as compared with one of 39%. This means that participation in the Mass by the reduced percentage of respondents is a *fuller participation* than it was when more people went to Mass without receiving Holy Communion.

The greatest crisis facing the Roman Catholic Church is in the practice of going to Confession. Unless something radical and urgent is done by the Catholic Church to stem this decline, the **Sacrament of Reconciliation** is in danger of becoming irrelevant for all but the minority of very serious and devout adults!

Part IV – Practice of Roman Catholics by Personal Variables

In this part of the chapter it is proposed to examine Mass attendance, reception of Holy Communion and going to Confession by personal variables. Table No. 17.10 presents the findings for Mass attendance by age, gender, marital status, area of birth, place of rearing, region of residence, education and occupational status.

Table No. 17.10: Mass Attendance, Reception of Holy Communion and Confession by Personal Variables

Variable	Mass Attendance		Reception of Holy Communion		Confession	
	Weekly or More Often	Never	Weekly or More Often	Never	Monthly or More Often	Never
Sample Average	**43.7%**	**9.3%**	**33.8%**	**16.9%**	**9.2%**	**33.7%**
(a) Age (p=<.001)						
1. 18-25 Years	19.7%	**17.6%**	9.4%	**26.6%**	2.1%	**43.7%**
2. 26-40 Years	27.8%	**13.0%**	22.7%	**21.2%**	4.4%	**44.9%**
3. 41-55 Years	39.9%	6.3%	30.5%	14.8%	6.8%	31.7%
4. 56-70 Years	**74.2%**	4.3%	**56.5%**	10.6%	**15.0%**	21.9%
5. 71 Years plus	**83.1%**	2.2%	**75.0%**	4.5%	**30.7%**	9.1%

Table No. 17.10 (Cont'd) Variable	Mass Attendance		Reception of Holy Communion		Confession	
	Weekly or More Often	Never	Weekly or More Often	Never	Monthly or More Often	Never
(b) Gender (p=<.001)	N/S				N/S	
1. Male	---	---	26.6%	**19.8%**	---	---
2. Female	---	---	**40.5%**	14.2%	---	---
(c) Marital Status (p=<.001)						
1. Single/Never married	32.0%	**13.6%**	22.1%	**21.5%**	6.1%	**39.8%**
2. Married	**52.6%**	5.8%	**41.8%**	10.1%	8.8%	27.6%
3. Separated / Divorced	23.7%	**13.2%**	18.9%	**37.8%**	5.3%	**42.1%**
4. Permanent Relationship	20.3%	**15.6%**	19.0%	**31.7%**	3.2%	**59.7%**
5. Widowed	**79.3%**	1.7%	**67.2%**	9.8%	**35.0%**	13.3%
(d) Area of Birth (p=<.001)						
1. City (100,000+)	29.5%	**13.4%**	22.9%	**23.5%**	6.4%	**44.2%**
2. Large Town (10,000+)	32.0%	**16.0%**	26.3%	**19.2%**	**10.3%**	**43.3%**
3. Town (1,500+)	43.3%	9.0%	**36.4%**	**18.2%**	**10.8%**	32.5%
4. Rural/Village	**62.7%**	2.8%	**47.2%**	8.2%	**11.7%**	18.6%
(e) Place of Rearing (p=<.001)						
1. Dublin (City / Co)	33.5%	**13.2%**	26.8%	**20.7%**	6.8%	**43.4%**
2. Rest of Leinster	45.2%	6.4%	**34.2%**	14.8%	5.8%	31.8%
3. Munster	**50.0%**	6.7%	**35.6%**	13.1%	**11.8%**	30.8%
4. Connaught Ulster	**54.7%**	5.0%	**46.5%**	15.9%	**12.9%**	19.4%
(f) Region of Residence	(p=<.001)					
1. BMW- Border Midlands West	**47.5%**	5.5%	**37.1%**	**83.0%**	6.6%	26.3%
2. Dublin	36.8%	**14.8%**	29.1%	**76.9%**	**9.7%**	**45.5%**
3. Mid-East & South-East	**43.8%**	**10.8%**	31.4%	**86.4%**	7.3%	27.2%
4. Mid-West & South-West	**47.3%**	5.3%	**38.3%**	**87.6%**	**13.1%**	33.0%
(g) Education (p=<.001)						
1. Primary or less	**75.7%**	7.8%	**65.0%**	**91.2%**	**20.4%**	20.4%
2. Incomplete Second-Level	**46.9%**	7.5%	**36.0%**	83.1%	**11.0%**	30.9%
3. Complete Second-Level	38.7%	9.1%	28.1%	82.1%	8.9%	**34.8%**
4. Third-level	34.1%	**11.1%**	26.3%	81.7%	4.4%	**39.2%**
(h) Occupational Status	(p=<.003)		(p=<.001)			
1 Unskilled/Semi	39.5%	**12.1%**	27.4%	**77.9%**	**9.8%**	31.7%
2. Skilled/Routine Non Manual	39.7%	9.1%	29.1%	**82.4%**	8.1%	**36.7%**
3.Inspectional/Supervisory	**53.8%**	6.7%	**44.8%**	**91.4%**	5.8%	**35.0%**
4. Professional/Executive	**45.7%**	4.9%	**38.7%**	**89.0%**	9.2%	30.1%

Note: Percentages above the sample average are in **bold**.

It is very interesting to note that with the exception of 'Gender' each of the other variables registered a statistically significant variation in Mass attendance. The range of percentages between the subsamples is fairly substantial in most variables. Because of these variations and their statistical significance, Table No. 17.10 is most discerning, and tells the observant reader much about the current state of religious practice of Irish adult Roman Catholics.

Table No. 17.10 merits very serious examination by readers interested in the variations in Mass attendance in each of the variables. It is in this way one finds out the factors which have an impact on the patterns of our religious behaviour. On the present Table there is an obvious cross-influence of other variables on most subsamples, for example, the cross-influence of age on education, of marital status on age, of urbanisation on region of residence, etc.

4.1 Mass Attendance by Personal Variables:

(a) Mass Attendance by Age [Table No. 17.10(a)]:
The correlation between age and Mass attendance is moderately high (r = +0.413). Only one-in-five of the 18 to 25 year-old Roman Catholics go to Mass once a week or more often, while more than four-in-five of those over seventy years attend so regularly. Many of this age cohort (18-25 years) are likely to be third-level students. A percentage of the subsample could be still among the extended adolescents, i.e. have not got a full-time job or settled down to raise a family. Some would see this phase in life as *transitional* between the dependence of childhood and the independence of adulthood. Behaviour during the transitional period tends to change on accepting responsibility in adult years. Should this occur in the case of Mass attendance frequency, the 18 to 25 year-olds will increase their frequency as they grow older.

Another interpretation of the low frequency of Mass attendance of the young age subsample would see it as a more radical withdrawal from religious practice. With such a reading of the figures it would be expected that as this age cohort ages it will bring its low Mass-attendance with it, with some exceptions, of course. This would mean that Irish youth are withdrawing from their religious cultural roots. This level of cultural de-radicalisation has happened earlier in other countries of Europe. Some would see the education system as an important 'agent of cultural de-radicalisation'. The weakening of the home and community culture as positive reference groups has had a negative effect on loyalty to weekly Mass and religious norms. Of course, the agents of cultural change who facilitate the modern economy would see cultural de-radicalisation as secular liberation!

Figure No. 17.3:
Mass Attendance by Age

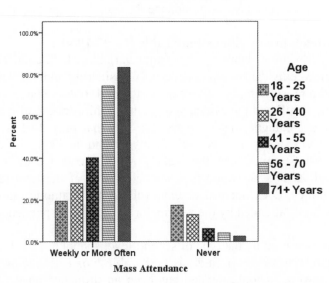

Mass Attendance

(b) Mass Attendance by Area of Birth [Table No. 17.10(d)]:
The impact of **urbanisation** on the decline in regular Church attendance is statistically significant and substantial. The reason for this is likely to be partially explained in the higher level of geographical and social mobility in the city and the weakness of kinship, neighbourhood and local community ties within large tracts of the city suburbia and exurbia. The **age** and **education** factors are also at play in the city population.

The negative correlation (r = -0.338) between urbanisation of area of birth and weekly Mass attendance is clear from Table No. 17.10(d) above. Those Roman Catholics born in a 'City' had less than half the frequency (29.5%) of weekly Mass attendance of the fellow Catholics born in 'Rural/Village' Ireland (63.0%). The 'Large Town' respondents registered 32.1%, while those born in a 'Town' were the national average of 43.5% attending Mass each week.

(c) Mass Attendance by Region of Current Residence [Table No. 17.10(f)]:

The value of the information given in Table No. 17.10(f) is that it provides the reader with information on Mass attendance near to his or her place of residence. The findings show the impact of the negative correlation between urbanisation and Mass attendance through the Republic of Ireland.

(d) Mass Attendance by Education [Table No. 17.10(g)]:

Next to age, education seems to be a major variable which contributes to a reduction in weekly Mass attendance. Considering that 35.4% of the Roman Catholic subsample (eighteen years and older) stated they had reached 'third level' and the evidence of growing third-level participation by the younger age-category 18-25 years, the fact that only **34.1%** attended Mass each week today means the negative trend is likely to continue. Again, it must be noted that the weekly Mass attendance of 'Complete Second-Level' at 38.7%, which is 4.8% below that of the total sample of Roman Catholics, does not reflect that well on the Catholic ethos of the secondary schools attended by the vast majority of these respondents.

When measured by the type of second-level school attended, there has been an interesting range of findings (see Table No. 17.11 below). It is quite clear that the school attended has been an influence on the people's frequency of Mass attendance.

Table No. 17.11:
Mass Attendance by Type of Second-Level School (Roman Catholics)

Type of Second-Level School Attended	Weekly Mass or More Often	Monthly Mass or More Often	Several Times a Year or More Often	Less Frequently or More Often	Never	No.
1. Secondary School (non-fee-paying)	36.1%	48.5%	67.5%	89.9%	10.2%	541
2. Secondary School (fee-paying)	46.5%	60.6%	80.3%	97.2%	2.8%	71
3. Vocational (VEC)	62.2%	72.9%	83.6%	92.3%	7.8%	103
4. Comprehensive School	32.2%	39.3%	50.0%	82.1%	17.9%	28
5. Community School	25.0%	46.9%	53.1%	87.5%	12.5%	32
6. Did not attend Second-Level	71.7%	84.9%	86.8%	93.4%	6.6%	106
Number	385	496	631	800	81	881

Those with the highest records of Mass attendance did not attend second-level schools and completed their education at Primary level or were

452

taught at home. Those attending Vocational Schools had the best Mass-attendance record of all the five second-level categories. This category of school refers to a period prior to the growth of comprehensive and community schools managed by the VECs. Fee-paying Secondary Schools were next highest in their regular Mass attendance. The non-fee-paying Secondary Schools alumni were below the national sample average of **43.7%** for weekly Mass attendance at **36.1%**. The non-fee-paying Secondary School respondents represent **61.4%** of the total Roman Catholic sample. Those attending Comprehensive and Community Schools recorded low weekly Mass attendance at **32.2%** and **25.0%** respectively. The age factor is also influential in the above variables.

4.2 Reception of Holy Communion by Personal Variables:

Table No. 17.10 gives a breakdown of reception of Holy Communion by personal variables. It is anticipated that variations will be close to those of Mass attendance. Older believers, who were reared in pre-Vatican II times, although devout, might be reluctant to receive Holy Communion except when they had been to Confession.

From a Catholic theological perspective, participation in the Eucharist, i.e. reception of Holy Communion, is the exercise of full membership of the Church. Failure to receive Communion is seen as a state of spiritual deprivation. Since the frequency of receiving Holy Communion follows the pattern of Mass attendance by Roman Catholics, it was decided not to provide a detailed commentary on reception by personal variables in this text. Such a commentary is available in the special Report on religion, i.e. *The Challenge of Indifference: A Need for Religious Revival in Ireland* (pages 36-45)[2].

4.3 Frequency of Sacramental Confession by Personal Variables:

The decrease of frequency of Confession by Roman Catholic respondents has been one of the most 'traumatic' findings of the current survey of religious practice in the Republic of Ireland. This is particularly noteworthy in the light of the fact that the development of regular Confession has been one of the contributions of the Irish believers *and leaders* to the whole Church, since medieval times.

---

[2] Mac Gréil, Micheál, *The Challenge of Indifference: A Need for Religious Revival in Ireland*, Maynooth, Survey and Research Unit, Department of Sociology, 2009.

The variations within the personal variables were as predicted, and are in line with other measures of religious (sacramental) practice. The range of variation is quite substantial in the case of age, marital status, area of birth, place of rearing and education. The range of difference between the education subsamples in the case of 'several times a year or more frequently', which is the accepted norm for the more devout practising Roman Catholics, is as great as 34.3% i.e. from 52.4% for respondents with 'primary or less' and 18.8% for 'third-level' respondents.

(a) Frequency of Confession by Age:
The age variable's performance in Table No. 17.10(a) was as anticipated. The following extract highlights the variation between the age sub-samples in the case of the expected norm and the percentages who no longer go to Confession.

Age Variable	Several times a year or More Often	Never go to Confession
1. 18 to 25 years	16.2%	43.7%
2. 26 to 40 years	19.8%	44.9%
3. 41 to 55 years	24.4%	31.7%
4. 56 to 70 years	32.9%	21.9%
5. 71 years plus	72.7%	9.1%
Total Number	248	297
(Sample Average)	(28.1%)	(33.6%)

Note: *Percentages above the sample average are underlined.*

Again, when analysing practice by age in relation to religion, it is important to discern the impact of maturation on the person's behaviour, i.e. as people grow older they tend to become more devout. That being allowed for, however, the above figures are so different, with slightly less than half of the 18 to 40 year-olds reporting that they had **given up going to Confession** altogether, it would be reasonable to assume that there is a move away from Confession for life for a substantial proportion of the junior middle-aged and also for many in the middle and senior middle-aged group. To bring about a return to Confession, therefore, presents a major practical challenge to the Roman Catholic Church in Ireland.

(b) Frequency of Confession by Area of Birth:

It is quite obvious that the greater the level of urbanisation the lesser the frequency of going to Confession. This is in harmony with the measures of religious practice. The relatively high percentage of 'City' and 'Large Town' born who said they **never** went to Confession is greater than anticipated.

(c) Frequency of Confession by Place of Rearing:

The findings of the place-of-rearing variable reflect the degree of urbanisation in the various provinces, and the impact of diocesan pastoral policy. The high level of frequency of going to Confession among those reared in Connaught/Ulster probably could reflect participation in three national pilgrimage shrines, i.e., Croagh Patrick, *Cnoc Mhuire* and Lough Derg. At each of these shrines the *Sacrament of Reconciliation* (Confession) is a central feature.

(d) Frequency of Confession by Education:

Table No. 17.10(g) gives the findings by education. Once again, frequency is negatively correlated with standard of education reached.

Education Variable	Monthly or More Often	Never go to Confession
1. Primary or Less	20.4%	20.4%
2. Incomplete Second-Level	11.0%	30.9%
3. Complete Second-Level	8.9%	34.8%
4. Third-Level	4.4%	39.2%
Number	79	287
(Sample Average)	(9.2%)	(33.6%)

Note: *Percentages above the sample average are underlined.*

The evidence of the above and other findings of the current national survey has confirmed that education in Ireland today (and for some time) has tended to be a force for secularisation, and has resulted in making religion less relevant for those who have succeeded in advancing in educational achievement in a time of great emphasis on educational participation.

Part V – Personal Prayer

In the previous part of this chapter, the levels of public worship and sacramental participation were measured. In the case of Mass, Holy Communion and Sacramental Confession, the practice of Roman Catholic respondents was examined. In Part V, the subject of the findings reported and commented on will be *personal prayer* and in Part VI *perceived closeness to God*. The latter is taken as an indication of the person's belief and religiosity.

5.1 Changes in Frequency of Prayer:
Table No. 17.12 gives the frequency of personal prayer reported by the total sample.

Table No. 17.12:
Frequency of Prayer of Total Sample (2007-08 and 1988-89)

Reported Frequency	A. 2007-08	B. 1988-89	Change (A – B)
1. Several Times Daily	21%	37%	-16%
2. Daily or More Often	47%	71%	-24%
3. Several Times Weekly or More Often	65%	82%	-17%
4. Weekly or More Often	72%	90%	-18%
5. Less Frequently	18%	} 10%	} +18%
6. Never	10%		
Number	1,011	1,001	---

The above findings show a moderately high level of personal prayer in the adult population of the Republic of Ireland in 2007-08. The decline in frequency of prayer since 1988-89, while substantial and statistically significant, is proportionately less than the reported decline in the frequency of public worship. More than in the case of public worship and practice, prayer is largely the product of the influence of family, friends and training in spiritual exercises.

In the past, the *Family Rosary* was a very strong form of non-sacramental prayer for Roman Catholics in Ireland. *Morning* and *night prayers, Grace* before and after meals, the *Angelus* and visits to *Sacred Shrines* and *Holy Wells* were common occasions of personal prayer. *Parish Missions, Retreats* and *Novenas* also were sources of inspiration to pray.

Other devotional services in Churches, Synagogues, Mosques and Temples all raise the mind to God and call the faithful to pray.

The possible causes for the decline in personal prayer would include social and cultural changes in the family and the non-domestic lifestyle of the people. The intrusions of television and Internet websites, which occupy and frequently distract the people, leave little time for family or private prayer. Personal religion (and its practice) is the product of primary socialisation in the home and among friends. In the past in Ireland, i.e. up until the 1960s, religion permeated all of social and personal life. Holidays were holy days. First names were nearly always called after Christian saints. Religious objects were displayed in the people's homes. Greetings were forms of blessings. All these practices and expressions were conducive to regular personal prayer. The advance of commercialisation in all aspects of life and the demands of modern industrial and post-industrial society have been agents of secularisation whose ultimate function seems to make religion, worship and prayer irrelevant. This will respond to the material **interests** of the people but is less likely to satisfy the people's need for **meaning**. The period leading up to 2007-08 was marked in Ireland by strong economic growth, consumerism and materialism. In such an environment, it was not surprising to see a decline in worship and prayer. It would be interesting to monitor the effects on prayer of the post-2008 economic downturn and the demise of endless material progress even beyond the reasonable needs of the people!

5.2 Frequency of Prayer by Personal Variables:

Table No. 17.13 gives the frequency of personal prayer by six personal variables, i.e. age, gender, marital status, area of birth, place of rearing and education.

Table No. 17.13: Frequency of Prayer by Personal Variables (Total Sample)

Variable	Several Times Daily	Daily or more often	Several times a week or more often	Once Weekly or more often	Less than once weekly or more often	Never	No.
Total Sample	**21.1 %**	**47.3 %**	**64.6 %**	**71.8 %**	**89.8 %**	**10.2 %**	**1,011**
Number	213	479	654	726	907	104	1,011
(a) Age	(p=<.001)						
1. 18-25 Years	7.2 %	23.4 %	37.2 %	42.0 %	74.9 %	25.1 %	167
2. 26-40 Years	13.4 %	34.2 %	56.2 %	64.6 %	89.4 %	10.6 %	322
3. 41-55 Years	14.2 %	45.8 %	66.0 %	78.1 %	92.7 %	7.3 %	247
4. 56-70 Years	35.8 %	72.7 %	88.0 %	91.4 %	95.9 %	4.0 %	176
5. 71 Years plus	60.8 %	90.7 %	93.8 %	95.8 %	99.0 %	1.0 %	97
Range of Variation	---	---	*56.6%*	---	---	*24.1%*	*1,009*

457

Table No. 17.13 (Cont'd.) Variable	Several Times Daily	Daily or more often	Several times a week or more often	Once Weekly or more often	Less than once weekly or more often	Never	No.
(b) Gender	(p=<.001)						
1. Male	17.3 %	37.0 %	55.3 %	63.5 %	85.2 %	**14.7 %**	497
2. Female	**24.7 %**	**57.4 %**	**73.7 %**	**79.7 %**	**93.9 %**	6.0 %	514
Range of Variation	---	---	*18.4%*	---	---	*8.7%*	*1,011*
(c) Marital Status	(p=<.001)						
1. Single/Never married	15.6%	34.3%	49.4%	56.4%	84.6%	**15.4%**	358
2. Married	**22.0%**	54.2%	**73.6%**	**82.8%**	**94.1%**	6.0%	469
3. Separated/Divorced	**25.0%**	40.9%	61.4%	65.9%	86.4%	**13.6%**	44
4. Permanent relationship	7.0%	38.0%	60.5%	60.5%	81.6%	**18.3%**	71
5. Widowed	**55.9%**	**83.8%**	**89.7%**	**94.1%**	**98.5%**	1.5%	68
Range of Variation	---	---	*40.3%*	---	---	*16.8%*	*1,010*
(d) Area of Birth	(p=<.001)						
1. City (100,000+)	16.8%	40.6%	61.0%	65.8%	86.2%	**13.7%**	416
2. Large Town (10,000+)	16.0%	32.8%	54.6%	63.8%	81.4%	**18.5%**	119
3. Town (1,500+)	**23.1%**	**56.2%**	**67.7%**	**73.9%**	**93.1%**	6.9%	130
4. Rural/ Village	**27.0%**	**57.2%**	**71.2%**	**81.1%**	**95.6%**	4.4%	344
Range of Variation	---	---	*10.2%*	---	---	*14.1%*	*1,009*
(e) Place of Rearing	(p=<.003)						
1. Dublin (City / Co)	12.1%	41.5%	63.4%	70.2%	**90.6%**	9.4%	265
2. Rest of Leinster	**29.3%**	**57.3%**	**67.1%**	**75.0%**	89.6%	**10.4%**	164
3. Munster	**26.0%**	**53.7%**	**70.6%**	**79.3%**	**94.0%**	6.1%	231
4. Connaught / Ulster	**26.8%**	**59.1%**	**68.2%**	**76.7%**	**91.9%**	7.9%	164
Range of Variation	---	---	*7.2%*	---	---	*4.3%*	*824*
(f) Education	(p=<.001)						
1. Primary or less	**44.8%**	**81.0%**	**90.5%**	**93.1%**	**96.5%**	3.4%	116
2. Incomplete Sec.-Lev.	**24.8%**	**55.7%**	**67.9%**	**77.1%**	**90.8%**	9.2%	262
3. Complete Second-Level	16.1%	37.3%	53.4%	62.0%	86.7%	**13.3%**	255
4. Third-level	14.5%	38.0%	62.0%	68.3%	88.9%	**11.1%**	379
Range of Variation	---	---	*37.1%*	---	---	*9.9%*	*1,012*

Notes: Percentages above the sample average are **in bold**.   Range of Variation in *italics*.

The six variables examined in Table No. 17.13 elicited a statistically significant variation and repeated the pattern of responses which Frequency of Public Worship produced.   This shows that public worship and personal prayer are indicators of each other and validate each other as evidence of the perceived transcendence of God in the mind of those who worship and pray!

A full commentary on this Table is given in the Report: *The Challenge of Indifference: A Need for Religious Revival in Ireland* (2009), pages 58-69.   The findings clearly point to the sections of the population where the level of prayer is extraordinarily high and where it is relatively weak.   The weakest subsamples include: young people, males, single/never married, the more urbanised and those with higher education.   The combination of these variables' results could form a trend which would greatly reduce society's religious practice in the years ahead.

The following extract from Table No. 17.13 highlights the variables' range of variation:

Several times a Week or More Often (Sample average 64.6%)	Range of Variation	Between			
		Highest Practice		Lowest Practice	
1. Age	56.6%	71 years plus	(93.8%) and	18 to 25 yrs	(37.2%)
2. Education	37.1%	Primary or Less	(90.5%) and	Complete 2nd Lev.	(53.4%)
3. Marital Status	40.3%	Widowed	(89.7%) and	Single/Never Mar.	(49.4%)
4. Gender	18.4%	Females	(73.7%) and	Males	(55.3%)
5. Area of Birth	10.2%	Rural/Village	(71.2%) and	Large Town	(54.6%)
6. Place of Rearing (ROI only)	7.2%	Munster	(70.6%) and	Dublin City/Co.	(63.4%)

Never Pray (Sample average 10.2%)	Range of Variation	Between			
		Highest Non-Practice		Lowest Non- Practice	
1. Age	24.1%	18-25 yrs.	(25.1%) and	71 yrs. Plus	(1.0%)
2. Marital Status	16.8%	Perm. Rel'p	(18.3%) and	Widowed	(1.5%)
3. Area of Birth	14.1%	Large Town	(18.5%) and	Rural/Village	(4.4%)
4. Education	9.4%	Complete 2nd Lev. (13.3%) and		Primary or Less	(3.4%)
5. Gender	8.7%	Males	(14.7%) and	Females	(6.0%)
6. Place of Rearing (ROI only)	4.3%	Rest of Leinst.	(10.4%) and	Munster	(6.1%)

The above extract highlights the diversity of prayer practice within the Irish adult population at the end of the *Celtic Tiger Era*, which was characterised by the supremacy of the economic institution and a growing (as it worked out to be) disastrous level of consumerism and reckless borrowing, all of which enhanced the move towards greater secularism.   It will be interesting to speculate if the collapse of economic consumerism will lead to a return to prayer and spiritual priorities among the people!

While the range of variations may seem dramatic, the overall level of prayer in the Republic was still quite substantial, with two-thirds praying several times a week or more often and 'only' one-in-ten who had given up the practice altogether.

Perhaps the clearest way to summarise the findings of Table No. 17.13 is to take two measures of frequency of prayer, i.e. 'daily or more often' and 'never', as is given in Table No. 17.14 below.

Table No. 17.14: Range and Direction of Variation of Practice of Prayer within Personal Variables

Variable	Daily or More Often	Never	Variable	Daily or More Often	Never
(a) Age			**(d) Area of Birth**		
1. 18-25 Years	23.4%	**25.1%**	1. City (100,000+)	40.6%	**13.7%**
2. 26-40 Years	34.2%	**10.6%**	2. Large Town (10,000+)	32.8%	**18.5%**
3. 41-55 Years	45.8%	7.3%	3. Town (1,500+)	**56.2%**	6.9%
4. 56-70 Years	**72.7%**	4.0%	4. Rural/Village	**57.2%**	4.4%
5. 71 Years plus	**90.7%**	1.0%	*Range of Variation*	*24.4%*	*14.1%*
Range of Variation	*67.3%*	*24.1%*	**(e) Place of Rearing**		
(b) Gender			1. Dublin (City/Co.)	41.5%	9.4%
1. Male	37.0%	**14.7%**	2. Rest of Leinster	**57.3%**	**10.4%**
2. Female	**57.4%**	6.0%	3. Munster	**53.7%**	6.1%
Range of Variation	*20.4%*	*8.7%*	4. Connaught /Ulster	**59.1%**	7.9%
(c) Marital Status			*Range of Variation*	*17.6%*	*4.3%*
1. Single/Never Mar'd	34.3%	**15.4%**	**(f) Education**		
2. Married	**54.2%**	6.0%	1. Primary or Less	**81.0%**	3.4%
3. Separated / Divorced	40.9%	**13.6%**	2. Incomplete Sec.-Level	**55.7%**	9.2%
4. Perm. Relationship	38.0%	**18.3%**	3. Complete Sec.-Level	37.3%	**13.3%**
5. Widowed	**83.8%**	1.5%	4. Third-Level	38.0%	**11.1%**
Range of Variation	*49.5%*	*16.8%*	*Range of Variation*	*43.7%*	*9.9%*
Total Sample	**47.3%**	**10.2%**	**Total Sample**	**47.3%**	**10.2%**

Notes: Percentages above the sample average are in **bold**. Range of variation *in italics*.

The above findings clearly show the patterns of religiosity within the adult population in 2007-08 and the challenge facing those in Irish society who wish to promote a high frequency of prayer. The variable with the largest range of variation is age. Respondents under 40 years of age are substantially less prayerful than their fellow respondents above that age. The impact of the age-factor on other variables is quite obvious, e.g. marital status and education.

The negative influence of education on age is a likely contributor to the low level of prayer of the under-forties, who have a relatively high level of educational achievement at complete second-level and third-level. The combination of both of these variables point to continued decline in religious participation in the years ahead unless a radical return to prayer takes place among the under-forties! The effects of the relative failure of the economy throughout the world and Ireland since 2008 could well undermine the young people's belief in materialist prosperity and consumerism and result in a return to spiritual values and religious practice! It was not possible to measure the impact of the economic downturn in the 2007-08 National Survey since the major collapse in the United States did not occur until the summer of 2008.

The results of gender and marital status are as anticipated and repeat previous research (see Mac Gréil, 1977 and 1996)[3]. Females' frequency of prayer is significantly and substantially greater than that of males. In the case of 'marital status', married and widowed were well above average in their level of prayer frequency. When linked with the performances of the 'gender' variable, it is likely that the mothers and grandmothers are the most committed to prayer.

The geographic influence on regular prayer practices points to greater frequency by respondents from the rural and small-town communities than those from cities and large towns. It seems that the more urbanised environments in Ireland are not as conducive to religious practice as are the more rural communities at present. This could well reflect the influence of personal and community life on prayer practice. This finding presents a real challenge to religious leaders in a society that seems to be becoming more urbanised and secularised over the recent past!

Part VI – Perceived Closeness to God

The perceived level of a sense of 'closeness to God' is a very important measure of people's relationship with God, which is both the product and source of one's life of prayer and worship. The full significance of closeness to God is outside the capacity of empirical research. Religion, of its nature, can only be understood in the context of faith, which is a metaphysical phenomenon. Sensed 'closeness to God' is evidence of the believer's understanding of God as personal.

---

[3] Mac Gréil, Mícheál, (1) *Prejudice and Tolerance in Ireland*, Dublin, CIR, 1977.
(2) *Prejudice in Ireland Revisited*, Maynooth, St. Patrick's College, 1996, page 165.

Table No. 17.15: Perceived Closeness to God of Total Sample

Level of Closeness	Percentage	Number
1. Extremely Close	21.7%	219
2. Somewhat Close	49.2%	498
3. Not Very Close	14.8%	151
(1 + 2 + 3)	(85.7%)	(868)
4. Don't Know	3.7%	37
5. Not Close at all	6.8%	69
6. Does Not Believe in God	3.9%	39
Number	100.1%	1,012

One of the most interesting findings in Table No. 17.15 is the relatively small percentage **(3.9%)** who said they *'did not believe in God'*[4] Six of every seven respondents reported some level of 'closeness to God'! When compared with the findings of 1988-89, there is a decline in the perceived level of closeness, i.e.:

Table No. 17.16: Perceived Closeness to God in 2007-08 and in 1988-89

Degree of Closeness *	1988-89	2007-08	Change
1. Extremely Close	24.5%	22.5%	-2.0%
2. Somewhat Close	61.2%	51.0%	-10.2%
3. Not Very Close	9.8%	15.5%	+ 5.7%
(1 + 2+ 3)	**95.5%**	**89.0%**	**-6.5%**
4. Not Close at all	2.9%	7.0%	+ 4.1%
5. Do Not Believe in God	1.6%	4.0%	+ 2.4%

* Excluding **'Don't Knows'**

The changes since 1988-89 are significant but quite moderate when compared with the differences in religious practices. There has been a slight reduction in perceived closeness, and an increase in the percentage 'not believing in God'. This shows a time- lag between loss of faith and ceasing to practise of religion. How long will it take lack of faith to catch up with decline in religious practice?

Table No. 17.17 gives the levels of perceived closeness to God by personal variables:

---

[4] For respondents reared in the Rep. of Ireland the percentage stating 'they did not believe in God' is **2.1%**.

Table No. 17.17:
Perceived Closeness to God by Personal Variables

Variable	Extremely Close (1) %	Somewhat Close (2) %	Not Very Close (3) %	(1+2+3) %	Don't Know (4) * %	Not Close At All (5) %	Does Not Believe in God (6) * %	No.
Total Sample	21.7	49.2	14.8	(85.7)	3.7	6.8	3.9	1,013
(a) Age	(p<.001)							
1. 18-25 Years	8.8	33.5	25.9	(69.2)	11.8	11.8	8.2	170
2. 26-40 Years	14.6	52.0	16.4	(83.0)	2.8	9.2	5.0	323
3. 41-55 Years	19.8	57.5	15.0	**(92.3)**	1.6	4.5	1.6	247
4. 56-70 Years	30.3	52.8	8.4	**(91.5)**	2.2	3.4	2.8	178
5. 71 Years plus	56.2	38.5	2.1	**(96.8)**	1.0	2.1	0.0	96
Number	219	498	151	(868)	38	69	38	1,014
(b) Gender	(p<.001)							
1. Male	16.7	46.6	18.5	(81.8)	4.4	7.8	6.0	498
2. Female	26.5	51.7	11.3	**(89.5)**	2.9	5.8	1.8	513
Number	219	497	150	(866)	37	69	39	1,011
(c) Marital Status	(p<.001)							
1. Single/Never married	16.2	45.0	18.2	(79.4)	6.7	9.8	4.2	358
2. Married	24.0	52.6	14.5	**(91.1)**	2.3	3.8	2.8	470
3. Separated/Divorced	18.2	43.2	13.6	(74.1)	2.3	20.5	2.3	44
4. Permanent relationship	2.8	59.2	12.7	(74.7)	2.8	8.5	14.1	71
5. Widowed	55.1	40.6	2.9	**(98.6)**	0.0	1.4	0.0	69
Number	219	497	150	(866)	38	69	39	1,012
(d) Area of Birth	(p<.001)							
1. City (100,000+)	15.5	49.2	17.9	(82.6)	4.3	7.9	5.3	419
2. Large Town (10,000+)	21.7	40.8	19.2	(81.7)	3.3	8.3	6.7	120
3. Town (1,500+)	23.1	49.2	11.5	(83.8)	6.9	5.4	3.8	130
4. Rural/Village	28.4	51.9	11.0	**(91.3)**	1.7	5.5	1.4	345
Number	219	498	151	(868)	37	69	40	1,014
(e) Place of Rearing	(p<.001)							
1. Dublin (City / Co)	17.4	47.5	21.5	**(86.4)**	5.3	6.4	1.9	265
2. Rest of Leinster	24.1	49.4	10.8	(84.3)	3.6	10.2	1.8	166
3. Munster	23.4	55.0	13.0	**(91.4)**	1.3	5.6	1.7	231
4. Connaught/Ulster	25.8	52.8	9.2	**(87.8)**	2.5	6.7	3.1	163
Number	182	421	120	(723)	27	58	17	825
(f) Region of Residence	(p<.001)							
1. BMW	23.3	50.4	11.5	(85.2)	5.6	4.4	4.8	270
2. Dublin	20.8	39.9	22.2	(82.9)	5.2	8.3	3.5	288
3. Mid-East & South-E	22.9	46.3	14.7	(83.9)	2.8	10.1	3.2	218
4. Mid-West & South-W	19.4	61.6	9.7	**(90.7)**	0.4	4.6	4.2	237
Number	219	498	150	(867)	37	69	40	1,013

Table No. 17.17 Cont'd. Variable	Extremely Close (1) %	Somewhat Close (2) %	Not Very Close (3) %	(1+2+3) %	Don't Know (4) * %	Not Close At All (5) %	Does Not Believe in God (6) * %	No.
(g) Education	(p<.001)							
1. Primary or less	47.0	40.2	6.8	**(94.0)**	0.9	2.6	2.6	117
2. Incomplete Sec.-Lev.	26.0	46.9	13.0	**(85.9)**	2.7	10.3	1.1	262
3. Complete Sec.-Level	20.4	43.9	17.6	(81.8)	5.5	9.0	3.5	255
4. Third-level	11.8	56.8	16.8	(85.4)	3.9	4.2	6.3	380
Number	220	498	151	(869)	37	69	39	1,014
(h) Occupational Status	(p<.02)							
1 Unskilled/Semi	22.2	46.9	16.9	**(86.0)**	4.3	3.9	5.8	207
2. Skilled/Routine non-m.	18.7	48.8	15.3	(82.8)	4.0	8.9	4.3	326
3.Inspectional/Supervisory	19.7	53.0	17.4	**(90.1)**	4.5	4.5	0.8	132
4. Professional/Executive	17.8	59.7	7.3	(84.8)	2.6	9.9	2.6	191
Number	167	440	122	(729)	33	62	32	856
(i) Take-Home Personal Income	(p<.001)							
1. Up to €119 per week	19.4	59.7	13.4	**(92.5)**	1.5	3.0	1.5	67
2. €120-€459 per week	27.3	39.6	16.9	(83.8)	3.5	7.7	5.0	260
3. €460-€1,149 per week	21.3	52.2	17.6	**(91.1)**	2.4	3.4	3.4	207
4. €1,150 plus per week	8.1	49.5	20.2	(77.8)	5.1	15.2	2.0	99
Number	136	300	109	(545)	44	24	20	633

Note: Percentages above sample averages in (1+2+3) column are in **bold**.
* Statistical variations of small cells are limited.

The findings of Table No. 17.17 provide a valuable and detailed insight into the current state of this 'perceived closeness to God' of a random and representative sample of the adults living in the Republic of Ireland. It is probably the nearest one can get to an empirical measure of the spiritual awareness of God's presence at the personal level.

One particular item of information contained in the above Table is the proportion of the respondents who said they *"did not believe in God"*. Because of the context in which this response has been given, its validity, i.e. representing the actual situation of conscious disbelief, is that much greater. By any standards, the proportion of the sample who stated 'they did not believe in God' is relatively low at *3.9% or 4.0%*, (when "don't knows" are removed) which means that 96% of adults have a place for God in their lives, however tenuous it may be for some respondents.

A fuller examination of the above findings is given in the special Report on Religious Practice and Attitudes, *The Challenge of Indifference: A Need for Religious Revival in Ireland*, pages 72-80.[5]

In general it is clear that older, female, rural/village-born, married and widowed and respondents with primary and incomplete second-level education reported the highest levels of perceived closeness to God. It must be noted that the average of perceived closeness for the total sample was higher than expected and challenges the extent to which secularisation has penetrated Irish society at this stage in its history.

Part VII – Religious Social Distance in Ireland

Six religious stimulus categories were selected to measure the level of social distance in this regard, i.e. 'Agnostics', 'Atheists', 'Jews', 'Muslims', 'Protestants' and 'Roman Catholics'. These six categories were deemed to cover a wide spectrum and variety of religious traits, *et cetera*.

Table No. 17.18 gives the social-distance-measurements towards each of the categories. The categories are placed in their rank order of prejudice.

Table No. 17.18:
Social Distance towards Religious Categories

R/O	Category	Kinship (1)	Friendship or closer (2)	Neighbour or closer (3)	Co-Worker or closer (4)	Citizen or closer (5)	Visitor only (6)	Debar / Deport (7)	MSD (1-7)	No.
1	Roman Catholics	**91.1 %**	96.8 %	97.5 %	98.9 %	99.4 %	0.1 %	0.5 %	**1.17**	1,012
2	Protestants	**78.4 %**	88.5 %	92.7 %	95.3 %	97.5 %	1.9 %	0.7 %	**1.48**	1,012
3	Jews	**60.7 %**	72.7 %	79.4 %	85.6 %	88.6 %	6.6 %	4.9 %	**2.18**	1,009
4	Atheists	**52.5 %**	68.8 %	76.5 %	83.1 %	89.0 %	3.7 %	7.3 %	**2.37**	1,003
5	Agnostics	**50.3 %**	64.8 %	72.7 %	79.5 %	85.7 %	5.8 %	8.4 %	**2.55**	1,002
6	Muslims	**42.9 %**	54.5 %	62.9 %	70.9 %	76.8 %	8.6 %	14.6%	**3.07**	1,010

---

[5] Mac Gréil, Micheál, *The Challenge of Indifference: A Need for Religious Revival in Ireland*, Maynooth, Survey and Research Unit, Department of Sociology, 2009, pages 72-80.

Two of the categories, i.e. Roman Catholics and Protestants are among the in-group (mean-social-distance of less than **1.500**). The MSD score for **'Muslims'** was quite negative at **3.07,** which should be a matter of concern for people seeking pluralist integration of members of this category living in Ireland. 'Muslims' living in Ireland have been very positive in their industrious work ethic, their law-abiding behaviour, their religious practice and their overall contribution to social and community life. The prejudice indicated in their relatively high social distance score is a reflection of *vicarious bias* from other 'Western societies' and a reaction to the ongoing Middle-East conflict. The current attitudes towards 'Muslims' are not that unlike the twentieth-century Western bias against Communists.

The position of **'Jews'**, while having improved substantially since 1988-89 (see Table No. 17.19), is still not satisfactory at **2.18** (MSD). This score has been influenced by the **11.5%** who would deny 'Jews' citizenship. Although slightly less than half of the **24.0%** who would deny 'Muslims' citizenship in 1988-89, it is significantly negative and shows an unacceptable degree of anti-Semitism in the sample. This negative dimension of the findings on Table No. 17.18 should not overshadow the relatively high percentage who would admit 'Jews' into kinship in the 2007-08 survey, i.e. **60.7%,** and the **79.4%** who would welcome 'Jews' as next-door neighbours. These results are to be greatly welcomed.

There has been an improved score for both **'Atheists'** and **'Agnostics'** when the findings of 1988-89 and 2007-08 are compared. The rank-order of the two categories has been reversed. 'Atheists' are more preferred than 'Agnostics' in the 2007-08 findings (see Table No. 17.19).

Table No. 17.19 monitors the changes in religious prejudice (as measured by social distance) between 1972-73, 1988-89 and 2007-08. Five of the six stimulus categories were measured in each of the three surveys. **Muslims** were introduced as a category in the 1988-89 National Survey.

The three measures selected for monitoring change have been Admit to Kinship, Deny Citizenship and Mean-Social-Distance score. The overall level increase in admitting members of stimulus categories Nos. 2 to 6 shows an increase in religious tolerance at the level of admission to kinship. The positive changes in denial of citizenship could have been more generous!

Table No. 17.19:
Changes in Social Distance towards Religious Categories (1972-73 to 2007-08)

Category	Year	National Sample				Dublin Subsample / Sample 2007-08			
		Kinship	Deny Citizenship	MSD	No.	Kinship	Deny Citizenship	MSD	No.
Roman Catholics	A. 1972-73	---	---	---	---	96.2%	0.2%	1.07	2,288
	B. 1988-89	96.8%	0.3%	1.06	1,001	97%	0.0%	1.04	254
	C. 2007-08	91.1%	0.6%	1.17	1,012	89.1%	1.5%	1.25	286
	Change*	**-4.3%**	**+0.3%**	**+0.11**	---	**-7.9%**	**+1.5%**	**+0.21**	---
Protestants	A. 1972-73	---	---	---	---	73.4%	.06%	1.38	2,286
	B. 1988-89	62.2%	1.4%	1.66	1,002	79%	1%	1.40	254
	C. 2007-08	78.4%	2.6%	1.48	1,012	80.1%	1.8%	1.45	286
	Change*	**+16.2%**	**1.2%**	**-0.18**	---	**+1.1%**	**+0.8%**	**+0.05**	---
Jews	A. 1972-73	---	---	---	---	57.0%	3.1%	1.80	2,293
	B. 1988-89	39.5%	12.1%	2.60	1,003	53%	5%	1.97	254
	C. 2007-08	60.7%	11.5%	2.18	1,009	67.1%	9.0%	2.03	285
	Change*	**+21.2%**	**-0.6%**	**-0.42**	---	**+14.1%**	**+4.0%**	**+0.06**	---
Atheists	A. 1972-73	---	---	---	---	37.7%	12.5%	2.52	2,300
	B. 1988-89	28.5%	19.8%	3.15	1,002	40%	12%	2.52	254
	C. 2007-08	52.5%	11.0%	2.37	1,003	57.5%	5.2%	2.05	283
	Change*	**+24.0%**	**-8.8%**	**-0.78**	---	**+17.5%**	**-6.8%**	**-0..47**	---
Agnostics	A. 1972-73	---	---	---	---	40.9%	10.9%	2.42	2,303
	B. 1988-89	31.1%	16.9%	3.02	997	44%	12%	2.49	254
	C. 2007-08	50.3%	14.2%	2.55	1,002	51.6%	11.0%	2.45	285
	Change*	**+19.2%**	**-2.7%**	**-0.47**	---	**+7.6%**	**-0.1%**	**-0.04**	---
Muslims**	A. 1972-73	---	---	---	---	---	---	---	---
	B. 1988-89	20.6%	24.0%	3.42	1,000	26.0%	---	2.95	254
	C. 2007-08	42.9%	23.2%	3.07	1,002	47.6%	24.2%	3.06	285
	Change*	**+22.3%**	**-0.8%**	**-0.35**	---	**+21.6%**	---	**+0.11**	---

*   Change between percentages of 1988-89 and 2007-08.
** 'Muslims' were not included in the 1972-73 survey.

The position of the **Roman Catholics** is still extremely strong with **91.1%** welcoming them into the family and **0.6%** who would deny them citizenship. The slight drop of **4.3%** 'admitting to kinship' from the 1988-89 survey, which was **96.8%**, is barely significant and is probably explained by demographic changes between the two National Surveys of 1988-89 and

2007-08. Roman Catholics are still the most preferred stimulus category of all the 51 reported on Table No. 4.1 (pages 62-4 above). Because of the exceptionally low MSD score of **1.17** on a range of 1 to 7, changes of significance are unlikely. (The MSD in 1988-89 was **1.06**.)

As already noted, the change of public attitudes towards Atheists and Agnostics have been substantial and significant, i.e. from **28.5%** to **52.5%** (admit to kinship) between 1988-89 to 2007-08 for 'Atheists' and from **31.1%** to **50.3%** in the case of 'Agnostics'. The decrease in the percentages denying citizenship was also welcomed for 'Atheists' and 'Agnostics' but it is still seriously high at **11.0%** and **14.2%** respectively.

In both the 1972-73 and 1988-89 surveys 'Agnostics' were preferred to 'Atheists', while in 2007-08 the rank-order position of the two categories was reversed. This result was not anticipated since it goes against the *principle of religious propinquity*. The reduction of prejudice towards 'Atheists' and 'Agnostics' is to be welcomed in that it represents a more tolerant religious attitude syndrome. That much being said, there is still need for further improvement in Irish attitudes towards non-believers. Being tolerant does not mean agreement with those expressing different religious views. It recognises the right of religious freedom.

While the improvement in social distance scores towards 'Muslims' is to be welcomed and acknowledged, the current scores are still unacceptable in a society aspiring to be pluralist and integrated. Many negative stereotypes come from politicised militant extremism. All 'Muslims' suffer from these stereotypes propagated by western media. In addition, certain prescriptions curtailing the freedom of women in societies dominated by Muslim governments are totally unacceptable to modern societies (such as Ireland) and are also likely to influence negative attitudes towards 'Muslims' as a whole.

The findings of the Dublin subsamples in the 1988-89 and 2007-08 National Surveys and the Survey of Greater Dublin in 1972-73 on Table No. 17.19 show the changes in religious society distance over thirty-five years. With the exception of 'Roman Catholics', Dubliners were more tolerant than the national samples from the other five stimulus categories, i.e. 'Protestants', 'Jews', 'Atheists', 'Agnostics' and 'Muslims'. Also, percentages 'admitting to kinship' were higher for the latter five and those 'denying citizenship' were significantly and substantially lower for 'Atheists' (a nominal minus of 7.3% between 1972-73 and 2007-08).

7.1 Religious Social Distance by Personal Variables:

Table No. 17.20 below measures religious social distance by personal variables. This is a fairly large Table with the possibility of one hundred and forty-four sub-Tables. Only 12.5% (18) of the 144 sub-Tables failed to elicit a statistically-significant variation, i.e. *chi-square* of *p<.05*. This means that religious social distance is a 'live issue' in the adult population as Table No. 17.20 shows. The ranges of variations are quite substantial in the case of 'admit to kinship' and 'denial of citizenship'. A close examination of Table No. 17.20 will give the reader a detailed profile of Irish religious prejudice and tolerance as expressed in social distance by multiple variables[6]. Such a close examination will give the reader a more complete grasp of the current state of religious prejudice.

7.2 Variable Performance:

In addition to the **nominal** personal and social variables, three specifically religious independent variables are added, namely, 'Church Attendance', 'Perceived Closeness to God' and 'Frequency of Prayer'. Each of the three elicited statistically significant variations in the case of the six stimulus categories. The seven ordinal variables, i.e. age, area of birth, education, occupational status, social class position, church attendance, closeness to God and frequency of prayer, produced a variety of responses, some of which were not anticipated.

7.2.1 Roman Catholics: Because of the limited range of variation due to their very high percentage 'admitting to kinship' (91.1%) and very low percentage 'denying citizenship', 'Roman Catholics' unexpectedly produce score variations between 9.2% and 16.6% in seven of the variables. The following extract (on page 473) from Table No. 17.20 gives the extremes of these variations for 'admission to kinship':

---

[6] **Note on Tabulation**: The late **Professor James Kavanagh**, Social Sciences, U.C.D. once remarked that "a good table was worth many pages of text". Readers of this text will at this stage realise the abundance of tables presented. The Professor of Sociology, King's College, Cambridge, **Anthony Giddens** cautions the reader "not to succumb to the temptation to skip over tables: they contain information in concentrated form, which can be read more quickly than would be possible if the same material were expressed in words. By becoming skilled in the interpretation of tables, you will also be able to check how far the conclusions drawn by a writer actually seem justified". (Giddens, Anthony, *Sociology*, Cambridge, Polity Press, 2006, page 96.)

Table No. 17.20:
Religious Social Distance by Personal Variables

Personal Variable	Roman Catholics Admit Kinship	Roman Catholics Deny Citiz.	Protestants Admit Kinship	Protestants Deny Citiz.	Jews Admit Kinship	Jews Deny Citiz.	Atheists Admit Kinship	Atheists Deny Citiz.	Agnostics Admit Kinship	Agnostics Deny Citiz.	Muslims Admit Kinship	Muslims Deny Citiz.	Number
Total Sample	**91.1%**	**0.6%**	**78.4%**	**2.5%**	**60.7%**	**11.4%**	**52.5%**	**11.0%**	**50.3%**	**14.3%**	**42.9%**	**23.2%**	**1,015**
A. Age	P<.001		P<.004		P<.001		P<.001		P<.001		P<.001		
1. 18-25 years	82.2%	1.8%	67.5%	6.5%	53.6%	11.9%	47.6%	10.8%	45.2%	13.9%	38.5%	26.6%	168
2. 26-40 years	93.3%	0.3%	79.6%	1.9%	68.3%	11.2%	63.4%	6.6%	61.2%	7.5%	52.5%	17.7%	325
3. 41-55 years	91.9%	0.4%	78.9%	2.4%	55.9%	10.5%	51.0%	11.4%	45.6%	17.0%	40.2%	24.0%	245
4. 56-70 years	92.7%	0.6%	83.1%	1.1%	57.9%	14.0%	48.0%	11.3%	48.0%	16.4%	36.5%	23.0%	178
5. 71 years plus	94.8%	0.0%	83.5%	1.0%	64.6%	8.3%	37.1%	24.7%	38.5%	27.1%	38.1%	34.0%	96
Score Variation	*12.6%*	*1.8%*	*16.0%*	*5.5%*	*14.7%*	*5.7%*	*26.3%*	*18.1%*	*22.7%*	*19.6%*	*16.0%*	*16.3%*	*(1,012)*
B. Gender	N/S		P<.005		N/S		P<.033		P<.002		N/S		
1. Males	---	---	78.6%	2.2%	---	---	55.3%	10.5%	54.0%	13.7%	---	---	499
2. Females	---	---	78.2%	2.9%	---	---	49.8%	11.4%	46.7%	14.9%	---	---	516
Score Variation	---	---	*0.4%*	*0.7%*	---	---	*5.5%*	*0.9%*	*7.3%*	*1.2%*	---	---	*(1,015)*
C. Marital Status	P<.018		P<.001		N/S		P<.001		P<.019		P<.001		
1. Single/Never Married	87.5%	0.6%	73.7%	3.6%	---	---	51.3%	13.0%	49.4%	16.6%	41.3%	26.3%	356
2. Married	94.7%	0.4%	82.6%	1.7%	---	---	53.0%	9.2%	50.4%	12.8%	45.1%	19.2%	468
3. Separated/Divorced	86.6%	0.0%	84.1%	2.3%	---	---	63.6%	6.8%	57.5%	10.0%	46.5%	23.3%	44
4. Permanent Relation'p	84.5%	1.4%	66.7%	2.8%	---	---	54.9%	4.2%	50.0%	5.7%	43.7%	15.5%	72
5. Widowed	92.6%	1.5%	84.1%	1.4%	---	---	46.3%	19.4%	50.0%	23.5%	33.3%	42.0%	69
Score Variation	*10.2%*	*1.5%*	*17.4%*	*2.2%*	---	---	*17.3%*	*15.2%*	*8.1%*	*17.8%*	*13.2%*	*26.5%*	*(1,009)*
D. Area of Birth	P<.046		P<.011		P<.001		P<.001		P<.001		N/S		
1. City (100,000+)	87.8%	1.2%	79.2%	1.4%	62.8%	9.4%	56.1%	5.1%	52.7%	9.7%	---	---	419
2. Large Town (10,000+)	94.1%	0.8%	82.4%	5.0%	66.9%	5.9%	63.8%	6.9%	65.8%	6.8%	---	---	119
3. Town (1,500+)	92.2%	0.0%	78.3%	0.8%	64.8%	10.2%	61.7%	6.2%	57.4%	9.3%	---	---	132
4. Rural/Village	93.3%	0.0%	75.7%	3.8%	54.4%	16.3%	40.8%	21.1%	39.2%	24.1%	---	---	345
Score Variation	*6.3%*	*1.2%*	*7.0%*	*3.0%*	*12.5%*	*10.4%*	*23.0%*	*16.0%*	*26.6%*	*17.3%*	---	---	*(1,015)*

Table No. 17.20 Cont'd.	Roman Catholics Admit	Roman Catholics Deny	Protestants Admit	Protestants Deny	Jews Admit	Jews Deny	Atheists Admit	Atheists Deny	Agnostics Admit	Agnostics Deny	Muslims Admit	Muslims Deny	Number
E. Place of Rearing ROI	N/S		P<.018		P<.001		P<.001		P<.001		P<.001		
1. Dublin (City & Co.)	---	---	80.5%	0.8%	63.4%	9.4%	54.9%	5.3%	48.3%	12.5%	46.4%	24.5%	243
2. Rest of Leinster	---	---	79.4%	1.2%	57.1%	17.8%	44.2%	17.8%	43.3%	18.9%	38.4%	34.1%	157
3. Munster	---	---	79.2%	3.5%	64.6%	14.7%	55.8%	13.0%	57.6%	18.6%	47.0%	20.0%	219
4. Connaught/Ulster	---	---	72.6%	3.0%	53.0%	4.9%	41.0%	13.0%	36.5%	14.5%	33.1%	15.3%	154
Score Variation	---	---	*7.9%*	*2.7%*	*11.6%*	*12.9%*	*14.8%*	*12.5%*	*21.1%*	*6.4%*	*13.9%*	*18.8%*	*(773)*
F. Region of Residence	N/S		P<.001		P<.001		P<.001		P<.001		P<.001		
1. B.M.W.	---	---	74.9%	1.8%	48.0%	13.7%	38.7%	17.1%	36.0%	20.1%	31.4%	26.2%	269
2. Dublin	---	---	80.1%	1.7%	67.0%	9.1%	57.4%	5.3%	51.6%	10.9%	47.7%	24.2%	284
3. Mid-East & South-E.	---	---	74.4%	6.8%	55.3%	18.0%	53.2%	13.9%	51.9%	16.2%	45.6%	24.0%	218
4. Mid-West & Sth-West	---	---	84.0%	0.4%	72.2%	5.9%	61.7%	8.1%	63.1%	10.2%	48.1%	17.7%	234
Score Variation	---	---	*9.6%*	*6.4%*	*24.2%*	*12.1%*	*23.0%*	*11.8%*	*27.1%*	*9.9%*	*16.7%*	*8.5%*	*(1,005)*
G. Education	P<.001		P<.007		P<.001		P<.001		P<.001		P<.001		
1. Primary or Less	97.4%	0.9%	80.5%	0.0%	64.1%	12.0%	45.8%	22.0%	41.4%	25.9%	45.8%	33.1%	117
2. Incomplete Sec-Level	94.7%	0.8%	80.6%	2.3%	54.4%	16.5%	47.9%	13.2%	45.6%	15.7%	41.0%	24.9%	262
3. Complete Sec.-Level	89.4%	0.4%	71.8%	4.7%	59.4%	13.8%	55.1%	12.2%	51.4%	16.6%	40.9%	28.0%	255
4. Third-Level	87.6%	0.5%	79.0%	1.9%	65.0%	6.1%	56.0%	5.3%	55.6%	8.1%	44.8%	15.6%	381
Score Variation	*9.8%*	*0.5%*	*17.1%*	*4.7%*	*10.6%*	*10.4%*	*10.2%*	*16.7%*	*14.2%*	*17.8%*	*4.9%*	*17.5%*	*(1,015)*
H. Occupational Status	P<.001		P<.005		P<.001		P<.001		P<.005		P<.005		
1. Unskilled/Semi-Skill.	90.8%	0.5%	74.5%	4.8%	51.2%	20.0%	43.2%	17.0%	42.5%	19.0%	38.2%	30.4%	207
2. Skilled/R. Non-Man.	91.4%	0.9%	78.8%	3.4%	62.0%	9.5%	56.1%	9.7%	53.6%	9.9%	46.2%	21.8%	328
3. Inspect./Supervisory	90.2%	2.8%	81.2%	0.0%	65.2%	8.3%	51.1%	13.0%	46.2%	19.7%	34.8%	21.2%	133
4. Professional/Exec.	94.3%	0.0%	83.2%	0.0%	70.7%	5.2%	59.2%	4.2%	56.5%	12.0%	50.5%	18.4%	191
Score Variation	*3.5%*	*0.9%*	*8.7%*	*4.8%*	*19.7%*	*14.8%*	*16.0%*	*12.8%*	*14.0%*	*9.8%*	*15.7%*	*12.0%*	*(859)*
I. Social Class Position	P<.031		P<.012		P<.001		P<.001		P<.001		P<.001		
1. Class I "Upper Class"	87.2%	0.0%	79.5%	0.0%	71.8%	2.6%	47.4%	2.6%	51.3%	17.9%	50.0%	31.6%	38
2. Class II "Upr-Middle Cls"	95.7%	0.0%	87.1%	0.0%	73.2%	2.2%	63.8%	2.2%	59.4%	7.2%	51.4%	10.1%	140
3. Class III "Mid-Middle Cl"	88.2%	0.4%	75.9%	2.2%	61.7%	9.3%	54.9%	9.3%	52.7%	13.3%	40.3%	19.0%	226
4. Class IV "Working Class"	92.0%	1.1%	76.5%	3.3%	57.1%	14.4%	48.3%	13.8%	46.1%	15.4%	40.3%	28.2%	361
5. Class V "Lower Class"	96.4%	0.0%	88.1%	3.5%	58.3%	17.9%	50.0%	20.2%	47.6%	20.7%	47.1%	30.6%	83
Score Variation	*9.2%*	*1.1%*	*12.2%*	*3.5%*	*16.1%*	*15.7%*	*16.4%*	*18.0%*	*13.3%*	*13.5%*	*11.1%*	*21.5%*	*(848)*

Table No. 17.20 Cont'd. Personal Variable	Roman Catholics		Protestants		Jews		Atheists		Agnostics		Muslims		Number
	Admit Kinship	Deny Citiz.	Admit Kinship	Deny Citiz.	Admit Kinship	Deny Citiz.	Admit Kinship	Deny Citiz.	Admit Kinship	Deny Citiz.	Admit Kinship	Deny Citiz.	
J. Church Attendance	P<.001		P<.001		P<.001		P<.001		P<.001		P<.003		
1. Never	88.0%	0.9%	78.0%	2.5%	66.9%	11.9%	71.8%	3.4%	68.4%	6.8%	52.5%	26.3%	118
2. Less Frequently	87.7%	1.0%	78.1%	4.6%	59.0%	6.2%	58.9%	8.4%	57.2%	11.3%	44.1%	21.5%	196
3. Several Times a Year	87.3%	0.0%	70.9%	2.2%	64.2%	9.7%	56.0%	10.4%	48.5%	10.4%	40.3%	21.6%	134
4. 1-3 Times Monthly	97.6%	0.8%	89.5%	0.0%	69.9%	10.6%	59.7%	12.1%	61.2%	17.6%	53.7%	21.1%	125
5. Weekly or More Often	92.5%	0.5%	77.0%	2.6%	55.4%	14.9%	40.6%	14.4%	39.0%	18.4%	36.9%	24.2%	426
Score Variation	*10.3%*	*1.0%*	*18.6%*	*4.6%*	*14.5%*	*8.7%*	*31.2%*	*11.0%*	*29.4%*	*11.6%*	*16.8%*	*4.9%*	*(999)*
K. Closeness to God	P<.006		P<.001		P<.001		P<.001		P<.001		P<.001		
1. Do Not Believe in God	94.5%	0.0%	77.5%	0.0%	69.2%	2.6%	71.8%	0.0%	74.4%	0.0%	71.1%	5.3%	39
2. Not Close at all	77.9%	0.0%	67.6%	0.0%	55.9%	13.2%	47.8%	13.0%	48.5%	10.3%	39.7%	33.8%	69
3. Not Very Close	86.8%	2.0%	78.7%	2.7%	61.6%	9.3%	67.8%	5.4%	60.4%	5.4%	39.7%	20.5%	151
4. Somewhat Close	93.0%	0.4%	80.5%	2.6%	61.5%	13.7%	49.7%	12.0%	47.4%	18.2%	40.1%	24.6%	498
5. Extremely Close	93.2%	0.5%	77.1%	3.7%	57.3%	10.5%	45.4%	12.8%	45.7%	15.5%	45.7%	22.4%	219
Score Variation	*16.6%*	*2.0%*	*12.9%*	*3.7%*	*13.3%*	*11.1%*	*26.4%*	*13.0%*	*28.7%*	*18.2%*	*31.4%*	*28.5%*	*(976)*
L. Frequency of Prayer	P<.001		P<.001		P<.006		P<.001		P<.001		P<.001		
1. Never	85.6%	1.9%	76.7%	1.9%	61.2%	5.8%	66.3%	3.0%	61.2%	2.9%	50.5%	17.5%	101
2. Less than Weekly	86.2%	0.0%	72.4%	2.8%	58.3%	15.6%	53.3%	10.4%	56.7%	15.6%	36.7%	31.1%	182
3. Weekly	95.8%	0.0%	78.1%	1.4%	56.9%	8.3%	53.6%	13.0%	47.9%	22.5%	43.1%	31.9%	263
4. Several Times a Week	84.6%	0.6%	71.3%	6.3%	56.6%	15.0%	49.4%	12.2%	48.0%	12.1%	43.4%	20.8%	182
5. Daily	95.5%	0.8%	85.3%	1.5%	63.0%	12.1%	52.8%	11.3%	49.2%	16.5%	41.5%	20.8%	71
6. Several Times a Day	95.8%	0.5%	81.6%	1.4%	65.1%	7.1%	46.4%	12.8%	43.0%	14.5%	46.5%	20.7%	212
Score Variation	*11.2%*	*1.9%*	*14.0%*	*4.9%*	*8.5%*	*8.5%*	*19.9%*	*10.0%*	*18.2%*	*19.6%*	*13.8%*	*14.4%*	*(1,011)*

Notes: 1. Percentages above the sample average are **in bold**.
2. Variations are in *italics*

Personal Variable	*Nominal Variation	Variation of Admit to Kinship Between			
		Highest % (Most Favourable)		Lowest % (Least Favourable)	
1. Closeness to God	16.6%	Non-Believers	(94.5%)	and	"Not close at all"	(77.9%)
2. Age	12.6%	71-year-plus	(94.8%)	and	18 to 25 years	(82.2%)
3. Frequency of Prayer	11.2%	Several times daily/Weekly	(95.8%)	and	Several times weekly	(84.6%)
4. Church Attendance	10.3%	1 to 3 Times Monthly	(97.6%)	and	Several times annually	(87.3%)
5. Marital Status	10.2%	Married	(94.7%)	and	Permanent Relation'p	(84.5%)
6. Education	9.8%	Primary or Less	(97.4%)	and	Third Level	(87.6%)
7. Social Class Posit.	9.2%	"Lower Class"	(96.4%)	and	"Upper Class"	(87.2%)

Note: These nominal variations are between very high favourable percentages.

The above extract from Table No. 17.20 gives the reader some insight into the study of 'Roman Catholics' within the variables. It is interesting to note the extremely positive attitudes of non-believers toward this category, i.e. **94.5%** would welcome 'Roman Catholics' into kinship. Age is negatively correlated with admit to kinship scores, while education and social-class position were negatively oriented. The responses of religious practice showed those with moderately-high levels of participation were most favourably disposed.

7.2.2 Protestants: The variable responses to 'Protestants' were statistically significant in the case of all twelve personal variables. The range of score variations were quite substantial in a number of cases considering again that 'Protestants', like 'Roman Catholics', were considered in-groups in Irish society, i.e. mean-social-distance score of under **1.500**. The following extract from Table No. 17.20 spells out the variables with a score variation of over 9%:

Personal Variable	Nominal Variation	Variation of 'Admit to Kinship' Between			
		Highest % (Most Favourable)		Lowest % (Least Favourable)	
1. Church Attendance	18.6%	1-3 times Monthly	(89.5%)	and	Several times annually	(70.9%)
2. Marital Status	17.4%	Sep.Divorced /Widowed	(84.1%)	and	Permanent Rel'ship	(66.7%)
3. Education	17.1%	Primary or Less	(88.9%)	and	Complete 2nd Level	(71.8%)
4. Age	16.0%	71-years plus	(83.5%)	and	18 to 25 years	(67.5%)
5. Frequency of Prayer	14.0%	Daily	(85.3%)	and	Several times weekly	(71.3%)
6. Social Class Position	12.2%	"Lower Class"	(88.1%)	and	"Middle-Middle Class"	(75.9%)
7. Region of Residence	9.6%	Mid-W & Sth-West	(84.0%)	and	Mid-East & Sth-East	(74.4%)

The patterns of replies in the case of 'Protestants' are fairly close to those expressed on the previous extract in relation to 'Roman Catholics'. Again, the greater tolerance and respect of those with greater age, lower education and "lower class" and the lesser tolerance of those who were young, better educated and enjoying higher 'social class' points to the more open-mindedness of those who benefit least from society. Normally one would expect such people to be **more** rather than **less** prejudiced. Perhaps it expressed a less generous or compassionate ethos in the subculture of the stronger and more privileged classes today!

The findings in relation to the religious personal variables are also interesting. Moderate regular religious practice seems to result in greatest tolerance towards Ireland's main minority denomination, i.e. 'Protestants'. This has optimistic connotations for future advancements in Christian Ecumenism.

7.2.3 Jews: The history of religious prejudice has shown that Anti-Semitism has been one of the most widespread of all particular prejudices. In the earlier two surveys[7], i.e. 1972-73 and 1988-89, a special *Anti-Semitic Scale* was included in the questionnaire. Unfortunately, it was not possible to include this scale in the 2007-08 questionnaire (because of lack of resources). The stimulus category **'Jews'** was included and its variable performance is reported on Table No. 17.20.

The standing of Jews in Ireland has always been favourable (allowing for the occasional bigoted and, thankfully, isolated occasion of hostility). Professor **Dermot Keogh's** history of the Jews in Ireland, *Jews in Twentieth-Century Ireland*[8], is essential reading for people interested in anti-Semitism in this country. In his foreword to Keogh's history, **Chaim Herzog, President of Israel (1983-93)**, made the following complimentary comment on the positive role of the members of the Jewish minority to Irish life:

> "The quality and involvement of the (Jewish) community can best be gauged by the fact that this very small group of people has produced representatives in the *Dáil* representing the three major parties in Ireland, one of whom achieved a ministerial appointment in the Irish government." (Keogh, 1998, p.viii)

---

[7] Mac Gréil, Micheál, *Prejudice and Tolerance in Ireland*, Dublin CIR, 1977.
　　　　　Prejudice in Ireland Revisited, Maynooth, St Patrick's College, 1996.
[8] Keogh, Dermot, *Jews in Twentieth-Century Ireland*, Cork, Cork University Press, 1998.

As was shown in the findings of the 1988-89 National Survey, the standing of **'Israel'** was perceived to be lower than anticipated and its strong correlation with social distance towards Jews probably reduced the pace of tolerance towards 'Jews'. The current social-distance scores towards 'Jews' and 'Israeli' (in the 2007-08 findings) are given in Table No. 17.21:

Table No. 17.21: Social Distance towards Jews and Israelis

Stimulus Category	'Jews' A.	'Israelis' B.	Nominal Change (A – B)
1. Admit to Kinship	**60.7%**	**47.9%**	**+12.8%**
2. Have as a Close Friend or Closer	72.7%	61.4%	+11.3%
3. Have as Next-Door Neighbour, or Closer	79.3%	67.0%	+12.3%
4. Work in the Same Workplace, or Closer	85.6%	74.1%	+11.5%
5. Welcome as an Irish Citizen, or Closer	88.5%	77.8%	+10.7%
6. Have as Visitor Only	6.6%	9.7%	-3.1%
7. Debar or Deport	4.9%	12.5%	-7.6%
6 + 7 (Deny Citizenship)	**(11.5%)**	**(22.2%)**	**(-10.7%)**

Table No. 17.21 shows the difference in social-distance scores between 'Jews' and 'Israelis' among Irish adults. Because of the relatively high correlation (0.64) between the responses towards these two categories, the relatively low rating of 'Israeli' as an ethnico-religious stimulus category, there is a real danger that the public image of the 'Israeli' can lead to an increase in Anti-Semitism. Hence, the need for a solution to the Israeli-Palestinian conflict that will be judged fair and just by the non-Jews for the sake of the public standing of Jewish people.

Returning to Table No. 17.20, 'Jews' as a stimulus category elicited a statistically significant variation in ten of the twelve variables. Gender and marital status produced consensus. Nine of the remaining variables had score variations of over 9% in the case of 'admit to kinship', while seven variables recorded a +9% variation in relation to 'denying citizenship'. The following extract from Table No. 17.20 spells out the plus 9% variation in respect of both 'admit to kinship' and 'denial of citizenship'.

Personal Variable	Nominal Variation	Variation of 'Admit to Kinship' and 'Denial of Citizenship' In the case of 'Jews', i.e. between			
A. Admit to Kinship		**Highest % (Most Favourable)**		**Lowest % (Least Favourable)**	
1. Region of Residence	24.2%	Mid-West/Sth.West	(72.2%)	and BMW	(48.0%)
2. Occupational Status	19.7%	Prof./Executive	(70.7%)	and Unskilled/Semi-Skilled	(51.2%)
3. Social Class Position	16.1%	"Upper-Middle Class"	(73.2%)	and "Working Class"	(57.1%)
4. Age	14.7%	26-40 years	(68.3%)	and 18-25 years	(53.6%)
5. Church Attendance	14.5%	1-3 Times Monthly	(69.9%)	and Weekly	(55.4%)
6. Closeness to God	13.3%	Non-Believers	(69.2%)	and "Not Close at all"	(55.9%)
7. Area of Birth	12.5%	Large Town (10,000+)	(66.9%)	and Rural/Village	(54.4%)
8. Place of Rearing	11.6%	Munster	(64.6%)	and Connaught/Ulster	(53.0%)
9. Education	10.6%	Third Level	(65.0%)	and Incomplete Second Lev.	(54.4%)
B. Denial of Citizenship		**Highest % (Least Favourable)**		**Lowest % (Most Favourable)**	
1. Social Class Position	15.7%	"Lower Class"	(17.9%)	and "Upr. Middle Class"	(2.2%)
2. Occupational Status	14.8%	Unskilled/Semi-Skilled	(20.0%)	and Professional/Executive	(4.2%)
3. Place of Rearing	12.9%	Rest of Leinster	(17.8%)	and Connaught/Ulster	(4.9%)
4. Region of Residence	12.1%	Mid.East & Sth.East	(18.0%)	and Mid-West & Sth.West	(5.9%)
5. Closeness to God	11.1%	Somewhat Close	(13.7%)	and Non-Believer	(2.6%)
6.5 Education	10.4%	Incomplete Sec.-Level	(16.5%)	and Third Level	(6.1%)
6.5 Area of Birth	10.4%	Rural/Village	(16.3%)	and Large Town (10,000+)	(5.9%)

The above figures show the extremes within each of the personal variables with substantial score-variations. The readers can see for themselves the direction of prejudice against 'Jews' in the population. Some of the variations are very significant, e.g. the geographic factor and social class stand out as the most significant influences.

7.2.4 Atheists and Agnostics: The improvement in the social distance scores of 'Atheists' and 'Agnostics' is something to be welcomed both from religious and social points of view. In the case of the former, it acknowledges the fact that "faith in God" is a gift. The neighbour is loved irrespective of his or her professed belief. The standing of 'Atheists' improved more than that of 'Agnostics' and this, in itself, is of interest. 'Atheists', it would seem, are not perceived as being pro-actively anti-religion.

The ranges of variation in the 'admission to kinship' and 'denial of citizenship' scores are quite substantial in relation to both categories and seem to follow similar patterns. The following extract from Table No. 17.20 gives the range of variation by personal variables for both categories in relation to 'admission to kinship'.

Personal Variable	Nominal Variations		Variation (Admit to Kinship) Between		
	Atheists	**Agnostics**	<u>Highest %</u> **(Most Favourable)**		<u>Lowest %</u> **(Least Favourable)**
1. Age	26.3%	22.7%	26 to 40 year olds	and	71 years plus
2. Gender	5.5%	7.3%	Males	and	Females
3. Marital Status	17.3%	8.1%	Separated/Divorced	and	Widowed
4. Area of Birth	23.0%	26.6%	Large Town (10,000+)	and	Rural/Village
5. Place of Rearing	14.8%	21.1%	Munster	and	Connaught/Ulster
6. Region of Residence	23.0%	27.1%	Mid-West & Sth.-West	and	Border/Midlands/West
7. Education	10.2%	14.2%	Third Level	and	Primary or Less
8. Occupational Status	16.0%	14.0%	Professional/Executive	and	Unskilled/Semi-Skilled
9. Social Class Position	16.4%	13.3%	"Upr.Class/Mid.-M. Class"	and	"Working Class"
10. Church Attendance	31.2%	29.4%	Never	and	Weekly or More Often
11. Closeness to God	26.4%	28.7%	Do Not Believe in God	and	Extremely Close to God
12. Frequency of Prayer	19.9%	18.2%	Never	and	Several Times a Day

The above findings are as anticipated for ordinal variables except in the case of age where the findings were mixed. The patterns in the case of 'denial of citizenship' followed a similar pattern in reverse, i.e. where highest percentages expressed 'least favourable'. Despite the substantial improvement in the standing of both 'Atheists' and 'Agnostics', their current position has plenty of room for improvement.

7.2.5 Muslims: This religious stimulus category is still in a precarious position in the social distance findings of the sample, although the level of prejudice towards them has reduced substantially in the percentages 'admitting to kinship' (i.e. from **20.6%** in 1988-89 to **42.9%** in 2007-08). Unfortunately the percentage 'denying citizenship' has remained more or less the same at **23.2%**.

The following extracts from Table No. 17.20 show the pattern of responses between the personal variables. They merit very serious concentration.

477

Personal Variable	Nominal Variation	Between			
A. Admit to Kinship		<u>Highest %</u> (Most Favourable)		<u>Lowest %</u> (Least Favourable)	
1. Age	16.0%	26 - 40 years	(52.5%) and	56 - 70 years	(36.5%)
2. Gender	N/S	---	and	---	
3. Marital Status	13.2%	Separated/Divorced	(46.5%) and	Widowed	(33.3%)
4. Area of Birth	N/S	---	and	---	
5. Place of Rearing	13.9%	Munster	(47.0%) and	Connaught/Ulster	(33.1%)
6. Region of Residence	16.7%	Mid-West & Sth.West	(48.1%) and	Border/Midlands/West	(31.4%)
7. Education	4.9%	Primary or Less	(45.8%) and	Complete 2nd Level	(40.9%)
8. Occupational Status	15.7%	Professional/Exec.	(50.5%) and	Inspect./Supervisory	(34.8%)
9. Social Class Position	11.1%	"Upr. Middle Class	(51.4%) and	"Middle & Work. Class	(40.3%)
10. Church Attendance	16.8%	1-3 Times Monthly	(53.7%) and	Weekly or More Often	(36.9%)
11. Closeness to God	31.4%	Do Not Believe in God	(71.1%) and	Not Very Close and Not Close at all	(39.7%)
12. Frequency of Prayer	13.8%	Never	(50.5%) and	Less Than Weekly	(36.7%)

B. Denial of Citizenship		<u>Highest %</u> (Least Favourable)		<u>Lowest %</u> (Most Favourable)	
1. Age	16.3%	71 years plus	(34.0%) and	26 – 40 years	(17.7%)
2. Gender	N/S	---	and	---	
3. Marital Status	26.5%	Widowed	(42.0%) and	Perm. Relationship	(15.5%)
4. Area of Birth	N/S	---	and	---	
5. Place of Rearing	18.8%	Rest of Leinster	(34.1%) and	Connaught/Ulster	(15.3%)
6. Region of Residence	8.5%	Border/Midlands/West	(26.2%) and	Mid-West & Sth.West	(17.7%)
7. Education	17.5%	Primary or Less	(33.1%) and	Third Level	(15.6%)
8. Occupational Status	12.0%	Unskilled/Semi-Skilled	(30.4%) and	Prof./Executive	(18.4%)
9. Social Class Position	21.5%	"Upper Class"	(31.6%) and	"Upr.Middle Class"	(10.1%)
10. Church Attendance	4.9%	Never	(26.3%) and	1-3 Times Monthly	(21.1%)
11. Closeness to God	28.5%	Not Close At All	(33.8%) and	Do Not Believe in God	(5.3%)
12. Frequency of Prayer	14.4%	Weekly	(31.9%) and	Never	(17.5%)

The above results are very negative and require serious attention. One thing which gives some degree of hope is the personal variable responses which point to possible improvement in the future, allowing for the absence of anti-'Muslim' propaganda! Some of the variables were mixed. The level of willingness to 'deny citizenship' is alarming for some variables.

Part VIII – Attitudes to Christian Church Unity

Ever since the Second Vatican Council there has been a serious dialogue between the leaders of the Roman Catholic Church and the World Council of Churches. Work towards the achievement of greater Christian Unity has been on the official agenda of the various Churches. Progress to date has been uneven, and the issue seems to have receded from the measure of seriousness it had in the 1960s and 1970s. Students of intergroup relations in Ireland, and in other countries with poor Roman Catholic-Protestant-Orthodox relations, would rank Christian unity as a *primary goal* in the achievement of integrated pluralist unity in these societies in the long term. The ongoing progress in the relations between the Orthodox Church and the Roman Catholic Church after centuries of "mutual excommunication" is a source of optimism for genuine ecumenists. Professor Finbar Clancy, S.J. has traced this progress between Rome and Constantinople in a most scholarly and informative manner in his recent article in the *Milltown Studies*[9].

8.1 Overall Findings:
Richard Rose, in his study of intergroup relations in Northern Ireland (see Rose, *Governing Without Consensus*, London, Faber, 1971), reported on an interesting survey of religious and political attitudes carried out in 1968 (in Northern Ireland). Two *opinion* questions were asked in relation to the *desirability* and practical *possibility* of 'Christian Church Unity'. These two questions have been replicated by the present author in the Greater Dublin Survey (1972-73), the National Survey (1988-89) and in the National Survey (2007-08). These four dates are very significant for the monitoring of the people's opinions towards Christian Unity in the Republic of Ireland, and the development of integrated pluralist relations in both Northern Ireland and the Republic.

It should not be forgotten, however, that already there is a whole range of pastoral and spiritual projects which are being pursued in an ecumenical manner. Much credit is due to the different Church leaderships for this advance in real unity. Such working together is essential to provide for favourable contact which leads to a reduction in inter-Church prejudice.

---

[9] Clancy, Finbar G., "Sailing to Byzantium: Three Papal Visits to Turkey", in *Milltown Studies* (No. 63) Milltown Park, Dublin, 2010 (pages 1–84).

This cooperation is also *necessary* for local community integration and for the protection of the good name of the Christian faith.

Table No. 17.22:
Desirability and Practicality of Christian Church Unity by Total Sample

A. Question: *"Do you think that in principle uniting the Protestant and Catholic Churches is Desirable or Undesirable?"*			
			Number
1. Desirable	22.8%	53.9%	230
2. Depends	31.1%		315
3. Don't Know/No Opinion		31.3%	318
4. Undesirable		14.7%	149
Number		99.9%	1,012

B. Question: *"Do you think that in practice uniting the Churches is Possible or Impossible?"*			
			Number
1. Possible	15.8%	46.5%	159
2. Depends	30.7%		310
3. Don't Know/No Opinion		28.3%	287
4. Impossible		25.2%	255
Number		100.0%	1,011

When compared with the findings of 1968 in Northern Ireland, those of Greater Dublin in 1972-73 and the National (Republic of Ireland) Survey of 1988-89, the trends are less than hopeful.

Table No. 17.23 gives a measure of change in the ecumenical level of optimism in the Republic of Ireland since 1972-73 when **83%** of Dublin respondents favoured the unity of the Catholic and Protestant Churches in principle, as compared with only **23%** of the National sample which would agree with that opinion in 2007-'08.

Table No. 17.24 traces the change in the Dublin subsample since 1972-73.

Table No. 17.23:
Changes in Opinions on the Desirability and Practicality of
Christian Church Unity (1968 to 2007/08)

Degrees of Agreement	1968* N. Ireland (1)	1972-73** Dublin (2)	1988-89** National (3)	2007-08 National (4)	Change (3) – (4)	Change (2) – (4)
A. Desirable in Principle						
1. Desirable	45%	83%	45%	23%	-22%	- 61%
2. Depends	7%	5%	27%	31%	+3%	+26%
3. Don't Know	7%	4%	18%	31%	+12%	+26%
4. Undesirable	42%	8%	11%	15%	+4%	+ 7%
B. Possible in Practice						
1. Possible	27%	62%	30%	16%	-14%	- 46%
2. Depends	7%	11%	27%	31%	+3%	+20%
3. Don't Know	7%	5%	14%	28%	+14%	+23%
4. Impossible	59%	22%	29%	25%	-4%	+ 3%
Number	1,291	2,083	1,003	1,000	-	-

* Richard Rose   ** Micheál Mac Gréil

Table No. 17.24:
Changes in Opinion on Church Unity in Dublin Sample since 1972-73

Church Unity	1972-73	2007-08	Change
(a) Desirable in Principle			
1. Desirable	83%	16%	-67%
2. Depends	5%	30%	+25%
3. Don't Know	4%	35%	+31%
4. Undesirable	8%	19%	+11%
(b) Possible in Practice			
1. Possible	62%	13%	-49%
2. Depends	11%	28%	+17%
3. Don't Know	5%	34%	+29%
4. Impossible	22%	25%	+3%

The above is one of the most substantial changes in the findings of this 2007-08 survey, i.e. a nominal drop of **67%** (i.e. from 83% to 16%) in support for Christian Church unity **in principle**, over thirty-six years. Something very radical has happened to the great idealism of the 1970s. It would appear that there is need for **serious research** with this virtual collapse in the proportion supporting the **desirability** of Church unity in principle. One could speculate as to why this has happened. Has there been a retrenchment in the ecumenical policies of the major Churches? This is another example of the late **Professor John Jackson's** (Sociology in TCD) view of the difficulty of bringing about change in society because of the *"dynamic conservatism of the institutions".* He implied that it was of the nature of institutions to maintain the *status quo.* Prophetic leaders can sometimes bring about change, which in time will be institutionalised. The other way change takes place is when the institution loses public support and a new 'modified' replacement of norms takes over. The latter manner of change can be painful. The prophetic leadership way of change can be more satisfactory in that it maintains more continuity. These ideas are mentioned to help the Christian Churches out of the current loss of support for Church Unity in Ireland among their congregations.

8.2 Responses by Personal Variables:

The following Table (No. 17.25) gives a breakdown of responses to the two ecumenical questions by eight personal variables:

Table No. 17.25:
Church Unity in Principle and in Practice by Personal Variables

Variable	Desirable in Principle					Possible in Practice				
	Desirable	Depends	Don't Know/No Opinion	Undesirable	No.	Is Possible	Depends	Don't Know/No Opinion	Impossible	No.
Total Sample	22.7%	31.1%	31.3%	14.7%	1012	15.8%	30.7%	28.3%	25.2%	1012
Number	230	315	318	149	---	160	310	287	255	----
(a) Age	(p<.001)									
1. 18-25 Years	12.5%	26.2%	**44.0%**	**17.3%**	168	12.6%	21.0%	**41.9%**	24.6%	167
2. 26-40 Years	19.5%	26.0%	**36.8%**	**17.6%**	323	12.4%	24.5%	**32.2%**	**31.0%**	323
3. 41-55 Years	20.2%	**40.1%**	26.3%	13.4%	247	13.4%	**39.3%**	25.1%	22.3%	247
4. 56-70 Years	**35.4%**	**33.7%**	23.6%	7.3%	178	**24.2%**	**38.2%**	21.3%	16.3%	178
5. 71 Years plus	**34.4%**	29.2%	18.8%	**17.8%**	96	**22.9%**	**32.3%**	13.5%	**31.3%**	96
Number	230	315	318	149	1012	159	310	287	255	1011
(b) Gender										
1. Male	Variations Not Statistically Significant					15.2%	29.1%	**32.7%**	23.0%	499
2. Female						**16.3%**	**32.3%**	24.1%	**27.2%**	514
Number						160	311	287	255	1013
(c) Marital Status	(p<.001)									
1. Single/Never Married	19.3%	28.0%	**36.7%**	**16.0%**	357	**16.2%**	25.1%	**34.1%**	24.6%	358
2. Married	**26.2%**	**33.9%**	27.3%	12.5%	472	15.7%	**36.2%**	23.7%	24.4%	472
3. Separated/Divorced	18.6%	25.6%	**44.2%**	11.6%	43	**18.6%**	18.6%	**41.9%**	20.9%	43
4. Permanent Relation'p	12.7%	29.6%	**39.4%**	**18.3%**	71	7.0%	29.6%	**35.2%**	**26.2%**	71
5. Widowed	**30.4%**	**33.3%**	14.5%	**21.7%**	69	**33.8%**	13.2%	**29.4%**	23.5%	68
Number	231	315	317	149	1,012	161	310	286	255	1012

Table No. 17.25 Cont'd. Variable	Desirable in Principle					Possible in Practice				
	Desirable	Depends	Don't Know/ No Opinion	Undesirable	No.	Is Possible	Depends	Don't Know/ No Opinion	Impossible	No.
(d) Area of Birth	(p<.001)									
1. City (100,000+)	17.5 %	26.1 %	**37.8 %**	**18.7 %**	418	13.7 %	22.3 %	**36.0 %**	**28.1 %**	417
2. Large Town (10,000+)	**24.4 %**	**33.6 %**	**31.9 %**	10.1 %	119	**16.0 %**	**33.6 %**	26.9 %	23.5 %	119
3. Town (1,500+)	20.9 %	**32.6 %**	25.6 %	**20.9 %**	129	**17.7 %**	29.2 %	20.0 %	**33.1 %**	130
4. Rural/Village	**29.4 %**	**36.2 %**	25.1 %	9.3 %	343	**17.7 %**	**40.6 %**	22.3 %	19.4 %	345
Number	230	315	315	149	1009	160	311	285	255	1011
(e) Place of Rearing	(p<.001)									
1. Dublin (City / Co)	16.6%	**32.1%**	**34.9%**	17.0%	265	14.3%	25.2%	**32.0%**	**28.6%**	266
2. Rest of Leinster	**26.2%**	**32.3%**	29.3%	12.2%	164	13.3%	**36.4%**	15.2%	**35.2%**	165
3. Munster	**33.2%**	30.2%	17.7%	**19.0%**	232	**20.8%**	**33.8%**	16.9%	**28.6%**	231
4. Connaught/Ulster	15.2%	**43.9%**	26.8%	14.0%	164	11.6%	**39.0%**	**29.3%**	20.1%	164
Number	189	280	224	132	825	127	269	197	233	826
(f) Region of Residence	(p<.001)									
1. B.M.W.	18.1%	**36.2%**	**33.6%**	12.2%	271	14.4	**31.0%**	**31.0%**	23.6%	271
2. Dublin	15.8%	29.8%	**35.3%**	**18.9%**	285	13.3%	27.7%	**33.7%**	**25.3%**	285
3. Mid-East & Sth.-East	**27.9%**	**31.1%**	**32.9%**	8.2%	219	**18.8%**	**33.9%**	27.1%	20.2%	218
4. Mid-West & Sth-West	**31.6%**	27.0%	22.8%	**18.6%**	237	**17.7%**	30.8%	20.3%	**31.2%**	237
Number	230	315	318	149	1,012	160	310	287	254	1011
(g) Education	Variations Not Statistically Significant					(p<.02)				
1. Primary or less						**20.3 %**	**35.6 %**	25.4 %	18.6 %	118
2. Incomplete Second-L.						17.3 %	30.8 %	**33.8 %**	18.1 %	260
3. Complete Second-L.						14.1 %	28.2 %	**31.8 %**	**25.9 %**	255
4. Third-Level						14.5 %	30.9 %	23.2 %	**31.1 %**	379
Number						160	311	287	254	1012
(h) Occupational Status	(p<.005)									
1 Unskilled/Semi	**24.3 %**	28.6 %	**37.9 %**	9.2 %	206	14.4 %	30.8 %	**38.0 %**	16.8 %	208
2. Skilled/Routine non-m.	19.6 %	**36.2 %**	**31.3 %**	12.9 %	326	**16.9 %**	30.8 %	28.9 %	23.4%	325
3.Inspectional/Supervisory	**24.2 %**	30.3 %	28.0 %	**17.4 %**	132	**18.9 %**	**31.1 %**	21.2%	**28.8 %**	132
4. Professional/Executive	**29.7 %**	26.6 %	24.5 %	**19.3 %**	192	**18.2 %**	**36.1 %**	17.3 %	**30.4 %**	191
Number	203	268	264	121	856	141	274	234	207	856

Note: Percentages above sample average are **in bold.**

The information given in Table No. 17.25 is quite straightforward and should be examined by the reader at his or her leisure. The commentary and interpretation do not exhaust the valuable information and detail given above.

The correlations and variations between the subsamples seem to be, at times, in the opposite direction to what one would expect, i.e. that the young, more urbanised and more highly educated would be more open to the desirability of Church Unity. In fact, there was a higher level of support for Church Unity among the more devout subsamples, i.e. the older, the widowed, the rural/village born etc. If this reflects the situation, it means that resistance to Church Unity is more 'institutional' than coming from the believers and Church attendees.

For a fuller discussion on the performance of each of the personal variables see *The Challenge of Indifference* (2009) pages 141-147.

8.3 Conclusion:

For those interested in the promotion of Christian Church Unity, the above findings are quite disappointing. The downward trend was to be seen in the results of the 1988-89 findings. A reduction of interest would seem to be yet another symptom of an overall decline in the perceived importance of religion in the lives of the people. This should raise questions for the leaders of the Churches within the Christian family of churches. Their co-operation and solidarity will be necessary to raise the levels of faith and religious practice which have suffered so much over the past thirty years or so. It is interesting to note that religious indifference once again becomes a relevant factor. The **late Professor Brian Wilson,** Sociologist of Religion in Oxford University, held the view that the advance of secularisation was marked by the **irrelevance** of Religion in Society. We could interpret the findings of this 2007-08 survey as indicating that Irish society was moving toward secularisation! It has not yet arrived at that state.

Most authorities on ecumenism are aware that its seeds must be sown *within each of the Churches*. It is erroneous to assume that if all children of different Churches are raised together they will inevitably end up ecumenical. What would be most likely to emerge in such a rear-together environment (all the time) is that there would be no distinctive Churches to unite, and the children would be assimilated into the religious values and norms of the most dominant denomination. Whereas, if knowledge, respect and reverence for the beliefs and practices of *sister* Churches is cultivated within individual Churches, it will find fruitful expression in genuine **integrated Christian pluralism** which is likely to be the most just form of Christian Unity.

Part IX – Overall Conclusion

This chapter began with a comment on the historical background of the current religious profile of Ireland and the importance of religion in intergroup relations in Irish society for a number of centuries, especially, since the Reformation. It was shown that the demographic predominance of **Roman Catholics** had been maintained in the Republic of Ireland since 1861. Of those who declared their religion in the *2006 Census*, **92.4%** were **Roman Catholic**, **3.2%** were **Church of Ireland**, **0.6%** were **Presbyterians**, **0.3%** were **Methodists** and **3.5%** belonged to **other religions**. Some 4.4% of the total population declared they had **no religion**, while **1.7% did not state** their religious affiliation. The big change in Protestant denominations in Northern Ireland since 1911 was dramatic (see extract from Table No. 17.3, page 441 above).

This change in proportions is likely to have had an impact on the socio-political balance of power in Northern Ireland and makes the current power-sharing devolved Government a most viable political solution. Despite its overwhelming demographic strength, the Roman Catholic Church in the Republic has not adopted a status of State or Established Church and exercises relatively little, if any, mass media dominance, as is obvious from current (2011) religious reporting in the major print and electronic media.

Religious practice has shown a relatively serious decline in public worship between 1988-89 and 2007-08, i.e. monthly (or more frequent) worship went from **87.9%** in 1988-89 to **54.4%** in 2007-08. Roman Catholic participation in the Sacrament of Penance dropped from **80%** 'several times a year' in 1988-89 to **27%** in 2007-08. The latter may be, in part, due to a 'change in norm' in the Roman Catholic pastoral advice. The decline in personal prayer was less dramatic, i.e. from **90%** 'weekly or more often' in 1988-89 to **72%** in 2007-08.

Social distance toward religious stimulus categories recorded significant improvements towards 'believers' and 'non-believers'. The religion eliciting the most severe prejudice is that of the **'Muslims'**, who are suffering from the negative stereotypes picked up from the media and the unresolved justice and peace problems of the Middle East. There is need for greater Christian – Muslim ecumenism.

The position of **'Jews'** has improved but they still suffer from the relatively negative standing of **'Israelis'** among the Irish adult population. An equitable solution to the Israel-Palestine conflict is very important for the prevention of a return to dangerous anti-Semitism. **'Atheists'** and **'Agnostics'** have gained more tolerance between 1988-89 and 2007-08.

Finally, the reasons given for the decline in regular public worship were four-fold, i.e.

	Total Sample	Roman Catholics
1. "Just Don't Bother"	64.8%	68.1%
2. "Working"	10.0%	10.3%
3. "Illness"	4.5%	3.4%
4. "Other"	20.7%	18.2%

Some **14%** were *not free* to participate because of work or illness, which confirms that on any one Sunday, only ± **86%** of the adult population are free to worship. This raises the **54.4%** participating in monthly (or more often) worship to **63.3%** of those *'free to worship'*. The main cause given by respondents for not taking part was plain **indifference**, hence, the title of the special Report: *The Challenge of Indifference* (2009)! Despite the negative trends reported above, there is still a strong core of respondents for whom their religion is a real support and source of continuous commitment. The negativity, cynicism and preoccupation with weaknesses in religious groups in many of the mass media of communication, rarely, if ever, report on the positive and newsworthy aspects of the Irish people's faith.

***

CHAPTER XVIII
Authoritarianism and Social Anomie

Part I – Introduction

In 1897 the sociologist, *Emile Durkheim*, published his work on *Suicide*[1] and introduced the concept of **social anomie** as a sociological condition which characterised a certain type of suicide, which he classified as 'anomic suicide'. In 1936 the psychologist, *Eric Fromm*, published his view that ethnocentrism, which was prevalent in Germany at the time, was influenced by a personality trait which he called **authoritarianism**[2]. These two concepts, i.e. 'social anomie' and 'authoritarianism' have contributed very significantly to our understanding of social prejudice and many other personality and societal dysfunctions, including social deviance.

In the 1972-73 survey, a *new 'authoritarian scale'* was in the questionnaire and proved to be a most significant 'personal variable' in explaining variations in the different measures of types of prejudice. This established clearly an important psychological dimension in the causality of prejudice. But it raised a further question, namely, what were the 'causes' of authoritarianism, assuming it was the product of nurture rather than *nature*? This does not deny that human beings have a capacity to become authoritarian, given the favourable socio-cultural background and environment. Another established feature of the authoritarian personality is the absence of a correlation between intelligence (which is to a degree inherited) and authoritarianism. In other words, the most intelligent person in the group could be the most authoritarian or least authoritarian member of the group! For further information on the *New Authoritarian Scale*, see Mac Gréil (1977)[3]. It was based on the Adorno, *et al* text[4]. An adaptation of the 1972-73 'authoritarian scale' has been included in both the 1988-89 and the 2007-08 national surveys.

One important variable, which was left out of the 1972-73 survey, was added to the 1988-89 and 2007-08 questionnaires, namely, an adaptation of

[1] Durkheim, Emile, *"Le Suicide", Etude de Sociologie*, Paris, Universitaires de France, 1897.
[2] Fromm, Eric, "Sozialpsychologisher Teil" in Horkheimer, M.(Ed.) *Studien uber Autorität und Familie Forschungsberichte aus dem Institut fur Sozialforschung*, Parijs, Felix Allen, 1936.
[3] See: Mac Gréil, Micheál, *Prejudice and Tolerance in Ireland*, Dublin, C.I.R., 1977, pages 112-115, 503ff.
[4] Adorno, T.W., Frankel-Brunswick, E., Levinson, D.J. and Sandford, R.N., *The Authoritarian Personality*, New York, Harper & Row, 1950.

Leo Srole's *Anomie Scale*[5]. This added to the explanation of prejudice scores through its influence on authoritarianism. This scale was an important addition to the 1988-89 survey that was inadvertently omitted from the 1972-73 survey questionnaire. Apart from the value of **anomie** and **authoritarianism** as 'independent variables', they were also important as 'dependent variables'. The level of each characteristic in Irish society gives the reader a valuable insight into the sociological and psychological health of the people.

During the 1950s a serious disagreement and 'argumentative cross-fire' took place between the authors and researchers who supported the **psychological** approach to the explanation of various forms of social prejudice, i.e. those who advocated that prejudice was the product of certain personality traits such as 'authoritarianism', and the proponents of the primacy of the **sociological** cause, i.e. such as social 'anomie'. The former camp was led by Adorno *et al* and his colleagues, while the latter was championed by Leo Srole. In fact, the findings of the University of Nijmegen (Holland) research into prejudice in Holland (published in 1987 by Felling, Albert; Peters, Jan; Schreeuder, O; Eisinga, R., and Scheepers, Peer) found that "the effects of anomie on ethnocentrism are for the major part mediated by authoritarianism"[6]. This result was confirmed in the 1988-89 Irish survey. A similar result was expected to be evident in the findings of the current (2007-08) survey but with a rise in the influence of 'social anomie'. The cooperation of the University of Nijmegen was very valuable to the present author when devising the *Anomie Scale* for the 1988-89 questionnaire.

In this Chapter (XVIII), it is proposed to present the findings of the 2007-08 survey in relation to the levels of authoritarianism and anomie in Irish society (Republic of Ireland). It is also proposed to compare the present findings with those of 1972-73 and 1988-89 in the case of authoritarianism and with the results of the 1988-89 national survey in respect of the degrees of anomie among the population. The results of the findings (on anomie and authoritarianism) will have some serious consequences for certain aspects of modern Irish society!

---

[5] Srole, Leo, "Social Integration and Certain Corollaries, An Explanatory Study" in *American Sociological Review*, Vol.21, No.4, 1956, pages 709-716.
[6] See: Peer Scheepers, Albert Felling and Jan Peters, "Anomie, Authoritarianism and Ethnocentrism: Update of a Classic Theme and an Empirical Text", in *Politics and the Individual*, Vol.2, No.1, 1992.

Leo Srole and Robert K. Merton developed the concept of anomie originally proposed by Emile Durkheim in his work on *suicide* in 1897. Srole's linking of anomie with minority relations was in his 'controversial' article published in 1956[7], "Social Integration and Certain Corollaries: An Explanatory Study". Robert K. Merton has interpreted anomie as a state of *normlessness* created by a situation where the society's cultural goals are being promoted without the possibility of achieving them within the accepted norms, i.e. *the inadequacies of the norms for sections of society to achieve the cultural goals*. He devoted a special chapter, "Social Structure and Anomie", to the topic in his very popular textbook, *Social Theory and Social Structure*[8]. Some authors challenge Merton's interpretation of Durkheim's concept[9].

Accepting the diversity of views by serious authors in relation to the understanding of Durkheim's concept of anomie, the present author accepts the Srole version as tested in his special scale, i.e. with its five components *"that could be labelled as: political powerlessness, social powerlessness, generalised socio-economic regression, normlessness and meaninglessness and social isolation* (Srole 1956, pages 712-3)" as quoted by Scheepers *et al*[10]. As already stated, the *Social Anomie Scale* used in this text is adapted from Srole's original scale. Authoritarianism (as a psychological trait) and social anomie (as a sociological phenomenon) are of interest both as 'dependent' and 'independent' variables. In the context of the psycho-socio-cultural approach to causality (explaining social prejudice), 'authoritarianism' would be a psychological cause and 'anomie' would be a sociological cause. The following model highlights the multiple nature of causality:

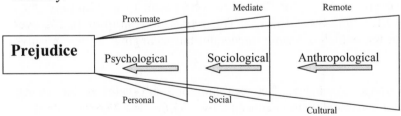

Figure 18.1: Filtered-Causation Model

---

[7] Srole, Leo, (1956), *Op.Cit.*
[8] Merton, Robert K., *Social Theory and Social Structure*, Glencoe Ill., Free Press, (1949) 1957.
[9] See Mestrovic, G., and Brown, Hèléne M., "Durkheim's Concept of Anomie as Dérèglement" in *Social Problems*, Vol.33, No.2, University of California, December 1985, pages 81ff.
[10] Scheepers, P., (1992) *et al*, *Op.Cit*, page 44.

The value of the above model is to emphasise the complexity of causation behind patterned behaviour and social dispositions. The individual person's prejudices and discrimination are expressions of social and cultural biases picked up by him or her in addition to his or her personality traits and passing moods. The human personality itself is largely the product of social norms and cultural values internalised by the individual during the process of socialisation and social interaction.

Part II – Authoritarianism in Irish Society

2.1 General Findings:

The original (new) *Authoritarian Scale* was devised (by the present author) for the 1972-73 social survey of Greater Dublin. It was based on "an adaptation of the more elaborate scales composed by Adorno *et al* (1950)" and was replicated in the 1988-89 National Survey. The four sub-scales are: Religious Fundamentalism, Pro-Establishment Conservatism, Fascist-type Submission and Aggression and Moralism and related issues.

A perusal of the performance of each item on Table No. 18.1 (below), taking each item singly as an expression of public opinion, may be of interest to the reader (see Table No. 18.3 below). Also, when compared with the opinions expressed by the 1988-89 sample, the 2007-08 sample views have changed in the direction of becoming less authoritarian. Only two of the sixteen items registered higher A-Scores in 2007-08 than those of 1988-89, i.e. Items Nos. B.1 and C.2.

The overall A-Score for 2007-08 was **88.1** which was **17.0** lower than the A-Score for 1988-89 at **105.1**. This represents a drop of **16.2%** over nineteen years, which is quite moderate but changing in the positive direction.

The range of changes between the four sub-scales is interesting. Religious Fundamentalism reduced by **31.6** or **25.6%**; Political Conservatism by 7.5 or 5.1%; Fascist-Type Submission and Aggression by **4.0** or **6.1%**; and Moralism and Miscellaneous Authoritarianism by **24.6** or **22.7%**. The change in Religious Fundamentalism could also be due to a decline in religious conviction and practice over the period from 1988-89 and 2007-08 as much as to a reduction in authoritarianism. The lack of substantial change in the two middle categories must be interpreted as

Table No. 18.1:
Authoritarian Scale – Sixteen Items* (2007-08 and 1988-89)

	Item	Agree	Neither Agree nor Disagree	Disagree	A-Score 0-200	Number
	A. Religious Fundamentalism:					
1.	"Everything that happens must be accepted as the Will of God"	35.1% (52.6)	21.0% (12.3)	43.8% (35.1)	91.3 (117.5)	1,013 (1,003)
2.	"Miracles in the Bible happened just as they are described there"	33.9% (60.0)	23.1% (21.2)	43.0% (18.7)	90.7 (141.3)	1,009 (1,003)
3.	"Men whose doctrines are false should not be allowed to preach in this country"	37.6% (48.2)	21.4% (17.9)	41.0% (33.9)	97.1 (114.3)	1,006 (997)
4.	"A thing is either right or wrong and none of this ambiguous woolly thinking"	34.1% (51.9)	21.3% (16.9)	44.6% (31.3)	90.5 (120.6)	1,012 (996)
	Sub-scale A-Score				91.8 (123.4)	
	B. Political Conservatism:					
1.	"Our system of Government is good because it is traditional"	49.4% (43.9)	18.4% (17.8)	32.1% (38.3)	117.4 (105.6)	1,010 (1,005)
2.	"It keeps things peaceful here"	57.6% (67.5)	17.8% (12.5)	24.6% (20.0)	132.8 (147.6)	1,008 (998)
3.	"Its goals are usually good ones"	52.2% (56.2)	19.7% (17.7)	28.2% (26.1)	124.0 (130.0)	1,008 (999)
4.	"It is in the hands of people who are good leaders"	31.6% (44.0)	22.4% (18.4)	45.9% (37.6)	85.6 (106.4)	1,009 (998)
	Sub-scale A-Score				114.9 (122.4)	
	C. Fascist-Type Submission and Aggression:					
1.	"There should be very strict control of RTÉ"	31.0% (40.0)	31.4% (17.9)	37.6% (42.1)	96.1 (97.9)	1,015 (998)
2.	"Gardaí should be armed always"	30.4% (29.6)	19.6% (12.5)	50.0% (57.9)	80.3 (71.7)	1,012 (1,000)
3.	"Student protest should be outlawed"	12.9% (21.1)	17.0% (15.3)	70.1% (63.6)	42.8 (57.5)	1,015 (992)
4.	** "Black people should be sent back to Africa and Asia where they belong and kept there" (Punks and Skinheads should be locked up)	8.4% (13.3)	11.3% (9.4)	80.2% (77.2)	28.1 (36.1)	1,013 (997)
	Sub-scale A-Score				61.8 (65.8)	
	D. Moralism and Miscellaneous Authoritarianism:					
1.	"Communism should be outlawed in Ireland"	37.0% (52.5)	32.0% (15.0)	30.9% (32.5)	106.0 (120.0)	1,014 (1,000)
2.	"Prostitution should be a prosecutable crime"	42.0% (63.9)	24.4% (14.7)	33.6% (21.5)	111.0 (142.4)	1,012 (996)
3.	"Homosexual behaviour between consenting adults should be a crime"	17.5% (35.1)	17.9% (20.9)	64.6% (43.9)	53.0 (91.2)	1,015 (999)
4.	"The more active you are in politics the harder it is to be a good Christian"	18.0% (31.2)	31.2% (18.4)	50.8% (50.4)	67.1 (80.9)	1,013 (999)
	Sub-scale A-Score				84.0 (108.6)	
	Total A-Scale Score				88.1 (105.1)	

Note: Figures in brackets are the 1988-89 scores. * The above items were spread through lists of items in the questionnaire to avoid **unidirectionality**. ** This item replaced: "Punks and Skinheads should be locked up" (from the 1988-89 survey) because these categories were no longer topical.

disappointing; the 24.6% decline in Moralism etc. is to be welcomed and marks a move towards greater overall tolerance!

2.2 Authoritarianism by Personal Variables:

When testing the sixteen-item Authoritarian Scale by factor analysis, it was discovered that three items failed to cluster as in the 1988-89 scale, i.e.:

C.2	*"Gardaí should be armed always";*
C.4	*"Black people should be sent back to Africa and Asia where they belong and kept there";*
D.4	*"The more active you are in politics, the harder it is to be a good Christian".*

The five items, i.e. C.1, C.3, D.1, D.2 and D.3 all clustered into one factor which was labelled: 'Fascist Repression/Moralism', i.e.

C.1	*"There should be very strict control of RTE";*
C.3	*"Student protest should be outlawed";*
D.1	*"Communism should be outlawed in Ireland";*
D.2.	*"Prostitution should be a prosecutable crime";*
D.3	*"Homosexual behaviour between consenting adults should be a crime".*

This meant that the whole scale was reduced to three factors and thirteen items[11]. Table No. 18.2 gives a breakdown of the A-Score (0-200) by personal variables.

Table No. 18.2: Adjusted Authoritarian Scale (Thirteen Items) by Personal Variables

Personal Variable	Total Scale Score (0 – 200)	Religious Fundamentalist Sub-Scale (0 – 200)	Political Conservatism Sub-Scale (0 – 200)	Fascist Repression/ Moralism Sub-Scale (0 – 200)	No.
Total Sample	**94.69**	**91.81**	**114.91**	**80.76**	**993**
A. Age	P<.001	P<.001	P<.001	P<.001	
1. 18-25 years	81.26	66.66	105.46	72.59	165
2. 26-40 years	87.15	86.55	101.14	76.60	318
3. 41-55 years	90.61	85.43	**119.02**	73.03	242
4. 56-70 years	**108.48**	**112.94**	**128.75**	**87.58**	170
5. 71 years plus	**128.64**	**131.43**	**141.02**	**116.31**	96
Score Variation	*47.38*	*64.77*	*39.88*	*43.72*	---

---

[11] The Three Factors include: (a) **Religious Fundamentalism**: Items Nos.: A1, A2, A3 and A4;
(b) **Political Conservatism**: Items Nos.: B1, B2, B3 and B4;
(c) **Fascist Repression/Moralism**: Items Nos.: C1, C3, D1, D2 and D3.
[See Table No.18.1]

B. Marital Status	P<.001	P<.001	P<.007	P<.001	
1. Single/Never Married	91.29	86.32	112.07	78.46	353
2. Married	**96.16**	**94.55**	**116.46**	**81.06**	457
3. Separated/Divorced	82.94	79.45	92.61	77.31	43
4. Permanent Relationship	80.80	68.75	108.88	69.80	71
5. Widowed	**124.15**	**133.50**	**139.59**	**104.31**	68
Score Variation	*32.86*	*64.75*	*46.98*	*34.51*	---
C. Area of Birth	P<.001	P<.001	P<.001	P<.001	
1. City (100,000 plus)	86.76	80.99	107.53	74.62	414
2. Large Town (10,000 +)	84.99	77.27	103.26	76.99	115
3. Town (1,500 plus)	93.62	91.79	**117.36**	75.98	128
4. Rural/Village	**108.09**	**110.11**	**126.75**	**91.15**	334
Score Variation	*23.10*	*32.84*	*23.49*	*16.53*	---
D. Place of Rearing in ROI.	P<.001	P<.001	N/S	P<.02	
1. Dublin (City & County)	92.51	84.38	---	76.51	265
2. Rest of Leinster	**103.10**	**102.64**	---	**82.66**	162
3. Munster	**105.95**	**113.07**	---	**90.07**	223
4. Connaught/Ulster	**92.47**	81.79	---	**81.19**	162
Score Variation	*13.44*	*33.79*	*---*	*13.56*	---
E. Region of Residence	P<.04	P<.001	N/S	N/S	
1. BMW (Border Mids. West)	89.88	79.28	---	---	266
2. Dublin	93.44	88.58	---	---	284
3. Mid-East & South-East	**100.56**	**102.17**	---	---	216
4. Mid-West & Sth-West	**96.31**	**100.57**	---	---	226
Score Variation	*10.68*	*22.89*	*---*	*---*	---
F. Education	P<.001	P<.001	P<.03	P<.001	
1. Primary or Less	**121.88**	**124.09**	**133.12**	**110.93**	113
2. Incomplete Sec.-Level	**105.95**	**109.51**	114.87	**95.10**	257
3. Complete Second-Level	89.15	86.18	110.37	75.28	251
4. Third-Level	82.29	77.33	112.33	65.38	370
Score Variation	*39.59*	*46.76*	*22.75*	*45.55*	---
G. Occupational Status	N/S	N/S	P<.001	P<.001	
1. Unskilled/Semi-Skilled	---	---	94.78	**89.56**	205
2. Skilled/Routine Non-M.	---	---	**117.34**	78.22	318
3. Inspectional/Supervisory	---	---	**113.45**	71.88	130
4. Professional/Executive	---	---	**129.31**	72.12	165
Score Variation	*---*	*---*	*34.53*	*17.68*	---
H. Social Class Position	P<.001	P<.004	P<.001	P<.043	
1. Class I: "Upper Class"	94.52	73.20	**129.99**	83.20	39
2. Class II: "Upr-Mid Class"	88.98	82.75	**127.48**	62.59	139
3. Class III: "Mid.-Mid. Cl"	88.11	84.87	**115.56**	68.77	227
4. Class IV: "Working Class"	**97.21**	**98.24**	110.75	**85.56**	362
5. Class V: "Lower Class"	**99.22**	**105.49**	93.82	**99.50**	85
Score Variation	*11.11*	*32.29*	*36.17*	*36.91*	*852*

Notes: Authoritarian scores above sample average **in bold**. Variations are in *italics*.
   Cronbach Alpha = 0.737

The above results are of special interest because the mean scores admit the possibility of a very high level of variation. On a score range of 0 – 200, an A-Score of 100 is the equivalent of 50% of the maximum score, i.e. making a PQ = 2.500. Since the four mean-scores are close to 100, i.e. **94.68, 91.81, 114.91** and **80.76**, the possibility of a significant and substantial variation for all three factors and the whole scale exists.

Despite the high PQ scores (P=100-Q), **Gender** did not produce a statistically significant variation for the scale or factor scores. In each of the four Tables, males and females recorded consensus in relation to the authoritarian personality trait. This in itself is further evidence that authoritarianism is socio-culturally, rather than genetically-determined. As noted already on a number of occasions in this text, the homogenisation of attitudes between males and females weakens the subcultural differences between men and women. Because of the growth of women in the workforce, their sharing similar indoor and outdoor recreational experiences and exposure to common television and media programmes and commentaries, it is likely that both men and women are being absorbed into the dominant (heretofore male) culture. The increase in gender-amalgamated primary and second-level schools must also contribute to this homogenisation of male and female attitudes and values. To the extent that male and female attitudes and opinions are becoming **uniform,** rather than **complementary,** is not necessarily a culturally-enriching development!

2.2.1 Age: The correlation between age and authoritarianism is as anticipated in the total scale and each of the factor scales. The older age-groups have higher A-Scores than the younger ones. The 18 to 25 year-olds were least authoritarian in three of the four scales which, in the light of their performance in previous scales, is to be welcomed. The frustrations caused by old age can see expression in authoritarianism and prejudice!

The score variations have been significant and quite substantial across the age groups. The following extract from Table No. 18.2(a) points this out:

Scale	Score Variation	Between Lowest A-Score		Highest A-Score	Scale Mean (0-200)
1. Total A-Scale	47.38	'18-25 yrs.' (**81.26**)	and '71 yrs.plus'	(**128.64**)	94.69
2. Religious Fundamentalism	64.77	'18-25 yrs.' (**66.66**)	and '71 yrs.plus'	(**131.43**)	91.81
3. Political Conservatism	39.88	'26-40 yrs' (**101.14**)	and '71 yrs.plus'	(**141.02**)	114.91
4. Fascist Repression/Moralism	43.72	'18-25 yrs.' (**72.59**)	and '71 yrs.plus'	(**116.31**)	80.76

Scale No. 4 which represents hard-core authoritarian Items is the most discerning of the four scales. This is because there is always the possibility of ideological elements influencing the score in the *'Religious Fundamentalist'* and *'Political Conservatism'* factors. Such an intrusion would be slight since the *Cronbach Alpha* score at **0.737** is quite significant and confirms the validity of the scale.

2.2.2 Marital Status: It is obvious from the findings of Table No. 18.2(b) that the age variable has influenced the variations between the 'Marital Status' sub-variables. Once again, the score variations were significant and substantial as seen in the following extract:

Scale	Score Variation	Between Lowest A-Score	Highest A-Score	Scale Mean (0-200)
1. Total A-Scale	32.86	'Perm.Rel'ships' (**80.80**) and 'Widowed' (**124.15**)		94.69
2. Religious Fundamentalism	64.75	'Perm.Rel'ships' (**68.75**) and 'Widowed' (**133.50**)		91.81
3. Political Conservatism	46.98	'Separated/Divor.'(**92.61**) and 'Widowed' (**139.59**)		114.91
4. Fascist Repression/Moralism	34.51	'Perm.Rel'ships' (**69.80**) and 'Widowed' (**104.31**)		80.76

Once again, the influence of old age with the added pain of widowhood seems to add to the support for authoritarian-type attitudes and views. The two groups least authoritarian are the 'Separated/Divorced' and those in 'Permanent Relationships'. As is seen on Table No. 18.2(b), the 'Single/Never Married' had below-average A-Score in each of the four scales.

2.2.3 Area of Birth: Those born in 'Rural/Village' areas had the highest A-Scores. The 'Large Town (10,000+)' sub-variable was the least authoritarian in three of the four scales. The overall trend of the findings of Table No. 18.2(c) indicates that the more urbanised respondents have lower A-Score than have those with 'Rural/Village' background. Score variations were moderate but significant.

2.2.4 Area of Rearing and Region of Residence: These are two 'nominal' variables. One of the scales, i.e. *'Political Conservatism'*, recorded the absence of statistically significant variations between the sub-variables of both variables. 'Region of Residence' also produced consensus in relation to the *'Fascist Repression/Moralism'* factor sub-scale.

The influence of the urbanised background has become clear in the responses of both variables. The score of those living in the BMW regions was lower than average, despite the predominantly rural/village composition. The relatively high A-Scores for 'Munster-reared' and those living in the 'Mid-West and South West' regions were against the trends in other scales! The score-variations were relatively moderate.

2.2.5 Education: The performance of education was as anticipated. Respondents with least education recorded highest A-Scores. The 'score-variations' were both significant and substantial.

Scale	Score Variation	Between Lowest A-Score	Highest A-Score	Scale Mean (0-200)
1. Total A-Scale	39.59	'Third Level' (**82.29**)	and 'Primary or Less' (**121.88**)	94.69
2. Religious Fundamentalism	46.76	'Third Level' (**77.33**)	and 'Primary or Less' (**124.09**)	91.81
3. Political Conservatism	22.75	'Comp.2nd Lev.'(**110.37**)	and 'Primary or Less' (**133.12**)	114.91
4.Fascist Repression/Moralism	45.55	'Third Level' (**65.38**)	and 'Primary or Less' (**110.93**)	80.76

The above extract from Table No. 18.2(f) highlights the negative correlation between authoritarianism and education. This was to be expected. The influence of **age** on these scores is also a factor producing the pattern of replies. This must be seen as a positive contribution of education to the development of a more *open-minded* personality trait in the graduates. The lowest A-Score in the above extract are still significant and should reduce further as participation in education increases!

2.2.6 Occupational Status: Both the 'Total Scale' and the *'Religious Fundamentalist'* scale elicited a consensus response between the sub-samples of the 'Occupational Status' variable. This is very significant in itself, i.e. that each of the four occupational grades has more or less similar A-Scores in each Table centred around the scales' mean scores of **94.6** and **91.81** respectively.

The results for the *'Political Conservatism'* factor were mixed and did not follow an expected pattern. 'Professional/Executive' sub-variable was the highest A-Score at **129.31** while the 'Unskilled/Semi-skilled' had the lowest score at **94.78**. In the case of Factor No.3 *('Fascist Repression/Moralism')* the results were more or less as anticipated, i.e. those with the lowest status had the highest A-Score.

2.2.7 Social Class Position: This variable elicited significant variations in all four scales. In the case of the Total Scale and *'Religious Fundamentalism'* the results were as anticipated. The following extract from Table No. 18.2(h) spells out the results:

Scale	Score Variation	Between Lowest A-Score		Highest A-Score	Scale Mean (0-200)
1. Total A-Scale	11.11	"Mid.Mid.Class" (**88.11**) and		"Lower Class" (**99.22**)	94.69
2. Religious Fundamentalism	32.29	"Upr. Class" (**73.20**) and		"Lower Class" (**105.49**)	91.81
3. Political Conservatism	36.17	"Lower Class" (**93.82**) and		"Upper Class" (**129.99**)	114.91
4. Fascist Repression/Moralism	36.91	"Upr.Mid.Class" (**62.59**) and		"Lower Class" (**99.50**)	80.76

With the exception of the *'Political Conservatism'* factor, the general trend in the scores is as expected. The score variation for the total scale was only moderate. This was in part due to the responses to Factors Nos. 1 ("Religious Fundamentalism") and 2 ("Political Conservatism") going in opposite directions. These internal diversities add to the complexity of such phenomena as authoritarianism!

2.2.8 Conclusion: It is hoped that the above commentary on the examination of the findings of *the Authoritarian Scale* and its three internal factors by personal variables has given the reader a better understanding of authoritarianism and how it is determined by age, education, rural-urban background etc.

The younger, more highly educated and more urbanised respondents had lower A-Scores as was anticipated. This is a positive result for young people (18-25 years) and for education. Both variables had not performed positively in numerous other scales dealing with intergroup attitudes.

Overall, the level of authoritarianism (as measured by the *Authoritarian Scale*) is still relatively high, especially, as measured by Factor No. 3. At times of economic and other crises there is always a danger of authoritarian, i.e. closed-minded and dogmatic, leaderships appealing for popular support from an anxious public's desire for drastic action, in the hope of alleviating the passing problems and "running the trains on time"! Such a reaction took place right across Europe in the wake of the *'1929 financial crash'* and the penal consequences of the *Treaty of Versailles*. As the Western World faces the painful outcome of the 2008 'financial crisis', there is a need to prevent a 1930s type of reaction! Hopefully, the West has learned the lessons of what happened eighty years ago; hence, the importance of monitoring authoritarianism in society and of challenging simplistic mono-causality and 'closed-minded' appeals for immediate action.   The emergence of strong demagogic leaders with authoritarian personality traits are a real danger in times of crisis (see Adorno *et al*, 1950).   The current findings refer to a survey carried out prior to the 2008 'financial collapse'.   The scale performance has been quite conventional.

Part III – Social Anomie

3.1 Introduction:

Despite the continued discussion and divergence of opinion by well-intended and learned sociologists and social psychologists over the past sixty years, the theory of social anomie is still valid and useful when measuring and explaining intergroup attitudes.   It is possible to define social anomie as*: A state of normlessness and perceived powerlessness resulting largely from a situation where society's culturally-prescribed goals are not realisable by significant sections of society within the confines of socially-acceptable norms.*   Failure to internalise *the necessary basic norms* required to cope with personal and social crises in the course of daily living in society leads to social anomie.

The above definition is the best the present author can offer after reviewing the recent literature.   The 'primary' sources from which the above definition has been based are **Emile Durkheim** (1897), **Robert K. Merton** (1938) and **Leo Srole** (1956).   The application of the 'theory of social anomie' is quite broad, i.e. in explaining suicide, social deviance, inter-group relations and other social phenomena.   The more complex society becomes, the greater the danger of acceptable social norms failing to achieve cultural goals.   This increases the likely level of social anomie in its society!

The influence of globalised mass media (print and electronic) and the continuous promotion of consumerism, individualism and dissociative competition, as opposed to collectivist and associative cooperation, seem to have helped to change the cultural priorities of many peoples.   The advanced cultural priority "to eat to live" is being reversed to the more primal   priority of "living to eat", if one may speak metaphorically.   In such a society, it is to be expected that *the insatiable goal of the pursuit of wealth* is certain to lead to a high level of *social anomie* because of the limited capacity of the socially acceptable norms to enable the people to achieve this goal. In feudal times and in social-class structured societies, only the elite were expected to be rich! In modern society it is expected that all people can be rich, which is a myth in the light of limited resources and restrictive norms. Not everyone can go from the *log cabin* to the *millionaire's penthouse*! A more equitable society would reduce anomie-producing conditions! The norm of *maximum income levels* would reduce anomic pressures.

Those who try to pursue the priority goal of pursuing wealth **outside** the acceptable norms end up as *society's deviants*. Emile Durkheim, in his classic text, *Suicide*[12], as far back as 1897 commented on the avarice of the wealthy and the pursuit of wealth by noting: "Religion has lost most of its power. And government, instead of regulating economic life, has become its tool and servant" (quoted from Chamblin, M.B. and Cochran, J.K. (1995)[13]. Looking at Western Society over one hundred and thirteen years later, Durkheim's comment would still be fairly accurate!

One of the most influential scholars and social researchers to develop the Durkheimian concept of anomie was Leo Srole of Cornell University Medical College in his seminal study and article published in the *American Sociological Review* in December, 1956[14]. In that article, Srole describes his new *Anomie Scale* devised to give "an operational formulation of the anomie concept. This formulation was broader however than that specified by Durkheim"[15]. The five-item scale devised by Leo Srole was as follows:

1.   *"There is little use writing to public officials because they aren't really interested in the problems of the average man."*

2.   *"Nowadays a person has to live pretty much for today and let tomorrow take care of itself."*

3.   *"In spite of what some people say, the lot of the average man is getting worse, not better."*

4.   *"It's hardly fair to bring children into the world with the way things look for the future."*

5.   *"These days a person doesn't really know whom he can count on."*

---

[12] Durkheim, Emile, *Suicide*, New York, Free Press (1897), 1951.

[13] Chamblin, M.B. and Cochran, J.K. "Assessing Messner and Rosenfeld's Institutional Anomie Theory: A Partial Test, in *Criminology*, Volume 33, No. 3, 1995, pages 411-429.

[14] Scrole, Leo "Social Integration in Certain Corollaries: An Exploratory Study, in *American Sociological Review,* Vol. 21, No. 6 (December), 1956, pages 709-716.

[15] *Ibid*, page 709.

Four out of five of Srole's components above are included in the *Anomie Scale* devised for the 1988-89 Irish National Survey and replicated in the present 2007-08 survey, i.e. components Nos. 1, 3, 4 and 5. The sense of unpredictableness and normlessness, expressed in component No. 2 is captured in the three new items included in the anomie scale, i.e.:

1. *"Everything changes so quickly that I often have trouble deciding what the right rules to follow are."*
2. *"People were better off in the old days when everyone knew how he/she was to act."*
3. *"You sometimes can't help wondering whether any effort is worthwhile."*

Some of the language has been changed in the Srole original components used in the *Anomie Scale* in order to adapt to current Irish cultural concepts in the English language.

There has been a decrease in the mean scale anomie score over the nineteen years between the two national surveys, i.e. from **103.9** in 1988-89 to **94.4** in 2007-08 (a drop of 9.5). This moderate improvement in the level of social anomie in the adult national population is largely due to changes in the socio-cultural environment in Ireland over the period, such as changes in the Northern Ireland Peace Process, more security because of the marked improvement in the people's standard of living and increased participation in education.

In a mean scale score of **94.4** on a scale of 0 to 200 still present in 2007-08, the level of social anomie is still a matter of concern, despite the changes listed above in the socio-economic environment. As was noted by Emile Durkheim, economic and material gains do not necessarily reduce social anomie[16]. Religion, family and community are probably the institutions with the most positive influence in reducing the levels of 'social anomie'.

Looking at Table No. 18.3 (below), the welcome decline in the percentages agreeing with the anomie items or components has been somewhat neutralised by the consistent rise in the percentages "neither agreeing nor disagreeing" which is indicative of delayed change or the possibility of reversal in the event of negative changes in the socio-cultural environment supporting 'social anomie'. The item (No. 5) to experience greatest improvement between 1988-89 and 2007-08 has marked a

---

[16] See Durkheim, Emile, *Suicide*, New York, The Free Press (1897), 1951.

substantial degree of optimism in the sample.   In light of the changes since March 2008, it is likely that such optimism has been reduced somewhat!

Table No. 18.3:   The Social Anomie Scale

	Item / Component	Year	Agree	Neither Agree nor Disagree	Disagree	Anomie Score (0-200)	Number
1.*	"These days a person doesn't really know whom he/she can count on."	2007-08 1988-89	42.2% (54.2%)	17.2% (10.7%)	40.6% (35.1%)	104.6 (119.1)	1,008
	Change (2007-08) – (1988-89)		**-12.0%**	**+6.5%**	**+5.5%**	**-17.5**	
2.	"Everything changes so quickly that I often have trouble deciding what are the right rules to follow."	2007-08 1988-89	46.3% (52.8%)	19.2% (13.4%)	34.5% (33.8%)	111.8 (119.0)	1,013
	Change (2007-08) – (1988-89)		**-6.7%**	**+5.8%**	**+0.7%**	**-7.2**	
3.	"People were better off in the old days, when everyone knew how he/she was expected to act."	2007-08 1988-89	35.0% (41.8%)	23.5% (13.0%)	41.5% (45.3%)	93.5 (96.6)	1,012
	Change (2007-08) – (1988-89)		**-6.8%**	**+10.5%**	**-3.8%**	**-3.1**	
4.*	"There is little use in writing to public officials for anything."	2007-08 1988-89	46.8% (55.3%)	27.6% (15.2%)	25.6% (29.5%)	121.1 (125.8)	1,013
	Change (2007-'08) – (1988-'89)		**-8.5%**	**+12.4%**	**-3.9%**	**-4.6**	
5.*	"The lot of the average person is getting worse not better in Ireland today."	2007-08 1988-89	34.0% (56.9%)	25.7% (14.5%)	40.3% (28.6%)	93.7 (128.3)	1,012
	Change (2007-08) – (1988-89)		**-22.9%**	**-11.2%**	**-11.7%**	**-34.6**	
6.*	"It is hardly fair to bring children into the world with the way things look for the future."	2007-08 1988-89	16.8% (20.2%)	19.2% (11.1%)	64.0% (68.7%)	52.8 (51.5)	1,009
	Change (2007-08) – (1988-89)		**-3.4%**	**+8.1%**	**-4.7%**	**+1.3**	
7.	"You sometimes can't help wondering whether any effort is worthwhile."	2007-08 1988-89	29.4% (37.2%)	22.2% (12.7%)	48.4% (50.1%)	81.0 (87.1)	1,013
	Change (2007-08) – (1988-89)		**-7.8%**	**+9.5%**	**-1.7%**	**-6.1**	
8.**	"With everything so uncertain in these days, it seems as though anything could happen."	2007-08 1988-89	67.5% ---	20.8% ---	11.7% ---	155.8 ---	1,015
	Change (2007-08) – (1988-89)		---	---	---	---	---
	Total Scale (Anomie Score) **Change 2007-08 and 1988-89**	2007-08 (A) 1988-89 (B)				94.4 103.9	
	Change	A - B	---	---	---	**-9.5**	

Notes: * Components of the original Srole scale.   ** A new item.
The changes in the various responses are **in bold**.   *Cronbach Alpha* = 0.651.

3.2 Social Anomie by Personal Variables:

The measure used to examine social anomie by personal variables is the Mean Anomie Scale-Score for the new eight-item Scale.

Table No. 18.4:   Social Anomie Scale-Score by Personal Variables

Personal Variable	Mean Anomie Scale-Score (0-200)	Number
Total Sample	**101.20**	**1,001**
A. Area of Birth	P<.008	
1. City (100,000 plus)	**106.54**	417
2. Large Town (10,000 +)	98.21	119
3. Town (1,500 plus)	92.69	129
4. Rural/Village	98.90	335
Score Variation	*13.85*	*(999)*
B. Place of Rearing in ROI.	P<.001	
1. Dublin (City & County)	**112.56**	267
2. Rest of Leinster	93.38	162
3. Munster	**104.30**	224
4. Connaught/Ulster	92.26	161
Score Variation	*20.30*	*(814)*
C. Region of Residence	P<.001	
1. BMW (Border Midlands West)	86.82	269
2. Dublin	**115.38**	286
3. Mid-East & South-East	100.14	217
4. Mid-West & Sth-West	**101.36**	229
Score Variation	*28.56*	*(1,001)*
D. Education	P<.001	
1. Primary or Less	**114.36**	117
2. Incomplete Sec.-Level	**113.02**	254
3. Complete Second-Level	**106.74**	253
4. Third-Level	85.40	376
Score Variation	*28.96*	*(1,001)*
E. Occupational Status	P<.001	
1. Unskilled/Semi-Skilled	**112.23**	204
2. Skilled/Routine Non-M.	100.11	324
3. Inspectional/Supervisory	98.09	132
4. Professional/Executive	87.88	187
Score Variation	*24.35*	*(847)*
F. Social Class Position	P<.001	
1. Class I: "Upper Class"	74.14	39
2. Class II: "Upr-Mid Class"	89.03	139
3. Class III: "Mid.-Mid. Cl"	89.59	234
4. Class IV: "Working Class"	**110.45**	357
5. Class V: "Lower Class"	**113.23**	85
Score Variation	*39.09*	*(843)*

Table No. 18.4 (Cont'd.) **Personal Variable**	**Mean Anomie-Scale Score (0-200)**	**Number**
G. Political-Party Preference (excluding Won't Vote/Don't Know)	P<.001	
1. Fianna Fáil	100.07	300
2. Fine Gael	91.27	188
3. Labour Party	**107.15**	64
4. Green Party	81.69	60
5. Sinn Féin	**116.11**	48
6. PDs/Independents	**110.66**	44
Score Variation	*34.42*	*(702)*

Note: Scores above sample average are **in bold**.

One of the most surprising findings of the above Table (No. 18.4) has been the failure of 'Age', 'Gender' or 'Marital Status' to elicit a statistically significant variation which would indicate that there was more or less a consensus across the 'age' spectrum and between the 'genders' and the five sub-variables under 'Marital Status'. In a sense this is disappointing as one would have anticipated evidence of positive influences in younger age groups.

The territorial and geographic backgrounds have all recorded significant and substantial variables. 'Education' and 'Occupational Status' responded in line with expectations. 'Social Class Position' brought out the class factor quite clearly, while 'Political Party Preferences' may have yielded surprises in relation to some readers' expectations!

3.2.1 Area of Birth: 'Social Anomie' seems to be significantly higher in respondents born in 'Cities (100,000 plus)' than in small urban areas and 'Rural/Village' backgrounds. This is quite significant when one remembers that over 40% (41.7%) of the national sample were born in cities. People born in (small) 'Towns' are the least anomic. This could indicate a greater degree of community support in these areas. This would seem to confirm Durkheim's own finding on the lower levels of anomie in rural areas where family, religion and community were stronger (see Durkheim, Emile, 1897).

3.2.2 Place of Rearing and Regions of Residence: Both of these variables recorded substantial and significant score-variations between the sub-samples. They repeat the high level of city 'anomie' in the case of the

Dublin responses for each of the two variables. The relatively lower level of social anomie recorded by the Connaught/ Ulster-reared and those living in the BMW regions produced the lowest levels of 'social anomie'. The findings show that the 'quality of life' still present in rural and remote Ireland has some positive bearing on the respondents reared in and living in these geographic environments.

3.2.3 Education: There is quite a moderate negative correlation between educational standard and the levels of 'social anomie' in the population. The 'score-variation' is substantial between those with 'Third Level' and the rest of the grades – all of whom scored above the sample average!

3.2.4 Occupational Status: The security of higher-statused occupations has had a significant and positive impact on the levels of 'social anomie'. The mutual impact of education and occupational status is probably at work here.

3.2.5 Social Class Position: The combined influence of Education and Occupational Status, which determines Social Class Position (page 189, footnote 7 above), has produced an impressively negative correlation between 'Social Class Position' and 'social anomie'. The reasons for the relatively high levels of 'social anomie' among members of the 'Working Class" and those in the "Lower Class" merit research. The combined demographic strength of these two classes is over half of the adult population (52.4%).

3.2.6 Political Party Preference: The findings of the levels of 'social anomie' among supporters of the various political parties have been influenced by the Social Class Position of the respondents (See Table No. 15.4, page 389). *Fianna Fáil* comes closest to representing the 'social-anomie' scores of the total sample. Labour and *Sinn Féin* are strongly represented in the "Working and Lower Classes" with above-average anomie scores. The Green Party supporters are very much "Middle Class".

3.2.7 Summary and Conclusion: The following extract from Table No.18.4 summarises the intra- and inter-variable findings:

R/O	Variable	Score Variation (0-200)	Between Lowest Anomie Score			Highest Anomie Score	
7	Area of Birth	13.85	'Town'	**(92.69)**	and	'City'	**(106.54)**
6	Place of Rearing	20.30	'Connaught/Ulster'	**(92.26)**	and	'Dublin City/Co.	**(112.56)**
4	Region of Residence	28.56	'BMW Regions'	**(86.62)**	and	'Dublin'	**(115.38)**
3	Education	28.96	'Third Level'	**(85.40)**	and	'Prim. or Less'	**(114.36)**
5	Occupational Status	24.35	'Prof./Exec.'	**(87.88)**	and	'Unsk../Semi'	**(112.23)**
1	Social Class Position	39.09	"Upper Class"	**(74.14)**	and	"Lwr. Class"	**(113.23)**
2	Political-Party Preference	34.42	'Green Party'	**(81.69)**	and	'Sinn Féin'	**(116.11)**

Note: Mean social-anomie score variation = **101.20**

The above extract from Table No. 18.4 gives the reader a good over-picture of the possible socio-cultural factors which seem to influence the levels of social anomie in Irish society. The four ordinal factors are 'Urban-Rural background', 'Educational Achievement', Occupational Status' and 'Social Class Position'. In other words, respondents from more urban backgrounds, lesser-educated, least-skilled occupations and lower social status tend to be most anomic. This places an extra urgency on society and community to increase education and improve the socio-cultural condition of those at the bottom of the scales. Society should examine and research the factors in city life which are conducive to 'social anomie'. Geographic and territorial backgrounds producing low anomie scores are worth examining, especially, to discover those non-economic influences which *reduce anomie* and its very negative social and personal consequences! The strength of family and community seem to be positive influences in the case of 'Place of Rearing' and 'Region of Residence'.

Part IV – Conclusion

As stated earlier, **Authoritarianism** and **Social Anomie** are both 'dependent' and 'independent' variables. As *dependent variables* the extent of their presence in society is very important as they can exercise very negative influences on the quality of life for all the citizens and for vulnerable sections in particular. They reflect a certain level of psychological/sociological/anthropological dysfunction which needs to be addressed. Not only do these two phenomena tell much about individual societies like the Republic of Ireland, they also reflect the impact of international ideologies, cultural goals, superstructures and accepted policies and norms, which are only in the best interests of the more powerful (for the time being) and injurious to the more vulnerable, many of whom have become quite powerless, normless and discriminated against.

As independent variables, 'authoritarianism' and 'social anomie' influence intergroup and other social attitudes. The link between **social anomie** and **ethnocentrism** has been studied widely ever since Leo Srole's[17] very important article was published in 1956. The relation between anomie and social deviance has been accepted ever since Emile Durkheim[18] published his seminal work on *Suicide* in 1897 and, later, the article of Robert K. Merton[19] in 1938. Many other well-known students of social deviance and intergroup relations have added to our understanding of this important independent variable.

Authoritarianism, as a personality trait, has been a significant independent variable in explaining levels of social prejudice and tolerance ever since the comprehensive work of Adorno T.F. *et al*[20], in 1950. The work was an attempt to examine the personality types or traits which underpinned the totalitarian rule of the Nazi leadership of the *Third Reich* in Germany in the 1930s and 1940s. In the previous studies of social prejudice directed by the present author in 1972-73 and in 1988-89, fruitful use of authoritarianism as an independent variable was made[21]. It will be interesting to examine its use again as an independent variable in this current (2007-08) research project.

***

---

[17] Srole Leo (1956) *Op.Cit.*
[18] Durkheim, Emile (1897) *Op.Cit.*
[19] Merton, Robert K. (1957) *Op.Cit.*
[20] Adorno, T.F., Frankel-Brunswick, E., Levinson, D.J. and Sandford, R.N., *The Authoritarian Personality*, New York, Harper & Row, 1950.
[21] See Mac Gréil, Micheál, 1977 and 1996, *Opera Cit.*

CHAPTER XIX
General Summary of Findings [1]

Part I – Introduction

In the course of this text, from Chapters IV to XVIII, an extensive range of findings relating to intergroup attitudes among a representative sample of the adults of the Republic of Ireland has been presented and discussed. The findings refer to those of a National Survey carried out from November 2007 to March 2008 and how they compared with the findings of two previous surveys, i.e. the Greater Dublin Survey of 1972-73 and the National Survey of 1988-89. All three surveys were processed, analysed and interpreted under the direction of the present author. In this and the following chapter it is proposed to provide a **descriptive summary** of the major findings. In Chapter XXI further analysis of these findings will be discussed.

1.1 Independent and Dependent Variables:

To facilitate the measuring of change in intergroup attitudes over the thirty-five years (from 1972-73 to 2007-08), the original questions were replicated in each of the three surveys. The scales used were mainly the *Bogardus Social Distance Scale* and a number of *Likert-type scales*. The *Bogardus* scale measured **behavioural-tendency**, while *Likert-type* scales gauged **evaluations** and **feelings**. In this way it was possible to arrive at valid and reliable measures of intergroup attitudes because of the consistency between the three components of social attitudes, i.e. behavioural tendencies, feelings and evaluations. As the *Cronbach Alpha* scores have indicated and the patterns of responses have confirmed, the author is satisfied that the findings have validity and reliability.

The independent variables used to explain differences in intergroup attitudes include the standard personal variables, i.e. age, gender, marital status, education, occupation and social-class position. Geographic factors such as 'Area of Birth' (classified according to the degree of urbanisation), 'Place of Rearing' and current 'Region of Residence' have proven quite significant in the case of inter-group attitudes. Religious practice, ethnic self-identity and political preference were also used as independent variables where relevant. Levels of 'authoritarianism' and of 'social anomie' have been treated both as 'dependent' and 'independent' variables.

The range of 'dependent variables' in this study covers the various types of social prejudice, i.e. ethnic, racial, religious, gender, sexual-orientation, political and a range of social prejudices (e.g. people with disabilities). Special categories have received more extensive analysis, i.e. Prejudice against Travellers, Anti-Semitism and Anti-British Prejudice. Attitudes towards Northern Ireland and issues related to community conflict arising out of the partition of Ireland at the foundation of the Irish Free State have been researched and discussed in each of the previous texts[1], i.e. in relation to the surveys of 1972-73 and 1988-89.

The two main cultural traits of the Irish people studied in the three surveys with obvious relevance for intergroup attitudes have been **Religion** and the **Irish Language**. Two special Reports have already been published (in 2009) on those topics, i.e. *The Irish Language and the Irish People* and *The Challenge of Indifference: A Need for Religious Revival in Ireland*. Relevant extracts from these Reports are included in Chapters XVI and XVII above.

The **Irish Travelling Community** constitute Ireland's main indigenous ethnic minority and have suffered much deprivation as victims of social prejudice and discrimination for generations. Attitudes towards Irish Travellers have been measured in each of the three surveys. Again, a special Report has been published in 2010 on the current (2007-08) state of Irish attitudes towards this minority, i.e. *Emancipation of the Irish Travelling People*. This Report is summarised in Chapter XIII above which deals mainly with changes in Irish people's attitudes over the thirty-five years.

1.2 Socio-Cultural Change:

In Chapter I the aim and scope of the research on which this book (text) is based were outlined. These included the aim of monitoring change in intergroup attitudes in the Republic of Ireland as part of the overall socio-cultural change which had taken place in two decades prior to 2007-08. One of the most radical demographic changes had been that from being an **emigrant society** to becoming an **immigrant** one. Up until the mid-nineteen-nineties, there were relatively few in-migrants to the Republic of

---

[1] Mac Gréil, Micheál: *Prejudice and Tolerance in Ireland*, Dublin, CIR, 1977.
  Prejudice in Ireland Revisited, Maynooth, St Patrick's College, 1996.

Ireland while there was a continuous stream of out-migration to the United Kingdom and other so-called Western 'Developed Societies'. The composition of the new immigrants is given in Table No. 2.1. The in-migration of workers has had a positive impact on ethnic tolerance in the Republic of Ireland as the findings of later chapters will show.

A second important socio-political change took place in the nineteen-nineties, namely, the cessation of paramilitary violence in Northern Ireland and the arrival at a mutually acceptable agreement between Nationalists and Unionists supported by the Irish and British Governments, i.e. the *1998 Good Friday Agreement*. This enabled the concentration on economic development on both sides of the Border and facilitated necessary cooperation. The full significance of this achievement has not been (so far) adequately assessed. It was shown in various findings that these changes have prepared the way for *pluralist coexistence* or *integrated pluralism* at the socio-political level on the island of Ireland!

The advance of *materialism and consumerism* with the corresponding decline in the relative position of the religious institution continued during the period between 1988-89 and 2007-08. The weakening of the *socialist ideology* after the 'fall of the Berlin Wall' in 1989 was likely to have affected the findings of the 2007-08 survey as well as bolstering the rise of *neo-liberal capitalism* in Europe, the United States and elsewhere, which probably contributed to the crisis in Western financial operations in 2008. The rise of globalisation was very evident in the last quarter of the twentieth century.

The thirty-five years over which Irish intergroup attitudes are measured coincide with the membership of the Republic of Ireland in the European Union, i.e. from 1972-73 until 2007-08. The 2008 collapse of the banking system in New York and throughout the capitalist world had **not** happened before the completion of interviewing in March 2008, just as the fall of the 'Berlin Wall' in 1989 occurred after the fieldwork of the 1988-89 survey had been completed.

1.3 Ethnic and Other Minorities in the Republic of Ireland:
Table No. 2.1 gives a breakdown of Ethnic Minorities in the Republic of Ireland as reported in the *2006 Census of Population*. Some **86.5%** of the national population were born in the island of Ireland, i.e. **85.3%** in the Republic and **1.2%** in Northern Ireland. Of those born abroad, **5.3%** were

born in Great Britain and **3.4%** were of Eastern European origin. The remaining **4.8%** are represented by **1.3%** from the Rest of Europe, **1.3%** from Asia, **1.0%** from Africa, and **1.1%** from the Americas and Australasia. This goes to confirm that, apart from Great Britain and Europe, relatively few 'foreign nationals' had, so far, come to live and work in Ireland. Any idea of excessive in-migration of foreigners, especially from outside the European Union, coming to live in the Republic of Ireland is grossly exaggerated, as the *Census of Population 2006* figures confirm. The European Union's *'fortress' immigration policy* has, if anything, prevented an adequate flow of population from countries suffering from severe deprivation coming to the relatively prosperous countries of Western Europe. Such a negative and inhumane policy has helped to ensure the continuity of gross inequality between the so-called 'developed' and 'developing' countries of the world in the 21st century. It is also a cause of ongoing international injustice and a threat to world peace and stability. Ethnic and racial prejudices often function to rationalise the restriction of the free movement of deprived people.

For Irish people with a sense of history, the current policy of restricting in-migration to migrant workers from poorer countries must raise a serious question of conscience. For over one hundred and fifty years, numerous Irish were forced to go abroad to earn a living in Britain, the United States, Canada, Australia and elsewhere and send home money to their economically struggling parents and relations in Ireland. Today "the shoe is on the other foot" and we seem to 'go along' with the European Union fortress immigration policy. How ironic?

Between the years 1996 and 2006 the population of the Republic of Ireland increased by **16.4%**, i.e. from 3,596,543 in 1996 to 4,172,013 in 2006. The natural increase in the Irish-born was only **6.6%** over the same decade, which points to the very significant demographic impact of immigration from abroad. The percentage increase in foreign-born persons over the ten years was **165.2%**, i.e. from 212,057 in 1996 to 562,457 in 2006. In 1996, the foreign-born persons constituted **5.9%** of the national population as compared with **14.7%** in 2006. This level of demographic change presented an enormous challenge to the State's national and local services, i.e. housing, schooling, etc.

In general, Irish society succeeded in coping with challenges arising from such abnormal proportions of population increase and in-migration without serious disruption and diminution of services. We were fortunate that it coincided with an ambitious programme of housing renewal. This is not to imply that everything went off smoothly. The distribution of in-migrants to various towns and cities (see Table No. 2.3) had helped to avoid a concentration of proportionately large numbers in particular districts and, thereby, prevent the growth of large ghettoes.

The experience of members of the in-migrants, particularly asylum-seekers, was researched by McGinnity, F. *et al* and published in 2006 by the ESRI. Table No. 2.5 records the experience of 'racism' and discrimination of a sample of asylum seekers. The most frequent negative experience was harassment in public and at work by one-third of those interviewed. The distribution of 'work permits' to in-migrants between 1995 and 2005 (Table No. 2.6) shows that two-thirds (67.2%) were for work in the service industry (42.8%) and in catering (24.4%).

The respondents in the 2007-08 national sample who were non-Irish-born were more highly educated than the Irish-born but were over represented in occupations with lower occupational status (relative to their educational qualifications). Table No. 8.12 (page 181) gives the occupational status and educational achievement of the Irish-born and the non-Irish-born. These findings go to show that members of minorities tend to need higher qualifications than members of the dominant group to get the same job. Of course, the average age of in-migrants was younger than that of Irish-born respondents.

In Part III of Chapter II, the *"sequential cycle of acting-out prejudice"* by Gordon Allport is discussed in some detail. Allport suggests that it is important to correct the behavioural expression of social prejudice at the earliest possible stage of this 'vicious cycle' which goes from "anti-locution or ridicule" to "expulsion or annihilation". Down through the history of intergroup conflict there is evidence of 'genocide' and 'ethnic cleansing' in practically every generation somewhere in the world which has resulted from the unchecked expressions of prejudice along the Allport five-point scale, i.e. anti-locution – avoidance – discrimination – physical attack – expulsion/annihilation. Hence, the importance of public awareness of the path leading to the extermination of groups or categories of people because of who they are or perceived to be!

1.4 Conceptual and Theoretical Frameworks:
The conceptual and theoretical frameworks used by the author in the current text are mainly the same as had been developed by him (in consultation with other authors) and presented in the texts published in 1977 and 1996[2]. The approach has been based on a *Psycho-Socio-Cultural Theory of Social Prejudice*. While the personality of the prejudiced person is the proximate cause of his or her prejudices, he or she is also a 'filter' through which the social and cultural influences on the person's attitudes are given form. The patterned nature of our attitudes (be they biased or tolerant) points to the predominance of socio-cultural determinism at work not only in our attitudes but also in our behavioural patterns (see Figure No. 18.1, page 489).

In all exercises of quantitative and qualitative research, it is very important that the researcher has a tightly defined set of concepts which delineate the subject matter being measured. Loose or indistinct conceptual frameworks lead to unnecessary imprecision in relation to the findings. Not only is a consistent and precise (as possible) network of concepts required for the accurate measurement of data, it is equally necessary for the correct diagnosis of issues to be measured. For these reasons it was felt necessary to insist on strict definitions for the major concepts used in this text, e.g. 'race', 'ethnic group', 'prejudice', 'discrimination', etc.

The theoretical framework attempts to provide a basis for the explanation of variations in results. At the macro-theory level, a structuralist approach has been adopted. The *"momentum model of society"* was originally proposed in 1977. It was an attempt to integrate the structural-functional and conflict-structural approaches. It suggests a new synthesis of conflict and equilibrium models. The *"momentum model"* sees society in the perpetual process of becoming and declining but never fully being. *Societas semper reformanda.* The "vacillating social-situation model" demonstrates the dynamic tension between forces of conflict (giving 'meaning') and of equilibrium (satisfying 'interests')[3].

Seven middle-range theories are proposed which help to explain social prejudice. These include: 'frustration-aggression', 'labelling and stereotyping', 'scapegoating', 'social prestige', 'in-group cohesion *versus* out-group hostility', 'the apostate complex' and 'fear and anxiety'. 'Social

---

[2] Mac Gréil, Micheál: *Prejudice and Tolerance in Ireland*, Dublin, CIR, 1977.
    Prejudice in Ireland Revisited, Maynooth, St Patrick's College, 1996.
[3] See Figure No. 3.2 and commentary, pages 50-51 above.

security/insecurity' could be added to the above seven middle-range theories. It was further hypothesised that there would be a causal link between authoritarianism, social anomie and social prejudice.

Two further theoretical models were proposed which would help to explain the position of a 'minority group' *vis-à-vis* the dominant group. These were the *'Park Cycle'* model which suggest that a minority group goes through a patterned-sequence-cycle, i.e. 1° 'contact'; 2° 'competition'; 3° 'accommodation' and 4° 'assimilation'. Some would challenge that **assimilation** was necessarily the terminal stage for every minority group. *'Integrated Pluralism'* can be a more satisfactory end status. At the time that Robert E. Park devised his "race-relation sequence-cycle" in 1926, the 'Melting Pot' model dominated integration expectations in the United States, which seemed to accept assimilation as an acceptable end-condition. The 'integrated pluralist' approach has since become more acceptable to ethnic minorities. This is very much the approach of the present author as expressed in the title of this book, i.e. ***Pluralism and Diversity in Ireland***.

The **Dominant Posture/Minority Response Paradigm** (see Figure No. 3.3, page 57 above) provides a most useful theoretical framework by which to explain or explore the state of intergroup behaviour or structures in societies at different times. The basic assumption of this paradigm is that the dominant group has the power to determine the level of recognition and equity of the dominant/minority relationship.

The **'Vicious-Circle Theory'** gives a most useful insight into the possibility of improving or worsening dominant/minority relations (see Figure No. 13.2). The 'vicious circle' refers to the causal link between attitudes–behaviour–conditions. The 'conditions' of the minority will in turn affect (positively or negatively) the attitudes of the dominant group.

Recent literature (not infrequently) emphasises the importance of favourable or unfavourable contact for intergroup relations. This relates to the nature of attitudinal change. Negative attitudes cannot be removed because an attitudinal vacuum is impossible. In effect, the only way to change a prejudice or negative attitude is to replace it with a tolerant or positive disposition. **Favourable contact** between members of the dominant group and those of the minority groups seems to be the most effective way of 'replacing' negative attitudes and prejudices with positive or tolerant dispositions. There is evidence in the findings of the 2007-08 survey which confirm the above view.

Part II – Social Distance in Ireland in 2007-08

2.1 Bogardus Scale:

The main scale used to measure and monitor social prejudice in the three surveys, i.e. 1972-73, 1988-89 and 2007-08, was the *Bogardus Social Distance Scale*[4]. It measured 'social distance' which is a measure of behavioural tendency and is a prime indication of social attitudes. Social prejudice is defined as a particular type of social attitude (see pages 34 to 36 above). Respondents were asked to indicate the closest level of intimacy or social distance to which they would be prepared to admit a member of each of fifty-one stimulus categories, i.e. ethnic, political, racial, religious and social categories. The seven levels of social distance were: kinship, friendship, next-door neighbour, co-worker, citizen, visitor (to Ireland) only and debar/deport. This scale has proven to be highly valid and most reliable.

Forty-six of the fifty-one 'stimulus categories' included in the 2007-08 questionnaire were also in the 1988-89 survey (which had fifty-nine categories). The five new stimulus categories added to the 2007-08 survey questionnaire were: 'Heavy Drinkers', 'Iranians', 'Lithuanians', 'Palestinians' and 'Romanians'. The reasons for including the new categories were three-fold, i.e. public concern about abuse of alcohol, the growing international relevance of the Middle East and the in-migration to Ireland of Romanian and Lithuanian citizens following their countries becoming members of the European Union. Categories dropped from the 1988-89 list were: 'Belgians', 'Church of Ireland', 'Danes', 'Ex-Prisoners', 'Greeks', Hare Krishna', 'Methodists', 'People of Luxembourg', 'People with AIDS', 'Portuguese', 'Presbyterians', 'Provisional IRA', and 'Sinn Féin'. Reasons for excluding the above thirteen stimulus categories included limitations of interviewing time (due to costs) and response to socio-cultural change in Ireland and elsewhere. It is possible to gauge the social-distance responses towards a number of the ethnic and religious categories from the findings in relation to religious and ethnic categories replicated on the 2007-08 social-distance scale.

---

[4] See Mac Gréil, Micheál, *Prejudice in Ireland Revisited*, Maynooth, St Patrick's College, 1996, pp 63-4.

Table No. 4.1 (pages 62-4) gives the social-distance scores of the total national sample for all fifty-one stimulus categories in *rank order* according to their mean-social-distance score (1 – 7). Categories with a MSD (mean-social-distance) of less than **1.500** could be classified as 'in-group' categories.

Table No. 19.1 shows the ranking of the fifty-one stimulus categories by Mean-Social-Distance (MSD) scores. Percentages admitting members of each category to kinship/family are also given. The first fifteen categories were deemed 'in-groups', i.e. with MSD scores under 1.500 on a continuum of one-to-seven.

Table No. 19.1: 'Admit to Kinship' and MSD of all Stimulus Categories by Rank Order

R/O	Stimulus Category	Admit to Kinship	MSD (1-7)	R/O	Stimulus Category	Admit to Kinship	MSD (1-7)
1st	'Roman Catholics'	91.1%	1.168	27th	'Socialists'	67.0%	1.990
2nd	'Working Class'	85.6%	1.228	28th	'Lithuanians'	65.5%	2.044
3rd	'People-Physical Dis.'	83.0%	1.268	29th	'Russians'	63.9%	2.091
4th	'Irish Speakers'	84.4%	1.324	30th	'Coloureds'	58.7%	2.164
5th	'Unmarried Mothers'	82.4%	1.339	31st	'Jews'	60.7%	2.179
6th	'Welsh'	82.4%	1.388	32nd	'Indians'	57.2%	2.276
7th	'Gardaí'	81.4%	1.392	33rd	'Capitalists'	60.8%	2.297
8th	'Euro-Americans'	81.3%	1.416	34th	'Afro-Americans'	52.7%	2.342
9th	'English'	81.0%	1.422	35th	'Blacks'	52.6%	2.348
10th	'Canadians'	80.0%	1.430	36th	'Atheists'	52.5%	2.373
11th	'Scottish'	81.7%	1.436	37th	'Africans'	52.3%	2.440
12th	'Unemployed'	80.9%	1.446	38th	'Agnostics'	50.3%	2.554
13th	'Protestants'	78.4%	1.4827	39th	'Romanians'	55.6%	2.566
14th	'French'	78.5%	1.4829	40th	'Heavy Drinkers'	41.9%	2.626
15th	'British'	77.2%	1.488	41st	'Pakistanis'	49.4%	2.682
16th	'Trade Unionists'	77.8%	1.552	42nd	'Palestinians'	49.4%	2.709
17th	'Northern Irish'	75.1%	1.603	43rd	'Nigerians'	50.5%	2.726
18th	'People-Mental Dis.'	74.4%	1.612	44th	'Israelis'	47.9%	2.842
19th	'Dutch'	74.2%	1.632	45th	'Iranians'	47.5%	2.850
20th	'Germans'	73.9%	1.644	46th	'Arabs'	45.6%	2.908
21st	'Spaniards'	75.4%	1.660	47th	'Communists'	45.9%	2.920
22nd	'Italians'	73.0%	1.703	48th	'Alcoholics'	32.7%	2.937
23rd	'Polish'	69.6%	1.790	49th	'Travellers'	39.6%	3.030
24th	'Gay People'	62.8%	1.923	50th	'Muslims'	42.9%	3.066
25th	'Chinese'	63.0%	1.924	51st	'Drug Addicts'	19.7%	4.194
26th	'Unionists'	66.2%	1.944	---	---	---	---

It is difficult to read these results in a meaningful manner without having certain criteria for appraising the attitudes they reflect. One of the general rules governing intergroup preferences is the *'Principle of*

Propinquity'. People tend to prefer those categories which they perceive to be closest to their own groups or categories in terms of nationality, religion, political ideology, racial grouping, geographic proximity, social-class position, etc. This has been borne out in the above findings for most sub-lists of stimulus categories, with notable exceptions.

The changes in social distance between 1988-89 and 2007-08 are given on Table No. 4.2 (pages 65-6) for the forty-six stimulus categories replicated in the 2007-08 survey. In forty-one of the forty-six stimulus categories there were significant decreases in Mean-Social-Distance (MSD) scores which reflect a welcome increase in social tolerance and **a** corresponding decline in social prejudice. The average mean change for the forty-six categories was **-0.399**, which represents more than a third of a stage on the *Bogardus Scale*, i.e. it dropped from **2.204** in 1988-89 to **1.805** in 2007-08. When the percentages 'admitting to kinship' are compared, there has been an average mean (nominal) increase of **16.4%**, which is quite substantial.

The reasons for such an overall improvement in social distance between 1988-89 and 2007-08 can be attributed to a number of causes. The general personal security resulting from a decade of economic prosperity as well as the removal of collective anxiety following a peaceful resolution to the 'Northern Troubles' would have reduced the level of frustration in the population, compared with 1988-89 when there was high unemployment, forced emigration and regular acts of relentless violence in Northern Ireland, with some offshoots of it in the Republic of Ireland and in Britain. The personal contact with in-migrants coming to Ireland to live and work had for the most part been favourable. This seems to have resulted in greater ethnic and racial tolerance. The Republic of Ireland was developing a more tolerant ethos towards the stranger and most deprived categories – according to the evidence of Tables Nos. 4.1 and 4.2 (pages 62-4 and 65-6 respectively).

While the above improvements in the overall social distance scores are to be welcomed, there is no room for complacency. The levels of ethnic, racial and social prejudice are still far too high for a mature and civilised society. Also, as was seen in 1988-89, the situation can disimprove when socio-cultural conditions change; hence, the need for perpetual vigilance and social alertness to symptoms and signs of prejudice and discrimination against vulnerable minorities in Irish society in times of socio-economic difficulties. The experience of Germany in the late 1920s, 1930s and early 1940s is a lesson every generation should study and see that it does not recur in that country or elsewhere!

2.2 Intergroup Definition:
In order to understand intergroup behaviour, it is necessary to find out how people define groups other than their own. Nominally a group may be defined in a particular category according to abstract criteria, i.e. racial, ethnic, religious, political, class, etc. In the concrete situation, most groups are seen differently by members of other groups, e.g. **Jews** can be seen as religious, economic, political, ethnic and so forth; **Northern Irish** as ethnic, political, religious or economic. Intergroup definition is as much (if not more) *subjective* as it is *objective!*

In each of the three surveys respondents were asked for the main reason for not admitting members of certain stimulus categories into kinship. Seven possible reasons were suggested, i.e. religious beliefs and/or practices; racial – colour of skin, etc.; political views and/or methods; nationality or culture; economic danger to us; not socially acceptable; or way of life. Should none of these reasons be the main one, respondents were asked to specify it. The findings of the *rationalisation scale* are dealt with in Chapter V above (pages 85-102).

One of the most significant findings was the relatively small percentage giving **racial** as their main reason for not admitting members of various stimulus categories into kinship, even in the case of members of racial or ethnico-racial groups. Groups with racial traits were seen more as **ethnic** rather than racial in the respondents' rationalisation. This 'colour blindness' was a welcome development but unfortunately it did not always lead to the removal of racial prejudice, e.g. in the case of the different social distance scores for *'Euro-Americans'*, i.e. White Americans and *'Afro-Americans'*, i.e. Black Americans. Does this mean that people continue to be racialist and are willing to discriminate against certain racial minorities while, at the same time, denying to themselves that they are racialist? It is by the behavioural tendencies and actual behaviour that racialism is really tested!

This question, which might be aptly defined as "the racial dilemma" has been discussed in some detail in Chapter IX, pages 193-218, where some of the recent debate on the *concept of race* has been summarised. The real problem is the myth of **"racial essentialism"** which seems to survive the commendable work of leaders such as the late **Martin Luther King, Nelson Mandela** and many others. *The virus of racism is chameleon in nature.* Political correctness alone will not remove it. The Enlightenment Movement of the 17th and 18th centuries may have *unwittingly perpetuated* radical racism by restricting liberation to white Europeans and doing so in an elitist manner. It is time to re-examine the legacy of the European Enlightenment (which followed the European expansionists into Africa and Asia) and purify it of its implicit racist premise. Otherwise it will be difficult to remove "racial essentialism" from Western culture.

The decline of "not socially acceptable" as a rationalisation for not admitting members of certain groups into kinship has been seen as progress in the reduction of stigma and social snobbery. Table No. 5.6 (page 93) gives the list of stimulus categories still perceived to be 'not socially acceptable' by over **5%** of those not admitting them to kinship. The changes since 1988-89 are very interesting. Categories representing those with compulsive behaviour problems, i.e. 'Drug Addicts' and 'Alcoholics', experienced an increase in this type of rationalisation. 'Travellers' have a slight reduction in this rationalisation, i.e. from **20.3%** in 1988-'89 to **17.8%** in 2007-08, in the proportion of those not 'admitting to kinship' who gave 'not socially acceptable' as their main reason. This is still far too high for a society "who cherishes all its children equally"!

The findings of Table No. 5.5 (page 92) merit serious study in that it measures the role of religion as a negative classification. In the case of those stimulus categories nominally classified as religious categories (i.e. 'Atheists', 'Agnostics', 'Jews', 'Muslims', 'Protestants', and 'Roman Catholics') there has been a very substantial drop in "religious beliefs and/or practices" as the main reason for not admitting members of these groups to kinship. Does this mean a growth in "religious indifference" in adult Irish society, as was noted in the special Report on religious practice and attitudes?

Ethnic or Cultural rationalisation, while still relatively high, was substantially lower than in the 1988-89 survey [see Table No. 5.7 (page 95)]. This decline could mean a reduction in ethnic endogamy for adults in the Republic of Ireland, which could lead to a degree of amalgamation or miscegenation between Irish and non-Irish citizens. The growth in cultural diffusion between Irish and other cultures would also be a likely reduction in

Irish endogamy. On the positive side, 'cultural diffusion' would inevitably enrich Irish culture provided the unique Irish ethos is not dissipated by the process. The best way to defend against the latter would be to strengthen Irish cultural ethos.

The most popular (main) rationalisation for not admitting members of most of the stimulus categories was *'Way of Life'*. This reason could mean different things, i.e. cultural/national dress, rituals, etiquette, dietary customs, deviant and objectionable behaviour, etc. This creates a certain ambiguity in relation to 'way of life', which can only be interpreted in the context of the place of the stimulus category in society. Table No. 5.8 (page 98) lists the twenty-nine categories with over **30%** 'Way of Life' rationalisation.

Part III – Ethnic and Ethnico-Racial Prejudices

3.1 Introduction:
Chapters VI and VII examine ethnic and ethnico-racial social prejudices as measured by social distance. Some twenty-nine of the fifty-one stimulus categories fall under this broad ethnic umbrella. They include categories classified nominally as ethnic, ethnico-racial and racial. All of these categories had significantly high 'nationality or culture' rationalisations (see Table No. 5.1, pages 86-7).

The twenty-nine stimulus categories (see Table No. 6.1, pages 104-5) were further *sub-classified* into four groupings:

(1)　*Irish, British and American Stimulus Categories*: 'Irish Speakers', 'Welsh', 'Euro-Americans', 'English', 'Canadians', 'Scottish', 'British', 'Northern Irish' and 'Afro-Americans'.

(2)　*Continental European Nationalities*: 'French', 'Dutch', 'Germans', 'Spaniards', 'Italians', 'Polish People', 'Lithuanians', 'Russians' and 'Romanians'.

(3)　*African, Asian and Racial Stimulus Categories*: 'Chinese', 'Coloureds', 'Indians', 'Blacks', 'Africans', 'Pakistanis' and 'Nigerians'.

(4)   *Middle-East Stimulus Categories:* 'Palestinians', 'Israelis', 'Iranians' and 'Arabs'.

Since Ethnic and Ethnico-Racial prejudices are the widespread areas of intergroup problems through most of the modern world, the reader is recommended to read Chapters VI and VII with special care. It is hoped that the relatively detailed findings presented in the various Tables will not be over-burdensome. The commentary is intended to point out a number of very significant and, often, positive findings.

The changes in Ethnic and Ethnico-Racial social distance between the findings of the 1988-89 and 2007-08 national surveys in the case of the *twenty-five stimulus categories replicated* are substantially positive (four of the twenty-nine stimulus categories were included in the 2007-08 survey for the first time, i.e. 'Iranians', 'Lithuanians', 'Palestinians' and 'Romanians'). Three indicators were selected to measure the changes, i.e. 'admission to kinship', 'denial of citizenship' and 'mean-social-distance (MSD)' (see Table No. 6.2, pages 108-9).   *Increase* in 'admission to kinship' and *decrease* in 'denial of citizenship' and 'mean-social-distance' are signs of a reduction in prejudice and an improvement in social tolerance.

3.2 Inter-Category Correlations:
The importance of inter-category correlations is what they tell the researcher and the reader about the patterns of dispositions in relation to stimulus categories.   Table No. 6.3 correlates the Irish, British and American Categories and clearly shows the presence of the **racial factor**, e.g. 'Afro-Americans', and the political factor in the case of 'Northern Irish', when the nine stimulus categories are cross-correlated.   The **ethnic factor** dominates for seven of the nine 'Irish, British and American' categories.

Table No. 6.4 correlates the 'Continental European Nationalities'. The strength of the correlations between Western European categories and between Eastern European categories is somewhat stronger than between Eastern and Western European categories.   This would show that in the disposition of respondents there is evidence of a residue of the period of insulation of Eastern European nationalities during the 'Iron Curtain' days!

Despite the very strong correlations between all of the seven 'African, Asian and Racial Categories', there is some evidence of the racial factor at work. This finding confirms both the validity and reliability of the *Bogardus Scale* as a measure of intergroup prejudice. Such consistency and patterned correlations were anticipated.

Table No. 6.7 (page 119) is the correlation matrix for all of the twenty-nine 'ethnic and ethnico-racial' stimulus categories. In all, there are 406 correlations in this Table. The patterns are quite clear. The categories are placed by rank order of 'mean-social-distance' scores. All scores over **0.50** are in bold. The patterns of preference are generally along the lines of the *'principle of propinquity'*.

3.3 Ethnic, Ethnico-Racial and Racial Social Distance by Personal Variables:

The main aim of Chapter VII is to carry out an analysis or examination of the influence of personal variables on the 'mean-social-distance' scores of each of the four groupings of stimulus categories, i.e.:

    (1)   Irish, British and American Stimulus Categories;
    (2)   Continental European Nationalities;
    (3)   African, Asian and Racial Stimulus Categories;
    (4)   Middle-East Nationalities.

The findings of this chapter, while confirming progress in overall tolerance, produced some unexpected results.

Age was the personal variable which went against the expected trends in each of the four groupings of categories. The youngest age group '18 to 25 year-olds' were among the most prejudiced sub-variable, while the '26 to 40 year-olds' were the most tolerant sub-variable. The reason for the '18 to 25 year-olds' being relatively intolerant, despite the higher standards of education and their experience of job security and high standard of living during the decade of economic prosperity has raised some serious questions which were addressed in Part VIII of Chapter VII. Among the possible causes raised of the '18 to 25 year-olds' performance were: extended adolescence, failures in the liberating qualities of current education programmes, exclusive peer-socialisation, the possible effects of excessive use of certain types of cyber-technology resulting in the 'personal isolation' of the virtual community and the possible decline of the influence of family and local community in the socialisation of the youth.

While the performance of a substantial minority of the young age group should be a matter of real concern in relation to ethnico-racial prejudice, it was very important to avoid alarmism. The majority of youth were quite tolerant. Hopefully, their above-average social distance is a transitional aberration, which will be corrected as the '18 to 25 year-olds' move on in years and assume more adult responsibility. Otherwise, it would be regressive for Irish society if a return to some of the 1988-89 measures of intergroup prejudice were to return – beginning with Irish youth!

Other variables tested in Chapter VII were: gender, marital status, area of birth, place of rearing, region of residence, education and occupational status. The performance of the 'age' variable was influenced by and in turn influenced, other variables, especially 'education' and 'marital status'. The commentary after each of the Tables (Nos. 7.1 to 7.6, pages 126ff) deals with inter-variable potential influence.

The performance of 'gender' as a personal variable was also not as anticipated. It failed to elicit a statistically significant variation in any of the Tables. This is evidence of a homogenisation of gender ethnic and racial attitudes. This may be a product of the *Feminist Movement*. Whether it means the 'feminisation' of male attitudes or the 'masculinisation' of female attitudes would be a matter for a new research project!

Chapters VI and VII are probably two of the most informative chapters on intergroup relations in this text. In addition to giving the reader an insight into the explanation of differences in the attitudes of various sub-variables, he or she is also given very valuable information on the current state of Irish (Republic of Ireland) prejudices in the wake of the welcome in-migration of people from diverse national (ethnic) and racial groups and the arrival at a satisfactory solution to the Northern Ireland Troubles. Trends and signs of concern are also detected. The substantial percentages of respondents 'denying citizenship' to certain categories is, as always, an extreme expression of intergroup prejudice.

Part IV – Ethnic Prejudice and Irish Ethnic Self-Identity

4.1 Irish Ethnic Self-Identity:
The increase of ethnic diversity in modern societies raises serious issues concerning the level and nature of the people's ethnic self-identity.

Economic and bureaucratic pressures are of their nature *culturally assimilationist* with the ultimate result of removing ethnic differences in a *global melting pot* with all people conforming to the cultural criteria of one macro-culture with one set of symbolic meaningful systems, values, norms and practices based on a pragmatically defined global set of beliefs and convictions. We are still very far from reaching such a global-village culture. The rise of support for *cultural pluralism* is a major counter-response to the pressure towards the 'global melting pot'!

The current state of ethnic self-identity in the Republic of Ireland is measured on a scale devised by Professor **Richard Rose** of Strathclyde University and used in his study of Northern Irish ethnic self-identity in 1968[5]. Respondents were asked: *"Which of these terms best describes the way you usually think of yourself?"* The terms proposed were:

1. Irish;	5. Southern Irish;
2. County/City where you grew up;	6. British;
3. Anglo-Irish;	7. Northern Irish;
4. European;	8. Other (specify).

Respondents' first and second choices were asked for by the interviewers. A follow-up question was asked concerning the strength of the respondent's ethnic self-identity, i.e. *"Would you say you are strong or average in thinking of yourself in these terms"* (referring to the first choice). Rose interpreted *average* to mean 'security' of self-identity and *strong* to mean more 'uncertainty' about self-identity.

4.2 Changes in Ethnic Self-Identity:
The findings of the Rose question which was replicated in the 1972-73, 1988-89 and 2007-08 questionnaires are reported on in Part I of Chapter VIII. Table No. 8.2 gives the summary findings which showed that **95.7%** of the 'Irish-Born' saw themselves as primarily Irish (**87.3%**) and Internal Irish (**8.4%**). Compared with previous findings there were fewer seeing themselves as County/City people primarily, which reflected "Working Class" ethnic self-identity in previous studies. This move in identity was interpreted as a sign of *embourgeoisement* of the majority of the Irish people. 'European' primary self-identity for the Irish-born is still insignificant at **0.5%**. One-third (**34.3%**) gave European as their second

---

[5] See Rose Richard, *Governing Without Consent*, London, Faber, 1971, pages 207-8.

choice.   Table No. 8.3 records the changes in Irish (Primary) Ethnic Self-Identity.   Primary/Ethnic Self-Identity by personal variables (Table No. 8.7) has elicited significant variations by all variables.   The presence of the Non-Irish Born has widened the spread.   The one variable exclusively Irish-reared, i.e. Place of Rearing (in the Republic of Ireland), shows how few saw themselves as non-Irish.   Differences within the variables are therefore largely due to the impact of **15.8%** of the sample who were born outside Ireland.

The findings with regard to 'strong' or 'average' self-identity were interesting (if not surprising).   The percentage emphasising the level of assertion of Ethnic Self-Identity was 'strong' increased from **41%** in 1988-89 to **77%** in 2007-08, while those stating it was 'average' dropped from **57%** to **21%** over the nineteen years.   In accordance with Richard Rose's interpretation, the findings reveal a degree of uncertainty about their Ethnic Self-Identity among a large majority of adults in the Republic of Ireland (see Table No. 8.5, page 166).   Table No. 8.6 confirms that the 'Irish-born' are more 'insecure' (going on Rose's interpretation) than the 'non-Irish-born'! Such insecurity of Ethnic Self-Identity could be problematic, especially as the world for most people seems to be becoming more culturally diverse despite the pressures towards global cultural assimilation.   How to help the people to feel more secure in their ethnic self-identity would be an interesting subject for psycho-cultural research!   Greater competence in and more regular use of the Irish language by the adult population in general may enable the people to have a higher degree of security in their Irish ethnic self-identity!

4.3 Reaction to Immigration:
One of the most significant changes in Irish society since the late 1980s was the end of involuntary emigration during the 1990s.   This was followed by a very substantial influx of in-migrants between 1996 and 2007.   Therefore, the reaction of the population of the Republic of Ireland to the new Irish phenomenon of immigration from Europe and elsewhere abroad was to become an important goal of the current research (reported on in this book). This immigration from Eastern Europe and elsewhere abroad has taken place in a relatively short period of time.

It has already been pointed out that the level of intergroup tolerance improved significantly and for many categories substantially between the national survey of 1988-89 and the (recent) one in 2007-08.   This reflects the level of favourable contact which resulted from this new influx of people from different ethnic and racial groups.   Taking into account the degree of intergroup difficulties experienced by some in-migrants (as reported in Chapter II, pages 20-25 above), credit is due for improved attitudes, in part, to the manner in which the authorities facilitated workers and citizens from abroad.

It should be remembered that the Irish people (in the past) have had experience of being migrant workers abroad over a very long period.   This should, in some way, enable them to empathise with economic migrants coming to Ireland in pursuit of work, when the country needed extra workers to expand the economy.   Many of the in-migrants came to Ireland to fill the vacancies in building, catering, nursing, etc.   They contributed greatly to Irish prosperity.

In addition to the *Bogardus Scale*, three special questions (taken from the European Social Survey, Round 3, 2006-07) were asked of the respondents to get their reaction to "people coming to Ireland from other countries", i.e.:

1. *"Would you say it is generally bad or good for Ireland's economy that people come to live here from other countries?"*
2. *"Would you say that Ireland's cultural life is generally undermined or enriched (by people coming to live here from other countries)?"*
3. *"Is Ireland made a worse or a better place to live (in) by people coming to live here from other countries?"*

Respondents were asked to place a mark on a continuum of 0 to 10 from *negative to positive* in relation to each question.   Table No. 8.10 (page 173) gives the overall response, which was *relatively positive*, i.e.:

Good for the economy	=	**6.67**,
Enriched the culture	=	**6.44**, and
Made Ireland a better place to live in	=	**6.46**.

When the sample was divided between the 'Irish-born' and the 'Non-Irish-born' the result was as expected i.e.:

	A Irish-Born (0-10 continuum)	B Non-Irish- Born (0-10 continuum)	A – B (0-10 continuum)
1. Good for the Economy	6.46	8.02	-1.56
2. Enriched the Culture	6.18	7.97	-1.79
3. Made Ireland a Better Place to Live in	6.26	7.93	-1.67
Number	832	133	---

The net value of in-migrants to the Republic of Ireland was significantly and substantially greater in the view of those who were not born in Ireland and the native Irish respondents.   The very positive responses of in-migrants themselves in relation to their worth to the host country is greatly to be welcomed.   They have a true sense of their self-worth, i.e. averaging $\pm$ **8.0** on a **0 – 10** continuum.   The moderately positive responses of the Native Irish in relation to the value of in-migrants, i.e. averaging **6.3** on the **0 to 10** continuum, was disappointing and reflects a short memory when the Irish migrant workers contributed so much to the development of their host countries, e.g. the rebuilding of Britain after the 1939-45 War!

Table No. 8.11 gives a breakdown of the responses to each of the three statements for the Total Sample, Irish-Born and Non-Irish-Born by personal variables.   The reader is recommended to read this table closely. The commentary tried to interpret the variations.   It was encouraging to note that the youngest age-group (18 to 25 years) were the most appreciative in the case of the 'Total Sample' and the 'Irish-Born', which was a corrective to this subsample's performance in other tables!   The young, females, the married, the urban-born, the more educated and those with the more highly-statused occupations tended to be most appreciative of the positive worth to Ireland of the in-migrants. This was more or less as anticipated.

4.4 Ethnic Social Distance ('Admission to Kinship' and 'Denial of Citizenship') by   Personal Variables:

The final section of Chapter VIII measures the social distance scores towards a selection of five ethnic stimulus categories, i.e. 'English', 'Canadian', 'Dutch', 'Spaniards' and 'Poles'.   These categories represent five ethnic regions of Britain, America, Northern, Southern and Eastern Europe. They were also chosen for their very low *'racial'* rationalisation in order to isolate the *ethnic* factor. Table No. 8.13 (pages 184) measures the social distance scores towards the five representative Ethnic Stimulus Categories by personal variables. The findings, therefore, will give the reader the level of ethnic prejudice against the categories and also give an insight into the variations between the scores of the sub-variables. The latter, it is hoped, will help the reader to understand the causes of prejudice and tolerance in Irish society towards 'purely' ethnic categories, i.e. without significant 'racial' connotations.

One of the most interesting findings of Table No. 8.13 was the failure of 'Gender' or 'Marital Status' to elicit statistically significant variations in the case of any of the six ethnic stimulus categories. This level of consensus is rare in survey research. The homogenisation of male and female attitudes has been very frequent in the course of this text, while marital status has frequently produced significant variations.

Age, once again, did not perform as anticipated. It had statistically significant variations in regard to each of the five stimulus categories. The '18 to 25 year-olds' were the least tolerant in their social distance towards each of the five categories, i.e. below the sample average in 'admitting to kinship' and above average in 'denial of citizenship'. 'Education' did not perform as expected, i.e. those with lowest education were the most tolerant. The mutual influence of 'age' on 'education' contributed to the lower-than-expected levels of tolerance among those with 'Complete Second-Level' and 'Third-Level'. These results were not anticipated! Occupational Status was close to what was anticipated, while 'Social Class Position' returned a mixed result.

Part V – Racial Prejudice

5.1 The Concept of Race:
Chapter IX reports on and discusses the level of racial prejudice in the Republic of Ireland in 2007-08 and comments at some length on the fairly complex debate on 'race, racism and racialism' among social scientists over the past two decades. Despite the fact that the pseudo-scientific arguments for poly or multiple human races have been shown to be void of scientific validity for over one hundred years, the myth of racism still continues to be used to justify maltreatment of whole populations of people in our divided

world. The political and social concepts of race are still seriously negative factors in intergroup relations.

In this text the concept of racism or racialism is strictly reserved to a *negative attitude (prejudice) towards a person perceived to belong to a group or category deemed to be inferior because of genetically inherited physical or physiognomic traits such as colour, shapes of eyes or lips, texture of hair, size, etc.* It is based on a false perception that there are a number of races and they are essentially different from one another. The truth is that there is but one human race and "the colour of one's skin is no more important than the size of one's boots" in human terms.

The first section of Chapter IX is devoted to a review of a selection of the considered opinions of a number of anthropologists, sociologists and psychologists and an historian. As noted already, biological racism is no longer being professed but 'the chameleon nature of the virus of racism' in human society enables it to continue with its socially destructive effects on the lives of countless people and institutions. It may be politically correct to present oneself as being 'colour-blind', while at the same time, fail to act for or even accept total equality for people with different physiological or physiognomic features from those of one's own group. The clearest example of racism in Irish attitudes is borne out in the different levels of social distance between *Euro-Americans* (i.e. White Americans) and *Afro-Americans* (i.e. Black Americans).

In the opinion of the present author, the concept 'race' is being used too widely, even by people who wish to promote the rights of minorities. Ethnocentrism, anti-Semitism, political prejudice and social prejudice are not infrequently referred to as racism or racialism. This is at best careless and inaccurate and at worse perpetuating one of the most dangerous myths of 'post-Enlightenment Europe'!

Slavery is older than racism but racialist slavery was the most invidious of all its forms. It denied the human dignity of the Black Slaves and viewed them as a lesser form of 'high primates', when compared with White Europeans.

5.2 Racial Prejudice in Ireland:
One of the most welcome findings from the 2007-08 National Survey has been the continued decline of racial prejudice in the Republic of Ireland as

measured by the *Bogardus Social Distance Scale*. The findings of the *Racialist Scale*, however, did not show a similar level of improvement. This was disappointing, although the level of racial prejudice was relatively low at a **p-score** of **36.8** on a **0 to 200** range. The 1988-89 findings for the same scale were also relatively low at **35.4**. Some might argue that it would only be reasonable to expect little or no movement at such a comparatively low mean racial score. Such a view must be resisted as we strive for a racist-free society.

Table No. 9.2 (page 202) gives the findings of the *Racialist Scale* for the 2007-08 and 1988-89 National Surveys. The *Cronbach Alpha* score of **0.768** was very satisfactory and confirms the validity of the findings. The two items to elicit significantly negative changes, i.e. *"...there should be a stricter control on Black People who enter this country than on Whites"* and *"...Black People should be sent back to Africa and Asia where they belong and kept there"*, may be influenced by the EU fortress policy! There was appreciably more support for the former (with **32.3%** agreeing) than for the latter (with only **8.4%** agreeing).

The nine-item *Racialist Scale* divided into two factors, i.e. *Exclusion Factor* and *Pure-Racialist Factor*. The mean sample *p-score* for the 'Exclusion Factor' was **47.2** (out of 200) while the 'Pure Racialist' factors score was much less at **23.6**, just half of the former. Table No. 9.4 gives the Racial Scale variations by personal variables, i.e. for the *Total Scale* and the two factors. The findings were more or less as anticipated, which was refreshing in the light of the unexpected performance of young and more-educated respondents in the social-distance scales. The range of scores for such low mean scale numbers is interesting and points to the dynamic state of racial tolerance and prejudice. The role of negative stereotyping of categories such as 'Nigerians' and 'Afro-Americans' can delay the decline of racialism in Ireland!

Table No. 9.5 is of particular interest in that it shows that the 'social-class position' variable performed as anticipated with a negative correlation in each of the three scales, i.e. Total Scale, Factor I and Factor II. This is a very important and interesting result in that it shows greater tolerance among the "Middle and Upper Classes" towards Black People. The higher prejudice scores among the "Working and Lower Classes" is very disappointing because of the lack of solidarity at these levels with minorities likely to be themselves at the lower end of the "social ladder"!

Table No. 9.6 gives the changes in social-class position between 1988-89 and 2007-08. There was a decrease in "Lower Class" (from **21.2%** in 1988-89 to **9.9%** in 2007-08) and an almost corresponding increase in the "Working Class" percentages. The upward movement in the "Middle Class" categories were smaller. It is interesting to note that changes between "Working Class" and "Middle Class" percentages were less than 2% (nominally).

The second measure of racial prejudice in Chapter IX is social distance towards five racial stimulus categories. The findings of Table No. 9.7 are mixed. The failure of gender to elicit a significant statistical variation between males and females further confirms the homogenisation of gender attitudes. Age, once again, produced a negative result for the 18 to 25 year-olds and a very positive one for the 26 to 40 year-olds.

Social distance towards 'Afro-Americans' and 'Africans' followed a similar pattern, which confirms the high *Pearson Product-Moment Coefficient* of **0.89** on Table No. 6.7 (page 119) above. Here the racial and ethnic prejudices reinforce each other. The interplay of these two types of prejudice in stimulus categories, perceived to be related to both race and nationality, is of interest. Ideally, a reduction in, or an undermining of, racism and/or ethnocentrism will speed up the path to tolerance towards those of non-European origin or background.

***

CHAPTER XX
General Summary of Findings [2]

Part I – Attitudes towards Northern Ireland and Britain

1.1 Northern Ireland:
The changes in the situation in Northern Ireland during the thirty-five years from 1972-73 until 2007-08 have been extraordinary. The paramilitary violence ended in a mutually acceptable resolution in the *1998 Good Friday Agreement.* The attitudes towards Northern Ireland and Britain as measured in the 2007-08 National Survey bear out the positive effects of this development.

Because of the improved intercommunity relations within Northern Ireland and between Northern Ireland and the Republic of Ireland, it was not necessary to have questions on possible or desirable solutions. The latter were part of the earlier two surveys, i.e. 1972-73 and 1988-89. Chapters X and XI deal with Northern Ireland and Britain respectively.

The *Special Northern Ireland Scale*, measures *opinions* more than *attitudes,* although the former often reflect attitudes that are pre-reflective while opinions are post-reflective. It is possible to divide the 'Northern Ireland Scale' with three areas of interest, i.e.

(1) *Catholic-Protestant Identity;*
(2) *National and Community Unity; and*
(3) *Cooperation and Violence.*

1.2 Social Distance toward Northern Irish Stimulus Categories:
In the fifty-one stimulus categories, three were of particular relevance to attitudes in the Republic of Ireland towards Northern Ireland, namely, 'Northern Irish', 'Protestants' and 'Unionists'. The changes in social-distance scores between 1988-89 and 2007-08 have been substantially positive especially in the case of 'Unionists'. The following extract from Table No. 10.1 highlights the extent of change in the percentages willing to admit members of each of the three stimulus categories to kinship between 1988-89 and 2007-08:

| Stimulus Category | Admit to Kinship | | |
| | 2007-08 | 1988-89 | Change (A – B) |
	A	B	
1. 'Northern Irish'	75.1%	70.9%	**+4.2%**
2. 'Protestants'	78.4%	62.2%	**+16.2%**
3. 'Unionists'	66.2%	33.4%	**+32.8%**

While the percentage admitting 'Northern Irish' into kinship is high, it is lower than where the *'principle of propinquity'* would place them. This shows a need for more favourable contact across the Border. The improvement in the scores of 'Protestants' (in a sample who are 90% 'Roman Catholic' and 5% 'Protestant') is substantial and significant. The most substantial improvement was reserved for 'Unionists' whose percentage 'admitting to kinship' improved by **98.2%** in a period of nineteen years, i.e. from **33.4%** in 1988-89 to **66.2%** in 2007-08. This is a most significant peace dividend for the people of Ireland, which is likely to improve further if mutual trust and cooperation are to continue. Of course, the reverse could happen should there be a serious reversal to this mutual cooperation!

Table No. 10.2 (pages 225-6) gives the findings of social distance as measured by 'Admission to Kinship' and 'Denial of Citizenship' by personal variables. Once again, the youngest age group (18 to 25 year-olds) recorded unanticipated results in their relatively high level of intolerance, i.e. below average in 'admission to kinship' and above average for 'denial of citizenship'. This, in turn, is reflected in the case of 'Marital Status' and 'Education'. 'Occupational Status' was more or less as anticipated. 'Rural'-born and reared seemed to be more tolerant towards Northern Irish categories than their city fellow-citizens!

1.3 Findings of Special Northern Ireland Scale:

"The perception of *Catholic-Protestant* identity **versus** *common cross-community* identity" is measured in Items Nos. 1, 2 and 3 (see page 231 above). The changes since 1972-73 are also monitored (see Table No. 10.3, page 231). Figure No. 10.1 (page 221) gives the current "Cross-Border/Cross-Nation/Cross-Denomination Perceptions".

In the replies to Items Nos. 4, 5, 6 and 8, which related to issues of national and community unity, there was less support for the "Two-Nations view" in 2007-08 than in 1988-89. The perceived divisive role of separate Catholic and Protestant schools and of the Roman Catholic Church in the Republic of Ireland was moderately reduced during the nineteen years between the surveys. The respondents' perception of the Irish language as "a good basis of Irish unity" was given more support in the 2007-08 findings. There was a moderate drop in support for the view that Irish National Unity was an essential condition of the solution to the 'Northern Irish problem'. There was overwhelming support for the *Good Friday Agreement of 1998*, i.e. **75.4%** for and **3.2%** against.

Overall, there was improvement in attitudes in the Republic of Ireland towards Northern Ireland. Further occasions of **favourable contact** are needed between people from the Republic and Nationalists and Unionists in Northern Ireland. Such things as sport, recreation and other non-political occasions of favourable contact need to be increased. The possibility of a single All-Ireland (international) Soccer team would be an obvious occasion for greater friendly solidarity between "working-class people" from Northern Ireland and the Republic. Currently the All-Ireland Rugby (international) team seems to provide occasions of solidarity for the "middle classes" from both sides of the 'Border'.

1.4 Attitudes towards the British:
By degrees, the long process of reconciliation between the people of the Republic of Ireland and Great Britain has continued to improve between 1988-89 and 2007-08. In the surveys of 1972-73 and 1988-89 there was evidence that the people of England, Scotland and Wales were among the most preferred of the non-Irish ethnic categories. This improved even further in the current survey.

Apart from the high status of the (ordinary) people of Great Britain, the process of reconciliation of Irish-British attitudes went even further. The hostility towards the *British Establishment* reduced significantly and substantially. Three items on the *Special Anti-British Scale* (page 251) brings out this point:

Item	Year	Agree	Don't Know	Disagree	Anti-British Score (0-200)
No. 4 *"The British have been even-handed when dealing with Northern Ireland since 1969."*	1988-89	22.4%	21.1%	56.5%	134.1
	2007-08	19.8%	41.9%	38.2%	118.3
	Change	-2.6%	+20.8%	-21.7%	**-15.8**
No. 9 *"I don't object to the British people but I don't like the British Government."*	1988-89	49.4%	20.6%	30.0%	119.4
	2007-08	19.2%	29.6%	51.3%	68.0
	Change	-30.2%	+9.0%	+21.3%	**-51.4**
No. 13 *"The British have little respect for the Irish people."*	1988-89	48.1%	18.9%	33.0%	115.1
	2007-08	18.9%	31.7%	49.4%	69.5
	Change	-29.2%	+12.8%	+16.4%	**-45.6**

The *Anti-British score* (0 - 200) in the case of each of the three items dropped significantly and in the case of Nos. 9 and 13 the drop was quite substantial. The likely cause of this change has been the positive involvement of the British Government in the bringing about of the power-sharing in Northern Ireland and an end to the major paramilitary strife.

One of the features of the findings of the *Special Anti-British Scale* in the 1972-73 survey was the absence of a positive correlation between the two factors (within the Anti-British scale), i.e. "low esteem" and "hostility towards the British". This result was suspected to be the product of a long period of colonial rule over the Irish and was named *'post-colonial attitudinal schizophrenia'*. Some of the respondents who held the British in high esteem were, in fact, looking down on themselves! In the 2007-08 survey this disposition has been greatly reduced as more and more Irish people have gained self-confidence *vis-à-vis* the British.

The attitudes of a minority of younger respondents were less tolerant than anticipated (see Table No. 11.2, page 245 and Table No. 11.5, page 255). Older and middle-aged respondents were more positive towards the British. The performance of those with 'Complete Second-Level' and 'Third-Level' education were also disappointing. The residue of 'post-colonial attitudinal schizophrenia' could be partly responsible for these anomalous findings!

Part II – Prejudices towards Social Categories

Chapter XII examines the prejudice of respondents towards nine *'social'* stimulus categories. These nine categories were subdivided into three special groupings, i.e.:

(a) *Personal/Domestic Categories*: 'Gay People', 'People with Physical or Mental Disabilities' and 'Unmarried Mothers';

(b) *Compulsive Behaviour Categories*: 'Alcoholics', 'Drug Addicts' and 'Heavy Drinkers'; and

(c) *Socio-Economic Categories*: 'Unemployed' and 'Working Class'.

2.1 General Findings:

Each of the stimulus categories' social-distance was reported on Table No. 12.1 (page 264) under two headings, i.e. *'admit to kinship'* and *'denial of citizenship'*. Comparisons with the findings of the 1988-89 survey in the case of eight of the nine categories are also given ('Heavy Drinkers' was added in the 2007-08 survey). There was an overall reduction of prejudice against social stimulus categories, with the exception of "Working class" whose performance remained more or less the same with minor changes below the accepted margin of error. "Working class" retained its overall social standing of **2ⁿᵈ position** with **85.6%** welcoming members of the category into kinship. At such a low level of social distance, i.e. **1.228** (on a 1 to 7 scale) the possibility of significant change is limited.

2.2 'Personal' and 'Domestic' Social Categories:

These stimulus categories have changed their scores substantially between 1988-89 and 2007-08. As was noted when reporting on the changes in MSD scores and in rank order of the forty-six categories measured in the 1988-89 and 2007-08 surveys (see Table No. 4.2, pages 65-6), 'Gay People' was the category to experience greatest positive change, i.e. from 45ᵗʰ in 1988-89 to 24ᵗʰ in 2007-08 (-21 places) and a change in mean social-distance score from **3.793** to **1.923** (-1.870) over the same period. This marks a very substantial decrease in homophobia and a corresponding improvement in tolerance of 'Gay People'.

The following extract from Table No. 4.2 (page 65) gives the changes for each of the four personal/domestic categories:

Stimulus Category	Mean-Social-Distance			Rank Order Position		
	2007-08	1988-89	Change	2007-08	1988-89	Change
1. People with Physical Dis.	1.268	1.581	-0.313	3rd	9th	-6
2. Unmarried Mothers	1.339	1.684	-0.345	5th	15th	-10
3. People with Mental Dis.	1.612	2.010	-0.398	18th	19th	-1
4. Gay People	1.923	3.793	-1.870	24Th	45th	-21

The above extract reports on the substantial improvement in the social-distance scores of all four stimulus categories over a period of nineteen years. This is something greatly to be welcomed in the light of the biases and bigotry of the past in most societies.

Table No. 12.2 (pages 266-7) gives the 'admission to kinship' and 'denial of citizenship' scores by personal variables. 'Age', 'Education' and 'Occupational Status' did not perform as anticipated which, again, is problematic. 'Social Class Position' produced a mixed result. Only **three** of the thirty-two sub-Tables recorded consensus, i.e. no statistical significance. This indicates that there is likely to be further movement in the level of tolerance toward these four categories.

The prejudice against 'Unmarried Mothers' is practically dead in the Republic of Ireland according to the findings of the 2007-08 survey. The percentage welcoming 'Unmarried Mothers' into kinship had increased by **34.9%** over the nineteen years (from **61.1%** in 1988-89 to **82.4%** in 2007-08). Their rank ordering went from **15th** in 1988-89 to **5th** in 2007-08 (out of the forty-six stimulus categories replicated in the 2007-08 survey). These changes are greatly to be welcomed in the interest of 'Unmarried Mothers' and their children.

The improvements in the social-distance of 'People with Physical Disability' and 'People with Mental Disability' are significant and substantial. This is also greatly to be welcomed. The response of the 'Education' and 'Occupational Status' variables to the disability categories was not as anticipated, while 'Age' was in accordance with expectations in the case of 'People with Mental Disability'. 'Social Class Position', as a variable, returned an unanticipated result with the "Middle and Upper

Classes" being less tolerant than the "Working Class" and "Lower Class" respondents. Are these *meritocratic* biases?

The responses by personal variables towards 'Gay People' on Table No. 12.2 (pages 266-7) show substantial score variations on seven of the eight variables. The variation in 'Education' was moderate. The middle-aged and more urbanised respondents and those with more prestigious occupations were less homophobic. 'Social Class Position' and 'Education' reported mixed results. The bigger the score variation between sub-variables the more likely those attitudes will continue to change in relation to 'Gay People'. Should such changes go in the direction of the trends between 1988-89 and 2007-08, it is likely that they will continue to improve. On the other hand, should the score variations represent a negative reaction to the signs of progress for 'Gay People' (and mixed scores may point towards such reaction), society must be vigilant in protecting the *rights* of Gay citizens!

2.3 Compulsive Behaviour Categories:

Because of advances in psychology and other behavioural sciences, there has been serious progress in our understanding and rehabilitation of those suffering from compulsive behaviour and addiction. Looking back over a long period of history, such behaviour has been defined variously as immoral, criminal and a manifestation of illness or the product of socio-cultural pressures. During the 'immoral' phase, i.e. demonisation phase, persons identified as suffering from compulsive behaviour were/are seen as being influenced by the 'devil' and were assigned to asylums, etc. The 'criminalisation' phase was/is marked by severe punishment, imprisonment, mutilation and even death. When the condition is seen as an 'illness' or the product of socio-cultural pressures, the public reaction is to cure and rehabilitate. This is not to ignore the extent of the role of free will or to underestimate, in any way, the intolerable level of hardship and pain caused to innocent victims by the compulsive behaviour and addiction of others.

Areas of compulsive behaviour take different forms, i.e. addiction to alcohol and drug, gambling, certain forms of sexual 'deviance', including 'paedophilia' (which seems to be moving from phase one to phase two at present) and others. Hopefully, all forms will reach the third phase in order to deal with the problems more constructively. The three stimulus categories examined in the 2007-08 survey were 'Alcoholics', 'Drug Addicts' and 'Heavy Drinkers' (which could be defined as a category *en route* to becoming 'Alcoholics'). The latter category, 'Heavy Drinkers', was added to the 2007-08 survey because of the growing problem of drinking to excess in Ireland over the previous two decades, especially among young people (including minors) of both genders.

The members of the three categories tested require public support for their rehabilitation and need to have the primary definition of their behaviour changed from one of *deviance* to that of *illness*. Severely negative attitudes would tend to isolate members of these categories and very likely contribute to a greater surrender to their addiction. Regrettably, the results of Table Nos. 12.1 and 12.3 (pages 264 and 274-5) clearly show a strongly negative response in the case of each of the three 'compulsive behaviour' categories, i.e. 'Heavy Drinkers', 'Alcoholics' and 'Drug Addicts'. This is very non-rehabilitative! Society itself has a major responsibility to control access to drugs and alcohol to ensure that vulnerable citizens are duly protected from their menacing effects!

The responses of the personal variables were quite mixed. Seven of the sub-Tables (out of a total of twenty-four sub-Tables) recorded a non-significant (N/S) response, i.e. indicating a consensus among the sub-variable. Six of the seven were in the case of 'Gender' (2), 'Marital Status' (2) and 'Area of Birth' (2). Variations in the levels of 'denial of citizenship' were relatively high which is indicative of a polarisation of attitudes towards members of these addictive/compulsive-behaviour categories. The 'lower classes' and those with lesser education seem to be more positively disposed towards members of the three categories than were their co-respondents at the top of the class and education spectra!

2.4 Socio-Economic Stimulus Categories:
The two categories in this group were 'Working Class' and 'Unemployed'. Both categories had mean-social-distance scores of less than **1.500**, i.e. 'Working Class' at **1.228** and 'Unemployed' at **1.446**, which ranked them within the in-group categories. Because of such a high level of social acceptance, there was a limit to significant or substantial variations in their scores when tested by personal variables (see Table No. 12.4, pages 282-3).

Where statistical significance was achieved, variations were not as anticipated in the case of age, area of birth, education and social class position. This, once again, raises serious questions about the relative intolerance of a minority of young people from '18 to 25 years of age', and the failure of higher education (at 'Complete Second-Level' and 'Third Level') to socialise young people to be less prejudiced!

Part III – The Irish Travelling People

Chapter XIII reports on Irish attitudes (in the Republic) towards the country's native ethnic minority, the Irish Travelling People. A special Report, *Emancipation of the Travelling People* was published in July 2010, based on the findings of the 2007-08 survey. Chapter XIII of this text presents the main findings of the published Report on the Travellers.

3.1 Demographic Profile of Travellers:
In all there were 22,369 Travellers at the time of the *2006 Census of Population.* This constituted **0.5%** of the population of the Republic of Ireland. A profile of this minority (see Table No. 13.1, page 298) shows the demographic indicators of the relative deprivation of Travellers, i.e., lower life-expectancy, poorer education participation, massive unemployment, and low community involvement. The findings of the 2007-08 National Survey were both optimistic and pessimistic. Some **39.6%** would 'admit Travellers into kinship' while, at the same time, as many as **18.2%** would 'deny Travellers citizenship'. This polarisation of attitudes is indicative of a change in the relationship between the 'Settled Community' and the 'Travelling Community'.

In the past, Irish Travellers were associated with Rural Ireland. The *2006 Census* shows that only **25.9%** of Travellers live in Rural/Village environments, while **53.0%** live in large towns and cities and **21.2%** live in **towns** between 1,500 and 9,999 citizens. They live in houses, serviced sites, unserviced sites and in campsites. The *2002 Housing (Miscellaneous) Act* criminalised camping on publicly owned land, which had been the normal right of Travellers for up to two hundred years. The distribution of Travellers by province in 2006 was also most interesting, i.e. **50.6%** in Leinster (19.4% in Dublin), **24.1%** in Munster and **25.3%** in Connaught/Ulster (3.4% in Cavan/Monaghan and Donegal). Settlements in the cities are at times close to the marginalised.

3.2 Social Distance Scores of Travellers:
Table No. 13.3, page 309, shows the change in social distance between 1988-89 and 2007-08. 'Admission to kinship' went from **13.5%** to **39.6%**,

i.e. a nominal increase of **+26.1%**, while 'denial of citizenship' went from **10.0%** in 1988-89 to **18.2%** in 2007-08, i.e. a nominal increase of **8.2%**. This polarisation is probably indicative of the rising claims of Travellers for their rights and also a negative response to the much publicised negative behaviour of a minority of Travellers (some of whom are treated as *outcasts*).

Social Distance by Personal Variables is given on Table No. 13.5, page 313-4. The older respondents (71 years plus) were most tolerant towards Travellers. The younger respondents (18 to 25 years) and the middle-middle-aged (41 to 55 years) were the least tolerant. Females, Dubliners, lower educated and middle occupations were also more tolerant. Overall, the variable responses were not as anticipated.

The reasons given for not admitting Travellers to kinship were interesting, i.e. 'Way of Life' (63.7%), 'Not Socially Acceptable' (17.8%) and Cultural (9.6%). This rationalisation is due in great part to the *Culture of Poverty* which Travellers are forced to accept in a relatively rich society. Are Travellers being seen more as nuisances than as people in need of help in Irish society?

3.3 The Special Anti-Traveller Scale:
This scale, adapted from the late Professor Earl Davis and colleagues' (ESRI) 1977 Scale which was used in the 1988-89 survey and replicated in the 2007-08 survey, retained a high *Cronbach* rating of **0.83**. This is quite a discerning scale. The overall scale's mean negative score of **3.56** (on a 1 to 6 scale) in 2007-08 was only marginally lower than the 1988-89 mean negative score of **3.61** (-0.05).

The two positive items of opinion were:

1. *"I would be willing to employ a Traveller"*   Agree (59.0%)   Disagree (41.1%)
2. *"I consider a Traveller competent to serve on a jury"*   Agree (73.2%)   Disagree (26.8%)

The fact is that almost three-fifths of the sample would be willing to employ a Traveller. This percentage had been growing steadily (if moderately) since 1977, i.e. 1977 (54.8%) and 1988-89 (56.9%). Of course, the sad fact that **41.1%** would not agree to employ a Traveller is still a very serious reflection on Irish society!

That almost three-quarters of the sample (73.2%) agreed that Travellers were *competent to serve on a jury*, should be reassuring for members of the Travelling Community. This positive percentage has grown steadily and substantially over thirty-two years, i.e. 1977 (31.4%) and 1988-89 (51.7%). Hopefully, members of the Travelling Community will be invited to serve on juries, especially in cases where Travellers are involved in cases before the Courts.

The recognition of Travellers as a separate ethnic group (within Irish society) has been an issue of importance for many Travellers and their leaders. What Travellers want is **pluralist integration** into Irish Society rather than assimilation (which seemed to be at the core of public policy over the past forty years). Respondents were asked for their views on the issue and responded most favourably in support of integrated pluralism, i.e. *"Travellers should be facilitated to live their own way of life decently"*: Agree **(72.3%)**, Don't Know **(16.9%)**, Disagree **(10.8%)**. It must be underlined that this does not mean that the *'culture of poverty and deprivation'*, which Travellers in general are forced to endure, should be facilitated. The first prerequisite of enabling Travellers *"to live their way of life decently"* would be to remove the 'culture of poverty and deprivation' from this minority of Irish citizens.

While the social distance findings were quite positive in having Travellers as 'Next Door Neighbours' or closer (61.7%) in 2007-08 (an improvement of a nominal 20.7% since 1988-89), the vast majority (79.6%) would *"be reluctant to buy a house next door to a Traveller"*. When examined by personal variables the more urbanised, those with better education and higher occupations were above average in *"being reluctant to buy a house next door to a Traveller"*. This would seem to point to a class or 'property value' reason for such reluctance. The inconsistency between the social-distance response and the scale-item opinion highlights the 'fair-weather liberalness' of many respondents when there is a clash of values!

The overall position of the Travelling People is very serious and will not improve without a new initiative from the State at the national and local government levels. In the special Report *Emancipation of the Travelling People* a number of recommendations have been proposed which were likely to enable the Settled People to give members of this minority 'a stake in Irish society' on an integrated pluralist basis.

Part IV – The Irish Family and Attitudes towards Women

4.1 Introduction:

Chapter XIV examines selected facts about the Irish family from the *Report of the 2006 Census*. It also examines the findings of the *Special Feminist Scale*, which was replicated in the 2007-08 survey from the questionnaire of the 1988-89 National Survey. The changes in the role and status of women in Irish society have been closely related to changes in the role and status of the family in Ireland today. The family, as a social institution, has lost its pivotal position in Irish society, which has become more and more economy-centred. **Patriarchy** and, to a certain degree **Matriarchy**, have both lost their authoritative position. This has, in part, led to a rise in **Filiarchy**, where young people assume individualist and consumerist dominance.

With a degree of decline in the central role of the family, other changes have also taken place including the decline of the local community and neighbourhood. There has been a big advance in the commercialisation of Irish life over the past seventy years, which has had its effects on family life, e.g. including waged employment for both men and women and the 'commercialisation' of leisure. Serious attempts to revive community spirit throughout Ireland have helped to counter the flow towards 'cosmopolitan individualism'. The success of such efforts, however, is very limited without the strengthening of the family as an institution.

4.2 Demographic Profile by Marital Status of Fifteen Years and Over:

The *2006 Census of the Population* in the Republic of Ireland shows that there were over three million people over 15 years of age (i.e. 3,118,136). One-third (**32.6%**) were single while almost one-half (**49.0%**) were married and one-in-twenty (**5.5%**) were widowed. The remaining **12.9%** were divided between separated/divorced (**5.1%**) and those living in permanent relationships (**7.8%**)[1].

Over two-thirds of Married Couples (**69.6%**) had children, while **30.5%** were without children. The distribution for cohabiting couples was almost two-thirds (**63.9%**) without children and **36.1%** with children.

---

[1] This national distribution of the *Census Report* of the '15 years and over' was matched closely by the **sample distribution** of the 18 years and over, i.e. Single (35.3%), Married (46.6%), Separated/Divorced (4.3%), Permanent Relationships (7.0%) and Widowed (6.7%).

Of the total of 189,240 lone parents in the *2006 Census Report*, **85.9**% were lone mothers and **14.1%** were lone fathers. It is interesting to note the age-distribution of the children of 'lone mothers' and 'lone fathers'. The majority **(71.8%)** of the children of lone fathers were over 15 years of age, while the majority of lone mothers' children **(55.9%)** were less than 15 years of age (see Table No. 14.5). The fact that **43.1%** of 'lone mothers' children were nine years or less, as compared with only 16.6% of the children of 'lone fathers', points to the cases of 'lone fathers' being predominantly post-marriage/partnership and a significant number of 'lone mothers' being pre-marriage/partnership.

Some **55.4%** of the population of 15 years or over are couples (married or cohabiting) while **6.1%** of the same population (15 years plus) are lone parents. The latter is greater than the proportion separated or divorced **(5.1%)**. Almost two-thirds of married and cohabiting couples had children, i.e. 560,697 couples. The demographic importance of lone parents (189,240) in Irish society today merits serious awareness. These figures from the *2006 Census Report* are key to understanding the domestic needs of Irish society (in the Republic of Ireland today).

4.3 The Feminist Scale:
The *Feminist Movement* has contributed to the substantial progress in gender equality in Ireland and elsewhere throughout the world. The liberation of women has been successful in most social institutions in Western Society, i.e. family, polity, law, education, recreation and economy. It has also advanced the status of women in the religious institutions, but most critics would feel that further advance is still necessary in some religions and denominations! Certain aspects of the Feminist Movement would seem to limit its effect of achieving gender and class equality. A more inclusive ideology of gender equality with a stronger **social** dimension would be required at this stage in Irish society!

Table No. 14.6 (page 344) gives the results of the *Feminist Scale* for 2007-08 and 1988-89. *Anti-feminism* (as measured by the scale) has not changed substantially over the nineteen years between 1988-89 and 2007-08. The reduction in the mean scale anti-feminist score from **46.3** in 1988-89 to **43.0** in 2007-08 is barely significant. At the same time it has decreased from a very low level, i.e. **46.3** on a **0-200** range of scores.

There was a substantial increase in opposition to confining women to the house and in support for the ordination of women to the priesthood (in the Roman Catholic Church). On the negative side, there was less support for the necessity of the *Feminist Movement*, i.e. **64.1%** agreed with its necessity in 1988-89 while **42.1%** agreed in 2007-08. Other changes in different **opinions** can be seen on Table No. 14.6, page 344. Each Item (of opinion) is examined by personal variables on Table No. 14.7 (pages 348-9). While there was a consensus of opinion in 35 of the 108 sub-Tables **(32.4%),** there were quite a divergence of opinion in the case of some personal variables, i.e. relatively high score variations. There may be signs of a change of public opinion in relation to feminism coming out of these variations. All major variations are commented on in the text (see pages 346-356).

A factor-analysis of the *Feminist Scale* results in three discernible factors within the scale, i.e.

    (a)   'Fundamentalist Sexism';
    (b)   'Domestic and Religious';
    (c)   'Political and Equality'.

The unit of measurement in the scale was the mean anti-feminist score (on a scale of 0-200). Eight of the twenty-six sub-Tables (22.2%) recorded a consensus between the sub-variables, i.e. they failed to elicit a statistically significant variation. Most of the score variations in the case of the twenty-eight sub-Tables with significant variations were substantial and show that feminism is still a live issue.

Table No. 14.9 (pages 358-9) gives the results of the Feminist Scale and Sub-Scales' Scores by Personal Variables. In the case of the ordinal variables, i.e. age, area of birth, education, occupational status and social-class position, responses were as expected except for age, where the youngest sub-variable, 18 to 25 year-olds, were more anti-feminist than the two middle-aged groups – 26 to 40 years and 41 to 55 years. Commentary on the score variations between sub-variables is given on pages 356-366 above.

Part V – Political Attitudes

Chapter XV examines the current state of a selection of Irish (Republic of Ireland) political attitudes and prejudices. The chapter begins by tracing the historical, geographic and ideological contexts of the current Irish political systems. The Northern Ireland conflict and recent moves to resolve it have dominated internal political developments, while reaction to the continuous campaign for greater European integration by the Irish political and socio-economic establishments (with the support of the Irish print and electronic media) has been a feature of recent external political developments, where public opinion is very evenly balanced, i.e. the Maastricht and Lisbon Referenda!

5.1 Political Social Distance:

The social distance in relation to six political stimulus categories is measured and analysed. The six political categories are: 'Capitalists', 'Communists', 'Gardaí', 'Socialists', 'Trade Unionists' and 'Unionists'. These six categories were also measured in the 1988-89 National Survey, which, in turn, enables the researcher and the reader to note the changes which had taken place over the nineteen years between the two surveys.

Table No. 15.1 (page 372) measures the percentages 'admitting to kinship' of and 'denying citizenship' to members of each of the six political stimulus categories. The findings are quite positive when compared with the 1988-89 scores. Five of the six political stimulus categories experienced substantial and significant increases in the percentages who would be admitted to kinship, i.e.

	A 1988-89	B 2007-08	B - A
'Unionists'	33.4%	**66.2%**	+32.8% (**+98.2%**)
'Socialists'	44.9%	**66.2%**	+21.3% (**+47.4%**)
'Communists'	24.4%	**45.9%**	+21.5% (**+88.1%**)
'Trade Unionists'	63.7%	**77.8%**	+14.1% (**+22.1%**)
'Capitalists'	47.8%	**60.8%**	+13.0% (**+27.2%**)
'Gardaí'	84.0%	**81.4%**	-2.9% (**-3.5%**)

Note: Proportionate increases are in brackets.

The significance of the nominal percentage increase (B-A) is determined by the 1988-89 findings where most of the 'admit to kinship' scores were quite low, i.e. under 50%. Proportionate percentage increases are given above (in brackets). 'Gardaí' was the only political stimulus category to experience a very slight disimprovement while still retaining in-group status.

Political social distance by personal variables is reported in Table No. 15.2, pages 376-7. The measures given for each of the six stimulus categories were admission to kinship and denial of citizenship. Eleven of the sixty sub-Tables failed to record a statistically significant variance, i.e. produced a consensus between the sub-variables. Readers should find it of interest to examine the performance of the categories for themselves and gauge the public support or hostility towards them. Political Party preference is included as a personal variable. Commentary and some interpretation are given on pages 375-388 above.

A second measure by personal variables of political social distance is reported on Table No. 15.3, namely, MSD scores (which incorporate all levels of social distance – 'kinship', 'friendship', 'next-door neighbour', 'co-workers', 'citizenship', 'visitor only' and 'debar/deport'). Twenty of the sub-scales have recorded a level of consensus. Table No. 15.3 gives a clear indication of performance of the variables, which helps the reader to predict changes in attitudes. Age, education, area of birth, education, occupation and social-class position did not perform as anticipated. In most cases results have been mixed.

5.2 Political Party Preference:
The Republic of Ireland could be classified as a liberal democracy. Under the above title an attempt was made to classify the social class of the supporters of the main political party. Table No. 15.4 (page 389) and Figure No. 15.1 (page 390) places party support on a spectrum from "Upper Class" (5) to "Lower Class" (1). The mean sample score was **2.7**, (on a social-class continuum of one-to-five), which is between "Working Class" and "Middle-Middle Class". The mean score for each of the parties was as follows:

Party	Score		Classification		
Sinn Féin	1.9	Between	"Working Class"	and	"Lower Class"
Labour Party	2.4	Between	"Working Class"	and	"Middle-Middle Class"
Fianna Fáil	2.8	Between	"Middle-Middle Class"	and	"Working Class"
Fine Gael	2.9	Between	"Middle-Middle Class"	and	"Working Class"
Green Party	3.0		"Middle-Middle Class"		

Fianna Fáil supporters are closest to the sample (national) mean of **2.7** (on a scale of 1 to 5) with *Fine Gael* and the **Green Party** to the 'right' of it and the **Labour Party** and *Sinn Féin* to the left of it! This supports a centrist position for the Irish population's range of ideology. **Political pragmatism** rather than **political ideology** seems to determine Irish political party support to a significant extent.

Political party loyalty has often been the source of public debate. Table No. 15.5 (page 391) gives the levels of regular voting support for their current party of choice. (Some 15% said "they would not vote".) The level of **party loyalty** was higher than was expected, i.e. excluding those who "would not vote" or "did not know" the party they would vote for. The following was the result of the total sample of Irish born:

Frequency of Voting for Party of Choice	Percentage	Number
1. Regularly	75.0%	486
2. Occasionally	20.5%	133
3. Never	4.5%	29

This seems to bear out a view once expressed by a former British Prime Minister, the late Mr Harold Wilson, M.P., that Governments were changed more by **selective abstentionism** rather than changing party allegiance. Of course, this is only possible where voting is voluntary, as it is in Ireland. The variations in party loyalty are reflected on Table No. 15.5 (page 392). The changes in levels of party preferences between 1988-89 and 2007-08 show a moderate drop in the case of *Fianna Fáil* (from 52% in 1988-89 to 44% in 2007-08) and no change for Labour. The drop of 2% for *Fine Gael* was well within the margin of error (see page 392). The percentages preceded the economic downturn of mid-2008. The collapse of the *Fianna Fáil* support in the General Election of 25th February 2011 would seem to mark a deviation from the 75% loyalty indicated above. It highlights the impact of the recession and the unpopular measures taken to deal with it.

5.3 Conclusion:

The social distance scale indicated greater overall tolerance of diverse political categories, notably: **'Unionists', 'Socialists'** and **'Communists'**. These results reflect the positive effects of the Peace Process in Northern Ireland and a reduction in ideological prejudice against 'left-wing' ideologies! The distribution of political preferences in the 2007-08 findings was close to the voting patterns of the **2007 General Election**.

Part VI – The Irish Language

Public support for Irish has been maintained at over 90% in favour of the language. The level of reasonable competence in Irish (of Irish-born respondents) was 47%. This marks an increase of 6% since 1988-89. This level of competence is the highest among the Irish population since the mid-19th century. The level of regular use of Irish was disappointing at 23%, while the status of the language proved to be very high in Irish society in 2007-08. The overall conclusion of Chapter XVI on pages 435-6 above, gives a summary account of the main findings in relation to the Irish language.

Part VII – Religious Attitudes and Prejudices

7.1 Introduction:

Chapter XVII examines religious attitudes and practices in the Republic of Ireland and comments on changes which have taken place since the 1988-89 National Survey. A special Report on Irish Religious Attitudes and Practices was published in 2009 entitled: *The Challenge of Indifference: A Need for Religious Revival in Ireland.* This Report includes a fairly detailed examination of liturgical worship, prayer and the perceived importance of religion in the lives of the people. The findings of the Religion Report were both positive and negative. The level of divine worship declined in Ireland over recent years, while belief in God seemed to hold firm. Reasons given for greater public worship were expressing **indifference rather than hostility**.

It was during the period between 1988-89 and 2007-08 that serious revelations and exposure of child abuse by a minority of clergy and religious came to the notice of the public. The negative impact of such revelations was likely to have been a partial contribution of decline in certain religious practices. The rise in individualism, materialism and consumerism was also likely to have contributed to the decline in religious practice and devotion between 1988-89 and 2007-08. The reduction in average personal wealth because of the downturn in the economy since 2008 may result in a questioning of materialism and facilitate a return to greater spiritual values!

7.2 Demographic Profile of Religious Affiliation in Ireland:
The predominance of Roman Catholicism in the Republic of Ireland has been maintained, ranging from 89.4% in **1861** to 86.8% in **2006**. Of those who declared a religious affiliation, **Roman Catholic** percentages are still in the nineties, i.e. 92.4% in 2006. In-migration to Ireland in recent years has been largely Christian in affiliation and mainly Roman Catholic.

The relative position of Protestant denominations has fluctuated over the years since Independence (in 1922). **Church of Ireland** constituted **3.2%** of the population in 2006.

When affiliations of respondents were compared to those of their parents, it was found that there was **little evidence of significant leakage**. This was confirmed by the *Census Reports*. A most significant, if surprising, finding (in the light of so much negative and adversarial media opinion on religious affairs) was that only **4%** denied believing in God in the 2007-08 survey. This was confirmed also in the Census findings.

7.3 Religious Practice:
The measures of religious practice reported in Chapter XVII included: public worship, Mass, Holy Communion, Confession and personal prayer. Table No. 17.5 and Figure No. 17.1 show clearly the decline in religious practice over the period 1981 to 2008. **Monthly** (or more often) worship went from **87.9%** to **54.4%** which is a very substantial decline by any standards, although the current level of practice is still considered relatively high. The problem has been that the change came from a very high level. **Weekly Mass attendance** for Roman Catholics dropped from **91%** in 1974 to **43%** in 2007-08. Monthly Mass attendance had dropped to **55%** in 2007-08.

The practice to suffer greatest change for Roman Catholics was in the participation in **Sacramental Confession,** i.e. Confession 'Several Times a Year' dropped from **80%** in 1988-89 to **27%** in 2007-08. Such a collapse in regular Sacramental Confession marks a crisis in this area of public worship for Roman Catholics in the Republic of Ireland. The reception of **Holy Communion** did not decline as severely as 'Weekly Mass Attendance' or 'Regular Sacramental Confessions', i.e. monthly Holy Communion declined from **63%** in 1988-89 to **43%** in 2007-08. Some **79%** of Roman Catholics who went to Mass once a month received Holy Communion.

Frequency of **personal prayer**, while down on the 1988-89 findings (90% weekly in 1988-89 to 72% in 2007-08), was still relatively high. Only **10%** of respondents stated they had given up the practice of prayer. When asked **'how close to God'** respondents felt, as high as **89%** felt some level of closeness, which would reinforce the relatively low level of those who had given up prayer.

When religious practices were measured by **personal variables,** it was found that those with **lowest participation** tended to be younger, more urbanised, male and more highly educated. 'Occupational Status' produced a more mixed result. Such trends reflect the secularising influences of education, youth culture and urbanised living. The major reason given for not attending weekly worship was: "just did not bother", **or indifference.**

On the question of **secularisation**, the evidence of religious practice and "perceived closeness to God" would challenge the opinion that religion had so far "become irrelevant" for the majority of the Irish people (which would mark the advance of secularisation). At the same time, there are definite signs of certain **tendencies towards 'secularisation'**, of which religious "indifference" is one. Attitudes towards Christian Unity were not as optimistic as in the 1972-73 survey.

7.4 Social Distance towards Religious Categories:
In Chapter XVII, six religious stimulus categories are measured for their current social distance, i.e. **'Agnostics', 'Atheists', 'Jews', 'Muslims', 'Protestants'** and **'Roman Catholics'**. The findings of the changes in mean-social-distance (MSD) scores show an all-round increase in religious tolerance between 1988-89 and 2007-08. The following extract from Table No. 17.19 highlights the change:

Stimulus Category	Admit to Kinship			Deny Citizenship		
	2007-08	1988-89	(Change)	2007-08	1988-89	(Change)
1. 'Roman Catholics'	91.1%	96.8%	**(-5.8%)**	0.6%	0.3%	**(+0.3%)**
2. 'Protestants'	78.4%	62.2%	**(+16.2%)**	2.6%	1.4%	**(+1.2%)**
3. 'Jews'	60.7%	39.5%	**(+21.2%)**	11.5%	12.1%	**(-0.6%)**
4. 'Atheists'	52.5%	28.5%	**(+24.0%)**	11.0%	19.8%	**(-8.8%)**
5. 'Agnostics'	50.3%	31.1%	**(+19.2%)**	14.2%	16.9%	**(-2.7%)**
6. 'Muslims'	42.9%	20.6%	**(+22.3%)**	23.2%	24.0%	**(-0.8%)**

While there was a substantial improvement in overall social-distance scores for religious categories, the relative position of **'Muslims'** is still very negative. It reflects a severe level of religious prejudice towards this very important world religion. The **23.2%** who would be willing to 'deny citizenship' to 'Muslims' bodes badly for **Christian-Muslim pluralism** in Ireland. Because of the relatively small numbers of Muslims in Irish society and their positive history of constructive harmony in Ireland, it is obvious that anti-Muslim prejudice in Ireland is vicarious and is imported from Western propaganda emanating from Israeli-Muslim hostility and the Western hostility towards Middle-East Muslim countries.

Table No. 17.20 measures religious social distance by personal variables, i.e. age, gender, marital status, area of birth, place of rearing, region of residence, education, occupational status, social-class position, Church attendance, closeness to God and frequency of prayer. Two measures for each of the six stimulus categories are used, namely, 'Admit to Kinship' and 'Deny Citizenship'. This means that there are one hundred and forty-four sub-scales on Table No. 17.20. Only fourteen of the sub-Tables (or 9.7%) failed to elicit a statistically-significant variation. This indicates that religious attitudes are dynamic within the population. The fairly extensive commentary on Table No. 17.20 merits reading in full and cannot be adequately summarised in a few sentences.

The range of variations was greatest in the case of responses to 'Atheists' and 'Agnostics'. Those most favourably disposed towards these two categories were young middle-aged (26 to 40 years), males, more urbanised, more highly educated, "upper" and "upper-middle classes", respondents with lower frequency of public worship and those who prayed less frequently. Respondents with higher frequency of prayer tended to be better disposed to 'Roman Catholics', 'Protestants' and 'Jews'. Occupational status was positively correlated with tolerance towards 'Roman Catholics', 'Protestants', 'Jews' and 'Muslims'. Other correlations tended to be mixed.

Part VIII – Authoritarianism and Social Anomie

8.1 The Concepts of Authoritarianism and Social Anomie:
Chapter XVIII examines the level of 'authoritarianism' and 'social anomie', which constitutes two important concepts that are significant in themselves and are shown to be related to social prejudice. **Authoritarianism** refers to

a particular 'personality type'[2] which tends to be closed-minded, dogmatic, intolerant, conventionalist, moralistic and religiously fundamentalist.   It might be argued that there is a degree of authoritarianism in most people, depending on their socio-cultural background.   It is not correlated with intelligence.   After experiencing the totalitarian regime of the German Fascist authorities (1933-1945), rationalised by anti-Semitism, racism and other forms of prejudice, a group of scholars from Berkeley University in the United States produced a definitive work on the role of authoritarianism and the psycho-socio-cultural factors contributing to the personality typology of the characters dominating the Third Reich Regime.   Their text, *The Authoritarian Personality*, has become a classic in the literature on this subject.   The special authoritarian scale used in this study is based on the scale of Adorno, *et al*[3].

Social Anomie is a concept which owes its origin to the well-known French sociologist, **Emile Durkheim** (1858-1917), one of the 'founding fathers' of modern sociology.   Two other sociologists developed the Durkheimian concept and theory in later years, namely, **Robert K. Merton** (1938) and **Leo Srole** (1956).   The latter produced a five-item scale in 1956, on which the Anomie Scale in the current study has been based (see pages 500-1).   The descriptive definition of social anomie proposed by the present author in the current text is as follows:

> Social Anomie is *a state of normlessness and perceived powerlessness, resulting from a situation where society's culturally-prescribed goals are not realisable by significant sections of society within the confines of socially acceptable norms.*

This definition draws heavily on Robert Merton's understanding of social anomie.   Leo Srole's **Anomie Scale** was seen by him as giving "an operational formulation of the anomie concept" (see pages 498ff above). Again, it is a matter of degree whether our accepted norms adequately match our cultural goals and enable us to cope with the demands of normal living. It is generally accepted that some suicides are related to social anomie.

At times of **widespread social change**, the functional link between goals and norms is inadequate and leads towards a greater degree of 'social

---

[2] T.W. Adorno, E. Frenkel-Brunswick, D.J. Levinson and R.N. Sandford, *The Authoritarian Personality*, New York, Harper and Row, 1950.
[3] *Ibid.*

anomie'. Failure of the socialisation process to transmit basic social norms and appropriate cultural goals also contributes to rising levels of 'social anomie'.

With regard to the correlation between social anomie and social prejudice, it will be shown that the former is, once again, (as it was in the 1988-89 national survey) a valuable independent variable "in both its direct and indirect influence"[4]. The path-analysis in the following chapter spells out the extent and direction of social anomie's influence.

8.2 The Authoritarian Scale:

The 1988-89 (sixteen item) Authoritarian Scale has been replicated in the 2007-08 National Survey. Table No. 18.1 (page 491) gives the findings of both surveys. When compared with 1988-89, the level of authoritarianism had decreased by a score of **17.0** on a scale of **0 to 200**, i.e. from **105.1** in 1988-89 to **88.1** in 2007-08. This is a significant, if moderate, drop in the total-scale **A-Score**. The four sub-scales had decreases in their scores, namely,

Sub-Scale	1988-89	2007-08	Change
1. **Religious Fundamentalism**	123.4	91.8	**-31.6**
2. **Political Conservatism**	122.4	114.9	**-7.5**
3. **Fascist-Type Submission & Aggression**	65.8	61.8	**-4.0**
4. **Moralism & Miscellaneous Authoritarianism**	108.6	84.0	**-24.6**

The above four sub-scales were based on the factors identified by Adorno *et al*[5]. It is interesting to note that the sub-scale with the greatest drop in the *A-Score* (**-31.6**) was in the 'Religious Fundamentalism' factor, which reflects the rise in religious tolerance and in religious indifference commented on in Chapter XVII.

When the sixteen-item scale was retested for the 2007-08 survey, it was discovered that three of the items failed to cluster in the factor analysis. A thirteen-item scale divided into three factors, i.e. 'Religious Fundamentalism', 'Political Conservatism' and 'Fascist Repression/ Moralism' emerged. The new authoritarian scale of thirteen items was

---

[4] See Mac Gréil, Micheál, *Prejudice in Ireland Revisited*, St Patrick's College, Maynooth, Department of Social Studies, 1996, page 462.
[5] Adorno, T.W. *et al, Op.Cit.*

examined by personal variables with its three Factors (see Table No. 18.2, pages 492-3).

The overall results have shown that the young, urban-born, and more highly educated recorded the least authoritarian scores which confirmed the anticipations of the findings. This positive result for age and education was to be welcomed in the light of the reverse of the trends in numerous other scales, which may, in part, be due to the complexity of the A-Scale. While there was a significant reduction in authoritarianism since 1988-89, its level is still relatively high at **94.69** (on a 0 to 200 scale). An authoritarian reaction to the post-2008 economic downturn (as happened in Europe after the post-World War I and post-1929 crashes) could easily exploit the fears of the people under charismatic, demagogic political leaders! The volatility of the socio-political situation in times of insecurity is conducive to exploitation by populist authoritarian political and community leaders!

8.3 Social Anomie Scale:
Table No. 18.3 gives the findings of the two national surveys held in 1988-89 and in 2007-08. The favourable changes brought about in Ireland over the intervening years enabled more people to achieve their cultural goals by acceptable social norms. Such changes as those which have taken place in Northern Ireland since 1994, have contributed to greater security and 'normality'. Still, at **94.4**, the level of social anomie in the adult population is too high for complacency. As can be concluded from Emile Durkheim's findings, economic and material gains alone do not necessarily reduce anomie. Religion, family and community support are probably the institutions with the most positive influence in reducing the levels of 'social anomie'[6].

Table No. 18.4 (pages 502-3) gives the findings of the *'Mean Social Anomie Scale-Score by Personal Variables'*. Age, gender, or marital status failed to elicit a statistically significant variation. In other words, there was consensus between the sub-variables in the case of these key personal variables! This tells its own story. Urban-born, lower-educated, lower-skilled and lower social-class-positioned registered the highest mean anomie scores. The range of score variations was greater in the case of social-class position, political-party preference, education and region of residence.

---

[6] Durkheim, Emile, *Suicide, A Study in Sociology*, New York, The Free Press, (1897), 1951.

In the following chapter, the influence of **authoritarianism** and **social anomie** on various types of social prejudice will be examined. It will be seen that different categories of prejudice react differently to authoritarianism as measured by the scale used in this survey because of the range of components selected for inclusion in the list of items and the complex nature of prejudice. Nevertheless, the consistency between the three factors on Table No. 18.2 (pages 492-3) and the relatively high *Cronbach Alpha* score of 0.737 point to the validity and reliability of the scale.

Part IX – Conclusion of Summary

The above wide-ranging summary (in Chapters XIX and XX) is intended to give the reader an overview of the content and findings reported in this text. It is not intended to be either a review of, or substitute for, the various chapters. Without reading and studying each chapter, the summary on its own provides the reader with a very superficial understanding of the attitudes and prejudices of the people of the Republic of Ireland as gathered from a forty-minute interview of a representative sample of 1,015 adults (18 years and over) between November 2007 and March 2008. The data from the previous National Survey of 1,005 adults, which was carried out in 1988-89, provided a basis for comparison. Also it should be noted that the findings and discussion do not exhaust the content of the data collected in the current survey (2007-08)!

The socio-economic conditions prevailing in Ireland at the time of both surveys were quite different. In the case of the earlier research (1988-89), and in the decade leading up to it, there was high unemployment, forced emigration and ongoing paramilitary violence and counter-violence in Northern Ireland, with overflows in the Republic and in 'mainland' Britain. In the decade leading up to the 2007-08 National Survey, Ireland had experienced relative prosperity, high employment, an end to forced emigration with notable numbers coming to Ireland for work. There was an end to violent conflict in Northern Ireland and the overwhelming support for power-sharing between Unionists and Nationalists.

The results of the 2007-08 research clearly record the positive effects of the growing socio-economic security and the significant increase in intergroup tolerance, when compared with the pattern of attitudes in the 1988-89 survey. In-migration of workers from Europe, Asia, Africa and elsewhere, created opportunities of favourable contact and this also contributed to a welcome reduction of social prejudice and a corresponding improvement in intergroup tolerance. Positive developments in Northern Ireland between 1994 and 1998 leading to the *Good Friday Agreement (1998)* and the experience of consensus regional government has also been a major factor in increasing social tolerance.

Among the most disappointing results have been the mixed findings in relation to the impact of **age** and **education** on a wide range of intergroup attitudes and **polarisation** of attitudes in relation to a number of categories. The latter requires focused research. Attitudes to a number of categories including 'Travelling People', 'Muslims', compulsive behaviour categories and others lower down in the Bogardus Rank Order of Preference need vigilant monitoring by those responsible for promoting and protecting minority rights.

***

CHAPTER XXI
The Final Analysis

Part I – Introduction

The completion of this text will mark the end of a long and complex process of social survey research into the intergroup attitudes and related issues in Ireland over a period of thirty-five years plus.   Three major representative samples of adults were interviewed, i.e. in 1972-73 (Greater Dublin sample), in 1988-89 (National Sample of the Republic of Ireland) and in 2007-08 (a similar National Sample).   An enormous amount of data has been collected, presented and examined in the three major surveys.   This book, then, is the third in a trilogy on prejudice and tolerance in Ireland by the current author[1].

According as the population of Ireland becomes more diverse, i.e. ethnically, 'racially', religiously, politically and socially, the need for and value of ongoing monitoring and greater analysis of intergroup relations become more important.   The analysis, presentation and monitoring of such relations has been the primary aim of this book and that of its predecessors. Hopefully, by 2024-25 a fourth major national survey of intergroup attitudes will be carried out and subsequently reported in a fourth publication.   This ongoing analysis and surveying of attitudes every fifteen to twenty years is necessary to ensure tolerant coexistence between diverse groupings and collectivities in Irish society.

In the course of this text an effort has been made to achieve a number of separate but related goals, which include the following:

(a) An accurate and objective presentation of the findings is given so that the reader has sufficient information to gauge the level of current intergroup attitudes (2007-08) in the Republic of Ireland.
(b) The text is written in such a way that it is accessible to the widest possible readership while, at the same time, of use and interest to students of the human sciences.

---

[1] Mac Gréil, Micheál, *Prejudice and Tolerance in Ireland*, Dublin CIR, 1977;
Prejudice in Ireland Revisited, Maynooth, St Patrick's College, 1996;
Pluralism and Diversity in Ireland, Dublin, The Columba Press, 2011.

(c) Since social attitudes change in response to social and cultural change, it is important to point towards indicators of patterns of and trends in the findings, when examined by personal variables and monitored over time (i.e. from 1972-73 to 1988-89 to 2007-08).

(d) The commentary and interpretation of various findings (presented by the author) are provided to enable the reader to understand the current state of Irish intergroup attitudes, prejudices and opinions.

(e) It is hoped that the critical reader will feel free to challenge the author's interpretations from a different theoretical point of view.

(f) Because of the wide and diverse range of stimulus categories and issues dealt with in the course of this text, each chapter has its own autonomy within the overall text to enable the reader to select separate areas of interest, i.e. broad categories of prejudice such as ethnic, ethnico-racial, racial, religious, political and social categories, and in that way cover the whole text by stages.

Chapters XIX and XX give **a general summary** of the text and an abridged abstract of the previous chapters. The reader is advised, however, not to depend on the summary provided as an adequate presentation of the findings examined in the body of the text. The reason why this descriptive summary is placed towards the end of the book is to help the reader **'pull the different strands together'** into a meaningful unity.

Part II – Path of Causation

The aim of this part is to attempt a 'final analysis' of the findings and, later in the chapter, make a number of recommendations arising out of such an analysis. As in all scientific research, the principal objective is to try and provide **explanation of the causes** through statistical correlations and measures of changes over time.

2.1 Ordinal Variable Path Analysis:

When trying to establish the direct influence of ordinal variables, use has been made of the **path analysis technique**. This relation between the variables (themselves) and the direct *Beta score* between each variable and **area of prejudice**, degree of **authoritarianism** and **level of social anomie** is reported. Table No. 21.1 and Figure No. 21.1 give the *Beta scores* for the inter-variable path analysis, i.e. the correlation between the variables themselves.

Table No. 21.1:
Ordinal Variables' Direct Beta Scores in Path Analysis

Ordinal Variables	Age 1.	Area of Birth 2.	Educ. 3.	Occupat. 4.	Religiosity 5.	Anomie 6.	Authorit-arianism 7.
1. Age	1,000	-.224	-.432	+.077	+.451	+.062	+.316
2. Area of Birth		1,000	+.134	+.011	+.251	+.082	-.223
3. Educational Achieve.			1,000	+.363	-.250	-.256	-.320
4. Occupational Status				1,000	+.029	+.025	+.001
5. Religiosity					1,000	+.029	+.437
6. Anomie						1,000	+.248
7. Authoritarianism							1,000

Note: Statistically significant *Beta scores* in **bold**, i.e. scores of **.070** plus.

The above table presents the *Beta scores* for **Authoritarianism as a function of Age, Area of Birth, Education, Occupation, Religiosity and Social Anomie**. The mutual impact of variables on each other gives the reader an insight into the relative influence they have on the 'dependent variables', (the various forms of prejudice), i.e. ethnic, ethnico-racial, racial, political, social, religious, sexist prejudice, *et cetera*. This matrix tells the reader much about the interdependence of the various personal variables in the path of multiple causality. Figure No. 21.1 presents the above matrix in diagrammatic form.

Age registers a significantly **negative** *Beta score* **(-.224)** in relation to 'area of birth' which reflects the demographic differences between urban and rural populations. Those born in more urbanised background tend to be proportionately younger on average. The younger respondents tend to be more educated, i.e. in terms of schooling **(-.432)**. Those with more senior occupational status have a slightly older age profile **(+.077)**.

The substantially higher *Beta score* of **0.451** points to the relatively older age-profile of respondents with the **highest religiosity** measures. The *Beta score* between **age** and **social anomie** is not statistically significant **(+.062)** which may, in part, be explained by the erratic performance of age in many of the tables measuring social prejudice and the spread of social anomie through the age groups. Age's direct score for **authoritarianism** is

Pluralism and Diversity in Ireland

Figure No. 21.1: Path Analysis of Personal Variables

Authoritarianism as a function of: Age, Area of Birth, Education, Occupation, Religiosity and Anomie

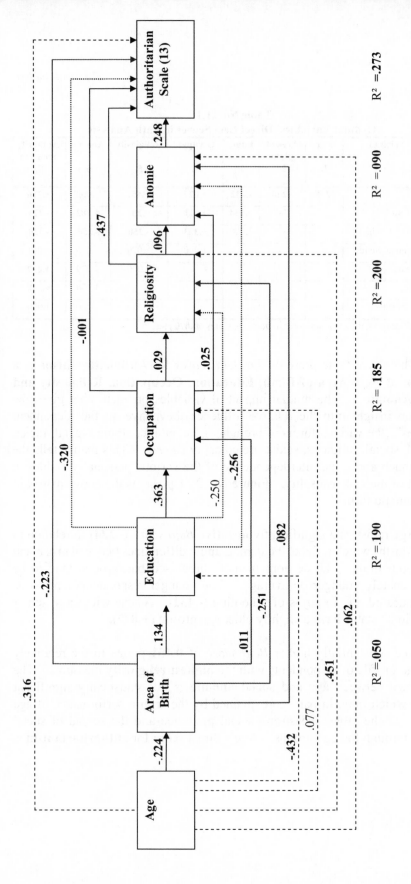

Age (1) 18-25 years, (2) 26-40 years, (3) 41-55 years, (4) 56-70 years and (5) 71 years and older
Where born (Area of Birth) (1) Rural/ Village (2) Town (1,500+), (3) Large Town (10,000+), (4) City (100,000+)
Education (1) Primary or less, (2) Incomplete Second-Level, (3) Complete Second-Level, (4) Third-level
Occupational Status (1) Unskilled / Semi-Skilled, (2) Skilled/ Routine Non-Manual, (3) Inspectional / Supervisory, (4) Professional / Executive

significant and substantial at **+.316**. Of course, it is more complex to gauge the **indirect** influence of age on **authoritarianism** via the intervening variables (see Figure No. 21.1).

Area of birth, which measures the influence of urbanisation on the different variables, elicited statistically significant scores in five of the six variables. Apart from **age** and **authoritarianism**, the other *Beta scores* were positive. The more urban-born respondents were more educated **(+.134)**, less religious **(-.251)**, more anomic **(+.082)**. They were younger **(-.224)** and less authoritarian **(-.223)** according to above direct *Beta scores*.

Educational achievement registered direct *Beta scores* which were both statistically significant and substantial in the case of each of the other six personal variables. They were positive only in the case of two variables, i.e. area of birth **(+.134)** and occupation **(+.363)**. The more highly educated were younger **(-.432)**, less religious **(-.250)**, less anomic **(-.256)** and less authoritarian **(-.320)**. These results were more or less as anticipated except for religiosity. The negative *Beta score* for 'religiosity' could result in a greater degree of religious fundamentalism in a fervent minority.

Occupational status failed to produce a significant *Beta score* in the case of four of the six personal variables, i.e. area of birth **(+.011)**, religiosity **(+.029)**, anomie **(+.025)** and authoritarianism **(+.001)**. The two variables which registered significant scores were age **(+.077)**, which was quite moderate, and education **(+.363)**, which was very substantial. The function of occupational status has proven to be a moderating influence throughout most of the tables in this research and tended to neutralise the negative impact of the age variable!

Religiosity has been measured by combining a number of variables, i.e. **'practice of prayer'**, **'perceived closeness to God'** and **'frequency of worship'**. It failed to elicit statistically significant *Beta scores* in the case of occupational status **(+.029)** and anomie **(+.029)**. The four personal variables with significant scores were quite substantial. Religiosity tends to be highest among older, more rural-born, lesser educated and the more authoritarian respondents.

The high direct *Beta score* **(+.437)** between **'Religiosity'** and **'Authoritarianism'** could mark a degree of **fundamentalism** among believers and active worshippers. It is also (as already noted) a reflection on the relatively negative influence of **education** on religious formation and practice. (See Chapter XVII, page 452.) People's level of sophistication in their religious teachings may not be commensurate with their level of rational self-consciousness and sophistication in knowledge and understanding of secular issues. Too great a separation between **education** and **religious teaching** can lead to an unacceptable level of religious fundamentalism, with its inevitably negative consequences for social cohesion and stability. Higher-level religious education of believers would contribute to lower levels of religious fundamentalism.

Social Anomie elicited a statistically significant *direct Beta score* in the case of three of the seven ordinal variables, i.e. 'area of birth' (**+.082**), 'educational achievement' (**-.256**) and 'authoritarianism' (**+.248**). It will be shown in the Tables reporting the *direct Beta scores* in relation to different measures of social prejudice that **social anomie** has become the most significant independent variable in the overall (see Tables Nos. 21.2, 21.3 and 21.4).

Authoritarianism is the variable at the end of the path in the above table. As already stated, when dealing with the previous personal variables, 'authoritarianism' had statistically significant and substantial *Beta scores* in the case of five of the six variables. Occupational status (**+.001**) failed to elicit a significant direct score. Age, religiosity and social anomie registered positive scores, i.e. **+.316**, **+.437** and **+.248** respectively. Area of birth and education have negative *Beta scores*, i.e. **-.223** and **-.320** respectively. There will be further commentary on the function of 'authoritarianism' later when dealing with the path analyses of a number of prejudice scores.

The findings of Table No. 21.1 tell the reader much about the **social and psychological profile** of a representative sample of the Irish adult population. The socio-cultural environment in the Republic of Ireland has been the dominant influence creating such a profile. The table measures the **interdependence** between the different ordinal variables. This always challenges the **illusion of singular causality** in relation to social attitudes and prejudices in society.

Part III – Path Analysis[2] of Different Areas of Prejudice

3.1 Beta Scores:

The application of path analysis of ordinal variables to different areas of social prejudice (as measured by social distance and *Likert-type scales*) is presented by combining the findings of Tables No. 21.1 and No. 21.2. This combination is presented in diagrammatic form on **Figure No. 21.2**, which gives the reader **an example** of how to link the two tables' findings in the case of 'ethnic prejudice'. Hopefully the reader will be able to envisage a diagrammatic presentation of each of the other ten special areas of prejudice (following the model presented in Figure No. 21.2).

Table No. 21.2[3] presents a most informative set of findings in relation to eleven areas of social prejudice. The measure of each area is arrived at by creating a dependent variable of *the collective mean-social-distance* scores of the various stimulus categories (in the subclass of categories), e.g. the collective mean-social-distance score of 'Arabs', 'Iranians', 'Israelis' and 'Palestinians' provide the variable for the subclass of categories designated **Middle-East Categories**. In the case of scales, the total scale prejudice scores are used, i.e. columns D, J and K. Statistically significant *Beta scores* (**0.070** and greater) are printed **in bold** on Table No. 21.2.

The above Table's findings are quite different to what was anticipated. This seems to be due largely to the unanticipated performance of the **age** and **education variables** and the weaker influence of the adjusted **authoritarian scale**. **Religiosity** had a weaker direct influence on prejudice than would be expected, considering the relatively positive *Beta score* (**+.451**) between age and religiosity, and the negative influence of education on religiosity (**-.250**) as shown in Figure No. 21.1 (page 560). **Social anomie** has been a quite significant positive (direct) influence (i.e. in the sense of increasing

---

[2] "**Path analysis** is a method for presenting a causal model in which a series of independent variables is used to predict a series of dependent variables… a set of computations needs to be done for each step of the model but the entire model can be shown in one diagram. The dependent variable changes with each phase of the process. The actual computations involve solving several sets of simultaneous equations formed by all or some of the correlations of the independent variables with each other and the correlations of each independent variable with the dependent variable. The results of these computations yield a numerical estimate of the effect of the independent variable on the dependent variable. The method of computation means that each estimate of direct effect, or path, is given with the effects of the other independent variables controlled." (Spaeth and Greally, 1970, quoted from Mac Gréil, 1977, page 501.)
[3] **Tables Nos. 21.3 and 21.4** (pages 572 and 576 below) give the *direct Beta scores* for specific stimulus categories.

Table No. 21.2:

Direct Beta Scores of Ordinal Variables in relation to Path Analysis of Social Prejudice

Independent Variable ↓ \ Dependent Variable →	Ethnic Prejudice A	Ethnico-Racial Prejudice B	Racial Stimulus Categories C	Racialist Scale D	Middle-East Categories E	Political Stimulus Categories F	Social Stimulus Categories G	Compulsive Behaviour Categories H	Religious Stimulus Categories I	Anti-Feminist Scale J	Anti-Traveller Scale K
Age	-.055	+.026	+.028	**+.130**	+.007	-.021	+.008	+.056	**+.070**	+.049	+.064
2. Area of Birth	-.013	**-.105**	**-.118**	-.058	-.057	-.053	-.013	-.013	**-.133**	-.003	**-.102**
3. Educational Achievement	-.041	**-.134**	**-.148**	**-.264**	**-.109**	**-.072**	+.015	-.031	**-.132**	**-.245**	+.010
4. Occupational Status	**-.136**	**-.129**	**-.122**	**-.180**	**-.158**	**-.172**	-.067	-.061	**-.173**	**-.161**	+.029
5. Religiosity	-.029	-.022	+.043	+.074	+.003	+.001	-.062	-.030	+.060	**+.094**	+.008
6. Social Anomie	**+.214**	**+.195**	**+.180**	**+.222**	**+.186**	**+.181**	**+.127**	**+.074**	**+.225**	**+.270**	+.003
7. Authoritarianism	+.054	**+.183**	**+.203**	**+.214**	**+.137**	**+.091**	+.042	+.040	**+.195**	**+.188**	**+.164**
R² =	*0.073*	*0.080*	*0.082*	*0.109*	*0.060*	*0.050*	*0.038*	*0.011*	*0.105*	*0.112*	*0.025*

Note: Statistically significant scores in **bold**, i.e. *Beta scores over .070*

The Final Analysis

Figure No. 21.2 Path Analysis: Ethnic Prejudice as a function of Age, Where Born, Education, Occupation, Religiosity, Anomie & Authoritarianism

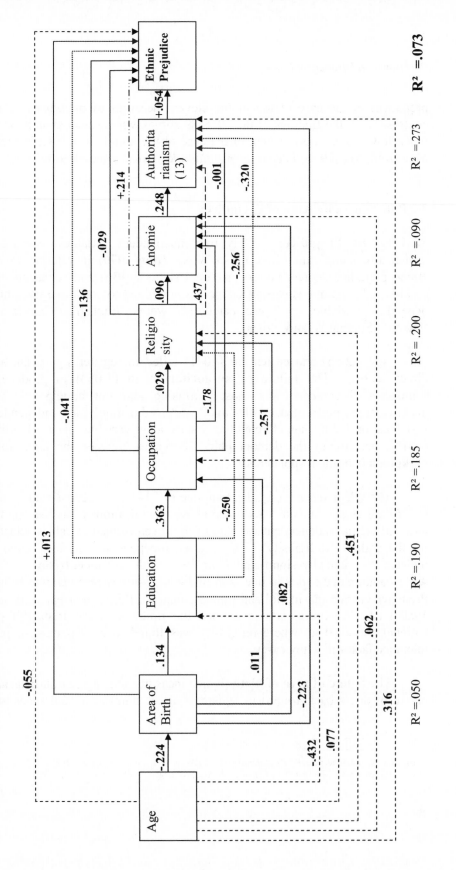

Note: Each area of prejudice reported on Tables Nos. 21.2, 3 and 4 may be presented in diagrammatic form by replacing the *direct Beta scores* on the lines above the centre inter-independent variables' path.

565

prejudice) in the case of ten of the eleven measures of prejudice. This contrasts with the findings of the 1988-89 survey when social anomie had a much lower *Beta score* except in the case of the anti-Traveller scale. (See Mac Gréil, M., (1996) *Prejudice in Ireland Revisited*, pages 459-462).

3.2 Beta Scores by Area of Prejudice:

3.2.1 Ethnic Prejudice: Only two independent variables recorded a statistically significant (direct) *Beta score* (**plus .070**) in relation to the ethnic prejudice scores, i.e. occupational status (-.136) and social anomie (+.214). The stimulus categories' scores combined to constitute the ethnic dependent variable. These categories were: 'English', 'Canadians', 'Dutch', 'Spaniards' and 'Poles'.

Age (-.055) and **education** (-.041) failed to register significant and direct scores. The failure of **authoritarianism** (+.054) to produce a significant *Beta score* was most surprising and not anticipated. The unanticipated performance of 'age' and 'education', as independent variables, probably has affected the independent variable **area of birth** (-.013), because of the demographic differences between the urban/rural backgrounds of the respondents.

The *Beta scores* of social anomie (+.214) and occupational status (-.136) are as anticipated. As noted above, **social anomie** has become the most influential independent variable of the seven ordinal variables selected for the path. 'Religiosity' (-.029), as an independent variable, failed to register a statistically significant *Beta score* with '**ethnocentrism**'. This was as anticipated and is in line with findings of survey research into Ethnic Prejudice carried out in Holland by R.N. Eisinga, P.L.N. Scheepers[4] (in the 1980s) and R. Konig[5] who examined the findings of the Irish 1988-89 national survey data, where religiosity was found to be a neutral or pro-tolerance factor in many cases.

The failure of **area of birth** (which measures the degree of urban/rural nature of one's background) to register a direct significant *Beta score* was

[4] Eisinga, R.N. and Scheepers, P.L.N., *Ethnocentrism in Nederland*, Nijmegen, I.T.S, 1989.
[5] Konig, Ruben, *Ethnocentrisme in Nederland en Ireland*, Nijmegen, Dept. of Sociologie, 1990.

not anticipated. These findings point to the very complex nature of causality in social and psychological research.

3.2.2 Ethnico-Racial Prejudice: This dependent variable consists of the mean-social-distance collective score of a group of seven stimulus categories classified as ethnico-racial, i.e. 'Chinese', 'Coloureds', 'Indians', 'Blacks', 'Africans', 'Pakistanis' and 'Nigerians'. The direct *Beta scores* are statistically significant in five of the seven independent variables, i.e. area of birth **(-.105)**, education **(-.134)**, occupational status **(-.129)**, social anomie **(+.195)** and authoritarianism **(+.183)**. The former three are negatively related to 'Ethnico-Racial Prejudice', while the latter two independent variables indicate a positive correlation. These findings confirm the author's anticipation (or hypotheses).

The failure of the age **(+.026)** and religiosity **(-.022)** independent variables to register statistically significant *Beta scores* are noteworthy. The performance of age was not anticipated while the neutrality of **religiosity** was expected in the light of previous research findings.

The difference in the path-analysis findings in relation to **Ethnic** and **Ethnico-Racial Prejudice** is significant. It highlights the impact of the 'racial factor' in the respondents' attitudes. Of course, the mean-social-distance scores of the former (Ethnic Prejudice) are **lower** than the latter (Ethnico-Racial Prejudice).

3.2.3 Racial Prejudice (Racial Social Distance): The two racial stimulus categories combined to create this dependent variable were: 'Blacks' and 'Coloureds'. Five of the seven independent variables elicited a statistically significant response. 'Area of birth', 'education' and 'occupation' produced direct negative *Beta scores*, i.e. **-.118, -.148** and **-.122** respectively. These were as anticipated. The more urbanised, the more educated and those with more highly statused occupations were less **racialist** than their opposites.

The failure of 'age' **(+.028)** and 'religiosity' **(+.043)** to register a statistically significant direct correlation with racial prejudice is noteworthy. The performance of age was not anticipated, while religiosity seemed to perform according to previous research [see Eisinga, *et al*, (1989) and Rubens (1990)].

3.2.4 Racialist Scale: This dependent variable (The Racialist Scale) has elicited statistically significant *Beta scores* in six of the seven independent variables. 'Area of birth' **(-.058)** has been the only exception. 'Religiosity' recorded a moderately positive correlation **(+.074)** with the findings of the 'Racialist Scale'. This was not anticipated.

'Education' **(-.264)** and 'occupational status' **(-.180)** registered negative *Beta scores* (i.e. the more educated and higher statused occupations meant the **lesser** the racialist prejudice as measured by the scale). These findings were anticipated.

'Age' **(+.130)**, 'social anomie' **(+.222)** and 'authoritarianism' **(+.214)** were as anticipated. It should be noted that the positive correlation between 'age' and 'racialism' was more moderate than anticipated because of the higher level of educational achievement of younger respondents than was the situation of older respondents. The performance of 'anomie' and 'authoritarianism' were very significant, especially the former. In the light of the level of 'social anomie' in the sample and its potentially negative effects on the personal and social lives of the people, there is a *prima facie* case for further research into this phenomenon!

3.2.5 Middle-East Stimulus Categories: This dependent variable combines the collective mean-social-distance of four stimulus categories, i.e. 'Arabs', 'Iranians', 'Israelis' and 'Palestinians'. Despite the relatively high MSD scores, three of the dependent variables failed to register statistically significant *Beta scores*, i.e. age **(+.007)**, area of birth **(-.057)** and religiosity **(+.003)**. The result with regard to 'age' and 'area of birth' were not anticipated.

The levels of significant direct *Beta scores* in the case of 'education' **(-.109)** and 'occupational status' **(-.158)** were negative as anticipated but lower than expected. 'Social anomie' **(+.186)** and 'authoritarianism' **(+.137)** were also anticipated, confirming the growing influence of 'social anomie' on social prejudice in Ireland.

3.2.6 Political Social Prejudice: This dependent variable has been made up of the collective mean-social-distance scores of six varied political stimulus categories, i.e. 'Capitalists', 'Communists', 'Gardaí', 'Socialists', 'Trade Unionists' and 'Unionists'. This group of categories has elicited a wide range of MSD scores as has already been noted (see Table No. 15.2, pages 376-7).

Three independent variables failed to elicit statistically significant (direct) *Beta scores* in relation to political prejudice, i.e. 'age' **(-.021),** 'area of birth' **(-.053)** and 'religiosity' **(+.001).**   This result has been influenced by the wide **range** of categories and the mutual influence of 'age' and 'area of birth'.   The finding in relation to 'religiosity' was anticipated.

There was a very moderate negative *Beta score* between 'education' **(-.072)** and political prejudice.   The low level of the score was not expected. 'Occupational status' **(-.172)** negative score was more substantial than 'education' and was in line with expectations.   The substantially positive scores for 'social anomie' were higher than expected once again, confirming the growing significance between 'social anomie' *direct Beta score* **(+.181)** and   another   class   of   social   prejudice.   The   performance   of 'authoritarianism' **(+.091)** was anticipated with regard to direction but not expected to be so moderate.

3.2.7 Social Stimulus Categories: This dependent variable consists of the collective MSD scores of nine social stimulus categories, i.e.

'Alcoholics',	*'People with Mental Disability'*
'Drug Addicts',	*'People with Physical Disability'*
'Gay People'	*'Unemployed'*
'Heavy Drinkers'	*'Unmarried Mothers'* and
	'Working Class

Their range of mean-social-distance goes from 'in-group' to 'out-group', i.e. from **under 1.500** to **over 3.500** (in a 1 to 7 range).

Six of the seven independent variables failed to get a statistically significant *direct Beta score*, i.e. 'age' **(+.008),** 'area of birth' **(-.013),** 'education' **(+.015),** 'occupational status' **(-.067),** 'religiosity' **(-.062)** and 'authoritarianism' **(+.042).**   This performance goes to emphasise that prejudice and tolerance are **selective** dispositions in response to stimulus categories.   The nine categories are so varied (as the above list shows) that they seem to neutralise each other in regard to social distance as an indicator of social prejudice when treated as a single dependent variable.   In column H on Table No. 21.2 three of the nine stimulus categories classified as *social* are combined into one 'dependent variable' and commented on in the next paragraph, i.e. 3.2.8.

The one independent variable to register a significant *Beta score* has been **Social Anomie** (+.127) which, in itself, is significant and re-emphasises the importance of the direct link between prejudice and 'social anomie'. The prominence of 'social anomie' as an independent variable has increased from what it was in the 1988-89 national survey. In a sense, prejudice seems to be *a symptom of social anomie*!

3.2.8 Compulsive Behaviour Categories: This dependent variable is made up of the mean collective MSD of three (social) stimulus categories, i.e. 'Alcoholics', 'Drug Addicts' and 'Heavy Drinkers'. Of the fifty-one stimulus categories on the *Bogardus Social Distance Table*, these three ranked extremely low on the rank order of preference list, i.e. 'Heavy Drinkers' (**40th**), 'Alcoholics' (**48th**) and 'Drug Addicts' (**51st**).

The performance of 'Compulsive Behaviour Categories' as a dependent variable on Table No. 21.2 replicated that of the 'Social Stimulus Categories' variable with only one independent variable eliciting a statistically significant variation in the *Beta scores*, i.e. Social Anomie. The reasons in this case are probably different. Does this indicate a high degree of negative consensus in relation to Compulsive Behaviour Categories? It would appear so!

Independent variables failing to reach the level of significance **(.070 plus)** almost replicated the previous independent variables, i.e. age **(+.056)**, area of birth **(-.013)**, education **(-.031)**, occupational status **(-.061)**, religiosity **(-.030)** and authoritarianism **(+.040)**. These findings were not anticipated. Are we seeing here a high degree of negative consensus?

The performance by **'Social Anomie'** (**+.074**) was significant but moderately low. The overall relevance of these *direct Beta scores* for the rehabilitation of the three 'Compulsive Behaviour' stimulus categories raises very serious questions with regard to the impact of public attitudes enabling the recovery of persons who may become addicted to alcohol and drugs! This confirms the performance of the individual stimulus categories, i.e. 'Heavy Drinkers', 'Alcoholics' and 'Drug Addicts' on the correlation matrix, Table No. 12.5 (page 289), where 'Compulsive Behaviour Categories' failed to cluster with other social categories.

3.2.9 General Religious Prejudice: In this dependent variable, the mean-social-distance scores of religious groups and non-believers are combined, i.e. 'Agnostics', 'Atheists', 'Jews', 'Muslims', 'Protestants' and 'Roman Catholics'.   The level of *direct Beta scores* is expected to be reduced because of the possible difference of attitudes towards 'believers' and 'non-believers'.   The following Table No. 21.3 gives the *direct Beta scores* for 'Christians', 'Muslims' and 'Non-believers', while Table No. 21.4 gives the *direct Beta scores* for 'Jews'.

Returning to Table No. 21.2, it is shown that only one independent variable failed to register a statistically significant *direct Beta score* in the case of Religious Categories measured together namely, **Religiosity** (+.060), which was not anticipated.   The performance of the variable on Table No. 21.3 gives an insight into its neutrality in relation to the mix of religious categories on Table No. 21.2.

While significant, the *Beta score* for 'age' **(+.070)** was much lower than expected.   The performance of the **18 to 25 year-olds** in the various social distance tables was against the trends anticipated and probably contributed to the low *Beta score* of 'age' on Table No. 21.2.   'Area of birth' **(-.133)**, 'education' **(-.132)** and 'occupational status' **(-.173)** were also more moderate than expected, although they were **in the direction** anticipated.   The more urbanised, more highly educated and those with more highly statused occupations proved to be more tolerant in their attitudes toward diverse religious stimulus categories taken together.

'Social anomie' **(+.225)** and 'authoritarianism' **(+.195)** returned moderately strong *direct Beta scores* on Table No. 21.2, which confirms the importance of both independent variables in explaining some of the causes of religious prejudice in society.   When one reflects on the mutual influence of 'social anomie' on 'authoritarianism' **(+.248)** on Table No. 21.1 (page 559), the importance of the two variables is confirmed.   Further research into the **causes** of 'social anomie' (as a sociological trait) and 'authoritarianism' (as a psychological trait) should be a priority objective for those interested in promoting and maintaining a tolerant and pluralist society.

3.2.10 Special Religious Categories: Before leaving the dependent variable measuring Religious Social Distance, it is worthwhile to examine the subject in greater detail.   Table No. 21.3 reports the **direct** *Beta scores* of Christian categories, 'Muslims' and Non-Believers ('Agnostics' and 'Atheists'). The findings show a relatively dynamic result, which tell the reader some valuable information about religious prejudice and tolerance in Ireland.

Table No. 21.3: Direct Beta Scores of Christians, Muslims and Non-Believers by Ordinal Independent Variables

Dependent Variable → / Independent Variable ↓	Christian Categories	'Muslims'	Non-Believers
	'Protestants' And 'Roman Catholics' A.	B.	'Agnostics' and 'Atheists' C.
1. Age	-.151	+.080	+.132
2. Area of Birth	+.026	-.060	-.196
3. Education	+.057	-.109	-.180
4. Occupational Status	-.119	-.110	-.150
5. Religiosity	-.113	+.004	+.143
6. Social Anomie	+.184	+.179	+.181
7. Authoritarianism	+.001	+.148	+.246
R^2	$R^2 = .081$	$R^2 = .049$	$R^2 = .117$

Notes: 1. Statistically significant scores in **bold**, i.e. score **.070 plus**.
2. *Direct Beta scores* for 'Jews' are reported on Table No. 21.4 (see page 576).

(a) Christian Categories: There are moderately high negative *Beta scores* for 'age' **(-.151)**, 'occupational status' **(-.119)** and 'religiosity' **(-.113)**. In regard to 'age', the older are more tolerant. In the case of 'occupational status', the result was as expected. Those with a higher occupational status were better disposed to Christian Categories. 'Religiosity' confirmed that the more religious were more tolerant. 'Social anomie' **(+.184)** once again, established its strong negative influence on social (religious) tolerance. 'Area of birth' **(+.026)**, 'education' **(+.057)** and 'authoritarianism' **(+.001)** did not produce statistically significant scores.

(b) 'Muslims': The *direct Beta scores* for 'Muslims' are as anticipated. Area of birth **(-.060)** and religiosity **(+.004)** failed to register statistically significant *direct Beta scores*. Social anomie **(+.179)** and authoritarianism

(**+.148**) produced moderately high pro-prejudice scores against 'Muslims'. 'Age' (**+.080**), 'education' (**-109**) and 'occupational status' (**-.110**) produced significant *Beta scores* in line with anticipations. The scores were more moderate than expected. Younger respondents, the better educated and those with higher-statused occupations tended to be more tolerant towards 'Muslims'.

(**c**) **Non-Believers**: This has been the dependent variable to elicit the strongest *direct Beta scores* with trends as expected. Each of the seven independent variables reacted strongly to **'Agnostics' and 'Atheists'** as a combined religious variable. Irish society (as represented by the respondents) is much divided in their attitudes here. It is one of the rare times that religiosity (**+.143**) produced so definite a pro-prejudiced response. Area of birth (**-.196**), education (**-.180**) and occupational status (**-.150**) were strongly negative towards this form of prejudice. Age (**+.132**), social anomie (**+.181**) and authoritarianism (**+.246**) were strongly positive.

In summary, therefore, those most tolerant towards **'Agnostics'** and **'Atheists'** tend to be younger, more educated, more urbanised, with higher statused occupations, less religious, less anomic and less authoritarian. This result is in line with expectations. The level of difference indicated in the *direct Beta scores* is such as to raise concern about the level of intolerance towards non-believers at a time when more people seem to profess their non-belief publicly. Tolerance towards 'non-believers' needs to be on the agenda of religious groups and associations in a country where faith is still a seriously held part of most people! Prejudice is a poor expression of any religion! For some believers religious endogamy is a genuinely held disposition but will be more difficult to maintain in a more diverse society.

3.2.11 The (Anti) Feminist Scale: Returning to Table No. 21.2, the 'Anti-Feminist Scale' has elicited an interesting response. Five of the independent variables, i.e. 'education' (**-.245**), 'occupational status' (**-.161**), 'religiosity' (**+.094**), 'social anomie' (**+.270**) and 'authoritarianism' (**+.188**), registered statistically significant *direct Beta scores*. Apart from **religiosity**, which has a moderately **low anti-feminist score**, the remaining four variables were moderately high. Again, 'social anomie' and 'authoritarianism' were quite influential **anti-feminist** independent variables. 'Education' recorded a moderately strong **pro-feminist** score, which was to be expected. 'Occupational status' returned a moderately high

pro-feminist score. 'Age' (**+.049**) and 'area of birth' (**-.003**) failed to elicit a significant *direct Beta score* with 'anti-feminism'.

The above findings indicate that **feminism** is still a live issue in Ireland today. The indications are that the levels of anti-feminism are likely to reduce in the future. The relatively **high** *direct Beta score* for 'social anomie' (**+.270**) is a matter of concern at a time when it is likely to increase[6]. Also the direct influence of authoritarianism (**+.188**) and anti-feminism is as anticipated. As in the case of attitudes towards 'non-believers' ('Agnostics' and 'Atheists'), the results of the **Anti-Feminist Scale** on Table No. 21.2, indicate a dynamic set of attitudes which need to be monitored. The Feminist Movement should take them on board and foster institutional (normative) support!

3.2.12 Anti-Traveller Scale: The relatively low direct *Beta scores* in response to the 'Anti-Traveller Scale' were not anticipated. This would seem to point, once again, to *a level of consensus in the negativity of Irish attitudes towards Travellers*, i.e. prejudices towards the country's oldest indigenous ethnic minority, 'The Travelling People'. This could add to the difficulty facing the Travellers' emancipation.

The independent variables failing to score .070 or higher were: 'age' (**+.064**), 'education' (**+.010**), 'occupational status' (**+.029**), 'religiosity' (**+.008**) and 'social anomie' (**+.003**). The failure of **'social anomie'** to register a statistically significant *direct Beta score* in relation to the 'Anti-Traveller Scale' has been unique. It was the only measure of social prejudice on Table No. 21.2 not to do so! From examining Table No. 12.5 on page 289, one gets a similarly **unique** pattern of attitudes towards Travellers.

'Area of birth' (**-.102**) and 'authoritarianism' (**+.164**) were the two independent variables to register statistically significant *direct Beta scores*. The negative score for 'area of birth' confirms the finding that the more positive attitudes towards Travellers are among those born in cities and towns rather than among respondents of rural origin. The trend in

---

[6] In times of rapid social change and a weakening of institutional norms to support people through social and personal problems, *a sense of normlessness* tends to become more prevalent. The weakening of *family*, *local community* and *religion* (as institutions) in society can result in an increase in 'social anomie', especially among the youth and young adults.

'authoritarianism' scores is as expected establishing the moderately positive correlation between this personality trait and anti-Traveller prejudice.

3.2.13 Conclusion: In the course of the above twelve sub-paragraphs the direct influence on variations is examined in the case of ten main areas of social prejudice (with two measures of racism, i.e. prejudice against **racial stimulus categories** and that measured by the special **Racialist Scale**). The findings of Table No. 21.2 give the path-analysis *direct Beta scores* of seven independent ordinal variables, i.e. 'age', 'area of birth' (rural-urban), 'education', 'occupational status', 'religiosity', 'social anomie' and 'authoritarianism'. The examination of **three special religious** dependent variables proved most enlightening.

The *Beta scores* give the direct correlation between independent and dependent variables, i.e. the areas of prejudice, having controlled the influence of other intervening independent variables. The information provided gives the researcher a better insight into the **multiple causes** of particular areas of prejudice and of prejudice in general. Without some understanding of **the actual causes of social prejudice** it is not possible to bring about changes in institutions and behaviour likely to replace it with tolerant norms and favourable social behaviour. Hopefully the above information and analysis will help bring about necessary changes that will lead to an increase of tolerance.

3.3 Path Analysis of Specific Prejudices:
Because of their importance in the history of social prejudice, it was decided to examine the direct *Beta scores* of three specific categories, i.e.

(1) Jews (Anti-Semitism);
(2) Gay People (Homophobia);
(3) Romanians (incorporating Anti-Romany prejudice).

Anti-Semitism has been one of the most enduring of all intergroup prejudices. As a minority, Jews have suffered enormously. They have provided an **ideal scapegoat** to be exploited by ruthless political leaders down the ages, e.g. their 'genocidal slaughter' by the German Third Reich in the 1940s.

Homophobia, i.e. prejudice against homosexual or 'Gay People' is also a pernicious form of social prejudice which has led to the persecution of homosexuals by political and religious authorities throughout the world. Incidents of **'Gay Bashing'** and **'blackmail'** of 'Gay People' have resulted in gross injustice. In addition, psychological pain and frustration are also suffered by 'Gay People' relating to personal sexual self-identity. For these and other reasons, the marked improvement in public attitudes reported in this text is to be greatly welcomed.

Romanians are citizens of a member country of the European Union. **Romany Gypsies** come from Romania and elsewhere in Eastern Europe. It would appear from the findings of the 2007-08 survey that attitudes towards 'Romanians' were quite negative and in breach of the *principle of propinquity* (see pages 108 and 144). Because of the precarious position of Romany migrants to Ireland and throughout Europe (especially France where many have been deported) it was necessary to find out the *direct Beta scores* of the stimulus category, 'Romanians'[7].

Table No. 21.4:
Direct Beta Scores for 'Jews', 'Gay People' and 'Romanians'

Dependent Variable → / Independent Variable ↓	'Jews' A	'Gay People' B	'Romanians' C
1. Age	.000	+.061	+.010
2. Area of Birth	**-.092**	**-.165**	**-.077**
3. Education	**-.121**	**-.079**	-.060
4. Occupational Status	**-.178**	**-.101**	**-.078**
5. Religiosity	+.018	+.052	-.016
6. Social Anomie	**+.200**	**+.125**	**+.191**
7. Authoritarianism	**+.136**	**+.157**	**+.152**
R^2	$R^2 = .079$	$R^2 = .062$	$R^2 = .066$

Note: Statistically significant *Beta scores* (.070 plus) are in **bold**.

---

[7] See: *The Irish Times*, 30.9.2010 reporting on the response of the **European Union** to the unilateral behaviour of France in relation to Roma people.

3.3.1 Direct Beta Scores with 'Jews':   Table No. 21.4 gives the *direct Beta scores* for 'Jews' as a stimulus category.   Two of the seven independent variables failed to register a statistically significant *direct Beta score*, i.e. age **(.000)** and religiosity **(+.018)**.   The former was not anticipated, as a significantly negative score was expected.

This neutral result by **age** is probably due to the surprise finding of the youngest subsample (18 to 25 year-olds) being more prejudiced in the social distance scores than other age groups (see Table No. 17.20, pages 470-2). The response of **religiosity**, being not significant, may help to remove or weaken the popular association of Christian belief (or Roman Catholic belief in the case of the Republic of Ireland) with anti-Semitism!

With regard to the independent variables registering statistically significant *Beta scores*, they performed as expected, i.e. area of birth **(-.092)**, education **(-.121)**, occupational status **(-.178)**, social anomie **(+.200)** and authoritarianism **(+.136)**.   The negative scores for 'area of birth' and 'education' were not as high as expected, probably because of the score for 'age'.   In the overall it means that younger people, those of urban background, better educated and those with higher occupational status tend to be less anti-Semitic.

Social anomie's relatively high positive score **(+.200)** in relation to anti-Jewish prejudice is yet another manifestation of the (growing) importance of this independent variable's influence on social prejudice.   (It is replacing **authoritarianism** as the major independent variable in influencing social prejudice in most of the dependent variables tested in this chapter.)   This is not to say that 'authoritarianism' **(+.136)** has not been a moderately high influence on the *anti-Semitism* of respondents.   Because of the reduction of the proportion of the Irish population who are 'Jews', the people's favourable contact is of necessity reduced.   The concentration of Europe's Jews in Israel, while understandable, may make the Irish people's attitudes towards Jews more dependent on Israel's public reputation (in Ireland)!

3.3.2 Homophobia: One of the stimulus categories to experience a very substantial increase in tolerance has been **'Gay People'** (see Table Nos. 12.1 and 12.2, page 264 and pages 266-7).   That being noted, there still remains an unacceptable level of homophobia in the findings, i.e. only **62.3%**

'welcoming into the family' and **5.3%** 'denying citizenship'. There is room for improvement in the above percentages.

Two of the independent variables failed to reach a *direct Beta score* of *Rho = 0.070*, i.e. 'age' **(+.061)** and 'religiosity' **(+.052)**. The performance of 'age' was not expected. This is probably due to the more prejudiced attitudes of the '18 to 25 year-olds' in Table No. 12.2 (pages 266-7). The fact that religiosity's score was, once again, not significant, was interesting and should help to deflate somewhat the association of this independent variable with anti-gay attitudes. The now-repealed 'Victorian' legislation criminalising homosexual behaviour between consenting male adults seemed to have religious undertones in the views of many!

Of the five independent variables with significant *direct Beta scores* in column B above, 'education' **(-.079)** was quite moderate as was 'occupational status' **(-.101)**. 'Area of birth' **(-.165)**, 'social anomie' **(+.125)** and 'authoritarianism' **(+.157)** were moderately high in their *Beta scores*. These results are fairly standard. Respondents, who were more urbanised, more educated, with more highly statused occupations, less anomic and less authoritarian, were more tolerant towards 'Gay People'.

3.3.3 'Romanians': The position of 'Romanians' as a stimulus category was placed below its expected position on the rank order of categories (see Table No. 4.1, pages 62-4). At 39th (out of 51), this category was placed eleven places below **'Lithuanians'** (28th) and sixteen places below **'Poles'** (23rd). This breach of the *principle of propinquity* and relatively negative MSD score of **2.566**, i.e. only **55.6%** 'welcoming to kinship' and **16.7%** willing to 'deny citizenship', must raise the alarm bells of **serious ethnic prejudice** against citizens of a fellow-member state of the European Union.

It has been less than seventy years since **Romany Gypsies**, who are seen as of Romanian origin, were persecuted as a result of the violent xenophobic policies of the German Third Reich. Are we in Ireland showing signs of a milder form of these same prejudices against Romany people, expressed in our heavy ethnic prejudice against 'Romanians'? The findings of this research should put us on our guard.

Column C of Table No. 21.4 gives the *direct Beta scores* of seven independent variables towards 'Romanians'. Three of the seven variables, i.e. 'age' **(+.010)**, 'education' **(-.060)** and 'religiosity' **(-.016)** failed to reach statistical significance. In the case of 'age' and 'education', this consensus in heavy prejudice is a most disappointing result. It was anticipated that these variables would produce significantly negative direct scores against prejudice towards 'Romanians', with younger, better educated and more religious respondents more tolerant. The neutrality of 'religiosity', nevertheless, was anticipated. Many committed religious believers will be disappointed at the neutrality of 'religiosity', considering the positive role of Religious throughout the world in the liberation of minorities!

'Area of birth' **(-.077)** and 'occupational status' **(-.078)** produced **moderately low** negative direct scores, which indicated the more urbanised and the higher statused occupations were (moderately) less prejudiced against 'Romanians'. 'Social anomie' **(+.191)** and 'authoritarianism' **(+.152)**, once again, registered relatively high *direct* (positive) *Beta scores*, which points to the strong influence between 'social anomie' and 'authoritarianism' and anti-Romanian prejudice. It would appear from these findings that one of the most effective ways to contribute to the increase of tolerance would be to address the causes of 'social anomie' and 'authoritarianism'.

Part IV – Patterns of Social Distance

In this part of Chapter XXI it is proposed to examine the patterns of social distance between the **fifty-one stimulus categories**. Some readers, not familiar with correlation coefficients, may have some difficulty with the full meaning of the findings given on Table No. 21.5. The score range goes from zero to one. The minimum required for statistical significance is *Rho = 0.20*. Scores below that are reported on the tables as **n/s** (not significant). The higher the *Rho* score, the more similar the patterns of social distance between the two stimulus categories correlated. For example, the patterns of social distance in relation to 'Iranians' and 'Israelis' appear to be almost identical with their *Rho = 0.90*.

4.1 Overall Correlations:

In Part II of Chapter VI, the inter-category correlations for *Ethnic, Ethnico-Racial* and *Racial stimulus categories* were presented on Table No. 6.7 [following the more specific presentation of the sub-classes of categories (see pages 106 to 111)]. In Part V of Chapter XII a similar exercise was carried out in the case of *Political, Religious* and *Social stimulus categories* (see Table No. 12.5, page 289). Table No. 6.7 examined the mutual correlations of 29 categories, while 22 are contained in Table No. 12.5.

The Table presented in ***Appendix B*** brings together **all** of the fifty-one stimulus categories tested by the *Bogardus Social Distance Scale* and reported on Table No. 4.1 (see pages 62-4). Stimulus categories are presented in **alphabetical order**, i.e. as listed on the questionnaire originally. The findings presented in Appendix B tell the social researcher much about the patterns of attitudes of respondents towards the different categories. Their (the categories') clustering together in their *Rho* scores confirms a number of interesting issues. Three factors are confirmed, i.e. the *principle of propinquity*, the importance of *intergroup perception* and the survival of the *racial issue* in Irish people's prejudices and preferences. The latter is confirmed, despite the low level of racial rationalisation (see Chapter V, pages 85 ff).

4.1.1 High Correlations: Ten of the correlations recorded very high *Rho* **scores of 0.80 plus**. The following **extract** from Appendix B identifies the highly correlated stimulus categories.

Stimulus Categories Correlation			Rho Score	Stimulus Categories Correlation			Rho Score
1. 'Iranians'	with	'Israelis'	0.90	6. 'Blacks'	with	'Coloureds'	0.82
2. 'Afro-Americans'	with	'Blacks'	0.89	7. 'Agnostics'	with	'Atheists'	0.81
3. 'Pakistanis'	with	'Palestinians'	0.89	8. 'Iranians	with	'Palestinians'	0.81
4. 'Africans'	with	'Afro-Americans'	0.84	9. 'Israelis'	with	'Palestinians'	0.81
5. 'Africans'	with	'Blacks'	0.83	10. 'Afro-Americans'	with	'Coloureds'	0.80

The groupings which dominate the above shortlist of very high *Rho* scores *(0.80 plus)* are **Ethnic/Racial** (5) and **Middle-East** (4) categories. The correlation between **'Agnostics'** and **'Atheists'** were the only other pair to join the ranks of the *0.81 plus* categories. Racial, ethnico-political and religious **propinquity** is also confirmed in the findings of the above extract from Appendix B.

Despite respondents' relatively high level of 'colour blindness', as expressed in their low degree of racial rationalisation (see Table No. 5.1, pages 86-7), it is clear that **race** is still a serious factor in the dispositions of the respondents.   The contrast between the correlations between 'Afro-Americans' and 'Euro-Americans (**0.37**) and that between 'Afro-Americans' and 'Africans'/'Blacks' (**0.84/0.89**) confirms the implicit influence of race on Irish attitudes.   This is part of the dilemma between *explicit 'colour blindness'* and *'implicit racialism'* which may have its origin in the **European Enlightenment** of the 18th century!

The clustering of the **Middle-East categories** was already discussed in Chapter VI (pages 103ff).   The similarity of attitude patterns towards 'Israelis', 'Palestinians', 'Iranians' and 'Arabs' reflects the closeness of negative scores in respondents' willingness to *deny them citizenship*, i.e. 'Israelis' (**22.2%**), 'Iranians' (**22.1%**), 'Arabs' (**20.8%**) and 'Palestinians' (**19.1%**).   The latent negative impact of the Middle-East Troubles is its inevitable effect on attitudes towards 'Jews' and 'Muslims'. The correlation *Rho scores* between 'Iranians' and 'Muslims' was high at **0.78** while the correlation between 'Israelis' and 'Jews' was moderately high at **0.64**.

These results call for greater constructive dialogue between *Christians, Jews* and *Muslims* and for greater urgency in arriving at a just and peaceful resolution to the current Israeli-Palestinian problem.   The possibility of a revival of *anti-Semitism* and continued *'Muslim phobia'* are likely unless the **United Nations** exercises greater effective influence in bringing about a lasting and fair settlement of the *Middle-East conflict*.   It is the opinion of this author that Irish attitudes expressed in this text are fairly representative of attitudes and opinions throughout Europe and the whole Western World.   It has already been shown that non-Irish-born respondents had similar attitudes in a number of related areas.

4.1.2 Low Correlations: At the other end of the spectrum (cases of *Rho scores* under **0.20**) four stimulus categories account for 90% of the non-significant (N/S) scores.   In all there were **fifty-nine** correlation coefficients in the NS range.   This represents **4.6%** of the 1,275 correlation coefficients in Appendix B.

The four stimulus categories with the highest numbers of non-significant scores were: 'Roman Catholics', 'Drug Addicts', 'Alcoholics' and 'Heavy Drinkers'.

		Scores under 0.20	Scores over 0.50
	'Roman Catholics'	18	0
Compulsive	'Drug Addicts'	20	2
Behaviour	'Alcoholics'	8	2
Categories	'Heavy Drinkers'	6	2

The above **extract** from Appendix B points to the special pattern of attitudes (negative) towards members of the **'compulsive behaviour categories'**. Serious psychological and sociological research is required to explain such a unique attitudinal phenomenon. As pointed out in Chapter XII when examining Irish attitudes towards 'compulsive behaviour categories' (who were **victims** of addiction) very negative attitudes were reported in Table No. 12.1 (page 264), i.e. 'Heavy Drinkers' (deny citizenship = **13.6%**), 'Alcoholics' (deny citizenship = **14.5%**) and 'Drug Addicts' (deny citizenship = **33.7%**). These attitudes are likely to impede rehabilitation. The two cases of **+0.50** score for each category were **internal** to the three compulsive-behaviour categories.

The lack of higher correlation scores between **'Roman Catholics'** and other stimulus categories points to the unique pattern of attitudes to this **most preferred** stimulus category. The exceptionally low mean-social-distance of **1.168** (on a 1 to 7 scale) with **91.1%** welcoming Roman Catholics into kinship and less than **1%** (**0.6%**) willing to deny them citizenship means that the range for variation is very limited (see Table No. 4.1, pages 62-4). Some public commentators may find this result **strangely positive** towards 'Roman Catholics' in the light of recent clerical abuse scandals and negative media reporting by commentators in relation to the Roman Catholic Church since the early 1990s!

4.2 Correlation Coefficients' Scores over Rho = 0.50 plus:
Correlations with *Rho scores* 0.50 plus could be classified as moderately high and higher. In all some 401 (or **31.5%**) of the correlation coefficients in Appendix B had a *Rho score* of **0.50 plus**. Table No. 21.5 lists the stimulus categories registering these scores by the number of pairings in question.

An examination of this table tells the reader and the researcher much about the patterns of the respondents' social-distance scoring. For instance, stimulus categories with *multiple rationalisations* would be expected to attract higher numbers of **0.50 plus** scores (see Table No. 5.8, page 98). The *principle of propinquity* should also be confirmed in the findings of Table No. 21.5. Finally, the *level of mean-social-distance* would also affect the number and levels of correlation scores.

Table No. 21.5: Stimulus Categories by Number of Correlation Scores 0.50 plus

	Stimulus Category	Number		Stimulus Category	Number
1	'Jews' +	28	26	'Capitalists' o	17
2	'Russians' *	28	27	'French' *	17
3	'Lithuanians' *	26	28	'Welsh' *	17
4	'Chinese' **	25	29	'Canadians' *	15
5	'Indians' **	25	30	'Protestants' +	15
6	'Spaniards' *	25	31	'Scottish' *	15
7	'Afro-Americans' **	24	32	'Trade Unionists' o	15
8	'Palestinians' *	24	33	'Euro-Americans' **	14
9	'Atheists' +	23	34	'Italians' *	14
10	'Nigerians' **	23	35	'Working Class' oo	14
11	'Pakistanis' **	23	36	'Germans' *	13
12	'Romanians' *	23	37	'Unemployed' oo	12
13	'Africans' **	22	38	'English' *	10
14	'Arabs' *	22	39	'British' *	7
15	'Blacks' ***	22	40	'Gardaí' o	7
16	'Poles' *	22	41	'Irish Speakers' *	7
17	'Unionists' o	22	42	'Unmarried Mothers' oo	6
18	'Communists' o	22	43	'People with Physical Disab.' oo	4
19	'Iranians' *	21	44	'Gay People' oo	3
20	'Muslims' +	21	45	'Northern Irish' *	3
21	'Agnostics' +	21	46	'Alcoholics' oo	2
22	'Coloureds' ***	20	47	'Drug Addicts' oo	2
23	'Dutch' *	20	48	'Heavy Drinkers' oo	2
24	'Israelis' *	20	49	'Travellers' oo	1
25	'Socialists' o	18	50	'People with Mental Disab.' oo	0
			51	'Roman Catholics' +	0

TOTAL = 802 (or 401 correlations)

Note:
*	=Ethnic	+ = Religious	
**	=Ethnico-Racial	o = Political	
***	=Racial	oo = Social Category	

583

The distribution of correlations with *Rho scores* of 0.50 plus on Table No. 21.5 is more or less as expected.

General Distribution of Scores

Range		No.	Percentage	
25 – 29	=	6	11.8%	} 47.1%
20 – 24	=	18	35.3%	
15 - 19	=	8	15.7%	} 27.5%
10 - 14	=	6	11.8%	
5 - 9	=	4	7.8%	} 21.5%
1 - 4	=	7	13.7%	
0	=	2	3.9%	} 3.9%
Total	=	**51**	**100%**	

The distribution of scores as shown on the above extract from Table No. 21.5 reflects the predominance of *ethnic* (20), *ethnico-racial* (7) and *racial* (2) categories, i.e. a total of 29. The three remaining general classifications, i.e. *political* (6), *religious* (6) and *social* (10), account for the remaining 22 stimulus categories and are quite diverse in their popularity (MSD scores) and in character.

'Jews' and 'Russians' produced the highest number of correlations of 0.50 plus (28). This reflects their multi-rationalisation on Table No. 5.1 where 'Jews' were perceived primarily as a 'religious' category (31.3%), as an 'ethnic/cultural' category (25.1%) and as a category with a special 'way of life' (25.3%). This would give them an association with a broad range of categories, as in the case of 'Russians' who had four significant rationalisations, i.e. 'political' (10.5%), 'ethnic/cultural' (36.0%), 'economic' (10.1%) and 'way of life' (26.1%).

The categories with ethnico-racial identities seemed to feature predominantly in the score range of 23-25, i.e. six of the seven ethnico-racial categories ['Euro-Americans' seemed to cluster with European (white) ethnic categories]. The Middle-East stimulus categories, i.e. 'Palestinians' (24), 'Arabs' (22), 'Iranians' (21) and 'Israelis' (20), all cluster closely together.

The European Ethnic stimulus categories seemed to cluster on the middle range of numbers, i.e. 'Lithuanians' (26), 'Spaniards' (25), 'Romanians' (23), 'Poles' (22), 'Dutch' (20), 'French' (17), 'Welsh' (17), 'Scottish' (15), 'Italians' (14), 'Germans' (13), 'English' (10), 'British' (7), 'Irish Speakers' (7) and 'Northern Irish' (3). The latter four categories are somewhat out-of-line with the eight European ethnic categories. It is interesting to see how close the numbers of **0.50 plus** score of 'Canadians' (15) and 'Euro-Americans' (white Americans) (14) are to those of the English, Scottish and Welsh in the minds of the Irish respondents. The position of 'Northern Irish' is quite unique and does not seem to cluster with any group except the Celtic Ethnic categories.

The performance of the various stimulus categories is obviously determined by the numbers of categories sharing similar classification. Hence, the proportionately high numbers for ethnico-racial and multiple classifications. The factor analysis on Table No. 21.6 regroups the stimulus categories in line with their correlations.

Part V – Clustering of Stimulus Categories into Factors

The following Table (No. 21.6) reports on the findings of a Factor Analysis of the mean-social-distance responses to 51 stimulus categories.

Table No. 21.6 confirms the validity and reliability of the *Bogardus Social Distance Scale* and the consistency of respondents' replies through the bringing together of stimulus categories according to the *principle of propinquity* in most cases. When compared with the Factor Clusterings of the stimulus categories in the 1988-89 national survey, the main patterns are repeated with a number of exceptions (see Mac Gréil, M., *Prejudice in Ireland Revisited*, 1996, Table No. 10, page 90).

5.1 *Factor One*: brings together fifteen 'ethnico-racial' categories largely from Africa, Asia, Middle-East and Eastern Europe, including Afro-Americans and two 'racial' categories, i.e. 'Blacks' and 'Coloureds'. This, once again, highlights the significant presence of the *implicit racial factor* present in the respondents' attitudes/prejudices over a wide range of (ethnic) rationalisations. The inclusion of four **religious** and two **politico-economic** categories (i.e. ideologies) repeats the 1988-89 pattern in the case of the former (religious) group of categories. In the perception of respondents there are probably some common features not easy to detect very clearly. Of course, the level of MSD scores can also influence the clustering of categories.

Table No. 21.6: Factor Analysis Clusterings of Stimulus Variables
(Rotated Component Matrix – + 0.5 correlations)

Factor I		Factor 2		Factor 3		Factor 4		Non-Clustering Categories
Ethnico-Racial/ Religious/ Politico-Economic		Ethnic (White)/ Social		People with Handicap/ Miscellaneous		Compulsive Behaviour		
(al) Ethnico-Racial (E-R)		**(a) Ethnic (White)**		**(a) People with Handicap**				
Africans	0.814	British	0.623	Physical h/c	0.656	Alcoholics	0.725	Gay Ppl *(5)
Afro-American	0.802	Canadians	0.765	Mental h/c	0.563	Drug Ad.	0.748	Northern Irish
Blacks	0.825	Dutch	0.712			H. Drinkers	0.815	Polish
Chinese	0.588	English	0.719	**(b) Miscellaneous**				Protestants
Coloureds	0.770	French	0.728	Gardaí	0.626			Socialists*(6)
Indians	0.751	Germans	0.614	Irish Speak.	0.645			Travellers
Nigerians	0.852	Italians	0.613	R. Catholic	0.619			Unionists
Pakistanis	0.821	Scottish	0.748					
		Spaniards	0.726					
		Welsh	0.750					
(a2) E-R Middle-East		Euro-Amer.	0.727					
Arabs	0.788							
Iranians	0.865	**(b) Social**						
Israelis	0.835	Trade Union	0.676					
Palestinians	0.820	Unemployed	0.587					
		Unmar.Moth	0.555					
		Work Class	0.606					
(a3) E-R East. Europe								
Lithuanians	0.642							
Russians	0.648							
Romanians	0.764							
(b) Religious								
Agnostics	0.648							
Atheists	0.652							
Jews	0.622							
Muslims	0.834							
(c) Politico-Economic								
Capitalists	0.533							
Communists	0.685							
21		**15**		**5**		**3**		**7 (51)**

Notes:

(1) The sub-division of categories clustered in Factors 1, 2 and 3 is according to nominal classification.

(2) The above rotated component matrix is (a) seven components extracted. Factors 5 and 6 identified one category each*, i.e. 'Gay People' in Factor 5 and 'Socialists' in Factor 6, at a 0.50 plus score.

5.2 *Factor Two*:   The pulling together of the main Ethnic European (white) stimulus categories is totally logical and in line with the *principle of propinquity*.   The 'Polish People' and the 'Northern Irish' failed to 'cluster' with other categories.   This would seem to confirm that Northern Irish are not perceived primarily as British or European people in the Republic of Ireland.   In an earlier correlation matrix, Northern Irish scores a *Rho = 0.50 plus* with the other three Celtic categories, i.e. 'Irish Speakers', 'Welsh' and 'Scottish' (see Table No. 6.7, page 119).

The failure of the 'Polish' category to 'cluster' with any other ethnic or ethnico-racial category points to its special standing in the attitudes of the people of the Republic of Ireland.   In Table No. 6.7, this category produced *Rho = 0.5 plus scores* with seventeen of the twenty-nine ethnic and ethnico-racial categories.   This makes it more surprising that the 'Polish' category failed to cluster on the above Table (No. 21.6).

The inclusion of the four social categories, i.e. 'Trade Unions', 'Unemployed', 'Unmarried Mothers' and 'Working Class' with 'Ethnic (white)' categories is probably little more than a 'statistical coincidence'. Some readers may be able to discern some significant common traits between the four social categories and the ethnic partners in 'Factor Two'!

5.3 *Factor Three*:   The two 'sub-clusters' under 'factor three' are interesting.   The bringing together of the two categories of people with handicap makes sense.   Both of these categories increased their level of tolerance and rank relatively high on the order of preference.   A growth in *meritocratic bias* could well militate against people with perceived handicap.   This was part of the **'super-race' ideology** of the German Third Reich eugenists.   In some societies today, the detection of handicap is being used as a reason for prenatal termination of the life of the potentially handicapped child.   This action denies the inalienable right of the handicapped child to life.   The rise in the status of people with handicap in the Republic of Ireland, as confirmed by the findings of the 2007-08 survey, is, therefore, greatly to be welcomed and reassuring for people with physical or mental handicap.

The three 'miscellaneous categories', i.e. 'Gardaí', 'Irish Speakers' and 'Roman Catholics', which clustered also under 'Factor Three' are very much 'in-groups' in Irish society.   The three categories were within the top seven, i.e. 'Roman Catholics' – **1**[st], 'Irish Speakers' – **4**[th] and 'Gardaí' – **7**[th], at the core of Irish groups!

5.4 *Factor Four:* This factor brings together the three 'compulsive behaviour' categories whose standing is low down on the rank order (out of 51) in the 2007-08 survey, i.e. 'Alcoholics' – **48**[th], 'Drug Addicts' – **51**[st] and 'Heavy Drinkers' – **40**[th]. As already noted in Chapter XII, the social distance scores against these categories are likely to be counterproductive in that they impede the necessary personal and social support for rehabilitation from addiction to alcohol and drugs.

5.5 *The Seven Non-Clustering Categories*: These stimulus categories on Table No. 21.6 are quite significant in a study of intergroup attitudes in Ireland today. Their **unique** standing, i.e. not bunching with other categories, merits attention. It indicates that efforts aimed at increasing tolerance and reducing prejudice towards each of them need to be tailored to the category's particular position. This non-clustering was expected in the case of some of the categories. With the exception of 'Polish People', the remaining six categories, i.e. 'Gay People', 'Northern Irish', 'Protestants', 'Socialists', 'Travellers' and 'Unionists', also failed to cluster in the 1988-'89 survey [see Mac Gréil, (1996), Table No. 10, page 90]. The implicit perception of the stimulus category in the mind of respondents is likely to determine with which set of categories it clusters or whether it stands alone as a unique expression of prejudice and tolerance!

Part VI – Concluding Comments and Suggestions

Before concluding this text it might be useful to note some of the **main findings** of the 2007-08 national survey of Irish (Republic of Ireland) intergroup attitudes and prejudices. These findings have been both positive and negative, when compared with those of the two previous surveys, i.e. 1972-73 (Greater Dublin) and 1988-89 (Republic of Ireland). In the course of previous chapters it was quite obvious that the findings reflect the impact of ongoing cultural, economic and social changes in Irish society. It is accepted that the people's intergroup attitudes and prejudices are largely *socio-culturally determined*, i.e. without excluding the particular influence of individual *personality traits*.

6.1 Utility of this Research:
The self-therapeutic benefit of any research making explicit the people's implicit social prejudices is generally beneficial. *A prejudice exposed is a prejudice undermined!* It is a primary function, i.e. objective consequence, of serious human science research to undermine prejudices and, thereby, liberate societies from the debilitating effects of false 'myths' of racism, ethnocentrism, anti-Semitism, sexism, homophobia, political bias, religious bigotry and the various forms of social and class prejudices. Hopefully, *Pluralism and Diversity in Ireland* will succeed in continuing the process of undermining social prejudice and promoting in its place greater social tolerance.

There is a danger that at times of serious **economic recession** the immediate concrete economic problems (local and international) understandably tend to **monopolise** public debate. This can lead to the neglect of deeper social issues such as intergroup prejudice and tolerance. Such preoccupation was characteristic of the two decades which followed the Wall Street Crash of 1929 and led to terrible consequences for minorities right across continental Europe. It could also be argued that the 1930s' recession in the United States of America delayed serious moves to emancipate Afro-Americans and other minorities.

It is in the shade of another **national and international recession** that the findings of this text are being released. It is expected that they will receive a positive response resulting in continued support for progress made over the previous two decades and elicit an energetic commitment to those minorities suffering the effects of unacceptable prejudice in Irish society. If this reaction happens, the publication of *Pluralism and Diversity in Ireland* at this time (the spring of 2011) will be very timely and help to reverse the tragic outcome for minorities following the recession of the 1930s! In times of economic recession and crisis, minorities are most at risk, e.g. the scapegoating of the Jews in Germany in the 1930s and 1940s. Populist and demagogic leaders can direct the aggression and anger of the people on to the minorities they have scapegoated.

In the light of the unexpected level of social prejudice of a significant minority of the '18 to 25 year-olds' in the present findings and the apparent failure of the education system to make them more tolerant, it may be necessary to include *'minority relations'* as part of the curriculum of the senior cycle in second level and undergraduate third level. It is a naïve illusion to believe that human beings are tolerant 'by instinct'! We learn our tolerant attitudes as part of our socialisation. In a multicultural society it is necessary to learn how to relate to different 'groups' in a tolerant and mutually respectful manner.

6.2 Significant Social Changes in Ireland since 1988-89:

Among the social changes and developments in Irish society since 1989, which were conducive to a decrease in intergroup prejudice and a consequent increase in social tolerance, were (a) *the success of the Northern Irish Peace Process;* (b) *the decade of sustained economic growth 1996-2007;* and (c) *the immigration of workers and residents to the Republic of Ireland* (from elsewhere in Europe and outside it). It was anticipated by the author that these three changes would have a positive effect on the attitudes on the ground of **greater security** and the creation of occasions of **favourable contact**. The security provided by the peace and economic prosperity removed the **frustration** generated by the Northern conflict and depressed economic activity. Frustration creates **tension** which, in turn, seeks release in **aggression**. Social prejudice is an easily accessible form of psychological aggression.

6.2.1 Northern Ireland:

During the fieldwork of the 1972-73 Greater Dublin survey, violence and conflict in Northern Ireland was very much an issue of daily headlines in Irish and world news media. It was to continue until the ceasefire in 1994. After a number of efforts seeking negotiated resolutions, e.g. the *Anglo-Irish Agreement of 1985*, a mutually acceptable agreement was approved by the people of Northern Ireland and the Republic of Ireland (by referendum) and ratified by Dáil Éireann and the Westminster Parliament in 1998. The *Belfast Agreement* (popularly known as the *'Good Friday Agreement'*) set up a joint-administration for Northern Ireland. This was clarified further by the *St Andrew's Agreement* in 2006. The findings of the current research (2007-08) have confirmed a significant and substantial improvement in the attitudes of respondents towards Northern Irish and the British (see Chapters X and XII). This is a most valuable peace dividend!

6.2.2 Period of Economic Prosperity:

A second environmental factor expected to reduce social prejudice has been the unprecedented improvement in the economy during the twelve years from 1996 until summer of 2008. The Irish workforce went from 1.3 million to 2 million plus (2,068,329). The material standard of living increased substantially. This brought with it a higher level of security and satisfaction. The anticipated effects of such improvements in material standards of living on intergroup attitudes were a reduction in prejudice and a rise in tolerance, which the findings seem to confirm!

Just as economic prosperity and security are likely to result in greater tolerance towards different stimulus categories in society, it is also possible for the **reverse** to happen when socio-economic conditions deteriorate (as has happened since the summer of 2008)[8]. This text does not report on the people's attitudes after the economic downturn. Community leaders should be aware of the current economic climate's potential for inciting displaced aggression against minorities and ascribing to them blame for the current crisis – of which they are totally innocent.

6.2.3 In-Migration of Workers: The third factor expected to bring about an increase in intergroup tolerance was the **favourable contact** generated between diverse ethnic groups as a result of the in-migration of workers from elsewhere in Europe and further afield. A most dramatic demographic change took place in the Republic of Ireland between 1996 and 2006 (see Chapter II). The policy of spreading the immigrants throughout the country seemed to have added to the facilities suitable for 'favourable contact'. The outcome of significant and substantial decreases in ethnic and ethnico-racial scores confirms the positive impact of in-migration of large numbers of workers from outside Ireland (i.e. representing an increase of ± **10%** of the population in the decade 1996-2006).

When asked to rate the effects of in-migrants on Irish society, respondents were, for the most part, positive. What was of special significance was the positive self-esteem of migrants themselves *vis-à-vis* their contribution to the economy of the host society, to Irish culture and quality of life. Of course, there were some problems (as reported in Chapter II) but, by and large the in-migration experience seems to have been a

---

[8] It should be noted that the fieldwork (i.e. interviewing) for this research took place between November 2007 and March 2008, i.e. before the collapse of banking systems and the downturn in the Irish economy.

positive one for the Republic and has contributed to greater maturity in intergroup relations in the country.

6.3 Areas of Concern in the 2007-08 Findings:

Just as it happens when the 'tide of economic growth fails to make all boats float', it has also happened that the 'wave of greater tolerance' (between 1988-89 and 2007-08) has left a number of minorities or categories 'still stuck in the quagmire of serious social prejudice'. The net result is to make the position of the members of these minorities relatively worse off.

6.3.1 Categories Scoring 2.500 plus (MSD): The stimulus categories who

scored 2.500 (Mean-Social-Distance – MSD) and higher on Table No. 4.1, pages 62-4, could be classified as being below the acceptable level of social tolerance in the light of the positive social environment at the time of interviewing, i.e. between November 2007 and March 2008. These categories (with MSD scores in brackets) include:

'Agnostics' (2.554),	*'Iranians' (2.850),*
'Romanians' (2.566),	*'Arabs' (2.908),*
'Heavy Drinkers' (2.626),	*'Communists' (2.920),*
'Pakistanis' (2.682),	*'Alcoholics' (2.937),*
'Palestinians' (2.709),	*'Travellers' (3.030),*
'Nigerians' (2.726),	*'Muslims' (3.066),*
'Israelis' (2.842),	*'Drug Addicts' (4.194).*

While all of these categories experienced some improvement in their mean-social-distance, their scores are still far too high for a society in good times aspiring to be liberal and tolerant.

In the course of the text, each of these performances is analysed. Categories which could be classified as **'compulsive behaviour'**, i.e. 'Heavy Drinkers', 'Alcoholics' and 'Drug Addicts', are in a more precarious position since they need public support to rehabilitate themselves. Current negative attitudes are more likely to push them further into their addiction (see Chapter XII).

The three ethnic categories, i.e. 'Romanians', 'Pakistanis' and 'Nigerians' are significantly higher (MSD) then their place should be according to the *principle of propinquity*.   **'Romanians'** are apparently suffering from the irrational stigma against Romany people.   **'Pakistani'** people's association with 'Muslims' (who have high MSD scores) and the vicarious negative stereotypes 'imported' into Ireland from the English 'Paki-bashing' ridicule through returned emigrants and popular British media are likely to have contributed to their relatively high MSD scores. The relatively high prejudice score of **'Nigerians'** is difficult to accept.   The link between Ireland and Nigeria has been positive throughout almost a century of pro-Nigerian Roman Catholic Missionaries and progressive overseas lay development.   In addition to *implicit racialism* there must be particularly negative stereotyping focusing on allegedly deviant behaviour of a minority of this fine people.   The media in Ireland needs to be wary not to add to such negative stereotyping.

It is interesting to observe how Irish respondents have 'lumped together' (which is a feature of ethnic prejudice) the four **Middle-East Ethnic groups**, i.e. 'Palestinians', 'Israelis', 'Iranians' and 'Arabs' at such a relatively high MSD range of scores (from 2.709 to 2.908).   These results raise a number of very serious questions for those engaged in the 'Western' versus 'Middle-East' international geo-politics.   Irish attitudes are unlikely to be much different from those of the 'Western' societies.   The findings point to an unacceptable level of prejudice or 'hate-attitudes' towards our Middle-East neighbours.   The inclusion of 'Muslims' at an even higher MSD score (3.066) is more alarming still.   It is necessary to repeat that a serious effort is called for to promote a positive programme of **Christian-Jewish-Muslim dialogue** to generate greater respect between these three world religions of common 'Semitic' background!   Such reconciliation would do much to prepare the way for Middle-East peace and reduce the level of prejudice towards it recorded in the findings of this text.

The position of **'Travellers'** (Travelling People) at the third lowest rank-order position (49th out of 51) is a serious embarrassment to the good name of the Republic of Ireland.   As an indigenous ethnic minority of 0.5% of the population (22,369), coming from the nomadic tradition, their position in the rank order of preference is totally out of kilter with the *principle of propinquity*.   A special chapter (XIII) entitled "The Travelling People – Ireland's Apartheid", covers many aspects of this minority's status and the very urgent need for Irish society to address their 'emancipation' in a pluralist manner.

The attitudes towards **'Atheists'**, **'Agnostics'** and **'Communists'** had improved substantially between 1988-89 and 2007-08 although they are still out of line with expectations. The momentum needs to continue in the direction of greater tolerance.

With the emerging negative correlation between **education** and **religiosity** (see Table No. 21.2, page 564) there is an obvious danger that the neglect of religion by the educational institution could (unwittingly) be contributing to a growth of religious fundamentalism. This would not be good for Irish society. So far, 'religiosity' is not a significantly negative independent variable in relation to most forms of prejudice (see Table No. 21.2).

6.3.2 Age as a Personal Variable: The performance of the **'age' variable** in relation to most of the categories on the *Bogardus Social Distance Scale* was not as expected. 'Young adult respondents' (18-25 year-olds) sub-variable prejudice score was higher than their older fellow-respondents. This was the more surprising because of the higher educational achievement of this age group in a time of relative economic prosperity and security (see Table No. 7.8, page 158).

Serious questions were raised in Part VIII of Chapter VII (pages 156-160) about the performance of the youngest adult age group. Assuming that the causes were more structural than personal, it is reasonable to expect that they are to be found in the socialisation norms and processes. Did the **education process** focus too much on career preparation to the neglect of personal development, i.e. lacking the primacy of the humanities? Were the phenomena of **extended adolescence** and **exclusive peer-socialisation** proving to be dysfunctional? The fact that the age group '26-40 years' proved to be the most tolerant of the five age sub-variables, would seem to point to the relatively recent change in the '18-25 year-olds' attitudes. This might raise questions in relation to the decline of the positive role of **the family** in the socialisation of the young. The findings of this research make a *prima facie* case for serious research into the socialisation of our young people in what some commentators call 'post-modern' Ireland. The levels of intolerance expressed in the findings in the case of the '18 to 25 year-olds' age group are quite worrying!

6.3.3 Authoritarianism and Social Anomie[9]: The findings of the 2007-08 survey have confirmed quite clearly the positive correlation between both *'authoritarianism'* and *'social anomie'* and various forms of social prejudice. What was new in the current research (2007-08) has been the substantial increase (since 1988-89) in the influence of 'social anomie' in the causal path of prejudice. The levels of correlation with prejudice are now higher (with rare exceptions) than those of 'authoritarianism'.

The levels of 'social anomie' (a sociological trait) and 'authoritarianism' (a psychological trait) are given in Chapter XVIII of this text. Because of the links between these two independent variables and numerous social and personality problems in modern society, it would appear reasonable that serious resources should be made available to investigate the **causes** of 'social anomie' and 'authoritarianism'. The link is so strong between them and prejudice that the latter is largely **a major symptom** of them in most cases (see Tables Nos. 21.2, 21.3 and 21.4, pages 564, 572 and 576)!

Part VII – Further Research and Concluding Remarks

In these final paragraphs of *Pluralism and Diversity in Ireland* it is proposed to identify a number of areas which merit **further research** and theoretical reflection. These proposals arise out of issues raised but not fully answered in the course of this study. A number of research questions have already been raised in the body of this text following findings requiring further knowledge and understanding in relation to social prejudice and tolerance and the performance of particular independent variables.

In addition to proposed areas of further research, a number of **concluding remarks** will be made in relation to the overall findings. It is clear from the findings that the role of local, national and international administrations in promoting, maintaining and *protecting* minorities is *crucial* to *pluralist coexistence* in Ireland and throughout the world.

---

[9] (a) **Authoritarianism** is a personality trait characterised by a degree of closed-mindedness, religious fundamentalism, moralism, dogmatism, repressive and pro-establishment dispositions.
(b) **Social Anomie** is a state of normlessness and perceived powerlessness resulting largely from where society's culturally prescribed goals are not realisable by significant sections of society within the confines of socially acceptable norms.

7.1 Areas of Further Research:
The following areas of research are deemed necessary as part of society's responsibility in seeking to secure just intergroup relations within its various communities and to provide necessary information to explain questions raised by the above findings:

(i) Overall Ongoing Monitoring of Prejudice in Ireland: In response to continuous social and cultural change in Ireland, it is advisable and worthwhile to repeat this current survey-research project every fifteen to twenty years. Ideally, such survey-research should cover the whole island of Ireland, i.e. Northern Ireland and the Republic of Ireland. A similar national survey-research exercise should be carried out in other countries focusing on the dominant-minority relations within each country. This would be distinct from trans-national research.

(ii) The Causes of 'Social Anomie' and 'Authoritarianism': Because of the prominence of these two independent variables in the findings of the 2007-08 study, it is very necessary to find out more about the *causes* of these phenomena. Such information is required to enable society to adopt the necessary structural and other measures aimed at reducing the levels of social prejudice towards minorities and between them.

(iii) Extended Adolescence and Social Prejudice: It is evident from the findings of this study that a significant and substantial proportion of *18 to 25 year-olds* are relatively more prejudiced than their education and economic security would warrant. The influence of 'extended adolescence' on such unexpected findings should be researched.

(iv) Education and Social Tolerance: The performance of 'educational achievement' as an independent variable was less positive than expected. This raises serious questions about the philosophy, curricula and pedagogy of education in the Republic of Ireland today. It is hypothesised that the shift in emphasis from the *'humanities'* to the *more pragmatic subjects* such as applied science, technology, economics, communications and other career subjects at the higher levels has resulted in weakening education's 'liberating' function.

(v) Integrated Pluralism: Serious research is required into the structural and attitudinal conditions conducive to 'integrated pluralism' in Ireland in the major social institutions, i.e. economy, education, family, law, polity and religion. By 'integrated pluralism' is meant intergroup coexistence which respects and promotes cultural and religious differences within the context of social integration based on social equality. It will require a degree of **institutional duplication** in areas of religious and cultural diversity.

(vi) The Role of the Media and Intergroup Prejudice: Mass media of communications play a very important role in the presentation of social minority groups to the public. Such presentation can aid or hinder just and pluralist integration in society. It is, therefore, very important that ongoing objective monitoring (through serious research) is carried out of print and electronic media available to the public in relation to social prejudice and tolerance in Ireland today.

(vii) Protection of Minority Rights in Irish Law: It is very important to carry out comprehensive research into the protection of minority rights in Irish law. This should include the study of the enactment, enforcement and application of *Irish Minority Rights' legislation*, adequate to the needs of all minority groups. Such research should be updated at regular intervals. Vigilant enforcement of adequate Minority Rights' Legislation is essential to protect members of minority groups and categories from negative discrimination.

(viii) Intergroup Favourable Contact: Most serious students of intergroup relations conclude that *favourable contact* between members of different groups and categories contributes to a reduction in social prejudice and a corresponding increase in intergroup tolerance. It is worthwhile, therefore, to carry out research into the conditions supportive of 'favourable contact' while also concentrating on those opposed to it. The findings of this text indicate the significant influence of 'favourable contact' in the sample's increase in social tolerance.

The above eight areas proposed for further research do not exhaust relevant issues worthy of serious study by human scientists. In the opinion of the present author, these eight areas should be given a degree of priority.

7.2 *Focail Scoir* (Concluding Remarks):

The findings of the 2007-08 survey are more positive than they are negative. When taken as a whole, adults of the Republic of Ireland are a fairly open and tolerant people. This does not overlook the evidence of unacceptable intolerance in the case of attitudes towards a number of stimulus categories. The trends are in the direction of greater tolerance when compared with the findings of 1972-73 and 1988-89. The period of *economic prosperity* during the late 1990s and up until 2008 (June) and the arrival at a viable *resolution to the Northern Ireland conflict* contributed to significantly greater tolerance. The *in-migration* of workers from Europe and elsewhere abroad created a situation of 'favourable contact' between the Irish and other ethnic groups. This, in turn, reduced levels of ethnic and racial prejudice.

Evidence with regard to ethnic self-identity raised questions about Irish people's ambiguity in relation to their own self-perception. On the other hand, the findings in relation to the Irish language were quite positive, especially in the areas of aspiration and competence in their fluency. Unfortunately, people are not using the language commensurate with their ability and this could, in part, explain their ambiguity towards their self-identity.

While welcoming the positive results and recognising the improvements in Irish social attitudes towards a large number of ethnic and other categories in the findings, it is more urgent to draw attention to those with unacceptable negative prejudices. Included among the latter are our Irish attitudes and behaviour towards Ireland's native ethnic minority, the *Travelling People*. This Irish minority requires an immediate and positive response from those with power and influence in Irish society.

Other categories needing serious support and attention are *victims of addiction and compulsive behaviour*, i.e. 'Heavy Drinkers', 'Alcoholics' and 'Drug Addicts', against whom social attitudes are very negative. This means their rehabilitation is impeded by the lack of public sympathy and compassion. It is understandable, however, that people living closely to those with serious addictive problems, can have negative dispositions towards them. Alcohol plays a very large part in Irish recreational life and is being promoted as if it were not addictive. These findings call for greater control of alcohol and drugs, especially, in relation to youth.

Negative stereotypes of *Middle-East ethnic groups* have resulted in the very negative attitudes towards 'Arabs', 'Israelis', 'Iranians', 'Palestinians' and 'Pakistani'. These are partly due to Irish exposure to the stereotypes of Middle Eastern countries in the populist media. Some such stereotypes may also be coming from our European Union association.

The position of *'Muslims'* on Table No. 4.1 is unjustified and unacceptable. The status of *'Jews'* also failed to improve as much as was anticipated. The continuation of the Middle East conflicts is polarising Irish attitudes and calls for a more 'reconciliatory' and less violent approach to Mid-East *versus* West confrontation. The current situation only ferments extremism and fundamentalism! *Christian–Jewish–Muslim dialogue* is necessary to facilitate a new tolerant order. **Anti-Semitism** and **Islamaphobia** are two dangerous religious prejudices in modern society and feed negatively of each other!

Attitudes to *'Nigerians'*, *'Africans'* and *'Afro-Americans'* still highlight the level of *implicit racialism* of the adults in the Republic of Ireland. The legacy of the failure of the **Enlightenment Movement** to be racially inclusive still affects Western negative attitudes towards African and Asian peoples. Its failure to defend Black People who were being enslaved in the 'New World' in the 18th and 19th centuries has limited its positive influence for human liberation. The current standing of 'Afro-Americans' *vis-à-vis* 'Euro-Americans' in this study bears out this point. There is an additional problem in relation to Irish attitudes towards 'Nigerians' whose position is not in line with the *principle of propinquity*, probably due to particular negative stereotyping of them.

With the above remarks, *Pluralism and Diversity in Ireland* draws to a close. Hopefully, the reader will have found the text informative, of interest and of benefit for the ongoing improvement of intergroup relations in Ireland and elsewhere abroad. Like all major social surveys, the findings are the fruit of *a consultation* with a random sample (1,015) of the adult population living in the Republic of Ireland between November 2007 and March 2008. Through their willingness to give forty minutes of their time to the interviewers, it has been possible to get the information on which to base the findings reported in the numerous tables and figures presented throughout the text. Our primary debt of gratitude is due to these respondents.

While every effort was made to report and explain the findings according to accepted survey-research conventions, the author apologises for any shortcomings in presentation and explanation. As is accepted, the interpretation of findings is subjective and open to discussion. An interesting outcome of this publication would be a wide and genuine discussion.

Tá súil ag an údar gur fiú an iarracht seo: ***Iolrachas agus Éagsúlacht in Éirinn***.

***

Bibliography

ACTON, C., and MILLER, R.L., *SPSS for Social Scientists,* 2nd Edition, Palgrave Macmillan, London, 2009.

ADAMS, RICHARD N., "The Evolution of Racism in Guatemala: Hegemony, Science and Antihegemony" in *Histories of Anthropology Annual,* Vol. 1, pp.132-180, 2005.

ADORNO, T.W., FRENKEL-BRUNSWICK, E., LEVINSON, D.J. and SANDFORD, R.W. (in collaboration with B. Aron, M.H. Levinson and W. Morrow), *The Authoritarian Personality,* New York, Harper, 1950.

ALLPORT, GORDON W., *The Nature of Prejudice,* Boston, Beacon, 1954.
Pattern and Growth in Personality, London, Holt Rinehart and Winston, (1963) 1969.

ALTINORDU, ATES, (2008), see Gorski, Philip S. *et al.*

ANOBY, STAN J., "Reversing Language Shift: Can Kwak'wala be Revived?" in Cantoni, St Clair and Yazzie (editions), *Revitalising Indigenous Languages,* North Arizona University Press, 1999.

ARENDT, HANNAH, *Eichmann in Jerusalem: A Report on the Banality of Evil,* Barcelona, Lumen, 3rd Ed., 2000.

ARENSBERG, C.M. and KIMBALL S.T., *Family and Community in Ireland,* Boston, Harvard University Press (1940), 1965.

ARON, B. (1958), see Adorno *et al.*

ARONSON, ELLIOT, *The Social Animal,* San Francisco, Freeman, 1980 (3rd Edition).

AVERROES / IBN RUSHD, (1126-1198) *On the Harmony of Religion and Philosophy,* (Translation: G. Hourani), London, 1961.

BACK, L. (1994) see Solomos, J. *et al.*

BALLACHEY, E.L. (1962) see Krech D. *et al.*

BANTON, MICHAEL, *Race Relations,* New York, Basic Books, 1967.
- *Race and Ethnic Competition,* Cambridge, University Press, 1983.

BARRETT, A., BERGIN A. and DUFFY, D., "The Labour Market Characteristics and Labour Market Impact on Immigrants in Ireland", Dublin, *ESRI Seminar Paper,* 2005.

BAUM, G. (1977), see Greeley, Andrew M., *et al.*

BENCHY, DANIEL, "Adolf Hitler" in *Studies,* Dublin, Jesuit Publications, March 1933, pages 29-47.

BENDIX, R. and LIPSET, S.M. (Editors), *Class, Status and Power,* London, Routledge and Kegan-Paul (1953), 1960.

BENEDICT, RUTH, *Patterns of Culture,* London, Routledge and Kegan-Paul, (1935), 1961.

BERGIN, A., (2005), see Barrett, A. *et al.*

BERKOWITZ, LEONARD, *Aggression, A Psychological Analysis,* New York, McGraw-Hill, 1962.

BERRY BREWTON, *Race and Ethnic Relations*, Boston, Haughton-Milflin, 1965.

BIEMER P. and LYBERG L., *Introduction to Survey Quality*, Wiley, New Jersey, 2003.

BLEAKLEY, DAVID, *Crisis in Ireland,* London, Fabian Society (Ser. 318) 1974.

BOGARDUS, EMORY, "Measuring Social Distance", in *Journal of Applied Sociology*, 1925.
- *Immigration and Race Attitudes*, Boston, Heath, 1928.
- "A Race Relations Cycle" in *American Journal of Sociology*, 1930.
- "A Social Distance Scale" in *Sociology and Social Research*, 1933.
- "Changes in Social Distance" in *International Journal of Opinion and Attitudes Research*, 1947.
- "Stereotypes versus Sociotypes" in *Sociology and Social Research*, 1950.
- *"A Forty Year Racial Distance Study"*, Pasadena, University of South California Press, 1967.

BONILLA SILVA, EDUARDO, *White Supremacy and Racism in the Post-Civil Rights Era*, Boulder, C.O., Lynne Reinner, 2001.
- *Racism without Racists: Colour-Blind Racism and Persistence of Racial Inequality in the United States*, Lankam, MD, Rowman and Littlefield, 2003.

BOWMAN, JOHN, *DeValera and the Ulster Question,* Oxford University Press 1982.

BOYD, ANDREW, *Brian Falkner and the Crisis in Ulster,* Tralee, Anvil, 1969.

BRAUER, MARKUS (1995), see Kraus, Susan *et al.*

BREEN, RICHARD, HANNAN D., ROTHMAN, D.B. and WHELAN, C.T., *Understanding Contemporary Ireland: State, Class and Development in the Republic of Ireland,* Dublin, Gill and Macmillan, 1990.

BRIGHAM, JOHN C., *Social Psychology*, New York, Harper Collins, 1991.

BRODY, HUGH, *Inishkillane, Change and Decline in the West of Ireland,* London, Penguin Press, 1973.

BROWN, H.M., (1985), see Mestrovic, G. *et al.*

BROWN, W.O., "Culture, Contact and Race Conflict" in Reuter, E.B. (Edition), *Race and Culture Contacts*, New York, McGraw-Hill, 1934.

BRYMAN, ALAN, *Social Research Methods,* Oxford University Press, 2004.

BURKE, WILLIAM P., *Irish Priests in Penal Times 1660-1760*, Waterford, 1914.

BUXTON, S., *Handbook to Political Questions*, London, 1880, pp. 41-2, (quoted in Farmur, Tony 2010 pp 43-4).

CALLAN, T. (2009), see Russell, H. *et al.*

CANADIAN ROYAL COMMISSION ON BILINGUALISM AND BICULTURALISM, *Report of the Royal Commission on Bilingualism and Biculturalism, Book 1, The Official Languages,* Ottawa, Canada, Queen's Printer, 1967.

CENTRAL STATISTICS OFFICE, *Census 2006 Report,*
Vol. 5, *Ethnic or Cultural Background,*
Vol. 9, *Irish Language,*
Vol. 13, *Religion,*
Principal Socio-Economic Results, Dublin, C.S.O., 2007.

CHAMBLIN, M.B. and J.K. COCHRAN, "Assessing Messner and Rosenfeld's Institutional Anomie Theory: A Partial Test", in *Criminology*, (pages 411-429), 1995.

CHEJNE, ANWAR G., *Muslim Spain, Its History and Culture,* Minneapolis, University of Minnesota Press, 1974.

CHUBB, BASIL, *The Government and Politics of Ireland,* Stanford University Press, 1970.

CLANCY, FINBAR G., "Sailing to Byzantium: Three Papal Visits to Turkey", in *Milltown Studies*, (No. 63), Milltown Park, Dublin (pages 1-84), 2010.

CLÁR (Committee on Irish Language Research), *Tuarascáil,* Baile Átha Cliath, Oifig Dhíolta Foilseacháin Realtais, 1975.

COCHRAN, J.K. (1985) see Chamblin, M.B. *et al.*

COMPTON, PAUL, "The Demography of Religious Affiliation" in *Demographic Review: Northern Ireland, 1995,* Belfast, NIEC, 1995.

CONNELLY, STUART, (2011) see Jones, Clarence B. *et al.*

CONNOLLY, PAUL and MICHAELA KEENAN, *Racial Attitudes and Prejudice in Northern Ireland,* Belfast, NISRA, 2000.

CONWAY, BRIAN, "Who Do We Think We Are? Immigration and Discursive Construction of National Identity in an Irish Daily Mainstream Newspaper, 1996-2004", in *Translocations*, Vol. 1, No. 1 (Pages 76-93), 2006.

COOLEY, CHARLES H., *Social Process*, New York, Scribners, 1918.

CORCORAN, MARY, *Irish Illegals: Transients between Two Societies*, Westport (Connecticut), Greenwood Press, 1993.

CORISH, PATRICK, *The Irish Catholic Experience*, Gill & Macmillan, Dublin, 1985.

COSER, LEWIS, *Continuities in the Study of Social Conflict*, New York, Free Press, 1967.

COULTER, COLIN and MURRAY, MICHAEL, *Northern Ireland after the Troubles, a Society in Transition*, Manchester University Press, 2008.

CRONBACH, L.J., "Coefficient Alpha and Internal Structure of Tests", in *Psychometrica*, Vol. 16 (pages 297-334), 1951.
- "Processes Affecting Scores on 'Understanding Others' and 'Assumed Similarity' ", in *Psychological Bulletin*, Vol. 52 (pages 177-193), 1955.

CRUTCHFIELD, R.S. (1962) see Krech, D. *et al.*

CUMMINS, JIM, *"Immersion Education for the Millennium: What we have Learned from 30 Years of Research on Second Language Immersion"*, Ontario Institute for Studies in Education of the University of Toronto, 2007.

DAHRENDORF, RALF, *Class and Class Conflict in Industrial Society,* London, Routledge and Kegan-Paul, 1961.

DAVIE, GRACE, *Religion in Britain since 1945: Believing without Belonging (Making Contemporary Britain)*, Blackwell, London, 1994.

DAVIS, EARL, GRUBE, J.W. and MORGAN, M., *Attitudes towards Poverty and Related Issues in Ireland*, Dublin, ESRI, 1984.

DAVIS, E. and SINNOTT R., *Attitudes in the Republic Relevant to the Northern Problem*, Dublin, ESRI (No. 17), 1984.

DeBLAGHD, EARNÁN, *Trasna na Bóinne, Sáirséal agus Dill*, 1955.

DeBOIS, W.E.B., *The Negro, Black Reconstruction in America*, New York, The World, 1962.

DeFRÉINE, SEÁN, *The Great Silence*, Baile Átha Cliath, Foilseacháin Nais. Teo., 1965.

DELAP, BREANDÁN, "Mí-Ionracas Daltaí agus a dTuismuitheoirí", ar www.beo.ie/alt-mi-ionracas-daltai-agus-a-dtuismitheoiri.aspx 2008.

DePAOR, LIAM, *Divided Ulster*, London, Penguin, 1971.

DEPARTMENT OF JUSTICE, EQUALITY AND LAW REFORM, *Report of the High level Group on Traveller Issues*, Dublin, March 2006.

DeVAUS, D.A., *Surveys in Social Research, 4th Edition*, UCLA Press, London, 1996.

DEVLIN, PADDY, *Straight Left: An Autobiography*, Belfast, The Blackstaff Press, 1993.

DICKENS, CHARLES, *David Copperfield*, London, Penguin, 1850.
   - *Great Expectations*, London, Penguin, 1861.

DOANE, ASHLEY, "What is Racism? Racial Discourse and Racial Politics" in *Critical Sociology*, No. 32, (pages 255-274) 2006.

DOBBELAERE, KAREL, "Some Trends in European Sociology of Religion: The Secularization Debate", in *Sociological Analysis*, Vol. 48:2 107-137, 1987.
   - "Towards an Integrated Perspective of the Processes related to the Descriptive Concept of Secularisation", in *Sociology of Religion*, Vol. 60:3, 229-247, 1999.
   - "Bryan Wilson's Contribution to the Study of Secularization", in *Social Compass*, Vol. 53:2, 141-146, 2006.

DOLLARD, JOHN, *Caste and Class in a Southern Town*, New York, Harper & Row, 1957.

DOLLARD, JOHN, DOOB, L.W., MILLER, N.E., MOWRER, O.H. and SEARS, R.R., *Frustration and Aggression*, New Haven, Yale, 1939.

DOMINGUEZ, VIRGINIA, *White by Definition: Social Classification in Creole Louisiana*, New Brunswick, N.J., Rutgers University Press, 1986.
   - *People as Subject, People as Object: Selfhood and Peoplehood in Contemporary Israel*, Madison, University of Wisconsin Press, 1989.
   - "The Racialist Politics of Concepts, or Is It the Racialist Concepts of Politics?" in *Ethos*, Vol. 21, No. 1 (pages 93-110), 1997.

DONAHOE, M., McVEIGH, R., and WOOD M., *Misli, Crush, Misli: Irish Travellers and Nomadism*, Dublin, Irish Travellers' Movement, 2009.

DOOB, L.W., (1939), see Dollard, J. *et al.*

DOUTHWAITE, RICHARD, *The Growth Illusion: How Economic Growth Enriched the Few, Impoverished the Many and Endangered the Planet,* Dublin, The Lilliput Press, 1992.
- *Short Circuit: Strengthening Local Economics in an Unstable World,* Dublin, The Lilliput Press, 1996.

DUFFY, D. (2005), see Barrett, *et al.*

DURKHEIM, EMILE, *On the Division of Labour,* New York, Macmillan (1893), 1933.
- *Suicide, A Study in Sociology,* New York, Free Press (1897), 1951.
- *Rules of the Sociological Method,* New York, Free Press (1895), 1964, 1959.

EISINGA, R.N. and SCHEEPERS, P.L.N., *Ethnocentrisme in Nederland,* Nijmegen, ITS, 1989.

ENGELS, FRIEDRICH, (1848) see Marx, Karl *et al.*

EQUALITY AUTHORITY, *Traveller Ethnicity,* Dublin, E.A., 2006.

ESTROFF, SUE, "A Cultural Perspective of Experiences of Illness, Disability and Chronic Illness" in *The Social Medicine Reader,* Durham, N.C., Duke University Press, 1997.

EVANS, ESTYN, *The Personality of Ireland, Habitat, Heritage and History,* London, Cambridge University Press, 1973.

FAHEY, TONY, "Trends in Irish Fertility Rates in Comparative Perspective" in *The Economic and Social Review,* Vol. 32, No. 2, pp153-180, 2001.

FAHEY, TONY, (2006), see Hayes, Bernadette, *et al.*

FAIRCHILD, HENRY PRATT, *Immigration,* New York, Macmillan, 1925.

FANNING, B., *Racism and Social Change in the Republic of Ireland,* Manchester, Manchester University Press, 2002.

FARMUR, TONY, *Privileged Lives: A Social History of Middle-Class Ireland 1882-1989,* Dublin A&A Farmur Ltd., 2010).

FELLING, A. (1992), see Scheepers, P. *et al.*

FENNELL, DESMOND, *Heresy, The Battle of Ideas in Modern Ireland,* Belfast, The Blackstaff Press, 1993.

FITZGERALD, GARRET, *Towards a New Ireland,* Dublin, Gill and Macmillan, 1973.
- *All in a Life,* Dublin, Gill and Macmillan, 1993.

FITZGERALD, GRETCHEN, *Repulsing Racism: Reflections on Racism and the Irish,* Dublin, Attic Press, 1992.

FORD, ALAN, *The Protestant Reformation in Ireland,* Frankfurt-am-Main, 1987.

FORD, ROBERT, "Is Racial Prejudice declining in Britain?" in *British Journal of Sociology,* (59)4, 2008.

FOUCAULT, MICHEL, *The Order of Things,* London, Tavistock, 1970.

FRENKEL-BRUNSWICK, E. (1958), see Adorno *et al.*

FREUD, SIGMUND, *Civilisation and Its Discontents,* London, Hogarth Press, (1933), 1949.

FROMM, ERIC, "Sozialpschologisher Teil" in Horkheimer, M. (Ed.), *Studien Uber Autoritat und Familie Forschungbericht aus den Institut fur Sozialforschung*, Parijs, Felix Allen, 1936.

GAL, S., *Language Shift: Social Determinants of Linguistic Change in Bilingual Austria*. New York, Academic Press, 1979

GALWAY TRAVELLER MOVEMENT, *Traveller Health Matters: Retrospective Impact Assessment of Low-Grade Traveller Accommodation*, Galway, 2009.

GARFINKEL, HAROLD, *Studies in Ethnomethodology*, New Jersey, Prentice-Hall, 1967.

GARNER, STEVE, "Ireland and Immigration: Explaining the Absence of the Far Right" in *Patterns of Prejudice*, London, Routledge, 2007.

GIDDENS, ANTHONY, *Sociology*, Cambridge Polity Press, 2006.

GILROY, PAUL, *There Ain't No Black in the Union Jack*, London, Hutchinson, 1987.

GLOCK, CLARENCE E., "Social Roles and Types in Race Relations" in *Race Relations in World Perspective*, Honolulu, University of Hawaii, 1955.

GOFFMAN, ERVING, *Presentation of Self in Everyday Life*, New York, Doubleday/Anchor, 1959.
-   *Asylums*, New York, Doubleday (1961), 1968.

GOLDBERG, DAVID H., *Foreign Policy and Ethnic Interest Groups: American and Canadian Jews Lobby for Israel*, Greenwood Press, USA, 1988.

GOLDTHORPE, J and WHELAN, C (eds.), *The Development of Industrial Society in Ireland,* Oxford: Oxford University Press, 1992.

GORSKI, PHILIP S. and ALTINORDU, ATES, "After secularization?" in *Annual Review of Sociology*, Vol. 34, 55-85, 2008.

GREELEY, A.M. (1970), see Spaeth, J.H., *et al.*

GREELEY, ANDREW M., and BAUM, G. (Editors), *Ethnicity*, New York, The Seabury Press, 1977.

GRUBE, J.W. (1984), see Davis E. *et al.*

HABERMAS, JÜRGEN, *Theory and Practice*, Boston, Beacon Press, 1973.

HAMILTON, THOMAS, *History of Presbyterianism in Ireland,* Belfast, Ambassador, (1986), 1992.

HANNAN, DAMIAN, (1990), see Breen, Richard, *et al.*

HARRIS, MARVIN, *Culture, People, Nature*, New York, Harper & Row, 1988.

HARRIS, ROSEMARY, *Prejudice in Ulster,* Manchester University Press, 1972.

HAYES, BERNADETTE C., FAHEY, TONY, and SINNOTT, RICHARD, *Conflict and Consensus: A Study of Values and Attitudes in the Republic of Ireland and Northern Ireland,* Institute of Public Administration, 2006.

HAYES, NICKY, *Foundations of Psychology, An Introduction*, London, Routledge, 1994.

HESSE, BARROR and S. SOYGID (Editors), "Narrating the Post-Colonial Political and Immigrant Imaginary" in *A Post-Colonial People – South Asians in Britain*, London, Hurst & Co., 2006.

HESSE, BARROR, "Im/Plausible Deniability: Racism's Conceptual Double Bind" in *Social Identities*, Vol. 10, No. 1, (pages 9-29), 2004.

HILL, PETER C. and KENNETH I. PARGAMENT, "Advances in the Conceptualization and Measurement of Religion and Spirituality" in *American Psychologist*, Vol. 58, No. 1, January 2003, pages 64-74.

HILLIARD, BETTY and NIC GHIOLLA PHÁDRAIG, MÁIRE (eds.) *Changing Ireland in International Comparison*. Dublin: The Liffey Press, 2007.

HIRSCHFELD, LAWRENCE, "The Conceptual Politics of Race: Lessons from our Children" in *Ethos*, 1997.

HISTORY IRELAND, Nov./Dec. 2008, p.13.

HITLER, ADOLF, *Mein Kampf*, (Berlin) London, Anchor Press (1933), 1969.

HOLLINGSHEAD, AUGUST DE BELMONT, *Elmstown Youth, the Impact of Social Classes on Adolescents*, New York, Wiley, 1949.

HOLLINGSHEAD, A.B. and REDLICK, F.C., *Social Class and Mental Illness,* New York, Wiley, 1958.

HORAN, JAMES, *James Horan: Memoirs 1911-1986,* (Editor M. Mac Gréil), Dingle, Brandon Books, 1992.

HURLEY, MICHAEL, (Editor), *Irish Anglicanism 1869-1969,* Dublin, Alan Figgis, 1970.

IGNATIEV, NOEL, *How the Irish Became White*, New York, Routledge, 1995.

IMMIGRANT COUNCIL OF IRELAND, *Background Information and Statistics on Immigration to Ireland*, Dublin, 2005.

INGLIS, TOM, *Moral Monopoly of the Catholic Church in Modern Ireland*, Dublin, Gill and Macmillan, 1987.

JOHNSON, HARRY, *Sociology, a Systematic Introduction*, London, Routledge and Kegan-Paul, 1961.

JONES, CLARENCE B. and CONNELLY, STUART, *Behind the Dream*: *The Making of the Speech that Transformed a Nation*, Hampshire, England, Palgrave Macmillian, 2011.

JOWELL, R. (and the Central Co-ordinating Team), *European Social Surveys 2002/2003, 2004/2005* and *2006/2007: Technical Reports*, London: Centre for Comparative Social Surveys, City University, 2003, 2005, 2007.

JOYCE, NAN, *Traveller, An Autobiography,* Dublin, Gill and Macmillan, 1985.

JUDD, C.M., RYAN, C.S. and PARK, BERNADETTE, "Accuracy in the Judgements of In-Group and Out-Group Variability" in *Journal of Personality and Social Psychology*, Vol. 61 (pages 366-379), 1991. See also Kraus, Susan (1995) *et al.*

JUNG, CARL G., *Psychological Types*, London, Routledge and Kegan-Paul, 1923.

KATZ, David, "Functional Approach to the Study of Attitudes", in *Public Opinion Quarterly*, 1960;
- "Nationalism and Strategies of International Conflict Resolution" in *International Behaviour*, New York, Holt, Rinehart and Winston, 1965.

KEANE, CLAIRE, (2009), see Russell, H. *et al.*

KEARNEY, RICHARD, (Editor), *Migrations, the Irish at Home and Abroad*, Dublin, Wolfhound Press, 1990.

KEENAN, MICHAELA, (2000), see Connolly, Paul, *et al.*

KELLEHER, MICHAEL J., *Suicide and the Irish*, Cork, Mercier Press, 1996.

KELMAN, HERBERT C., (Editor*), International Behaviour: A Social-Psychological Analysis*, New York, Holt, Rinehart and Winston, 1965.

KEOGH, DERMOT, *Jews in Twentieth Century Ireland*, Cork University Press, 1998.

KIMBALL, S.T., (1965), see Arensberg, L.M., *et al.*

KINGSTON, WILLIAM, *Interrogating Irish Policies*, Dublin University Press, 2007.

KLUCKHOHN, CLYDE, *Mirror for Man,* New York, McGraw-Hill (1949), 1971.

KONIG, RUBEN, *Ethnocentrisme in Nederland en Ierland*, Nijmegan Dept. of Sociology, 1990.

KRAUS, SUSAN, JUDD, CHARLES M., PARK, BERNADETTE, RYAN, CAREY S., and BRAUER, MARKUS "Stereotypes and Ethnocentrism: Diverging Interethnic Perceptions of African American and White American Youth" in *Journal of Personality and Social Psychology,* Vol. 69 (3), 1995.

KRECH, D., CRUTCHFIELD, R.S. and BALLACHEY, E.L. *Individual in Society*, New York, McGraw-Hill, 1962.

KRINGS, TORBEN, "Equal Rights for All Workers: Irish Trade Unions and the Challenge of Labour Migration", in *Irish Journal of Sociology*, (Vol. 16.1), Dublin, pages 43-61, 2007.

KROEBER, A.L., *Anthropology, Culture Patterns and Processes*, New York, Harpinger, 1948.

KRYSAN, MARIA, "Prejudice, Politics and Public Opinion: Understanding the Sources of Racial Policy Attitudes" in *Annual Review of Sociology,* Vol. 26, pp.135-168, 2000.

LECKY, W.E.H., *The History of England in the 18th Century*, London, Longmans, 1890.

LEE, JOSEPH J., *Ireland 1912-1985: Politics and Society*, Cambridge University Press, 1989.

LEMERT, EDWIN M., *Social Psychology*, New York, McGraw-Hill, 1951.

LEVINSON, D.J. (1958), see Adorno, *et al.*

LEVINSON, M.H. (1958), see Adorno, *et al.*

LEWIN, KURT, *A Dynamic Theory of Personality*, New York, McGraw-Hill, 1935.

LIEBERSON, STANLEY, "A Societal Theory of Race and Ethnic Relations", in *American Sociological Review,* 1961.

LIPSET, S.M., (1960), see Bendix R., *et al.*

LOMBROSO, CESARE, *The Criminal Man*, 1876.

LYBERG L. (2003), see Biemer P.

LYNCH, CATHERINE, *ENAR Shadow Report: Racism in Ireland*, Brussels, ENAR, 2008.

LYNCH, PATRICK, *Investment in Education*, Dublin, OECD, 1966.

McCANN, M., Ó SIOCHÁIN, S. and RUANE, J., *Irish Travellers: Culture and Ethnicity*, Belfast, Institute of Irish Studies, Q.U.B., 1994.

McCLELLAND, DAVID, *Personality*, New York, Holt, Rinehart & Winston, 1951.

McGINNITY, F., (2009), see Russell, H. *et al.*

McGINNITY, FRANCES, (2008), see O'Connell, Philip J. *et al.*

McGINNITY, F., O'CONNELL, P.J., QUINN, E. and WILLIAMS, J. *Migrants' Experience of Racism and Discrimination in Ireland*, Dublin, ESRI, 2006.

Mac GRÉIL, MICHEÁL, *Psycho-Socio-Cultural Theory of Prejudice* (unpublished M.A. Thesis), Kent State University, 1966.
- *Prejudice and Tolerance in Ireland*, Dublin, CIR, 1977 & New York Praegar, 1980.
- (Editor) *James Horan: Memoirs 1911-1986*, Dingle, Brandon Books, 1992.
- *Prejudice in Ireland Revisited*, Maynooth, St Patrick's College, 1996 and 1997.
- *Quo Vadimus*, Tuam, Archdiocese, 1998.
- *Our Living Faith: Report on the Pastoral Needs and Resources of the Diocese of Meath*, Maynooth, St Patrick's College, 2005.
- *The Irish Language and the Irish People*, Má Nuad, Aonad Taighde, 2009A.
- *The Challenge of Indifference: A Need for Religious Revival in Ireland*, Maynooth, Dept. of Sociology, 2009B.
- *Emancipation of the Travelling People*, Maynooth, Dept. of Sociology, 2010.

McVEIGH, R., (2009), see Donahoe, M., *et al.*

MAIER, NORMAN, R.F., *Frustration: A Study of Behaviour Without a Goal*, Ann Arbor, PB, (1949), 1961.

MALINOWSKI, BRONISLAW, *The Dynamics of Culture Change: An Enquiry into Race Relations in Africa*, New Haven, Yale U.P., 1945.

MANDELBAUM, DAVID S., *Selected Writings of Edward Sapir on Language, Culture and Personality*, University of California (1949), 1958.

MANNHEIM, KARL, *Man and Society in an Age of Reconstruction*, New York, Routledge and Kegan-Paul, 1942.
- "The Problem of Generations" in *Essays on the Sociology of Knowledge*, New York, Oxford University Press, 1952.
- *Ideology and Utopia*, London, Routledge and Kegan-Paul (1929), 1960.

MARX, KARL and ENGELS, FRIEDRICH, *The German Ideology (*1846), Marx-Engels Institute, Moscow, 1932.
-*The Communist Manifesto*, 1848.

609

MASLOW, AMBROSE H., *Motivation and Personality*, New York, Harper, 1954.

MEERTONS, R.W., (1995), see Pettigrew T.F., *et al.*

MERTON, ROBERT K., "Discrimination and the American Creed" in *Discrimination and National Welfare*, New York, Harper, 1949.
- *Social Theory and Social Structure*, New York, Collier Macmillan, 1957.

MESTROVIC, G. and H.M. BROWN, "Durkheim's Concept of Anomie as Dérèglement", in *Social Problems*, (pages 81ff), 1985.

MILES, ROBERT, *Racism after Race Relations*, London, Routledge, 1993.

MILL, JOHN STUART, *Principles of Political Economy*, London, 1848 (First Edition).

MILLER, N.E. (1939), see Dollard, J. *et al.*

MILLER, PATRICK, H., "The Anatomy of Scientific Racism: Racialist Responses to Black Athletic Achievement" in *The Journal of Sport History*, (pages 119-151), 1998.

MILLER, R.L., (2009), See Acton, C., *et al.*

MISCHEL, WALTER, *Introduction to Personality*, New York, CBS College Publishing, 1981.

MOLONEY, RAYMOND, "The Dialectics of History: Doran, Lonergan, Boegelin", in *Milltown Studies*, No. 65, Dublin, Milltown Park, 2010.

MONTAGUE, ASHLEY, *Man's Most Dangerous Myth: The Fallacy of Race*, Cleveland, The World Publishing Company, 1964.

MORGAN, M., (1984), see Davis E. *et al.*

MORROW, W., (1958), see Adorno, *et al.*

MOWRER, O.H., (1939), see Dollard, J. *et al.*

MURRAY, MICHAEL, (2008), see Coulter, Colin.

MYRDAL, GUNNAR, *The American Dilemma: The Negro Problem and Modern Democracy*, New York, Harper &Row (1944), 1962.

NIC GHIOLLA PHÁDRAIG, MÁIRE, (2007), see Hilliard, Betty, *et al.*

NORTHERN IRELAND STATISTICS & RESEARCH AGENCY, *Northern Ireland Census 2001- Key Statistics for Settlements*, Stationery office, Belfast, 2005.

O'CONNELL, P.J., (2006), see McGinnity, F. *et al.*

O'CONNELL, PHILIP J. and McGINNITY, FRANCES, *Immigrants at Work: Ethnicity and Nationality in the Irish Labour Market,* The EA and ESRI, Dublin, 2008.

Ó GRÁDA, CORMAC and WALSH, BRENDAN, "Fertility and Population in Ireland, North and South" in *Population Studies,* Vol. 49, No. 2, pp259-279, Population Investigation Committee, 1995.

OIREACHTAS, *Prohibition of Incitement to Hatred Act*, 1989, Baile Átha Cliath, 1989.

OIREACHTAS, *Stráitéis Fiche Bliain don Ghaeilge, 2010-2030*, Baile Átha Cliath, Oifig Dhíolta Foilseachán Rialtais, 2010.

O'MAHONY, EOIN, "Mind the Gap: Measuring Religiosity in Ireland", in *Studies*, Issue 385, Vol. 97, Dublin, 2008.

O'MAHONY, PAUL, *Crime and Punishment in Ireland*, Dublin, The Round Hall Press, 1993.

OMOTO, KEIICHI, "The Rise and Fall of the Biological Concept of Race" in *The Japan Review*, 1997.

ORWELL, GEORGE, *Animal Farm*, A Fairy Story, London, Secker & Warburg, 1945.
   Nineteen Eighty-Four, London, Secker & Warburg, 1949.

O'SÍOCHÁIN, SÉAMUS, (1994), see McCann, M. *et al.*

PAOLUCCI, PAUL, "Race and Racism in Marx's Camera Obscura" in *Critical Sociology*, (pages 618-648), 2006.

PARGAMENT, KENNETH I., see Hill (2003) *et al.*

PARK, BERNADETTE, (1991), see Judd, C.M. *et al.* and Kraus, Susan (1995) *et al.*

PARK, ROBERT E., "Our Racial Front on the Pacific", in *Survey Graphic*, Vol. 9, 1926.
   - *Race and Culture*, New York, McGraw-Hill, 1950.

PARK, ROBERT E., and E.W. BURGESS, *Introduction to the Science of Sociology*, Chicago, University of Chicago Press (1921), 1969.
   - *The Structure of Social Actions*, New York, McGraw-Hill, 1937.

PARSONS, TALCOTT, *The Social System*, Glencoe, Illinois, Free Press, (1951), 1964.

PAVEE POINT, *Traveller Inclusion in a New National Agreement*,
   http://www.paveepoint.ie/pdf/SocialInclusion.pdf., 2005 (a).
   Assimilation Policies and Outcomes: Travellers' Experience
   http://www.paveepoint.ie/publications-racism.html, 2005 (b).

PEILLON, MICHEL, *Contemporary Irish Society: An Introduction*, Dublin, Gill and Macmillan, 1982.

PEILLON, MICHEL and SLATER, ÉAMONN, *Encounters with Modern Ireland*, Dublin, I.P.A, 1998.

PETERS, J., (1992), see Scheepers, P. *et al.*

PETTIGREW, THOMAS F., "Reactions toward the New Minorities of Western Europe" in *Annual Review of Sociology*, Vol. 24, pp.77-103, 1998.

PETTIGREW, T.F. and MEERTENS, R.W., "Subtle and Blatant Prejudice in Western Europe" in *European Journal of Social Psychology*, Vol. 25, 57-75, John Wiley & Sons, 1995.

QUINN, E., (2006), see McGinnity, F. *et al.*

RADCLIFFE-BROWN, A.R., *Structure and Function in Primitive Society*, London, Routledge, 1952.

RAJECKI, D.W., *Attitudes,* Sunderland, Mass., Sinauer (2nd Ed.), 1990.

REDLICK, F.C., (1958), see Hollingshead, A.H. *et al.*

REX, JOHN, *Race Relations in Sociological Theory*, London, Weidenfeld and Nicolson, 1970.

RHODES, A.L., "Authoritarianism and Alienation and the Srole Scale as Predictions of Prejudice", in *Sociological Quarterly*, Vol. 3 (pages 193-202), 1961.

ROGERS, CARL, *Counselling and Psychotherapy*, Boston, Houghton-Milflin, 1942.

ROSE, RICHARD, *Governing without Consent*, London, Faber, 1971.

ROTHMAN, D.B., (1990), see Breen, Richard, *et al.*

RUANE, J., (1994), see McCann, M., *et al.*

RUHS, M., *Managing Immigration and Employment of European Non-Nationals in Ireland*, Dublin, T.C.D., 2005.

RUSHD, IBN (1126-1198), see Averroes.

RUSSELL, HELEN, McGINNITY, F., CALLAN T. and KEANE, CLAIRE, A *Woman's Place: Female Participation in the Irish Labour Market*, Dublin, E.A. & ESRI, 2009.

RYAN, C.S., (1991), see Judd, C.M. *et al* and Kraus, Susan (1995) *et al.*

RYAN, LIAM, "Irish Emigration to Britain since World War II" in *Migrations: The Irish at Home and Abroad,* (Ed. R. Kearney), Dublin, Wolfhound Press, 1990.

SANDFORD, R.N., (1958), see Adorno, *et al.*

SAPIR, EDWARD, see Mandelbaum, David S. (Editor), 1958.

SCHEEPERS, P., FELLING A., and J. PETERS, "Anomie Authoritarianism and Ethnocentrism: Update of a Classical Theme and an Empirical Text" in *Politics and the Individual*, Vol. II, No. 1, 1992.

SCHEEPERS, P.L.N., (1989), see Eisinga, R.N., *et al.*

SCHEFF, THOMAS, *Being Mentally Ill*, London, Weidenfeld & Nicolson, 1966.

SEARS, R.R., (1939), see Dollard J. *et al.*

SIMMEL, GEORG, *Conflict and the Web of Conflict Affiliations*, New York, Free Press (1908), 1953.

SIMPSON, G.E. and J.M. YINGER, *Racial and Cultural Minorities: An Analysis of Prejudice and Discrimination*, New York, Harper & Row, 1965.

SINNOTT, RICHARD, (2006), see Hayes, Bernadette C., *et al.*

SKINNER, B.F., *Science and Human Behaviour*, New York, Macmillan, 1953.
- *About Behaviourism*, New York, Knopf, 1974.

SLATER, ÉAMONN, (1998), see Peillon, Michel, *et al.*

SMELSER, NEIL J., *Theory of Collective Behaviour*, New York, Free Press, 1962.
- (Editor) *Handbook of Sociology*, London, Sage, 1988.

SMITH, TOM W., "Social Identity and Socio-Demographic Structure" in *International Journal of Public Opinion Research 2007,* Vol. 19, No. 3, Oxford University Press, 2007.

SOLOMOS, JOHN and LEO BACK, "Conceptualising Racisms: Social Theory, Politics and Research" in *Sociology*, 1994.

SOYGID, S. (2005), see Hesse B. *et al.*

SPAETH, J.L. and GREELEY, A.M., *Recent Alumni and Higher Education: A Study of College Graduates*, New York, McGraw-Hill, 1970.

SPENCER, MARTIN E., "Multiculturalism, 'Political Correctness' and the Politics of Identity" in *Sociological Forum,* Vol. 9, No. 4, pp.547-567, Springer, 1994.

SROLE, LEO, "Social Dysfunction, Personality and Social Distance Attitudes", paper read to the *American Sociological Society*, 1951.
- "Social Integration and Certain Corollaries: An Explanatory Study", in *American Sociological Review*, (pages 709-716), 1956.

STEWART, A.T.Q., *The Narrow Ground: the Roots of Conflict in Ulster*, London, Faber & Faber (1977), 1989.

SUMNER, W. GRAHAM, *Folkways: A Study of the Sociological Importance of Usages, Manners, Customs and Morals*, New York, Ginn, 1906.

THOMAS, W.I., and F. ZNANIECKI, *The Polish Peasant in Europe and in America*, Boston, Badger, 1918-20.

TONNIES, FERDINAND, *Community and Association*, London, Routledge and Kegan-Paul, 1955.

TYLOR, EDWARD BURNETT, *Primitive Culture*, London, Murray, 1871.

VANDER ZANDEN, JAMES W., *American Minority Relations*, New York, Ronald Press, 1972.

VEBLEN, THORSTEIN, *The Theory of the Leisure Class*, New York, Vanguard Press, 1928.

VISWESWARAN, KAMALA, "Race and the Culture of Anthropology", in *American Anthropologist*, Vol. 100, No. 1, pp.70-83, 1998.

WALSH, BRENDAN (1995), see Ó Gráda, Cormac, *et al.*

WEBER, ANN, *Social Psychology*, New York, Harper Perennial, 1992.

WEBER, MAX, *Essays in Sociology* (Edited by Garth & Mills), London, Routledge and Kegan-Paul, (1948), 1970.

WHELAN, CHRIS. (ed.) *Values and Social Change in Ireland,* Dublin, Gill & Macmillan, 1990.
- (1990), see Breen, Richard, *et al.*
- (1992), see Goldthorpe, J. *et al.*

WHITE, LESLIE, *The Evolution of Culture: The Development of Civilisation until the Fall of Rome*, New York, McGraw-Hill, 1959.
- *The Science of Culture, A Study of Man and Civilisation*, Toronto, Doubleday (1959), 1969.

WILLIAMS, J. (2006), see McGinnity, F. *et al.*

WILSON, BRYAN, "Aspects of Secularization in the West"*,* in *Japanese Journal of Religious Studies,* Vol. 3:4, 264-276, 1976.

WINANT, HOWARD, "Race and Race Theory" in *Annual Review of Sociology,* Vol. 26, pp.169-185, 2000.

WOOD M., (2009), see Donahoe, M., *et al.*

WORSLEY, PETER, *et al, Introducing Sociology*, Harmondsworth (England), Penguin, 1970.

WYNDHAM ACT 1905.

YINGER, J. MILTON, *The Scientific Study of Religion*, New York, Schocken Books, 1970.

YINGER, J.M. (1965), see Simpson, G.E., *et al.*

ZANGWILL, ISRAEL, *The Melting Pot: Drama in Four Acts*, New York, Macmillan, 1921.

ZNANIECKI, F. (1918-20), see Thomas, W.I. *et al.*

***

Appendix A

Survey Questionnaire 2007 / 2008

SURVEY OF ATTITUDES IN IRELAND 2007 / 2008

SRI

Area Code: ____ ____ ____   Respondent Code:____ ____   Interviewer No: ___ ___ ___ ___ ___

Interviewer Name: _____

Date of Interview: ____(day) _____ (Month) _____ (year)   Time began (24 hour clock) ____ : ____

Introduction: Hello, my name is _____. I am a member of a research team from _____ (Fieldwork Agency). We have been commissioned by the ESRI and the Research Unit at NUI Maynooth to carry out a social survey of a representative sample of adults in the Republic.

The main purpose of the survey is to find out people's opinions, attitudes and values, so that we can get a better understanding of how people see the problems and challenges facing Irish society.

Your address has been chosen as part of a random sample of the Irish residents. It is very important for us that you co-operate so that our sample will be completely representative. I can assure you that strict confidentiality and anonymity will be maintained with regard to all of your answers.

I would be most thankful if you could spare me about 40 minutes of your time to answer a questionnaire.

1.   *[INTERVIEWER: RESPONDENT'S SEX IS:]*   Male.......☐1   Female.......☐2

2a.   Perhaps I could begin by asking a few questions about you. Could you tell me where you were born? Perhaps you could tell me the size of the town or city and the county or country.
[INTERVIEWER: COMPLETE LINE A, BELOW]

Who	City 100,000+	Large town, 10,000-99,000	Town 1,500 to 9,999	Rural or town under 1,500	County or Country [Write in]
		Size of Place [Tick one box]			
a) Respondent	☐1	☐2	☐3	☐4	
b) Spouse or partner	☐1	☐2	☐3	☐4	
c) Father	☐1	☐2	☐3	☐4	
d) Mother	☐1	☐2	☐3	☐4	

2a1   If you are married or live with a partner, where was your spouse or partner born? *[INTERVIEWER: COMPLETE LINE B, ABOVE. IF NO SPOUSE OR PARTNER, WRITE 'NOT APPLICABLE']*

2a2   And where were your parents born? *[INTERVIEWER: COMPLETE LINES C AND D, ABOVE]*

2b.   Where did you grow up? (i.e. principal county or country of residence up to 16 years)

_____

2C: [IF RESPONDENT NOT BORN IN THIS AREA] How many years have you been living here? _____ (years).

3a.   Which of these terms best describes the way you usually think of yourself?
(SHOW CARD A AND TICK ONE BOX IN FIRST COLUMN BELOW).

How see self...	3A First Choice	3B Strong or average	3C Second choice
Anglo-Irish	☐1		☐1
British	☐2		☐2
County/city where I grew up	☐3	Strong.............☐1	☐3
European	☐4	Average............☐2	☐4
Irish	☐5	(Don't know).....☐3	☐5
Northern Irish	☐6		☐6
Southern Irish	☐7		☐7
Other (please specify)	☐8		☐8

3b.   Would you say you are strong or average in thinking of yourself in these terms? *[TICK ONE AT 3B ABOVE]*

3c.   Of the remaining categories, which would be closest to the way you see yourself? *TICK ONE BOX IN COLUMN 3C ABOVE.*

3d.   Of which country are you a citizen? _____
(COUNTRY, IF MORE THAN ONE, LIST ALL).

Social Distance

4a. People have different views about certain groups in society. I am going to read out a list of groups and I would like you to tell me, for each group, how close you would be willing to allow them. The idea is to get your first reaction. Therefore, it would be better if we went through the list fairly quickly. *(SHOW CARD B AND EXPLAIN IT).*

	A. Closest Social Distance							B. Reason, if not kin
	KIN	FRND	NBR	WORK	CITZ	VISIT	DEBAR	[READ TEXT 4B, ENTER LETTER]
1. Africans	1	2	3	4	5	6	7	_____
2. Agnostics	1	2	3	4	5	6	7	_____
3. Alcoholics	1	2	3	4	5	6	7	_____
4. American Blacks	1	2	3	4	5	6	7	_____
5. Atheists	1	2	3	4	5	6	7	_____
6. Arabs	1	2	3	4	5	6	7	_____
7. Blacks	1	2	3	4	5	6	7	_____
8. British	1	2	3	4	5	6	7	_____
9. Canadians	1	2	3	4	5	6	7	_____
10 Capitalists	1	2	3	4	5	6	7	_____
11 Chinese	1	2	3	4	5	6	7	_____
12 Coloureds	1	2	3	4	5	6	7	_____
13 Communists	1	2	3	4	5	6	7	_____
14 Drug Addicts	1	2	3	4	5	6	7	_____
15 Dutch	1	2	3	4	5	6	7	_____
16 English	1	2	3	4	5	6	7	_____
17 French	1	2	3	4	5	6	7	_____
18 Gardaí	1	2	3	4	5	6	7	_____
19 Gay people	1	2	3	4	5	6	7	_____
20 Germans	1	2	3	4	5	6	7	_____
21 Someone with physical disability	1	2	3	4	5	6	7	_____
22 Heavy Drinkers	1	2	3	4	5	6	7	_____
23 Indians (non-Am)	1	2	3	4	5	6	7	_____
24. Iranians	1	2	3	4	5	6	7	_____
25 Israelis	1	2	3	4	5	6	7	_____
26 Italians	1	2	3	4	5	6	7	_____
27 Travellers	1	2	3	4	5	6	7	_____
28 Irish speakers	1	2	3	4	5	6	7	_____
29 Jews	1	2	3	4	5	6	7	_____
30 Lithuanians	1	2	3	4	5	6	7	_____
31 Someone with mental disability	1	2	3	4	5	6	7	_____
32 Moslems	1	2	3	4	5	6	7	_____
33 Nigerians	1	2	3	4	5	6	7	_____
34 Northern Irish	1	2	3	4	5	6	7	_____
35. Pakistanis	1	2	3	4	5	6	7	_____
36 Palestinians	1	2	3	4	5	6	7	_____
37 Polish people	1	2	3	4	5	6	7	_____
38 Protestants	1	2	3	4	5	6	7	_____
39 Roman Catholics	1	2	3	4	5	6	7	_____
40 Russians	1	2	3	4	5	6	7	_____
41 Romanians	1	2	3	4	5	6	7	_____
42 Scottish	1	2	3	4	5	6	7	_____
43 Socialists	1	2	3	4	5	6	7	_____
44 Spaniards	1	2	3	4	5	6	7	_____
45 Trade Unionists	1	2	3	4	5	6	7	_____
46 Unemployed	1	2	3	4	5	6	7	_____
47 Unionists	1	2	3	4	5	6	7	_____
48 Unmarried Mothers	1	2	3	4	5	6	7	_____
49 Welsh	1	2	3	4	5	6	7	_____
50 Working class	1	2	3	4	5	6	7	_____
51 White Americans	1	2	3	4	5	6	7	_____

4b. Looking over your answers to this question, there are a number of categories which you would not welcome into kinship. Which of the following would you say was your main reason for placing them at the distance indicated?

[SHOW CARD C AND EXPLAIN IT. THEN ENTER LETTER UNDER REASON FOR EACH GROUP NOT CIRCLED 1 IN TABLE ABOVE. DO NOT CIRCLE LETTERS HERE]

A	Religious Beliefs and/or Practices	E	Economic danger to us
B	Racial – colour of skin, etc	F	Not socially acceptable
C	Political views and/or methods	G	Way of life
D	Nationality and culture.	H	Other (specify in table above)

Background and views on Family

5a Let's go back and talk about yourself again.
What is your date of birth? ___ ___ / ___ ___ / ___ ___ ___ ___ (dd/mm/yyyy)

5b Could you tell me whether you are …
Single/Never Married.. ☐1
Married.. ☐2
Separated or Divorced.. ☐3
Living in permanent partnership .... ☐4
Widowed .... ☐5
Other, specify _____ ..... ☐6

5c How many children do you have (including adopted), if any? _____ [IF NONE, GO TO 5E]

5d And how old is the eldest? _____ and the youngest_____

5e How many children were there in your family of origin?
(count in yourself and all your brothers and sisters (incl. any adopted)_____

6. With regard to the role of men and women in society, I would be interested to know if you would agree or disagree with each of the following statements:

	Agree	Neither agree nor disagree	Disagree	(Don't know)
1.A woman's proper place is in the home	☐1	☐2	☐3	☐4
2. It is bad that there are so few women in government in this country	☐1	☐2	☐3	☐4
3. Generally speaking, women think less clearly than men	☐1	☐2	☐3	☐4
4. Women work better than men in the caring professions	☐1	☐2	☐3	☐4
5. People should be employed and promoted strictly on the basis of ability, regardless of sex or gender	☐1	☐2	☐3	☐4
6. The feminist movement is very necessary in Ireland	☐1	☐2	☐3	☐4
7. Some equality in marriage is a good thing, but by and large the husband ought to have the main say in family matters	☐1	☐2	☐3	☐4
8.Education and vocational training is less important for girls than boys	☐1	☐2	☐3	☐4
9. A woman should be as free as a man to propose marriage	☐1	☐2	☐3	☐4
10.Husbands and wives should have an equal say in how to spend the family money, irrespective of who earns it	☐1	☐2	☐3	☐4
11. Women should be allowed to become priests in the Roman Catholic Church	☐1	☐2	☐3	☐4
12. The emigration of young women from Ireland is less serious for the country than the emigration of young men	☐1	☐2	☐3	☐4

Religion

8a Now, I would like to ask you a number of questions relating to religion.
Could you tell me the religion or denomination to which you, your spouse/partner and your parents belong?

[INT: PLEASE SPECIFY DENOMINATION, WHERE RELEVANT. IF NONE, WRITE IN 'NONE']

Respondent Self _____

Spouse _____ Not applicable (no spouse or partner) ... ☐₀

Father _____

Mother _____

8b Is this the religion in which you (and your spouse) were brought up?

INTERVIEWER: IF YES FOR BOTH, GO TO Q.9.

	8b. Same religion brought up?	8c. If no at 8b, religion in which brought up	8d. If no at 8b, main reason for change
a. Self	Yes.. ☐₁ No.....☐₂		
b. Spouse	Yes.. ☐₁ No.....☐₂		

8c. If NO please give religion in which you and your spouse were brought up *[enter above in table]*

8d What was the main reason for change? *[enter above in table]*

9 How would you say that the religious beliefs in which you were brought up influenced your growth or development as a person? *[SHOW CARD D AND TICK ONE BOX]*

An essential help to me...☐₁
Important but not essential..☐₂
Helped me somewhat ....☐₃
Neither a help nor a hindrance..☐₄
Hindered me somewhat ....☐₅
A serious hindrance ....☐₆
A grave hindrance ....☐₇

10 Would you say that being a _____ (Respondent's Religion) is an advantage to you in getting on?
[SHOW CARD E AND TICK ONE BOX]

A great advantage...☐₁
A slight advantage...☐₂
Neither an advantage nor disadvantage ....☐₃
A slight disadvantage ....☐₄
A great disadvantage ....☐₅

11a How often do you attend Church or place of Worship? *[SHOW CARD F AND TICK ONE BOX]*

Daily..☐₁
Several times a week...☐₂
At least once a week..☐₃
Once to three times a month ....☐₄
Several times a year..☐₅
Less frequently ....☐₆
Never ....☐₇
(No answer) ....☐₈
Not applicable ....☐₉

11b *IF CODES 4 TO 6 AT (11A)* Is there any particular reason why you don't go more often?
[SHOW CARD G AND TICK ONE BOX]

Illness..☐₁
Working..☐₂
Just don't bother ....☐₃
Other reason (specify) _____ ....☐₄

12. *FOR ROMAN CATHOLICS ONLY:* Could you say how often you go to Mass, to Holy Communion and to Confession? *(TICK ONE BOX IN EACH COLUMN – USE CATEGORIES AS PROBES AS NECESSARY)*

	Mass	Holy Communion	Confession
Daily	□1	□1	□1
Several times a week	□2	□2	□2
At least once a week	□3	□3	□3
Once to three times a month	□4	□4	□4
Several times a year	□5	□5	□5
Less frequently	□6	□6	□6
Never	□7	□7	□7
(No answer)	□8	□8	□8

ALL

13   How often do you pray ?
    [SHOW CARD I AND TICK ONE BOX]

Several times a day	□1
Once a day	□2
Several times a week	□3
Once a week	□4
Less than once a week	□5
Never	□6

14   How close do you feel to God most of the time?   Please look at this card.
[SHOW CARD J AND TICK ONE BOX]

Extremely close	□1
Somewhat close	□2
Not very close	□3
Not close at all	□4
Does not believe in God	□5
(Don't know)	□6

15   Now, I would like to read you a few statements about beliefs that some people hold.
    After I read each statement could you tell me whether you agree or disagree?

	Agree	Neither agree nor disagree	Disagree	(Don't know)
Everything that happens must be accepted as God's will	□1	□2	□3	□4
The more active you are in politics, the harder it is to be a good Christian	□1	□2	□3	□4
The miracles in the Bible happened as they are described there	□1	□2	□3	□4
People whose doctrines are false should not be allowed to preach in this country	□1	□2	□3	□4
My religion has a great deal of influence on my political ideas	□1	□2	□3	□4
If I have to make an important decision my religion would play an Important part in it	□1	□2	□3	□4

16   How important would you say it is for children (USE CATEGORIES AS PROBES IN EACH CASE)

	Very Important	Fairly important	Not very important	Let them make up their own minds	(Don't know)
To be brought up with the same religious views as their parents	□1	□2	□3	□4	□5
To be brought up with the same views as parents on the Border question	□1	□2	□3	□4	□5
To be brought up to vote for the same party as their parents do	□1	□2	□3	□4	□5

17a Imagine, If you had a son, and he came to you and told you that he had decided to become a priest, how do you think you would respond? *(TICK ONE BOX ON FIRST LINE BELOW)*

17b And if you had a daughter and she came to you and said she had decided to become a nun, how do you think you would respond? *(TICK ONE BOX ON SECOND LINE BELOW)*

	Greatly Welcome	Welcome with reservation	Neither welcome nor discourage	Would discourage	(Don't know)
Son's decision to become a priest	☐1	☐2	☐3	☐4	☐5
Daughter's decision to become a nun	☐1	☐2	☐3	☐4	☐5

ALL

18a There's a lot of talk these days about uniting the Protestant Church and the Roman Catholic Church into one. What do you think of this idea? (Let us make sure I have this clear). Do you think that in principle uniting the Protestant and Catholic churches is ....*[READ AND TICK ONE]*

Desirable	Depends	(Don't know, no opinion)	Undesirable
☐4	☐3	☐2	☐1

18b Do you think that in practice uniting the churches .... *[READ AND TICK ONE]*

Is possible	It depends	(Don't know, no opinion)	Impossible
☐4	☐3	☐2	☐1

General Views

19. That's very interesting. Before going on to the next subject, I would like to get your opinions on a number of general views held by some people. Would you agree or disagree or have no opinion about each of the following statements: *[READ AND TICK ONE BOX ON EACH LINE]*

		Agree	Neither agree nor disagree	Disagree	(Don't know)
a	With everything so uncertain in these days, it seems as though anything could happen	☐1	☐2	☐3	☐4
b	These days a person doesn't really know whom he/she can count on	☐1	☐2	☐3	☐4
c	Most people can still be depended on to come through in a pinch	☐1	☐2	☐3	☐4
d	Everything changes so quickly that I often have trouble deciding what are the right rules to follow	☐1	☐2	☐3	☐4
e	Everywhere in the world Irish people are loved	☐1	☐2	☐3	☐4
f	If you try hard enough, you can usually get what you want.	☐1	☐2	☐3	☐4
g	In striving for international co-operation we have to take care that no typically Irish customs get lost	☐1	☐2	☐3	☐4
h	People were better off in the old days when everyone knew just how (s)he was expected to act	☐1	☐2	☐3	☐4
i	Irish people are always willing to put their shoulders to the wheel	☐1	☐2	☐3	☐4
j	There is little use writing to public officials for anything	☐1	☐2	☐3	☐4
k	The lot of the average person is getting worse not better in Ireland today	☐1	☐2	☐3	☐4
l	It's hardly fair to bring children into the world with the way things look for the future	☐1	☐2	☐3	☐4
m	Generally speaking, Ireland is a better country than most other countries	☐1	☐2	☐3	☐4
n	Most people don't care what happens to the next fellow	☐1	☐2	☐3	☐4
o	You sometimes can't help wondering whether any effort is worthwhile	☐1	☐2	☐3	☐4
p	Irish people have reason to be proud of their history	☐1	☐2	☐3	☐4
q	Parents are not strict enough with their children in Ireland today	☐1	☐2	☐3	☐4
r	Nowadays, more and more people are prying into matters that should remain personal and private	☐1	☐2	☐3	☐4
s	What this country needs most, more than laws and political programmes, are a few courageous, fearless, devoted leaders in whom the people can put their faith	☐1	☐2	☐3	☐4

Education

20a Thank you, I wonder if we could now talk about how you get on in school/college?
What age were you when you left school/college (for the first time)?

Age _____ Years   Still in school/college ... ☐₀

20b Did you return to school/college later   Yes......☐₁   No........☐₂

20c What was the total number of years spent in full-time education_____

21a What type of second-level school did you attend [READ AND TICK ONE]
(for the last two years of your times in second-level education)?

Secondary School ....☐₁
Secondary fee Paying………….................☐₂
Vocational………….………. ....☐₃
Comprehensive………….……. ....☐₄
Community ....☐₅
Did not attend second level........................☐₆

21b What was the name of the second Level School _____

22a So what level did you reach? [TICK ONE BOX UNDER 'SELF', BELOW]
22b How was it in the case of your wife/husband/ partner? [TICK ONE BOX UNDER 'SPOUSE', BELOW]
22c Could you tell me about your parents? [TICK ONE BOX UNDER 'FATHER' AND ONE UNDER 'MOTHER', BELOW]

[SHOW CARD K AND TICK ONE BOX IN EACH COLUMN]

	Self	Spouse	Father	Mother
0. None	☐₁	☐₁	☐₁	☐₁
1. Incomplete Primary	☐₂	☐₂	☐₂	☐₂
2. Complete Primary	☐₃	☐₃	☐₃	☐₃
3. 1-2 years of Second Level school, no exam	☐₄	☐₄	☐₄	☐₄
3. Group Cert	☐₅	☐₅	☐₅	☐₅
3. 3-4 years of Second Level (Inter or Junior Cert or equivalent)	☐₆	☐₆	☐₆	☐₆
4. Completed Second Level (Leaving Cert or equivalent)	☐₇	☐₇	☐₇	☐₇
5. Some University/Third Level, no qualification	☐₈	☐₈	☐₈	☐₈
5. Third Level Certificate or Diploma	☐₉	☐₉	☐₉	☐₉
6. Completed University/Third Level Primary Degree (e.g. BA)	☐₁₀	☐₁₀	☐₁₀	☐₁₀
7. Post Graduate (M.A., Ph.D., etc.)	☐₁₁	☐₁₁	☐₁₁	☐₁₁
9. Not applicable (spouse, father, mother only)		☐₁₂	☐₁₂	☐₁₂

22d Please list the highest educational (i.e. certificates, diplomas, degrees, etc) and/or professional qualifications you received.

Degrees_____

Diplomas_____

Certificates_____

Professional Qualifications_____

Other _____

22e Have you attended adult education courses since finishing your formal education?

Yes........☐₁   No.............☐₂ → Go to 23

22f (If yes) What was important course in adult education you completed.

_____

Black People

23. Thank you. Now I would like to get your views in relation to Black people. Could I ask you a number of questions?

		Yes	No	(Don't know)
a	If you had a boarding house would you refuse digs (accommodation) to Black people?	□₁	□₂	□₃
b	Do you think that because of their basic make-up Black people could never become as good Irish people as others?	□₁	□₂	□₃
c	Do you believe there should be a stricter control on Black people who enter this country than on Whites?	□₁	□₂	□₃
d	Do you believe that the Black person is basically or inherently inferior to the White person?	□₁	□₂	□₃
e	Would you stay in a hotel or guest house that had Black guests also?	□₁	□₂	□₃
f	Do you believe that the Black person deserves exactly the same social privileges as the White person?	□₁	□₂	□₃
g	Do you hold that by nature the Black and White person are equal?	□₁	□₂	□₃
h	Do you believe that Black people are naturally more highly sexed than White people?	□₁	□₂	□₃
i	Would you hold that Black people should be sent back to Africa and Asia where they belong and kept there?	□₁	□₂	□₃
j	Do you agree that it is a good thing for Whites and Blacks to get married where there are no cultural or religious barriers?	□₁	□₂	□₃

Community and Social Involvement

24a That's fine, the next thing I'd like to talk about is community involvement.
Are you a member of any voluntary organisation/association/society ?

Yes.........□₁   No..............□₂ → Got to 25a

24b If yes, are you a member of any of the following types of voluntary organisations?
(SHOW CARD L AND TICK ALL THOSE THAT APPLY).

1. Tenants' /Residents Committee ....□₁	9. Prayer Group.....................................□₉
2. Golf Club...□₂	10. Other Church/Religious Group.....□₁₀
3. Political Party/Movement..................□₃	11. Sports Club/Association ....□₁₁
4. Peace Movement..............................□₄	12. Snooker/Darts Club ....□₁₂
5. Pro-Environment Society..................□₅	13. Irish Language Group...................□₁₃
6. Trade Union......................................□₆	14. Social/Leisure Group...................□₁₄
7. ICA/Women's Groups.......................□₇	15. Social Action Group......................□₁₅
8. Music/Dance/Drama Group..............□₈	16. Other (Specify) ....□₁₆

Immigration

25a Thank you.   Now I would like to get your opinion about people coming to Ireland from other countries.

Would you say it is generally bad or good for Ireland's economy that people come to live here from other countries? Please use this card *(CARD M).*

Bad for the economy _____ Good for the economy   (Don't Know)

$\square_0$ $\square_1$ $\square_2$ $\square_3$ $\square_4$ $\square_5$ $\square_6$ $\square_7$ $\square_8$ $\square_9$ $\square_{10}$ $\square_{88}$

25b   And, using this card, would you say that Ireland's cultural life is generally undermined or enriched by people coming to live here from other countries? *(CARD N).*

Cultural life Undermined _____ Cultural life enriched   (Don't Know)

$\square_0$ $\square_1$ $\square_2$ $\square_3$ $\square_4$ $\square_5$ $\square_6$ $\square_7$ $\square_8$ $\square_9$ $\square_{10}$ $\square_{88}$

25c   Is Ireland made a worse or a better place to live by people coming to live here from other countries? Please use this card *(CARD O).*

Worse place to live _____ Better Place to live   (Don't Know)

$\square_0$ $\square_1$ $\square_2$ $\square_3$ $\square_4$ $\square_5$ $\square_6$ $\square_7$ $\square_8$ $\square_9$ $\square_{10}$ $\square_{88}$

Languages

26a Could I now ask you a few questions about the Irish Language.
With regard to the future of Irish which of the following would you like to see happen?
(SHOW CARD P AND TICK ONLY ONE OF THE FOLLOWING).

The Irish language should be discarded and forgotten..$\square_1$
It should be preserved for its cultural value as in music and art...............................$\square_2$
Spoken Irish should be preserved only in the Gaeltacht...$\square_3$
Ireland should be bilingual, with English as the principal language............................$\square_4$
Ireland should be bilingual, with Irish as the principal language...............................$\square_5$
Irish should be the principal language of use (like English is now)............................$\square_6$
Other, please specify _____..........$\square_7$

26b   Which of the following best describe the way you felt about Irish while in school?
26c   And the way you feel now? (USE CATEGORIES AS PROBES)

	When in school	Now
[TICK ONE BOX IN EACH COLUMN]		
Strongly in favour	$\square_1$	$\square_1$
Somewhat in favour	$\square_2$	$\square_2$
No particular feelings	$\square_3$	$\square_3$
Somewhat opposed	$\square_4$	$\square_4$
Strongly opposed	$\square_5$	$\square_5$
Not applicable (Did not go to school where Irish was taught)	$\square_6$	

26d   *(IF CHANGE RECORDED BETWEEN 'WHEN IN SCHOOL' AND 'NOW')*
What brought about this change? _____

26e   Have you studied any other language besides Irish and English?

Yes........$\square_1$ No..............$\square_2$ → Go to 26g

26f   If yes, Which ones ? _____

26g   What would you say your standard is in these languages? (USE CATEGORIES AS PROBES)

Language	Very Fluent	Fluent	Middling	No so Fluent	Only a Little	None
Irish	☐1	☐2	☐3	☐4	☐5	☐6
French	☐1	☐2	☐3	☐4	☐5	☐6
German	☐1	☐2	☐3	☐4	☐5	☐6
English	☐1	☐2	☐3	☐4	☐5	☐6
Spanish	☐1	☐2	☐3	☐4	☐5	☐6
Italian	☐1	☐2	☐3	☐4	☐5	☐6
Other (Specify_____)	☐1	☐2	☐3	☐4	☐5	☐6

27a   How frequently would you say you use Irish?   (i.e. read, listen to or speak)

Daily	Weekly	Occasionally	Rarely	Never
☐1	☐2	☐3	☐4	☐5 → Go to 27c

27b   (If codes 1-4 circled at 27a)   When would you normally use Irish? Would you use it when ....
[READ LIST AND TICK 'YES' OR 'NO' FOR EACH.]

	Yes	No
1. When meeting Irish-speaking friends	☐1	☐2
2. At work	☐1	☐2
3. All possible opportunities	☐1	☐2
4. At home	☐1	☐2
5. Listening to programmes TV/RADIO	☐1	☐2
6. Reading (specify)	☐1	☐2
7. Communicating with officials	☐1	☐2
8. Other (specify)	☐1	☐2

27c   INTERVIEWER: CHECK 26G
RESPONDENT'S COMPETENCE IN IRISH IS 'VERY FLUENT', 'FLUENT' OR 'MIDDLING' ....☐1 → GO TO 27d
RESPONDENT'S COMPETENCE IN IRISH IS 'NOT SO FLUENT', 'ONLY A LITTLE' OR 'NONE' ....☐2 → GO TO 28

27d   Could I have your personal reaction to using Irish?
(Please answer yes or no to the following statements)
[READ LIST AND TICK 'YES' OR 'NO' FOR EACH.]

	Yes	No
1 I am committed to using as much as I can	☐1	☐2
2 I am reluctant to begin a conversation in Irish with a person whose ability in Irish I am not sure of	☐1	☐2
3. I would also be reluctant to speak Irish to an Irish-speaking person when others who do not know Irish are present	☐1	☐2

Northern Ireland

28. Northern Ireland is a topic of interest and concern for many people. I would like to get your views on some aspects relating to the Northern problems.
Would you agree or disagree with each of the following statements?

	Agree	Neither agree nor disagree	Disagree	(Don't know)
Catholics in Northern Ireland have more in common with Northern Protestants than they have with Catholics in the Republic	□1	□2	□3	□4
Northern Irish Protestants have more in common with the rest of the Irish people than they have with the British	□1	□2	□3	□4
Northern Ireland and the Irish Republic are two separate nations	□1	□2	□3	□4
Having separate Catholic and Protestant schools (Primary and Secondary Schools) has been a major cause of division in the Northern Irish community.	□1	□2	□3	□4
The use of violence, while regrettable has been necessary	□1	□2	□3	□4
A return to the Irish language and culture could provide a good basis for Irish unity in the long term (even though it might present difficulties in the short term)	□1	□2	□3	□4
The position and influence of the Catholic Church in the Republic is a real obstacle to Irish unity	□1	□2	□3	□4
National unity is an essential condition for the just solution of the present Northern problems.	□1	□2	□3	□4
Protestants in the Republic have more in common with Catholics here than they have with Protestants in Northern Ireland	□1	□2	□3	□4
There should be increased co-operation across the Border with the people in Northern Ireland	□1	□2	□3	□4
Northerners on all sides tend to be extreme and unreasonable	□1	□2	□3	□4
The 'Good Friday' Agreement (1998) provides a good basis for community co-operation	□1	□2	□3	□4

Political Parties and Government

29a If there were a General Election today and you were voting, which Party would you be inclined to vote for (first preference)

_____ (party name)   Would not vote ... □0

29b Have you voted for this party in the past?

Regularly......□1   Occasionally......□2   Never......□3

30. Can you remember which party you voted for in the last General Election in June 2007 (first preference) ?

1. Fianna Fail......□1
2. Fine Gael......□2
3. Labour Party......□3
4. Progressive Democrats....□4
5. Green Party......□5

6. Sinn Fein......□6
7. Independent......□7
8. Other (specify)......□8
9. Can't remember......□9
10. Did Not Vote......□10

31. Now, I'd like to read you a few things that people sometimes say in favour of our system of government. After each statement please tell me whether you agree, disagree or have no opinion.

	Agree	Neither agree nor disagree	Disagree	(Don't know)
Our system of government is good because...				
a. It is traditional	□1	□2	□3	□4
b. It keeps things peaceful here	□1	□2	□3	□4
c. Its goals are usually good ones	□1	□2	□3	□4
d. It is in the hands of people who are good leaders	□1	□2	□3	□4

Views of Other Groups and Organisations

32. Now, I would like to read you a number of statements about the opinions that some people hold. After I have read each statement could you tell me whether you agree or disagree or have no opinion?

		Agree	Neither agree nor disagree	Disagree	(Don't know)
a	If Ireland did not have its own team in the Olympic games or International sports, I would cheer for the British	□1	□2	□3	□4
b	The British are pretty decent people	□1	□2	□3	□4
c	Some British qualities are admirable but on a whole I don't like them (the British).	□1	□2	□3	□4
d	I'd rather live in Britain than any other place abroad.	□1	□2	□3	□4
e	The British are inferior in every way.	□1	□2	□3	□4
f	British people are slow and unimaginative	□1	□2	□3	□4
g	I don't object to the British people but I don't like the British Government.	□1	□2	□3	□4
h	The world owes a lot to Britain	□1	□2	□3	□4
i.	I am happy to see British people get on in Ireland	□1	□2	□3	□4
j.	I would never marry a British person	□1	□2	□3	□4
k.	I would be happy if Britain were brought to its knees.	□1	□2	□3	□4
l.	The British Government has been even-handed when dealing with Northern Ireland since 1969	□1	□2	□3	□4
m.	The British have little respect for the Irish	□1	□2	□3	□4

33. In recent years, the problem of the Travellers has been discussed widely in Ireland. I would be very thankful if you would let me know if you agree or disagree in relation to each of the following statements referring to an average member of the Travelling People.
(USE CATEGORIES AS PROBES)

		Agree Strongly	Agree moderately	Agree slightly	Disagree Slightly	Disagree moderately	Disagree Strongly	(Don't Know)
a.	I would respect a Traveller	□1	□2	□3	□4	□5	□6	□7
b.	I would be reluctant to buy a house next door to a Traveller	□1	□2	□3	□4	□5	□6	□7
c.	I would be hesitant to seek out a Traveller's company	□1	□2	□3	□4	□5	□6	□7
d.	I would be willing to employ a Traveller	□1	□2	□3	□4	□5	□6	□7
e.	I would exclude a Traveller from my close set of friends	□1	□2	□3	□4	□5	□6	□7
f.	I would consider a Traveller competent to serve on a jury	□1	□2	□3	□4	□5	□6	□7
g.	I would avoid a Traveller in social situations	□1	□2	□3	□4	□5	□6	□7

628

34. Thank you, again, I would like to read you various statements about people's attitudes and opinions on a wide range of issues. After I have read each statement could you tell me whether you agree or disagree.

		Agree	Neither agree nor disagree	Disagree	(Don't know)
a	There should be a very strict control of RTE	□1	□2	□3	□4
b	Communism should be outlawed in Ireland	□1	□2	□3	□4
c.	An applicant's religion should be considered when considering him or her for a responsible public position.	□1	□2	□3	□4
d.	Mothers are the best family builders	□1	□2	□3	□4
e.	Catholic priests should be free to marry	□1	□2	□3	□4
f.	Homosexual behaviour between consenting adults should not be a crime	□1	□2	□3	□4
g.	Obedience to the directives of the clergy should be the hallmark of the true Catholic	□1	□2	□3	□4
h.	Gardaí should be armed always.	□1	□2	□3	□4
i.	Travellers should be facilitated to live their own way of life decently	□1	□2	□3	□4
j.	The dole should be abolished	□1	□2	□3	□4
k.	A thing is either right or wrong and none of this ambiguous woolly thinking	□1	□2	□3	□4
l.	Premarital sex is always wrong	□1	□2	□3	□4
m.	Prostitution should remain a prosecutable offence	□1	□2	□3	□4
n.	Student protests should be outlawed	□1	□2	□3	□4

Occupation, Standard of Living and Household

35a That is very interesting. Now, could you tell me something about your occupation and employment. Which of the following would best describe your present situation?
(SHOW CARD Q AND TICK ONE BOX)

Employee, Permanent /open ended .... □1

Employee, temporary / fixed term .... □2

Self-employed on your own .... □3

Self-employed with paid employees .... □4 →(**How many employees ?** _____)

Self-employed with others in a co-op or partnership .... □5

Self-employed working for somebody else on a contract or fee-paid basis .... □6

Permanently ill/disabled .... □7

Retired .... □8

Student (full-time) .... □9

Home (domestic) duties .... □10

Unemployed (seeking work) .... □11

35b How long have you been in this situation? ____ Years/ Months

If currently at work, please answer the following (35c to 35j) in relation to your main job. If not currently at work, please answer in relation to your most recent job.

35c Could you describe exactly what your occupation is?
(IF NOT CURRENTLY AT WORK, PLEASE GIVE OCCUPATION IN MOST RECENT JOB.
IF NEVER WORKED, WRITE 'NEVER WORKED' AND GO TO 35E]
IF FARMER, STATE ACREAGE AND FARM TYPE IF MANAGER/SUPERVISOR STATE NUMBER SUPERVISED. IF ON
OCCUPATION WITH DISTINCT RANK OR GRADE – GARDAI, ARMY, CIVIL SERVICE – PLEASE STATE RANK)

_____

_____

35d Where do you work? _____

35e What job or occupation would you be <u>most suitably qualified for</u>? (Please describe exactly)

_____

_____

35f Which sector of the economy do you work in ?
IF NEVER WORKED, WRITE 'NEVER WORKED' AND GO TO 36

Agriculture/Forestry/Fisheries .... ☐₁
Mining/Quarrying/Turf, etc.............. ☐₂
Building & Construction.................. ☐₃
Industry... ☐₄

Distribution (wholesale, retail, shop, pub, etc)..☐₅
Commercial/Business services.........................☐₆
Other services...☐₇

35g Do you work in the   Public Sector.........☐₁   or Private Sector ....☐₂

35h Are you a member of a Trade Union?   Yes....☐₁   No......☐₂

35i About how many hours per week do you work on average? _____Hours.
[NOTE: INCLUDE USUAL PAID OVERTIME.]

35j Do you supervise others at work?   Yes.........☐₁   No.........☐₂

35k How old were you when you got your first full-time job?
(exclude vacation employment while a student)   _____ Years.

**36. Now I would like to ask you about the kind of work your husband/wife/partner and your parents are
or were <u>*ideally qualified to do*</u>. In each case, please describe as fully as possible.**

IF FARMER, STATE ACREAGE AND FARM TYPE IF MANAGER/SUPERVISOR STATE NUMBER SUPERVISED. IF ON OCCUPATION
WITH DISTINCT RANK OR GRADE – GARDAI, ARMY, CIVIL SERVICE – PLEASE STATE RANK)

Husband/wife or partner: _____

_____

Father: _____

_____

Mother : _____

_____

37a How about your material standard of living ?
Would you say that your (family's) income at present is :

Very satisfactory	Fairly satisfactory	Not very satisfactory	Poor	Very Poor
☐₁	☐₂	☐₃	☐₄	☐₅

37b Where would you place yourself on the following social class scale ?

Lower Class.. ....☐₁
Working class..☐₂
Middle class ....☐₃
Upper middle class ....☐₄
Upper class..☐₅
(No answer or Don't know)..☐₆

38. Thank you very much for your views.   I would now like to ask you a few questions about your income.

38a Could you tell me what your <u>personal income</u> has been over the past three months,
i.e. your average weekly.
(SHOW CARD R AND TICK INCOME CODE FOR BOTH BEFORE AND AFTER TAX/PRSI)

	A	B	C	D	E	F	G	H	I	J	K	L
Before Tax:	☐₁	☐₂	☐₃	☐₄	☐₅	☐₆	☐₇	☐₈	☐₉	☐₁₀	☐₁₁	☐₁₂
After Tax:	☐₁	☐₂	☐₃	☐₄	☐₅	☐₆	☐₇	☐₈	☐₉	☐₁₀	☐₁₁	☐₁₂

38b Are you the householder?   Yes....☐₁ → Go to 38c   No......☐₂→ Go to 38d

38c Could you tell me the total average <u>household income</u> per week over the past three months?
(SHOW CARD R AND TICK INCOME CODE FOR BOTH BEFORE AND AFTER TAX)

	A	B	C	D	E	F	G	H	I	J	K	L
Before Tax:	☐₁	☐₂	☐₃	☐₄	☐₅	☐₆	☐₇	☐₈	☐₉	☐₁₀	☐₁₁	☐₁₂
After Tax:	☐₁	☐₂	☐₃	☐₄	☐₅	☐₆	☐₇	☐₈	☐₉	☐₁₀	☐₁₁	☐₁₂

38d Could you tell me how many persons living in the household are …

(a) aged less than 18 years   _____

(b) aged 18 to 64years   _____

(c) 65 years or more   _____

38e So that means there are *[TOTAL]*   _____ persons in the household. *[CHECK & AMEND IF NECESSARY]*

39a With regard to your accommodation, would you tell me if it is….

Owner occupied (fully paid for) .... ☐₁
Being bought out (by mortgage).. ☐₂
Tenant Purchase Scheme (from Local Authority) .... ☐₃
Privately rented .... ☐₄
Local Authority Rented.. ☐₅
Other (please specify_____)........... ☐₆

39b Is your accommodation …

Detached house ....☐₁	Other Apartment Flat..............................☐₅
Semi-detached house ....☐₂	Caravan................................☐₆
Terraced ....☐₃	Other (specify) _____ ☐₇
High-rise Apartment Flat ....☐₄	

39c How many rooms are there in your home (excluding toilets, bathrooms and kitchenettes) _____

40 Time Interview Ended (24 hour clock): ____: ____

Thank you very much for taking part in this survey.

THESE QUESTIONS ARE FOR THE INTERVIEWER TO ANSWER

41a. **Where interview took place:**

Living Room................. ☐₁
Hallway .... ☐₂

Kitchen .... ☐₃
Doorstep.. ☐₄
Other place (specify) _____ ☐₅

41b. **How would you describe the respondent's reception of the survey?**

Excellent .... ☐₁
Very good .... ☐₂
Good............................. ☐₃
Fair .... ☐₄

Fair, improving later .... ☐₅
Cool .... ☐₆
Hostile .... ☐₇

41c. **How would you describe the amount of explanation needed.**

General introduction only .... ☐₁
Gen. Introduction & further explanation at beginning.................... ☐₂
Gen. Introduction & further explanation at certain points.............. ☐₃

41d. Had the respondent heard of the survey?

Had heard of survey from person previously interviewed....................................... ☐₁
Had heard of survey from other sources (specify) _____ ☐₂
Had not heard of survey... ☐₃
(Don't know) .... ☐₄

41e. On which visit was the Interview as Obtained?

1	2	3	4	5	6	7	8	9	10	11	12	13
☐₁	☐₂	☐₃	☐₄	☐₅	☐₆	☐₇	☐₈	☐₉	☐₁₀	☐₁₁	☐₁₂	☐₁₃

Appendix B

Pearson Product-Moment Correlation Coefficients of Bogardus Social Distance Scale

(51 Stimulus Categories)

Pearson Product-Moment Correlation Coefficients

	Stimulus Category	1	2	3	4	5	6	7	8	9	10	11	12	13	14	15	16	17	18	19	20	21	22	23	24
1	Africans	1	.67	.35	.84	.63	.69	.83	.36	.38	.50	.61	.75	.60	.26	.45	.35	.37	.31	.49	.42	.25	.58	.70	.31
2	Agnostics		1	.37	.67	.81	.65	.66	.33	.31	.59	.52	.57	.61	.24	.39	.29	.32	.25	.44	.36	.25	.59	.58	.28
3	Alcoholics			1	.33	.38	.41	.34	NS	.20	.31	.29	.30	.36	.50	.20	NS	NS	.22	.27	NS	.65	.31	.36	.22
4	Afro-Americans*				1	.67	.69	.89	.42	.39	.50	.64	.80	.60	.26	.48	.37	.35	.30	.52	.44	.20	.71	.67	.27
5	Atheists					1	.67	.68	.36	.30	.60	.53	.59	.66	.26	.39	.28	.30	.27	.50	.36	.25	.64	.57	.28
6	Arabs						1	.70	.35	.35	.63	.55	.63	.68	.32	.41	.32	.36	.27	.40	.38	.33	.65	.75	.30
7	Blacks							1	.41	.35	.48	.65	.82	.60	.28	.40	.32	.25	.27	.50	.36	.22	.70	.68	NS
8	British								1	.59	.39	.44	.38	.31	NS	.56	.76	.45	.41	.35	.44	NS	.40	.32	.38
9	Canadians									1	.42	.56	.42	.35	NS	.73	.57	.69	.46	.36	.61	.24	.45	.36	.45
10	Capitalists										1	.51	.45	.60	.24	.48	.38	.43	.38	.37	.44	.31	.64	.60	.32
11	Chinese											1	.74	.57	.26	.56	.46	.44	.40	.45	.44	.30	.69	.56	.27
12	Coloureds												1	.57	.27	.44	.41	.34	.29	.47	.41	.21	.66	.66	.20
13	Communists													1	.31	.40	.28	.34	.20	.39	.36	.27	.65	.65	.23
14	Drug Addicts														1	NS	NS	NS	NS	.25	NS	.52	.26	.30	NS
15	Dutch															1	.57	.71	.52	.41	.70	.22	.50	.43	.48
16	English																1	.60	.48	.32	.49	NS	.41	.33	.46
17	French																	1	.55	.30	.66	.20	.43	.34	.60
18	Gardai																		1	.29	.48	.21	.34	.24	.54
19	Gay people																			1	.42	.26	.49	.35	.26
20	German																				1	NS	.49	.39	.46
21	Heavy Drinkers																					1	.28	.26	NS
22	Indians																						1	.74	.27
23	Iranians																							1	.22
24	Irish Speakers																								1
25	Israelis																								
26	Italians																								
27	Jews																								
28	Lithuanians																								
29	Mental Disability																								
30	Muslims																								
31	Nigerians																								
32	Northern Irish																								
33	Pakistanis																								
34	Palestinians																								
35	Phys Disability																								
36	Poles																								
37	Protestants																								
38	Roman Catholics																								
39	Romanians																								
40	Russians																								
41	Scottish																								
42	Socialists																								
43	Spaniards																								
44	Trade Unionists																								
45	Travellers																								
46	Unemployed																								
47	Unionists																								
48	Unmar. Mothers																								
49	Welsh																								
50	Euro-Americans*																								
51	Working Class																								

Notes: (1) * 'Afro-Americans' were labelled 'American Blacks' and 'Euro-Americans' were labelled 'White Americans' on the Questionnaire.
(2) Scores under *Rho=0.20* were not significant (statistically) and are noted NS.
(3) Scores *Rho=0.50* and higher are printed **in bold**.

of the Bogardus Social Distance Scale (51 Categories)

26	27	28	29	30	31	32	33	34	35	36	37	38	39	40	41	42	43	44	45	46	47	48	49	50	51	
.41	.60	.66	.30	.68	.77	.44	.70	.69	.29	.57	.44	.21	.70	.64	.32	.47	.45	.33	.42	.39	.52	.31	.34	.36	.29	1
.35	.55	.57	.25	.59	.56	.40	.53	.52	.21	.46	.39	NS	.52	.55	.27	.49	.43	.31	.29	.31	.45	.27	.28	.78	.23	2
.25	.27	.25	.34	.39	.31	.28	.32	.30	.20	.20	.25	NS	.29	.28	.21	.28	NS	NS	.32	.24	.29	.26	.21	NS	.21	3
.43	.67	.70	.24	.65	.75	.43	.65	.66	.27	.63	.46	NS	.71	.67	.35	.51	.51	.36	.41	.33	.55	.32	.34	.37	.25	4
.35	.59	.60	.28	.59	.60	.45	.57	.56	.24	.49	.44	NS	.55	.59	.30	.51	.41	.33	.35	.30	.52	.25	.27	.27	.23	5
.39	.60	.55	.28	.75	.67	.43	.72	.72	.21	.48	.38	NS	.65	.58	.34	.52	.42	.34	.36	.31	.51	.27	.34	.32	.21	6
.36	.60	.65	.26	.65	.75	.42	.67	.64	.23	.57	.41	NS	.70	.60	.25	.46	.42	.31	.39	.29	.50	.27	.26	.30	.22	7
.40	.44	.45	.33	.27	.32	.41	.31	.33	.36	.51	.48	.34	.40	.42	.45	.39	.55	.51	NS	.47	.45	.42	.47	.50	.46	8
.58	.42	.45	.37	.30	.33	.41	.35	.37	.48	.50	.48	.33	.41	.49	.61	.44	.57	.55	.24	.48	.44	.52	.63	.63	.54	9
.44	.56	.48	.26	.57	.49	.43	.56	.57	.29	.44	.43	.22	.48	.54	.42	.61	.52	.45	.31	.37	.49	.34	.42	.45	.30	10
.47	.59	68	.32	.51	.58	.41	.58	.55	.32	.63	.47	.26	.61	.62	.38	.50	.53	.46	.31	.45	.53	.40	.43	.38	.36	11
.37	.62	.70	.23	.59	.70	.36	.63	.62	.23	.59	.39	NS	.69	.68	.29	.43	.46	.35	.34	.32	.49	.30	.31	.33	.27	12
.42	.54	.57	.26	.65	.61	.40	.65	.64	NS	.45	.34	NS	.60	.54	.32	.56	.42	.36	.39	.30	.52	.24	.29	.31	.21	13
NS	.24	.23	.22	.33	.32	NS	.32	.32	NS	.20	NS	NS	.27	.24	NS	.26	NS	NS	.38	NS	.24	NS	NS	NS	NS	14
.66	.53	.57	.37	.39	.45	.48	.45	.48	.48	.58	.59	.40	.50	.56	.60	.48	.65	.58	.25	.47	.49	.49	.69	.61	.51	15
.47	.46	.45	.33	.26	.31	.44	.32	.35	.43	.48	.48	.34	.39	.45	.56	.40	.57	.57	NS	.56	.45	.44	.60	.49	.54	16
.66	.44	.45	.37	.32	.34	.53	.35	.37	.46	.47	.50	.36	.40	.53	.66	.44	.62	.56	.26	.51	.41	.45	.69	.57	.53	17
.40	.35	.33	.38	.22	.27	.48	.28	.25	.57	.41	.51	.49	.30	.36	.44	.29	.35	.49	.20	.44	.46	.40	.60	.40	.50	18
.36	.48	.49	.28	.38	.45	.36	.42	.41	.32	.42	.44	.23	.42	.44	.24	.44	.36	.30	.36	.28	.51	.34	.28	.29	.31	19
.57	.50	.53	.31	.40	.47	.44	.42	.46	.45	.58	.57	.34	.48	.56	.56	.46	.60	.52	.32	.40	.45	.40	.63	.56	.45	20
.21	.27	.22	.32	.30	.24	.23	.29	.29	.20	NS	.23	NS	.22	.24	.21	.31	NS	.20	.35	.27	.30	.29	.22	.20	.22	21
.53	.71	.70	.31	.67	.72	.47	.73	.71	.26	.63	.49	NS	.70	.73	.38	.56	.56	.40	.41	.37	.56	.30	.37	.43	.29	22
.42	.62	.58	.22	.78	.77	.38	.79	.81	NS	.46	.38	NS	.69	.64	.35	.53	.44	.34	.38	.28	.48	.25	.34	.37	NS	23
.48	.30	.48	.23	.25	.51	.28	.27	.54	.38	.49	.44	.28	.34	.28	.58	.28	.41	.47	NS	.49	.39	.47	.53	.40	.52	24
.45	.64	.59	.22	.78	.75	.36	.77	.81	.20	.47	.37	NS	.69	.62	.36	.54	.46	.35	.39	.30	.49	.28	.35	.38	.21	25
1	.53	.51	.37	.38	.39	.58	.47	.46	.37	.47	.45	.30	.45	.54	.60	.56	.65	.49	.25	.44	.48	.41	.55	.55	.46	26
	1	.75	.31	.60	.64	.45	.65	.66	.28	.62	.52	.23	.67	.73	.42	.64	.62	.44	.39	.42	.61	.36	.43	.46	.32	27
		1	.32	.57	.66	.41	.64	.63	.29	.74	.50	.20	.70	.76	.38	.55	.60	.46	.38	.43	.59	.37	.40	.44	.31	28
			1	.29	.28	.39	.33	.28	.47	.35	.42	.34	.30	.31	.35	.23	.28	.37	.27	.43	.37	.45	.40	.32	.43	29
				1	.78	.37	.78	.76	NS	.46	.35	NS	.67	.60	.30	.50	.38	.28	.43	.26	.44	.23	.30	.32	NS	30
					1	.40	.75	.76	.23	.54	.41	NS	.76	.69	.32	.46	.44	.34	.51	.29	.50	.26	.34	.34	.21	31
						1	.49	.40	.39	.41	.52	.41	.43	.45	.49	.47	.47	.47	.22	.41	.53	.32	.47	.37	.44	32
							1	.89	.22	.55	.44	.20	.69	.66	.32	.52	.46	.33	.44	.32	.52	.30	.34	.37	.23	33
								1	.23	.54	.43	NS	.69	.67	.37	.55	.48	.38	.44	.32	.52	.29	.39	.39	.23	34
									1	.36	.49	.38	.27	.30	.48	.24	.34	.44	NS	.51	.35	.55	.57	.47	.65	35
										1	.64	.28	.63	.66	.47	.46	.64	.50	.32	.52	.55	.43	.46	.47	.37	36
											1	.43	.47	.52	.54	.47	.59	.48	.30	.51	.60	.43	.60	.46	.51	37
												1	NS	..23	.35	.23	.27	.30	NS	.35	.32	.36	.45	.34	.46	38
													1	.69	.40	.48	.50	.38	.43	.34	.54	.31	.40	.38	.27	39
														1	.48	.56	.61	.48	.40	.42	.60	.38	.49	.51	.34	40
															1	.48	.65	.59	.23	.60	.46	.55	.78	.60	.55	41
																1	.62	.51	.33	.40	.67	.34	.42	.42	.37	42
																	1	.62	.25	.58	.54	.45	.60	.57	.50	43
																		1	.21	.60	.59	.46	.60	.55	.52	44
																			1	.24	.36	.28	.21	.22	NS	45
																				1	.53	.65	.57	.41	.58	46
																					1	.46	.46	.41	.40	47
																						1	.52	.55	.62	48
																							1	.66	.65	49
																								1	.60	50
																									1	51

List of Tables and Figures

639

List of Figures

Index

A

acceptance 31, 414

accommodation 6, 55ff, 182, 202, 205, 293ff, 297, 310ff, 328, 336, 513

Acht na dTeangachta Oifigula (2003) 398, 401, 423

Act of Settlement (1654) 31, 240

action-tendency (see behavioural-tendency)

Acton, C. 601

Adams, Gerry, MP, 220

Adams, Richard N. 193, 601

admit-to-kinship (see Bogardus Scale)

Adorno, T.W. 11, 52, 228, 487f, 490, 498, 506, 552f, 601

adolescence 135, 156ff, 160, 177, 188, 191, 300, 521, 594, 596

adulthood 157, 450

affiliation (see Religious Affiliation)

Africa 15ff

'Africans' 22, 59, 63, 66, 69, 72f, 87f, 92, 95, 100, 104f, 109f, 115ff, 119ff, 144ff, 191, 201, 213f, 217f, 515, 519, 530, 567, 580f, 583, 586, 599

'Afro-Americans' (Black Americans) 22, 59, 63ff, 72f, 82f, 87, 100, 104ff, 133ff, 190, 194, 201, 210, 213ff, 515, 517, 519ff, 528ff, 580ff, 589

age (variable) (see Personal Variables)

aggression 7, 52ff, 57, 153, 157, 188, 209, 375, 412, 490f, 512, 553, 589ff

agitators 173

'Agnostics' 11, 46, 59, 63, 66, 69, 74, 87, 90, 92, 98, 100f, 287ff, 465ff, 486, 515, 518, 550f, 571ff, 580, 583, 586, 592, 594

agri-business 179

agriculture 6, 24, 409

Ahern, Bertie, T.D. 220, 388

alarmism 522, 160

'Alcoholics' 59, 63, 66, 68f, 78, 80, 87, 93, 98, 263ff, 272ff, 287ff, 515, 518, 535, 537ff, 569ff, 581ff, 586, 588, 592, 598

alienation 54, 57, 221, 336

all-Ireland structures 233

all-weather liberals 318

Allport, Gordon 25f, 30ff, 34ff, 42, 52, 328, 511, 601

Allport's Sequential Cycle 25, 27, 30, 511

Altinordu, Ates 601

amalgamation 34, 57, 96f, 518,

America 15, 17, 20, 31, 34, 60, 67, 105, 106, 112, 118ff, 123ff, 183, 190ff, 237, 240, 321, 405, 499, 510, 519ff, 589

Anglicans 240

Anglo-Irish 162ff, 168, 170ff, 254, 414, 523

Anglo-Irish Agreement (1922) 392

Anglo-Irish Agreement (1985) 220, 590

annihilation 34, 57, 511

Anoby, Stan J. 409, 601

anomie 8, 11f, 52, 123, 487ff, 498ff, 551ff, 558ff, 595f

Anomie Scale 12, 489, 499ff, 552, 554

Anti-British Scale 221, 249ff, 255f, 262, 533f, 573

Anti-Feminist Scale 573f

anti-locution 25ff, 147, 511

anti-Romany 575

anti-Semitism 10, 31, 45f, 74, 218, 466 474f, 486, 508, 528, 552, 575, 577, 581, 589

Anti-Traveller Scale 294, 319ff, 330ff, 540, 566, 574

anxiety 52f, 55, 214, 512, 516

apartheid 9, 28f, 198, 216, 240, 293, 307, 336, 593

apostate complex 54, 512

Aquinas, Thomas (St.) 75

'Arabs' 59, 70f, 83, 88, 90, 92ff, 100f, 105, 109, 111, 117, 121, 149, 152ff, 191, 515, 520, 563, 568, 581, 583f, 586, 592f, 599

archives 18

area of birth (variable) (see Personal Variables)

areas of concern 592

armed struggle 235f, 239

Arendt, Hannah 601

Arensberg, C.M. 601

Aron , B. 11, 601

Aronson, Elliot 35, 47, 601

Asia 3, 15, 17, 19ff, 31, 202, 204, 491f, 510, 518, 529, 555, 585, 599

Asian categories 105, 109f, 115, 118ff, 121, 123f, 126ff, 144ff, 191, 519ff

aspirations (Irish Language) 10, 399ff, 416, 418

assimilation 28, 34, 55ff, 96, 310, 312, 336, 397, 513, 523f, 541

atavistic 27, 104, 204

'Atheists' 11, 46, 59, 63, 66f, 69, 74, 83, 87, 92, 287f, 289, 465ff, 469ff, 476, 486, 515, 518, 550f, 571ff, 580, 583, 586, 594

attitudes, 1, 13, 15ff, 36ff, 45ff, 174ff, 194, 219ff, 239ff, 243, 261, 301f, 319ff, 337ff, 366ff, 369ff, 394, 399ff, 427ff, 429ff, 435, 437ff, 465ff, 479ff, 513, 531f, 533, 542f, 545f, 555ff, 599

attitudes and behaviour 39ff, 160, 191, 194, 598

attitudinal neutrality 38

attitudinal vacuum 40, 513

authoritarianism 8, 10ff, 52, 123, 157, 228 487ff, 505ff, 513, 551ff, 558f, 566ff, 595ff